D0068680

THE PAPERS OF
WOODROW WILSON
VOLUME 51
SEPTEMBER 14–NOVEMBER 8, 1918

SPONSORED BY THE WOODROW WILSON
FOUNDATION
AND PRINCETON UNIVERSITY

THE PAPERS OF
WOODROW
WILSON

ARTHUR S. LINK, *EDITOR*

DAVID W. HIRST, *SENIOR ASSOCIATE EDITOR*

JOHN E. LITTLE, *ASSOCIATE EDITOR*

FREDRICK AANDAHL, *ASSOCIATE EDITOR*

MANFRED F. BOEMEKE, *ASSISTANT EDITOR*

DENISE THOMPSON, *ASSISTANT EDITOR*

PHYLLIS MARCHAND AND MARGARET D. LINK,
EDITORIAL ASSISTANTS

Volume 51
September 14–November 8, 1918

PRINCETON, NEW JERSEY
PRINCETON UNIVERSITY PRESS
1985

Note to scholars: Princeton University Press subscribes
to the Resolution on Permissions of the Association of
American University Presses, defining what we regard
as "fair use" of copyrighted works. This Resolution, intended to encourage scholarly use of university press
publications and to avoid unnecessary applications for
permission, is obtainable from the Press or from the
A.A.U.P. central office. Note, however, that the scholarly
apparatus, transcripts of shorthand, and the texts of Wilson documents as they appear in this volume are copyrighted, and the usual rules about the use of copyrighted
materials apply.

Publication of this book has been aided by a grant from
the National Historical Publications and Records Commission.

Printed in the United States of America
by Princeton University Press
Princeton, New Jersey

INTRODUCTION

THE opening of this volume finds the Allied armies moving rapidly in a great counteroffensive on the western front, while the A.E.F.'s First Army, under General Pershing, has just undertaken its first military operation on its own against the so-called St. Mihiel Salient. Unknown to the Allied Supreme War Council, which still plans for Germany's defeat in 1919, the combined Allied and American drives will be near to piercing Germany's frontier by the time that this volume ends.

In the United States, mobilization and war production are mounting daily, and Wilson has few major concerns about the war effort. One is the threat of a major shipyard strike on the Pacific Coast, which causes him to think in the direction of imposing an umbrella-like national labor policy. Second, Postmaster General Burleson's heavy-handed dealings with the press and the behavior of zealous federal district attorneys still raise problems in the field of civil liberties with which Wilson has to deal personally. In addition, Wilson continues to encounter stubborn Democratic opposition in the Senate to the woman-suffrage amendment, which has already passed the House of Representatives. In a step still unprecedented in American history, Wilson appears before the Senate on September 30, 1918, to plead for the passage of the amendment as essential to the successful prosecution of the war.

Abroad, Wilson's initial primary preoccupation is the constant demand by Allied leaders for the dispatch of substantial American reinforcements to bolster Allied forces in northern Russia and to succor the Czech Legion in Siberia, which is under heavy pressure from the Red Army. In conversations with Allied Ambassadors in Washington, and in a firm note to the Allied governments on September 27, Wilson declares, somewhat unceremoniously, that no more American troops will be sent to northern Russia, and that the scattered units of the Czech legion should be withdrawn to eastern Siberia. Wilson also once again affirms that the United States will not become involved in the Russian Civil War.

Meanwhile, on the other side of the world, events occur that hold out to Wilson the hope of great opportunity and the portent of mortal danger to the Allied and American armies. On September 29, William II and his advisers agree that Germany's desperate military situation demands the immediate pursuit of peace negotiations. Internal reforms, looking toward the establishment of a parliamentary form of government in Germany, follow quickly, and, on October 6, 1918, a new government under Prince Max von Baden appeals to Wilson for an armistice based upon the Fourteen Points and Wilson's "subsequent pronouncements." The British, French, and Italian Prime Ministers, in conference in Paris, panic in the fear that Wilson will be beguiled into going it alone in peace negotiations. Without consulting Wilson, they send him the terms for an armistice which they will demand. Wilson replies to the Germans on October 8, asking for clarification of the German note and warning that there would be no talk of an armistice unless the Germans agree to withdraw their armies "everywhere from invaded territory." The German government replies on October 12, accepts Wilson's demand for evacuation, and affirms that it speaks for the great majority in the Reichstag. Meanwhile, demands for unconditional surrender, led by Senator Henry Cabot Lodge and Theodore Roosevelt, sweep the country and threaten to jeopardize Wilson's ability to engage in any kind of peace parleys. In fact, he tells Ambassador Jusserand on October 11 that he doubts the wisdom of concluding an armistice at this time, since talk of peace could only undermine the élan of the Allied and American troops. However, he does reply, on October 14, to the latest German note, but he makes it clear that he will not enter into any "arrangements" which do not guarantee the absolute "present military supremacy of the armies of the United States and of the Allies in the field." When the Germans respond affirmatively on October 20, Wilson at once sends Colonel House to Paris to confer directly with the Allied leaders. From October 27 through November 4, House hammers out political and military agreements with the Allied statesmen, generals, and admirals. Wilson, who is in daily telegraphic communication with House, approves.

While these epochal events in Europe promise the early end of the war, the people of the United States have been convulsed by a biennial political campaign. Wilson pours out a stream of letters in support of Democratic candidates for Congress. At the urging of Tumulty and other advisers, he issues, on October 25, an appeal to Americans for the return of a Democratic Congress. Such a vote of confidence, he says, is necessary, because a Republican victory would be interpreted "on the other side of the water" as a repudiation of his leadership on the very eve of peacemaking. For a variety of reasons, many of which have nothing to do with Wilson's leadership, the voters elect a Senate with a slim Republican majority and a House of Representatives with a substantial one.

"VERBATIM ET LITERATIM"

In earlier volumes of this series, we have said something like the following: "All documents are reproduced *verbatim et literatim*, with typographical and spelling errors corrected in square brackets only when necessary for clarity and ease of reading." The following essay explains our textual methods and review procedures.

We have never printed and do not intend to print critical, or corrected, versions of documents. We print them exactly as they are, with a few exceptions which we always note. We never use the word *sic* except to denote the repetition of words in a document; in fact, we think that a succession of *sics* defaces a page.

We usually repair words in square brackets when letters are missing. As we have said, we also repair words in square brackets for clarity and ease of reading. Our general rule is to do this when we, ourselves, cannot read the word without having to stop to puzzle out its meaning. Jumbled words and names misspelled beyond recognition of course have to be repaired. We correct the misspellings of names in documents in the footnotes identifying those persons.

However, when an old man writes to Wilson saying that he is glad to hear that Wilson is "comming" to Newark, or a semiliterate farmer from Texas writes phonetically, we see no reason to correct spellings in square brackets when the words are perfectly understandable. We do not correct Wilson's misspellings unless they are unreadable, except to supply in square brackets letters missing in words. For example, he frequently spelled "belligerent" as "belligerant." Nothing would be gained by correcting "belligerant" in square brackets.

We think that it is very important for several reasons to follow the rule of *verbatim et literatim*. Most important, a document has its own integrity and power, particularly when it is not written in perfect literary form. There is something very moving in seeing a Texas dirt farmer struggling to express his feelings in words, or a semiliterate former slave doing the same thing. Second, in Wilson's case it is crucially important to reproduce his errors in letters which he typed himself, since he usually typed badly when he was in an agitated state. Third, since style is the essence of the person, we would never correct grammar or make tenses consistent, as one correspondent has urged us to do. Fourth, we think that it is very important that we print exact transcripts of Charles L. Swem's copies of Wilson's letters. Swem made many mistakes (we correct them in footnotes from a reading of his shorthand books), and Wilson let them pass. We thus have to assume that Wilson did not read his letters before signing them, and this, we think, is a significant fact. Finally, printing typed letters and documents *verbatim et literatim* tells us a great deal about the educational level of the stenographic profession in the United States during Wilson's time.

We think that our series would be worthless if we produced unreliable texts, and we go to considerable effort to make certain that the texts are authentic.

Our typists are highly skilled and proofread their transcripts carefully as soon as they have typed them. The Editor sight proofreads documents once he has assembled a volume and is setting its annotation. The Editors who write the notes read through documents several times and are careful to check any anomalies. Then, once the manuscript volume has been completed and all notes checked, the Editor and Senior Associate Editor orally proofread the documents against the copy. They read every comma, dash, and character. They note every absence of punctuation. They study every nearly illegible word in written documents.

Once this process of "establishing the text" is completed, the manuscript volume goes to our editor at Princeton University Press, who checks the volume carefully and sends it to the printing plant. The galley proofs are read against copy in the proofroom at the Press. And we must say that the proofreaders there are extraordinarily skilled. Some years ago, before we found a way to ease their burden, they queried every misspelled word, inconsistencies in punctuation and capitalization, absence of punctuation, or other such anomalies. Now we write "O.K." above such words or spaces on the copy.

We read the galley proofs at least three times. Our copyeditor gives them a sight reading against the manuscript copy to look for remaining typographical errors and to make sure that no line has been dropped. The Editor and Senior Associate Editor sight read them against documents and copy. We then get the page proofs, which have been corrected at the Press. We check all the changes three times. In addition, we get *revised* pages and check them twice.

This is not the end. The Editor, Senior Associate Editor, and Assistant Editor give a final reading to headings, description-location lines, and notes. Finally, our indexer of course reads the pages word by word. Before we return the pages to the Press, she comes in with a list of queries, all of which are answered by reference to the documents.

Our rule in the Wilson Papers is that our tolerance of error is zero. No system and no person can be perfect. There may be errors in our volumes. However, we believe that we have done everything humanly possible to avoid error; the chance is remote that what looks at first glance like a typographical error is indeed an error.

We thank our editor at Princeton University Press, Mrs. Alice Calaprice, for her help in the preparation of this volume. We are grateful to Professors John Milton Cooper, Jr., William H. Harbaugh, Richard W. Leopold, and Betty Miller Unterberger—all members of our Editorial Advisory Committee—for reading the manuscript of this volume and for being, as before, constructively critical.

THE EDITORS

Princeton, New Jersey
April 9, 1985

CONTENTS

Introduction, vii
Illustrations, xxiii
Abbreviations and Symbols, xxv

News Reports

Collateral Materials

Political correspondence, reports, memoranda, and aide-mémoire

Diplomatic correspondence, reports, memoranda, and aide-mémoire

ILLUSTRATIONS

Following page 326

Marching in the Fourth Liberty Loan Parade in New York
Library of Congress

Prince Maximilian von Baden
Princeton University Library

Wilhelm Solf
Princeton University Library

General Maurice Janin
National Archives

Herbert Hoover
Princeton University Library

Wartime Diplomats
> *Clockwise, from upper left: John William Davis,*
> *William Graves Sharp, Pleasant Alexander Stovall,*
> *Thomas Nelson Page*
Princeton University Library

Unconditional Surrender!
> *Theodore Roosevelt and Henry Cabot Lodge*
Princeton University Library

Thomas William Lamont
Princeton University Library

ABBREVIATIONS

ALI	autograph letter initialed
ALS	autograph letter signed
ASB	Albert Sidney Burleson
CC	carbon copy
CCL	carbon copy of letter
CCLS	carbon copy of letter signed
EBWhw	Edith Bolling Wilson handwriting, handwritten
EMH	Edward Mandell House
FR	*Papers Relating to the Foreign Relations of the United States*
FR 1918, Russia	*Papers Relating to the Foreign Relations of the United States, 1918, Russia*
FR-WWS 1918	*Papers Relating to the Foreign Relations of the United States, 1918, Supplement, The World War*
HCH	Herbert Clark Hoover
Hw, hw	handwriting, handwritten
HwLS	handwritten letter signed
HwS	handwritten signed
JD	Josephus Daniels
JPT	Joseph Patrick Tumulty
MS, MSS	manuscript, manuscripts
NDB	Newton Diehl Baker
RG	record group
RL	Robert Lansing
T	typed
TC	typed copy
TCL	typed copy of letter
TCLS	typed copy of letter signed
TI	typed initialed
TL	typed letter
TLI	typed letter initialed
TLS	typed letter signed
TS	typed signed
TWG	Thomas Watt Gregory
WBW	William Bauchop Wilson
WGM	William Gibbs McAdoo
WHP	Walter Hines Page
WJB	William Jennings Bryan
WW	Woodrow Wilson
WWhw	Woodrow Wilson handwriting, handwritten
WWsh	Woodrow Wilson shorthand
WWT	Woodrow Wilson typed
WWTL	Woodrow Wilson typed letter
WWTLI	Woodrow Wilson typed letter initialed
WWTLS	Woodrow Wilson typed letter signed

ABBREVIATIONS FOR COLLECTIONS
AND REPOSITORIES

Following the National Union Catalog of the
Library of Congress

ADM	British Admiralty
AzU	University of Arizona
CSt-H	Hoover Institution on War, Revolution and Peace
CtY	Yale University
DGU	Georgetown University
DLC	Library of Congress
DNA	National Archives
FMD-Ar	French Ministry of Defense Archives
FO	British Foreign Office
InNd	University of Notre Dame
IOR	India Office Library and Records
JFO-Ar	Japanese Foreign Office Archives
KyU	University of Kentucky
LDR	Labor Department Records
MH	Harvard University
MH-Ar	Harvard University Archives
MH-BA	Harvard University Graduate School of Business Administration
MiDbF	Ford Motor Company
NcU	University of North Carolina
NjP	Princeton University
PRO	Public Record Office
RSB Coll., DLC	Ray Stannard Baker Collection of Wilsoniana, Library of Congress
SDR	State Department Records
ViU	University of Virginia
WC, NjP	Woodrow Wilson Collection, Princeton University
WDR	War Department Records
WP, DLC	Woodrow Wilson Papers, Library of Congress

SYMBOLS

[September 19, 1918]	publication date of published writing; also date of document when date is not part of text
[*October 4, 1918*]	composition date when publication date differs
[[October 9, 1918]]	delivery date of speech if publication date differs
**** ***	text deleted by author of document

THE PAPERS OF

WOODROW WILSON

VOLUME 51

SEPTEMBER 14–NOVEMBER 8, 1918

THE PAPERS OF
WOODROW WILSON

To John Joseph Pershing

[The White House] 14 September 1918.

Accept my warmest congratulations on the brilliant achievements of the army under your command.[1] The boys have done what we expected of them and done it in the way we most admire. We are deeply proud of them and of their chief. Please convey to all concerned my grateful and affectionate thanks.

Woodrow Wilson.

T telegram (Letterpress Books, WP, DLC).
    [1] Wilson referred to the reduction of the St. Mihiel salient by the American First Army on September 12-13 in the first major military operation in which largely American forces had been deployed under American leadership. See Edward M. Coffman, *The War to End All Wars: The American Military Experience in World War I* (New York, 1968), pp. 262-84.

From Robert Lansing, with Enclosure

My dear Mr. President: Washington September 14, 1918

Allow me to send you a copy of a letter which, in Mr. Creel's absence from town, I have addressed to Mr. Edgar S. Sisson. The proposed action of the Committee on Public Information was brought to my attention late yesterday afternoon and a copy of the text to be given out was handed me this morning.

I am unwilling at so late an hour to refer to you, but there seems no other course in the circumstances which attend the perilous situation of Mr. Poole and his Allied colleagues at Moscow and the American men and women who have remained in Moscow and Petrograd.   Faithfully yours,   Robert Lansing.

TLS (WP, DLC).

E N C L O S U R E
Robert Lansing to Edgar Grant Sisson

My dear Mr. Sisson: [Washington] September 14, 1918.

In the absence of Mr. Creel I am addressing myself to you in an urgent matter. I have just been offered an opportunity this morning to read the first installment of the data which the Committee proposes to release for publication tomorrow and which contains a scathing arraignment of Lenine and Trotsky and the Bolsheviki leaders.[1] It is not likely that the Germans will fail to bring this attack, published by a Committee of which three of the President's cabinet are members, to the attention of the Bolsheviki.

Mr. Poole, American Consul at Moscow, with the Department's approval, has courageously remained at his post to give countenance to his colleagues of the Allied Governments who are under arrest.[2] Mr. Allan Wardwell and Mr. Andrews[3] of the Red Cross and two Y.M.C.A. secretaries have remained at Moscow. At least two American women are reported to be still either at Moscow or Petrograd.

The publication of the data against the Bolshevik leaders includes an arraignment of their personal integrity. In my judgment it goes further, therefore, than any of the political activities which have been charged by the Bolsheviki against the British and French representatives now under arrest. In other words, what the Committee proposes will not only tend to arouse bitter animosity against Mr. Poole and the other Americans in Russia—where hitherto they have occupied a somewhat special position owing to the attitude of this Government—but will not unlikely imperil their lives and jeopardize further the already precarious position of the official representatives of the Allies.

If the data against the Bolshevik leaders is released on the date which I understand is proposed, namely tomorrow, September 15th, it will be impossible to communicate with Mr. Poole in time to secure the departure of himself and the remaining Americans in Russia. In the circumstances, I am unwilling to share responsibility for the consequences which may result from the publication of these documents.

On April 23, 1918, I telegraphed the American Ambassador at London that no publication of this data was desired at that time or pending further conference.[4] I assume, therefore, that the Committee's proposed action has been taken only after the British authorities at London have been properly informed of the Committee's intention. Please inform me definitely on this point.

I am, my dear Mr. Sisson,
Sincerely yours,   [Robert Lansing]

CCL (WP, DLC).
[1] That is, the so-called Sisson Documents, about which see D. R. Francis to RL, Feb. 13, 1918, n. 1, Vol. 46.
[2] The intervention of the Allies at Archangel in early August had led to greatly increased hostility toward their representatives and citizens in Russia on the part of both the Soviet government and pro-Bolshevik Russians in general. The situation became very critical on August 30, when Moisei Solomonovich Uritski, the head of the Petrograd

branch of the Cheka, the Bolshevik police organization, was assassinated in Petrograd and Lenin himself was shot and seriously wounded in Moscow by a Left Social Revolutionary, Fania Efimovna Roidman Kaplan. The fury of the Bolsheviks over these two unrelated incidents brought about the Red Terror, directed against all persons suspected of counterrevolutionary activity and which was ultimately responsible for the deaths of thousands of persons throughout Russia. Allied nationals were soon victims of the frenzy. On August 31, a Bolshevik mob invaded the British embassy building in Petrograd and shot to death the former Assistant Naval Attaché, Capt. Francis N. A. Cromie, when he resisted the invasion and killed two of the intruders. In the following days, numerous British and French diplomatic and consular officials, members of military missions, and civilians were imprisoned in Moscow and Petrograd. The most notable of these was Robert Hamilton Bruce Lockhart, who was placed in military confinement in the Kremlin, charged with being the master mind of a plot to kill Lenin and Trotsky and overthrow the Soviet government. Significantly, Lansing, on September 14, had sent a telegram to DeWitt C. Poole, Jr., ordering him to leave Moscow at once and go to Stockholm, Archangel, or Omsk. This communication ultimately reached Poole through the kindness of Chicherin. See George F. Kennan, *The Decision to Intervene* (Princeton, N. J., 1958), pp. 453-66; Richard H. Ullman, *Anglo-Soviet Relations, 1917-1921: Intervention and the War* (Princeton, N. J., 1961), pp. 285-96; and William Henry Chamberlin, *The Russian Revolution, 1917-1921* (2 vols., New York, 1935), II, 63-80.

[3] Capt. James W. Andrews of the American Red Cross, who was seriously ill at this time.

[4] See Lord Reading to A. J. Balfour, April 25, 1918, Vol. 47.

From the White House Staff

The White House.
14 September, 1918.

Memorandum for the President:

Senator Smith, of South Carolina, telephoned to ask if the President will see on Monday morning if possible, or Monday afternoon if it is not possible in the morning, a committee consisting of six senators and a delegation from the House representing the cotton-growing States concerning the cotton situation.[1]

Representative Bell, of Georgia, subsequently telephoned making the same request, and expressed the very earnest hope that the appointment could be made for Monday *morning*.

TL (WP, DLC).

[1] Bernard Baruch had announced on September 4 that, as a result of the rapidly rising prices for cotton products, the War Industries Board would soon create a committee to consider ways to bring about "a reasonable stabilization of prices" for raw cotton. This announcement brought an immediate storm of protest from senators and representatives from cotton-growing states. Wilson himself issued a statement on September 13 to clarify the objectives of the proposed committee. The principal object, he said, was to satisfy the great demand for cotton of both the United States and its associates by finding ways to market lower grades of cotton which were presently unsaleable. However, he did admit that it might become "part of this committee's duty to recommend basic prices on cotton." This statement led to a sharp drop in the price of cotton on September 14, as well as to the above request for an immediate conference between Wilson and interested senators and representatives. At a conference held at the White House at 5 p.m. on Tuesday, September 17, Wilson told the group that he would fix the price of cotton. After this decision was made public on September 20, there was another strong price decline in the cotton market. The furor died down following a statement issued on September 27 by the chairman of the War Industries Board's committees on cotton and on cotton distribution which declared that they "would not recommend that a price be fixed on raw cotton at the present time." *New York Times*, Sept. 5, 14, 15, 21, 22, and 28, 1918.

From Scott Ferris

Washington, D. C.

My dear Mr. President: September 14th, 1918

I beg to hand you herewith a note just received from Mr. Gifford Pinchot, together with a copy of my reply.[1]

By a combination of circumstances we were defeated[2] by five votes. They were: (1st) bitter partisanship on the part of Republican members; (2nd) apathy and absenteeism due to the fact that the water power bill had been up so long; (3rd) jealousy on the part of certain members to the Flood Control and Rivers and Harbors Committees who felt they should have been placed on this special Water Power Committee; (4th) intense activity on the part of the Water Power people, who have flooded all the desks with ass[a]ults on those who believe in conservation and the public interest side of the question, and a firm insistence upon wheedling the Government out of its rights, and giving the water power interests precisely what they wanted. It may be worth while to mention that they knew precisely what they did want.

It is most too bad to trouble you with this matter, but I know you were interested in it, and you stood by us so loyally in the matter, that I have dared to make a little explanation to you of why we lost the fight.

You will pardon this intrusion, I am sure.

Sincerely, Scott Ferris

TLS (WP, DLC).
[1] Pinchot's letter to Ferris of Sept. 11, 1918 is missing. S. Ferris to G. Pinchot, Sept. 14, 1918, CCL (WP, DLC), is an acknowledgment of Pinchot's letter.
[2] Ferris referred to the latest action taken by the House of Representatives on the water-power bill (S. 1419), about which see the index references in Vols. 45 and 49 of this series. Ferris, on September 5, had proposed a motion to recommit the bill to the Committee on Water Power with instructions to amend it to include a clause which permitted the federal government to regain control of water-power projects upon the payment of the fair market value of those projects. The motion was defeated by a vote of 133 to 128. The House then proceeded to pass the bill as it stood. *Cong. Record*, 65th Cong., 2d sess., pp. 10051-53.

Sir William Wiseman to Arthur Cecil Murray

My dear Murray, [New York] 14 September 1918.

I have so many letters from you unanswered that I feel ashamed of myself. You must, however, make excuses for me. For the last month I have been up on the North Shore with House and have been trying to keep my work going under rather difficult conditions. It has been well worth the time spent because I saw so much of House and the President and had an opportunity of getting at their inner minds on important questions. I think I was also able to establish an even closer relation with them than before.

I have now returned to New York, but find a pile of work to get through. Practically the arrears of a month.

I have not been down to Washington at all since Reading left and feel that I ought to go there as soon as possible and exchange news with Barclay. Otherwise I am afraid he may feel that I am purposely keeping away from him. I hope that you will not revenge yourself by writing any less to me. Some of your letters I show to House and discuss the substance of them all with him. He feels as I told you that through you he is being kept in close touch with what is going on in Europe and he is really very grateful for it and of course it enables me to get information from him in exchange. You are doing exactly what I could never get them to do before— that is, send me inside information about everything that is going on. In this way House and the President have come to regard me as perhaps their chief source of information and surely this is or could be of some advantage. I presume you are seeing all the cables I send to Reading and those he sends to me.

I see by the last cable that Reading has decided to continue his present position under the same conditions as before. Perhaps this is the line of least resistance and if he is satisfied, I do not think we ought to object. It is of course quite unthinkable that he should give up the job. There is no one else who could approach his value. I still think, however, that he should make arrangements to visit England fairly frequently. You know all the reasons in favour of it and I think agree they are sound.

As soon as possible after Reading returns I shall try to get over. For your very private information it is not impossible that House may come over this winter. In fact the one thing at present which prevents him making definite plans is the feeling that the situation is changing so rapidly that it would be better for him to wait until we reach something like a definite pause for the winter. Also he thinks it likely that German peace proposals may be sprung on us at any time and he would like to discuss them with the President and then come over to Europe. If he goes of course I should go with him. But if he decides to postpone his trip indefinitely, he will probably want me to take a short trip over there, say in November.

I am glad to hear that a satisfactory job has been found for Swinton[1] and I should think that his really great ability would find scope in that department of the Ministry of Munitions.

Your letter of the 13th about Imperial Preference is particularly

---

[1] Maj. Gen. Ernest Dunlop Swinton, best known as the principal inventor of the military tank. He had recently been in Washington on the staff of Lord Reading.

interesting. We must watch this situation very carefully. The President seems to think that the Allies, particularly England, want to form an economic alliance against Germany after the war. The thing has evidently been put to him in quite the wrong way and he thinks that we want to smash German trade permanently. He is determined that America shall be no party to this policy and would very quickly and definitely disassociate himself with any pronouncement along those lines. At the same time he is quite willing that economic pressure should be used, if necessary, after the war to force Germany to live up to the terms of the Treaty of Peace. He really has very much the same idea as our people, but the extremists of the Tariff Reform League have scared him a bit.

I should like you to keep me well informed as to the developments of our economic policy and I will try and do the same by you. I am making a start by sending you by this mail some confidential memoranda giving the American viewpoint.

It is also interesting to receive your notes on the situation in France. I do not think the U. S. Government are very well informed by their agents about political conditions in France and the French Embassy here is, as you know, far from being in close relations with the Administration.

I am puzzled about the situation in Siberia. All our advices seem to show that the Czecho-Slovaks are in grave danger. Yet Dr. Masaryk who is in Washington does not seem to take a very serious view of the position and all the advices the American Government receive tend to show that the Czechs are reasonably secure. I hope now that General Graves[2] has reached Vladivostock and that Knox and Eliot[3] are there we may be able to get more reliable information. As far as the President's position is concerned he has lost faith and curiously enough, practically lost interest in the Bolsheviks and is, I think, much more inclined to fall in with our programme than he was a few months ago.

I have just cabled Reading[4] regarding cable which Barclay sent

[2] Maj. Gen. William Sidney Graves, commander of the American expedition which had arrived at Vladivostok on September 3, 1918. Newton D. Baker had met Graves secretly in Kansas City, Missouri, on August 3, and, handing Graves his orders in a sealed envelope, had said: "This contains the policy of the United States in Russia which you are to follow. Watch your step; you will be walking on eggs loaded with dynamite. God bless you and good-bye." The orders were a copy of Wilson's *aide-mémoire* printed at July 17, 1918, Vol. 48. See W. S. Graves, *America's Siberian Adventure, 1918-1920* (New York, 1931), pp. 3-4.

[3] That is, Col. Alfred William Fortescue Knox and Sir Charles Norton Edgecumbe Eliot.

[4] W. Wiseman to Lord Reading, Sept. 14, 1918, T telegram (W. Wiseman Papers, CtY). It reads as follows: "Have just seen copy of cable No. 4070 from Barclay to F.O. I think Barclay's phrasing is unfortunate and am satisfied U.S.G. had no intention of issuing a peremptory ultimatum."

the F. O. about Gen. Poole at Archangel.[5] This is a good example of how real trouble can be manufactured out of nothing. Undoubtedly the U.S.G. rather resent the way in which Poole is running things at Archangel and I should imagine that he is not getting on particularly well with the American representatives there—probably he is rather impatient with them. It is only necessary, however, to explain to the Administration the necessity of the action which Poole has taken and to promise to do everything possible to respect Russian independence and the authority of the Local Board. I have no doubt that Lansing spoke quite sharply to Barclay and then Barclay rushed off and sent this cable. We have enough real difficulties without making unnecessary trouble for ourselves.

Reference to your letter of August 10th: I do not think that Lippmann has given you quite the right impression. He was employed by House in his Enquiry Bureau because he is undoubtedly a very able young man and represents a certain section of the more intelligent radicals in this country. House, however, has not very much confidence in his judgment and would certainly not think of letting him organize a political intelligence department for him in Europe. As a matter of fact House has no idea of setting up any political intelligence department on your side. Baker, who knows Lippmann well and thinks a lot of him, asked House for the loan of his services chiefly, as far as I can make out, to report on the American propaganda in Europe. Since he has been over there Lippmann has sent various reports, which I have seen, criticising rather violently everyone connected with the American propaganda. He sent some of these by cable through the State Department—in due course they reached Creel's Department—with the result you can imagine. Finally House has had to send Lippmann a sharp cable telling him to confine himself to reports by mail and advising him not to criticise people quite so freely.

As for Lippmann's views on the League of Nations—he has never discussed the matter with the President and I do not think he knows much of House's opinion on the subject. Personally I liked Lippmann and there can be no doubt that he is a clever writer with original ideas—and a way of expressing them which appeals in this country. He ought to have done quite well at his present job—and I thought that he would, but he does not seem to have the knack of fitting into a Government Department.

Reference your letter of August 20th, to which was attached a letter from Herron: I do not think you ought to take Herron too seriously. He is one of the many people who pose as an agent of

[5] C. A. de R. Barclay to the Foreign Office, Sept. 9, 1918, Vol. 49.

the Administration with very little justification. It is rather amusing to hear that Herron has obtained the President's sanction for his reports to be sent to A.J.B.[6] The President has probably forgotten all about Herron—certainly he does not know that Herron is sending reports to anybody. House gets all Herron's reports and reads them and finds most of them rather nonsense. Anyone can see Herron's reports as far as the Administration is concerned.

With reference to your letter of August 23rd, I can tell you where the distinguished Americans you mention get most of their information regarding labour conditions in England: It is through a man called Buckler who is attached to the American Embassy in London. I spoke to Eric[7] about him last time I was in London and warned him that Buckler is an alarmist and more or less of a Bolshevist. There are, of course, many other Americans, journalists and others, travelling through England and France, and they most of them seem to me to take an unnecessarily gloomy view about labour conditions. Of course they take care not to get their information from anybody connected with the Government. If, however, you continue to keep me informed about the real labour situation, I can guarantee that House and the President will get the right information. For the rest, an occasional article by one of the American correspondents in London can help to give the public here a true view.

I am greatly interested in the proposal for a Mission of American business men which you outlined in your letter of the 30th. Please let me know how the scheme progresses. House has not heard anything about it, but thought the idea a good one.

Lyle[8] sent me your long letter to him of the 16th of August which I found extraordinarily interesting and only wish that I could give you an equally illuminating account of the situation here. I must try and do so one of these days.   [William Wiseman]

CCL (W. Wiseman Papers, CtY).
  [6] That is, Arthur J. Balfour.
  [7] That is, Sir Eric Drummond.
  [8] Probably Maj. Charles Henry Lyell, M.P., who had replaced Arthur Murray as Assistant Military Attaché at the British embassy in Washington.

To Robert Lansing

My dear Mr. Secretary,   The White House. 16 September, 1918.

This is the reply which I think we ought to make to the Austrian note,[1] and I hope that you will make it public so soon as we have officially received the note:

The Government of the United States appreciates the spirit in which the suggestion of the Imperial Austro-Hungarian government is made, but feels that there is only one reply it can make. It has repeatedly and with entire candour stated the terms upon which the United States would consider peace and can and will entertain no proposal for ⟨confidential⟩[2] *a* conference ⟨of any kind about⟩ *upon* a matter ⟨about⟩ *concerning* which it has made its position and purpose so plain.[3]   Faithfully Yours,   W.W.

WWTLI (R. Lansing Papers, NjP).

[1] This very long and rambling communication had already appeared in the newspapers of September 16. It summarized many of the peace proposals and statements of war aims made by the Central Powers, the Entente Allies, and the United States Government since December 1916. However, it said, most of these proposals and statements had been made in speeches and other public statements by political leaders of the belligerent nations. What was really needed in order to arrive at a "compromise peace" satisfactory to all parties was a direct dialogue among official representatives of all the warring states at some private meeting place so that the complex problems of a peace settlement might be thoroughly aired and possible solutions gradually worked out. The substantive paragraph reads as follows: "The Imperial and Royal Government therefore comes again to the governments of all the belligerent states with a proposal shortly to send to a neutral country, upon a previous agreement as to the date and place, delegates who would broach a confidential non-binding conversation over the fundamental principles of a peace which could be concluded. The delegates would be commissioned to communicate to one another the views of their respective governments on the aforesaid principles and very freely and frankly interchange information on every point for which provision should be made." W. A. F. Ekengren to RL, Sept. 16, 1918, *FR-WWS 1918*, I, I, 306-309.

When this note was made public on September 15, it was prefaced by a lengthy preamble which stressed the need for peace in all the warring nations. This statement is printed in the *New York Times*, Sept. 16, 1918.

[2] Words in angle brackets deleted by Lansing; words in italics added by him.

[3] On September 16, Lansing issued the following press release: "I am authorized by the President to state that the following will be the reply of this Government to the Austro-Hungarian note proposing an unofficial conference of belligerents: The Government of the United States feels that there is only one reply which it can make to the suggestion of the Imperial Austro-Hungarian Government. It has repeatedly and with entire candor stated the terms upon which the United States would consider peace and can and will entertain no proposal for a conference upon a matter concerning which it has made its position and purpose so plain." T MS (R. Lansing Papers, NjP).

To Raymond Poincaré

[The White House] 16 September, 1918

Your gracious message about the recent victories of the army under General Pershing[1] has touched me very much. The personal feeling of which you speak makes me feel near to you, and the scenes of the recent fighting very real, and I want you to know how cordially and entirely I share your feeling of pride in the association of the French and American forces and in what has been effected for the relief of the regions recently occupied, and the repulse of the invaders.   Woodrow Wilson

T telegram (Letterpress Books, WP, DLC).

[1] R. Poincaré to WW, Sept. 13, 1918, Vol. 49.

To Albert Sidney Burleson

My dear Burleson: [The White House] 16 September, 1918

I know the principal writer for this paper,[1] Norman Thomas. He was once a pupil of mine at Princeton. I have just had a talk with Nevin Sayre about the whole matter of the holding up of this particular issue[2] and have urged views upon him which I hope and believe will alter the policy and, to some extent, the point of view of men like Thomas; but I write this only to suggest that you treat these men with all possible consideration, for I know they are absolutely sincere and I would not like to see this publication held up unless there is a very clear case indeed.[3]

Always faithfully yours,   Woodrow Wilson

TLS (Letterpress Books, WP, DLC).
[1] *The World Tomorrow*, of which Thomas was editor, sponsored by the Fellowship of Reconciliation.
[2] *Ibid.*, I (Sept. 1918). There were numerous items in this issue which the Post Office Department might have found objectionable, most notably John Haynes Holmes, "The Search—A Parable," p. 207, and Norman Thomas, "The Acid Test of Our Democracy," pp. 219-26, which was highly critical of American and Allied actions in Russia.
[3] The September issue of the magazine was released by the Post Office Department. For brief descriptions of John Nevin Sayre's meeting with Wilson, see Harry Fleischman, *Norman Thomas, A Biography: 1884-1968* (New York, 1969), p. 69, and W. A. Swanberg, *Norman Thomas: The Last Idealist* (New York, 1976), pp. 63-64.

To William Procter Gould Harding

[The White House]
My dear Governor Harding: 16 September, 1918

I am very much obliged to you for sending me a copy of the letter of Mr. Fred I. Kent, Director of the Federal Reserve Board's Division of Foreign Exchange.[1]

As to the policy with regard to the exportation of gold to Mexico, I feel that I am hardly entitled to a judgment in the matter, and in answer to the question of the last part of your letter of September 14th,[2] I would say that I am quite willing to accept the judgment in that matter of the Gold Exports Committee. Certainly any action advantageous to Mexico is advantageous also to the United States at this time, because our relations with Mexico remain unsatisfactory, partly because of the impression of the Carranza Government that we are illiberal and unfriendly.

Cordially and sincerely yours,   Woodrow Wilson

TLS (Letterpress Books, WP, DLC).
[1] F. I. Kent to W. P. G. Harding, Sept. 12, 1918, TCL (WP, DLC). Kent discussed the great need for silver bullion as a means of payment to China for necessary imports and for loan to the British government.
[2] Harding had suggested that the best way to stimulate silver production in Mexico

and its export to the United States was to increase gold shipments to Mexico. The last paragraph of his letter follows: "It is probable that the Mexican demand for gold from this country, both for the reimportation of 25% of the value of the silver exported and for the payrolls at the mines, would not exceed in any event, 40% of the value of the silver brought into the United States from Mexico, and if, after considering the matter, you would prefer to have the Gold Exports Committee, which is composed of two members of the Federal Reserve Board and a representative of the Treasury, adopt a more liberal policy with respect to shipments of gold to Mexico for mining purposes, I would be grateful if you would have me advised accordingly." W. P. G. Harding to WW, Sept. 14, 1918, TLS (WP, DLC).

To Edward Nash Hurley, with Enclosure

My dear Hurley: [The White House] 16 September, 1918.

I am sending you the enclosed, because I know how keen you are on keeping everything within proper control, and I would be very much obliged if you would read the enclosures and let me know what you think about them, at the same time, if you will be kind enough, returning the papers for my files.

Cordially and faithfully yours,   Woodrow Wilson

TLS (Letterpress Books, WP, DLC).

E N C L O S U R E

From Thomas Watt Gregory

Dear Mr. President: Washington, D. C. September 13, 1918.

I deem it important to bring to your attention a question of the future operations at Hog Island.

Originally, the enterprise was organized with only a rather nominal control by the Fleet Corporation. When, in January, the Hog Island expenditures had created "a public scandal,"[1] as Mr. Hurley phrased it, the Fleet Corporation sent its representative to the plant to "assume direct supervision" and to "exercise the powers of the Fleet Corporation" under the contract. Under this new regime, plans and expenditures were checked with due care and a very wholesome reorganization of the enterprise was effected.

Recently the Fleet Corporation discontinued its intimate personal control of affairs upon the theory that it was paying the American International Shipbuilding Corporation a very substantial fee as its agent to manage the enterprise; hence, that such agent should be held responsible, and if it failed in its responsibility a new agent should be appointed.

In so far as this may represent a general administrative policy of the Fleet Corporation, there is no occasion for my commenting upon it; but to the extent to which this policy affects this particular enterprise I cannot help but feel a very considerable concern.

Hog Island is exclusively a Government yard, built with $60,000,000 of Government funds and in the process of spending $250,000,000 more of Government moneys. The agent in this case has not convinced us that it has managed the enterprise with due regard to economy and the public interest. In fact, Mr. Baldwin,[2] senior vice-president of the American International Corporation, in the hearings at my department, stated that since this was a war job, it was "entirely immaterial" whether it cost too much, and that "it is perfectly immaterial what it did cost as long as the result was produced." Similar thoughts were expressed by Mr. Muhlfeld,[3] one of the vice-presidents of the American International Shipbuilding Corporation.

In view of the large Government expenditure at this plant, and in view of our past experience, I am wondering whether the Government can feel safe in leaving, without intimate direct supervision, the management of the enterprise in the hands of an organization which expresses itself so frankly on the subjects of costs and economy.   Sincerely yours,   T. W. Gregory

TLS (WP, DLC).
    [1] About this matter, see EMH to WW, Feb. 16, 1918, n. 1, Vol. 46.
    [2] George Johnson Baldwin, who was actually chairman of the board of directors of the American International Shipbuilding Co.
    [3] George Oscar Muhlfeld.

To Bainbridge Colby

My dear Colby: The White House 16 September, 1918

Thank you warmly for your letter of the 13th.[1] The complexities of the labor situation are multiplying rather than decreasing, and I am heartily glad that your judgment approves of my action in the Bridgeport case.

                    Cordially and sincerely yours,   Woodrow Wilson

TLS (B. Colby Papers, DLC).
    [1] B. Colby to WW, Sept. 13, 1918, Vol. 49.

To Joseph Patrick Tumulty

Dear Tumulty: [The White House] 16 September, 1918

Please make it plain to these gentlemen that I will in no circumstances assent to my History of the American People being used in this way.[1] And please drop a line to Harper & Bros. and ask them if there is anything in this.   The President

TL (WP, DLC).
[1] Baumer Films, Inc., of New York, had proposed to make a motion picture out of Wilson's *History of the American People*. N. J. Baumer to E. E. Prussing, Sept. 10, 1918, TLS (WP, DLC).

To Joseph Patrick Tumulty, with Enclosure

Dear Tumulty: [The White House] 16 September, 1918

I don't like to answer this letter myself and would be very much obliged if you would reply to this effect: that while fully recognizing the right of the people of our own country to know everything there is to know about the airplane or any other programme, I am clearly of the judgment, though I knew nothing of this particular matter, that editorials such as this from the Outlook can serve no useful purpose on the other side of the water, but might on the contrary furnish useful material to the enemy.   The President

TL (WP, DLC).

E N C L O S U R E

From Lawrence Fraser Abbott

My dear Mr. President: New York September 12th, 1918.

The Post Office Department officially informs us that the entire foreign edition of The Outlook of September 4 has been held in the Post Office here as unmailable because of an editorial which that issue contained on the airplane situation. I attach the editorial to this letter.[1] Our foreign edition amounts to about six thousand copies, and is sent very largely by paid-for subscriptions to American soldiers, Y.M.C.A. workers, and other patriotic Americans abroad.

The editorial was based on the published reports of the investigation of the Senate Committee on Military Affairs. If the editorial reveals any military secrets to our enemies we cheerfully accept the ban which has been laid upon us, for we wish to aid in every possible way in the winning of the war by a decisive victory. If the prohibition of censorship is merely based upon the criticism of Government officials, it seems to us both unjust and un-American, for we cannot rid ourselves of the conviction that constructive criticism is one of the means of winning the war.

I venture to lay the facts of this particular act of censorship, as well as our own attitude in the matter, before you, confidently relying both upon your sense of justice and upon the wisdom of your judgment as to what may be done to preserve the freedom of public opinion in our democracy, while at the same time we are gladly sacrificing temporarily certain democratic rights for the sake of a victorious prosecution of the struggle in which every loyal and patriotic American desires to play his part.

I am,   Respectfully yours,   Lawrence F. Abbott

TLS (WP, DLC).

[1] "The Airplane Scandal," *The Outlook*, CXX (Sept. 4, 1918), 10-11. As Abbott indicates in his letter, the editorial was largely a summary of published reports of the investigation of aircraft production carried out by a subcommittee of the Senate Committee on Military Affairs, especially the testimony of Gen. William L. Kenly. The conspicuous exception was a statement from an anonymous "young American aviation officer" who, after being seriously injured in the crash of an American-built airplane, told one of the editors of *The Outlook* that "all the American fliers on this side distrust the structural strength of this particular machine." "To supply our fliers," commented the editorial, "with machines in which they have no faith because they have tried them and discovered their weakness is nothing less than a crime." The editorial continued as follows: "We regret to have to say that the country will hold Secretary Baker personally responsible for the collapse of our aircraft programme. He has resisted the formation of a single department with a Cabinet head. The President ought not to permit this resistance any longer. . . . We wish that the President might . . . create a special department with a man of power and authority at its head. This is the only effective remedy for the War Department's present failure in airplane production."

To Mark Allison Matthews[1]

My dear Dr. Matthews: [The White House] 16 September, 1918

Of course, I appreciate the desire of service expressed in your letter of September 7th,[2] but I must frankly say that I do not think it would be wise to do what you suggest. While I have the highest opinion of the abilities of Dr. van Dyke, I did not know that his appointment was "at large," and I must frankly say that I do not approve of appointments "at large." I was not informed about the appointment of Dr. van Dyke, or I might have given it a modified form.

I know that you will understand that I write in the greatest haste but with sincere appreciation.

Cordially and sincerely yours,   Woodrow Wilson

TLS (Letterpress Books, WP, DLC).

[1] Pastor of the First Presbyterian Church of Seattle.

[2] M. A. Matthews to WW, Sept. 7, 1918, TLS (WP, DLC). Matthews asked that he be appointed a "Chaplain at large" so that he could visit and preach in military and naval camps and stations on the Pacific Coast. He cited Josephus Daniels' appointment of Henry van Dyke as a naval chaplain in December 1917 as a precedent. Although Van Dyke's appointment was irregular in that he was long past the normal age limit for chaplains and did visit many different naval facilities during his active duty, the Editors have found no evidence that he ever held the formal title of "chaplain at large" or anything like it.

From Robert Lansing, with Enclosure

My dear Mr. President: Washington September 16, 1918.

The enclosed has just been received in my confidential cipher from London. The Clemenceau request to which reference is made has not reached the Department.

Faithfully yours,   Robert Lansing

TLS (SDR, RG 59, 763.72/13456, DNA).

E N C L O S U R E

London September 15, 1918

1899 The Secretary of War requests that the following urgent and extremely confidential message be given to the President immediately:

The message from Clemenceau which has been sent you through the Department of State requests sending of five additional _____ [American][1] battalions to Murmansk. The French profess themselves unable to send any further forces but have (?) further[2] secured Foch's indorsement to Clemenceau's request. You will observe however that Foch stipulates that they be sent direct from America and not detached from forces now in France. The military advisers at Versailles considered the subject yesterday and unanimously but informally agreed that in future no further forces of any kind should be sent to Murmansk this year, English and French representatives concurring. Bliss says Foch consents only out of deference for Clemenceau and will not misunderstand your declining. Bliss and I agree that yielding to this request would only open the door to further diversion of American forces as French and British will not send theirs and will join in requests upon us. Could you not decline on ground that all our energy is to be devoted to early and decided success on western front?

Our men are thus [superb] in battle and in both France and England their success is on every tongue. Pershing really won a great fight and his army is impatient to go on. Our losses are about five thousand wounded and sick sent to hospital; but very few dead or mortally hurt. Of those I saw most were slight injuries. Prisoners numbered fifteen thousand when I left. Full details of casualties and captures not available for some days.   Page.

T telegram (SDR, RG 59, 763.72/13456, DNA).
[1] Corrections from NDB to RL, Sept. 15, 1918, T telegram (N. D. Baker Papers, DLC).
[2] Not in the copy in the Baker Papers.

From Robert Lansing

My dear Mr. President: Washington September 16, 1918

As I took the liberty of sending you a copy of the letter I wrote Mr. Sisson on Saturday afternoon, allow me to enclose to you a copy of his reply which you may be interested to note, both as to character and statement.[1]

I have also attached a report from the Swedish Consul General at Moscow[2] which indicates that there may be a larger number of Americans and of Allied officials and citizens there still, than we had previously believed.

Faithfully yours, Robert Lansing

TLS (WP, DLC).
[1] E. G. Sisson to RL, Sept. 14, 1918, TCL (WP, DLC). Sisson suggested that DeWitt C. Poole, Jr., Allen Wardwell, and James W. Andrews place themselves under the protection of the Swedish Consul in Moscow if they were unable to get out of the Bolshevik-controlled area. He added the following comments: "That publication [of the Sisson Documents] will add anything to their present peril is difficult to conceive. You will put them in actual danger of being connected with the exposure (in which they have no part whatever) by pointing them out as your reason for urging an abnormal action. A story that has been in the newspaper offices of the country for 24 hours cannot be suppressed by normal means."
[2] Sheldon Whitehouse to RL, Sept. 14, 1918, TC telegram (WP, DLC), printed in *FR 1918, Russia*, I, 670-71. This telegram was based upon a report to his government of the Swedish Consul General at Moscow, C. A. Asker. Asker estimated that there were eight hundred persons in the English "colony" in Moscow, a thousand in the French, and seven hundred and fifty Italians. Roughly half of these were willing to leave, either immediately or soon. Of the diplomatic, consular, and military representatives of these nations, seven Englishmen, including Lockhart, at least forty-eight Frenchmen, and fourteen Italians were imprisoned by the Bolsheviks for alleged political offenses. At least twenty English and twenty-eight French civilians were being detained as hostages. There were about fifteen Americans in Moscow, of whom ten were about to leave for Petrograd, and all of whom would leave as soon as possible.

From Herbert Clark Hoover

Dear Mr. President: Washington 16 September 1918

If your overcrowded time has permitted you to look over my memorandum upon the Trade Commission's report on the Packers,[1] I would be glad if you could give me your view as to whether it would be desirable to issue it to the press. It not only supports the critical recommendations of the Commission, but approaches the subject from other angles and would possibly stimulate discussion and lend support to such action as you might desire to take.

Faithfully yours, Herbert Hoover

TLS (WP, DLC).
[1] H. C. Hoover to WW, Sept. 11, 1918, Vol. 49.

From Harry Augustus Garfield

Dear Mr. President: Washington, D. C. September 16, 1918

I understand that the mine workers in part of the anthracite field have voted to strike, because of my refusal to consent to increase of wages.

For your information, I send copies of my letter of September 6th, an original of which I sent to the officers of each of the 29 Districts including, of course, the anthracite field, and of a telegram to Mr. Hayes, President of the United Mine Workers,[1] in response to a message requesting an interview with me here today.

I shall say to the representatives when they call that if this strike is with their consent I must refuse to confer with them until the men return to work. If they say it is not with their consent, I shall wire the strikers that their particular case will receive no consideration as long as they are out on strike.

I propose also to request Mr. Bielaski of the Attorney General's office at once to send representatives into the field to report the names of agitators.

Further, I shall respectfully recommend that you send a message to the strikers similar to the Bridgeport message.

The importance of immediate action is obvious. I am, therefore, submitting this recommendation and outlining my proposed course of action, without waiting to confirm the newspaper reports. If I do not hear from you meanwhile, I will call Mr. Tumulty and make sure of your approval, before I take action.[2]

Cordially and faithfully yours,   H. A. Garfield.

TLS (WP, DLC).
[1] H. A. Garfield to F. J. Hayes, Sept. 6, 1918, CCL, and H. A. Garfield to F. J. Hayes, Sept. 13, 1918, TC telegram, both in WP, DLC.
[2] "Please say that the President, of course, approves of this." G. F. Close to [White House Staff], c. Sept. 16, 1918, ALI (WP, DLC).

From Grenville Stanley Macfarland

My dear President Wilson,   Boston September Sixteenth 1918

I am informed that a proposal has been or is about to be submitted to you concerning the appointment of a so-called Federal Administrator or a Federal Commission for the relief of the street railways.

If the plan is, as I believe it to be, one to extend financial relief to the street railways through the mediation of the Federal Government, I think it very ill advised.

I understand, of course, that the bankers and those financially interested in the street railways have made the most of an alleged fear that their bankruptcy may impair the financial ability of the nation to wage the war. But this is the old and regulation talk of the gentlemen who seek to avoid the just penalties of high finance and other forms of financial dissipation from which the street railways are now suffering. I venture the assertion that there is not a single street railway in the country today which is not earning a fair return upon the value of the plant devoted to the public uses. Their difficulties lie wholly in the fact that not only is the stock of nearly all of them largely watered but even their bonds in some cases. For example, Dr. Maltby,[1] who was recently a member of that section of the New York Public Service Commission that had charge of the New York Street Railways in their recent receivership proceedings, told me last week that not only was the common stock of these street railways watered but at least one class of their bonds was watered.

This street railway problem is a local problem. It ought not to be added to the already too great burdens of the National Government. The local communities can and will take care of this problem if the Federal Government indicates that it does not intend to assume the burden. The street railway situation in Boston and Chicago was just as accute [acute] as it is any where else in the country. I aided in solving it in both cases satisfactorily to the companies and I think to the citizens. Of course the companies had to surrender possession of the property for public operation for all time before an increase of fare was granted.

I am now in the process of aiding Mayor Hylan to bring about this form of relief in New York City. The representatives of the surface, elevated and subway companies profess to be ready to surrender their property to the city upon reasonable terms. Of course, the private managers will not give up their profitable relations with the companies so long as there is hope that they may be saved to them by Federal intercession.

If you are inclined to give favorable consideration to granting relief to the street railways I ask for the opportunity to make further representations to you on the subject, for I think I can claim without immodesty to have especial knowledge of the situation.

Yours sincerely,   G. S. Macfarland

TLS (WP, DLC).
   [1] Milo Roy Maltbie.

From William Kent

My dear Mr. President: Washington September 16, 1918.

I hold copies of two letters addressed to Mr. Sims, Chairman of the joint Water Power Committee, by you dated August 22 and

August 26[1] respectively. I quote therefrom: "I am very much in hopes that it will be the judgment of the House to reject the committee amendment and recur to the original bill in the form in which it was delivered to Mr. Pou, of the Rules Committee." This in the letter of August 22d. In the letter of August 26: "it is my earnest hope that the Congress will see fit to pass the bill as it was originally drafted and provisionally agreed upon in our informal conference." I feel sure that it was not your intention to strike out of the bill as it finally passed the House certain amendments that added strength to the features of the bill that go to preserve public rights, and there were a number of such amendments.

I spoke to Secretary Lane over the telephone, and he stated that he was sure that your objection went only to the "net investment" feature as opposed to "actual value," and that you did not have in mind cutting out the additional safeguards that appear in the bill as amended and passed.

In looking over the Committee of Commerce having charge of the bill, I fail to find, in the absence of Senator Lenroot, anyone who seemed especially qualified to look into this matter. I therefore telephoned to Senator Pomerene, in whom I have the greatest confidence and who in turn seems to have confidence in me, and asked him if he would go over the changes in the bill with Mr. Merrill,[2] and be prepared to express his opinion as to the amendments introduced and passed. He has kindly assented, and I would suggest that, with the bill pending tomorrow, it might be well for you to confer with him as to his view on this important matter.

Yours truly,   William Kent

TLS (WP, DLC).
    [1] Printed in Vol. 49 at these dates.
    [2] Oscar Charles Merrill, Chief Engineer of the United States Forest Service.

From William Graves Sharp

My dear Mr. President: Paris, September 16, 1918

While transmitting to-day a despatch on certain phases of conditions existing in France, in answer to the Department's instructions, I am enclosing a copy with the thought that possibly you might also be interested in perusing it, in whole or in part, despite its length.[1] Some of the observations therein made will not be modified by subsequent events—particularly those based on the fundamental characteristics of the French people; others will probably need a re-casting as the war progresses.

It is my desire, as it is my duty, to soon write you of a situation which the recent successes of the Allied troops has projected for consideration, as I believe, ahead of its time. Even in a confidential despatch to the Department I have not thought best to discuss it. The situation, however, is not one involving France alone, but rather pertains to what I believe is the insensibly changing attitude of all the European Allies toward the original purposes of the war. I have briefly hinted at such a possibility in this despatch.

May I take this opportunity to tell you how pleased I am to know of your selection of Mr. Davis for the London post. He was a former colleague of mine in Congress for several years, and from my knowledge of his attainments I am sure no better choice could have been made.

I am, dear Mr. President,

Very sincerely yours,   Wm. G. Sharp.

TLS (WP, DLC).
    ¹ W. G. Sharp to RL, Sept. 14, 1918, TC telegram (WP, DLC). Sharp devoted the first twelve of the thirty-four pages of this dispatch to a discussion of what he considered the significant aspects of the French national character. Then he turned to specific questions asked by the State Department. Asked to describe the "Imperialist Forces" in France, that is, individuals or groups who favored the continuation of unrestricted competition among nations, the aggrandizement of France without regard to the welfare of other countries, and opposed all endeavors to create a supranational authority such as a league of nations, Sharp declared that, at the moment, there was "no such concrete force" in France. However, such a movement might appear as a result of "the cupidity" excited by a desire for heavy indemnities, which was growing as the prospect of a crushing victory over Germany came nearer realization. Sharp considered the widespread demand for the return of Alsace-Lorraine to France to be reasonable. He felt that a less desirable and imperialistic kind of territorial aggrandizement might take the form of demands that France's eastern boundary should be the Rhine River and/or that former German colonies should come under French control.
    Sharp was somewhat ambiguous in his analysis of the "forces of Liberalism" in France, that is "nationalists" who insisted that every nation had a "right to be treated as an end in itself" and who therefore hoped to see the establishment of a "super-national authority as justiciar between peoples." Sharp believed that Wilson's Fourteen Points address was widely accepted in France as the program of liberalism and quoted Foreign Minister Stéphen Pichon who had said that France would follow Wilson in any course which he might advocate. On the other hand, Sharp noted that some members of the government, notably Clemenceau, were skeptical of the practicability of a league of nations, even though they favored such an organization in theory. Moreover, Sharp warned that there was widespread sentiment for severely restricting Germany's freedom of trade following the war.
    Sharp declared that the "Social-Revolutionary Forces"—those frank internationalists who hoped for a class war in every nation and for rule of the world by the international proletariat—were more negligible in influence in France then than at any time since the beginning of the war. He attributed this to the example of the weak, yet despotic, Soviet regime in Russia; to Clemenceau's firm hand in removing all socialist influence from the French government; and, above all, to the fact that the Allies now seemed clearly on the way to a thorough defeat of Germany.
    Under the heading of "Suggestions for Strengthening the Forces of Liberalism," Sharp only reemphasized his belief that France had "a child-like confidence in the wisdom and foresight of President Wilson to so shape 'after-the-war' conditions as to bring to her [France] an abiding peace and security."
    In the final section of his dispatch, Sharp briefly characterized some of the current leaders of France. Clemenceau, he believed, was unquestionably the dominant figure in the government. Vigorous, forceful, cynical, skeptical of high ideals as applied to European politics, and a man of intense prejudices, Clemenceau, Sharp declared, would finally be "ranged on the side of the forces of Liberalism." He dismissed most of the socialist leaders rather contemptuously, although he did profess respect for the character and ability of Albert Thomas. He believed that President Poincaré was seriously under-

estimated: although lacking in charisma and personal popularity, he had been an important steadying force in the French government.

From the Diary of Colonel House

September 16, 1918.

The Austrian proposal has been the sensation of the day. Everyone is talking of it. Late in the afternoon Gordon told me that the President had sent his sixty-eight word reply. He did this, so Gordon says, largely at the suggestion of Tumulty who thought that haste should be used in order that a political advantage might be reaped. It was understood that Lodge and some of the republicans intended making speeches in the Senate tomorrow, and this was to anticipate them. Lansing told Gordon that they had in mind also forestalling the British and French. I was inexpressably shocked to think that the President would act thus hastily for two such unworthy reasons. It places him on a level with Lloyd George and his kind.

We have been endeavoring to bring about political unity among the Allies in order not to be wholly at the mercy of Germany. The President and Lansing both seem determined that it shall be known to the world that this country is acting independently of our allies. They blazon the fact to the entire world. This is well enough if it is our purpose to stand aloof from world politics, but in view of the fact that I have prepared, and the President has accepted, a covenant for a league of nations, the essence of which is that there shall be close political and economic unity throughout the world, their position is wholly wrong.

In my opinion, the President should not have answered this Austrian peace proposal for at least two weeks. He should have had the entire world on tip-toe in expectation of his reply. He should have then declined it in a way which would have given the Central Empires the reasons why we cannot make peace with their present rulers. The same people are in control now who made the Brest-litvosk and Roumanian and Ukrainian Treaties. They, and their kind, sank the Lusitania, committed all the atrocities on land and sea, ravished Belgium and brought the moral standard of the world to what it is.

He should also have said that we did not desire to go into a closed session to discuss peace terms, that they did not seem to know the world had changed and the fundamentals of peace must be known to the world, after which the details could be worked out in more intimate council. If Lloyd George had the vision and ability he could use this opportunity and take the liberal leadership away from the President.

Speaking of team-work and "common counsel," while Lansing was in one room preparing the President's answer for the press, Billy Phillips was in another assuring Barkley,[1] the British Chargé, that no immediate action was contemplated. Barkley sent this information to his Government, but almost simultaneously his Government must have read the President's answer to Austria.

T MS (E. M. House Papers, CtY).
    [1] That is, Colville Barclay.

From Samuel Lavit[1]

Bridgeport, Conn., Sept. 17, 1918.

Men voted to return to work this morning and abide by your orders. Manufacturers refuse to reinstate former employees. Immediate action on your part will prevent another strike this afternoon.   Samuel Lavit.

T telegram (WP, DLC).
    [1] Enclosed in WBW to JPT, Sept. 17, 1918, TLS (WP, DLC). In this same letter, Secretary Wilson also enclosed a draft of the telegram printed as the following document. Woodrow Wilson used W. B. Wilson's draft verbatim.

To the Remington Arms Company

[The White House] September 17, 1918

My attention has been called to the fact that several thousand machinists and others employed in connection with war industries in Bridgeport, Connecticut, engaged in a strike to obtain further concessions because they were not satisfied with the decision rendered by the umpire appointed under the authority conferred upon the National War Labor Board. On the 13th instant, I communicated with the workmen engaged in the strike, demanding that they accept the decision of the arbitrator and return to work, and stated the penalties which would be imposed if they refused to do so.[1] The men at a meeting voted to return to work this morning, but I am informed by their representative that the manufacturers refuse to reinstate their former employees. In view of the fact that the workmen have so promptly complied with my directions, I must insist upon the reinstatement of all these men.[2]

Woodrow Wilson

T telegram (Letterpress Books, WP, DLC).
    [1] WW to Members of District Lodge No. 55 and Other Striking Workers, Sept. 13, 1918, Vol. 49.
    [2] Apparently, all of the discharged workers were reinstated either on September 17

or shortly thereafter. Indeed, the companies involved issued statements on that day in which they denied that they had refused to reemploy the men. *New York Times*, Sept. 18, 1918.

Three Letters to Robert Lansing

CONFIDENTIAL

My dear Mr. Secretary: The White House 17 September, 1918.

It occurs to me to request you to make pointed inquiry of the British, French, and Italian governments as to what the so-called Allied Military Council at Vladivostok is, of whom it is composed, and by whose authority it was formed and is undertaking to act, intimating at the same time that we recognize the authority of no such body and would be very glad to have the situation at Vladivostok cleared of unnecessary complications.

                Cordially and faithfully yours,   Woodrow Wilson

TLS (SDR, RG 59, 861.00/2762½, DNA).

My dear Mr. Secretary: The White House 17 September, 1918

Do you not think it would be wise to ask Japan in some courteous but nevertheless plain way, what she is now proposing to do with the large army which she has sent to Siberia? Our advices are, as I understand it, that the railroad is open and under control of our friends from Vladivostok all the way to Samara, and that the hostile forces which were said to be in the intervening regions are dispersed or cowed and under control. In such circumstances I can see no necessity for a large Japanese force in Siberia, and think the purpose of its continuance there needs to be defined.

You will observe that some influence is at work to pull absolutely away from the plan which we proposed and to which the other governments assented, and proceed to do what we have said we would not do, namely form a new Eastern front. It may be that it will be necessary to leave some portion of the Czecho-Slovak troops in Western Siberia, in the neighborhood of the Urals, to prevent the Germans taking agricultural and other supplies which might be accessible there, but by the time the winter closes the country, it is my clear judgment that we should insist that the Czecho-Slovaks be brought out eastward to Vladivostok and conveyed to the Western front in Europe, if necessary, according to the original agreement made with them. I am clear that we should insist upon taking no part in attempting to form a new Eastern front and that any attempt to use the Czecho-Slovaks in conjunction with what is being attempted at Archangel would also be walking into the same trap.

Am I not right in my recollection that we have already prepared the Japanese and other governments for our insistence upon this view of the case?

Cordially and sincerely yours,   Woodrow Wilson

TLS (SDR, RG 59, 861.00/3009, DNA).

My dear Mr. Secretary: The White House 17 September, 1918

I am sorry to say I do not share your judgment about Professor Charles McCarthy,[1] and I think if you were to consult with Herbert Hoover you would find that he was delighted to end his association with McCarthy in the Food Administration. I have read this memorandum on Irish conditions[2] and am frank to say that I do not see any one of his suggestions that could be acted on with advantage. I am afraid that Mr. McCarthy is taking a too limited view of the whole subject.

Cordially and faithfully yours,   Woodrow Wilson

TLS (SDR, RG 59, 841D.00/16½, DNA).
 [1] See RL to WW, Sept. 13, 1918 (second letter of that date), Vol. 49.
 [2] It is printed as an Enclosure with the letter cited above.

To Bernard Mannes Baruch

My dear Baruch: The White House 17 September, 1918

You are hereby authorized to draw on the fund for National Security and Defence which Congress has placed at my disposal, in the sum of $1,500,000. for the purpose of sending to the Czecho-Slovaks the supplies mentioned in your letter of September 16th.[1]

I approve of the method of action suggested by you in that letter, for I am quite clear that the English should be asked to make their contribution to this end exactly as we are making ours, and I am happy to learn that they are in a position to do so.

I was very glad to learn from General March last evening that the winter overcoats and shoes which are so much needed can be supplied from stocks existing in Vladivostok itself.

I shall be ready to supply Professor Masaryk with the means which it may be necessary for him to use in getting together an organization of engineers to inspect supplies here.

Cordially and sincerely yours,   Woodrow Wilson

TLS (B. M. Baruch Papers, NjP).
 [1] B. M. Baruch to WW, Sept. 16, 1918, TLS (WP, DLC).

Three Letters to Scott Ferris

My dear Ferris: [The White House] 17 September, 1918

Thank you very much for your letter of the 14th explaining the vote on the Water Power bill. I am very glad to get it, and no apologies were needed for sending it to me.

Cordially and sincerely yours,   Woodrow Wilson

My dear Ferris: [The White House] 17 September, 1918

I am sincerely obliged to you for having let me see the enclosed,[1] which I return. We must keep on this job until it is finished.

Cordially and sincerely yours,   Woodrow Wilson

[1] See S. Ferris to WW, Sept. 14, 1918, n. 1.

My dear Ferris: [The White House] 17 September, 1918

The enclosed letter explains itself.[1] Will you not tell me what your own attitude is towards the legislation referred to? If it is all right, I shall be very glad to express my approval of it in any way that will be serviceable.

Cordially and sincerely yours,   Woodrow Wilson

TLS (Letterpress Books, WP, DLC).
[1] W. Kent to WW, Sept. 16, 1918.

To James Wilson Howe

My dear Wilson: [The White House] 17 September, 1918.

Of course I sympathize with the feelings expressed in your letter of September 11th,[1] but frankly I think that you are hardly justified in your impatience and uneasiness. I find that the thing that is taking the most moral courage on the part of most of our fellow-citizens is to remain at their ordinary duties and keep the whole civil life of the country on as normal and effective a basis as possible. I think it is a mistake for all of us to crowd into "war work" of one sort or another, and I beg most affectionately that you will look at the whole matter from that point of view.

In haste,   Affectionately yours,   Woodrow Wilson

TLS (Letterpress Books, WP, DLC).
[1] It is missing.

From Albert Sidney Burleson

My dear Mr. President: Washington September 17, 1918.

Enclosed herewith please find letter from Mr. Marbury.[1] As you know, he is the ablest lawyer in Maryland and has proven himself an unselfish and unyielding supporter of your policies. This letter has made a profound impression on me. Day by day from newspaper comments and interviews had with Members of Congress and other prominent men throughout the country, evidence of discontent and dissatisfaction arising out of this threat of further "dry" legislation as is embodied in the Agricultural Bill[2] is forced upon me.

A few weeks ago the outlook for success of our political party was quite favorable, every indication pointing to a victory for the Administration at the November election, but now, because of this vexatious prohibition issue, many of those who were formerly most optimistic have changed their attitude to one of deep pessimism. Whereas, before the offering of the Randall Amendment and the compromise resulting therefrom, every indication in Ohio, Rhode Island, Massachusetts, Delaware and New York gave assurance of increased Democratic strength, with a possibility of electing three Democratic Senators and a chance for the Governorship in New York, now the result is involved in gravest doubt. This change, beyond doubt, is largely chargeable to this threat of further dry legislation.

A glance at the editorial expressions of the influential newspapers, such as the Springfield Republican, the World, the Evening Post, the Dallas News, will convince anyone that there is a fixed belief in the minds of thoughtful people that the proposed legislation in fact is wholly unnecessary either for the conservation of food, coal, transportation capacity or any other real war purpose. Every man whose opinion is worthy of consideration knows that full authority to deal with this problem has heretofore been vested in you as President. You not only have the power under the law to reduce the alcoholic content of wine and beer, to limit the hours during the day within which same can be sold, but you can if deemed necessary make any City or Section of our Country bone-dry. You have authority to control the amount of grain and coal to be used for brewing purposes, limit the transportation facilities to be used in moving the product or material used in its manufacture, or if deemed wise prohibit its manufacture and sale altogether.

This being true, and it is known of all men that it is true, the inquiry naturally arises, Why should there be additional legislation? Any attempt at such action is not only unnecessary but is hypocritical and insincere,—an effort under the guise of an exercise of war power by legislation to bring about statutory prohibition which if dealt with on the basis of honesty would be beyond Constitutional authority. The action of the Federal Food Board in recommending reduction of the alcoholic content of beer, which you approved, the authority given you by law to deal with the amount of coal and transportation facilities to be used in the manufacture thereof, the Act of Congress giving you authority to establish and maintain dry zones, the action taken by you on September 7 in prohibiting the making of beer after December 1st has so strengthened your position that you are absolutely free to deal with this proposed legislation when it reaches you as it deserves.

I feel that I would be derelict in my duty to you if I did not once more urge that this insincere measure be vetoed. No one could argue that such action on your part was influenced in the slightest by a regard for the "liberal element." You have acted promptly to reduce the amount of alcohol in beer. You have prohibited its making after December first. You refused to throw your influence against the submission of the Constitutional Amendment when one word from you would have killed it. How could any one in the face of these incontestable facts argue against the virtue and force of such veto.

The whole country has accepted the action you have heretofore taken in this matter in perfect good faith as the part of an orderly effort to conserve food and grain in furtherance of the prosecution of the war. The bases of these orders were necessity and emergency. The people believe it was a question between bread and beer and that you promptly decided in favor of bread.

But, my dear Mr. President, no such issue is presented in the proposed Amendment. It is not a food conservation measure; it will not add to our man power, it will not increase our industrial efficiency. It is a prohibition measure pure and simple, forced upon the people by a timid Congress which has not the courage to meet the fanatical mob spirit behind it, notwithstanding the fact that the *Congress* has set in motion by its own act a Constitutional Amendment for the people themselves to pass on. A strong, vigorous veto disapproving this measure will do more to strengthen the morale of the people and call them back to sanity and tolerance than anything else you could do at this time. I am absolutely sure that the country will applaud your act in doing so.

Just one more word. The people are beginning to feel the burden of the tremendous taxes imposed as a result of the war. Within a few short weeks these taxes are to be further increased. I feel sure they will not complain, but if at the same time an additional burden is forced upon the tax payer in all the great municipalities of our

Country, brought about by the loss of excise taxes now being gathered from these liquor interests, especially when it is known that it was the result of unnecessary and unjustified action on the part of the Congress, I fear they will bitterly resent the fact that you did not protect them against it. My excuse for this long letter which I have written in great haste is my earnest desire that a mistake be not made.

It costs the govt $10 to overcome the resulting evils for every dollar received in liquor revenue. You now have full control of this situation. Why permit your hands to be tied so that you can not use *your own judgment* as to what is best.

I sincerely hope you may see the dangers of this situation as I see it. There is dynamite in it.

Faithfully yours,   A. S. Burleson

TLS (WP, DLC).
    [1] William Luke Marbury to ASB, Sept. 14, 1918, TLS (WP, DLC). Burleson's letter to Wilson is an expanded paraphrase of Marbury's letter.
    [2] About this matter, see JPT to WW, Sept. 7, 1918, Vol. 49. The Randall amendment, mentioned below, was an earlier version of the amendment described in n. 1 thereto.

From Key Pittman

My dear Mr. President: [Washington] September 17, 1918.

I consider this matter which I am about to write to you of such immediate importance that I would call upon you if it were not for the fact that I believe that I can explain the matter in this letter and thus avoid taking up any of your time.

A number of the Democratic Senators last night met with Mrs. Catt and other leaders of the National American Woman Suffrage Association. They canvassed the situation thoroughly. We are convinced that the action of Senator Benet[1] when the resolution comes up for a vote will determine its passage or defeat. Senator Benet will avoid voting, if possible. He would prefer that he be not put to the test. He realizes that in voting for the amendment he would offend his colleague Senator Smith and many other leading Democrats from South Carolina. On the other hand, he realizes that he owes you the highest allegiance, and will, I believe, if he considers it a matter of sufficient import to you, be present and vote for the amendment. If he votes for the amendment we believe that the new Senator from Kentucky, Mr. Martin, will follow suit. In that event, Senator Shields of Tennessee will undoubtedly also vote for the amendment. If Benet votes against it or does not vote Senator Martin of Kentucky will have reason to believe that the resolution will fail and will either not vote or vote against it.

The Governor or [of] Kentucky,[2] who appointed Mr. Martin, will be committed by Senator Martin's vote. From the information I gathered while in Kentucky, I believe that he would prefer that he be not committed until after the election for obvious political reasons. On the other hand, if the matter is forced to a vote I believe that he would favor Senator Martin of Kentucky voting for the resolution by reason of the attitude of the Courier Journal and other large Democratic papers in Kentucky.

By reason of this situation and the attitude of the Republican party in the Senate a number of us have determined to attempt to force the resolution to a vote on tomorrow week. Notice to this effect will probably be given this morning. The minute the notice is given those opposed to you and opposed to suffrage will bring every pressure to bear on Senator Benet to either commit him against suffrage or to induce him to be absent.

On the roll call Senator Benet votes third. If he votes for suffrage then we have no doubt of obtaining the other two doubtful votes and very probably others. It is asking a great deal of you, but all of us hope that you can find time to take this matter up with Senator Benet while he is in his present frame of mind. We are all so anxious to win this big fight that we do hope that you will understand and appreciate what would appear to be over-insistence.

Should you desire further information from me with regard to any phase of this matter I will respond in person or by letter immediately.   Very sincerely yours,   Key Pittman

TLS (WP, DLC).
[1] Christie Benet, Democratic senator from South Carolina, who had been appointed on July 6, 1918, to fill the vacancy created by the death of Senator Tillman.
[2] That is, Augustus O. Stanley.

From Robert Lansing

Mr. dear Mr. President: [Washington] September 17, 1918.

In my letter to you of September 9th,[1] I brought to your attention certain problems in regard to the present situation in Russia. These problems seemed to fall into three separate parts. The last of these concerns providing immediately for winter supplies for the civilian population of the Archangel district and I asked authority to state to the British Government that we would do our share and suggested that it might be met properly by the setting aside of five million dollars from your fund for the National Security and Defense.

Time presses, for the whole of the winter supplies so urgently needed, must be delivered at Archangel before that port is closed by ice. Shipments must start before October first. Mr. Francis is quite clear that the security of the military assistance offered at Archangel, and the support of the civilian population in that region, will depend upon whether the impending food shortage, approaching famine conditions, will be met by the Allies and ourselves.

The matter seems to me quite separate from any mere general plans to aid Russia and requires a decision before physical conditions preclude the possibility of any favorable action which might be planned. Perhaps you will, therefore, see your way clear to instructing me how I may answer the British proposal.

Faithfully yours,   Robert Lansing

CCL (SDR, RG 59, 861.48/680e, DNA).
  [1] RL to WW, Sept. 9, 1918, Vol. 49.

From Valentine Everit Macy

My dear Mr. President: Washington, D. C. Sept. 17, 1918.

At my request under date of August 20th, you were so kind as to confer with me and my associates on this Board, on Tuesday, August 27th, in reference to the need of a better co-ordination of the Labor Adjustment work of the Government.[1]

At your request Secretary Wilson called representatives of the different labor adjustment boards together in conference on September 12th. As this conference led to no definite decisions, a second conference will be held at the call of Secretary Wilson, but no date for this conference has as yet been fixed.

Pending these conferences we have withheld the decision in reference to wages and working conditions in Pacific Coast shipyards, which was already overdue. Owing to the continuing delay, we feel that either we should proceed at once with the issue of this decision or a public statement should be made, preferably by you, that pending wage adjustments will be held up until a better co-ordination of the wage adjusting agencies of the Government can be brought about.

As evidence of the growing impatience over the withholding of our decision, we enclose copies of telegrams typical of several that have come to our attention during the last few days.[2]

We shall appreciate your advice as to the course which you consider wise under all the circumstances.

Respectfully,   V. Everit Macy.

TLS (WP, DLC).
  [1] See V. E. Macy to WW, Aug. 20, 1918, n. 1, Vol. 49.
  [2] C. H. Hamilton to V. E. Macy, Sept. 16-17, 1918, and "Blain" to H. R. Seager, Sept. 14, 1918, both TC telegrams (WP, DLC).

From Benedict Crowell, with Enclosure

My dear Mr. President: Washington. September 17, 1918

I enclose herewith a copy of a cablegram just received from General Bliss, concerning sending extra American troops to Archangel. The War Department is in agreement with the opinion of the military representatives, as expressed in the last sentence of the cablegram.   Very truly yours,   Benedict Crowell

TLS (WP, DLC).

E N C L O S U R E

Versailles. September 15th [1918].

Number 219 Secret. For the Secretary of War and the Chief of Staff. Please inform the President that the Secretary of War showed me last night just at moment of his departure for London a note from Mr. Clemenceau to Mr. Pichon intended to be sent by the latter to the President asking for reenforcements of 5 American battalions to be sent to Archangel, Russia. The Secretary of War requests the President to defer action on this request until he hears from him at London. For your information I add that British Government several days ago requested military representatives to consider question of sending reenforcements to Archangel. After full and careful consideration the military representatives at meeting yesterday unanimously agreed that their professional judgement was opposed to sending more reenforcements to north Russia this year and they telegraphed this opinion last night to British Government.   Bliss.

CC telegram (WP, DLC).

From Benedict Crowell, with Enclosure

Dear Mr. President: Washington. September 17, 1918.

I am enclosing herewith copy of General Bliss' letter of August twenty-second which was received several days ago in the absence of Secretary Baker. You may be interested in reading it.

Sincerely yours,   Benedict Crowell

TLS (WP, DLC).

ENCLOSURE

Tasker Howard Bliss to Newton Diehl Baker

My dear Mr. Secretary: Versailles. August 22, 1918.

I received in due time your No. 5, dated in Washington July 28th,[1] which came by courier via Brest and Tours.

1. At first I was rather worried—and I suppose the misunderstanding is entirely my fault—by what you expected of me in the matter of ascertaining the assistance that the British would give us in cargo-tonnage for carrying out the 80-division Program, and the assistance from the British and French in the matter of artillery. As you know, the first official knowledge that I had of the original 100-division Program was in remarks made by M. Tardieu at the last meeting of the Supreme War Council, and which I have already reported. Mr. Lloyd-George seemed quite vexed at the idea, which he assumed, that anyone except the British were figuring on the matter of British tonnage. He cut the whole matter short very bluntly by saying that I could find out from the United States Government how much tonnage was needed for the 100-division Program, how much the United States could furnish, and that then the British Government would take up the question of whether it could supply the deficiency. There was no vote taken but the British Secretary[2] (who kept the Minutes) recorded that as the action of the Council.

2. When the 100-division Program went by the board, I was told that Washington was figuring on an 80-division Program, and I assumed that part of that figuring would be the determination through the usual expert agencies of how the necessary tonnage would be obtained. However, the British have got the figures and if there is any hope of their giving us the necessary assistance they are doubtless working at it with their experts and ours in London. The extract from the confidential cablegram of Mr. Lloyd-George to M. Clemenceau dated August 2, quoted to me in War Department No. 81, of August 19,[3] would seem to indicate that the British had already settled the matter adversely.

3. The British seem to take it very much to heart that we are not going to feed our man-power into their organizations in order to enable them to maintain their previous number of divisions; also, that we have not committed ourselves as a matter of policy to maintaining American divisions on the British Front. It is hard to believe that England, who is so vitally interested in the issue of the war,

[1] It is missing in all collections.
[2] That is, Lt. Col. Sir Maurice P. A. Hankey.
[3] P. C. March to T. H. Bliss, Aug. 19, 1918, Vol. 49.

would allow this to stand in the way of her furnishing tonnage assistance provided she could possibly furnish it.

4. In the matter of artillery, Mr. Stettinius' Commission immediately set some eight or ten experts to work in collaboration with General Wheeler[4] (Chief Ordnance Officer in France) and his Staff. They submitted to the French and British a complete statement of our needs and when I last saw him he hoped for an official reply to them, and a favorable one, by about last Tuesday. He also expected about the same time a reply from the British.

5. As I now understand the situation, we want to carry out at least the 80-division Program; we cannot do it unless we get assistance from the British in cargo-tonnage, varying in amount from a little over 1,200,000 tons in August to a little over 200,000 tons in February next, after which we expect to be able to take care of ourselves by our own shipping-construction program; and that the British have intimated that they can give us no further cargo-tonnage assistance and that they may be obliged to cut down the troop tonnage which they have given us. If that should prove to be the case, then we cannot carry out the 80-division Program by the approximate date desired. Nevertheless, despatches purporting to be dated in Washington and published in English and French newspapers here, state that the authorities in Washington are officially declaring that the 80-division Program will be carried out by the beginning of next summer and that we will then have enough troops here to finish the war on this front. If these despatches are not authentic, they ought to be censored, either in the United States or here, because it seems to me that they will make more difficult the getting of tonnage assistance if we need any, and my official telegrams from Washington are clearly to the effect that we do need it.

6. If Marshal Foch and his subordinates believe that the 80-division Program, carried out by the beginning of next summer, will give reasonable hope of ending the war on this front next year; and if, to carry out the 80-division Program we must borrow tonnage from our Allies, I am inclined to think that the only way that we can get it is to *force* it from them in some such way as suggested in Paragraph 3 *et seq*, of my No. 180.[5] I do not think that I exaggerate when I say that the thing you now have to fear is that the Germans may at any moment make some proposition (far less than what we would accept if we had our own way about it) that will cause the common people over here to force their Governments

[4] That is, Brig. Gen. Charles Brewster Wheeler.
[5] See T. H. Bliss to NDB, Aug. 14, 1918, Vol. 49.

into a consideration of it, or to overturn one or more of these Governments and put in another that will consider it. If such a proposition should be made and if any of the peoples here should be disposed to consider it favorably in order to put an end to their long-continued sacrifices, they would be very much helped in withstanding German allurements by the knowledge that a definitely and openly expressed hope was being held out to them, that if they endure these sacrifices a few months longer and even increase them if necessary, the war will end the way they want it and they can then demand their own terms.

7. You say that "the Port situation seems more or less insoluble" from your end of the line. I saw Mr. Day[6] a short time ago, after he had completed an inspection of at least part of the improved port facilities and he said that he was prepared to entirely change his view from the one entertained by him before he left the United States. Many difficulties exist and perhaps will continue to exist; but the French now feel so utterly dependent upon the United States that I am convinced that if we only have the necessary tonnage we will be able to carry out our problem so far as receipt of troops and stores at this end of the line is concerned. I have noticed heretofore that whenever an all-impelling emergency arises, facilities are made available, the very existence of which up to that moment was denied. There was a very illuminating discussion which threw light on this subject at the meeting of the Supreme War Council in London last March. It was just a week before the German drive began on March 21; it was known to be coming and everyone was in a state of grave anxiety as to the outcome. The British had become very much alarmed over the railroad situation in France and were tentatively discussing a proposition to suspend for a time all movements of American troops to France, pending the arrival of large numbers of railway cars and locomotives. M. Clemenceau made a very impassioned speech and said that in view of the impending emergency he would, if necessary, sign an agreement then and there to handle all American troops and supplies, so far as getting them from the sea coast to the front was concerned, without suspending the movement of a single man but rather increasing that movement. Of course he spoke somewhat hastily and rashly, but what he meant was that when an emergency was on them the people would stand a great deal more of inconvenience and hardship than they were then enduring.

8. I note what you say about the consultation and agitation at home over the two Russian expeditions. It is a pity that we cannot

[6] Charles Day, mechanical engineer of Philadelphia, then in France on a special mission for the Secretary of War.

get more exact information as to what is really happening in Russia. As to the size of the expedition via Vladivostok, the Allies here at Versailles have little hesitation in expressing their opinion that now that they are committed to the expedition it must be carried through. Just now my special interest is in learning as soon as we can whether the Allied movements in Russia will help the Germans in getting any man-power out of that country or out of its seceded territories. The British estimate that by March 1, Germany will have added 400,000 Russians to her military forces. They made that estimate some time before the Allies began their present movements of military intervention. In the estimate of relative strengths of the Allies and the Germans at the beginning of next summer, which I sent home some time ago,[7] I did not give consideration to this British estimate of Russians available for the German army. If their estimate should prove true, it is a very serious thing at a time when we are counting so much on deterioration in German strength.

9. The possibilities of the situation to which we have committed ourselves is shown by a note dated August 18, from the French General Staff to the French Section at Versailles, of which they furnished me a copy. Referring to the operations being conducted by the English General Poole from Archangel toward Vologda it speaks of General Poole's encountering positions which he could not attack with good chances of success on account of the weakness of his force. The note added "L'envoi de renforts est donc urgent." In none of the discussions at Versailles did we contemplate General Poole going further than he could go with the force at his disposition. His main object was to hold the port of Murmansk and later, if necessary, the port of Archangel. His own declaration was that if he moved south with a small force, a part only of that which has already been given him, he would rally to him en route to Vologda at least 100,000 friendly Russians. If the Russians prove friendly and rally to him, well and good; if they do not, and if they prove hostile, he will, by continuing his advance, put himself in the attitude of war with Russia. That is distinctly the attitude, so far as I can gather here, which our Allies expect to take if it should prove necessary to accomplish their purpose. That has not been my idea, but I suppose that it has all been discounted in the United States. If the Japanese and other Allies strengthen the Czecho-Slovaks, I cannot see that it can have any other object than to overturn the present so-called Government in Russia; because they cannot proceed with the consent of that Government to the West and establish

[7] See T. H. Bliss to NDB and P. C. March, Aug. 14, 1918; and T. H. Bliss to NDB, Aug. 7, 1918, printed as an Enclosure with NDB to WW, Aug. 23, 1918; both in Vol. 49.

a front against the Germans. If that Government should be over-turned, it looks to me as though a military dictatorship would have to be established for the remainder of the war.

10. You say that if I should have any opportunity to learn the estimate placed by the people in France on the de Haviland-4 aero-planes shipped from America, you would be glad to have it. I con-ferred with my colleague, General Belin, and learned from him that the French Aviation Technical Section of the War Ministry here has stated that it is not possible at present to report upon the qual-ities of the American-built de Haviland-4, as the trials of the ma-chine assigned to that section for test are still in progress. It stated, however, that the first flights of that machine gave results of "little brilliancy," clearly inferior, in particular, to those of the Breguet machine fitted with the Liberty motor. Other flights are to be held with a different type of propeller, a modification in the weights carried, and minute adjustment of the machine. On completion of these trials a report will be submitted by the French Technical Section as to the value of the machine, and this report will be transmitted to me by the French Military Representative General Belin. The latter informs me that the de Haviland squadrons sent to the front are reported as satisfactory by their pilots.

11. This information, incomplete as it is, is about what might have been expected. A Technical Section, making competitive tests and investigations, "fly-specks" everything. If one machine, in some one particular, is not so good as another, or as the others, it is "damned with faint praise." The same machine when it gets into the hands of the aviators at the front, who are not making com-petitive tests of it with others but who consider it on its own merits, are apt to be quite satisfied with it. I think that this gives us a good "pointer" in making contracts for war material. There are plenty of military weapons, of a particular type, each of which is quite good enough for our service, although one of them, perhaps, is better than any of the others. If our facilities for producing that one best type are sufficiently ample to give us all that we want of it in the time desired, we can accept that type and reject the others. But if, as is almost always the case in an emergency such as this war has been for us, we have to call on the manufacturers of different types in order to produce a sufficient number of the machines, I do not think that we ought to waste time in getting them merely because they are not all in every respect up to the same plane of excellence.

12. I have an officer specially assigned to pursue this subject and as soon as I get the report of the French Technical Section I shall forward it, or, if it should seem desirable, cable an abstract of it.

13. As I told you in my last letter[8] that I intended to do, I went on August 11th to Moulliens-au-Bois, the Headquarters of our 33d Division (Infantry only), commanded by General George Bell. There I met General Pershing who arrived an hour later. We talked about the next meeting of the Supreme War Council which I then expected to be held any day, and subjects that we thought would come up for discussion. He told me that he thought the English would make a strong fight for the retention of a certain part of the American Army on their front. The next morning the English King arrived and he almost immediately asked General Pershing and myself into a private room where he stated at considerable length, but not very clearly, his views about the situation. He referred once or twice to what Mr. Lloyd-George had said to him and I think that he was repeating the former's views. He said that if the English could not get help from us they would have to reduce the number of their divisions to 35 or else retain the present number at very greatly reduced strength, which all their military men thought would be very unwise. He seemed to be perturbed at the idea of the creation of an independent American Army which might remove American troops from the British Front. General Pershing stated in very general terms the object that he had in view, but carefully avoided saying anything that would commit him to a course which seemed to be in the King's mind. He thanked the King most cordially for all of the assistance that we had obtained from the British and expressed the determination of the Americans to cooperate with everybody on this front in whatever way the military men should agree was the best to end the war quickly and successfully. The King is rather blunt in his manner of speaking and General Pershing handled exceedingly well a subject which might have proved delicate.

14. The night that we stayed at Moulliens-au-Bois, it was heavily bombed by German aeroplanes. I am inclined to think that their spy-service may have given them a "tip" as to the intended visit of the King, and that they thought perhaps he was then there. Immediately after lunch on the 12th, I went to the front to see the Illinois regiment, commanded by Colonel Sanborn,[9] which was then in the attack being made by General Rawlinson's IVth British Army. I found Col. Sanborn's headquarters in a dugout on the north bank of the Somme, on the edge of the village of Chipilly. It had been

[8] T. H. Bliss to NDB, Aug. 7, 1918, printed as an Enclosure with NDB to WW, Aug. 23, 1918, Vol. 49.
[9] Col. Joseph Brown Sanborn, commander of the 131st Infantry Regiment, formerly the First Illinois Infantry Regiment.

used in the attack along the north bank and evidently had had a hard time of it, but had done exceedingly well, as for that matter all our troops have. The Somme here winds like a serpent. Corresponding to each inward fold a sharp limestone crest runs down to the marshy borders of the river. Between these crests are deep ravines pitted with excavations in the chalk and spotted here and there with a few trees or clumps of brush. Colonel Sanborn said, in a slight criticism of what they had had to do, that they had had to move from one of these crests to another without sufficient reconnaisance. When they attacked one they did not know what was behind it. When they crossed each crest they found in front of them a deep pocket and the forward slope of another crest, with nests of German machine guns scattered everywhere. In fact, the successive positions looked to me as though they were almost impossible to take except as they were flanked by the Australian troops to the right and left. The thing that surprised me is that our newest troops, apparently, do quite as well as those who have had very much longer training over here. But in the kind of warfare now being waged, it is not a question of maneuvering large masses of men but of pushing forward small units each of which goes as far as it can and then stops while those on the right or left of it free its further advance. This sort of work gives a splendid opportunity for the individual intelligence and courage of our men.

15. In our work here political questions are, as yet somewhat vaguely but more and more persistently, pushing themselves to the front, and I have a hard time in steering the American Section clear of them. It cannot be denied that in certain of the campaigns in which our Allies are deeply interested, world-politics play an important part. I have already told you that it has been more or less openly said by prominent political and military men that they look to the United States to settle the Balkan question and my colleagues were inclined to shrug their shoulders when I showed them my No. 66 of July 1st, from Washington,[10] which was to the general effect that the United States has no interest in the Macedonian question. Of course when the peace-terms come to be discussed, I suppose that questions relating to the Balkans will have to be considered by us, as well as other questions; but what people here are now interested in is getting the United States involved in these political questions for the purpose of enabling them better to shape their military campaigns. For their purpose, they want certain questions settled before peace comes, instead of after.

16. Moreover it would seem that the Allies are fearing that they

[10] See NDB to T. H. Bliss, July 1, 1918, Vol. 48.

cannot themselves agree on the settlement to be made of some of these questions after the war. I think that it is for this reason that my English colleagues are primarily anxious to have an Inter-Allied political agreement arrived at *now* when there is still enough pressure on them to keep them more or less together. But the English tell me quite plainly that they believe no one but the United States can lead them in this "get-together" political movement. They constantly refer to the situation in the Balkans as showing the necessity of an ante-peace agreement. They say that in the advance made a little while ago by the Italian Army west of Lake Ohrida the movement would have been far more successful and might possibly have caused a falling back of the entire Austro-Bulgarian line had it not been for disagreements between the Italians and the French. The French had put in a certain force to assist the Italians. After the movement began, the Italians said that the French must not go to the town of EL BASEN; or, if their natural line of advance took them there, they must agree to immediately surrender it to the Italians. They made this demand a *sine qua non* to further cooperation by the French, although they had themselves asked for this cooperation. The British tell me that the French commander telegraphed this demand to Paris and that M. Clemenceau then ordered the immediate withdrawal of the French contingent.

17. My colleagues have committees in their Sections here which interest themselves in such questions. Some days ago a representative of the British Section came to see me about the necessity, in his opinion, of the establishment of a politico-diplomatic representation on the Supreme War Council, in which all four Governments should take part, and which should serve to get the Allies together on political questions, precedent to the preparation of plans for campaigns. His idea, although not definitely stated, seemed to be that the Military Representatives should call attention to the necessity of this; at least I drew that inference because when I asked why Mr. Lloyd-George, M. Clemenceau, and Mr. Orlando did not get together on the matter, he said that he did not believe that the French would accede to a proposition emanating from the British and that the French and Italians would not, probably, agree. But he seemed to think that they could be made to work together under pressure from the United States.

18. I immediately foresaw all sorts of complications. I told him that, under instructions from my Government, I could not and would not mix myself up in any question which, although it might ultimately have a decidedly military bearing, was primarily political; that I was not in a position, nor was I expected to be in a position, to know the political views of my Government on these delicate

questions; and that, unless instructed so to do, I could take no part
in a Joint Note such as he seemed to contemplate. Later, he brought
me a paper on the subject of "Strategy without Policy," of which I
give you immediately below a paraphrase in order that you may
know the line of thought of some minds here.

Paraphrase. The paper begins with a statement that successful
war requires unity of direction and that successful military strategy
must carry out a definite unified policy,—both being controlled and
directed by a single executive authority; that for three years of
misfortune and mistakes there was an enforced unity in Allied
counsels only when fear of defeat and enemy pressure forced the
Allies to act together; "but directly the pressure is removed they
tend to drift apart, and to think first of their own interests which
are not always in harmony with the common aims";

That it required the misfortunes of three years to establish a
reasonable approach to unity of command and strategical direction;

But the paper goes on to say that the Allies have never had, even
now, "unity in policy"; that the Balkans, Austria, Russia, and Roumania, show the serious results of a want of united policy to guide
strategy;

That the idea that inconvenient political questions may be shelved
until a military victory is gained is a delusion because it postpones
military victory as the result of the military force not being employed
to the best advantage; that it will be *far more difficult to agree after
the enemy has sustained a defeat*, because when the enemy's power
is most in evidence is the time when the Allies have pulled together,
and that now that a new period of success is beginning they will
do well to discover what are the causes of dis-union and remove
them;

That it is necessary to find or invent some appropriate machinery
for the solution of political questions; that the problem cannot be
dealt with by the ordinary method of diplomatic procedure; that the
Allied nations have agreed to accept the decisions of the Supreme
War Council as binding them in the military sphere in which the
Council is advised by a single con-joint staff after consultation with
the Commander-in-Chief; but that the Council receives no advice
in the political sphere, which is necessary in order that strategy
should be properly based, and that there are no political advisers
to work out a common policy for the consideration of the Council;
that, therefore, when political questions arise, national divergencies
of view also tend to arise, and that the conduct of the war is hampered because the Council is unable to lay down a clear and agreed
statement of what it wants, for the achievement of which its military
advisers are to be called upon to work.

The paper goes on to ask—What is the policy of the Allies with regard to Poland? Is it their object to reconstitute the old, historic Kingdom of Poland as it existed before the first partition? Have the Allies got a policy in the matter at all? It states that it is evident that the whole future of Eastern Europe in general, and of the Balkan States in particular, depends upon this. If the Allies have, as yet, no agreed policy in the matter, it is necessary that there should be a Committee of national representatives permanently sitting together to work out a scheme for one. It will be for the Supreme War Council itself to accept or reject their results, but by no other means is it to be expected that definite, agreed schemes for the solution of this problem, and of all the other complicated problems of the Near East which hinge upon it, will be worked out. And unless they are worked out the objects to the attainment of which the military effort is to be directed will be left in vagueness.

The paper goes on to call attention to the hesitation of the Allies in deciding upon a common policy in regard to Siberia; the unedifying quarrels between the French and the Italians which have recently put a stop to promising operations in Albania; the inconsistent aspirations of the Italians and the Yugo-Slavs; the conflicting views of the different Allied Propaganda Organizations, etc., etc.,—all of which the writer thinks illustrate the necessity for the establishment of machinery to make definite con-joint political decisions.

The paper winds up with a definite recommendation for the establishment of a permanent body of diplomatic representatives in whom the Allies have confidence, to sit permanently together at some common center and work out schemes of Allied policy everywhere in co-operation with one another, just as the military staffs at Versailles work out military schemes. *End of Paraphrase.*

19. After reading the above-mentioned paper, I had another conference with the British officer who had submitted it, and asked him why the heads of the Allied Governments in Europe could not take this question up, if they so desired, through the regular diplomatic channels, with the Government in Washington. He said that he did not believe they would all agree to do so. I then said that the military Representatives were bound by the instructions they might receive from their Governments in a particular case; that if the political heads of the Governments could not agree to consult Washington through diplomatic channels, How could it be expected that they would agree to a Joint Note of their Military Representatives on the same subject? From his reply I gained the idea that he thinks that the political men of the Governments here *want* to agree, but that there is a certain political cowardice which prevents them from doing so; and that for this reason they might

welcome military pressure based on the ground that political agreement was a necessary condition to military success.

20. I called his attention to the fact that the Supreme War Council is made up of the political heads of the four great nations primarily engaged in the war on the Western Front; that each of them had already their political advisers in their political cabinets; that the political questions which worried him related to distant fronts and not to the Western Front; that the military operations on those fronts should be subordinated to those on this one; that, for example, an offensive in Macedonia or in Italy or elsewhere should be undertaken provided the Supreme Command said that it would facilitate the final decision on the Western Front; and that just now the common policy of the Allies should be a *military* policy to thoroughly beat the Central Powers.

21. The reply to all this was simply that if we did not agree on a policy before our decisive military success, the Allies will never agree on it afterwards. And that confirms me in the opinion which I have several times expressed to you, that what concerns some of the Allies is not so much a political agreement, as being a necessary basis for sound military strategy, as it is a pure and simple political agreement which they think can be arrived at only under enemy pressure and before the final victory. In other words, their apprehension increases the slower that victory comes without an antecedent political agreement having been reached as to what they will do *after* the war. Personally, I cannot see what military bearing a political agreement as to the future of Poland will have on the successful progress of a campaign to which the Allies are now devoting every possible effort. I cannot see the bearing a political agreement as to the future of Russia will have on the progress of the war except a possible unfortunate result from some such political agreement that would oblige the Allies to divert an increasing part of their strength from the Western Front. A political agreement as to the settlement of all European political questions after the war might have a bearing on the military conduct of the war; but an unsuccessful attempt at such an agreement might have an unfortunate effect; for example, it might be that, at the end, the Allies may be unwilling to grant to Italy all that was promised in the Secret Treaty of April 26, 1915, and if that fact should develop in an attempt to now reach a political agreement, it might seriously affect the attitude of Italy toward the war.

22. As I have said to you before, I shall take no part in these political matters, knowing that my sole function is to give what help I can in the immediate problem of *beating the Germans*. Of course I cannot abdicate the functions of my mind; these questions

are intensely interesting to anyone who is in the least concerned about the future of the world; but whilst I think about them and listen to discussions about them, I shall speak of them only in this personal way to you.

August 24, 1918.

23. Colonal Stead,[11] who has been representing the British War Office at Salonica and who tells me that in one capacity or another he has passed the last fifteen years in the Balkans, came to see me today on his way to London. He gave me a very complete statement about the situation on the Macedonian Front, from the British point of view. He confirmed what I said in paragraph 16, above. He tells me that with the Greeks the war is very unpopular; that Mr. Venizelos with difficulty raised a force of six weak divisions, the total amounting to something like 40,000 men; that under the guise of a service-of-the-rear force, he gradually accumulated at Salonica between 200,000 and 250,000 men; that these men are required to be fed by the Allies, and that the whole thing was a device of Mr. Venizelos to feed a lot of people who otherwise would make trouble at home; that their families get separation allowances. In addition to this, he says that there are about 70,000 refugees in Salonica over and above the usual civil population and the garrison. He thinks that an offensive on the Macedonian Front is desirable whenever proper preparations shall have been made for it, but that if undertaken under present conditions it might prove a failure. If the enemy should break through the present line, he thinks that the Italians would withdraw, for political reasons, to Valona, while the rest of the line would be forced to withdraw to Salonica, because practically all the supplies for the army are concentrated there. He says that the French have large financial interests at Salonica and that this fact controls to an unfortunate extent their military policy. A long time ago the Military Representatives recommended, and the Supreme War Council approved, that bases of supply be created in Old Greece with an improvement in the lines of communication to them, so that in the event of necessity the Allied Army of the East could fall back in such a way as to continue to protect Greece, even though Salonica might have to be abandoned or held as long as possible by a small force. We have repeatedly called attention to the small progress that has been made in this work but as all of the orders that go to the Italian contingent on the Macedonian Front are sent from Rome and those to the remainder of the Allied force there are sent by the French Government from Paris, it is

[11] Col. Alfred Stead.

difficult to enforce the decisions of the Supreme War Council in these remote theatres. I have sometimes thought that the only way to secure prompt and unified action in such cases would be to give Marshal Foch a strong Staff and give him *general* control on all other theatres as he now has detailed control on the Western Front.

24. Colonel Stead's fear is that the Germans may make a serious effort against the Macedonian front. He thinks that they will be unwilling to enter the winter with a knowledge on the part of the German people that they have been unsuccessful everywhere at the end of the year; and that, therefore, if they are able to stabilize their line on the Western Front they may send a certain number of divisions to the Balkans. Military operations there can be continued until at least into the month of January and unless a Winter Campaign can be fought on the Western Front, they might be able to withdraw a few Divisions for the above purpose. As you know, the last decision of the Supreme War Council was that preparations should be continued in Macedonia for an offensive somewhere about October 1st unless at that time the Supreme War Council should decide that it was unwise. I think that Colonel Stead has been summoned back to London to give his views on the situation to the British War Cabinet.

August 26th.

Marshal Foch has just sent word that he would like to have the Military Representatives come for a conference at his Headquarters, at 3.30 this afternooon. The courier for Washington leaves here to-day and I must, therefore, close this letter hastily. After I return from the Marshal's Headquarters to-night, I shall try to get word to you by the Navy courier as to the subject and result of the Conference.

I received yesterday another paper from the British Section on the same subject as the one outlined in my paragraph 18, above. Notwithstanding the success which the Allies are now having, the British talk a good deal about some form of German "Peace Proposals to which the Allies will be compelled to give a definite reply." They do not agree with Colonel Stead in the opinion that the Germans may attempt a serious movement on the Macedonian front; nor do they believe they will try it in Italy. The paper which I received yesterday expresses the general opinion that the German Armies are faced with the prospect of fighting indefinitely on the defensive against increasing odds, with famine at home and Allies ready to desert them at the first safe opportunity; that only an accident, such as a general strike in England and return of a Pacifist majority to Parliament in October, the fall of the French Cabinet, or a quarrel between some of the Allies, all unlikely contingencies, could delay the ultimate end; that under the circumstances the only course for Germany seems to be to purchase peace before her remaining manhood is destroyed and her country invaded. After a somewhat lengthy discussion of the "pros and cons" the paper concludes that Germany may propose peace without delay, *that is, in the course of the next few weeks*; that she may propose terms so alluring to one or another of the Powers here that the Governments will be forced to consider them; that no Government could give an independent reply without risking the breaking up of the Alliance; that, therefore, the Supreme War Council, or some other body representing the Allied nations would have to be hastily summoned and this body would find itself confronted with the necessity of hastily agreeing upon a policy on the many questions upon which, as yet, there is no agreement.

In other words, the paper reinforces the argument in the one which I paraphrased in paragraph 18, above. The paper then goes on to state some of the questions on which a broad policy would have to be agreed upon by the Allies before an answer could be given to any peace proposals. These questions are enumerated as follows:

(a) The future of Alsace-Lorraine;
(b) Compensation to Belgium;
(c) The rectification of the Italian Frontier;
(d) The future of Poland, the Czecho-Slovaks and the Yugo-Slavs;
(e) The future of Russia and Finland;
(f) The whole Balkan territorial settlement, including Roumania and Thrace;
(g) Turkey, Palestine, Persia;
(h) The German Colonies;
(i) The German Fleet;
(j) Economic Policy and the question of Raw Materials;
(k) "The Freedom of the Seas."

The paper goes on to say that the Allies would not only have to come to a decision with regard to these and other points, but in refusing (if they did refuse) the German offer they would have to state their own terms with sufficient definiteness to satisfy their own people at home who, it thinks, are already beginning to show signs of restlessness owing to the absence of any precise definition of war-aims by their respective Governments. The following is interesting as a British view and I quote it in full:

"Great Britain is in a peculiar position in regard to the terms of peace. In framing their peace proposals the German Government are likely to make great use of the fact that such territory as has been taken by the Allies is all in the hands of Great Britain, viz: The German Colonies, Mesopotamia and Palestine. By offering to exchange these territories for others in the hands of the Central Powers (Belgium and Northern France, Lorraine and the Trentino, etc) Germany will hope to cause dissension among the Allies and to create the impression that Great Britain is responsible for the prolongation of the war. Such tactics are likely to be a source of danger to the Allies and to Great Britain in particular, who will be placed in an embarrassing position if she has to put forward apparently selfish reasons for refusing a German offer. On the other hand, any attempt of this kind would be rendered abortive if the Allies had already agreed upon a policy with regard to the territories in question.

"To the Allies in general and to Great Britain in particular the actual terms of peace are not so important as the circumstances in which peace is made; from this point of view a peace made on good terms before the Prussian militaristic theory is discredited in the eyes both of Germany and of the whole world would be less desirable than a peace made on worse terms when Prussian "Militarism" has been crushed. On the other hand, the time will come when Germany will be ready to accept such terms of peace as of themselves will proclaim the defeat of her "militarism" and such terms if offered by her it would be impossible for the Allies to reject.

"It is not suggested in this paper that such circumstances have yet arisen or that such terms will be offered by Germany as will ensure for the Allies the achievement of the high aims with which they embarked on this struggle. But it is conceived that the time has come when it will no longer be possible for the Allies to subsist on catchwords and proclaim that the Germans must be beaten before peace terms can be discussed.

"The proposals put forward by Germany are certain to be attractive in form and their summary rejection would produce among the mass of the peoples concerned a state of feeling which the Governments would disregard at their peril. An offer of peace by Germany in the near future would, in fact, create a crisis in the fortunes of the Allies. Such an offer must be met with serious and honest consideration by the Allied Governments and a reasonable statement of their position.

"The possibility of a situation such as is indicated above arising in the very near future cannot safely be disregarded. Unless they have previously agreed on the main outlines of a policy such as will both be acceptable to the Allied Governments and win the approval and acquiescence of their peoples they will be in the position of a Commander who waits to formulate his scheme of defense until the enemy has attacked, and has also to obtain the approval of his subordinates to every detail of his plan. In such a situation agreement will be infinitely more difficult to obtain. The whole discussion will be conducted in an atmosphere of haste and mutual suspicion and the result is likely to be an unreasoned refusal with no agreed statement of alternative terms. This result would greatly strengthen the Pacifist Parties in all the Allied countries except in America, and would imperil the position of the Governments and the harmony of the Alliance. The only remedy is for the Supreme War Council without delay to decide on the broad outlines of a policy."

The above are the British views.

I am about leaving for the Marshal's headquarters and hope to write you tonight the result of the conference.

With kindest regards, believe me

Cordially Yours   Tasker H. Bliss.

TCL (WP, DLC).

Robert Worth Bingham to Joseph Patrick Tumulty

Louisville, K'y., Sept. 17, 1918.

Republican nominee for Senate[1] has declared for suffrage. Governor Stanley's appointee, Senator Martin, has not yet expressed himself, although I was assured by Governor Stanley he would vote for suffrage. I feel sure Martin will declare and vote for suffrage if the President will request him to do so as a part of his war program. Governor Stanley makes his opening speech as Democratic nominee on next Saturday. I believe it important that Senator Martin should declare for suffrage before Governor Stanley's opening speech.

Robert W. Bingham.

T telegram (WP, DLC).
[1] Ben Lone Bruner, M.D.

Isaac K. Russell[1] to Joseph Patrick Tumulty

Bridgeport, Conn., Sept. 17 1918.

You might tell the President, if you get a chance, that his message to the Bridgeport employees, to-day, had an effect it would be impossible to overstate on the machine workers. In a single stroke it wiped out all black memories of the Eidlitz award[2] and transferred sullen beaten workmen into a buoyant force, aware at last of a method of spontaneous cooperation that is all they could desire. I have never seen such a change in the spirit of men as that which

has occurred here since the President's message came at four o'-
clock. Regards to you. Isaac Russell

T telegram (WP, DLC).
    ¹ At this time a field representative of the National War Labor Board. For his earlier
relationship with Wilson, see the index references to him in Vol. 25 of this series.
    ² About which, see W. H. Taft and F. P. Walsh to WBW, Sept. 10, 1918, printed as
an Enclosure with WBW to WW, Sept. 11, 1918, Vol. 49.

To Robert Lansing

CONFIDENTIAL

My dear Mr. Secretary: The White House 18 September, 1918.

What has happened at Kazan in the defeat of the Czecho-Slovaks
by the Bolsheviks (said to number "more than 30,000"),¹ taken in
connection with the latest advices from Archangel, makes the situation in Northern Russia and Siberia quite clear, I think.

General Poole's predictions as to what would happen in Northern
Russia if we sent a small contingent of troops there to support the
handful of British already on the ground has been verified, so far
as I can see, in no particular. He predicted, you will remember,
that large forces of Russians would gather and that the only function of the Allied forces would be to hold Murmansk and Archangel
in their rear and see that they were accessible for the shipment of
supplies. Not only has this not happened, but you will notice from
Francis' most recent dispatches that they are finding it difficult
even by persuasion to make the local authorities function in any
independent way, and that the situation is not at all what it was
anticipated that it would develop into. Now come requests that we
send more troops to Archangel, which we will not do, the Military
Council at Versailles entirely concurring in the negative judgment.

So far as Siberia is concerned, things have reached this point.
We must either insist that the Czecho-Slovaks give up their purpose
of establishing an Eastern front, a purpose in which we never
concurred, and that they move eastward and unite with the Allied
forces in Eastern Siberia and ultimately be transferred to some other
front, or we must fall in with the design which has all along un-
derlain this matter, namely the design of drawing us into the formation of an Eastern front composed of troops of the Allied nations.

In both regions, of course, winter is at hand.

I am writing to beg that (if your judgment concurs) you call the
attention of all the governments concerned to the decision which
we made at the outset and can in no case alter; that we will not
be a party to any attempt to form an Eastern front, deeming it
absolutely impracticable from a military point of view and unwise

as a matter of political action, and that we give them kindly but definitively to understand that the most we are ready to do is to assist to hold Archangel or Murmansk, as the exigencies of the winter dictate, until the spring, and that in Siberia we shall insist, so far as our cooperation is concerned, that if the Czecho-Slovak troops cannot maintain themselves in Western Siberia, they withdraw to Eastern Siberia and there await the determination of the best military disposition of their forces.

I would be obliged if you would have an immediate conference with Professor Masaryk about this matter and acquaint him also with our position. In view of the enclosed,[2] we cannot act too soon or speak too plainly.

Cordially and faithfully yours,   Woodrow Wilson

TLS (SDR, RG 59, 861.00/3010, DNA).
    [1] Wilson was quoting from J. V. A. MacMurray to RL, Sept. 16, 1918, T telegram (SDR, RG 59, 861.00/2715, DNA). This dispatch relayed a telegram from Bohdan Pavlu, president of the Czecho-Slovak National Council in Siberia. Pavlu reported on the fall of Kazan, on September 10, to a "very well armed and strongly disciplined" force of over 30,000 Bolsheviks. He also noted that the Bolsheviks had taken Simbirsk on September 12. He pointed out that these defeats made critical the situation of the Czech armies on the Volga front and perhaps also at Ekaterinburg. The fall of Kazan cut off the possibility of a junction between the Czechs in Siberia and the Allied forces at Archangel. If "help from the east" did not come soon, the Czech forces would have to abandon Samara and retreat to Ufa.
    [2] J. K. Caldwell to RL, September 16, 1918, FR 1918, Russia, II, 383-84. It contained a summary translation of a telegram, dated Chelyabinsk, September 12, 1918, from Maj. Gen. Jan Syrovy, the recently appointed commander in chief of the Czechoslovak forces in Russia. It read as follows: "Our situation on Volga is critical. Kazan just fell enabling enemy to operate on Kama. Simbirsk is being evacuated which endangers Samar and Volga front. Our troops wearied by three months' uninterrupted fighting, tire incredibly fast, and transfer of troops from east will only delay catastrophe temporarily. It is impossible to continue to operate without immediate assistance of strong Allied force. Demand from Allies immediate and categorical reply following questions, if our common cause is dear to them: (1) Is it their intention to participate in any way in operations supporting us on Volga front; (2) if so do they intend to start at once an extraordinary transfer of troops and in what numbers? Failure to render immediate assistance will prevent us from clearing further than Urals. There is small hope for aid from Russian army in near future. There is no time for consideration and conference. Telegraph immediately answer of Allies."

To Peyton Conway March, with Enclosure

My dear General March: The White House 18 September, 1918

I am very much obliged to you indeed for letting me see the enclosed, which I have read with care. I think you know already that the judgments expressed are my own also.

With sincere regard,

Faithfully yours,   Woodrow Wilson

TLS (WDR, RG 120, Records of the American Section of the Supreme War Council, 1917-1919, File No. 366-6, DNA).

E N C L O S U R E

Tasker Howard Bliss to Peyton Conway March

No. 19.

My dear March: Versailles. September 7, 1918.

In my last letter (No. 18)[1] I told you about the question of reinforcements for the expeditions to Murmansk and Archangel coming up on a telegram received by the British War Cabinet in London
from the British Admiral Kemp at Murmansk. As the matter then
stood and now stands, it is somewhat extraordinary. The Supreme
War Council agreed to send to General Poole the reinforcements
which he then asked (a couple of months ago), and the reinforcements were sent or are enroute. The British War Cabinet then drew
up the instructions for General Poole's operations.[2] He was told that
he could get no more reinforcements this season. He was told that
with the force that he had, and that was enroute to him, he should
rally to himself the Russian volunteers that he had already assured
the War Council would come to him, that he was then to try and
get in touch with the Czechs in Russia. On the assumption that
he got the assistance of a sufficient force of friendly Russian volunteers, and also of the Czechs, he was to try and get possession
of the Archangel-Vologda-Ekaterinburg Railway; and also the line
of communications of the Dwina River, and the railroad to Viatka.
In case the Russians did not volunteer in sufficient numbers and
he could not get in touch with the Czechs, he was then to confine
himself to the defense of Archangel during the winter. The situation
has apparently arisen that was contemplated in his instructions.
The Russians have not volunteered in sufficient numbers and he
has not gotten in contact with the Czechs. We do not know whether
he is now obeying the remainder of his instructions and preparing
for the defense of Archangel during the winter.

We have not heard a word, as yet, from General Poole. As I told
you in my last letter, the British Admiral at Murmansk telegraphed
to London for reinforcements, the total number and composition
of which he did not state. The British War Cabinet, which had
drawn up General Poole's Plan of Operations, then took the extraordinary step of referring Admiral Kemp's telegram to us, asking
us, practically, what we recommended. They did not tell us whether
they desired to change their instructions already given to General
Poole. If they did not desire to change them, then of course there
is nothing that we need do. If they did desire to change them they
should tell us what change they want to make, what new plan they

---

[1] It is printed as an Enclosure with P. C. March to WW, Sept. 12, 1918, Vol. 49.
[2] See T. H. Bliss to NDB and P. C. March, Aug. 18, 1918, Vol. 49.

want to have carried out, and then we can decide whether we will make any new recommendation to the Supreme War Council. I think that the British possibly feel that they may have "bitten off more than they can chew" and want to throw the responsibility elsewhere. This they cannot do if I have anything to say about it. The only plan suggested by the Military Representatives, or contemplated by them, was to hold the ports of Murmansk and Archangel during the winter. We did not propose any campaign into the interior because we could not tell what obstacles might have to be overcome and what force had to be sent in order to overcome them. I told you on page 2 of my letter No. 18 that my remarks at the meeting of the Military Representatives (copy of which I inclosed to you) were embodied in a telegram and sent that same day to the British War Cabinet. The result of that was that the British have ordered a brigade of four battalions of Infantry and some additional artillery to be sent from England to Archangel. They also ask us to give general consideration to the subject. In order to do this we are still waiting to learn the views and wishes of General Poole.

Since writing my last letter to you, the situation has become still more curious. Two or three days ago Colonel T. Bentley Mott[3] come [came] to me from General Foch's Headquarters, where he had received a telegram from our Ambassador, Mr. Francis, now at Archangel. Mr. Francis urgently demanded reinforcements to be sent without telling us how many or what kind. He asked Colonel Mott to bring the matter to the attention of General Pershing and myself. After communicating with General Pershing, Colonel Mott brought the telegram to me and I went over the whole situation with him. I explained to him that General Poole had received everything that he had asked for and that we had heard nothing from him to the effect that he wanted anything more. I told him that General Poole was engaging in a campaign which we had never contemplated nor recommended and that it was up to him to obey his instructions and confine himself to the defense of the Arctic ports as soon as he found that he could not successfully conduct the campaign into the interior with the force that was being provided him.

To-day Major Riggs,[4] assistant to Colonel Ruggles at Archangel,[5] appeared upon the scene here. It seems that he and a member of the French Mission at Archangel have been sent to Paris by their respective Ambassadors to represent the situation. Major Riggs presented to me a letter addressed to me by Mr. Francis in which

[3] Thomas Bentley Mott, Gen. Pershing's representative on Gen. Foch's staff.
[4] Elisha Francis Riggs, Assistant Military Attaché with the American embassy in Russia.
[5] That is, James A. Ruggles.

he urges the sending of reinforcements. Major Riggs says that he wants five more battalions than those which the British Government have just decided to send. He can give me no satisfactory statement of what he believes will be accomplished by this force. In a general way he seems to think that with this additional force General Poole can force himself to parts of Russia where he will secure volunteers and where he can then get into contact with the Czechs and as a result of it they will practically conquer Western Russia and re-establish a front against the Germans. His talk sounds to me wild. But one thing which he said impressed me strongly because it reinforced what I have so often said in my dispatches to Washington. He says that if the Allies do not now go in with a sufficient force to re-establish the Eastern Front the Germans will get a great many recruits out of Russia. If we had stayed at Murmansk and Archangel, as I supposed we were to do, we would not have given German propaganda the opportunity of saying that the Allies were engaged in an invasion of Russia with a view to ulterior objects repugnant to the Russian people. If we were to invade Russia, either by way of Vladivostok or by way of Murmansk and Archangel, we ought, of course, to do it with a powerful force, but I have always supposed that an invasion of Russian [Russia] was repugnant to the intentions of the United States. The whole question at issue now is, "What are we in Russia for?" If we are there for the purpose of getting at Germany we must go with a force sufficient for that purpose. We have not the tonnage for it, either to get the force there or to maintain it after it is there, nor have we the time to do it.

This subject may reach such a stage that I shall have to send you a cable message about it before this letter reaches you. It will probably depend upon what General Poole says after we hear from him. The singular fact is that we have a British Admiral demanding reinforcements, Mr. Francis demanding reinforcements, Major Riggs and an officer from the French Mission at Archangel demanding reinforcements,—but thus far no demand from General Poole. It begins to look to me as though the explanation is that the diplomatic mission at Archangel is afraid of being captured by a German-Bolshevik advance, because if they do not get out of Archangel before the Port freezes up in November, they cannot get out by water before next summer. That may raise the question as to whether it may not be better for the Allies to order their diplomatic missions to entirely withdraw from Archangel before the winter closes them in.   Hastily but Sincerely yours,   Tasker H. Bliss

P.S. I forgot to say that in his letter to me, Mr. Francis makes the amazing statement that General Poole tells him that he had been promised at least 10,000 American troops. When I read it I told Major Riggs that if any one made such a statement to General Poole it was difficult to characterize it as other than a deliberate falsification of facts. The British Government knew perfectly well that the American Government went into the expedition with the greatest reluctance; they knew that under the proposed plan the greatest demand that could be made of the United States was one, or at most, two battalions; that when Lord Milner, of his own motion, without any authority of the Supreme War Council, telegraphed to Washington for three battalions, two batteries of artillery, and three companies of engineers,[6] the American Government held the whole thing up and that it cabled me for an explanation of this demand; that I had replied that Lord Milner's proposition was not the one approved here and that it was only with the greatest difficulty that the British extracted from the United States the agreement to send three battalions and three companies of engineers.[7]

I also omitted to say that after my conversation with him I asked Major Riggs to make a statement to the officers of the American Section here, of his views as to the situation in Russia and its requirements. They tell me that he made the same impression upon them that he did upon me, viz., that he is very confused in his ideas and has not made the situation any clearer to us than it was before.

TLS (WDR, RG 120, Records of the American Section of the Supreme War Council, 1917-1919, File No. 366-6, DNA).
  [6] See A. J. Balfour to Lord Reading, June 11, 1918, Vol. 48.
  [7] See the Enclosure printed with NDB to WW, June 20, 1918, Vol. 48.

To Joseph Patrick Tumulty, with Enclosures

Dear Tumulty: [The White House] 18 September, 1918

Please get into communication with Mr. Villard and tell him that I have gone over this matter[1] very thoroughly with the Postmaster General since Mr. Villard's interview with me and have counselled the Postmaster General in a way that was entirely friendly to Mr. Villard. Nothing more could be accomplished by a personal interview with me.   The President

TL (WP, DLC).
  [1] The Post Office Department informed Villard and the staff of the New York *Nation* on September 13 that the issue of that magazine dated September 14 was being withheld from the mail pending a decision concerning controversial material in the issue. At first, it was widely assumed that an editorial entitled "Civil Liberty Dead," CVII (Sept. 14, 1918), 282, was the item in question. However, when Villard made a hurried trip to Washington on September 14, he was informed by William H. Lamar, the Solicitor of the Post Office Department, that the offending editorial was "The One Thing Needful," *ibid.*, p. 283. This editorial, written anonymously by Albert Jay Nock, strongly criticized

the sending of Samuel Gompers to Europe to communicate American ideas to European labor groups. "The one thing needful at the present moment," the editorial said, "is that we should know the whole state of European labor." That is, if Americans were to be sent to European labor groups at all, they should go to listen to the whole spectrum of European labor opinion from right to left, rather than to propagate American views. However, the editorial lapsed into personal abuse of Gompers with such comments as the following: "When Mr. Gompers drops the sample case and mounts the tripod, the public will get from him at his best merely the kind of information that a sturdy partisan drummer, travelling continually in an atmosphere of sheer bagmanism, is able to furnish."

Villard later recalled that Lamar explained his objection to the editorial as follows: "Mr. Gompers has rendered inestimable services to this government during this war in holding union labor in line and while this war is on we are not going to allow any newspaper in this country to attack him." Lamar, as Villard remembered, offered to release the issue if the page containing the editorial was deleted. Villard refused to do so. Oswald Garrison Villard, *Fighting Years: Memoirs of a Liberal Editor* (New York, 1939), pp. 355-56.

The news that an issue of *The Nation* had been withheld by the Post Office Department created a furor in the American press. Villard later observed (*ibid.*, p. 356) that it gave *The Nation* much valuable free publicity. However, as it turned out, the incident was already closed, as Wilson indicates above. On his arrival in Washington on September 14, Villard first consulted Franklin K. Lane, who advised him to see Wilson at once. When Villard reached the White House, he found Tumulty "so incensed and so profanely desirous of helping" that he did not insist upon seeing Wilson. Tumulty told him to go see "that old boll weevil from Texas." Burleson refused to see Villard but sent Lamar, and the conversation took place which is quoted above. Villard returned to the White House to report, and Tumulty promised to take care of the matter. *Ibid.*, pp. 355-56. What ensued is explained in "Wilson Lifted 'Nation' Ban," *New York Times*, Sept. 20, 1918, as follows: "The sudden overruling of . . . Lamar of the Post Office Department, who excluded the New York Nation from the mails, was directly due to President Wilson. The matter was taken up at the Cabinet meeting Tuesday [September 17], and the President is understood to have expressed his unconditional disapproval of the action, sanctioned by Postmaster General Burleson, and directed that the order against *The Nation* be rescinded."

For further commentary on the whole affair, see " 'The Nation' and the Post Office," *The Nation*, CVII (Sept. 28, 1918), 336-37.

E N C L O S U R E   I

From Oswald Garrison Villard

My dear Mr. President: New York City September 17, 1918

It is three years since I have ventured to trespass upon your time, but I now respectfully ask that you give me an appointment for Thursday of this week, if it is in any way possible, in order to discuss with you the Post Office Department's treatment of the issue of The Nation of September 14th.

I believe that a very serious situation is arising with the liberal press of the country in connection with the Post Office Department. Secretary Lane is one of those who urges me to seek the opportunity to lay the matter before you personally, and acquaint you with certain things that are happening.

In the hope that you will be able to find a few minutes for me on Thursday, I am,

                    Very truly yours   Oswald Garrison Villard

TLS (WP, DLC).

ENCLOSURE I I[1]

New York, September 17, 1918.

I call your attention to Lamar's outrageous attack upon me in morning papers,[2] in which he condemns [me] at the moment that he states the matter is in the hands of the Postmaster General for adjudication. Please note also his use of anonymous letter from New York paper to classify me with Nearing and John Reed. This is an indefensible abuse of official power, moreover I gave no interview to the press whatever, except on Friday when I merely stated ignorance of what it was all about and am making my first statement for publication today.[3] I want also to call your attention to the fact that if decision is not rendered soon I am in danger of losing my second class mailing rights and can thus automatically be barred from the mails, as was done in the case of The Masses.

Oswald Garrison Villard.

T telegram (WP, DLC).
[1] The following telegram was addressed to Tumulty.
[2] Lamar issued a statement on September 16 in which he stated that the Post Office Department was "considering complaints against several articles" in the issue of *The Nation* for September 14 "in addition to the editorial entitled 'The One Thing Needful.' " He also mentioned that the department had received a telegram from "one of the leading New York daily papers" which suggested that it would be best for newspapers in the future not to quote seditious statements "in such cases as Reed and Nearing and The Nation." The telegram further suggested that it would be wise for editors merely to say that they had "attacked our Allies, or denounced the draft, or disparaged the war" and to add that the text had been forwarded to the governmental authorities. Lamar concluded his statement as follows: "The Postmaster General coincides with the view expressed in the foregoing telegram and suggests that it will be in the interest of the country at the present time for publishers generally to pursue the course suggested." *New York Times*, Sept. 17, 1918.
[3] "Villard Makes Protest," *ibid.*, Sept. 18, 1918.

Oswald Garrison Villard to Joseph Patrick Tumulty

New York, Sept. 18, 1918

Warmest thanks for wise and just decision.[1] Deeply appreciate your personal interest and aid.   Oswald Garrison Villard.

T telegram (WP, DLC).
[1] It was announced on September 18 that the ban on the mailing of the issue of *The Nation* for September 14 had been lifted. *New York Times*, Sept. 19, 1918.

To George Foster Peabody

My dear Mr. Peabody: The White House 18 September, 1918

I knew you would share our feeling of deep satisfaction at the results in Georgia, and I am very grateful for your friendship and for what you say in your kind letter of September 16th[1] about the maturing plans of the administration. They do, I am happy to say, seem to be maturing in a way that promises undoubted success. In great haste,

Cordially and sincerely yours,   Woodrow Wilson

TLS (G. F. Peabody Papers, DLC).
  ¹ It is missing in all collections.

From Carrie Clinton Lane Chapman Catt

My dear Mr. President: New York September 18, 1918.

It is now clear to us that if Senator Benet will vote "aye" on the Federal Suffrage Amendment on the *first* roll call, that the Amendment will not only pass, but that we may get several additional votes. Every Senator will know when and if he votes "aye" that the Amendment will pass. The psychology of this fact has been called to our attention by some of the Senators. The Roll Call will be:

Mr. Ashurst	aye
" Bankhead	no
" Baird	no
" Beckham	no
" Benet	?
" Borah	no
" Brandegee	no

Every Senator knows that the vote of the Amendment depends upon Mr. Benet and he, if voting "aye" on the first roll call, would virtually make the announcement that it will pass. If you can see your way clear to bring this to his attention and get his consent, we believe that it would ensure the passage of the Amendment, provided Mr. Martin of Kentucky will also vote "aye" as we are assured that he will.

We understand that Senator Ellison Smith is doing his utmost to get Senator Benet in opposition.

We are not unmindful that we shall owe our victory to you and are more grateful than words can express.

Yours sincerely,   Carrie Chapman Catt

TLS (WP, DLC).

To Carrie Clinton Lane Chapman Catt

My dear Mrs. Catt: [The White House] 18 September, 1918

Thank you for your letter of this morning. I am alive to the situation and am going to try at once to reach Senator Benet.

Cordially and sincerely yours,   Woodrow Wilson

TLS (Letterpress Books, WP, DLC).

To Christie Benet

My dear Senator Benet: [The White House] 18 September, 1918.

I know that you will forgive and justify me as leader of our party in making another direct and very earnest appeal to you to vote for the suffrage amendment.[1]

I need not assure you that I would not venture to make this direct appeal to you, were I not convinced that affirmative action on the amendment is of capital importance not only to the party, but to the country, and to the maintenance of the war spirit and the support of the administration which is indispensable to the winning of the war.

It would take me a long time, my dear Senator Benet, to tell you in detail upon what evidence I have reached this conviction. I am sure that you will not require of me that I should detail the evidence. I can say that my conviction is founded upon impressions received from many directions upon which I am sure I can rely, for I have tested them in many ways. If you would be generous enough to vote "Aye" on this question, I have reason to believe that your vote would be influential in leading at least two other doubting Senators to vote the same way, and that the amendment would be carried.

I know that I am asking a great deal, but I also know how generous you are in your purpose to accept leadership and serve the present unusual interests in an unusual way.

Cordially and sincerely yours, [Woodrow Wilson]

CCL (WP, DLC).
[1] The Editors have not found any evidence about Wilson's earlier appeal to Benet.

To Key Pittman

[The White House]
My dear Senator Pittman: 18 September, 1918

Thank you for your letter of yesterday. I have written as strong an appeal as I know how to make to Senator Benet, and hope with all my heart for a favorable response.

Cordially and sincerely yours, Woodrow Wilson

TLS (Letterpress Books, WP, DLC).

To Valentine Everit Macy

My dear Mr. Macy: [The White House] 18 September, 1918.

Thank you for your letter of yesterday, to which I hasten to reply. I think that the best way in which to act at present is for your Board to issue a formal statement to the men with regard to whose wages you are delaying the announcement of your decision, saying that at the earnest request of the President you have entered into conference with the other labor adjustment agencies of the government in an effort to arrive at some common policy which will be just to all the war labor forces, and that it is in response to the President's request that you are delaying your decision in this particular case until the conferences are concluded, which it is hoped will be in the near future.

I hope sincerely that this advice will meet with your approval. I am perfectly willing that you should say in the announcement that you are making it at my request.

Cordially and sincerely yours,   [Woodrow Wilson]

CCL (WP, DLC).

To James George Scripps[1]

CONFIDENTIAL

My dear Mr. Scripps: [The White House] 18 September, 1918

I warmly appreciate your letter of September 14th.[2] It assures me of just the kind of support which makes a man feel strong and confident amidst many difficulties.

You can without compunction afford to be consistent in the matter of the representation of the First Ohio District. Mr. Longworth[3] has supported the administration in the way that most of the active partisan Republicans have supported it. That is to say, with the purpose of making criticism tell as adversely as possible and also with the purpose, if it can be subtly enough managed, to take the direction of the war out of the hands of the administration and place it where the Republicans can control it more directly.

Allow me to say again how sincerely I appreciate the opportunity of giving you this confidential advice.

Cordially and sincerely yours,   [Woodrow Wilson]

CCL (WP, DLC).
  [1] Managing director of the Scripps-McRae chain of newspapers founded by his father, Edward Wyllis Scripps.
  [2] J. G. Scripps to WW, Sept. 14, 1918, TLS (WP, DLC).
  [3] That is, Nicholas Longworth, who was running on the Republican ticket for re-election to the House of Representatives.

To Louis Brownlow

My dear Mr. Chairman: The White House 18 September, 1918

I have kept your letter of September 9th[1] several days, because the question it raised was one upon whose decision many consequences would hang, and one, therefore, which I felt I had to consider with the utmost care and prudence.

As I have thought about it and conferred about it, I have come to the pretty clear judgment that it would not be wise, unless it should become absolutely necessary (and I don't think it will), to take over the trolley lines of the District. It would lead to similar action by the government in other places and amidst a great variety of conditions, and would ultimately put an additional burden upon the Treasury of the United States which it would be most unwise and imprudent to put upon it. I hope and believe that the salvation of these utilities can be worked out in a different way, and I know you are addressing yourself to the problem with all possible diligence.   Cordially and sincerely yours,   Woodrow Wilson

TLS (WC, NjP).
 [1] L. Brownlow to WW, Sept. 9, 1918, TLS (WP, DLC).

From John Joseph Pershing

[via] London, Sep. 18, 1918.

Please accept the most sincere thanks of the American Expeditionary Forces for your stirring message of congratulations. Your words of commendation have been received with deep appreciation by all ranks and will inspire in us a higher sense of our obligations to our country. I assure you that it shall always be the endeavour of the army in France to prove worthy of the confidence of the American people.   Pershing.

T telegram (WP, DLC).

From Robert Lansing, with Enclosure

Dear Mr. President: Washington September 18, 1918.

In view of the telegrams received yesterday revealing that a state of terrorism exists in Moscow and Petrograd through which thousands of innocent Russian citizens are being killed,[1] it occurs to me that it might be desirable for this Government to do what it can to prevent a continuance of this terrible state of affairs. I am anxious to avoid any semblance of political interference but rather to base

our action purely on the ground of humanity and as acting in behalf
of the Russian people themselves who are the victims of these
crimes.

There are two courses which seem practicable:

1. A circular telegram to the neutral countries of the world, as
   suggested in the accompanying draft,
2. A statement to be issued by you to the American people, a
   copy of which could be communicated to the various neutral
   governments as an expression of the views of the American
   people.

I might add that in the case of the Armenian massacres, this
Government sent an expression of its aversion through Ambassador
Morgenthau.[2] Then, however, we had a Government with which
to deal but in the case of Russia we are unable to act in so direct
a manner. The Armenian massacres, however, might nevertheless
be considered as a precedent to follow at the present time.

I would be grateful if you would kindly indicate your views.

Faithfully yours,   Robert Lansing

TLS (WP, DLC).
[1] One of them was D. C. Poole, Jr., to RL, Sept. 3, 1918, *FR 1918, Russia,* I, 681-82.
Poole reported that, since May, the "Extraordinary Commission against Counter-Revolution" had conducted "an openly avowed campaign of terror." "Thousands of persons,"
he continued, "have been summarily shot without even the form of trial. Many of them
have no doubt been innocent of even the political views which were supposed to supply
the motive of their execution. The assassination of Uritski and the attempt on Lenin
are the results of this high tyranny. Socialists, once coworkers with the Bolsheviki, have
turned against them the methods by which they formerly attacked the tyranny of the
Tsars. 'Mass terror' is the Bolshevik reply." Poole quoted the official press as reporting
that 500 persons had been shot in Petrograd alone as a result of the murder of Uritski.
    Poole's general description of the situation and his suggestions for action to counter
it were as follows: "In Moscow 'general searches' are being made under general orders
to arrest 'the better-to-do and all former officers.' The ill-administered prisons are filled
beyond capacity and every night scores are irresponsibly shot. Sentence is passed on
the slightest grounds, or the general charge, 'might be dangerous to the Bolshevik
power.' In sum, vengeful and irresponsible gangs are venting the desperation of their
declining power in the daily massacre of untold innocents. The situation cries aloud to
all who will act for the sake of humanity. It is possible that some stay might be put on
the Bolsheviks, if the Allied Governments could gain the adhesion of the neutrals to
joint action by which the representatives of the latter would inform the Bolsheviks that
the whole world, neutral and Allied, is revolted by the present inhuman and purposeless
slaughter, and unless this is stopped forthwith, Allies and neutrals alike will not only
deny members of the Bolshevik government future asylum but hold them jointly and
severally responsible for their present deeds. The other and truly efficacious course is
a rapid military advance from the north. Our present halfway action is cruel in the
extreme. Our landing has set up the Bolshevik death agony. It is now our moral duty
to shield the numberless innocents who are exposed to its hateful reprisals."
    [2] See WJB to H. Morgenthau, April 27 and 29, 1915, and RL to H. Morgenthau, Oct.
4, 1915, *FR-WWS 1915,* pp. 980, 988.

E N C L O S U R E

I am in receipt of information from reliable sources revealing that
the peaceable Russian citizens of Moscow, Petrograd and other

cities are suffering from an openly avowed campaign of mass terrorism and are subject to wholescale executions. Thousands of persons have been shot without even a form of trial; ill administered prisons are filled beyond capacity and every night scores of Russian citizens are recklessly put to death; and irresponsible bands are venting their brutal passions in the daily massacre of untold innocents.

It is the earnest desire of the people of the United States to befriend the Russian people and lend them all possible assistance in their struggle to reconstruct their nation upon principles of democracy and self-government. Civilization recoils at the crimes which are being committed against the innocent and helpless victims of wanton barbarism, and I know that my fellow citizens would wish me on their behalf to express publicly their horror at this existing state of terrorism, and their deep compassion for the Russian people.[1]

T MS (WP, DLC).
[1] About the final version of this document, see WW to RL, Sept. 20, 1918 (first letter of that date), n. 2.

From Joseph Patrick Tumulty

Dear Governor: The White House 18 September 1918.

In every mail, I receive letters from Scott Ferris, of the Democratic National Congressional Committee, urging me to have you write *particular* letters of endorsement of congressional candidates. I think you ought to refuse to do this. They ought to be willing to be the beneficiaries of a blanket endorsement, such as you intend to issue.

With reference to the Gubernatorial contests throughout the country. I think you ought to keep hands off, for just as soon as you take part in them by a letter of endorsement, you immediately make the question of the repudiation of your Administration the issue. I think the course for us to follow is to confine our efforts exclusively to congressional and senatorial contests, at the same time showing a kindly interest in Democratic Gubernatorial candidates, either by interviews or unofficial statements.

Sincerely,   Tumulty

I entirely agree with you. Close will show you a letter to Sen. Beckham.[1] Is that all right?   W.W.[2]

TLS (J. P. Tumulty Papers, DLC).
[1] WW to J. C. W. Beckham, Sept. 19, 1918.
[2] WWhw.

From Edward Mandell House, with Enclosure

Dear Governor: New York. September 18, 1918.

I am enclosing a telegram which has just come from Mr. Balfour to Wiseman.

There is a feeling in Entente circles that the Bulgarian Government are much strengthened by being able to announce that they are friends with the United States, and that the one thing they are afraid of is a declaration of war by the United States. They tell their countrymen that they have not only secured territorial expansion at the expense of Serbia and Greece, but they have done so while keeping on good terms with the United States, which will mean after war reconstruction and financing.

If you desire to make a threat I would suggest that you give it as wide publicity in Bulgaria as possible, so that the effect desired on the people may be had. The Government would naturally conceal it if possible.   Affectionately yours,   E. M. House

TLS (WP, DLC).

E N C L O S U R E

London. September 17, 1918.

Following from Mr. Balfour for Sir William Wiseman.

You may inform the President for his personal and most confidential information that a general offensive is about to take place on the Macedonian front, and that it would, in my opinion, be of value if a threat could be conveyed to Bulgaria without delay so as to weaken Bulgarian morale and resistance before the offensive matures.

T MS (WP, DLC).

From George Creel

My dear Mr. President: [Washington] September 18, 1918.

I have just talked with Mr. Baruch about the withdrawal of his appointment of Lindbergh of Minnesota.[1] I said to him, as I now take the liberty of saying to you, that honor and courage and common sense command the retention of Mr. Lindbergh. I can conceive of nothing more harmful to the Nation's interest than that we should be put in the position of backing down under the threat of a lot of reactionary politicians, willing at all time to put their party above their country.

Mr. Lindbergh and his associates are absolutely and entirely loyal, true to America in every respect, and the attack upon them is as false as it is base. It is the political power of the Non-Partisan League that the Democrats and Republicans fear, and it is out of this fear that their lies proceed.

May I get hold of Mr. Baruch and bring him to the White House for a conference with you? As you know, I have given time and sweat to straightening out this situation in the Northwest, and it is indeed bitter to have all my work undone by a single act of cowardice. Respectfully, [George Creel][2]

CCL (G. Creel Papers, DLC).
[1] About which, see G. Creel to WW, Sept. 12, 1918, Vol. 49.
[2] If Wilson ever replied to this letter, his reply is missing in the Creel Papers and in WP, DLC. In any event, Lindbergh was not reappointed to the War Industries Board.

From William Gibbs McAdoo

Dear Mr. President: Washington September 18, 1918.

I have carefully considered the recommendation dealing with the Mexican financial situation enclosed with your note of September 6,[1] and I return the recommendation herewith.

Appreciating the political importance of the matters presented the Treasury Department would be cordially in favor of the purchase of Mexican Government securities having the approval of our State Department by American bankers and the offer of the same to our investors. Any such offer should be arranged so as not to conflict with our Liberty Bond campaign. I fear, however, that Mexican Government bonds unless guaranteed by the United States would not prove attractive to our bankers and to our investors, even though the Department of State should go further in stating our policy than it did in the case of the proposed loan to China. The Mexican Government it appears does not wish financial aid from the United States Government, and in any event a United States guarantee of its bonds would no doubt be distasteful. Even if the Mexican Government consented to a guarantee of its bonds by this Government I am not disposed to consider that a satisfactory method to extend our financial aid to Mexico.

If the Mexican Government should overcome its objection to receiving financial aid from the United States, it occurs to me that it might be preferable to furnish financial assistance in another way.

The present troubles of the Mexican Government arise from two sources. One, the country has no circulating medium except gold. Two, the Government revenues are falling short of expenses and it is only a question of time as to when this deficit can no longer be met.

Recognizing the fact that to cut off gold shipments would be a particular hardship to Mexico by reason of the absence of any circulating medium except gold, the Federal Reserve Board has permitted certain limited amounts of gold to go to Mexico. The net amount of gold thus shipped from January 1, 1918 to August 20, 1918 amount[s] to over $16,000,000, which in present circumstances is, in my judgment, a very considerable sum. Refusal to permit the shipment of this gold might result in the shutting down of important mining and oil industries with resulting disorder and unsettlement. It is the recognition of this fact that has led to permission to ship gold. This course has been in accordance with the wishes of the State Department; as a mere Treasury matter, the shipment of gold to Mexico would have been embargoed in the same manner in which it has been embargoed to other countries.

Provision of a suitable circulating medium for Mexico is thus not only in the interest of Mexico itself but also of this country inasmuch as such provision will permit us to diminish the amount of gold that we are now allowing to go to that country.

Provision must be made for some means of meeting the monthly deficit in expenses until such time as revenues can be brought up to the point where they equal or exceed the expenditures.

I do not believe it necessary at the present time to undertake the reorganization of the Mexico debt. The world has become accustomed to the default on the Mexican obligations and does not expect any immediate resumption. In these circumstances it will, in my judgment, be more prudent to deal with the immediate pressing necessities and when these have worked out or are in a fair way to do so, to undertake the more ambitious program. In readjusting the debt of the Mexican Government it may well be advisable to institute a commission of inquiry as to the manner in which present holders of the debt acquired such debt and in the reorganization to allow to no holder a larger amount in new bonds than is necessary to cover the cost to him of the old. In other words, there will probably be no good reason for permitting the speculator who had bought his holdings at merely nominal prices to have them redeemed at their face amount. My suggestion for dealing with the situation is one that would require further careful consideration of present conditions in Mexico and consultation with people conversant with those conditions. If, on inquiry, some such plan as is suggested below should appear feasible, it may be advisable to send to Mexico some one in the confidence of this Government and who is likely to be acceptable to the Mexican authorities for the purpose of sounding the latter informally as to whether they would be willing to cooperate in some such plan.

The plan I am outlining is based on the idea suggested in the memorandum of the Russian Ambassador for dealing with a new currency for Siberia. That plan is based on the theory that any currency will be acceptable to any population if that currency can immediately demonstrate its power to purchase commodities. Mexico has been short of commodities and like Siberia would undoubtedly recognize a new currency if backed by commodities, in spite of the fact that the Mexican public has had bitter experience with the successive issues of paper put forth by one Government after another.

The suggestion is to form a Trading Corporation which in this case might perhaps better be denominated a Bank, with a capital subscribed by the United States Government which would be invested in commodities needed by the Mexican population. The Corporation would be empowered to issue circulating notes and would undertake to lend to the Mexican Government for the purpose of meeting its monthly deficit certain limited amounts of its circulating notes. The amount that is loaned to the Mexican Government would be loaned in return for obligations of that Government, repayable either out of specific revenues or out of a general surplus, whenever a surplus in the budget is established. Such a Trading Corporation or Bank would send to Mexico the commodities purchased and would make arrangements with retail, and if necessary, wholesale traders for supplying them with goods desired, stipulating, however, that they shall in selling such commodities, take in payment the circulating notes issued by the Corporation. Certain limited amounts of circulating notes could be put into circulation by making judicious loans to merchants against exportable commodities. In this way the notes would get into circulation. They would also get into circulation through being paid out by the Mexican Government for pay roll of troops, etc. out of sums the Mexican Government would have borrowed from the Corporation for the purpose of meeting its deficit. If the circulating notes of the Corporation can thus obtain currency, the first step would have been taken for the provision of a circulating medium and at the same time the Corporation would have dealt with the deficit of the Government.

It would undoubtedly be necessary for the Government of the United States to pay up the capital stock of this Corporation and probably the directorate of the Corporation should be composed of United States nationals and Mexican nationals nominated respectively by the two Governments. The Mexican Government should have the option at any time to purchase the stock of the Corporation from the Government of the United States, paying therefor the amount paid in, together with some moderate rate of interest for the time that the capital has been employed. A currency of this kind supported by commodities available for delivery in Mexico or by bank balances in the United States would, without difficulty, maintain itself at par in my judgment and without the necessity of shipping gold into Mexico.

If this plan works out as hoped the capital of the Corporation and its issue of notes could be increased from time to time and the Corporation or Bank could ultimately be transformed into the State Bank of the Mexican Republic.

The plan which I have outlined would have to receive further careful study. I recognize it may be difficult, if not impossible, to secure the adherence of President Carranza to the plan. If the plan outlined meets with your approval I should be glad to have authority from you to discuss it with a few people conversant with Mexican affairs, including, I should think, Mr. Bruère,[2] and if it meets with encouragement, I should expect to suggest to you the making of strictly informal inquiries as to whether such a plan, if put forward, would be likely to meet the adherence of the Mexican Government. It could I think be arranged so that the plan could be put forward by some thoroughly trustworthy American who has the confidence of the Mexican Government and in such a way as not to commit this Government to anything until it could be determined whether or not it will be possible for the two Governments to cooperate for the purpose of achieving the desired end.

Cordially yours,   W G McAdoo

The White House
Approved: [blank] September, 1918.

TLS (WP, DLC).
    [1] See WW to WGM, Sept. 6, 1918, Vol. 49.
    [2] That is, Henry Bruère, lawyer of New York, who was at this time a financial adviser to the Mexican government.

From Thomas Watt Gregory

My dear Mr. President: Washington, D. C. September 18, 1918.

You may remember that under date of August 27th, 1918, you referred to me a letter from Mrs. Vernon, the wife of Reverend Ambrose White Vernon, of Brookline, Massachusetts, on the subject of two German alien enemy seamen, Anton Slivinski and Carl Kluck.[1] Mrs. Vernon stated that these men had been paroled for the period of the war under the custody of her husband, and then had suddenly, without warning and without any breach of the parole on their part, but, as she feels, in violation of the terms of the parole, been interned at Hot Springs, North Carolina. You asked me to look into the facts of the case in order that we might form our own judgment as to whether the right course was pursued.

I find that, up to the time at least of their internment at Hot Springs, these cases were in the exclusive charge of the Department of Labor and that the proceedings complained of by Mrs. Vernon were taken by that Department, and not, as she seems to believe, by my Department. In order to answer your letter fully, however, I have undertaken to ascertain from that Department the facts of the matter and the basis of their proceedings.

The men were seamen on a German vessel interned at Boston. Previous to the taking over of the vessel, they had been employed as choremen for the Harvard Church at Brookline, of which the Reverend Vernon was the pastor. Upon the taking over of the vessel, the Department of Labor decided to parole the men to the Harvard Church. No intimation was given, however, either to the men or the Reverend Vernon, that the parole would be for the duration of the war. The parole agreement signed by the men contained the clause, "It is understood that this agreement will remain in force during the continuance of the present war." But the agreement referred to is that of the aliens, not of the government; and obviously the government must leave itself free to revoke a parole on any ground satisfactory to it.

Later, under the pressure arising out of accusations against Mr. Vernon of disloyalty to the United States, he resigned his pastorate, and thereupon requested of the Department of Labor that the men continue to be placed in his charge. At that time, the Department of Labor did not know the reasons for his resignation and advised him that the two aliens would be left under his supervision. This took place in February 1918. Later, in May 1918, the Department of Labor received strong protests against this use of the services of a man whose loyalty was under suspicion, and the Commissioner of Immigration at Boston[2] was requested to make a thorough investigation. In his report the Commissioner recommended the termination of the parole and the internment of the two men. By this time the internment station at Hot Springs had been established and all of the officers and seamen of the vessels interned at Boston, other than said Slivinski and Kluck, had been transferred to that station. On the basis of the report of the Commissioner of Immigration,[3] it was decided by the Labor Department to transfer these two men also to the internment station. It is true that the men were not charged with any breach of the parole or other misconduct, but their internment was not a violation of any implied or express conditions of the parole, and, regardless of the truth or falsity of the accusations against Mr. Vernon, was, I believe, a proper course for the Department of Labor to pursue under all the circumstances. The decision of that Department may have been somewhat abruptly executed; but this was due to the fact that the Department of Labor was in process of transferring the Hot Springs Camp to the Department of War, and quick action in the cases of these two seamen was necessary, so that the expenses of their transportation to the camp might be paid from the funds of the former Department.

I am returning Mrs. Vernon's letter herewith.

Faithfully yours,   T. W. Gregory

TLS (WP, DLC).
  [1] See WW to TWG, Aug. 27, 1918, and n. 1 thereto, Vol. 49.
  [2] Henry J. Skeffington.
  [3] That is, Anthony Caminetti.

From Herbert Clark Hoover, with Enclosure

Dear Mr. President: Washington 18 September 1918

Following up our conversation of last Saturday, I have had a discussion with Senator Kellogg as to the Act that he some years ago proposed for the curtailment of rampant business. I have today the enclosed letter from him, together with a copy of the original draft.[1] It appears to me there are some ideas in it that are extremely well worth while, more especially the difficulty of dealing with the whole problem of aggregate business instead of narrowing it to one individual class of business.

Yours faithfully,   Herbert Hoover

TLS (WP, DLC).
  [1] "FEDERAL LICENSE ACT," T MS (Hoover Archives, CSt-H). Kellogg summarizes its provisions well.

E N C L O S U R E

Frank Billings Kellogg to Herbert Clark Hoover

My dear Mr. Hoover: Washington, D. C. September 18, 1918.

Pursuant to our conversation last evening, I am writing this letter, giving a synopsis of the Federal License Act, to aid the President in his consideration of the subject. Very generally stated, the object to be accomplished by the proposed Federal License Act is to control large aggregations of capital engaged in Interstate Commerce, and while permitting the concentration of capital sufficient to handle the commerce of the country and to compete with foreign nations, to prevent such operations, by their power, from crushing out their competitors and monopolizing the trade.

I do not believe that the Sherman Act is a complete remedy and that breaking up large corporations into small parts will accomplish the object. What is needed is a License Act whereby large corporations may be licensed to engage in Interstate Commerce, on condition that they do not engage in those practices which result in the control of prices of output of markets and give them the power to crush out their competitors by unfair and oppressive means of competition. At the same time corporations should not be harassed by unnecessary law suits, should know whether they are doing legal business or not, and should be encouraged to invest capital in domestic and foreign commerce, for when the war closes we shall need all our resources to maintain the balance of trade which the war has thrown into our hands.

With these preliminary suggestions, let me, as briefly as possible, analyze the proposed bill. It was drawn before the Clayton Act or the Federal Trade Commission Act was passed, and hence might have to be changed to comply with the present status of the law. I have not had time to redraw the measure. In substance, it provides as follows:

SECTION 1 provides that all corporations having capital, stock or assets of $10,000,000 or more, shall be required to take out a license to engage in Interstate Commerce, and corporations having less than this may take out such license. It might be advisable to make this dividing line a higher capital. It is important not to require all of the small industries of the country to take out licenses in order to engage in business. It is only those large aggregations which can become dangerous to the independent traders.

SECTION 2 provides for the application for a license and the information to be given in such application.

SECTION 3 requires the Corporation Commission to examine the application to see if the corporation is legally organized and does not involve any unlawful restraint of trade or constitute a monopoly.

SECTION 4 provides that if the Corporation Commission should refuse a license, the applicant may bring a suit before the Court of Commerce, or any District Court of the United States, which could review the action of the Corporation Commission. When this Act was drawn, there was a Court of Commerce. It has since been abolished. This protects the corporation against the arbitrary action of the Corporation Commission.

SECTION 5 provides for a change in the name of the corporation or an amendment of its certificate.

SECTION 6 provides that said corporation shall not carry on the business of discounting bills, notes or other evidences of debts or receiving deposits, etc.

At this point it might be advisable to add a section providing that such corporation shall not engage in more than one kind of business. This would have to be carefully drawn, so as not to unduly limit the scope of the enterprise, for it is conducive to economy in production and to individual enterprise that corporations be permitted to integrate their business. For instance, a corporation engaged in the manufacture of iron and steel should be permitted to produce its raw material and to manufacture the products of the same. Those engaged in operating packing houses should be permitted to engage in all business incident thereto and the manufacture of all byproducts. This would have to be very carefully considered, because it is not advisable to unduly restrict the enterprise of the American people.

SECTION 7 requires a corporation organized after the passage of the law to demonstrate that its stock is issued whether for money or property equal to the face value thereof. But this provision shall not apply to a corporation organized before the passing of the law. The object of this provision is, as far as possible, to prevent the issuance of stock not represented by capital assets and to give security and confidence to the investor.

SECTION 8 provides that no corporation having more than 50% of the total business of the same character in the United States shall purchase the property or business of any of its competitors without the consent of the Corporation Commission. The object of this provision is to prevent the buying out of competitors, which was usually brought about in the old times after destructive competition. On the other hand, there may be cases where it is advisable to permit a large corporation to purchase its competitor. It may be that 50% is too high. This is a matter for consideration.

SECTION 9 provides for reports from the corporation so that the Corporation Commission can be fully informed.

SECTION 10 provides for the increase of capital.

SECTION 11 provides that if a corporation licensed shall enter into a contract or combination or engage in any conspiracy in restraint of trade, or shall monopolize or attempt to monopolize commerce, or engage in oppressive methods of competition, its license may be taken away.

SECTION 12 provides for the appointment of a Corporation Commission consisting of three persons. This was drawn before the Federal Trade Commission was organized and at a time when there was a Bureau of Corporations in the Department of Commerce, and it may be that this should be changed.

SECTION 13 gives the Commission the same power as the Bureau of Corporations under the act creating the Department of Commerce and Labor.

SECTION 14 provides that if a licensed corporation shall attempt to restrain or monopolize commerce or use oppressive methods of competition, or otherwise violate the law, any one may complain to the Corporation Commission and the Corporation Commission shall have power to investigate and to make an order requiring the licensed corporation to desist, and the Commission is authorized to institute proceedings in any District Court of the United States to forfeit the license of the corporation or to enjoin such violation.

The object of this section is to provide for a general supervision of the business of the licensee, and if corporations are licensed on condition that they obey the law, they will be much less liable to attempt a monopoly or use oppressive methods of competition and trade, because they are liable to lose their license and have their business stopped. On the other hand, they should be protected against harassing complaints of competitors and uncalled for investigations and prosecutions.

SECTION 15 provides for fees for issuing licenses.

SECTION 16 authorizes a licensed corporation to apply to the Commission for determination as to whether any proposed action of such licensee would unduly restrain or monopolize trade, etc. Heretofore corporations, especially in foreign countries, have been very greatly hampered because of their inability to determine in advance whether their proposed action was legal or not. Courts and lawyers necessarily differ on this subject. This would allow them to apply to the Commission and have the Commission decide in advance so that they may feel secure in their investments and transactions.

It must be borne in mind that especially in our foreign trade, we are going to require large aggregations of capital, and concentrations and cooperations will become more and more necessary after the war.

This somewhat inadequate analysis will give a general idea of the proposed legislation.

Yours very sincerely,   Frank B. Kellogg.

TCL (Hoover Archives, CSt-H).

From James McGranahan[1]

Dear President Wilson,   Londonderry 18th September, 1918.

I desire on behalf of the Irish Presbyterian Church to express our warm appreciation of the signal service which you and the people of the United States have rendered to civilisation and humanity in coming to the aid of the Allied Nations in this great struggle,—a struggle with forces that aim at the overthrow of that freedom for which the Anglo-Saxon race has always contended. The entrance of your nation into the arena came at the supreme moment in the history of the conflict. We have admired not only the rapidity of your preparations, the completeness of your organisation and the perfection of arrangements by which such large bodies of troops have been transported to these lands but also the splendid victories achieved by your men on the field of battle when either brigaded with their Allies or as recently when fighting as an independent section of the great Army.

Nor can we fail to admire the way in which your nation has risen up in its strength to grapple with the drink traffic and so sweep out of the way that which has been such a hindrance to the victory we all desire.

Our intense interest in your brave and noble action is increased by the remembrance that many of the founders of your great nation were members of the Presbyterian Church—chiefly Ulstermen—who, feeling the pressure of tyrannical powers such as their free spirits could not bear, betook themselves to a land where they helped to make liberty of conscience the watchword of settled government. They carried with them the faith, language and customs of the homeland and impressed them upon the country of their adoption.

Since our alliance with the United States then is not of recent origin we can all the more heartily and sincerely congratulate you on the great victories which your entrance into this contest has helped to secure, a contest which was not of our or your seeking.

We pray that you may be strengthened for the great work to which you have put your hand, that the people over whom you so worthily preside may be rightly guided in every step that is taken to hasten victory, and that we and all allied with us may soon rejoice in the peace that shall make democracy safe for all time.

I am, Sir,   Yours very sincerely,   James McGranahan

TLS (WP, DLC).
[1] Moderator of the General Assembly of the Presbyterian Church in Ireland and pastor of the First Presbyterian Church, Londonderry.

A Statement[1]

[Sept. 19, 1918]

Every day the great principles for which we are fighting take fresh hold upon our thought and purpose and make it clearer what the end must be and what we must do to achieve it. We now know more certainly than we ever knew before why free men brought the great nation and government we love into existence, because it grows clearer and clearer what supreme service it is to be America's privilege to render to the world. The anniversary of the discovery of America must therefore have for us in this fateful year a peculiar and thrilling significance. We should make it a day of ardent re-dedication to the ideals upon which our government is founded and by which our present heroic tasks are inspired.[2]

T MS (WP, DLC).
  [1] Members of the National Liberty Loan Committee had requested Wilson to issue a proclamation designating October 12, 1918, as "Liberty Day" in order to promote the Fourth Liberty Loan. This statement served as the preamble of the proclamation.
  [2] There is a WWsh draft of this statement in WP, DLC. The proclamation was published in the *Official Bulletin*, II (Sept. 20, 1918), 1, 3.

To Robert Lansing

[The White House]
My dear Mr. Secretary: 19 September, 1918.

I am ashamed to have overlooked the matter you call to my attention with regard to the population of the Archangel district.[1] Evidently, we shall have to "chip in" with the British Government, and I hope that you will say to them that we are willing to do so, to the extent of the five millions you name, though that seems to me, I must admit, a very large sum indeed. I assume that not so much as that will be needed.

I take it for granted that some part—perhaps the greater part— of the supplies can go from Great Britain. I hope so with all my heart. Shipments from here may be impossible under the exigencies of our present shipping programme in connection with the army.

In haste,   Faithfully yours,   Woodrow Wilson

TLS (Letterpress Books, WP, DLC).
  [1] See RL to WW, Sept. 17, 1918.

To John Crepps Wickliffe Beckham

My dear Senator: The White House 19 September, 1918

I understand you are leaving today to join Governor Stanley in opening the campaign in Kentucky. May I not say that my cordial best wishes go with you? It is of the utmost consequence that the administration should have the direct and unflagging assistance of its real friends at this time, and I bid you God speed.

Cordially and sincerely yours,   Woodrow Wilson

TLS (A. O. Stanley Papers, KyU).

To Grenville Stanley Macfarland

CONFIDENTIAL

[The White House]

My dear Mr. MacFarland: 19 September, 1918

My opinion about the public utilities situation is quite in accord with yours as expressed in your letter of September 16th, and I have not seen any reason to change it. I am from Missouri.

Cordially and sincerely yours,   Woodrow Wilson

TLS (Letterpress Books, WP, DLC).

To Robert Latham Owen

[The White House]

My dear Senator Owen: 19 September, 1918.

I am so deeply interested in the passage of the suffrage amendment that, learning that you are about to leave town, I am taking the great liberty of asking if you will not either postpone your absence or obtain a hard and fast pair. I know that you will pardon your party's leader for this liberty.

Cordially and sincerely yours,   Woodrow Wilson

TLS (Letterpress Books, WP, DLC).

From Robert Lansing

Dear Mr. President: Washington September 19, 1918.

I beg to call to your attention the attached copy of a confidential telegram from the American Legation at Berne.[1] It appears that Doctor Sulzer, Swiss Minister to the United States, is alleged to be representing that he returned to Switzerland with a special mission from you. The telegram quotes what purports to be a portion of an autographed letter from you to Doctor Sulzer, as follows:

"I authorize you to declare to some important German friends that there is now a possibility to start negotiations of peace on a basis satisfactory to both belligerents."

May I inquire what action you wish me to take on the Minister's telegram?   Faithfully yours,   Robert Lansing

TLS (SDR, RG 59, 763.72119/1897, DNA).
    ¹ P. A. Stovall to RL, Sept. 12, 1918, T telegram (SDR, RG 59, 763.72119/1897, DNA). Stovall reported that one "Arraga, formerly Uruguayan Minister at Berlin," had, on September 9, told "an agent" of the American legation that Hans Sulzer had "returned from Washington with special mission from President Wilson and autograph letter from President." Stovall then quoted the sentence which Lansing quotes in the above letter. Stovall added that Sulzer was alleged to have made the following comment: "The affair must be hurried since the authority of Wilson may soon diminish and his voice no longer be dominant among the Allies." Stovall also reported that the German Minister in Bern, Gisbert, Baron von Romberg, had sent the "letter and message" to General Erich Ludendorff on September 7. Finally, Stovall noted that "the agent" had been shown a photostatic copy of the alleged letter from Wilson but that he could remember no detail of it, such as the physical characteristics of the stationery or the date. The Editors have been unable further to identify Arraga.

From John Nevin Sayre

Dear Mr. President,   Suffern, N. Y. September 19, 1918.

I want to thank you sincerely for the very helpful way you talked with me the other evening. We had a meeting of the editorial board of the World Tomorrow in New York yesterday, and I explained to the editors the substance of your views. During our meeting word came from the New York Post Office that the magazine was released.

I cannot tell you how glad I am for aside from any personal reasons, I feel that suppression of the magazine would have done harm in creating the impression among our readers that the Government was unnecessarily restricting free speech. As the magazine is almost a cooperative venture, the subscribers know that its editors are not disloyal or unpatriotic, but that they are deeply religious, and speaking as preachers that which moral conviction impells them to say; that which they also believe will help our country and the world.

Since our talk I have a new appreciation of the stupendous work you are doing. May God guide and sustain you.

                    Your sincere admirer   John Nevin Sayre

P.S. Please remember me cordially to Mrs. Wilson and Miss Bones, and accept my thanks for your hospitality.

ALS (WP, DLC).

Two Letters to Robert Lansing

My dear Mr. Secretary,   The White House. 20 Sept., 1918

I think the first of the two courses you suggest[1] is the better and hope that you will send the enclosed telegram.[2]   W.W.

ALI (B. Long Papers, DLC).
  [1] In RL to WW, Sept. 18, 1918.
  [2] It is missing, but it was Wilson's revision of Lansing's draft telegram printed as an Enclosure with RL to WW, Sept. 18, 1918. Wilson's version was sent to all American diplomatic stations and was given to the press on September 21. It is printed, e.g., in *FR 1918, Russia*, I, 687-88, and in the *Official Bulletin*, II (Sept. 23, 1918), 1. Wilson's version (RL to Amlegation, The Hague, Sept. 18 [20], 1918, T telegram, SDR, RG 59, 861.00/2778a, DNA) reads as follows:
  "This Government is in receipt of information from reliable sources revealing that the peaceable Russian citizens of Moscow, Petrograd and other cities are suffering from an openly avowed campaign of mass terrorism and are subject to wholesale executions. Thousands of persons have been shot without even a form of trial; ill administered prisons are filled beyond capacity and every night scores of Russian citizens are recklessly put to death; and irresponsible bands are venting their brutal passions in the daily massacre of untold innocents.
  "In view of the earnest desire of the people of the United States to befriend the Russian people and lend them all possible assistance in their struggle to reconstruct their nation upon principles of democracy and self-government and acting therefore solely in the interest of the Russian people themselves, this Government feels that it cannnot be silent or refrain from expressing its horror at this existing state of terrorism. Furthermore it believes that in order successfully to check the further increase of the indiscriminate slaughter of Russian citizens all the civilized nations should register their abhorrence of such barbarism.
  "You will inquire, therefore, whether the Government to which you are accredited will be disposed to take some immediate action, which is entirely divorced from the atmosphere of belligerency and the conduct of war, to impress upon the perpetrators of these crimes the aversion with which civilization regards their present wanton acts."

CONFIDENTIAL

My dear Mr. Secretary: The White House 20 September, 1918.

Thank you for having let me see the enclosed.[1] I entirely agree with Baker's judgment in the matter of the expected request from Clemenceau. I say "expected" because I have not seen it and believe we have not yet received it, have we?

Cordially and faithfully yours,   Woodrow Wilson

TLS (SDR, RG 59, 763.72/13464½, DNA).
  [1] The Enclosure printed with RL to WW, Sept. 16, 1918 (first letter of that date).

To Robert Lansing, with Enclosure

CONFIDENTIAL

My dear Mr. Secretary: The White House 20 September, 1918.

These papers are, I suppose, out of date now, but I return them for your files, and also wish to say that I agree with the judgments expressed in your letter.

Cordially and faithfully yours,   Woodrow Wilson

TLS (SDR, RG 59, 861.00/3645, DNA).

ENCLOSURE

From Robert Lansing

My dear Mr. President: Washington September 13, 1918.

I venture to bring to your attention a communication from the Secretary of the Navy of the 20th ultimo transmitting a weekly report from the commanding officer of the u.s.s. olympia, dated July 6, 1918, enclosing a declaration and resolution of the District Council of Murmansk and a temporary agreement between the representatives of Great Britain, France and the United States and the Murmansk Region Council; the latter of which has been signed by the commanding officer of the olympia,[1] whose action in so doing has been provisionally approved by Vice Admiral Sims.

The Secretary of the Navy entertains the opinion that the agreement is sound in principle and should meet with the approval of this Government. As it sets forth clearly that all authority in the internal government of the region belongs to the Regional Council and that the representatives of Great Britain, France and this country do not interfere in the internal affairs of the region, it seems to me a good working arrangement. In view of the recent political developments in Archangel, however, I am inclined to reserve judgment as to whether it may be interpreted by some as entailing recognition of the Murmansk Council as a de facto government and it is for that reason that I should welcome an expression of your desires in this matter.

Faithfully yours,   Robert Lansing

TLS (SDR, RG 59, 861.00/3645, DNA).
    [1] JD to RL, Aug. 20, 1918, TCL (SDR, RG 59, 861.00/3645, DNA), which enclosed a report from the commanding officer of *U.S.S. Olympia*, Capt. Bion Barnett Bierer: B. B. Bierer to W. S. Sims, July 6, 1918, TC MS (SDR, RG 59, 861.00/3645, DNA). In this dispatch, Bierer transmitted a resolution adopted by the Murmansk Region Council on June 30, 1918, which welcomed the assistance of Great Britain, France, and the United States in defending Russia against the Germans and the Finns, in organizing a Russian army, and in improving the country's economic conditions. Bierer also enclosed a "temporary agreement," which he and his British and French colleagues had signed with the presidium of the Murmansk Region Council on July 6, 1918, and he asked that it be approved. In the agreement, the signatories pledged their "fullest mutual co-operation" in the defense of the Murmansk region against the powers of the "German coalition." The British, French, and American representatives promised to provide the Murmansk Region Council with foodstuffs for the entire population of the region, with

military equipment and supplies, and with all other necessary materials, goods, and "technical appliances." However, they would not interfere in the internal affairs of the region and would leave full authority over the region's internal government in the hands of the Murmansk Region Council. The representatives of Great Britain, France, and the United States affirmed that their respective governments did not intend to take possession of any part or region, and the council declared that the "sole reason" for concluding the agreement was "to save the Murmansk Region in its integrity for the great Undivided Russia."

In his letter to Lansing of August 20, 1918, Daniels recommended that the government endorse Bierer's course of action, and he pointed out that it had already received the support of Admiral Sims. Lansing, in turn, asked for Wilson's approval of the agreement, and he enclosed a draft of a reply to Daniels to that effect. RL to WW, Sept. 27, 1918, TLS (SDR, RG 59, 861.00/3679a, DNA). For a brief discussion, see Leonid I. Strakhovsky, *The Origins of American Intervention in North Russia (1918)* (Princeton, N. J., 1937), pp. 68-71.

Two Letters to Herbert Clark Hoover

My dear Hoover: [The White House] 20 September, 1918.

I have read the enclosed[1] with close attention and take the liberty of suggesting that perhaps it would not be wise to publish it. I particularly want to avoid even the appearance of a controversy between two agencies which really trust oneanother, and while I think the considerations you urge are of great weight, it seems to me best that we should thresh the matter out with as little appearance of public di[s]cussion as possible.

Cordially and faithfully yours,   Woodrow Wilson

TLS (Letterpress Books, WP, DLC).
  [1] See HCH to WW, Sept. 16, 1918.

My dear Hoover: The White House 20 September, 1918.

I have been as much interested as you evidently are in the enclosed bill and Senator Kellogg's discussion of it. I think with you that there are ideas in it which are thoroughly worth considering, and I would be very glad if Senator Kellogg or someone whom he could employ would redraft the bill in conformity with recent legislation, so that we might have a measure to which we could apply particular scrutiny.

Cordially and sincerely yours,   Woodrow Wilson

TLS (Hoover Archives, CSt-H).

To Jessie Kennedy Dyer

My dear Jessie: [The White House] 20 September, 1918.

I am very much interested in what you tell me of what you have been asked to do for the Liberty Loan Committee in Chicot County,[1] and I wish with all my heart I could write the little speech you want me to write, but it is literally impossible. I can only send you this message to deliver in any form you see fit.

Please tell the people for me that this seems to me to be a war in which the American people are privileged to play a singular and noble part because they have no selfish ends to serve and are fighting for the principles and ideals which have always lain at the very foundation of our own nation's life. We are trying to extend to the world the gift of liberty and conscience and disinterested service of mankind, which were intended to be the contribution of America to the world. If ever it was worth while to pour out blood and money and make every conceivable sacrifice, it is worth while now, and every dollar invested in the Liberty Loan is a dollar invested in the prosperity and liberty of men at home and throughout all the nations of the world. We can withhold nothing, and we should give everything with the ardor of those absolutely devoted to a great cause.

In haste,   Affectionately yours,   Woodrow Wilson

TLS (Letterpress Books, WP, DLC).
¹ She was then living in Dermott, Ark. Her letter was Jessie K. Dyer to WW, Sept. 15, 1918, ALS (WP, DLC).

To Frank Morrison

My dear Mr. Morrison: [The White House] 20 September, 1918.

I hope that you will not think that I am taking a liberty when I express the earnest hope that organized labor will not oppose the re-election of Congressman Sherley, of Louisville. I have tested Mr. Sherley in a great many ways and even when I did not agree with his opinions I have entirely honored and respected him. He is one of the most useful, not to say indispensable, members of the House, and I am disturbed by the rumor that the labor men in Louisville are trying to induce a man of their own ranks to run against Mr. Sherley. If you are willing, I would very much appreciate your advising the labor men in Louisville against this, for I believe that Mr. Sherley's retention in Congress is in the national interest.

Cordially and sincerely yours,   Woodrow Wilson

TLS (Letterpress Books, WP, DLC).

From Alexander Monroe Dockery

PERSONAL

My dear Mr. President: Washington September 20, 1918.

Referring further to your favor of the 9th ultimo,[1] will say that I would have made an earlier reply but for the absence from Kansas City of one gentleman whose opinion I desired in respect to the attitude of the Democratic nominee for Congress in the Kansas City District. He has just returned, and therefore I am able to make this belated response.

The gentlemen of whom I made inquiry are all positive that Mr. Bland will prove to be an earnest supporter of the war policies of the Administration. However, one of the number states that Mr. B. stood with Senator R.[2] in opposition to the food conservation policy of the Administration, and that he is a warm personal friend of the Senator.

I am still of the opinion that Mr. B. will loyally support the Administration in the conduct of the war, but at the first opportunity— either here or at Kansas City—I will put the question at rest by a personal interview on my o[w]n account.

Sincerely, your friend,   A M Dockery

TLS (WP, DLC).
   [1] WW to A. M. Dockery, Sept. 9, 1918, TLS (Letterpress Books, WP, DLC).
   [2] That is, James Alexander Reed of Missouri.

From Ellen Duane Davis

My dear Friend,   Philadelphia Sept. 20, 1918

Here I come to bother you again and this time it is a real personal bother which will count much, not only to me but to all the women in Pennsylvania. The National Woman's Suffrage Association, of which Mrs Catt is the Head, held a "conference" here yesterday with an executive meeting afterwards at which I was unanimously delegated to invite you to come here during the week beginning November 13th to speak to us. Mrs Catt seems to think Pennsylvania the pivotal State which will decide the ratification of the Ammendment (which please God will pass the Senate on Sept. 26th) but whether it passes or no, we shall go on with our Suffrage work in conjunction with our War work and we earnestly ask you to help us by coming. *Please* say yes and give me the date so that we can secure a big enough building to hold *you* and your audience. Will you please telegraph reply? Remember the Liberty Loan Drive will be over. The Elections will be over, and while the War will not be over and there will be many sad hearts among the women,

nothing can give them the encouragement to fight for our ratification in our Legislature as a word from you in the flesh. You spoke
in New York, in Baltimore and now we need you here[.] E.P. knows
I am writing this and while he thought it might be "difficult" yet
he did not say "don't bother him" & I truly think he has the feeling
that I am your greatest nuisance. Please give my best love to the
dear First Lady. If you come in the afternoon will you both take
luncheon here with us? Hoping for the benefit of American Democracy you will come believe me
    Always your sincere & respectful friend
Ellen Duane Davis

Do you pray for things to happen? I do and shall pray that you
will come.

ALS (WP, DLC).

From Robert Latham Owen

My dear Mr. President: [Washington] September 20, 1918.

I am very much gratified to see your active interest in the passage
of the Suffrage Amendment. I have determined to remain and have
persuaded Senator Sterling also to remain since we can strengthen
the vote by remaining.

I had never contemplated leaving the city without a hard and
fast pair, but even a hard and fast pair in this case will not suffice,
for we have two votes absent (Sens Hiram Johnson and Lafollette
both in California) for the amendment to one (Sen. Swanson) necessarily absent against the amendment. Senator Sterling and myself
have determined, upon an analysis of the vote, that we would not
leave the city as you seem to fear.
Very respectfully yours,

If Sterling & myself left one pair with Swanson[,] Hiram Johnson
and Lafollette would not be paired.

TL (WP, DLC).

From Valentine Everit Macy

Washington, D. C. September

My dear Mr. President: Twentieth Nineteen Eighteen.

Many thanks for your letter of September 18th. After its receipt
our Board met and decided it was wise to order the following notice
placed in all shipyards:

"Appreciating the natural impatience of shipbuilding employees at the delay in the issue of its forthcoming decision in reference to wages, hours and working conditions in the shipyards, the Shipbuilding Labor Adjustment Board announces that at the earnest request of the President, it has entered into conference with other labor adjustment agencies of the Government in an effort to arrive at some common policy which will be just to all the war labor forces, and in response to the President's request, it is delaying its decision until the conferences are concluded, which it is hoped will be in the near future."

Hoping that this meets with your approval,

Respectfully,   V. Everit Macy

TLS (WP, DLC).

Oswald Garrison Villard to Joseph Patrick Tumulty

Dear Mr. Tumulty: New York City September 20, 1918.

Thanks for your note. I know you helped a lot. Let me take the opportunity to say to you that I gave no interview to any newspaper about the matter. Those attributed to me, beyond a statement on Friday last that I did not know what the trouble was, are fictitious. This also applies to the story in today's Times, which they did not get from me. I have not even seen a reporter.

I shall write to the President next week, thanking him and submitting the memorandum which you suggested. I think we shall have a constructive suggestion or two to offer him, which may be of real service in solving this very difficult problem, for I realize, of course, that there are two sides to it and that it is difficult to draw the line. The trouble today is, chiefly, that the law is being administered by the wrong kind of man—boll-weevils!

Faithfully yours,   Oswald Garrison Villard.

TLS (WP, DLC).

A Translation of a Telegram from Jean Jules Jusserand to the Foreign Ministry

Washington, no date, received September 20 [1918].

I talked with the President[1] about the worrisome situation revealed by the last news from the region of Samara and of the necessity of acting in face of the danger.

Entirely absorbed by the idea that the decision of the war depends on the western front and that it is there that it is necessary to concentrate our effort without the least diversion, the President appears absolutely ready, on the contrary, to accept the hypothesis of a withdrawal of the Czechs from the Urals as soon as we can send them some increased military reinforcements.

I insisted upon the importance of maintaining positions which will prevent the Germans from obtaining food supplies and minerals. I observed that the Japanese commander could at least divert a part of the inter-Allied troops at his disposal and send them to Irkutsk, where they could liberate the Czech forces there who could then go to the aid of those in danger at the extremity of the line. They could perhaps find some help among Russian loyalists. The President made no objection.

General Janin thinks with me that it will be the only means of aiding our Czech allies in time and that it would be well if such suggestions were made without delay to the Japanese commander.

Jusserand.

T telegram (État-Major, l'Armée de Terre, Service Historique, 4 N 46, FMD-Ar).
  ¹ On September 18, to present him. Gen. Pierre Thiébaut Charles Maurice Janin, chief of the French military mission to Russia, 1916-1917, and, more recently, commander of the Czechoslovak forces in France. He was on his way to assume command of the Czechoslovak forces in Siberia. Janin signed himself simply "Maurice Janin."

Colville Adrian de Rune Barclay to the Foreign Office

Washington September 20th, 1918.

No. 4254. General Janin saw the President on September 18th and asked if he would send troops to Murman. The President refused. To a similar question regarding Western Siberia he would give no definite answer. His attitude towards Czecho-Slovaks was most sympathetic and he was apologetic for the delay there had been over the despatch of supplies.

T telegram (FO 371/3324, No. 160450, p. 572A, PRO).

To Alexander Monroe Dockery

CONFIDENTIAL

[The White House]

My dear Governor Dockery: 21 September, 1918.

Thank you for your letter of this morning about Mr. Bland of Kansas City. It gives me just the line on him which I desire.

Cordially and faithfully yours,   Woodrow Wilson

TLS (Letterpress Books, WP, DLC).

To Thetus Willrette Sims

My dear Mr. Sims: The White House 21 September, 1918

In view of the possibility of three-day adjournments by the House and the absence of a quorum from the city, I venture to write you this hurried note to urge that the Emergency Power Bill be pressed to passage, if possible, before adjournment, as it is of capital and immediate importance as a war measure. I hope that it will be possible for you to obtain the consent of the House to this action.

In haste,

Cordially and sincerely yours,   Woodrow Wilson

TLS (WC, NjP).

Four Letters from Robert Lansing

My dear Mr. President: Washington September 21, 1918.

I have made careful inquiry but as you may already have noted from the first telegram we received from Mr. Morris upon his arrival at Vladivostok,[1] it would seem that thus far the so-called Allied Military Council is merely an informal committee dealing with purely technical matters concerning the military forces.

I shall, however, make our position quite clear to the French and Italian Ambassadors and to the British Chargé d'Affaires, ad interim.   Faithfully yours,   Robert Lansing.

[1] R. S. Morris to RL, Sept. 18, 1918, T telegram (SDR, RG 59, 861.77/486, DNA). Morris reported that he had arrived at Vladivostok on September 17. Most of this telegram was concerned with a proposal to make John F. Stevens director general of the Russian railway system. However, the following sentence referred to the Allied Military Council: "General Graves advises me that there is no formal allied military council but merely an informal committee of military representatives who have met to arrange details of transportation of troops and material; that he has sent his quartermaster to meetings of this committee, and that no questions of general policy have been decided."

Lansing, on September 4, had instructed Morris to go to Vladivostok to undertake a "complete review" of the situation in Siberia. "Your inquiries and reports," Lansing said, "should cover the economic, social, financial, political, and military situations." RL to R. S. Morris, Sept. 4, 1918, *FR 1918, Russia*, II, 366.

My dear Mr. President: Washington September 21, 1918.

I have just had, this morning, a conversation with Professor Masaryk in regard to the Czecho-Slovak situation. He was very emphatic in agreeing with us that the restoration of an Eastern Front was absolutely out of the question. He also agreed that it was the wisest course for the Czecho-Slovaks on the Volga and in Eastern Russia to retire through Siberia as soon as that could be done with safety. He said, however, that it would be most dangerous for the forces at certain points near the Urals to withdraw in their defenseless condition; that the safety of their retirement depended upon getting them arms and ammunition. His advices were that there were at least fifty thousand Czecho-Slovaks without arms dependent entirely for their protection upon the small forces which were armed.

In every way he was most thoroughly in accord with our policy and told me that he would take up the matter of supplies immediately with Mr. McCormick, Mr. Baruch and Mr. Hurley.

Incidentally, in talking with him, he told me that he had information that the Germans had in Germany under training about 500,000 additional troops which would be used when they considered the time favorable.

Faithfully yours,   Robert Lansing.

TLS (WP, DLC).

Dear Mr. President: Washington September 21, 1918.

In your letter of the 18th regarding the Czecho-Slovaks you ask me, if my judgment concurred, to make a certain communication to the governments concerned. I am preparing to do so.

May I, however, call your attention to the accompanying extract from our Aide Memoire of July 17th[1] which was communicated to these same governments? I feel that we should be careful to do nothing which would open the door to possible criticism that we have not lived up to the assurances that we shall not seek, even by implication, to set limits to the action or to define the policies of our associates. It seems to me that we should make our position clear that we will not send forces into the interior to support the Czecho-Slovaks and that in our opinion they should proceed to a zone of safety; but I am a little embarrassed by the suggestion that we "insist" that they shall be brought out eastward to Vladivostok and conveyed to the Western Front in Europe if necessary.

In view of the statement in the Aide Memoire I do not see how we can go further than to call again to the attention of the Allied governments our policy and say to them that it has not been affected by recent events, particularly emphasizing the fact that we consider the restoration of an eastern front entirely impracticable.

If this course meets with your approval I will have a suggested draft of a note prepared at once.

Faithfully yours,   Robert Lansing

TLS (SDR, RG 59, 861.00/3010, DNA).
  [1] This enclosure is missing. The aide-mémoire is printed as an Enclosure with WW to F. L. Polk, July 17, 1918, Vol. 48.

My dear Mr. President: Washington September 21st, 1918.

I am laying before you a matter[1] which has been the subject of considerable study on the part of this Department, the Treasury and the War Trade Board, and which has been freely and fully discussed jointly. It appears in the form of a memorandum which I attach and to which are also attached, but which you may not find it necessary to read, a memorandum from the Russian Ambassador and several cables, one from Mr. Francis and one from Mr. Page, the latter dealing with a French suggestion.[2]

It was our idea that consideration of this matter might be delayed and determination in regard to it postponed until some definite plan had been adopted in regard to economic assistance in Siberia and in Russia. However, the practical side of economic aid is inextricably connected with a medium of circulation and the theory of economic operations is necessarily based upon some practical financial plan, the adoption of which must precede all commercial assistance. The other Governments concerned are already independently engaged in instituting each a separate plan. In as much as it has been felt highly desirable that the same scheme should under-lie operations in Russia and Siberia, because it is hoped that those two will ultimately be in practical co-operation if not in absolute harmony, it seems desirable that a general plan should be adopted by all those of the co-belligerents who will operate in that whole country.

Consequently I lay the matter before you and hope that it will have your approval in principle, so that we may suggest it to England, and France and Japan, and come to a mutual understanding and can operate each on the same plan instead of operating independently, and so that the pound, the yen, the dollar and various other units of value will not promiscuously circulate in different spheres, to the hopeless confusion of the Russians and to the detriment of the ruble.

I am, my dear Mr. President,

Yours very sincerely,   Robert Lansing.

TLS (WP, DLC).
    [1] The "matter" was the problem of creating a currency which people in northern Russia and Siberia would accept at face value and one which "a stable Russian Government" would take over.
    [2] [RL], memorandum; [B. A. Bakhmet'ev] memorandum dated "August, 1918"; and "MEMORANDUM FOR THE SECRETARY OF THE TREASURY," dated Aug. 28, 1918, all T MSS (WP, DLC); D. R. Francis to RL, Sept. 14, 1918, and W. H. Page to RL, Sept. 17, 1918, both T telegrams (WP, DLC).

From Herbert Clark Hoover, with Enclosure

Dear Mr. President: Washington 21-September-1918

We have now completed a preliminary programme of exports of food needed during the coming twelve months to support the Allies, the Belgian Relief, the American Expeditionary Forces and the minimum shipments of necessities to the Neutrals, which I attach hereto.

You will see the progression—

Average 3 year pre war exports—   5,533,000 Tons,
Last year,   11,820,000   "
Next year,   17,550,000   "

While our wheat situation is better this year than last, the draught [drought] has affected our grasses and corn to an extent that gives us on balance about the same food values as last year. It will, therefore, be a year of strenuous conservation.

The enlarged programme is due in part to increased Army shipments, but in the main to diversion of Allied tonnage to us instead of the Argentine, Australia and the East. The Allied countries will receive less total food from all sources than last year by some 3,000,000 tons, this reduction having been made largely in animal feeds in order to release tonnage for the American Army. This arrangement necessitates larger meat and fat exports from us and the killing of further capital in animals by them.

Yours faithfully,   Herbert Hoover

TLS (WP, DLC).

E   N   C   L   O   S   U   R   E

	Average 3-year Pre-war Shipments	Shipped Year ending July 1, 1918	Must ship Year ending July 1, 1919	Increase This year over Last Year
	TONS	TONS	TONS	TONS
Meats and Fats (Beef, Pork, Dairy, Poultry and Vegetable Oil Products)	645,000	1,550,000	2,600,000	1,050,000
Bread Stuffs (Wheat and substitutes in terms of grain)	3,320,000	6,800,000	10,400,000	3,600,000
Sugar (From United States and West Indies)	618,000	1,520,000	1,850,000	330,000
Feed Grains (Mostly Army Oats)	950,000	1,950,000	2,700,000	750,000
Totals,	5,533,000	11,820,000	17,550,000	5,730,000

T MS (WP, DLC).

From William Byron Colver

My dear Mr. President: Washington 21 September 1918

Efforts to prevent the Commission's report on the Meat Packers from going into the Congressional Record and being printed as a House or Senate document have thus far been entirely successful.

You were so good as to suggest that you might send it to Congress, thus insuring its official publication. You suggested that you be supplied with a copy for that purpose and there is, therefore, a copy attached hereto for such use as you may deem proper.[1]

Faithfully yours,   William B. Colver.

TLS (WP, DLC).
    [1] "The President asks if you will be kind enough to prepare for transmission this report from the Federal Trade Commission. It will be necessary to ask the Commission for another copy, as it is to be transmitted to both Houses of Congress." G. F. Close to R. Forster, c. Sept. 21, 1918, TL (WP, DLC). Wilson transmitted the "Summary of the Report of the Federal Trade Commission on the Meat-Packing Industry" to Congress on September 24, and it was printed in *Cong. Record*, 65th Cong., 2d sess., pp. 11051-63 and, separately, as 65th Cong., 2d sess., House Document No. 1297. The full report, transmitted by William B. Colver to Wilson on November 25, 1918, was printed as Part II of House Document No. 1297.

From Thetus Willrette Sims

My Dear Mr. President,   Washington, D. C. Sept 21st, 1918

The Committee on Interstate and Foreign Commerce has by unanimous vote reported favorably the Emergency Power Bill. I tried yesterday to get unanimous consent to take it up and pass it following action on the Agricultural appropriation bill and objection was made. Mr. Kitchin asked me to immediately take the matter up with you and urge you to either write me or him a letter urging immediate consideration of the bill as a war measure before taking any three day adjournments. He says he believes it will be necessary for you to do so in order to keep a quorum in the City for the passage of the bill. Will you kindly do so and if possible send letter to Capitol before noon today.   Sincerely yours,   T. W. Sims

ALS (WP, DLC).

From Robert Somers Brookings

My dear Mr. President: Washington Sept. 21, 1918.

At a meeting of the Price Fixing Committee with the representatives of the steel industries, on Thursday and yesterday of this week, while the cost of all steel products has been constantly mounting, owing to the increase in labor wage, cost of supplies, and advance in transportation rates, we have avoided making any advance in the price of steel.

Some minor adjustments, however, were necessary in the prices of ore and pig iron, in order to maintain absolutely necessary production and keep the industry in healthy condition.

Will you kindly approve the enclosed statement for publication,[1] and oblige,   Your respectfully,   Robt. S. Brookings

TLS (WP, DLC).
[1] It was published in the *Official Bulletin*, II (Sept. 24, 1918), 2.

Two Letters to Robert Lansing

My dear Mr. Secretary: The White House 23 September, 1918.

You are quite right about the enclosed, and I am perfectly willing that you should modify what I suggested so as not to "insist" that the Czecho-Slovaks be brought out eastward to Vladivostok, but merely to urge the advisability of that as, in our judgment, a wise and necessary course.

Cordially and faithfully yours,   Woodrow Wilson

TLS (SDR, RG 59, 861.00/3013, DNA).

My dear Mr. Secretary: The White House 23 September, 1918.

This is a very extraordinary and distressing matter. I cannot believe that Dr. Sulzer did anything so dishonorable. Of course, I gave him no such authorization and no such letter, and it is important that the Legation at Berne should inquire, I should say, directly of Dr. Sulzer about it, and take immediate steps to correct this outrageous statement, if necessary conveying the denial directly or indirectly to the German Minister there. I would be very much obliged if you would request them to do something of the sort.[1]   Cordially and faithfully yours,   Woodrow Wilson

TLS (SDR, RG 59, 763.72119/1959, DNA).
[1] Lansing paraphrased the above letter in RL to P. A. Stovall, Sept. 23, 1918, T telegram (SDR, RG 59, 763.72119/1897, DNA).

To Joseph Patrick Tumulty

Dear Tumulty: [The White House] 23 September, 1918

I would be very much obliged if you would write to the people in Minneapolis, thanking them for consulting us and telling them that I think the formation of clubs of this sort unnecessary and embarrassing.[1]   The President

TL (WP, DLC).
[1] Wilson was responding to O. E. Johnson to JPT, Sept. 14, 1918, TLS (WP, DLC).

Johnson, secretary and manager of the Calhoun Commercial Club of Minneapolis, had written to ascertain whether Wilson approved of the Unconditional Surrender Club of the United States of America. He wished to be sure that Wilson had in fact approved of the organization before he organized a branch of it in Minneapolis.

The Unconditional Surrender Club had been founded in Flint, Michigan, on July 29, 1918. Its members pledged "undying fealty" to the United States Government, unfailing support to "our soldiers," "all that we possess to the cause of winning the war," and "to make any and whatever sacrifices we may be called upon to make to the end that the central powers may be brought to realize that only an unconditional surrender will be acceptable to us and to the United States of America." These objectives were communicated to Wilson in Dwight T. Stone *et al.* to WW, July 29, 1918, T telegram (WP, DLC), and were widely publicized. Subsequently, the Flint club freely implied that Wilson had approved of the organization and its objectives, citing in support Tumulty's acknowledgment of the club's telegram of July 29. There is no copy of Tumulty's acknowledgment in WP, DLC. However, as quoted in Johnson's letter cited above, it reads as follows: "The President asks me to acknowledge the receipt of your telegram of even date and to tell you and all those concerned that he much appreciates your patriotic pledges and your heartening assurances."

To Winthrop More Daniels

My dear Daniels: The White House 23 September, 1918

Thank you for your letter of the 20th with the memorandum from Mr. Morris L. Cook.[1] I will take the matter up on Wednesday with my little war board and see if the cooperative idea suggested by Mr. Cook does not commend itself to them as it does to me.

Cordially and faithfully yours,   Woodrow Wilson

TLS (Wilson-Daniels Corr., CtY).
[1] W. M. Daniels to WW, Sept. 20, 1918, TLS, enclosing Morris Llewellyn Cooke, "Memorandum as to Federal Utilities Advisory Board," T MS, and M. L. Cooke to W. M. Daniels, Sept. 20, 1918, TCL, all in WP, DLC. Cooke, a consulting engineer, was at this time the executive assistant to Edward N. Hurley. All of these documents dealt with Cooke's proposal for a federal utilities commission or advisory board which would standardize agreements made between public utility companies and the various departments of the federal government.

To William Byron Colver

My dear Colver: [The White House] 23 September, 1918.

Thank you for the "big list" and other papers anent the activities of the Chamber of Commerce.[1] I hope the matter will be successfully brought out into the open by our friends on the hill.

In haste,

Cordially and faithfully yours,   Woodrow Wilson

TLS (Letterpress Books, WP, DLC).
[1] Wilson was responding to W. B. Colver to WW, Sept. 21, 1918, TLS, enclosing Allen Walker to C. C. Brown, Oct. 20, 1915, TCL; "Special List of 'One Hundred,' " T MS; Samuel W. Tator, "Special Report on Donation of $1000 to Martin B. Madden by Armour & Company," Aug. 31, 1918, T MS; F. W. Croll to M. B. Madden, Aug. 30, 1918, TCL; and M. B. Madden to F. W. Croll, Sept. 1, 1918, TCL, all in WP, DLC. Walker, a member of the executive committee of the Chamber of Commerce of the United States of America, had solicited from Brown, an official of the Victor Talking Machine Co., a subscription

of $1,000 a year for three years to the "Emergency Fund" of the Chamber of Commerce. He enclosed a list, complete as of October 20, 1915, of forty-six business and industrial firms which had made such donations. Neither these two enclosures nor the covering letter from Colver, reveal the exact purpose of this emergency fund. That it was probably political in nature is suggested by the three other enclosures which all deal with a contribution by Armour & Co. to the "Republican Publicity Association." Martin Barnaby Madden, a Republican congressman from Chicago, and the treasurer of the Republican Publicity Association, stated that the organization did not take part in campaigns for the nomination or election of candidates for office but merely gathered and disseminated information which would "demonstrate the superiority of Republican principles and accomplishments, and expose the defects and failures of Democratic policies and administration." However, there was no mention of the Chamber of Commerce in any of the three enclosures relating to the Republican Publicity Association.

To Ellen Duane Davis

My dear Friend: [The White House] 23 September, 1918

I wish with all my heart I could, but I can't. I am going to make a speech, which it is imperatively necessary that I should make for various reasons, this week in New York, but I know by the difficulty I have found in finding any time at all to prepare that speech that I cannot in conscience add another. It is a great distress to me to disappoint you in this or any other matter, but I simply cannot add any more to what I am doing, as I am sure you will believe.

In great haste, with affectionate messages to you both,
Cordially and sincerely yours,   Woodrow Wilson

TLS (Letterpress Books, WP, DLC).

From Robert Lansing

My dear Mr. President: Washington September 23, 1918.

As I told you the other day I am to receive a degree from the University of the State of New York at Albany on October 18th. and have to deliver a short address. I have taken as a live subject the peace overtures by the Central Powers. In view of the fact that it unavoidably deals with the policy of our Government toward such overtures I am sending you a copy of my proposed remarks.[1]

I dislike very much to bother you with such a matter but it seems to me that nothing should be said in an address of this sort which can in any way disagree with your views. The sum and substance of the address is that until Prussianism is blotted out discussions of peace are of no avail and that we can in no event enter into a treaty of peace which is tainted with the Prussian spirit as that has been demonstrated in the treatment of Russia. At this time it seemed to me wise to dwell upon our intention to save Russia from German domination.

I do not think it will take you very long to glance through the address beginning on page three. I am naturally anxious to have it in hand as soon as possible in order that I may put it into print.

Faithfully yours,   Robert Lansing.

TLS (WP, DLC).
   ¹ Not found. For House's reaction to the proposed speech, see EMH to WW, Sept. 25, 1918. In any event, the conferral of the degree was postponed until 1919, and Lansing never delivered the address.

From Newton Diehl Baker

CONFIDENTIAL.

General Headquarters, A.E.F., September 23, 1918.

Paragraph 1. The British have put the matter of cargo tonnage in the hands of Lord Reading who has been too ill to carry on the work. I saw him in London and arranged to have our experts prepare the preliminaries for our consideration the latter part of this week when he will be well enough to conclude the matter. In the meantime the British have definitely allotted to us for export use 200,000 dead weight tons and these ships will be immediately diverted to us.

Paragraph 2. The British view is that tonnage diverted to us is withdrawn from essential allied needs, principally cereal imports, and will be required to be made good later in the cereal year by assistance from us when our new ships make it possible. Their suggestion will be that America cooperate through Allied Maritime Transport Council and the existing program committees in using any surplus we develop for whatever may be agreed to be the most pressing allied need at the moment. They concede that the control of American tonnage must remain with America and that no vote of Allied Maritime Council can be permitted to control it but urge that the American representatives on the Maritime Council and program committees be authorized to make full display of American needs and facilities as representatives of other nations will do and that the relative needs of the various allies as they thus appear be sent to America for our information in determining our use of our ships.

Paragraph 3. This use of aggregate facilities for the paramount needs as they appear from time to time we would doubtless consent to in any case, but with your approval I would like to agree with Lord Reading as follows:

First. There can be no diversion of ships either American or British from American army supply use below the amount needed for constant maintenance of such American forces as are already in Europe from time to time.

Second. We will cooperate with the British, French and Italians in using their tonnage for our military program and our tonnage for the essential supply of their military and civil programs by counsel changing the use of ships as their needs become paramount, we reserving the right to use our own judgment when informed by common counsel as to the fact of any allied need being really greater than the next items in our own programs.   Baker.

T telegram (N. D. Baker Papers, DLC).

From Robert Lansing, with Enclosure

My dear Mr. President: Washington September 24, 1918.

On Saturday I saw Professor Masaryk and he assured me that he still held the view that it would be impossible to reestablish the Eastern Front; that he did not believe we could count upon the Russians reorganizing as a military force.

Today, however, I have received the enclosed communication from him sending me a cablegram from General Gaida and Dr. Girsa,[1] together with an agreement reached between Professor Masaryk and General Janin as to the general situation.[2]

Will you be good enough to indicate to me what reply you desire made to this communication?[3]

Faithfully yours,   Robert Lansing.

TLS (WP, DLC).

[1] Not found. However, the telegram undoubtedly contained the same information and warning as was included in the first and second paragraphs of the telegram from Morris printed as Enclosure I with the next document.

[2] This agreement, dated Sept. 21, 1918, and signed by Masaryk, is entitled "AGREEMENT WITH GENERAL JANIN ON THE SITUATION IN RUSSIA." TS MS (SDR, RG 57, 861.00/2920, DNA). The text follows:

"*Confidential*

"1. The front against the Germans in Russia cannot be restored without the whole Japanese Army.

"2. It is doubtful whether the Russians, left to themselves, can soon raise a large enough army to organize Russia on a non-Bolshevik platform.

"3. If the Bolsheviks have a military agreement with the Germans, the Germans will send an army against us. Though small, if better equipped and armed than ours, this army will try to organize the prisoners of war, of whom there may be a considerable number in Russia, even some hundred thousand.

"4. Under these circumstances it may be advisable that our army retire over the Ural; but even for such a retreat our men must get arms and ammunition.

"5. But what will be the fate of the Allied contingents at Archangelsk and Murman? And what will be the fate of the quite numerous Americans, English, French, Bohemians, etc., in Moscow and Russia in general? To save those, our army should not retire over the Ural before the Allied troops and citizens are saved. At any rate, arms and ammunitions must be sent to the Western part of our army.

"6. Archangelsk and Murman could easily become a second edition of Gallipoli.

"7. Archangelsk could be saved, if we could join forces there by occupying the line Tchelyabinsk-Yekaterinburg-Vjatka-Perm-Vologda. Murman could be evacuated; of course there is a danger of a German base for submarines.

"The saving of Archangelsk again presupposes that we are well armed; this region, I fear, is poor and without food.

"Then: Vologda can be easily attacked by the Germans from Petrograd and Moscow.

"And can we hold that line, if we lose the hold on the Volga, especially on Samara?

"8. How far to retreat over the Ural? That will depend on the strength of the enemy. I would expect that the Germans would try to get into touch with their prisoners in Siberia and therefore push towards the East.

"9. If we can hold Siberia, that should have the political effect of placing the whole of Siberia under one government and enabling the Russians there to organize an army.

"10. And what with Russia? I do not know whether the Allies have a definite plan about the near future of Siberia and Russia, and what this plan is; if Russia will be abandoned to her fate, then there is no reason for keeping our troops in Siberia, and they should in that case go to France. At least a part of our army.

"Vide on the whole quesiton my memorandum, Aug. 28.

T. G. Masaryk."

[3] See WW to RL, Sept. 26, 1918.

E N C L O S U R E

Thomas Garrigue Masaryk to Robert Lansing

Mr. Secretary,   [Washington] September 23, 1918.

I submit the enclosed cable, received today, to your kind attention.

The situation in Russia changes almost daily: now we have to face the fact of open hostility of the Bolsheviks to the Allies, and as it seems, mostly to the Americans. Their wrath against the Americans would indicate that the people favor the latter, and that the Bolsheviks are afraid of the American influence.

The other fact is that the Germans now openly side with the Bolsheviks and even the Kaiser speaks in favor of them.

Under these circumstances my suggestion to assist our Western Army by a larger contingent, as expressed in both of my Memoranda (of July 20[1] and August 28)[2] receives added weight; only by these means the part of Russia leading up to Archangelsk [Archangel] can be held, and Siberia saved from the Germans. I fear the retirement of our army could prove disastrous to the Allied nationals living in Russia.

This plan of course does not in any way imply the restoration of the Russian front; in this respect I refer to the enclosed minutes summarizing our agreement with General Janin, reached before I had the honor of discussing the question with you.

At this occasion I also venture to suggest that the Government of the United States could make the Germans and directly the German Emperor responsible for the Bolshevik outrages on their and Allied nationals; such a declaration would be in accordance with the Allies' Archangelsk proclamation.

Yours very sincerely,   T. G. Masaryk.

Powhatan Hotel

TLS (WP, DLC).
[1] "HELP OF THE ALLIES TO THE CZECHOSLOVAK ARMY IN RUSSIA NECESSARY," T MS (SDR, RG 59, 763.72/11171½, DNA).
[2] "THE SITUATION IN RUSSIA AND THE MILITARY HELP OF THE ALLIES AND THE UNITED STATES," T MS, *ibid.* In this memorandum, Masaryk said that negotiations with the Bolsheviks were now impossible and that it was necessary to secure control of Russia from Siberia and eastern Russia to the Volga River and from there to the northern ports of Archangel and Murmansk. Order had to be restored in Russia; a democratic republic should be created. Masaryk then went on at length about the danger that Germany and Austria-Hungaria, by using former prisoners of war, would continue to dominate Russia and, with Bolshevik help, would move into Siberia. The Czechs had never wanted conflict with the Bolsheviks; only when the Bolsheviks combined with the Germans had the Czechs begun to defend themselves. The Czechs in Siberia now needed help, and needed it at once. They still wanted to go to France to fight on the western front, but their transfer to the West would depend upon "developments of the Russian situation and on the plans of the Allies in Russia." Meanwhile, the Czechs would stay in Siberia and cooperate with the Allies.
    Wilson returned these memoranda to Lansing on October 7, 1918. G. F. Close to RL, Oct. 7, 1918, TLS, *ibid.*

From Robert Lansing, with Enclosures

My dear Mr. President: Washington September 24, 1918.

I know that you have read the enclosed telegram (23d, 10 pm) from Mr. Morris with the same anxiety that I have. It presents very clearly a situation full of difficulties because the Russian communities of the Volga region, which have been friendly to the Czecho-Slovaks, being unarmed, will be at the mercy of the Red Guards, who have committed such monstrous crimes within the past six weeks in Moscow and other cities, if the Czecho-Slovaks withdraw to the east of the Urals.

I must confess that I sympathize with the spirit of the Czecho-Slovaks when they say that they cannot abandon their helpless friends to certain massacre and pillage. I believe that the world would be disposed to condemn such a course, and that the Czecho-Slovaks with their high sense of honor would rather die on the Volga than bear the charge of such ingratitude.

It seems to me that we must assume that the Czecho-Slovak force west of the Urals will remain there and do the best that they can to protect the friendly Russian communities from Bolshevik excesses.

The question is what ought we to do in the circumstances and what can we do in case we feel it our duty to assist them? It is an extremely difficult question to answer because I think that we must

assume that, justly or unjustly, we will be blamed for the consequences unless we can show conclusively that it was utterly impossible to give aid to the Czecho-Slovaks in eastern Russia.

We could of course say, adhering rigidly to our announced policy,
that it is their duty, regardless of their Russian allies, to join their
compatriots in Siberia and that we ought not to be asked to come
to their assistance if they do not follow that course. But I fear that
such a declaration of attitude would be generally criticized and
would place the blame upon us if disaster should fall upon the
communities of eastern Russia.

Yet, assuming that we ought to aid these people if we can, what
can we do? I do not see how, with the small force which we have
in Siberia, we can do more than hasten arms and ammunition to
them and refrain from urging them to withdraw at the present
time. But, even with sufficient munitions and supplies, I doubt if
so small a body of troops can avoid final annihilation unless a considerable force is sent to cooperate with them in repelling the Bolsheviks. Where is such a force to come from? A few thousands
would appear useless. There seems to be only one course and that
is Japan, and I feel quite convinced that the Japanese Government,
even if it were physically possible, would hesitate to enter on so
hazardous an adventure.

The more I consider the matter the more perplexing and distressing it becomes. We cannot abandon the Czecho-Slovaks on
the ground that they will not abandon their Russian friends. Of
course that would never do. And yet, what is the alternative, or is
there any?

In view of the recent examples of the blood-thirsty character of
the Bolsheviks, which has introduced a new factor into the problem
of relieving the Czecho-Slovaks, I feel that we should give most
careful consideration to the suggestions of Mr. Morris.

I would be grateful for your instructions or opinion as to the
policy we should adopt in dealing with this new situation which
was not foreseen when the Aide Memoire of July 17th was prepared
and which has resulted from the extreme terrorism which has
recently been resorted to by the Bolsheviks.

Faithfully yours,   Robert Lansing.

TLS (WP, DLC).

ENCLOSURE   I

Vladivostok September 23rd, 1918.

September 23rd. Preliminary to our economic, social, and publicity program in Siberia, and second only to the question of the

railways, is the question of the future disposition of our military forces during the approaching winter. The significant factors in the military situation are: First; there are at present in Vladivostok and vicinity approximately 25,000 soldiers. Very few of these forces are now engaged in active military operations. The number in the city will be increased by new arrivals and is already excessive for the requirements maintaining order and protecting stores. Second; the Chinese Eastern and Trans-Siberian Railways are *particularly* open as far as Omsk and beyond and every report we receive indicates the lines to that point are in no way threatened. They are guarded by Japanese and Czech soldiers scattered at intervals along their entire length and are equal to the movements of troops under the present Russian management. Third; the advance guard of the third division of the Japanese army, which is reported mobilizing at Nagoya, has now reached Harbin on its way toward Manchuli and may possibly proceed directly to Chita or even to Irkutsk. Fourth; A small British force is now preparing to leave for the Volga region and will soon be followed by the French and Italian contingents. Fifth; reports from the Volga region all agree that the Czech forces there are seriously menaced from various directions. Their commanding officers are pleading earnestly for immediate assistance. General Gaida has come to Vladivostok for the avowed purpose of urging upon the Allies the necessity of some immediate help without which the Czechs will be compelled to fall back to a position east of the Ural Mountains possibly to Omsk. He fears that if they thus fall back, they will leave their supporters in the evacuated towns defenseless against the general massacres which are likely to follow.

The single question which confronts the Czech leaders is whether they can make some arrangement with the Allies which will permit them to hold the Volga region or failing that, the line of the Urals during the coming winter and thus keep the door open into European Russia. They are *clear* that this cannot be done unless reinforcements are sent to them promptly.

General Graves is of the opinion that he should go to Omsk with a substantial portion of his command and form a base there for the winter, cooperating, as necessity required with other Allied forces in supporting the Czechs to the west. The advantages of such a movement would be: First, it would give much needed support to the Czech forces in the Volga region and would therefore be consistent with the purpose of the present expedition. Second, it would make more certain the protection of the railway and thus secure a base from which economic and other activities might penetrate even into European Russia. Third, the presence of an Allied force and particularly of American troops in that part of Russia, would have a strong moral effect upon the entire population in a territory which so directly affects European Russia. Fourth, it would have the additional advantage of giving our own forces, during the winter, an opportunity for more valuable service than any that will present itself at Vladivostok where there is so little direct contact with Russian opinion.

The movement suggested is open to the possible objection that it might convey to the Czech commanders and to the Russian people, the impression that the United States Government in co-operation with the Allies, was preparing for much more extended military operations than are in fact contemplated. This objection could be met by a formal reaffirmation of the limitations clearly announced in the statement of August 3rd.[1] A further possible objection is that this movement of our troops might be interpreted as an indication of our intention to give direct support to the recently organized Siberian Government at Omsk.[2] No doubt such an interpretation would be fostered at the outset but I think could be fully corrected by our subsequent action.

Admiral Knight, General Graves and I have carefully weighed these facts. Admiral Knight is convinced that such an expedition, far from antagonizing the Russian people, would be generally welcomed and would form a very effective center for American activities in that part of Siberia. General Graves has studied carefully the strategic situation and feels that there are no serious military difficulties or dangers involved provided that the Chinese Eastern and Trans-Siberian Railways are protected and operated to the extent they now are. He is also of the opinion that *the* with the line of communication thus secured, their maintenance would not constitute a drain upon the resources of the country.

In my judgement such movement would be entirely consistent with the policy which has been adopted by our Government in reference to Siberia. In fact it seems to me to offer the only practicable way in which that policy can be applied during the winter, for it will accomplish the two main objects which we have in view, to render assistance to the Czech forces *represented* along the railway and concentrated at railway centers in the Volga region; and to open up the field for social and economic action. If these centers are not properly guarded, they will revert to a condition of anarchy which will prevent any effective service.

Finally I fear that our failure to come into closer contact with the Czech forces and with the Russian people in Western Siberia may have serious results. Already I find that the British and French representatives here, particularly General Knox and General Paris,[3] are influencing the Czech leaders with impracticable plans to create by force a new Russian Army and a new Eastern front. General

Gaida, who is very young, has been impressed by these schemes and misled by unauthorized suggestions of ultimate unlimited American support. I believe that General Graves presence in Western Siberia would steady the Czechs leaders and make clear to them and to the Russian people our policy and purpose.

I would therefore recommend for the consideration of the Department the wisdom of granting to General Graves, the privilege of proceeding, in his discretion and with a substantial portion of his forces, to a point in the vicinity of Omsk and wintering there if conditions all justify such action. I further suggest that when General Graves has decided upon the details of such a plan, they be submitted to the Japanese Government with the request that it co-operate by (#) a portion of its troops to the base selected.

In conclusion, I venture to urge that whatever action is decided upon be announced to the Czech commanders at the earliest practicable moment for the reason that as has been clearly pointed out to me by General Gaida, his plans for the winter are dependent upon the character and extent of the assistance which he can count on receiving from our own and the Allied Governments.

Morris

(#) Omission.

[1] That is, the press release printed at that date in Vol. 49.
[2] Morris apparently referred here to the Siberian Provisional Government, located at various times during this period either at Tomsk or at Omsk. Known earlier as the Western Siberian Commissariat, it was a successor regime to the Government of Autonomous Siberia (about which see n. 3 to the Enclosure printed with RL to WW, April 22, 1918, Vol. 47). The Siberian Provisional Government claimed control over all of Siberia and was strongly conservative in its political and social orientation. Its premier was Petr Vasil 'evich Vologodskii. It was about to be superseded, at least in part, by the Ufa Directorate, about which see n. 1 to Enclosure II below. About the Siberian Provisional Government, see Chamberlin, *The Russian Revolution*, II, 12-14; John Albert White, *The Siberian Intervention* (Princeton, N. J., 1950), p. 103; and Elena Varneck and H. H. Fisher, eds., *The Testimony of Kolchak and Other Siberian Materials* (Stanford, Calif., 1935), pp. 234n140 and 238n156.
[3] Gen. Robert C. Paris, the senior French officer in the Far East at this time.

ENCLOSURE II

Peking September 23rd, 1918.

Important. Following received from Harris, Irkutsk: "114, Twenty-fifth [Twenty-third]. For Department. Short resume present conditions Siberia based on personal observation. No enthusiasm shown among people for recruiting or for continuation war. All statements by the various Governments, no matter what nature, received with indifference. If Czechs were removed from any city in Siberia, Urals or Samara districts, Bolsheviki would immediately get control again. Time wasted in petty politics. No large grasp of whole situation or ability, even among intelligent classes, to view procedure from an all Russian standpoint. Their horizon bounded by what they can see from their village church steeples. Declarations of all Russian assembly just held at Ufa[1] read well from their allied standpoint and were framed for that purpose but policy for regeneration Russia internally so radically socialistic as concerns land question, private ownership, manufacturing and trade, that is practically the Bolshevik plan form and would only sink Russia deeper in the mire if practiced. No strong men have come forward in any of the Governments as yet. German agitations still fermenting strong. Swedish agents responsible for much of it. Unless Allies are prepared to assist Czechs in their present struggle against the Germans in European Russia, the Allies in all fairness to the Czechs should seasonably withdraw them from the whole country so they may not be needlessly sacrificed. Czechs doomed to failure if dependent alone upon help of Siberian and Russians. The presence of at least fifty thousand allied forces in company with Czechs at the front absolutely necessary for prestige and morale generally and to knit together the Russian troops. Presence of American troops in these operations is highly desirable. The Russian turn of mind at present is such that they think Americans lay a little too much stress upon sending of Y.M.C.A. agents, Red Cross representatives, labor advisers, agricultural experts and commissions of merchants. While appreciating all these things they express themselves at this moment as being strongly in favor of seeing a few thousand American soldiers marching through their cities."   MacMurray

T telegrams (WP, DLC).
    [1] In an effort to achieve some degree of unity among the anti-Bolshevik forces in Siberia, representatives of the Siberian Provisional Government, of a rival Socialist-Revolutionary government located at Samara, and of various other Siberian political organizations met in a so-called State Conference at Ufa from September 8 to 23, 1918. The result was the creation of an All-Russian Provisional Government, with executive power vested in a five-man directorate, usually referred to as the Ufa Directorate or Directory. Vologodskii, the Premier of the Siberian Provisional Government, headed the Directorate also. The new government, which soon moved to Omsk, was a shadow regime, torn by dissension between its Socialist-Revolutionary and its conservative members and by the obstructionist tactics of the rival Siberian Provisional Government, also located at Omsk. Both organizations effectively came to an end with the beginning of the dictatorship of Admiral Aleksandr Vasil'evich Kolchak on November 18, 1918. See Chamberlin, *Russian Revolution*, II, 20-21, 173-79; Varneck and Fisher, *Testimony of Kolchak*, p. 239n157; and George Stewart, *The White Armies of Russia: A Chronicle of Counter-Revolution and Allied Intervention* (New York, 1933), pp. 147-51, 239-43.

From the Diary of Colonel House

September 24, 1918.

I am just back from Washington. When I arrived there Sunday morning[1] and had had breakfast the President came to my room

    [1] September 22, 1918.

and asked me to come into Mrs. Wilson's apartment and sit with them while they had theirs.

He had been thinking, he said, of the letter I wrote him from Magnolia, September 3rd, and he had written a speech which he thought would cover the case, provided he could get the Allies to agree to it. He wished me to read the speech so as to get my judgment of it and also as to when and where it should be delivered. He said Benjamin Strong of the Federal Reserve Bank in New York had asked him to open the Liberty Loan Drive with a speech in New York but he had declined because he did not consider it a suitable occasion. He was wondering if the Economic Club of New York would do.

I thought the Liberty Loan Drive would be an admirable occasion. It could be arranged for Friday night of this week. He could devote one sentence to the Liberty Loan telling how necessary it was to raise the money because this country had in mind certain things which should be done to prevent future wars. He could then launch out on his subject and not refer to the loan again. It could be done as he did it in Baltimore last spring.[2]

The President agreed to this and asked me to make arrangements. We discussed who should speak with him, the length of time his speech should take, when it should begin and when it should end.

The President wanted me to go to church. I consented but when he gave me an opportunity to evade it I took advantage of it much to his disgust. While they were at church I had an hour each with Burleson and Lane. Burleson wished me to advise the President to veto the Prohibition Bill which is about to pass. Lane's trouble was the Returning Soldiers' Homestead Bill,[3] a measure I think well of if it is properly drawn.

[2] Wilson's address at Baltimore is printed at April 6, 1918, Vol. 47.

[3] Although several bills to provide homesteads for returning veterans had been introduced in Congress, House here referred to a much more detailed plan for legislation which was still being developed in the Interior Department. Lane had outlined his ideas in F. K. Lane to WW, May 31, 1918, TLS (WP, DLC). Since the fertile lands in the public domain most suitable for farming had long since been alienated, Lane wrote, the returning soldiers would have to make do with the vast acreage of arid or swamp lands still in the public domain, together with cutover lands in private hands, which might be reacquired by the federal government. The effective use of such areas would require extensive planning by the Interior Department. As the so-called "Lane plan" evolved in 1918 and 1919, it came to include a comprehensive scheme under which the Interior Department would direct the development of complete towns surrounded by agricultural lands. The veterans and their families would do much of the actual construction and reclamation work and would eventually own their homes and farm lands. The Lane plan was embodied in H.R. 487, the Lane-Mondell bill, introduced by Franklin Wheeler Mondell, Republican congressman of Wyoming, on May 19, 1919, during the first session of the Sixty-sixth Congress. Although reported out of committee and briefly debated, the bill did not pass, largely due to the opposition of commercial farmers and to the apathy of the veterans themselves. See Reports of the Department of the Interior for the Fiscal Year Ended June 30, 1918, I (Washington, 1919), pp. 3-13, 24-29; Keith W. Olson, Biography of a Progressive: Franklin K. Lane, 1864-1921 (Westport, Conn., 1979), pp. 149-54; and Bill G. Reid, "Franklin K. Lane's Idea for Veterans' Colonization, 1918-1921," Pacific Historical Review, XXXIII (Nov. 1964), 447-61.

After lunch the President and I went to his library where he read his speech. It was admirable except in places. I called his attention to these and, after some argument, he made the changes I suggested. He gave me the speech to read again on Monday, after he had made the changes, and it seemed to me without objections excepting one word for which he substituted another. The address concerns the League of Nations and while he does not go into it to the core, he makes it clear the kind of league we must have.

We discussed the sentiment for this measure as it exists throughout the world. I had some data upon this subject which I gave him to read aloud. In addition, I had the French conception of what a league should be, which he had not seen. I found him not at all up to date in regard to the subject.

We discussed Russia at some length, looking at the map and trying to find what was best for the Czech army, now there, to do in the circumstances. I asked why he had not gone ahead with his economic and relief policy regarding Russia. He replied that Redfield had so "messed the matter up" that it was impossible for him to do so; that he had now taken it out of his hands and placed it in that of the War Trade Board[4] and he hoped something would come of it. He did not know that Gordon had worked this out and arranged it.

I wondered why he had permitted the publication of the alleged Lenine-Trotsky documents,[5] and whether he was satisfied as to their authenticity. He expressed himself as being thoroughly satisfied. I told him I had my doubts, and I thought their publication meant a virtual declaration of war upon the Bolsheviki Government. He admitted this.

I found out from Lansing later that George Creel had persuaded the President to pubelish [publish] them and that the State Department knew nothing of it and disapproved entirely. They not only do not credit the authenticity of the documents, but they consider it a bad time to make the exposé. This is great teamwork. If Lansing were a strong man such things could not happen. Lansing

[4] On about September 18, Wilson had designated Vance C. McCormick, Bernard M. Baruch, and Edward N. Hurley as an informal committee to take charge, through their respective organizations—the War Trade Board, the War Industries Board, and the Shipping Board—of "the purchase, shipment, and distribution of supplies, including Red Cross supplies, for the Czecho-Slovak forces and possibly limited amounts of other supplies required by the communities in the neighborhood of which Czecho-Slovaks are operating." RL to J. K. Caldwell, Sept. 18, 1918, FR 1918, Russia, II, 385. The successor to this group—the Russian Bureau, Inc., of the War Trade Board, was incorporated on October 5, 1918, under the presidency of Vance C. McCormick. Its purpose, in the words of a recent authority, was "to facilitate private commercial intercourse between Russia and the United States and, where deemed advisable, to provide on a modest scale direct economic relief financed by the bureau itself." Linda Killen, The Russian Bureau: A Case Study in Wilsonian Diplomacy (Lexington, Ky., 1983), p. 49.

[5] That is, the so-called Sisson Documents.

said that Creel had, at one time, wanted the right of access to all the State Department cables so that he might use his judgment as to what should be given to the public. This Lansing refused.

The President and I took up on Sunday the desirability of declaring war on Bulgaria. I brought this up apropos of the despatch which Balfour had sent Wiseman for my attention.[6] The President was willing to declare war, but disliked to do so at this time when the Bulgarians were in full flight. He thought it might look as if we had waited until they were beaten. I did not agree with this conclusion and will take it up again in a few days.

He brought up the prohibition rider to the Agricultural Bill, which he said would be before him in a few days. Both Tumulty and Burleson are advising him to veto it. Burleson he paid but little attention to because he was an ardent anti-prohibitionist, but he declared Tumulty was not. This shows that Burleson is more sincere, for I am as certain as I am of anything that Tumulty is as much as anti-prohibitionist as Burleson. The President said he had given no expression whatever as to what he would do, but wanted to tell me he had in mind to veto the bill. He was led to this because of the financial difficulties which it involved, and which at this time might prove serious.

Monday, Tumulty made this same argument to me in a very passionate speech, so I could see where the President got his viewpoint. I advised him to discuss it with McAdoo and to be advised by him, provided the financial point was the only one bothering him. Personally, I said, I was in favor of letting it alone, without, however, knowing enough of the details to speak intelligently. He argued against my position and I did not press my point of view.

When I left last night and was bidding him goodbye, he asked me again if I had thought further about it. I told him I had and that I had mentioned the matter to Gregory, and that Gregory agreed with me that he had best not veto the bill. Coming over on the train today I spoke of it to McAdoo. He takes the same view that I do, and says if the President brings it to him he will advise letting it alone.

The President spoke of politics in general and expressed an earnest desire that a democratic Congress should be elected. He said he intended making a speech or writing a letter about two weeks before the elections, asking the people to return a democratic House. I did not express any opinion as to the wisdom of this.

I had a good opportunity of giving him a talk about the necessity of fighting Germany from within as well as from without; that it was as much a part of military tactics to do this as it was to handle

[6] See the Enclosure printed with EMH to WW, Sept. 18, 1918.

the armies in the field. He assented, and I wondered why he had sent in a message like the one to Austria if he had such a conviction. The speech he is to make on Friday had some ill advised sentences, sentences which if strictly adhered to, would make the negotiations for peace impossible. I did not tell him this, but I gave out the thought that he was making the same mistake the Allies had made from the beginning.

I took the opportunity to tell him that the German military situation was not so bad, but that the situation was much worse behind the lines and our every effort should be to aid our armies by diplomacy.

It should be stated here that there will be many apparent inconsistancies in this diary. Last year I thought actions unwise and impossible which this year I strongly approve—so rapidly do events move.

After we finished discussing domestic and foreign politics, the President began to play with a new stamp that he had had made with "Woodrow Wilson" on it. He used this on the fly-leaf of a number of books not having his name in them. He seemed as pleased as [a] child with a new toy and expressed himself as being so.

He was interested in the account I gave him as to why the New York Times had written their extraordinary editorial upon the Austrian Note.[7] I found he had no idea of what should be done with

---

[7] The editorial was "The Austrian Peace Overture," *New York Times*, Sept. 16, 1918. It hailed the Austrian proposal for a nonbinding conference of belligerents as "the first veritable peace offer . . . in a form which the Allies may honorably accept in the confident belief that it will lead to the end of the war." "The custom and practice of nations," the editorial continued, "demand that this invitation to enter upon the preliminaries of peace receive the most serious and respectful attention of the Governments to which it is addressed. . . . We are bound to accept it as the sincere expression of a desire for much needed peace, and we may assume with entire confidence that it is issued with the full knowledge and assent of the Imperial Government of Germany, after conference and deliberation." The cause of the peace proposal was obviously the recent defeats which the Central Powers had sustained on the battlefields. "It would be the worst of blunders," the editorial went on, "for us or for any of the Entente Allies to abate war preparations now. But reason and humanity demand that the Austrian invitation be accepted. . . . We cannot imagine that the invitation will be declined." Proper safeguards would have to be taken to insure that there would be no peace which would leave Germany in control of a vast new empire in the Near East and in Russia. "Entering a conference," the editorial concluded, "with definite instructions to yield no point that would leave Germany in a position to call to her armies and their support the men and the resources of the boundless Eastern lands she now holds in thrall, the delegates of the United States, Great Britain, France, Italy, and their co-belligerents may meet the representatives of the Central Powers without arousing among anxious peoples at home the fear that they are about to barter away the soul of the allied cause."
On September 17, in the wake of the news that Wilson had summarily rejected the Austrian proposal, the *Times* published another editorial which expressed disappointment that Wilson and the Allies had acted without any attempt to test the sincerity of the Central Powers. The Allies, it suggested, might, for example, have demanded that Germany evacuate its troops from Belgium, France, and Alsace-Lorraine as a preliminary to serious peace discussions. Had the Allies agreed to open discussions, they could then have set forth whatever terms they felt necessary. "Not Accepted," *ibid.*, Sept. 17, 1918.

Austria or how the Empire should be broken up if, indeed, it was to be broken up at all. Generally, he thought the League of Nations should settle many such problems and smooth over insuperable difficulties. He thought if nations knew they were in a protective league they would be willing to accept different boundaries and smaller areas.

He was interested to know that Gordon was the first man to suggest John W. Davis for Ambassador to England. The President does not know Davis any better than I do, but he took Gregory's estimate of him. Gregory in talking to me about Davis expressed the opinion that he was a clever and able lawyer with a decided turn for diplomacy.

In speaking of Page, the President spoke of his letter of resignation to which he has only replied by cable.[8] He said he did not dare write expressing cordial regrets fearing lest it might place him in Page's unfriendly hands. I did not think Page would write or say anything unfriendly while either of them was alive, but I did believe that, sooner or later, Page's criticism of him would be given to the world. The President did not believe his criticism would impress anyone provided the war went the way it was going now. He thought the world very generally accepted the fact that we went into the war at the psychological moment and that to have gone in earlier as Page desired would have been an error.

In speaking of himself and the estimate history would have of him, he thought this too depended largely on the result of the war and of what was accomplished by it. He spoke of Washington and of how little he seemed to have done on his own initiative which

---

The editorial of September 16, which was directly contrary to most American editorial opinion on the Austrian proposal, stirred up so much controversy that the editors of the *New York Times* felt obliged to print still a third editorial on the subject: "No Negotiated Peace," *ibid.*, Sept. 19, 1918. The editors admitted that the original editorial had been widely "misunderstood" but insisted that they had never suggested a "negotiated peace," that is, one in which both sides would bargain for acceptable peace terms. What they had really meant to say was that, in any preliminary peace talks, the Central Powers had to be presented with the Allied peace terms, that is, those embodied in Wilson's public statements on the subject, as an ultimatum which would have to be accepted before serious negotiations could begin. If the *Times* had erred, it was on the assumption that the Austrian proposal was in effect a surrender and, hence, an acceptance of those terms. The editors admitted that it was now clear that neither the Wilson administration nor the American public had shared that assumption.

There is nothing in the House Diary from September 15 to 24 to indicate the nature of the "account" of the writing of the first editorial which House gave to Wilson. However, on October 1, House lunched with Henry Morgenthau and Adolph Simon Ochs, the owner and publisher of the *New York Times*. Ochs insisted that he had had nothing to do with the editorial and had not even known of its publication until the afternoon of September 16, since he had been at that time at Lake George, New York. He declared to House that Charles Ransom Miller, the editor in chief of the *Times*, and Carr Vattel Van Anda, the managing editor, were "wholly responsible" for the editorial. House Diary, Oct. 1, 1918.

[8] That is, WHP to WW, Aug. 1, 1918, and WW to WHP, Aug. 24, 1918, both printed in Vol. 49.

had led some observers to think he was not a man of great parts. In reply to this I expressed the opinion I have expressed before that Washington's greatness was because of his ability to know good advice from bad, that every leader must necessarily depend largely upon the advice of others, and his final reputation depended upon whether he was able to distinguish good advice from bad.

After dinner, Sunday night, we talked of history, literature, art and what influences brough[t] forth the best. The President called attention to the fact that when Italy was broken up into small kingdoms and republics, literature and art flourished best, and that in England during the Elizabethan period when the country had become stabilized, but when adventure was still rife, Shakespeare and his contemporaries did their best work. We wondered what was in store for America in this direction and when it would come if ever.

Miss Bertha Bolling, Mrs. Wilson's sister, embarrassed me at dinner by telling of her visit to Virginia and the compliments paid me there. Among other things she said, "You are a maker of men." The President smiled dryly and remarked, "He ought to change his pattern." He said this with himself in view in order to be facetious.

Just before we went to bed the President said he had in mind contesting the tax on his income which the House has placed upon it.[9] His reason was that the makers of the Constitution had in mind that the President should not be punished or rewarded by Congress,

[9] The House Ways and Means Committee had, on August 7, decided to extend the income tax to include the salaries of the President, members of the Supreme Court and all other federal judges, and all state officials. Claude Kitchin, the chairman of the committee, declared that there was "a great sentiment all over the country that no one should be exempt from taxation." The question was immediately raised as to whether this action might be unconstitutional since the Constitution provided that the salary of the President could not be increased or decreased during his term of office and that the salaries of federal judges could not be diminished during their service on the bench. Kitchin stated that a majority of the committee believed that an income tax upon these officials did not constitute a diminution of their salaries, and that, in any case, the income-tax amendment to the Constitution permitted Congress to raise revenue from whatever sources necessary. It was estimated that the tax upon the President's annual salary of $75,000 would amount to some $24,000. *New York Times*, Aug. 8, 1918.

Wilson's idea of opposing the proposed tax upon his salary may have been either inspired or reinforced by a letter to the Editor of the *New York Times*, datelined Washington, Sept. 17, 1918, and signed with the initials "A.S.L." The writer argued that the proposal was not only clearly unconstitutional but also violated the important principle of the separation of powers. "No matter," he wrote, "what delicacy or reluctance the President and the Judges may feel toward testing the right of Congress to tax their salaries, it is clearly their duty to resist this tax—not only for their own benefit, but in the interest of this great and vital principle that underlies our government." *Ibid.*, Sept. 22, 1918, Sect. III, p. 1.

The Senate Finance Committee, on October 17, struck out the provision of the revenue bill which provided for the taxation of the salaries of the President, federal judges, and state officials. *Ibid.*, Oct. 18, 1918. However, at some subsequent date, a new provision to tax the salaries of the President, all federal judges, and all federal employees was added to the bill, and it remained in it at the time of its enactment on February 24, 1919. 40 *Statutes at Large* 1065.

and if he allowed this infringement of the Constitution to pass it might at some time have serious results. He said he intended to take some action by way of paying his income tax to show it was not the money he had in mind but the principle. I asked him not to take any action himself, but to let me handle it in my own way, to which he agreed. I sent for Gregory early Monday morning and advised with him about it.

Gregory thought there was some doubt as to its constitutionality. I advised him to take it up with someone in the Senate. I later asked McAdoo to take it up with some Senator and try to kill it there. I did not inform McAdoo that the President had talked to me on the subject, but let him go on his own initiative. It would not look well for the President to institute such a suit. His motives would certainly be misconstrued. Then, too, how could you get a court which would have jurisdiction? The Federal Judiciary are affected in the same way. I believe the matter can be adjusted.

On Monday, Herbert Hoover called at the White House by appointment to tell me of conditions in Europe and of the necessity for better coordination of our economic forces there. He was rather dispirited with affairs, both there and here, and was in his normal pessimistic frame of mind. I cheered him and he left feeling better.

Prof. William E. Dodd, of the Chair of Philosophy in Chicago University,[10] also called. He discussed the possibility of establishing a National University at Washington which would be free from the influences under which most of our universities work.

Lansing and I had a long conference at the State Department. We discussed the prospective peace conference. He thought the President, himself and myself should be the democratic members, and that Taft should be the republican member. He thoroughly disapproved of Root. He thought labor and liberals would be distrustful of him, while they would be satisfied with Taft. He told of a speech he was to make at Albany on the 18th of October, but he did not know that the President had already given me a copy of this speech to read and pass upon. I was not able to find time to read this while in Washington but brought it home with me. The President had read it and thinks it "too flat-footed" as he expressed it. That is the trouble with Lansing, he has never had, and never can have, a diplomatic touch. I do not suppose a stronger man would be willing to occupy the position he holds under the President.

McAdoo remakred [remarked] that he and the other Cabinet Members were nothing but clerks. This is not true of McAdoo, and

---

[10] Dodd was, actually, Professor of History at the University of Chicago.

that is why the President gets along with him less well. He prefers the Baker, Daniels, Lansing type as they are absolutely subservient to him.

Hurley of the Shipping Board gave an account of his activities. He wishes to come to New York in order to have a more extended conference with me.

The President, Mrs. Wilson and I went to the theater Monday evening. We had finished everything and he was very tired, having had a very hard day. He looks tired and I felt sorry for him. I wish he would allow me to better organize his work. If I were in Washington constantly I think he would let me act for him in many matters, but he seems entirely unwilling to have others do so.

He wanted me to go with him to Princeton on a special train this morning. He goes to vote in the primaries. I agreed to go, but when I found that McAdoo was going direct to New York on a later train, I decided to go with him. I came over with McAdoo and Eleanor reaching New York at 3.25.

From Josephus Daniels

Dear Mr. President: Washington, Sep. 25, 1918.

Permit me to suggest that if you will ask Senator Benet, of South Carolina, to call to-day and give him a letter which he can print at home, he will feel that he can vote for the suffrage amendment. I have not seen himself [him myself], but a gentleman who is very close to him and who talked with him two hours last night makes this suggestion, and, coming from a man who usually knows what he is talking about, I believe it will convince him. The Senator is at the University Club.   Sincerely,   Josephus Daniels

ALS (WP, DLC).

To Josephus Daniels

My dear Daniels: The White House 25 September, 1918.

I did write Senator Benet, of South Carolina, some days ago a letter[1] which is surely all he could wish for, and I had a talk with him and Governor Manning the other day, which I hoped and thought at the time was conclusive.

In haste,   Faithfully yours,   Woodrow Wilson

TLS (J. Daniels Papers, DLC).
  [1] WW to C. Benet, Sept. 18, 1918.

To Joseph Patrick Tumulty, with Enclosures

Dear Tumulty: [The White House] 25 September, 1918

I gathered from our talk yesterday about this matter that you and Garfield could think out a better way to handle it than for me to write to Garfield and ask about it. If there is some way in which Garfield could volunteer to inform me and clear it up, I think that that would be the bestm [best,] for I don't wish to seem to imply any criticism of Garfield.   The President

TL (WP, DLC).

E N C L O S U R E   I

From Joseph Patrick Tumulty

Dear Governor: [The White House] 23 September, 1918

The correspondence between Hard,[1] the magazine writer of the New Republic, and Mr. Morrow,[2] a member of the Fuel Administration, which correspondence by the way is already in the hands of Senator Lodge,[3] presents a situation that has many serious aspects. The fact, is, as admitted by Mr. Morrow and also admitted by Mr. Garfield in his testimony before the Appropriations Committee, that the Fuel Administration accepted from an association made up of coal operators throughout the country, the services of these allied associations and accepted from the funds of these associations something in the neighborhood of $2,000,000 which was used, to quote Mr. Morrow's words, as follows:

"Moreover, last winter when I took over this work, the Fuel Administration had no funds then available to develop independent organizations, so we asked the operators to let us use their trade associations as distributing agencies for the Fuel Administration, utilizing their information, personnel, offices, etc., with the operators paying all the expenses of the Association and the additional cost of the greater volume of work placed on them by our distribution program.

"The operators made no objection to this and we appointed the secretaries of these associations the representatives of the Fuel Administration, clothed them with the proper authority, and made plain to them that for the time being their associations, their machinery and everything else had become a part of the Fuel Administration, were to be so considered and so asministered [administered]. They have carried out that program faithfully and to date the operators have borne practically all the expenses.

"The Secretaries of associations thus taken over and the District Representatives specially employed in the fields where there were no trade associations which could be thus utilized, comprise men whose salaries range from #3000 to $15000 a year, these salaries being paid by the operators. We hope to pay a part of the expenses from the Fuel Administration appropriation, but for distribution and inspection at the mines, all of which are under the direction of the Distribution Division, our total expenses this year will be not less than $2,500,000. Dr. Garfield thinks that he will not have more than $1,000,000 available out of his appropriation, for these uses. However, the work must be done efficiently and thoroughly, and it cannot be so done without precisely the organization and information that you got some glimpse of. We have put the matter before the coal operators and asked them to foot the bill and they are doing it."

There is no doubt of the unfortunate impression this is bound to make on the country, for the coal operators, whether they are justly entitled to the reputation or not, are looked upon by the public at large, especially the consuming public, with grave suspicion, just as the packers of America are despised by the ordinary men on the street.

How we are to meet this situation is a difficult matter, without seeming to rebuke and repudiate Mr. Garfield, whose motives in the matter are the highest and who, being faced by a national emergency, did what he could to meet a grave situation. I have just finished reading the correspondence, and my judgment is that in order to outwit Senator Lodge, you should send a letter to Mr. Garfield, saying that these facts have been called to your attention and while you have no opinion to express regarding them, you ask for a full and complete report from Mr. Garfield at once. You might say in the letter that if it is true that Congress has not appropriated sufficient money with which to carry on this work, that you will be ready at once to make an appropriation out of your Defence fund, and that at all events the connection, if any exists, between the Fuel Administration and the National Association of Coal Operators must be severed at once.   Tumulty

TLS (WP, DLC).
    ¹ William Hard.
    ² John DeLorma Adams Morrow.
    ³ J. D. A. Morrow to W. Hard, Aug. 30, 1918; W. Hard to J. D. A. Morrow, Sept. 5, 1918; and J. D. A. Morrow to W. Hard, Sept. 13, 1918, all TCL (WP, DLC). Morrow's letter of August 30 was a general discussion of the Fuel Administration's regulation of the distribution of coal in the United States. He mentioned in passing that the coal operators were supplying, during the present year, over $1,500,000 toward the expenses of the Fuel Administration, and also were providing the services of many officials of the coal industry, who received no salaries and often paid their own expenses. Hard, in his reply of September 5, asked for more information on a number of points in Morrow's

letter. One of them was the matter of the coal operators' contributions to the work of the Fuel Administration. Hard added to this query the comment that he regretted that the government did not "meet its own proper bills." Morrow, in his response of September 13, provided answers to all of Hard's questions but devoted most of his space to a defense of the coal operators' donations of men and money to the Fuel Administration. Tumulty paraphrases and often directly quotes from this defense in the above letter.

E N C L O S U R E   I I

Robert Wickliffe Woolley to Joseph Patrick Tumulty

Dear Joe: Washington September 23, 1918.

Shortly after I handed you on Saturday last a copy of excerpts from a letter written by Mr. J. D. A. Morrow, Chief of the Division of Distribution of the Fuel Administration and Secretary of the National Coal Association, to Mr. William Hard, I received a call from Mr. Benjamin Allen,[1] Director of Publicity of the Food Administration and confidential adviser and personal friend of Dr. Harry A. Garfield, the Fuel Administrator. Mr. Allen was accompanied by Mr. T. M. Alexander,[2] of the Bureau of Education of the Fuel Administration.

These gentlemen were greatly disturbed over conditions in Dr. Garfield's Bureau, which they related to me, and after a conference of more than two hours I agreed to lay the matter before you for such action as you might deem necessary. Mr. Allen explained that his appeal to me was made only after he had tried personally to impress Dr. Garfield with the seriousness of recent developments in the Fuel Administration, and was due to the suggestion of Mr. Alexander, who was my Director of Motion Picture publicity in the campaign of 1916, and others that I might consent to take the matter up with the President.

Obviously, I could not and would not be placed in the attitude of filing charges against a fellow public official; Mr. Allen only asked that I try to help the Fuel Administrator and I assented. I was told that aside from the President, the only man in official life in Washington with whom Dr. Garfield would consent to discuss the affairs of his bureau was Mr. Herbert C. Hoover, for whose opinion he has the highest respect. Therefore, it was agreed that it was highly advisable to have Mr. Hoover confer with him and endeavor to impress him with the necessity of effecting a reorganization quickly and of issuing a public statement as to what had been done. You will readily understand the necessity for haste when I tell you that what Mr. Allen stated to me and I herewith repeat to you is in the possession of Senator Lodge, and that the latter plans, so I am informed, to make it public either through a Senate investigation or in the approaching campaign about a fortnight before election.

Mr. Allen's statement to me in substance was as follows:

He (Allen) was head of the London Bureau of the Associated Press at the time Mr. Hoover was made Food Administrator. The latter drafted him to return to this country to take charge of publicity of the Food Administration and to act as his confidential adviser. This he has done ever since. When Dr. Garfield was made Fuel Administrator he conferred with Mr. Hoover as to his organization and it was agreed that Mr. Allen would act also as his confidential adviser, especially in the matter of publicity. For a while, this arrangement worked satisfactorily and the coal producers were kept in their place. They were shown no special favors and received no information as to policy in advance of the newspapers or the public generally. So alive did Dr. Garfield seem to be to the character and resourcefulness of the men with whom he was dealing that shortly after he became Fuel Administrator he was reported to have likened, in a public speech, the coal barons to the robber barons of the Rhine. In due time, however, things changed. Allen says he finds that instead of information emanating from a single source, the Educational Bureau, it was given out through fourteen press agents attached to the staffs of dollar a year chiefs of divisions, not one of them on the payroll of the Fuel Administration. In other words, the coal producers were conducting their own propaganda from within the Fuel Administration. They practically ignored the Educational Bureau and all information was given to the Daily Coal Digest, the official organ of the coal producers, a day ahead of the daily newspapers.

The petroleum and gasoline publicity, so Allen alleges upon information furnished by the Educational Bureau, has been given out in New York by the Petroleum War Service Board, said to be a camouflage organization created and maintained by the Standard Oil Company. City editors of New York newspapers are said to have some specimens of this publicity marked as originating in Room 116, Fuel Administration. This is a file room and no office of any kind is or has been located there. Other specimens in their possession, so Mr. Allen is informed, are marked as from Room 958, War Industries Board. This also is a false address, as neither the Petroleum War Industrious [Industries] Board nor the Fuel Administration has an office in that building. Mr. Allen states that all petroleum and gasoline propaganda so given out in New York is distributed through the McCann agency, a Standard Oil concern. He says that a specimen of the result of such shifting of responsibility is "gasolineless Sunday," to support which Dr. Garfield and Petroleum Director Requa have admitted to him in the past few days that they have no authentic figures. He says Mr. Requa gave evidence of being "frightened out of his boots." It seems that the gasoline situation so far as war purposes are concerned depends upon the tonnage of oil carrying steamers available, and that there is no present likelihood of a sufficiently large tonnage being available to catch up with the supply of gasoline. Mr. Allen thinks Mr. Requa has found an alibi, however, in that the United States has just taken sides with France in the controversy with Great Britain over the specific gravity of gasoline used in aeroplanes, France contending for a finer specific gravity than Great Britain.

He says that the National Coal Association offered to Mr. Sartwell[3] and Mr. Alexander, the two men actually in charge of the Fuel Administration's Education Bureau, $100,000 for propaganda work and it was declined. This is said to be at the bottom of the criticism of the Educational Bureau contained in Mr. Morrow's letter to William Hard.

Mr. Allen stated that Mr. Noyes,[4] head of the Oneida Community, who has recently been placed in charge of the Educational Bureau, is a well meaning person who has no conception of the job before him. His sole contact with newspaper and periodical publications has been through the advertising columns. Believing that is the only way of securing results, Mr. Allen says he is now spending $875,000 in advertising, practically every dollar of which is wasted.

Mr. Allen said that upon seeing a copy of the Morrow letter he carried it directly to Dr. Garfield, that the latter turned white and expressed himself as being shocked, clearly showing that the receipt of this substantial financial assistance on behalf of the Government from one of the parties at interest to be regulated was wholly without his knowledge. Upon discussing the matter, however, he failed to be impressed with the significance of it and, of course, absolutely failed to appreciate its value as a weapon in the hands of a hostile critic.

As further indicating the further activities of Mr. Morrow, Mr. Allen cited the case of supplying coal to non-essential industries. A Mr. Ogle,[5] Assistant Director of the Division of Statistics of the Fuel Administration, without consulting any one, sent out a questionnaire to ascertain the exact amount of coal which each of these industries had been allowed to accumulate since last winter. They disclosed that in many instances a four year's supply has been permitted, in hundreds of cases two and three years supply and in thousands of cases, so Mr. Allen is informed, a year's supply. He says that Mr. Ogle laid the data before Mr. Morrow with the recommendation that these accumulations be used for releaving [relieving] potentially tense situations in a number of localities, but that Mr. Morrow pigeon-holed the data and directed that nothing futher be done.

May I not suggest that you send for Mr. Allen, if you think it necessary, and get further details from him. He would be very glad to discuss it with you and Mr. Hoover together. I know you will appreciate my hesitancy in bringing the matter to your attention, but I felt that I would be shirking a duty to the administration of the country if I did not.

Cordially and sincerely yours,   R. W. Woolley

TLS (WP, DLC).
   [1] Benjamin Shannon Allen.
   [2] Thomas Mathew Alexander.
   [3] Edward R. Sartwell.
   [4] Pierrepont Burt Noyes, actually the Director of the Bureau of Conservation of the Fuel Administration.
   [5] Alfred McCartney Ogle, Jr., Princeton 1904, actually the Director of the Bureau of State Distribution of the Fuel Administration.

From Harry Augustus Garfield

Dear Mr. President: Washington, D. C. September 25, 1918

I enclose, herewith, a copy of a letter which I am sending to Senator Walsh.[1]

Cordially and faithfully yours,   H. A. Garfield.

TLS (WP, DLC).
   [1] H. A. Garfield to T. J. Walsh, Sept. 25, 1918, CCL (WP, DLC). Garfield enclosed in this letter copies of the correspondence cited and summarized in n. 3 to Enclosure I printed with the previous document. He added the following comment: "Concerning the particular matter supposed to be damaging in this correspondence, namely, the intimation that the Fuel Administration has received money from the coal industry, I beg to say that the Fuel Administration has received no money from the coal industry. It has received, however, as stated by me to the Committee on Appropriations last May . . . and is receiving the services of men lent by the coal industry at my request and without cost to the Fuel Administration. It also has received and is receiving, statistical information from operators' associations, without compensation. The duties of the men referred to are to distribute coal, in accordance with the prices, rules, and regulations of the United States Fuel Administrator and the orders of State Fuel Administrators not connected with the coal industry. Final authority in no matters relating to price or policy or distribution rests with anyone interested in the coal industry."
   Garfield also enclosed to Walsh copies of correspondence which he believed proved that the Fuel Administration had not deferred to the Standard Oil Company in issuing its order prohibiting the nonessential use of gasoline on Sundays.

From Edward Mandell House

Dear Governor: New York. September 25, 1918.

I do not like Lansing's speech. It is intemperate and, in my opinion, is one that should not be made by a Foreign Secretary. It is the kind of speech to which we so strongly objected before we went into the war.

I do not believe the American people need that kind of stimulus now. If I am not mistaken, in their present temper, it will be more difficult to get them to stop at the proper time than to keep on. We should not forget that Europe is very tired of war, particularly labor circles, and they will not take kindly to any thought from us which tends to prolong it beyond reason.

I am looking forward with the keenest pleasure to seeing you on Friday. I am sorry that the "Follies"[1] has been taken to Boston but I hope we can make a satisfactory substitute.

Affectionately yours,   E. M. House

TLS (WP, DLC).
[1] The Ziegfeld Follies of 1918 had concluded its New York run on September 14. *New York Times*, Sept. 14, 1918.

From Joseph Patrick Tumulty

My dear Governor: [The White House] September 25, 1918

In the matter we discussed yesterday, I am a little bit apprehensive as to the effect on the public mind in its present temper of any affirmative expression such as "justice for friend and foe alike." You will recall that this is one of the phrases that I called to your attention yesterday. At the moment the Republican party is trying to alarm the country by harping on the danger of an incomplete peace, misrepresenting the Administration and trying to galvanize this bogey into partisan usefulness. Any phrase such as we discussed would be examined not with a view to interpreting rightly the magnanimous feeling which lies behind it, but with the hope of extracting color if not confirmation for a party slogan. The words would be compared with other sentences like "Peace without victory"; "too proud to fight," and the like, and would in certain quarters revive a feeling of criticism which refuses to be allayed. Therefore, I fear that the phrase would lend itself to disingenuous and hostile misconstruction.   [Tumulty]

CCL (J. P. Tumulty Papers, DLC).

Two Letters from George Creel

My dear Mr. President: Washington, D. C. September 25, 1918.

There is a grave chance that the Suffrage Amendment may lose by a single vote. Even if it goes through, more Republican votes will be cast for it than Democratic votes.

This morning I received the exact information, with proof, that the Republicans will make the entire matter a campaign issue in every one of the equal suffrage states.

I feel deeply that the passage of this Amendment is a war necessity for it will release the minds and energies of thousands of women for war work and war enthusiasm. I feel deeply also that it is necessary to have the Administration receive full credit for its consistently courageous and friendly attitude.

Is it not possible for you to go before the Senate in support of the Amendment as an urgent war measure? Aside from its effect in this country, there is a wonderful effect that it will have on the world at large.   Respectfully,   George Creel

My dear Mr. President: Washington, D. C. September 25, 1918.

It was a difficult matter indeed to get correct figures, and it is only now that the task has been finished.[1] In addition to the attached article from the larger agricultural papers, various smaller ones have been prepared.   Respectfully,   George Creel

TLS (WP, DLC).
    [1] Committee on Public Information, "Comparative Prices on What the Farmer Buys and Sells," T MS (WP, DLC). This consisted of a brief discussion followed by a lengthy series of charts which listed the increases in price between 1914 and 1918 of basic agricultural products and of many kinds of goods purchased by farmers. The charts by and large supported the contention in the introductory section that prices of agricultural products, such as wheat, oats, and raw cotton, had increased much more rapidly and to a higher point than the prices of most goods purchased by farmers.

From George Creel, with Enclosure

My dear Mr. President: Washington, D. C. September 25, 1918.

Captain Merriam,[1] our representative in Rome, is in very close touch with the Italian leaders by reason of his work, and has come to enjoy their confidence in a very large degree.

I attach herewith a confidential statement regarding the substance of one of his recent conversations with Sonnino.
                    Respectfully,   George Creel

TLS (WP, DLC).
    [1] Charles Edward Merriam, Professor of Political Science at the University of Chicago, at this time the head of the Italian office of the Committee on Public Information.

E N C L O S U R E

"Sonnino believes that the Czecho-Slavs have shown capacity in various ways, especially by action in Russia, and that they have demonstrated strong national spirit. He believes that they have irrevocably broken with Austria. He strongly favors Czecho-Slav independence. He is not certain in regard to the growth of the Jugo-

Slav group as an independent organized political body. He would let them have all opportunities possible and wait for developments. He gives me an intimation that they should give more definite proof than heretofore of their ability to conduct independent national existence. He intimates that we should delay talk of modification terms of London treaty until Jugo Slavs show more clearly their capacity and national unity and give unquestionable evidence of definite break with Austria. He is afraid of the possibility that certain groups might even now yield to autonomy under Austrian control in place of absolute independence. He lays emphasis on Italy's need for national security by means of better boundary lines, and says that Austria has drawn present lines so as to render Italy vulnerably [vulnerable] from military point of view. He admits importance of league of nations, but cannot entirely overlook the necessity of territorial equilibrium. Under any circumstances he considers it unfair to let Italy remain with wedge of Austrian territory driven toward her heart. He states that he was interested in negotiating treaties of London and in view of the fact that there was then under consideration division of territory, he could not overlook interests of Italy. Italian representatives had to do likewise as all the others were claiming territory. He is uncertain about possibility of dismembering Austria. That part of Austria which is German would in all likelihood join itself to Germany immediately or within a few years, or at least would submit to German leadership and control. In such case Germany would be strengthened and Italy would have an even more dangerous neighbor while all nations would be in the shadow of impending attack by greater Germany upon balkans. This constitutes all the more reason why new states carved out of Austria should have ability for resistance and vitality. I gained the impression that he intends to wait for development of Jugo Slavia; that if they make good showing he will give many concessions, but in any case certain territorial demands will be insisted upon by Italy although certain claims in London treaty may be waived. Of course in determining the Italian policy Sonnino is not the only factor, but in view of his ability and experience his attitude is important. He added that in any event the bear should be caught before his hide was divided. He warned that too much weight should not be given to the apparent heat of Italy's internal controversies, because although they may make bitter declarations, they will finally arrive at internal harmony."

T MS (WP, DLC).

From Frank Morrison

My dear Mr. President: Washington, D. C. Sept. 25, 1918

In a conference with Mr. Patrick Gorman[1] and Mr. Peter Campbell, A. F. of L. representatives at Louisville, Kentucky, I informed them that in a letter to me you had expressed the hope that organized labor in Louisville would not present a candidate against Mr. Shirley, and that it was your belief that Mr. Shirley's retention in Congress is in the national interest.[2]

Mr. Shirley's vote in favor of the Clayton bill and other measures beneficial to the wage workers has not been overlooked, but during the Sixty-fifth Congress, out of fourteen opportunities to vote upon labor questions, he is recorded nine times against, two in favor and three not voting. This recent record, aggravated by local conditions, resulted in organized labor of Louisville placing Mr. Gorman in the field as their candidate.

At the conference above referred to, it was agreed that the situation might result in the election of Mr. Shirley's opponent, an event which would be less desirable than the existing status, and in view of your expression, and as one more contribution of Louisville trade unionists to assist the President in his effort to secure a triumphant end of the present world war, Mr. Gorman stated that he would withdraw as a candidate.

Yours sincerely,   Frank Morrison

TLS (WP, DLC).
   [1] Patrick Emmet Gorman, president of the Louisville Union Trades and Labor Assembly and vice-president of the Kentucky Federation of Labor.
   [2] WW to F. Morrison, Sept. 20, 1918.

Joseph Patrick Tumulty to the Norman Foster Company

Gentlemen: [The White House] 25 September, 1918

The President asks me to return herewith the draft referred to in your letter of September 23rd,[1] with the request that you will cancel it. It was not at all a satisfactory settlement,[2] but the President does not care to do more than to return the draft with the above request.   Very truly yours,   [J. P. Tumulty]

CCL (WP, DLC).
   [1] Norman Foster Co. to JPT, Sept. 23, 1918, TLS (WP, DLC).
   [2] About which, see N. Foster to WW, June 10, 1918, Vol. 48.

To Robert Lansing

My dear Mr. Secretary,   The White House. 26 September, 1918.

Here are the memoranda I was to send you on Siberia and Russia.

I. For Morris at Vladivostock, information and instruction to the effect that we are giving General Graves authority to establish his headquarters at some such place as Harbin where he can be in touch with an open port during the winter and from whence he can make the best use of his force to safeguard the railways and keep the eastward routes open for the Czechs; but that we have definiterely [definitely] disapproved his suggestion that he establish himself at Omsk or any other point in the far interior, because, strongly as our sympathies constrain us to make every possible sacrifice to keep the country on the Volga front out of the hands of the merciless Red Guards, it is the unqualified judgment of our military authorities that to attempt *that* is to attempt the impossible. We mean to send all available supplies that we can spare from the western front forward as fast as possible for the use of the Czech forces, but we cannot undertake to send them west of the Urals. So far as our cooperation is concerned we must frankly say that the Czech forces should retire to the eastern side of the Urals to some point at which they will be certainly accessible to supplies sent from the east, preferably where they will be in a position to make it impossible for the Germans to draw supplies of any kind from western Siberia, but in any case where they can make themselves secure against attack. With the deepest regret but with perfect realization of compelling facts we must in frankness say that our assistance cannot be given in the carrying out of any other programme. All that the British commander at Archangel expected to happen upon the sending of allied and American troops to the northern ports has failed of realization and this Government cannot cooperate in an effort to establish lines of operation and defence through from Siberia to Archangel.[1]

II. For Francis, full information as to all of the above and, in addition instructions to act on the certain assumption that no more American troops will be sent to the northern ports. He should be told that, it being in our view plain that no gathering of any effective force by the Russians is to be hoped for, we shall insist with the other governments, so far as our cooperation is concerned, that all military effort in that part of Russia be given up except the guarding of the ports themselves and as much of the country round about them as may develop threatening conditions. We will, of course, do our utmost to send supplies, but cannot undertake general relief, and must presently, of course, be cut off from Archangel by the ice and able to go only to Murmansk.

Please commend the course he has taken,—a thoroughly American course which I have entirely admired,—and impress upon him the fact that we are following, not the course of our choice, but the course of stern necessity.[2]

I think the above furnish a sufficient outline of what it will be necessary to say to each of the governments concerned directly at their headquarters at London and Paris and Rome as well as through their representatives at Vladivostock and Archangel.[3]

Please make it clear to Morris that the ideas and purposes of the Allies with respect to what should be done in Siberia and on "the Volga front" are ideas and purposes with which we have no sympathy and that the representatives of the Allies at Vladivostock are trying their best to "work" General Graves and every other American in sight and should be made to understand that there is absolutely "nothing doing."   Faithfully Yours,   W.W.

WWTLI (B. Long Papers, DLC).
    [1] This message and the advice in the last paragraph were conveyed in RL to R. S. Morris, Sept. 26, 1918, *FR Russia, 1918*, II, 392-93.
    [2] This message was conveyed in RL to D. R. Francis, Sept. 26, 1918, *ibid.*, p. 546.
    [3] The substance of these two telegrams was also sent to London, Paris, Rome, Tokyo, and Peking. The telegram to London, for example, is printed as an Enclosure with RL to C. A. de R. Barclay, Sept. 27, 1918.

To Frank Morrison

My dear Mr. Morrison: [The White House] 26 September, 1918

Thank you for your letter of yesterday. Your response to my suggestion about Representative Sherley gratifies me very deeply, and I feel that both you and Mr. Gorman have acted with admirable public spirit.

With sincere appreciation,
                    Cordially yours,   Woodrow Wilson

TLS (Letterpress Books, WP, DLC).

To Christie Benet

My dear Senator Benet: [The White House] 26 September, 1918

It becomes my duty again to appeal to you for your vote in favor of the Suffrage Amendment.

I have every reason to believe that, if you vote for this measure, your action will influence at least two other Senators; so that there will be no doubt that the amendment will pass.

I assure you that prompt and favorable action in the premises is of vital importance both nationally and internationally; so much so, in fact, that I have no hesitation in stating that the passage of the Suffrage Amendment at this time is absolutely essential in bringing the war to a speedy and successful conclusion.

On this ground I appeal to you to hold up the President's hands at the time of all times when his responsibility to his own country and his obligations to the cause of world-democracy weigh most heavily upon him.

To give me your help in bearing that responsibility and discharging that obligation, I most earnestly ask your vote in favor of the Suffrage Amendment.

Cordially and sincerely yours,   [Woodrow Wilson]

CCL (WP, DLC).

To Park Trammell

My dear Senator: [The White House] 26 September, 1918.

I hope that you will permit me to make another earnest appeal to you to vote in favor of the suffrage amendment. I can assure you that I would not do this if I did not feel it to be my duty as the responsible leader of our party and the present leader of the nation. I can assure you from my own knowledge of affairs that it is of capital importance to us, both nationally and internationally that this amendment should be adopted. I would be glad at any time to discuss the matter with you very fully, but know that you will pardon me for not putting the whole argument into a brief note, which is after all only to appeal to you to act with a large part of our friends in the Senate in putting through this very necessary public reform.

Cordially and sincerely yours,   Woodrow Wilson

TLS (Letterpress Books, WP, DLC).

Two Letters from Josephus Daniels

My dear Mr. President: Washington. September 26, 1918.

I have your letter of the 25th instant with reference to Senator Benet, and later I understand you sent him a note which I hope will make things all right. He was a great deal troubled by the fact that most of our leaders from the South were opposed to the amendment, and hesitated somewhat about taking a position not in harmony with theirs, but I feel sure that your letter will settle it.

Sincerely yours,   Josephus Daniels

Personal

My dear Mr. President: Washington. September 26, 1918.

When Mr. Padgett[1] returned from abroad, he told me about a dinner given to the Naval Affairs Committee by Sir Eric Geddes. I spoke to you about it yesterday and about the speech made by Sir Eric Geddes at that dinner. I am enclosing you herewith the copy of the speech which was printed for private circulation only and which Mr. Padgett brought to me. I thought you would like to see it. I am sure you will read it with interest, and of course between the lines you will see its importance as well as in the printed text.[2]

If you do not wish to keep it, will you return it to me when you have read it.   Sincerely yours,   Josephus Daniels

TLS (WP, DLC).
    [1] That is, Representative Lemuel P. Padgett, chairman of the House Committe on Naval Affairs, who, with eight other members of his committee, had recently visited England.
    [2] Geddes spoke at a dinner given in London by the Board of Admiralty on August 2, 1918. Geddes was very frank. He compared the American naval effort in European waters very unfavorably to the British effort; called for greater construction by the United States of fast light cruisers, destroyers, and patrol craft; and closed with a strong plea for a greater American contribution. Arthur J. Marder, *From the Dreadnought to Scapa Flow: The Royal Navy in the Fisher Era, 1904-1919* (5 vols., London, 1961-70), V, 127.

From George Creel

My dear Mr. President: Washington, D. C. September 26, 1918.

I have just finished reading the advance copy of your Liberty Loan speech, and it has done wonders for my pride and strength and resolve. What with all the drudgery and the pettiness and the smother of small things, one is apt to lose sight of the tremendous truths that are our courage and our inspiration.

Everything that you say is always a tonic to me, but especially this Liberty Loan speech. More than anything before, it tears away the false and the selfish and the traditional, and gets right down to the heart of humanity.

Especially in Italy and England, it is going to make easy a task that has been very difficult and depressing.

I am very proud and happy to serve you.
                                        Devotedly,   George Creel

TLS (WP, DLC).

From William Kent

My dear Mr. President: Washington September 26, 1918.

You know and appreciate my reluctance to call to your attention minor matters, but I most urgently request your attention to the inclosed letter written by my son-in-law, Mr. G. S. Arnold.[1] Entirely apart from any feeling I have for one so nearly related, I wish to express my unbounded confidence in his rightness and good sense. It was at my request that he, while an attorney in California, became interested in the case of Miss Pollak. There has been no time when absolutely responsible relatives have not been willing to go every sort of bond for her loyalty and behavior.

I have taken the matter up with the Attorney General, who naturally dislikes to interfere with cases under local treatment. The official head of the prosecution in this case is a friend, Mr. John W. Preston, of California, a man in whom I have great confidence, but who, in the stress and strain of prosecuting, might feel himself hampered by discrimination. Mr. Arnold, of his own knowledge, cites a prejudice existing in one of his subordinates. I most urgently request your action in asking the Attorney General to order the quashing of the indictment, which differs from a pardon which would be urged, in being the avoidance of a wrong which could not be redressed once it was committed.

You can rely with entire confidence on the statements of Mr. Arnold, for whom Secretary Lane, Justice Brandeis, and many others of your trusted friends will vouch.

Yours truly,   William Kent

TLS (WP, DLC).

[1] George Stanleigh Arnold to WW, Sept. 26, 1918, TLS (WP, DLC). Arnold, a lawyer of San Francisco, who was at this time a member of the War Labor Policies Board, called Wilson's attention to the case of Theodora Pollak, a young educational and social worker in California, who had been included in a blanket federal indictment of members of the Industrial Workers of the World at Sacramento in February 1918. She was specifically charged with conspiracy to circulate I.W.W. literature and with writing and printing a pacifist poem. The poem, Arnold said, had in fact been written a year before America's entrance into the war and had never been published. The only actual charge against Miss Pollak, Arnold asserted, was that she was a member of the I.W.W., a charge which, given the current climate of opinion in California, was certain to result in conviction, despite the fact that membership in the organization was not in itself a crime. Preston, the United States District Attorney for the Northern District of California, had suggested that she plead guilty with the understanding that she would then be given a light sentence. She had refused to do so. Arnold stated that Miss Pollak had "a sensitive and exceedingly nervous temperament" and said that "a conviction in her case would be equivalent to a death sentence." Her case was called for October 10. Arnold urged Wilson to have Attorney General Gregory quash the indictment against her.

Kent also enclosed in the above letter an undated memorandum which Arnold had prepared for him about the case. The facts and arguments in the memorandum were very similar to those in Arnold's letter to Wilson. However, he did add the information that Miss Pollak was "tubercular" and requested that the case against her either be dismissed, or, if that was impossible, that it be separated from those of the others indicted at the same time and that her trial be delayed until a time when Arnold would be less pressed in his work for the government and, hence, better able to act as her attorney.

From Herbert Clark Hoover

Dear Mr. President: Washington 26-September-1918

During this week I have sat for 17½ hours in consultation with a group of 18 to 25 leading hog producers from various parts of the country, over the problem of stabilization of the price of hogs. The Committee has made the attached recommendations.[1]

These recommendations, coming from the agricultural community, enable us, by giving directions to the 55 packing firms who participate in export and Navy and Army orders, to curb the high and low price in the movement of pork products. There are some particulars as to the method of arriving at a formula of stabilization, which I propose to amend, that I will not trouble you with. The main issue on which I wish to consult you is that they wish, in order to maintain the stimulated production of pork, that we should give an "assurance" of a minimum of $15.50 per hundred pounds for hogs during the period of the war. The price recently has been as high as $21.00.

While I have little doubt of our ability, by the regulation of the large controlled purchases, to affect this, I do not wish to take any unnecessary responsibility in giving "assurances," even though they are carefully stated not to be guarantees. My suggestion is that we should extend the present minimum, which applies to hogs farrowed in the spring of 1918, also to hogs farrowed in the autumn of 1918. This will maintain the production for the present and we can before next spring consider whether we want to extend assurance again. I am confident that the assurances that we gave last fall have been the mainspring of the great increase in production, which production is of vital importance to us during the coming winter.

I have also had extensive conferences over the question of cattle, but we have been able to come to no particularly constructive suggestions, as the cattle business is infinitely more complicated than the production of pork.

If you approve, I will give the limited assurance as mentioned above. You will understand that this is a carefully guarded statement of assurance; that it is not a guarantee; that it is merely a statement of our intention within our abilities arising from purchases under government control, and the agricultural community well understands that physical situations may develop under which we could not make good.[2]

Yours faithfully, Herbert Hoover
Approved Woodrow Wilson
1 October, 1918.

TLS (Hoover Archives, CSt-H).
[1] T MS (Hoover Archives, CSt-H), printed in the *Official Bulletin*, II (Sept. 28, 1918), 14. Most of the "recommendations" were simply brief discussions of economic factors which would have to be considered in the effort to stabilize hog prices at a reasonable level. The only real recommendation was that the existing minimum price of $15.50 per hundred pounds for hogs be maintained "continuously during the war."
[2] Hoover's "limited assurance" was embodied in a letter to Henry Carter Stuart, Governor of Virginia and chairman of the Agricultural Advisory Committe, a subcommittee of the Food Administration, which was printed in *ibid.* (Oct. 14, 1918), 32.

An Address in the Metropolitan Opera House

Speaking copy 27 Sept., 1918[1]

My fellow citizens: I am not here to promote the loan. That will be done,—ably and enthusiastically done,—by the hundreds of thousands of loyal and tireless men and women who have undertaken to present it to you and to our fellow citizens throughout the country; and I have not the least doubt of their complete success; for I know their spirit and the spirit of the country. My confidence is confirmed, too, by the thoughtful and experienced cooperation of the bankers here and everywhere, who are lending their invaluable aid and guidance. I have come, rather, to seek an opportunity to present to you some thoughts which I trust will serve to give you, in perhaps fuller measure than before, a vivid sense of the great issues involved, in order that you may appreciate and accept with added enthusiasm the grave significance of the duty of supporting the Government by your men and your means to the utmost point of sacrifice and self-denial. No man or woman who has really taken in what this war means can hesitate to give to the very limit of what they have; and it is my mission here to-night to try to make it clear once more what the war really means. You will need no other stimulation or reminder of your duty.

At every turn of the war we gain a fresh consciousness of what we mean to accomplish by it. When our hope and expectation are most excited we think more definitely than before of the issues that hang upon it and of the purposes which must be realized by means of it. *For it has positive and well defined purposes which we did not determine and which we cannot alter.* No statesman or assembly created them; no statesman or assembly can alter them. They have arisen out of the very nature and circumstances of the war. The most that statesmen or assemblies can do is to carry them out or be false to them. They were perhaps not clear at the outset; but they are clear now. The war has lasted more than four years and the whole world has been drawn into it. *The common will of mankind has been substituted for the particular purposes of individual states.* Individual statesmen may have started the conflict, but neither they nor their opponents can stop it as they please. It has become a peoples' war, and peoples of all sorts and races, of every degree of power and variety of fortune, are involved in its sweeping processes of change and settlement. We came into it when its character had become fully defined and it was plain that no nation could stand apart or be indifferent to its outcome. Its challenge drove to the heart of everything we cared for and lived for. The voice of the war had become clear and gripped our hearts. Our brothers from many lands, as well as our own murdered dead under the sea, were calling to us, and we responded, fiercely and of course.

The air was clear about us. We saw things in their full, convincing proportions as they were; and we have seen them with steady eyes and unchanging comprehension ever since. We accepted the issues of the war *as facts*, not as any group of men either here or elsewhere had defined them, and we can accept no outcome which does not squarely meet and settle them. Those issues are these:

Shall the military power of any nation or group of nations be suffered to determine the fortunes of peoples over whom they have no right to rule except the right to force?

Shall strong nations be free to wrong weak nations and make them subject to their purpose and interest?

Shall peoples be ruled and dominated, even in their own internal affairs, by arbitrary and irresponsible force or by their own will and choice?

Shall there be a common standard of right and privilege for all peoples and nations or shall the strong do as they will and the weak suffer without redress?

Shall the assertion of right be haphazard and by casual alliance or shall there be a common concert to oblige the observance of common rights.

No man, no group of men, chose these to be the issues of the struggle. They *are* the issues of it; and they must be settled,—by no arrangement or compromise or adjustment of interests, but definitely and once for all and with a full and unequivocal acceptance of the principle that the interest of the weakest is as sacred as the interest of the strongest.

This is what we mean when we speak of a permanent peace, if we speak sincerely, intelligently, and with a real knowledge and comprehension of the matter we deal with.

We are all agreed that there can be no peace obtained by any kind of bargain or compromise with the governments of the Central Empires, because we have dealt with them already and have seen them deal with other governments that were parties to this struggle, at Brest-Litovsk and Bucharest. They have convinced us that they are without honour and do not intend justice. They observe no covenants, accept no principle but force and their own interest. We cannot "come to terms" with them. They have made it impossible. The German people must by this time be fully aware that we cannot accept the word of those who forced this war upon us. We do not think the same thoughts or speak the same language of agreement.

It is of capital importance that we should also be explicitly agreed that no peace shall be obtained by any kind of compromise or abatement of the principles we have avowed as the principles for which we are fighting. There should exist no doubt about that. I am, therefore, going to take the liberty of speaking with the utmost frankness about the practical implications that are involved in it.

If it be in deed and in truth the common object of the governments associated against Germany and of the nations whom they govern, as I believe it to be, to achieve by the coming settlements a *secure* and *lasting* peace, it will be necessary that all who sit down at the peace table shall come ready and willing to pay the price, the only price, that will procure it; and ready and willing, also, to create in some virile fashion the only instrumentality by which it can be made certain that the agreements of the peace will be honoured and fulfilled.

That price is impartial justice in every item of the settlement, no matter whose interest is crossed; and not only impartial justice but also *the satisfaction of the several peoples whose fortunes are dealt with*. That indispensable instrumentality is a League of Nations formed under covenants that will be efficacious. Without such an instrumentality, by which the peace of the world can be guaranteed, peace will rest in part upon the word of outlaws and only upon that word. For Germany will have to redeem her character, not by what happens at the peace table but by what follows.

And, as I see it, the constitution of that League of Nations and the clear definition of its objects must be a part, is in a sense the most essential part, of the peace settlement itself. It cannot be formed now. If formed now, it would be merely a new alliance confined to the nations associated against a common enemy. It is not likely that it could be formed after the settlement. It is necessary to guarantee the peace; and the peace cannot be guaranteed as an afterthought. The reason, to speak in plain terms again, why it must be guaranteed is that there will be parties to the peace whose promises have proved untrustworthy, and means must be found in connection with the peace settlement itself to remove that source of insecurity. It would be folly to leave the guarantee to the subsequent voluntary action of the governments we have seen destroy Russia and deceive Roumania.

But these general terms do not disclose the whole matter. Some details are needed to make them sound less like a thesis and more like a practical programme. These, then, are some of the particulars, and I state them with the greater confidence because I can state them authoritatively as representing this Government's interpretation of its own duty with regard to peace:

First, the impartial justice meted out must involve no discrimination between those to whom we wish to be just and those to whom we do not wish to be just. It must be a justice that plays no favourites and knows no standard but the equal rights of the several peoples concerned;

Second, no special or separate interest of any single nation or any group of nations can be made the basis of any part of the settlement which is not consistent with the common interest of all;

Third, there can be no leagues or alliances or special covenants and understandings within the general and common family of the League of Nations;

Fourth, and more specifically, there can be no special, selfish economic combinations within the League and no employment of any form of economic boycott or exclusion except as the power of economic penalty by exclusion from the markets of the world may be vested in the League of Nations itself as a means of discipline and control.

Fifth, all international agreements and treaties of every kind must be made known in their entirety to the rest of the world.

Special alliances and economic rivalries and hostilities have been the prolific source in the modern world of the plans and passions that produce war. It would be an insincere as well as an insecure peace that did not exclude them in definite and binding terms.

The confidence with which I venture to speak for our people in these matters does not spring from our traditions merely and the well known principles of international action which we have always professed and followed. In the same sentence in which I say that the United States will enter into no special arrangements or understandings with particular nations let me say also that the United

States is prepared to assume its full share of responsibility for the maintenance of the common covenants and understandings upon which peace must henceforth rest. We still read Washington's immortal warning against "entangling alliances" with full comprehension and an answering purpose. But only special and limited alliances entangle; and we recognize and accept the duty of a new day in which we are permitted to hope for a general alliance which will avoid entanglements and clear the air of the world for common understandings and the maintenance of common rights.

I have made this analysis of the international situation which the war has created, not, of course, because I doubted whether the leaders of the great nations and peoples with whom we are associated were of the same mind and entertained a like purpose, but because the air every now and again gets darkened by mists and groundless doubtings and mischievous perversions of counsel and it is necessary once and again to sweep all the irresponsible talk about peace intrigues and weakening morale and doubtful purpose on the part of those in authority utterly, and if need be unceremoniously, aside and say things in the plainest words that can be found, even when it is only to say over again what has been said before, quite as plainly if in less unvarnished terms.

As I have said, neither I nor any other man in governmental authority created or gave form to the issues of this war. I have simply responded to them with such vision as I could command. But I have responded gladly and with a resolution that has grown warmer and more confident as the issues have grown clearer and clearer. It is now plain that they are issues which no man can pervert unless it be wilfully. I am bound to fight for them, and happy to fight for them as time and circumstance have revealed them to me as to all the world. Our enthusiasm for them grows more and more irresistible as they stand out in more and more vivid and unmistakable outline.

And the forces that fight for them draw into closer and closer array, organize their millions into more and more unconquerable might, as they become more and more distinct to the thought and purpose of the peoples engaged. It is the peculiarity of this great war that while statesmen have seemed to cast about for definitions of their purpose and have sometimes seemed to shift their ground and their point of view, the thoughts of the mass of men, whom statesmen are supposed to instruct and lead, has grown more and more unclouded, more and more certain of what it is that they are fighting for. National purposes have fallen more and more into the background and the common purpose of enlightened mankind has taken their place. The counsels of plain men have become on all hands more simple and straightforward and more unified than the counsels of sophisticated men of affairs, who still retain the impression that they are playing a game of power and playing for high stakes. That is why I have said that this is a peoples' war, not a statesmen's. Statesmen must follow the clarified common thought or be broken.

I take that to be the significance of the fact that assemblies and associations of many kinds made up of plain workaday people have demanded, almost every time they came together, and are still demanding, that the leaders of their governments declare to them plainly what it is, *exactly what it is*, that they were seeking in this war, and what they think the items of the final settlement should be. They are not yet satisfied with what they have been told. They still seem to fear that they are getting what they ask for only in statesmen's terms,—only in the terms of territorial arrangements and divisions of power, and not in terms of broad-visioned justice and mercy and peace and the satisfaction of those deep-seated longings of oppressed and distracted men and women and enslaved peoples that seem to them the only things worth fighting a war for that engulfs the world. Perhaps statesmen have not always recognized this changed aspect of the whole world of policy and action. Perhaps they have not always spoken in direct reply to the questions asked because they did not know how searching those questions were and what sort of answers they demanded.

But I, for one, am glad to attempt the answer again and again, in the hope that I may make it clearer and clearer that my one thought is to satisfy those who struggle in the ranks and are, perhaps above all others, entitled to a reply whose meaning no one can have any excuse for misunderstanding, if he understands the language in which it is spoken or can get someone to translate it correctly into his own. And I believe that the leaders of the governments with which we are associated will speak, as they have occasion, as plainly as I have tried to speak. I hope that they will feel free to say whether they think that I am in any degree mistaken in my interpretation of the issues involved or in my purpose with regard to the means by which a satisfactory settlement of those issues may be obtained. Unity of purpose and of counsel are as imperatively necessary in this war as was unity of command in the battlefield; and with perfect unity of purpose and counsel will come assurance of complete victory. It can be had in no other way. "Peace drives" can be effectively neutralized and silenced only by showing that every victory of the nations associated against Germany brings the whole world nearer the sort of peace which will bring security and reassurance to all peoples and make the recurrence of another such struggle of pitiless force and bloodshed forever impossible, *and that nothing else can.* Germany is constantly intimating the "terms" she will accept; and always finds that the world does not want terms. It wishes the final triumph of justice and fair dealing.[2]

Printed reading copy (WP, DLC).
    [1] WWhw.
    [2] There is a brief WWT outline of this address in WP, DLC; also two pages with WWsh. A transcript of one phrase reads: "Justice which does not discriminate between friend and foe."

To Josiah Oliver Wolcott

(Personal and Confidential.)

New York, 27 September, 1918

I venture to make an earnest personal appeal to you to vote for the suffrage amendment, because I regard this as one of the most critical events in the history of the party not only, but in the history of our national policy and our international relations. I beg you to believe that I would not take this course if I were not sure of the embarrassing and distressing effects which would follow a defeat of the measure, particularly by the failure to obtain a sufficient number of Democratic votes. The support of the party is of particular consequence to me in this matter.   Woodrow Wilson

Same telegram to
Senator Shields, Washington, D. C.
Senator Benet
Senator Overman
Senator Martin (of Kentucky)

T telegram (WP, DLC).

From Robert Lansing, with Enclosure

My dear Mr. President: Washington, September 27, 1918.

I am enclosing to you five telegrams in regard to Bulgaria[1] which indicate that their spirit is entirely broken and that they are ready to break with the Central Powers. I felt that you should have these at once in order that you might consider the policy which we should adopt and could instruct the Department at your earliest convenience as to the course we should take.

You will observe by the papers that this situation is already known to the press, and I think it would be wise if Mr. Tumulty would call Mr. Patchin, who will be at the Department during the evening, as to how far we should go in giving out the fact that we are officially advised of Bulgaria's overtures. If you agree with this will you be good enough to ask Mr. Tumulty to be very definite as to the extent of the statement which is to be made? I think it is obvious that we will have to say something to the correspondents in regard to the matter and I do not wish to say anything until I have your views as to what should be said.

Faithfully yours,   Robert Lansing

TLS (WP, DLC).
¹ P. A. Stovall to RL, Sept. 26, 1918, and R. W. Bliss to RL, No. 4585, Sept. 26, 1918, and No. 4586, Sept. 27, 1918; all T telegrams (WP, DLC). The fifth telegram is printed as Enclosure I with W. Phillips to WW, Sept. 29, 1918.

E N C L O S U R E

The Hague, Sept. 27, 1918.

Urgent. 4587. Confidential. My 4585. Bulgarian Minister¹ has just written me the text of a telegram from Malinoff,² Bulgarian Premier, to Bulgarian Minister at Washington³ which he requests that I forward in cipher. Does Department desire me to accept it for transmission or express regrets at not being able to comply with Minister's request. The telegram instructs Bulgarian Minister at Washington to communicate textual message to the President and the Secretary of State, which is to the effect that Bulgaria's participation in the war was had only after exhausting all peaceful means of reaching agreement with neighbors for realization of national unity as well as emphasized in Bulgaria's answer to Austrian peace proposal of September 14; that Bulgarian cause is in conformity with principles which led the United States to intervene in war and Bulgarian Government therefore appeals to President Wilson to mediate to terminate bloodshed in southern theatre of war by an armistice to be followed by preliminary peace negotiations, the various questions regarding the Balkan peninsula to be left to General Peace Conference for final settlement.

I request instructions as soon as possible.   Bliss.⁴

T telegram (WP, DLC).
¹ Pantcho Hadji-Mischef, Bulgarian Minister to the Netherlands.
² That is, Aleksandŭr Malinov.
³ That is, Stefan Panaretov.
⁴ That is, Robert Woods Bliss, American Chargé at The Hague.

Two Letters from Robert Lansing

My dear Mr. President: Washington, September 27, 1918.

I cannot help but feel that we stand in a peculiar relation to the civilian population in the regions of France and Belgium occupied by the Germans. As we are fighting on their soil and as our own people and territory are, in a measure by that fact, spared the horrors of a German invasion, it seems to me that we should view the situation very much as if our own land had been occupied and our own people subjected to the privations and brutal treatment which for four years have been the portion of the Belgians and French.

We are receiving constant reports, the truth of which seems beyond question, that the retiring armies of Germany are destroying property and committing outrages in the territory which they are forced to evacuate, that the destruction is without any military benefit whatsoever, and that this deliberate lawlessness is inspired by malice and spite.

If these criminal acts were perpetrated against American citizens on American soil, I believe that we would be warranted in attempting to prevent it by threatening reprisals upon the territory and property of the Germans and by declaring that full reparation would be required for all property destroyed or carried away, which in no way contributed to the military advantage of the retreating armies.

If this view is correct, and I think that it is, our peculiar relationship to the French and Belgians, arising from the fact that our battlefields are on their territory and their non-combatants are suffering from German vindictiveness caused by the successes of our arms, raises the question whether it is not our right, if not our duty, to threaten reprisals unless this wanton destruction and ill-treatment by the retreating Germans cease.

We have been for some time, as you know, pressed to do this by the French and Belgian Governments, but up to now I have not had time to consider the subject except from their standpoint. I do it now from our standpoint, and would appreciate your determination as to our course of action.

Faithfully yours,   Robert Lansing.

My dear Mr. President: Washington, September 27, 1918.

The Italian Ambassador told me today that his Government telegraphed him that they would send no High Commissioner to Siberia though urged to do so by the British and French Governments, and that they desired to conform their policy to ours in such matters.

Faithfully yours,   Robert Lansing.

TLS (WP, DLC).

From William Christian Bullitt

My dear Mr President: Washington September 27, 1918.

May I respectively offer you my thanks for your address of this night. Never have you voiced more clearly or more simply the hopes which are in the hearts of the millions in every nation who care about the same things for which you care. Never have you moved more wisely through the nets of international politics.

More and more the political and moral leadership of the world is coming into your hands: more and more you are making us thank God that this is so.

Very respectfully yours   William C. Bullitt.

TLS (WP, DLC).

From Raymond Blaine Fosdick, with Enclosure

My dear Mr. President: Washington September 27, 1918

The enclosed memorandum on the negro problem at Newport News has just come to my hands from one of our representatives. It seems to me to be rather significant, and I thought you might like to look it over.   Cordially yours,   Raymond B. Fosdick

TLS (WP, DLC).

E N C L O S U R E

STATUS OF NEGRO PROBLEM AT NEWPORT NEWS
(Confidential)

While the situation at Newport News has greatly improved, there is still great danger that trouble may arise before the war is closed. Unfortunately the true attitude of the negro remains unseen. He must not be judged so much by what he says publicly, as by what he is thinking and doing in secret. This tendency towards secrecy is growing. The negroes are not telling the white man all the truth about what they think of present conditions, and what they expect when the war is over.

To appreciate the present situation and to guess what the future will bring, it is necessary to know some of the things he is thinking, and why he is thinking thus:

(a) They are very uneasy about the future. All are looking for a coming democracy in which the negroes will occupy a high position. This talk may be heard in street cars, on street corners and almost any place where two or three of them get together. The details of this democracy they do not discuss. It is enough for them that they are coming to their own. They grow uneasy when the thought occurs to them, that coming kingdoms do not always appear.

(b) They demand a better chance, industrially, socially and politically; they complain bitterly of a white man's oppression. They feel they have been discriminated against long enough. They say further that no sacrifice is too great to win a freedom, which was not gained by the Civil War. Here again is no attempt to state clearly what they want. As an illustration of this feeling, here are the exact words of a negro, with almost national reputation: "I come to the problem, with no race prejudice. My best friends in this world are white men. I have spent my life in trying to bring about a more friendly relation between the whites and the blacks. The negroes are not free to-day and have never been. I do not want them to have that for which they are not prepared, but I do want them to have a chance as human beings. If this war does not bring this chance, there is no hope, and I, for one, will feel that another course is necessary."

(c) There is a mistrust of the government. They feel that certain things could be accomplished, if the government would take a definite stand. Too many of them look upon the government as unfriendly, and seeking to do them harm, rather than look after their interests. For instance some of the women here will not engage in war service because they say it is a trick of the government's to get them into oversea service. Many of the mothers would not let their girls participate in our program for the same reason. They believe that as soon as they learn to do work here, they will be made to work over there. They speak often of the strong arm of the government.

(d) There is a widespread feeling, that negro troops are discriminated against and badly treated. They point to the attitude of some white officers, and regard that attitude as typical. They love to linger on isolated cases. Locally, this condition is improved, because some of them have learned that white men are subject to the same treatment and that after all bad treatment comes from individuals and not the government.

(e) There is a growing dissatisfaction that so many negroes are among the stevedores and Labor Units. They believe that there is a deliberate attempt to put the hard and nasty side of army life on the negro. I am told that this feeling is nation-wide.

(f) They want the mob-spirit put down. They point to the fact that lynching and brutal treatment of negroes has been increased, since we entered the war. Apparently our President's recent utterance on the mob-spirit[1] is doing good. Many local people have expressed great satisfaction.

(g) The most discouraging thing to me here is the fact that many ministers are preaching, and prominent men sent here are lecturing that the war cannot be won without the negroes. Time and again have they said in my hearing that the United States was failing, and had to call upon the negroes to win the war. When such utterances are made, whether in church or out, prolonged applause follows. With these men this is not idle talk. They believe it is actually so. This fact accounts for much of their arrogance and furnishes a reason for demanding great things when the conflict is over.

T MS (WP, DLC).
    [1] Wilson's statement to the American people, printed at July 26, 1918, Vol. 49.

From Harry Augustus Garfield

Dear Mr. President: Washington, D. C. September 27, 1918

In sending you, yesterday, a copy of my letter to Senator Walsh, I neglected to inform you that I called the Senator's attention to the fact that on May 4th of this year the relation of the Distribution Division of the Fuel Administration to the fuel industry was fully explained, Chairman Shirley inquiring for the Committee. I referred the Senator to the published document, Sundry Civil Bill 1919, Hearings before Sub-committee of House Committee on Appropriations, pages 2,025 to 2,033.

The Senator, at once, appreciated and commented upon the fact that the Congress was therefore duly informed and had taken no action, unless the subsequent cutting down of the appropriation asked for from four and one-half to three and one-half millions might be regarded as at least an acquiescence in the arrangement by which the industry was loaning men without cost to the Fuel Administration.

Cordially and faithfully yours,   H. A. Garfield.

TLS (WP, DLC).

From Scott Ferris

My dear Mr. President: Washington, D. C. September 27, 1918.

I have just returned from a trip to the West. I was on a speaking campaign in Missouri for two days with ex-Governor Folk, now Democratic nominee for the United States Senate. I also had a long conference with him in St. Louis.

He is very anxious that you arrange to give expression in some way of approval of his efforts as a part of your official family. Governor Folk is making a brilliant fight out there for United States Senator, and is helping the ticket all along the line. As you know, the newspaper situation is bad for us in that State, and it is also true the Republicans are quite active, and are making a good hard campaign. While I think Governor Folk's election is sure, yet a word from you that he could use for publication purposes, or otherwise, would make it a certainty.

He asked me, as a personal favor, and as a distinct one, to make this request of you immediately upon my return. I know you will think I am almost a public nuisance, for making so many appeals to you of this character, but I am trying to discharge my duties[1] as best I can, and I know you will bear with me.

Very respectively yours,   Scott Ferris

TLS (WP, DLC).
  [1] Ferris was chairman of the Democratic Congressional Campaign Committee in 1918.

Peyton Conway March to Tasker Howard Bliss

[Washington] September 27, 1918.

Number 94 Confidential.

The President is today informing all Allied nations that he will send no more troops to northern ports in Russia. March.

Harris.[1]

TC telegram (WDR, RG 407, World War I Cablegrams, DNA).
  [1] Maj. Gen. Peter Charles Harris had succeeded Maj. Gen. McCain as Adjutant General on September 1.

Robert Lansing to Colville Adrian de Rune Barclay, with Enclosure

My dear Mr. Chargé: Washington September 27, 1918.

I beg to hand you herewith a memorandum setting out the program of the United States with respect to the disposition for the winter of the American Expeditionary Forces in Siberia and in Russia and the sending of supplies for the use of the Czecho-Slovak Forces.

I am, my dear Mr. Barclay,

Very sincerely yours,   Robert Lansing

TLS (FO 115/2450, p. 141, PRO).

E N C L O S U R E

Washington, September 27, 1918.

MEMORANDUM.

After consideration of the matter of the disposition for the winter of the American Expeditionary Forces in Siberia and in Russia, the Government of the United States has decided that its forces in Siberia should not be established at Omsk or any other point in the far interior because, strongly as that Government's sympathies constrain it to make every possible sacrifice to keep the country on the Volga front out of the hands of the merciless Red Guards, it is the unqualified judgment of the military authorities of the United States that to attempt military activities west of the Urals is to attempt the impossible. The Government of the United States means to send all available supplies that can be spared from the western front as fast as possible for the use of the Czecho-Slovak forces, but it cannot undertake to send supplies west of the Urals. So far as United States cooperation is concerned, the Government thereof must frankly say that it is its view that the Czech forces should retire to the eastern side of the Urals to some point at which they will be certainly accessible to supplies sent from the east, preferably where they will be in a position to make it impossible for the Germans to draw supplies of any kind from western Siberia, but in any case where they can make themselves secure against attack. With the deepest regret, but with perfect realization of compelling facts, the Government of the United States must in frankness say that its assistance cannot be given in the carrying out of any other programme. All that some in authority expected to happen upon the sending of allied and American troops to the northern ports in Russia has failed of realization. The Government of the United States cannot cooperate in an effort to establish lines of operation and defence through from Siberia to Archangel.

However, authority is being given General Graves to establish his headquarters at some such place as Harbin provided the Chinese Government interposes no objection, so that he can be in touch with an open port during the winter and can make the best use of his force to carry out the plans for safeguarding the rear of the Czecho-Slovaks. The Government of the United States has asked the Chinese Government whether there would be any objection to this plan.

The Government of the United States has very carefully considered the situation which exists in north Russia and has informed the American Ambassador at Archangel that as it is, in the opinion of the Government of the United States, plain that no gathering of any effective force by the Russians is to be hoped for, it will insist with the other governments, so far as United States cooperation is concerned, that all military effort in northern Russia be given up except the guarding of the ports themselves and as much of the country round about them as may develop threatening conditions. The Government of the United States will, of course, do its utmost to send supplies, but it cannot undertake relief, and must presently, of course, be cut off from Archangel by the ice and able to go only to Murmansk.

No more American troops will be sent to the northern ports.

The course which the Government of the United States is following is not the course of its free choice, but that of stern necessity. Circumstances in European Russia, which have thrown that country into one of the saddest periods recorded in all history, and separation from the scenes of bloodshed and anarchy by the intervening hostile territory, render any efforts which the Government of the United States could make to bring succor to the distressed people of Russia inadequate and impracticable. The Government of the United States is constrained, consequently, to come to this decision.   Robert Lansing

TS MS (FO 115/2450, pp. 143-47, PRO).

From the Diary of William Phillips

Friday, Sept 27 [1918].

The press this morning announced that Bulgaria had asked for an armistice. When I reached the Department I found a despatch from The Hague had been received, dated September 27th, containing a note[1] which Bliss, who is now Chargé there, had received from his Bulgarian colleague stating that the Commander-in-Chief of the Bulgarian armies in the field[2] had been authorized yesterday to propose to the Commander of the British armies in Macedonia[3] immediate cessation of operations in order to permit of an armistice with a view to beginning negotiations for peace; and asking President Wilson to use his influence with the Allies to recognize the sincere efforts of the Bulgarian Government to stop the bloodshed. This was followed immediately by a further despatch from Bliss saying that the Bulgarian Minister at The Hague had sent him the text of a telegram from the Bulgarian Premier to the Bulgarian Minister in Washington to be forwarded. Bliss asks for instructions regarding the transmission.

The President left for New York this morning to deliver the opening Liberty Loan speech this evening. We reached him by telephone at Col. House's. He at once wrote a reply in his own hand which was read over the telephone to Auchincloss who gave it to me, and I put it in instruction form. It was to the effect that the President appreciated the confidence imposed in him and was willing to urge an armistice upon the entente if the Bulgarian Government will authorize him to say that the conditions of the armistice are left to him for decision and that Bulgaria will accept the conditions which he (The President) imposes. If the above conditions are accepted, then Bliss may forward the Premier's message to Washington.

It has been a day of excitement, because all hands feel that Bulgaria's move is in reality capitulation. The Allied armies have already practically retaken the disputed portion of Serbia in occupation by Bulgaria, and are advancing into Bulgaria itself.

T MS (W. Phillips Papers, MH).
  [1] That is, R. W. Bliss to RL, No. 4586, Sept. 27, 1918, cited in RL to WW, Sept. 27, 1918 (first letter of that date), n. 1.
  [2] The nominal commander in chief of the Bulgarian armies in the field was Prince Boris, heir to the Bulgarian throne. However, it was General Todorov, the deputy commander in chief, who proposed the cessation of hostilities. See British embassy to Department of State, Sept. 30, 1918, *FR-WWS 1918*, 1, I, 330, in which his name appears as "Doroff." The Editors have been unable to learn the given names of Gen. Todorov.
  [3] Lt. Gen. George Francis Milne.

From the Diary of Colonel House

September 27, 1918.

The usual confusion reigns today because of the President's coming visit. I have changed my telephone number and that, in itself, has added to the confusion for those who have the right to reach me have not yet gotten it. They therefore come in person and I cannot deny them.

Loulie and I met the Presidential party at 1.20. There was a great throng around the Pennsylvania Station when we arrived, and a greater one when the President came out. We drove directly to the Waldorf Hotel but before we left the train I had an opportunity to tell him of the Bulgarian debacle. He was intensely interested. Gordon had read me all the cables over the telephone from Washington, and I brought the President to our apartment so that he might have them read to him over the private wire.

We remained at the hotel scarcely a moment, and the President and I came up the Avenue to 115 East 53rd Street. The crowds were enthusiastic and I have never seen a better reception. After Gordon had read the cables to the President, and while he was doing so, I had the Manager kill our ordinary telephone in order that we might be perfectly quiet.

In coming up I had told the President of Lansing's idea that he should reply by saying he would intercede for an armistice provided the Bulgarians would evacuate Serbia and permit the Allies access to Bulgaria in the event it was necessary to help Bulgaria defend her territory against the Central Powers. The President evidently thought this was also my view, and he sat down at the desk and wrote the following:

"Appreciate the confidence reposed in me and am willing to urge an armistice upon the Entente if Bulgarian Government will agree now that the immediate terms of peace pending the final determinations of the general peace conference shall include the evacuation by the Bulgarian forces of Serbia and Macedonia and the Epirus and permission to the Entente Allies to enter Bulgaria if and when necessary to defend her territory against the Central Powers."

"W.W."

The President handed this to me for my opinion. I disapproved and told him he did not know enough about conditions to specify the terms. Not only that, no Bulgarian Government would dare go before their people having accepted such terms. I advised telling them he would be willing to act as they desired, provided they would leave it to his judgment as to the terms of the armistice.

He argued the matter for a few minutes, saying he was afraid it would look like leaving too much to him. I replied that they would prefer this rather than having to consent to such terms as he had outlined; that the Government could go before the Bulgarian people claiming that he, the President, had not been fair with them; that they had reposed confidence in him believing he was a friend of Bulgaria. In other words, they would make excuses they liked to their people. The President saw the force of this argument and wrote the following:

"I appreciate the confidence reposed in me and am willing to urge an armistice upon the Entente if the Bulgarian Government will authorize me to say that the conditions of the armistice are left to me for decision and that the Bulgarian Government will accept the conditions I impose. Otherwise, I should not be hopeful of result of mediation on my part at this juncture in so vital a matter."[1]

I telephoned this to Gordon and had him send it immediately to the Secretary of State for transmission.

The President returned to the Waldorf and I remained at the apartment to attend to the hundred and one matters which needed attention.

Gordon telephoned again to say that Lansing had sent at twelve o'clock the following cable to our Legation at the Hague:

[Blank]

It was necessary of course to send an urgent cable to the Hague killing this message and substituting the one the President and I had prepared. Lansing wanted to insert the word "unconditionally" in the message which the President authorized to be sent. The President was not here when I received this suggestion and I decided it must be sent as he had written it. The message is strong enough without inserting the word "unconditionally."[2]

The President, Mrs. Wilson, Margaret, Grayson, Gregory and Jesse Jones dined with us at seven o'clock. While we were having coffee, a messenger came from Washington with the despatches which Gordon had already read over the telephone. Nevertheless, the President asked the others to excuse us and we went into the study to read Lansing's letter.

Lansing wished to give out a statement concerning the despatches which both the President and I thought unwise. Lansing said that Philip Patchin of the State Department would remain in New York to receive anything the President might wish to communicate. I was sorry the President did not reply in some way, but he did not seem to consider it necessary. He remarked that Lansing was so stupid that he was constantly afraid he would commit some serious blunder. I could not but confess that he was stupid. He seems less alert than when he first became Secretary of State, and I wonder whether his health has not made this difference.

Governor Strong[3] called for the President at 8.15 and our entire party motored to the Metropolitan Opera House. It was an historic occasion. The house was beautifully decorated, and was crowded with the most important people of New York, including the Governor of the State[4] and other officials. Governor Strong made an excellent speech. He read it to me yesterday in order that there might be no jarring notes. I made one or two suggestions which he adopted. Strong did not finish writing his speech until late this afternoon and yet he delivered it with but few references to his notes. Not being a public speaker, this seemed to me quite a feat of memory.

The President read his address. Most of it seemed somewhat over the heads of his audience; the parts which were unimportant bringing the most vigorous applause.

We are all wondering how the press will receive it. After the speaking the President asked me to ride with him to the Waldorf. We went to the sitting room and discussed the address for some minutes. He was flushed with excitement and altogether pleased with the day's effort. The President seems to want me with him after one of these great speeches.

I had a very tiring day but was able to get back home by 10.30.

¹ WWhw drafts of these telegrams are in the E. M. House Papers, CtY.
² It was sent as RL to R. W. Bliss, Sept. 27, 1918, 3 p.m., printed in *FR-WWS 1918*, I, I, 324.
³ That is, Benjamin Strong.
⁴ That is, Charles Seymour Whitman.

Sir William Wiseman to Lord Reading

[New York] Sept. 27th. 1918.

No. 771 VERY urgent and secret.

HOUSE suggested I should send you the message contained in Paragraph B. He has seen and approved of it.

The PRESIDENT has been here today with HOUSE and while he was here a message arrived from the State Department that the BULGARIAN Minister at the HAGUE had requested U. S. Minister to ask his Government if the PRESIDENT would use his good offices as intermediary to obtain armistice for the BULGARIANS. The PRESIDENT's first inclination was to sketch out broadly terms of peace which he thought BULGARIA ought to accept and to tell them that if they were willing to agree to these terms he would use his good offices. HOUSE, however, pointed out that it might be some embar[r]assment to the ALLIES if the PRESIDENT were to state, even broadly, what he considered just terms should be and that perhaps it would be better for him to say he would act as intermediary, only if BULGARIAN Government would leave it to him to arrange on their behalf, just terms for armistice. The PRESIDENT agreed to this view and instructions to that effect have been sent to U. S. Minister at the HAGUE.

Above information is of course of the utmost secrecy and must on no account be communicated to anyone else until received through channel. Reason of sending it to you now is that there will be probably rumour and attempt to misinterpret the PRESIDENT's attitude and we think it necessary that you should know that his sole purpose is to for[e]stall any attempt on behalf of GERMANY to use situation for their own advantage by making trouble among the ALLIES on the question of peace terms to BULGARIA.

T telegram (Reading Papers, FO 800/225, PRO).

From the Diary of Colonel House

September 28, 1918.

I went to the Waldorf at ten o'clock and the President and I conferred for about a half hour. We discussed the Russian situation mainly. I urged him to give Vance McCormick considerable play in the economic and relief side of our efforts to aid that country. I found he had not read the paper which Hollis Godfrey had prepared on after war reconstruction.[1] I am sorry for I wished to discuss this with him. There were many other matters of minor importance which we took up before he left New York at 10.50. I did not go to the station with him but returned from the hotel to our apartment.

I forgot to speak to the President about urging the Italians to make an offensive at this time. In lieu of this I called Gordon over the telephone and asked him to see General March, Chief of Staff, and suggest that he send a cable to Pershing requesting him to see Foch and have him insist that the Italians start an immediate offensive. General Diaz is afraid to jeoparidze [jeopardize] the reputation he made in the last offensive, but he should be pushed into another in spite of this. In my opinion, the Austrians are so demoralized that any kind of push will succeed.

Yesterday I told Sir William Wiseman about Bulgaria's request that we should intercede in favor of an armistice and just what had been done. He asked permission to send a cable to his Government to which I consented. This cable is a part of the record. I spoke to the President this morning about the necessity of having some arrangement with the Allies, particularly England, as to the return of our troops after the war. He is fully alive to its importance and said he had the matter under consideration.

[1] Hollis Godfrey, "Proposal for the Organization of a *National Reconstruction Plan Commission* for the United States," T MS (E. M. House Papers, CtY).

A Statement

The White House [Sept. 28, 1918]

Again the Government comes to the people of the country with the request that they lend their money, and lend it upon a more liberal scale than ever before, in order that the great war for the rights of America and the liberation of the world may be prosecuted with ever increasing vigor to a victorious conclusion. And it makes the appeal with the greatest confidence because it knows that every day it is becoming clearer and clearer to thinking men throughout the nation that the winning of the war is an essential investment. The money that is held back now will be of little use or value if the war is not won and the selfish masters of Germany are permitted to dictate what America may and may not do. Men in America, besides, have from the first until now dedicated both their lives and their fortunes to the vindication and maintenance of the great principles and objects for which our Government was set up. They will not fail now to show the world for what their wealth was intended.

Woodrow Wilson[1]

Photocopy of WWhw MS (WC, NjP).
[1] This statement was printed in the *Official Bulletin*, II (Sept. 28, 1918), 1. It was also printed in facsimile in newspapers throughout the country.

From Robert Lansing

My dear Mr. President,   Washington September 28, 1918.

Your address last night is the greatest that you have ever made. I have studied it line by line and not a word could be added or subtracted without impairing the symmetry of the thought or weakening the structure of the message. It gives the country—the world—a very definite goal to attain.

For myself I wish to thank you for saying what I think but could never have said. It has cleared the international atmosphere in a most wonderful way.   Faithfully yours   Robert Lansing.

ALS (WP, DLC).

From William Kent

My dear Mr. President: Washington September 28, 1918.

From the bottom of my heart I thank you for your New York message. It is perfect in thought, feeling and expression. That you may know how timely it is, I enclose a pamphlet, and call your attention to the concluding paragraph and the names of endorsement on the back cover.[1]

Such stuff is not only vile from the standpoint of common humanity but is inherent sedition as interfering with matters of life and death in our own country. No pacifist can work greater harm.

If the Germans believe that they are to be starved and oppressed throughout the centuries, they will find, in lieu of their boldness for conquest, at a time when they are crumbling, a new resistance—that of the rat in a corner. Our boys may be killed in unnecessary fighting due to just such utterances.

I have already had discussion with Mr. Richard Hurd of the Board of Trustees of this amiable association,[2] and know that they are pledging eternal boycott of German goods as one means of bringing about the desired result.

I know that you have consistently refrained from talking back at the irrepressible Roosevelt. I would not advocate your paying personal heed to this infamous interference with statecraft, but somehow or other it should be brought home to these people that they are overstepping the bounds of private opinion, are interfering in the war, and should be subject to treatment in accordance with their deserts.   Yours truly,   William Kent

I am afraid it is asking too much to request you to read the entire pamphlet I therefore send the specific matter mentioned and will forward the entire booklet as soon as I get some copies.

TLS (WP, DLC).
    [1] It is missing but it was one of the pamphlet series issued by the American Defense Society, Inc. This organization issued at least thirty-five such pamphlets through June 1919. The Editors have been unable to locate a copy of any pamphlet in the series which fits the vague description given in the above letter. However, a copy of Pamphlet No. 24, *Unpatriotic Teaching in Public Schools* (New York, 1918), located in NjP, reveals that, as of the date of publication, Theodore Roosevelt was the "Honorary President" of the American Defense Society, and that the "Honorary Vice-Presidents" included David Jayne Hill, Robert Bacon, Perry Belmont, Charles Joseph Bonaparte, John Grier Hibben, Henry Bourne Joy, and Charles Stebbins Fairchild.
    [2] That is, Richard Melancthon Hurd.

From Robert Latham Owen

Washington, D. C., September 28, 1918.

Please permit me to extend my heartfelt thanks for your great message delivered at the Metropolitan Opera House, in New York City. I regard it as of the greatest advantage in clearing the path to permanent world peace, and thank you for the frankness and the courage and the vision with which you have pointed the way to the rule on earth of justice, humanity and righteousness.

Robert L. Owen.

T telegram (WP, DLC).

From Richard Lloyd Jones

Madison, Wis., Sept. 28, 1918.

Your New York address and statement of our peace plans is one of the broadest and biggest and most far seeing humanitarian declaration ever uttered, and puts you permanently in the class of Washington and Lincoln. My enthusiasm and admiration go to you with my thanks as an American citizen and my congratulations.

Richard Lloyd Jones.

T telegram (WP, DLC).

From Francis Edward Clark[1]

My dear President Wilson: Boston September 28, 1918.

Permit me to tell you how thrilled I was by the address you gave last night in New York, as reported in this morning's papers. I feel that it is the greatest and will be most far-reaching in its influence, of any of your great addresses. It makes the issues of the war so plain, that a way-faring man, though a fool, need not err therein.

I have been distressed that the leaders of the party with which I had formerly long been connected, seem to look askance at the League of Nations, which can alone secure for us a permanent peace. Your ringing words will be worth more than a Liberty Loan or an army at the front. I hope and pray that you may live to see the full consummation of your plans, and if I may in any measure speak for the three hundred thousand Christian Endeavor young men in the armies and navies of the United States and our Allies, and the millions who cannot go to the front, I am confident that I express their joy that the great causes for which we are fighting have been set forth so lucidly and so convincingly.

With great esteem, I am
                    Respectfully yours,   Francis E. Clark

TLS (WP, DLC).
  [1] Founder and president of the United Society of Christian Endeavor.

From Patrick Emmet Gorman

Honorable Sir: Louisville, Ky. Sept 28/18

At the Labor Day Celebration held in this city on September 2 1918 I was announced as a candidate for Congress, later the various labor unions of this locality endorsed my candidacy and the organized workers of this locality were of the opinion that I would be returned the winner. It was suggested to me that this was not the proper time to announce for this office because of the fact that it may to a certain extent interfere with the successfull prosecution of the war, inasmuch as my opponent Swager Sherley was so potent a factor in the prosecution of the war, so impressed was I with these statements that I, with Peter J. Campbell, journeyed to Washington to ascertain what attitude the American Federation of Labor and Government officials had, regarding my race.

On arriving in Washington we learned that the AF of L, the Department of Labor and the four great Railroad Brotherhoods did not deem it wise for me to make the race at this time, but even in the face of the position assumed by the organizations named above we were rather reluctant in with-drawing because of Sherleys Labor Record. However when Mr Morrison showed me the letter addressed to him by you, clearly stating *your* position in the matter I most readily and willingly quit the race, upon my return to Louisville the daily papers made known my withdrawal and I was almost instantly flooded with a rain of personal callers and telephone messages seeking to ascertain the truth of the news items, to some my position was plain and I was congratulated, while others doubted my stat[e]ments and left suspicious of my actions in Washington. As I was the candidate of the Federated Unions I am to make a detailed report to them of my with-drawal.

Now Mr. Wilson, I am a young man, ambitious, with my very heart enveloped in the cause of the workers I represent. I never in my life have been accused of a single act of dishonesty but in this case I have a fear that my action in with-drawing from this Congressional race will not meet with the unanimous approval of the working People of this Locality. I am of the firm opinion however that my class places as much confidence in you as I personally do and that you are really the President of *all* the people of the United States and not of any particular class. I feel that a copy of the letter addressed by you to Mr Morrison or a similar letter addressed to me, would relieve all doubt and suspicion from the minds of the people that nominated me. It cuts me deep to think that I am under suspicion by those who formerly idolized me.

Would you kindly let me hear from you at your very earliest convenience.

God granting you more power in leading our nation and the world to Victory and Freedom.

I Remain   Faithfully   Patrick E Gorman

ALS (WP, DLC).

From Elbert Henry Gary

My dear Mr. President: New York September 28th, 1918.

Recognizing that comment by an individual citizen concerning the Leader of the Nation is of little consequence, I am nevertheless impelled to write what appears to me will be the universal opinion of the people of this country regarding your address of last evening at the Metropolitan Opera House.

It was the greatest of all public utterances since the beginning of the war, clear, emphatic, explicit, comprehensive and convincing.

It was directed first to your own constituency, but, with equal force and effect, to all others of the Allies; and to the opposing Government as well.

It furnishes a fundamental basis, a world constitution, which must, in substance, be adopted and which will firmly establish the rights and fully protect the interests of every nation and every person in accordance with the principles of justice.

Of all your splendid addresses and papers this is the best and will be of the most benefit to mankind. Spoken at a critical time, to the multitudes, eager to read what you may say, its influence cannot be completely measured until the record of the times is written.

It will be the final judgment of those who, at the present time, are bitter foes of the United States and its Allies, that your decisions have been wise, your actions justified and your language classic. All then, if not at present, will better understand and appreciate how much is really intended by your speech. Everyone throughout the Universe, even now, should congratulate and thank you.

With great respect and admiration, I am,

Sincerely yours,   Elbert H. Gary

TLS (WP, DLC).

From Cleveland Hoadley Dodge

My dear President   Riverdale-on-Hudson Sept. 28th, 1918

I am broken hearted that I failed to see you or hear you yesterday. I tried to get in touch with Col. House but he had just changed his telephone number & I could not find out from him how to reach you. I am getting on, as far as my health goes, very well as long as I am careful but I have to shun late hours & was obliged, much against my inclination, to forego the satisfaction of hearing what I knew would be an epoch making speech. It certainly was—you hit the nail right on the head, so clearly & convincingly that it is bound to have a great effect, & I heartily thank & congratuate you.

We have been in the seventh heaven these past few days over the news from the Balkans & Palestine. It means so much to Grace & myself, and I realize now more than ever before how wise your policy has been towards Bulgaria & Turkey. If the Balkan states would now make peace and leave the settlement of their vexed boundaries & nationalities to a disinterested tribunal after the war is ended, there would be some hope for a permanent peace in that unhappy peninsula

At any rate Bulgaria & Turkey seem to be nearly at their end and I am correspondingly happy and grateful to you for your wise and patient course of action—or nonaction.

If you come on again for Columbus Day I surely hope you will stay long enough to make us another visit & in any event that I may not fail again to see you

Congratulating you as Commander in Chief on the superb conduct of your armies, with heartiest good wishes for you & Mrs Wilson from Mrs Dodge & myself

Ever cordially & affectionately yours   Cleveland H Dodge

ALS (WP, DLC).

A Translation of a Telegram from Jean Jules Jusserand to the Foreign Ministry

Washington, no date [Sept. 28, 1918]
Received 29 September 1918

URGENT. 1330. Further to my telegram 1309. As if to interdict any rejoinder to himself, the President has just sent to the embassies concerned a written note[1] in which, while insisting on the keen regrets he suffers in disagreeing with their governments, he lays down most rigorously the limitations which he persists in seeing imposed upon the American effort in Siberia and in Russia. He bases his position especially on the view of the American military authorities, which is clearly unfavorable. Secretary of War Baker's opinion on this will have had a determining influence.

Mr. Wilson has declared that these authorities have determined [1331] that "to risk a military action west of the Urals is to attempt the impossible." All that can be spared from the supplies destined for the western front will be sent to the Czecho-Slovaks, "but the United States cannot undertake to send anything west of the Urals." The American government believes it must "frankly say that the Czech forces must withdraw east of the Urals" to places where the supplies can reach them, and where they can eventually prevent products of western Siberia from reaching the Germans, but where, above all, they [the Czechs] will be secure.

"With very deep regret, but yielding to necessity, the American government does not believe that it can provide its aid to realize any other program whatsoever.

"None of the predicted benefits of sending American troops to northern Russia has been realized."

The American government cannot cooperate in any effort to link Archangel and Siberia (seven groups garbled, repetition requested) General Graves will establish his headquarters.

[1334] The English Embassy has telegraphed the original text of the American note on Siberia to London, where we can have a copy. I have just come from the Secretary of State. I have indicated to him the extremely painful impression such a document will have on us and the other Allies.

The President, I said, on this question, has always had opinions less optimistic than our own: each has a right to its own. But how can one justify decisions by which not only the hoped-for aid is refused but by which the realization of our hopes by our own methods is rendered more difficult. It is no longer a question of advancing or staying where we are but of abandoning what we now hold and have great interest in protecting.

And what will be the result of this abandonment? Along with great damage to our cause and immense encouragement to our enemies from such a retreat without a fight, we run the risk of a massacre analogous to the one in Astrakhan[2] of which M. Grunniije,[3] now here, [1335] has all the details. This blood will be on your head, not on ours, and it will be a grave responsibility to have caused these deaths.

Somewhat agitated, as it seemed to me, the Secretary of State barricaded himself behind the unanimous view of the American military authorities; the nonrealization of the Allies' prognostications (group garbled) refers especially to those of General Poole; and the necessity of letting nothing distract from the French front.

On this last point, I replied that if any nation is above suspicion here it is our own, and that, if Marshal Foch supports the request for aid in Russia, this surely can be granted without harm to our most cherished interests. It conforms, moreover, to his strategy that the Germans be given no rest in any quarters.

Along with an attitude which will cause the sharpest pain to the Allies, I said in conclusion, there is also the fact that your forces and your resources are not the only ones involved and that the circumstances [1336] may favor our views instead of justifying your pessimism. No doubt your present attitude reduces our chances extremely, but even so they are not an impossibility. We can, I hope, count on the President's not finding something from which to take umbrage in the efforts which we could make to take advantage of various circumstances (a Russian awakening, for example) and, in any case, to avoid the predicted misfortunes. Certainly, the Secretary of State replied without hesitation, and he added: moreover, it would be natural that, if circumstances changed, it would be followed by a reexamination of the problem.

Jusserand.

T telegram (État-Major, l'Armée de Terre, Service Historique, 6 N 53–2, FMD-Ar).
[1] That is, the Enclosure printed with RL to C. A. de R. Barclay, Sept. 27, 1918.

From William Phillips, with Enclosures

Dear Mr. President,   Washington Sunday A.M. [Sept. 29, 1918]

At the request of the Secretary I send you two important despatches just received regarding the Bulgarian situation *one* from *Berne* transmitting the text of Malinoff's message to the Bulgarian Minister here *the second* from The Hague suggesting that we endeavor to send your message to Malinoff through other channels than The Hague.

One of the points on which the Secretary would be grateful for an expression of your wishes is whether we shall attempt to answer the despatch from Berne.

We might make positive efforts to reach Bulgaria with your original message to Malinoff by wireless at Salonica.

                    Very respectfully   William Phillips

Malinoff apparently sent his appeal to you simultaneously through The Hague and Berne. Our Legation at The Hague held it pending instructions. The Berne Legation sent it through.

ALS (WP, DLC).

ENCLOSURE   I

Pontarlier, (Berne), September 27, 1918.

Urgent, 4946. In a formal note Bulgarian Legation hands me telegram in English from Malinoff to Bulgarian Minister, Washington. Telegram follows:

"Kindly transmit to the President of the United States, Mr. Wilson, and to the Secretary of State, Mr. Lansing, in Washington, the following:

The Bulgarian nation and Government were constrained to enter into the general conflict after they had exhausted all peaceful means possible for coming to an understanding with their neighbors and for realizing their race reunion. This fact Bulgaria reiterated in her note of September 20th last in answer to the peace proposition of Count Burian given out on September 14th. If the ideas of the President of the United States are to be crowned with success, and if their realization is that sought for no more in the old conception and methods of action, but in the path pointed out by the honored President of the American Republic, for the establishment of a new order of things guarantying freedom and justice among the nations, Bulgaria which feels that the idea and the cause for which she is struggling find place side by side with the principles in behalf of which America interfered in this war, is glad and ready to follow that path, in order to secure the fulfillment of justice desired by her. Having this in view, therefore, the Bulgarian Government turns to the friendly President of the Republic of the United States, with the request that its President use his good offices for putting an end to the bloodshed on the Macedonian front by the conclusion of an armistice, after which are to follow preliminary negotiations for peace, the final settlement of the Balkan questions being left to be decided in the general peace conference. Signed Malinoff."

Stovall

E N C L O S U R E   I I

The Hague September 28, 6 p m. 1918.

4601, urgent. Have today communicated to Bulgarian Minister views of President as contained in your 2132 September 27th 3pm. Shortly after receipt of this communication, Bulgarian Minister sent Secretary to this Legation to state that every possible means were being taken to forward to Sofia a communication containing the above mentioned views of the President; that although he had no reason to believe delays in its transmission would occur, he felt it essential in view of the urgency of matter, that nothing should be left undone to ensure its prompt delivery. He therefore suggested that this Legation take steps to have President's views transmitted to Bulgarian Government through channels other than those available to Bulgarian Legation here which telegraphs through Germany and Austria-Hungary. In this connection, he mentioned the possibility of communicating across Macedonian front. I transmit the foregoing for such action if any as the Department may think advisable.   Bliss

T telegrams (WP, DLC.)

From Carrie Clinton Lane Chapman Catt

My dear Mr. President: [Washington] September 29th 1918

We turn to you this morning in sheer desperation. As you doubtless know, Mr. Drew of New Hampshire[1] was won over by the

Massachusetts senators, and Mr. Benet by the group representing the solid South. Our vote is on for tomorrow and we are still two short.

Several senators on the floor, and in conversation, have said that they could not see that woman suffrage is in any sense a war measure. Mr. Benet said he would change his position if he thought it was. There is but one thing we can think of which could win those needed votes. I venture to suggest that a friendly senator might write you a letter and ask if, in your judgment, it is a war measure. If you could see your way clear to reply to the effect that it is, and *why*, so that the reply could be printed in tomorrow's papers, we feel sure it would greatly help. If it did not win the needed votes, at least it would still further clarify the war aims you have so wonderfully set forth, and especially in your masterly address of Friday. As the country has responded to your leadership in the material aids necessary to the victory of our armies, so must the country understand and endorse the principles of liberty for which this nation is supposed to be giving its life blood.

Many of us were shocked at the peace terms put forth by Senator Lodge.[2] He had much of the substance, but the spirit of humanity was not there. There was none of the thrill, the exaltation which your exposition of our aims produces. We shudder to think that should the reactionary element of either or both parties come uppermost at the end of the war, the world may lose the fruits for which a generation has been sacrificed.

It is therefore not alone to win two votes that we suggest this step. The country and especially the women recognize the need of constant direction of thought and feeling upward and onward. Our country is asking its women to give their all, and upon their voluntary and free offering may depend the outcome of the war. If the Amendment fails, it will take the heart out of thousands of women, and it will be no solace to tell them that "it is coming." It will arouse in them a just suspicion that men and women are not co-workers for world freedom, but that women are regarded as mere servitors with no interest or rightful voice in the outcome. The leaders in women's work in the Red Cross, Y.M.C.A., Liberty Loan, Food, are almost without exception women who have been trained to their work in our Association, so that my statement is no idle claim—these women by the thousands feel as do we here in Washington feel. If the Amendment wins, it will revitalize women, put new fire and fervor in all they do, enable them to do more. We have many war workers in our house and last night I asked a young woman, who for patriotic reasons only has been working in the

Ordnance Department, why woman suffrage should be called a war measure. She promptly replied, "Because it is an incentive to better and more work."

We are truly grateful for all you have done for our measure, but we believe that to hold the women to their best endeavors is so important at this time that you and the nation will find reward in their loyal gratitude. If, in addition to a letter of this nature, you could send for the men who we still believe are possibilities, and talk to them on these lines, it might win them. In addition to Senator Benet, who said yesterday on the floor of the Senate that he would change if convinced that it was a war measure, we suggest Senators Walcott [Wolcott], Shields, Overman and Trammell. The two latter are undoubtedly pledged to stand by the solid South, but two would be more willing to break way than one, and we hope that you who have proved yourself a miracle worker on many occasions may be able to produce another wonder on Monday—of putting vision where there was none before.

The hope and the fate of the women of the nation rest in your hands.   Sincerely yours,   Carrie Chapman Catt

TLS (WP, DLC).
    ¹ Irving Webster Drew, a Republican, who had been appointed to the Senate on September 2 to fill the vacancy caused by the death of Senator Gallinger.
    ² In his speech during the debate on the manpower bill in the Senate on August 23, Lodge declared that the time had come for the United States to state precisely what it meant when it said that it was fighting for the safety of democracy, the security of all nations, and the preservation of freedom and civilization. He argued that the Germans, in the face of certain defeat, would soon inaugurate an "insidious and poisonous peace propaganda." Thus, the United States could no longer afford to speak in mere generalities but had to define its peace terms. Lodge then laid down the conditions which he and his Republican colleagues regarded as the "irreducible minimum" for a "just and righteous peace": the restoration of Belgium; the unconditional return of Alsace-Lorraine to France; the transfer of Italia Irredenta, including Trieste, to Italy; independence for Serbia and Rumania; the creation of independent Yugoslav, Czechoslovak, and Polish states; security for Greece; the restoration of the provinces taken from Russia in the "villainous peace" of Brest-Litovsk; the establishment of Constantinople as a free port in the hands of the allied nations and the elimination of Turkey from Europe; freedom of Palestine from Turkish rule; the exaction of compensation from Germany, which could be obtained in part by the disposition of the German colonies. "It can not be a peace of bargain," Lodge continued, "of give and take, and of arrangement. It can not be a peace which rests on signed treaties alone, for no treaty is worth the paper it is written on when made with Germany, whom no agreement binds, to whom no signature has meaning, and whose pledges are as false as dicers' oaths. The only peace for us is one that rests on hard physical facts, the peace of unconditional surrender. No peace that satisfies Germany in any degree can ever satisfy us. It can not be a negotiated peace. It must be a dictated peace, and we and our allies must dictate it. The victory bringing such a peace must be won inside, not outside, the German frontier. . . . In one word, we must go to Berlin and there dictate peace. This purpose can be accomplished. We shall do it, but we must be above all propositions of a bargained peace, all suggestions of negotiations; deaf to every voice which would divert us from the path; deaf alike to the whimper of the pacifist and to the wheedling or truculent appeal of the helpers of Germany. When Germany is beaten to her knees and the world is made safe by the arrangements which I have suggested, then, and not before, we shall have the just and righteous peace for which we fight." *Cong. Record*, 65th Cong., 2d sess., pp. 9393-94. See also the *New York Times*, Aug. 24, 1918.

An Address to the Senate

Speaking Copy 30 Sept., 1918.[1]

GENTLEMEN OF THE SENATE: The unusual circumstances of a world war in which we stand and are judged in the view not only of our own people and our own consciences but also in the view of all nations and peoples will, I hope, justify in your thought, as it does in mine, the message I have come to bring you. I regard the concurrence of the Senate in the constitutional amendment proposing the extension of the suffrage to women as vitally essential to the successful prosecution of the great war of humanity in which we are engaged. I have come to urge upon you the considerations which have led me to that conclusion. It is not only my privilege, it is also my duty to apprise you of every circumstance and element involved in this momentous struggle which seems to me to affect its very processes and its outcome. It is my duty to win the war and to ask you to remove every obstacle that stands in the way of winning it.

I had assumed that the Senate would concur in the amendment because no disputable principle is involved but only a question of the method by which the suffrage is to be extended to women. There is and can be no party issue involved in it. Both of our great national parties are pledged, explicitly pledged, to equality of suffrage for the women of the country. Neither party, therefore, it seems to me, can justify hesitation as to the method of obtaining it, can rightfully hesitate to substitute federal initiative for state initiative, if the early adoption of the measure is necessary to the successful prosecution of the war and if the method of state action proposed in the party platforms of 1916 is impracticable within any reasonable length of time, if practicable at all. And its adoption is, in my judgment, clearly necessary to the successful prosecution of the war and the successful realization of the objects for which the war is being fought.

That judgment I take the liberty of urging upon you with solemn earnestness for reasons which I shall state very frankly and which I shall hope will seem as conclusive to you as they seem to me.

This is a peoples' war and the peoples' thinking constitutes its atmosphere and morale, not the predelections of the drawing room or the political considerations of the caucus. If we be indeed democrats and wish to lead the world to democracy, we can ask other peoples to accept in proof of our sincerity and our ability to lead them whither they wish to be led nothing less persuasive and convincing than our actions. Our professions will not suffice. Verification must be forthcoming when verification is asked for. And in this case verification is asked for,—asked for in this particular matter. You ask by whom? Not through diplomatic channels; not by Foreign Ministers. Not by the intimations of parliaments. It is asked for by the anxious, expectant, suffering peoples with whom we are dealing and who are willing to put their destinies in some measure in our hands, if they are sure that we wish the same things that they do. I do not speak by conjecture. It is not alone the voices of statesmen and of newspapers that reach me, and the voices of foolish and intemperate agitators do not reach me at all. Through many, many channels I have been made aware what the plain, struggling, workaday folk are thinking upon whom the chief terror and suffering of this tragic war falls. They are looking to the great, powerful, famous Democracy of the West to lead them to the new day for which they have so long waited; and they think, in their logical simplicity, that democracy means that women shall play their part in affairs alongside men and upon an equal footing with them. If we reject measures like this, in ignorance or defiance of what a new age has brought forth, of what they have seen but we have not, they will cease to believe in us; they will cease to follow or to trust us. They have seen their own governments accept this interpretation of democracy,—seen old governments like that of Great Britain, which did not profess to be democratic, promise readily and as of course this justice to women, though they had before refused it, the strange revelations of this war having made many things new and plain, to governments as well as to peoples.

Are we alone to refuse to learn the lesson? Are we alone to ask and take the utmost that our women can give,—service and sacrifice of every kind,—and still say we do not see what title that gives them to stand by our sides in the guidance of the affairs of their nation and ours? We have made partners of the women in this war; shall we admit them only to a partnership of suffering and sacrifice and toil and not to a partnership of privilege and right? This war could not have been fought, either by the other nations engaged or by America, if it had not been for the services of the women,— services rendered in every sphere,—not merely in the fields of effort in which we have been accustomed to see them work, but wherever men have worked and upon the very skirts and edges of the battle itself. We shall not only be distrusted but shall deserve to be distrusted if we do not enfranchise them with the fullest possible enfranchisement, as it is now certain that the other great free nations will enfranchise them. We cannot isolate our thought or our action in such a matter from the thought of the rest of the world. We must either conform or deliberately reject what they propose and resign the leadership of liberal minds to others.

The women of America are too noble and too intelligent and too devoted to be slackers whether you give or withhold this thing that is mere justice; but I know the magic it will work in their thoughts and spirits if you give it them. I propose it as I would propose to admit soldiers to the suffrage, the men fighting in the field for our liberties and the liberties of the world, were they excluded. The tasks of the women lie at the very heart of the war, and I know how much stronger that heart will beat if you do this just thing and show our women that you trust them as much as you in fact and of necessity depend upon them.

Have I said that the passage of this amendment is a vitally necessary war measure, and do you need further proof? Do you stand in need of the trust of other peoples and of the trust of our own women? Is that trust an asset or is it not? I tell you plainly, as the commander-in-chief of our armies and of the gallant men in our fleets, as the present spokesman of this people in our dealings with the men and women throughout the world who are now our partners, as the responsible head of a great government which stands and is questioned day by day as to its purposes, its principles, its hopes, whether they be serviceable to men everywhere or only to itself, and who must himself answer these questionings or be shamed, as the guide and director of forces caught in the grip of war and by the same token in need of every material and spiritual resource this great nation posesses,—I tell you plainly that this measure which I urge upon you is vital to the winning of the war and to the energies alike of preparation and of battle.

And not to the winning of the war only. It is vital to the right solution of the great problems which we must settle, and settle immediately, when the war is over. We shall need then in our vision of affairs, as we have never needed them before, the sympathy and insight and clear moral instinct of the women of the world. The problems of that time will strike to the roots of many things that we have not hitherto questioned, and I for one believe that our safety in those questioning days, as well as our comprehension of matters that touch society to the quick, will depend upon the direct and authoritative participation of women in our counsels. We shall need their moral sense to preserve what is right and fine and worthy in our system of life as well as to discover just what it is that ought to be purified and reformed. Without their counsellings we shall be only half wise.

That is my case. This is my appeal. Many may deny its validity, if they choose, but no one can brush aside or answer the arguments upon which it is based. The executive tasks of this war rest upon me. I ask that you lighten them and place in my hands instruments, spiritual instruments, which I do not now possess, which I sorely need, and which I have daily to apologise for not being able to employ.[2]

Printed reading copy (WP, DLC).
[1] WWhw.
[2] The WWT of this address, which Wilson sent to the Public Printer, is in WP, DLC. The spellings of "predelections" and "apologise" are Wilson's.

To Carrie Clinton Lane Chapman Catt

My dear Mrs. Catt: The White House 30 September, 1918.

Thank you for your letter of the 29th. I did not do what it suggested, but I hope that you think what I did do was better.

In great haste, and with the earnest hope that the amendment may pass,

Cordially and faithfully yours,   Woodrow Wilson

TLS (National American Woman Suffrage Assoc. Papers, DLC).

To Robert Lansing

My dear Mr. Secretary: The White House 30 September, 1918.

So far as I can see, the agreement[1] referred to in the enclosed is all right.[2]

Cordially and faithfully yours,   Woodrow Wilson

TLS (SDR, RG 59, 861.00/3680, DNA).
[1] Wilson was responding to RL to WW, Sept. 27, 1918. TLS (SDR, RG 59, 861.00/3679a, DNA). About this matter, see n. 1 to the Enclosure printed with WW to RL, Sept. 20, 1918 (third letter that date).
[2] Lansing conveyed Wilson's approval in RL to JD, Oct. 14, 1918, CCL (SDR, RG 59, 861.00/3680, DNA).

To William Kent

My dear Kent: The White House 30 September, 1918.

Your letter of the 28th about my speech in New York cheers me very much, and I entirely agree with your judgment as to the propaganda of the American Defence Society. It is astonishing to me that some of the responsible men whose names are given as Vice Presidents or Trustees should lend their authority to such damnable stuff—for it is nothing less.

Cordially and faithfully yours,   Woodrow Wilson

TLS (W. Kent Papers, CtY).

To George Creel

My dear Creel: The White House 30 September, 1918.

Please read the latter part of this letter from Kent, and the stuff which he attached. Will it not be possible for you to see to it that none of the stuff of this so-called American Defence Society gets out of the country?

Cordially and faithfully yours,   Woodrow Wilson

TLS (G. Creel Papers, DLC).

To William Christian Bullitt

My dear Mr. Bullitt: The White House 30 September, 1918.

Thank you warmly for your letter of the 27th about my speech in New York. It has given me genuine gratification.

Cordially and sincerely yours,   Woodrow Wilson

TLS (W. C. Bullitt Papers, CtY).

To Raymond Blaine Fosdick

My dear Fosdick: The White House 30 September, 1918

Thank you for the memorandum about the negro problem as it presents itself at Newport News. The report gives me a great deal of concern. Can you think of any proper means of correcting their impressions?

Cordially and sincerely yours,   Woodrow Wilson

TLS (WP, DLC).

Two Letters from Robert Lansing

Returned to me at Cabinet Oct 1/18
RL.

My dear Mr. President: Washington September 30, 1918.

The Bulgarian Minister, this morning, went through the rather farcical business of presenting the communication which we had read and handed to him last night. Before seeing him the announcement was made that the armistice had been signed at Salonika, so he said that he could see no object in making reply to the note.

The Minister seemed to be actually rejoiced at the surrender of his country. He said that when the change of ministry took place some weeks ago he was convinced Bulgaria would withdraw from the war because the new cabinet was anti-German. I told him in response to his inquiry, that I did not know the terms of the armistice but assumed that they would be demobilization of the Bulgarian armies, control of the railroads, and surrender of all occupied territory.

He then said, "Why do not the Allies impose the condition that the Bulgarians attack the Turks and take Constantinople?" Surprised at the suggestion I asked "Do you mean to say your Government would agree to do that?" He replied, "Gladly. They would send 250,000 men against the Turks for they hate them."

He further said that he was convinced that the capitulation was forced by the people and very likely by the army.

Faithfully yours,   Robert Lansing

TLS (SDR, RG 59, 763.72119/2024B, DNA).

Returned to me at Cabinet
Oct 1/18 RL

My dear Mr. President: Washington September 30, 1918.

It has occurred to me that the entire collapse of Bulgaria and the complete submission to the terms demanded for an armistice may create a situation which will require action.

It is possible that the Allied Governments may consider the time is opportune to negotiate with Bulgaria a definitive treaty of peace in order to forestall a possibly too generous treatment when the final peace is made. I believe that Serbia and Greece would favor a settlement of the Balkan Question now while Bulgaria is helpless, and that Roumania would not be loath to such an arrangement.

As we are not at war with Bulgaria, the Allies may take the position that a separate peace treaty with her is not our affair and that they can conclude it independently going as far as they please in drawing the boundaries of the Balkan States. If they do this there will be the future embarrassment of revising such a conqueror's peace. It will be hard to do it. And if it is harsh and unjust (as is very possible), it will not make for permanent peace.

In the circumstances ought we not to consider the advisability of intervening with the Powers and of insisting that as the Balkan Question must be included in the final settlement, all questions relating to territory in those regions should be, by agreement in the separate peace treaty, postponed for consideration to the general peace conference?

I am very fearful that now that Bulgaria is powerless the old political game in the Balkans will be renewed, and that the same pernicious jealousies, which prevented the kingdom from remaining neutral, if not friendly, will start the victors to quarreling again. If this can be prevented it ought to be because the consequences might be very serious.

We could act on the Bulgarian appeal to you for mediation, or we could act on the principle that no treaty relating to territory should be recognized if negotiated during the war but should be treated as the Brest-Litovsk and Bucharest Treaties will be treated.

If anything is to be done to anticipate an undesirable treaty with Bulgaria by the Allies, it will have to be done quickly, I think, if it is to be effective. It would be difficult to face a *fait accompli*.

Faithfully yours,   Robert Lansing.

TLS (SDR, RG 59, 763.72119/2024A, DNA).

From Gordon Auchincloss

My dear Mr President: Washington Sept. 30th, 1918

Mr House has asked me to send you the following cable which he has just received from Lord Robert Cecil.

"If not improper I should be very glad if you could convey to President Wilson my personal deep appreciation of his speech last night. It is, if I may say so, the finest description of our war aims yet uttered and will give us all renewed courage to face the horrors of war"   Faithfully yours   Gordon Auchincloss

ALS (WP, DLC).

From Edward Mandell House

Dear Governor: New York. September 30, 1918.

I am enclosing you a copy of the cable from Lord Robert Cecil which I asked Gordon to send you over today.[1]

It indicates the response which the British Government will make to your request for their opinion upon your Friday night speech. I think, taking it all in all, what you said has been received with more general favor than anything you have said before. It makes me very happy of course.

Affectionately yours,   E. M. House

TLS (WP, DLC).
[1] Enclosure not reprinted.

From Park Trammell

Dear Mr. President: Washington, D. C. September 30th, 1918.

I am in receipt of your letter of the 26th instant, urging me to support the Federal Amendment granting the right of franchise to women and wish to thank you for your views upon this subject. My high regard for your opinion and my earnest desire to give you my full and hearty co-operation has caused me considerable discomfort in dealing with this problem.

Unfortunately however, I have made a public statement to the people of Florida that I contemplated voting against the amendment. This being true I do not now feel that I can consistently change my attitude.

If I was only differently situated would be pleased to conform to your wishes.

Cordially and sincerely yours,   Park Trammell

TLS (WP, DLC).

From James Revell Lord and Samuel McCune Lindsay[1]

Dear Mr. President: Washington, D. C. September 30, 1918.

On behalf of the joint committee of the American Federation of Labor and the National Child Labor Committee which had the honor to confer with you on Thursday, July 18th, in respect to a proposed new federal child labor law,[2] we desire to report briefly what we have done since to carry forward the plans then agreed upon and approved by you. A new bill was drafted as a war emergency measure containing the standards of the federal child labor law which the United States Supreme Court recently held unconstitutional but making them operative as a direct prohibition or regulation under the war power of Congress for the period of the war and six months thereafter, and without making use of the instrumentalities of interstate commerce for the purpose of such prohibition and regulation.

This bill (H.R. 12767), copy of which we enclose herewith,[3] was introduced in the House of Representatives on August 15th, by Mr. Keating at our request and referred to the committee on labor. The committee by a five to three vote has just agreed to report this bill favorably. After careful canvass of the situation in the Senate we decided that the difficulties of a satisfactory reference of a war measure to a committee where the subject of child labor regulation or prohibition would have sympathetic consideration were so great that it would be better not to introduce the bill at all in the Senate at present, but to secure as speedy action as possible in the House and look forward to having the House Bill perhaps substituted for one of the child labor bills now in the committee on interstate and foreign commerce in the Senate.

We believe that there is a possibility of passing this war emergency child labor bill in this Congress before the 4th of March next and that substantial agreement among all the parties in interest on the draft of a permanent child labor measure which would meet all constitutional requirements can not be secured in time for its enactment by this Congress. We also believe that the inclusion of child labor standards in war contracts as approved by the War Policies Board while an excellent thing as far as it goes will not by any means take care of the war emergency until a permanent child labor law can be enacted. We are doing our utmost to cooperate with the Children's Bureau of the Labor Department and other organizations interested in child labor to devise a satisfactory permanent measure of federal child labor regulation and prohibition, but we are convinced that this is no light task and will not be easily or quickly achieved. We are therefore anxious to have the war emergency measure (the Keating bill) pressed vigorously upon the attention of Congress.

If this is your desire and the bill in its present form complies, as we believe it does, with your wishes as expressed at our conference with you on July 18th, will you be good enough to so advise us or the chairman of the committee on labor of the House of Representatives. The Children's Bureau seems to think that the emergency situation is sufficiently well taken care of and that the same effort that would be necessary to pass the emergency bill in this Congress would secure the enactment of the permanent measure. The lawyers appointed to draft a permanent measure which would be satisfactory to the conference called by the Children's Bureau, and in which we have been represented, have agreed upon a taxing measure taxing the products of mills, factories, mines, etc. which employ children contrary to the standards of the recently held unconstitutional federal child labor act, and the Children's Bureau has asked for an appointment for the representatives of its conference to lay this measure before you for your approval. Any permanent measure, and especially one relying on the taxing principle, will involve a debate in Congress which makes it seem to us improbable that such a measure can be passed by this Congress. In any event, we believe that pressing the emergency war power measure at this time would not interfere with our united active support of the permanent taxing measure, and if we succeeded in passing the war emergency measure it would hasten rather than retard the passage of the permanent measure.

We would like to have your decision, however, on the question of policy with respect to the best procedure in dealing with the war emergency measure and the permanent measure and we shall gladly unite with all the other friends of child labor legislation in support of whatever course of action you deem expedient in order that the national standards with respect to child labor which were enacted in one of the big measures of social legislation of your administration when you signed the first federal child labor law, may be maintained unimpaired during the present war emergency and may be reinstated as part of the permanent law of the land at the earliest possible moment.

Yours respectfully,   James Lord
Samuel McCune Lindsay

TLS (WP, DLC).
 [1] Lord was president of the mining department of the A. F. of L., chief of the mining division of the United States Employment Service, and a member of the advisory commission on labor of the Council of National Defense; Lindsay, Professor of Sociology at Columbia University, was chairman of the National Child Labor Committee and president of the American Association for Labor Legislation.
 [2] About this matter, see S. Gompers to WW, July 19, 1918, Vol. 49, and n. 1 thereto.
 [3] The enclosure is missing.

From Christie Benet

My dear Mr. President: [Washington] 30th Sept., 1918.

I had hoped to have a further conference with you before the Anthony Suffrage Amendment came up for a vote in the Senate, or at least to have an opportunity to write you in response to your letters and telegram to me. I had not expected to be ready to declare my position until today at least, but a situation arose on Saturday which made it necessary that I should state my decision. Your absence in New York on that day prevented my seeing or communicating with you.

I think it needless for me to state my reasons in detail, but I believe, Sir, that you will agree with me that when I once reached the conslusion [conclusion] that a fundamental right of the sovereignty of the States was being defeated by this Amendment, and needlessly, that I had no course left but to vote against it.

My desire to follow you, for whom I have such respect and whom I have followed so long was strong on the one hand; on the other my plain duty, as I saw it, forced me to the conclusion that I reached. No decision of my life has caused me the concern that this one brought, and I only solved it after the most searching and serious consideration.

With my sincere regards, I am

Yours respectfully,   Christie Benet

TLS (WP, DLC).

Remarks to a Group of American Blacks[1]

[Oct. 1, 1918]

I am very much obliged for your generous address. You have certainly interpreted my purposes correctly, but every man is surrounded by all sorts of limitations of which I am impatiently aware, and you may certainly be sure that everything in my power to accomplish justice will be accomplished. We all have to be patient with one another. Human nature doesn't make giant strides in a single generation. It is not as careful of our faults as we would wish that it were, and I have a very modest estimate of my own power to hasten the process, but you may be sure that everything that I can do will be accompished, and I thank you very much for your audience and wish you Godspeed.

T MS (WP, DLC).
    [1] Wilson received a delegation from the National Race Congress of the United States of America, an annual conference of black leaders from twenty-eight states, at the White House at 4:30 p.m. on October 1. The delegation included the Rev. William H. Jernagin, pastor of Mt. Carmel Baptist Church of Washington and president of the National Race Congress; Bishop Isaac Nelson Ross, of Washington, presiding bishop of the thirteenth episcopal district of the African Methodist Episcopal Church and vice-president of the congress; the Rev. J. C. Austin, D.D., of Pittsburgh, the "national organizer" of the congress; and William Harrison, an attorney of Chicago and the "national lecturer" of the congress. Their address is missing in WP, DLC. However, according to the *Washington Post* of October 2, 1918, Harrison addressed the President as follows: "We come in behalf of 12,000,000 of our race to direct your attention to the fact that discriminations on account of race and color and segregation and Jim Crowism are practiced in some of the departments. We believe the mere directing of your attention to the conditions is sufficient to have the conditions remedied." The delegates also submitted to Wilson a memorial, which is printed as an Enclosure with WW to JPT, Oct. 3, 1918.

To the Student Army Training Corps

October 1, 1918.

The step you have taken is a most significant one. By it you have ceased to be merely individuals, each seeking to perfect himself to win his own place in the world and have become comrades in the common cause of making the world a better place to live in. You have joined yourselves with the entire manhood of the country and pledged, as did your forefathers, "your lives, your fortunes and your sacred honor" to the freedom of humanity.

The enterprise upon which you have embarked is a hazardous and difficult one. This is not a war of words; this is not a scholastic struggle. It is a war of ideals, yet fought with all the devices of science and with the power of machines. To succeed you must not only be inspired by the ideals for which this country stands, but you must also be masters of the technique with which the battle is fought. You must not only be thrilled with zeal for the common welfare, but you must also be masters of the weapons of today.

There can be no doubt of the issue. The spirit that is revealed and the manner in which America has responded to the call is indomitable. I have no doubt that you too will use your utmost strength to maintain that spirit and to carry it forward to the final victory that will certainly be ours.   Woodrow Wilson

TS MS (C. R. Mann Papers, NcU).

A Memorandum by Robert Lansing

MEMORANDUM OF ORAL STATEMENT BY FRENCH
AMBASSADOR IN RE PEACE WITH BULGARIA.

Noon, October 1, 1918.

The Ambassador informed me that he had received a telegram from the Minister of Foreign Affairs advising him that the French Government considered it unwise to discuss terms of peace with Bulgaria, that the difficult settlement of the Balkan Question should be postponed until the general peace conference, and that the present armistice should be continued in force to that time.

He said that the terms of the armistice were evacuation of occupied Serbian and Greek territory by the Bulgarians, disarmament of the Bulgarian army, surrender of important strategic positions in Bulgaria to the Allies, and the use and control of Bulgarian Railways. I have an impression that he said that the Bulgarians were also to deliver over to the Allies all war supplies in their possession.

4:20 p.m. October 1, 1918.

I orally informed the President of the foregoing. He had previously handed me the annexed memorandum, which he had prepared on receipt of my letter of September 30th.   RL

T MS (SDR, RG 59, 763.72119/2024½, DNA).

A Memorandum

Handed me at Cabinet Oct 1/18 RL

Gov't of U. S. cannot be [but] regard every question that concerns any one of the Balkan States as an essential part of the general peace settlement, inasmuch as there is no part of Europe that is more likely to be a seed-bed of war than the Balkans. Peace with Bulgaria cannot be treated apart from the general Balkan settlement without embarrassing the consideration of such matters as the reopening of the treaties of Brest-Litovsk and Bucharest and making many matters of final consideration very difficult to handle. It would be very hazardous to treat separately any part of the whole.

WWhw MS (SDR, RG 59, 763.72119/2025½, DNA).

To Joseph Patrick Tumulty, with Enclosure

Dear Tumulty: [The White House] 1 October, 1918.

Would you be kind enough to send the enclosed letter, suggested by the War Department?   The President

TL (WP, DLC).

E N C L O S U R E[1]

Dear Sir: The White House September [blank] 1918.

The President directs me to acknowledge receipt of your letter of August 19, 1918, in which you refer to alleged discrimination against colored soldiers in the Army, and to advise you that investigation shows that no discrimination has been practiced by the War Department.

Steps have already been taken to provide colored Red Cross nurses for colored soldiers, and colored doctors are being called into the service as soon as there are organizations to which to assign them.

In the absence of detailed information on the various points covered by your communication, it is impossible to conduct a satisfactory investigation.

The President directs me to say that he feels a sincere appreciation of the loyalty of the members of the colored race, and of their services in helping to win the war, and he desires me to convey to you his assurance that colored men will be afforded [full] *the fullest possible*[2] opportunities for commissions, promotions and advancement on their merits.   Very truly yours,   J. P. Tumulty.

TCL (WP, DLC).

¹ The following letter, which Benedict Crowell had prepared at Wilson's request, was a reply to Nick Chiles to WW, Aug. 19, 1918, TLS (WP, DLC). Chiles was the editor and owner of the *Topeka Plaindealer*, a newspaper for blacks.
² Changes WWhw.

To Robert Lansing

My dear Mr. Secretary: The White House 1 October, 1918.

Your kind note,¹ which I have just seen today, about my address in New York has given me the greatest gratification, and I thank you for it with all my heart.

Cordially and sincerely yours,   Woodrow Wilson

TLS (RSB Coll., DLC).
¹ RL to WW, Sept. 28, 1918.

To Josiah Oliver Wolcott

My dear Senator,   The White House 1 Oct., 1918.

May I not have your support in this critical matter of the suffrage? I am deeply moved about it and meant what I said yesterday more deeply and solemnly than I was able to put into words. Your support would be of the greatest service to the administration and to the country.   Sincerely Yours,   Woodrow Wilson

ALS (received from Daniel F. Wolcott).

To Scott Ferris

My dear Ferris: [The White House] 1 October, 1918.

I have your letter of September 27th conveying ex-Governor Folk's request, and I need not tell you how gladly I would respond to it if I knew how to do it without creating a similar liability in a score of other quarters. I am hoping that some opportunity of a natural sort will occur or that the general efforts I have in mind will reach Missouri effectively.

Cordially and faithfully yours,   Woodrow Wilson

TLS (Letterpress Books, WP, DLC).

Two Letters to Thomas Watt Gregory

My dear Gregory: [The White House] 1 October, 1918.

William Kent, of the Tariff Commission, is, as you know, a very earnest and serious man, and I must say that the case of Theodora

Pollak as presented by his son-in-law, Mr. Arnold, appeals to me very much. Will you not be kind enough to have it looked into and tell me whether you think, or do not think, that she could be dealt with differently?

                    Cordially and faithfully yours,   Woodrow Wilson

My dear Gregory: [The White House] 1 October, 1918.

The enclosed letter[1] from his wife was handed to me this morning by a rather pitiful old German whom I see occasionally looking after the flowers around the club house at the Virginia Golf Course. I must say it appeals to me, and I am sending it to you to ask if there is any legitimate way in which the poor old fellow could be released from his present restrictions.

    In haste,   Faithfully yours,   Woodrow Wilson

TLS (Letterpress Books, WP, DLC).
    [1] It is missing. However, as a White House memorandum of October 1, 1918 (T MS, WP, DLC) reveals, it was a letter from Annie B. Leissler to Wilson of September 25, 1918. Mrs. Leissler had requested permission for her husband, George A. Leissler, a German alien, to enter the District of Columbia to pursue his business as a gardener and a tree specialist. See also TWG to WW, Oct. 8, 1918.

To Elbert Henry Gary

My dear Judge Gary: [The White House] 1 October, 1918.

Your kind letter of September 28th has given me a great deal of pleasure. It was certainly an act of generous kindness on your part to express to me your approval of my speech of the other evening in New York. The speech certainly came from the heart and represented the very deep anxiety I have that the whole temper of the nations engaged against Germany should be a temper of high-minded justice. In proportion as that is their temper, they are the more sure of the kind of triumph which will bring blessings to the world.

    With renewed expressions of appreciation,
                    Sincerely yours,   Woodrow Wilson

TLS (Letterpress Books, WP, DLC).

To William Harlowe Briggs[1]

My dear Mr. Briggs: [The White House] 1 October, 1918.

Mr. Tumulty has shown me your letter to him of September 25th[2] about the suggestion that my History of the American People be used in some way as material for moving pictures. I am complimented that you and the gentlemen of the Mayflower Company should think that its use in that way would be serviceable, but I am sorry to say that I can in no circumstances consent. I have been very much displeased myself recently by the use certain public men have made of their writings through the movies, and I believe that I follow the true instinct when I say that no such use of my History would be acceptable to the people of the country. I cannot afford to embark in commercial ventures of this or any other kind.

Pray do not regard this as a criticism. It is merely a decision.

Sincerely yours,   Woodrow Wilson

TLS (Letterpress Books, WP, DLC).
   [1] Editor in the book department of Harper and Brothers.
   [2] W. H. Briggs to JPT, Sept. 25, 1918, TLS (WP, DLC). In forwarding Brigg's letter to Wilson, Tumulty had commented as follows: "Dear Governor: Before you sign such an agreement, I hope you will let me speak to you about it. J.P.T." JPT to WW, Sept. 26, 1918, TL (WP, DLC).

To Winthrop More Daniels

My dear Daniels: The White House 1 October, 1918

Thank you for the joint views of yourself and Woolley about a federal utility board.[1] I am afraid that I cannot, without cutting across the necessary coordinations, create just such a board as you and he suggest, but my mind and my little war board that meets on Wednesdays are at work on the subject, and I hope that we can work out something sensible.

In haste, with warmest regard,

Faithfully yours,   Woodrow Wilson

TLS (Wilson-Daniels Corr., CtY).
   [1] See WW to W. M. Daniels, Sept. 23, 1918, n. 1.

From Robert Lansing, with Enclosures

My dear Mr. President: Washington October 1, 1918.

I enclose to you a letter to the French Ambassador in response to his of September 28th which I propose to send him if it meets with your approval.

As he has been very importunate in asking for a reply I hope you can return this to me as soon as possible.

Faithfully yours,   Robert Lansing

TLS (SDR, RG 59, 763.72/11659, DNA).

Jean Jules Jusserand to Robert Lansing

Dear Mr Secretary,   Washington, le September 28, 1918.

As I told you yesterday, it appears from information received by my Government that the military commander at Innsbruck had decided that extreme measures would be taken against allied aviators who should drop manifestoes or even should be found the bearers of such documents. This would be considered as a crime and punished by death. Il [It] will be remenbered [remembered], by the way, that those papers consist sometimes in nothing more noxious than President Wilson's addresses.

My Government considers that, in order to prevent such action, the Austrian authorities should be informed by radiogram that, if measures so contrary to international law and to humanity were carried into effect, retaliation would have unavoidably to be practised on Austrian officers in our hands; the number would be double and the punishment the same.

You kindly told me that, on first sight, it seemed to you that no other means but the threat of retaliation could be resorted to in order to prevent this new grievous breaking of accepted rules. I should be much obliged to you for letting me know whether I may consider this as your definitive opinion.

Believe me, dear Mr Secretary,

Very sincerely yours,   Jusserand

TLS (SDR, RG 59, 763.72/11659, DNA).

Robert Lansing to Jean Jules Jusserand

My dear Mr. Ambassador: [Washington] October 1, 1918.

I discussed with the President this afternoon your letter of September 28th in which you state that the military commander at Innsbruck had decided to treat the dropping or possession of documents by aviators as a crime punishable with death.

The President holds the opinion that, however abhorrent and indefensible the announced practice may be, he cannot consent that this Government should unite in a threat to retaliate by executing twice as many captured Austrian officers as aviators put to death under the reported military order.

The Government of the United States would, nevertheless, unite in announcing to the Austrian authorities, by such means as are available, that it denounces the proposed treatment of captured aviators, who are found bearing or to have dropped documents within the lines of the enemy, as utterly indefensible and violative of every principle of humanity and every rule of civilized warfare, and that, if the proposed practice is put into actual operation, the Austrian Government must realize that such barbarous and inhuman treatment of prisoners of war will invite extreme measures to prevent its continuance, deeply as this Government would deplore the consequences which would result.

I am, my dear Mr. Ambassador,

Very sincerely yours,   Robert Lansing

CCL (SDR, RG 59, 763.72/11659, DNA).

From Frank Lyon Polk

My dear Mr. President: Washington October 1, 1918.

Mr. Page asked me to deliver to you the enclosed letter.[1]

Permit me to congratulate you on your tremendously impressive speech at the Metropolitan Opera House. It struck a note that will give several of your friends in Europe more than a few serious moments.

Believe me,   Yours faithfully,   Frank L Polk

TLS (WP, DLC).
[1] T. N. Page to WW, Sept. 11, 1918, ALS (WP, DLC). It discussed the dissension within the Italian cabinet, and especially the dispute between Orlando and Sonnino with regard to Italy's policy in the Yugoslav and other Balkan and eastern Adriatic questions.

From George Creel

My dear Mr. President,   Washington, D. C. October 1, 1918

Mr. Gallauner[1] is a very bitter Hungarian Catholic and is also anything but well disposed towards the Czeko-Slovacs. Most of the charges that he makes[2] are absolutely false and yet it is important that we avoid these factional quarrels. I suggest that you write him the attached letter[3] amd [and] I will handle him when he calls to see me.

With regard to the American Defense matter, sent you by Mr. William Kent, I have already taken pains to see that none of it goes out of the country. Like the National Security League, this organization is one of our most difficult problems, and I think it is being solved very rapidly by my constant refusal to recognize either of them in any way.   Respectfully,   George Creel

TLS (WP, DLC).
[1] That is, Edmund Gallauner, a Hungarian-American leader.
[2] His letter is missing.
[3] WW to E. Gallauner, Oct. 2, 1918, TLS (Letterpress Books, WP, DLC).

From James Edgar Gregg[1]

My dear Mr. President: Hampton, Virginia October 1, 1918

I hesitate to intrude, even by letter, upon the crowded moments of your working time. But I can not forbear expressing the grateful satisfaction of mind and heart which I have felt in reading your noble message to the people of our country and of the whole world, in your address at the opening of the Liberty Loan campaign in New York last Friday night. I can truly say that every public utterance which you have made, from the beginning of the war, has thrilled me and given me still more faith in your leadership. And in this latest address, in your five-fold statement of our duty with regard to peace, you seem to me to have sounded just the note to which our conquering armies abroad and our exultant citizens at home most need now to listen, when you say: "First, the impartial justice meted out must involve no discrimination between those to whom we wish to be just and those to whom we do not wish to be just."

It is just this truth, as it seems to me, to which we ought now to be recalled. For we shall soon be facing the moral tests of victory, far severer than those of defeat and adversity. There are persons who would have us imitate our enemies in our treatment of the vanquished. But how can we dishonor our Republic and our sacred cause by any such crim[i]nal folly? The course which you point out, as I view it, is the only course of decency, of national self-respect, of righteousness, and of the true justice which is fundamentally merciful, as the truest mercy is fundamentally just.

We at Hampton are greatly pleased, I hardly need say, in the prospect of welcoming you here at the celebration of our Fiftieth Anniversary on November first and of listening to your words at that time. It will be an occasion of great good cheer and hope for the colored people and for all who are trying to help them.[2]

With sincere regard, I am

Faithfully yours,   James E. Gregg

TLS (WP, DLC).
    [1] Principal of the Hampton Normal and Agricultural Institute.
    [2] A mysterious reference. There is no record in WP, DLC, that Wilson was invited to speak at the Hampton Institute on the mentioned date, and he did not participate in the anniversary celebration.

From Atlee Pomerene

My dear Mr. President: Washington, D. C. October 1st, 1918

Your note of this date[1] received, expressing the hope that I might see my way clear to vote for the Suffrage Amendment.

I cannot tell you how it pains me to find myself in a position where I cannot agree with you.

The State which re-elected me, the only Democratic Senator, except Senator Thurman,[2] to succeed himself since the civil war, and which gave you two years ago 90000 majority, has three times in six years defeated Woman Suffrage by overwhelming majorities. I cannot ignore these votes. If I did so I would feel that I was misrepresenting the State that has so signally honored me. That I cannot do.

Again, and I say it with all due respect, I cannot understand how Woman Suffrage can be regarded as a war issue. It ought to be a sufficient answer to those who raise this question, to say that under our scheme of government all states now have women suffrage that want it, and all other states can have it as soon as they want it, without any amendment to the Federal Constitution. To pursue this method is the very essence of Democracy, and as I see it to attempt to enforce Woman Suffrage upon a State before its citizens are ready for it, violates the fundamental principles of our governmental system.   Very Sincerely   Atlee Pomerene

ALS (WP, DLC).
    [1] It must have been a personal letter, such as the one which Wilson wrote to Wolcott. There is no copy of Wilson's letter to Pomerene in WP, DLC.
    [2] Allen Granberry Thurman, Democratic senator from Ohio from 1869 to 1881.

From Josiah Oliver Wolcott

My dear Mr. President,   Washington, D. C. Oct. 1, 1918.

I acknowledge receipt of your note of this date urging upon me the support of the suffrage amendment. Permit me also to acknowledge receipt of your telegram the other day on the same subject.[1]

I am keenly aware of your great interest in the passage of the resolution and this fact is a source of great worry to me, for I am finding myself unable to go with you in your reasoning upon the matter; and, because I have in large questions uniformly found your views so admirably expressive of what I conceive to be the wisest and best in public thought, it is particularly painful to me that in this one regard I find myself in opposition. Yet feeling as I do, I must not disregard my own views and thus lose respect for myself, however unhappy I may be in making the decision. The time may come when my mind will undergo a change of attitude. But until it does so, I feel impelled to follow its present way of regarding the question. I remain

With great respect   Very sincerely yours   J. O. Wolcott

ALS (WP, DLC).
    [1] WW to J. O. Wolcott, Sept. 27, 1918.

Two Letters to Robert Lansing

My dear Mr. Secretary: The White House 2 October, 1918.

I return herewith your letter to the French Ambassador[1] with my approval.

Cordially and sincerely yours,   Woodrow Wilson

TLS (SDR, RG 59, 763.72/11660, DNA).
[1] Enclosure II printed with RL to WW, Oct. 1, 1918.

My dear Mr. Secretary: The White House 2 October, 1918.

I must say that I have very serious doubts about the American Slavic Legion which Francis has undertaken to organize.[1] Even if the $1,300,900 spoken of is used, it will go a very little way, and knowing certainly, as I do, that we cannot supply any more money for such purposes, I think that Francis ought to be definitely apprised of the fact that we can supply no more and asked to consider the consequences which may follow. We cannot maintain an army, our own or another, in Northern Russia, much as we should wish to do so, and while I would wish Francis to know how much we admire the spirit and success with which he has guided matters at Archangel, I think we ought to apprise him very definitely of the limiting facts.[2]

Cordially and faithfully yours,   Woodrow Wilson

TLS (SDR, RG 59, 861.00/2910, DNA).
[1] In two telegrams of September 29, Francis had informed Lansing, among other things, that the British and French had enlisted "several thousand Russians" in British-Slavic and French-Slavic legions. Since many Russians had expressed the desire to enlist under American auspices, Francis intended to follow the British and French examples and to organize an American-Slavic legion. He proposed to use for that purpose the approximately one and a half million dollars which had remained from the six million dollars allotted to him for the acquisition of supplies for the American troops in northern Russia. His reason for organizing a Slavic-American legion, Francis said, was to encourage the formation of a Russian army, which was essential for the establishment of a Russian government and the regeneration of the country. "Association of our soldiers," Francis concluded, "will convince Russians that an army is not inimical to liberty as our government has been model since the revolution for all democratic Russians except Bolsheviks." D. R. Francis to RL, No. 430, Sept. 29, 1918, T telegram (SDR, RG 59, 861.00/2831, DNA), and No. 431, T telegram (SDR, RG 59, 861.00/2840, DNA).
[2] RL to D. R. Francis, Oct. 3, 1918, TS telegram, *ibid.*: "Your four hundred and thirty and four hundred and thirty one September twenty nine. There are definite limiting facts which govern your proposal to organize American Slavic Legion. It is certain that no money additional to the balance of six million dollar fund, which balance, I understand, now approximates one million three hundred thousand dollars, is or will be available for this purpose. You must therefore consider the consequences of what may follow when fund is exhausted. The President wants you to know how much we admire the spirit and success with which you have guided matters at Archangel but has serious doubts about the undertaking. Please consider the foregoing carefully before you go further and report."

To John Wesley Wescott

My dear Judge: The White House 2 October, 1918.

I have your letters of September 21st about the First New Jersey Congressional District,[1] and of September 30th conveying your too generous appreciation of my speech in New York.[2] I accept such things from you as a token of affection, even when I cannot accept them as justified critical judgments, and they make my heart very warm.

As for the letter to Mr. Dickerson[3] that you suggest, I don't think you realize into what trouble you might be getting me. I am asked for a letter in almost every congressional district, and circumstances which I could easily expound to you if I had you by my side have made it so unwise for me to "hand pick" candidates in such a fashion, that I have been obliged to refrain from writing any such letters, except upon such extraordinary occasion as naturally called a letter forth.

I greatly admire what Mr. Dickerson has done. He has acted with the highest motives and I am sure could be most serviceable to the country in Congress. The administration certainly needs the support of such men.

If you have occasion to make a speech in Mr. Dickerson's behalf, please feel at liberty to quote that sentiment from me.

Cordially and faithfully yours,   Woodrow Wilson

TLS (J. W. Wescott Coll., NjP).
[1] It is missing.
[2] J. W. Wescott to WW, Sept. 30, 1918, TLS (WP, DLC).
[3] Edwin Stuart Dickerson, a businessman of Merchantville, N. J., and partner of Woodward and Dickerson, fertilizer merchants of Philadelphia. As the Democratic candidate in the first New Jersey congressional district, Dickerson lost to the Republican incumbent, William John Browning, by a vote of 23,785 to 10,627.

To Josephus Daniels

My dear Daniels: The White House 2 October, 1918.

For fear you have no other copy of the enclosed speech of Sir Eric Geddes, I am returning it. As I said to you the other day, I don't like it even a little bit.

Cordially and faithfully yours,   Woodrow Wilson

TLS (J. Daniels Papers, DLC).

To Cleveland Hoadley Dodge

My dear Cleve: The White House 2 October, 1918.

I am heartily sorry I did not see you in New York and am particularly sorry because it means that you have to take extra good
care of yourself. Your letter has given me a great deal of pleasure,
and I share your happiness about the apparent clearing up of the
situation in the Balkans. I hope with all my heart that we can now
work out some kind of justice for those distracted states.

In haste,   Affectionately yours,   Woodrow Wilson

TLS (WC, NjP).

To John Frost Nugent[1]

My dear Senator: [The White House] 2 October, 1918.

I learn with genuine gratificaiton of your nomination for the
Senate and write to express my earnest hope that you will be elected.
We have had a taste of your quality here which makes us all more
certain than ever that Idaho could not have a more loyal or trustworthy representative or the administration a more generous supporter.   Cordially and sincerely yours,   Woodrow Wilson

TLS (Letterpress Books, WP, DLC).
   [1] United States senator from Idaho, a Democrat. Nugent had been appointed on
January 22, 1918, to fill the vacancy caused by the death of Senator James Henry Brady,
a Republican. About the circumstances surrounding Nugent's candidacy, see F. T.
Dubois to WW, Aug. 1, 1918, and the Enclosure printed with WW to ASB, Aug. 1,
1918, both in Vol. 49.

To Frank Watterson Jackson[1]

My dear Mr. Jackson: [The White House] 2 October, 1918.

I am in hearty sympathy with every just effort being made by
the people of the United States to alleviate the terrible sufferings
of the Greeks of Asia Minor. None have suffered more or more
unjustly than they. They are bound by many ties to the rest of the
liberty loving peoples in the world who are fighting to free all weak
and oppressed nationalities from the cruelty and oppression of strong
and autocratic governments.

The Greeks in Asia Minor have by their thrift and enterprise
shown themselves to be possessed of qualities most essential to the
future economic development of that fertile country.

Their steadfast allegiance to their Christian faith in the face of
every inducement and threat to abandon it, commends them most
strongly to all who believe in the principles of religious freedom.

And their adherence to the ideals of Constitutional government should make them peculiarly the object of the cordial sympathy of the American people, the foundation stones of whose political structure are freedom and liberty.

For these reasons I warmly commend the efforts being made by the Relief Committee for Greeks of Asia Minor, to relieve the suffering Greeks of that country, and I bespeak for it the hearty and continued support of the Greeks and all lovers of Greece in America.

Sincerely yours,   Woodrow Wilson

TLS (Letterpress Books, WP, DLC).
[1] Businessman of New York and former United States Consul in Patras, Greece (1901-1903); at this time also general manager of the Greek Currant Company, general agent for the Greek Line, and chairman of the Relief Committee for Greeks of Asia Minor. The following letter was a verbatim copy of a draft prepared by the relief committee and transmitted to Wilson in F. W. Jackson and J. P. Xenides to WW, Sept. 2, 1918, TLS (WP, DLC). The letter from Jackson and Xenides and the enclosed draft were sent by the Greek Minister, Georges Roussos, to Lansing who, in turn, forwarded them to Tumulty. G. Roussos to RL, Sept. 16, 1918, TCL (WP, DLC), and RL to JPT, Sept. 25, 1918, TLS (WP, DLC). Wilson instructed Tumulty as follows: "Dear Tumulty: I am quite willing that these gentlemen should use this letter which they have proposed that I should sign, but I would be very much obliged to you if you would write them begging that they will make use of it only in such ways and at such times as may be approved by the Liberty Loan Committees of the communities in which they work. The President." WW to JPT, Sept. 30, 1918, TL (WP, DLC). Tumulty informed Jackson accordingly in JPT to F. W. Jackson, Oct. 2, 1918, TLS (Letterpress Books, WP, DLC).

From Ferdinand Foch

Monsieur le Président,[1]   [Supreme Headquarters] Le 2.10.18

J'ai eté particulièrement sensible à votre attention de m'envoyer votre photographie. Au milieu des abominations et des rigueurs de notre guerre, il me sera particulièrement réconfortant d'avoir l'image de l'homme qui a conduit son peuple à la guerre pour la défense unique des grands principes de Justice et de Liberté.

Recevez, Monsieur le Président, l'assurance de mes respectueux sentiments,   F. Foch

ALS (WP, DLC).
[1] Our translation follows:
"I have been particularly sensible of your attention in sending me your photograph. In the midst of the abominations and rigors of our war, it will be particularly cheering to have the image of the man who has led his people into a war for the sole defense of the great principles of Justice and of Liberty."

From the White House Staff

The White House.
Memorandum for the President   October 2, 1918

Mr. Kerwin of the Department of Labor asks if the President will fix an appointment to see Representative Keating, Miss Abbott of the Child Labor Division of the Department of Labor,[1] Mr. Owen Lovejoy[2] and Mr. Sterling[3] on the subject of the proposed child labor legislation.[4]

T MS (WP, DLC).
    [1] That is, Grace Abbott, author and social worker, formerly associated with Jane Addams at Hull-House; director of the Child Labor Division of the Children's Bureau of the Labor Department since 1917.
    [2] That is, Owen Reed Lovejoy, general secretary of the National Child Labor Committee.
    [3] Unidentified.
    [4] Wilson saw Representative Keating, Miss Abbott, Lovejoy, and Sterling at the White House at 5 p.m. on October 8, 1918.

Two Letters from Henry French Hollis[1]

Dear Mr. President: Paris, France October 2nd, 1918.

Since your inspiring speech in New York last week setting forth so clearly the spirit of the war and the issues which have forced themselves upon our attention, I have been buying English and French papers, and Paris editions of American papers, so that I might be informed of the attitude of our associates upon the points you emphasize. To my great surprise there has been absolutely no comment. All the papers gave the substance of your speech in the news columns, some of them printed it in full. But no editor has referred to it. The enclosed clipping from the Paris edition of the New York Herald[2] is all that I have found. Other Americans report to me the same experience.

I am forced to believe that it is a deliberate boycott under orders from the French and English governments. Through the censorship, the control of the print paper supply, publishing committees, and favors and threats of vario[u]s kinds, they maintain a strict control of the editorial columns of all journals. All the rest of your messages and speeches of the past three months have been played up enthusiastically in all the papers, particularly your recent reply to the Austrian peace feeler, which was called "curt and blunt" and was much approved.

What is the object of the present boycott?

I believe it represents the real attitude of Lloyd George and Clemenceau toward your proposal of a League of Nations, universal rights and an open and impartial peace. These two men are dominant in England and in France at present. They and a few friends have the entire control of the two governments. They expect to control at the peace conference.

They intend yo [to] get for their Nations, and for their supporters, very substantial advantages over the rest of the world out of the victory which we have made possible over Germany. They intend to get trade advantages and preferences of various kinds in the world's commerce, particularly in commerce with their own colonies and depemdencies [dependencies]. They intend to get ahead of us in this respect while we are using our ships to get our troops home to America. I am afraid that we shall not have the use of many English ships to transport our men westward.

You have in mind the attitude of the French and English leaders toward the principles set forth in your New York speech. You have told me that you believe that the people of England and of France are behind you on these principles, and that you must act through them to get their leaders into line. I agree with you in this, but I realize that it will be up-hill work. Your New York speech was evidently intended (1) to appeal to the people of our associates along the lines you have laid down, and (2) to persuade the people of Germany and of Austria-Hungary and of their allies, that they will get fair play from us. Realizing this, I watched with great interest for editorial comment. The fact that it was not permitted shows that Lloyd George and Clemenceau are determined in their opposition.

I report the facts for your consideration.

I think that we are likely in the peace conference to find ourselves in the awkward position of having Germany on our side on this point. She is naturally the one that England and France intend to handicap most heavily. They will not wish to agree to the return of her colonies. They are putting out stuff now to show that Germany would use them for submarine bases for further deviltry in future wars. They will not wish to agree to giving Germany equal rights of commerce with her former colonies or with their own.

It will be obviously to the advantage of a defeated Germany to insist on a League of Nations, universal rights to trade, and free access to the sea. We ought to be thinking of this probable alignment and be making up our minds how best to soften the effect of such a spectacle if it becomes a reality.

I believe that your speech had a great influence on Bulgaria's sudden capitulation. I believe that it will have a similar and early effect on Turkey and Austria and, in connection with defeats and other discouragements, a powerful effect on the German people. It would not surprise me if one of the large German armies should collapse and start a rout. The current American opinion is that the fighting will end this fall, but I think that is rather too optimistic. There can be no doubt, though, that the end is in sight.

I am delighted to see the wisdom of your stand vindicated regarding declarations of war against Bulgaria and Turkey. You may be sure that it was not forgotten when Bulgaria decided to capitulate.

I saw the King of Belgium last Thursday,—a tall, handsome man, rather shy and formal. He asked me to say to you that he very much appreciated your assistance and encouragement, and that he particularly admired your high-minded and advanced position toward the rights of the smaller nations.

He said further that you would be the dominating influence at the peace conference. I thupght [thought] it was diplomatic to say that you did not expect to be dominant, but that you hoped that the principles that you had set forth would be controlling.

He has no desire for peace, even if his country is restored with full indemnity, unless Germany is beaten and made harmless for the future. Without guaranties for the future he would not feel safe as Germany's neighbor. His attitude, as well as that of all the Belgians I saw, was very fine, grateful without too much humility, pruod [proud] without lack of appreciation.

I visited the Belgian front at Nieuport the day before the Belgian drive started. The Germans threw a few shells over my head at our automobile.

Along with our recent military successes, exchange with neutrals, including Spain and Switzerland, has much improved. Our plans in Spain are working out well and we shall get mules from there in about the number indicated in my former letter.[3] France has agreed to let us have some horses, but I doubt their value.

I am much pleased that Mr. Cravath has returned to Europe. He is very valuable. I hope you will talk to Mr. Norman Davis[4] who goes to America soon. Mrs. George Rublee[5] has asked me to express to you her admiration for your New York speech.

Sincerely yours,   Henry F. Hollis

[1] Hollis had been in Europe since July 1918 as a representative of the Treasury Department with the Interallied Council on War Purchases and Finance.

[2] "Final Settlement Must Not Be Made Secretly," undated clipping, WP, DLC. It stated that newspapers throughout the United States saw in Wilson's speech the "categorical abandonment of the old diplomatic methods and the engagement to form a League of Nations at the Peace Conference." It quoted the New York Herald to the effect that Wilson's address had shown that "this war of peoples" had raised questions which could not be settled by "statesmen or diplomatists in secret conclave." "It is absolutely essential," the editorial concluded, "that right should triumph over force in a definite and decisive manner, both on the battlefield and in the forum, and just as we fight in the open, we must make peace in the open."

[3] H. F. Hollis to WW, Sept. 12, 1918, CCLS (WP, DLC).

[4] Norman Hezekiah Davis, at this time financial adviser to the Secretary of the Treasury in connection with foreign loans. He had been sent on a special mission to Spain in July 1918 to purchase supplies for the A.E.F. in France.

[5] Juliet Barrett (Mrs. George) Rublee.

Dear Mr. President: Paris, October 2nd, 1918.

My only son,[1] a Lieutenant in the Army Aviation, shot himself through the head at Dayton, Ohio, September 4th. He had a serious fall of three hundred feet on July 3rd, and in his descent his machine hit and killed his bunk-mate. He was himself badly injured about the head, but we thought that he had recovered. We now learn that he had brooded over the unfortunate killing of his friend, although he was not at all at fault for it. He must have had some distorted views which drove him to suicide.

He was a brave, clean boy, much loved by his mates. He was not afraid to fly. He loved it and looked forward to success as an aviator on the front.

His death is the great tragedy of the war to me. Naturally I do not wish to come back to the publicity of the Senate at present.[2]

Sincerely yours,   Henry F. Hollis

TLS (WP, DLC).
[1] Henry French Hollis, Jr.
[2] Hollis did not run for reelection. He stayed in Paris until December 1918. After a brief trip to the United States, he returned to Europe in February 1919 as a member of the United States Liquidation Commission for the disposal of surplus American war materials.

From Raymond Blaine Fosdick

My dear Mr. President: Washington, October 2, 1918

With reference to the report on the negro problem at Newport News,[1] I am taking the matter up with Dr. Emmet J. Scott, Secretary Baker's advisor on matters relating to colored troops, to see what can be done. I believe it will be possible to secure a few large-calibred men, both white and colored, to carry on through the colored churches, etc., a definite propaganda which will counteract some of the mischievous impressions that are going around. Our Commission is itself placing in the camps men of understanding and sympathy in connection with our social work among colored troops, and I believe this step will be of some assistance. We are arranging, too, to bring the spirit of your recent utterance on mob rule[2] to the attention of colored people everywhere, so that they will realize that at least the government is friendly. Other steps will undoubtedly suggest themselves, and I think that with Dr. Scott's help we can make a very definite dent on this problem.

Cordially yours,   Raymond B. Fosdick

TLS (WP, DLC).
[1] The Enclosure printed with R. B. Fosdick to WW, Sept. 27, 1918.
[2] That is, the "Statement to the American People," printed at July 26, 1918, Vol. 49.

Robert Lansing to Joseph Patrick Tumulty, with Enclosure

My dear Mr. Tumulty: Washington October 2, 1918.

I beg to enclose herewith for the President a copy of a personal and confidential letter, dated September 20, 1918, addressed to me by the Honorable Albert G. Schemedeman [Schmedeman], American Minister to Norway.

I am, my dear Mr. Tumulty,

Very sincerely yours,   Robert Lansing

TLS (WP, DLC).

E N C L O S U R E

PERSONAL AND CONFIDENTIAL.

Sir: Washington, D. C., September 30, 1918.

In accordance with your request of Saturday I have the honor to repeat the remarks made to me by Mr. Ihlen on July 23, 1918, when I took leave of him before coming to the United States.

He requested me to inform the President and the Secretary of State that he wished to thank them over and over again for the fairness with which the American Government had treated Norway during the entire negotiations. He said that he was joined in these expressions of thanks by the whole cabinet and that they were all more than pleased with the interpretation of the agreement and in the way in which it is working now. He said, further: "It is hardly necessary for me to tell you of the feeling of sympathy and admiration that almost every Norwegian has for America and that the relationship between Norway and the United States is better today than it has ever been."

I also called on the Prime Minister[1] the same day. He asked me to say to the President a [sic] that the neutrals feel that the peace which President Wilson stands for will be a peace that all neutrals will be satisfied with.

I have the honor to be, Sir,

Your obedient servant,   A. G. Schmedeman.

TCL (WP, DLC).
[1] Gunnar Knudsen.

Robert Lansing to William Graves Sharp

Washington, October 2, 1918.

For your information. I am today addressing the following note to the French Ambassador:

Quote. My dear Mr. Ambassador: I told the President this afternoon[1] of the policy of your Government in relation to the postponement of all territorial questions in the Balkans until the conference for the negotiation of a general peace, which was contained in the telegram from M. Pichon which you were good enough to read me this morning.[2]

The President expressed himself as very much gratified with the announced attitude of your Government which is essentially in accordance with his judgment.

In order that there may be no misapprehension by the other interested Governments as to the views of this Government in relation to the situation created by the capitulation of Bulgaria, I am instructing our Ambassadors to Great Britain and Italy and our Ministers to Serbia and Greece to inform the Governments to which they are accredited as follows: Quote.

In connection with the recently arranged armistice entered into between the commander of the allied military forces operating in Macedonia and the commissioners of the Bulgarian Government, the Government of the United States, in expressing its gratification at the practical withdrawal of Bulgaria from her alliance with the German and Austro-Hungarian Empires and the consequent cessation of hostilities, feels that it should very frankly state that it cannot but regard every question which concerns the Balkan States as an essential part of the general peace settlement inasmuch as there is no region of Europe more likely to be a seed-bed for war than the Balkans. The Government of the United States is firmly convinced that peace with Bulgaria cannot be treated apart from a general Balkan settlement without embarrassing the consideration of such subjects as the reopening of the treaties of Brest-Litovsk and Bucharest and making very difficult many matters of final consideration. The Government of the United States desires to register the opinion that it would be very hazardous to treat separately any part of the whole subject which will be included in the final treaty of peace.

I trust, my dear Mr. Ambassador, you will be kind enough to advise your Government of the foregoing communication. Unquote.

Lansing

TS telegram (SDR, RG 59, 763.72119/2057a, DNA).
  [1] That is, October 1, 1918, the date on which Lansing dictated this telegram.
  [2] See the memorandum by Robert Lansing printed at Oct. 1, 1918.

Sir William Wiseman to Sir Eric Drummond

[New York] 2 October 1918.

No. CXP. 778.

Please deliver the following message to Lord Robert Cecil from Col. House.

The President wishes me to thank you cordially for your message.[1] He has read your letter of August 19th to Sir William Wiseman[2] and is highly gratified to find that you share his conviction as to the absolute necessity for a League of Nations and the principles on which the League should be founded.

T telegram (W. Wiseman Papers, CtY).
[1] That is, the message quoted in G. Auchincloss to WW, Sept. 30, 1918.
[2] It is printed as an Enclosure with EMH to WW, Sept. 13, 1918, Vol. 49.

Sir William Wiseman to Lord Reading

[New York] 2 Oct. 1918.

No. CXP. 779.

I understand Barclay has cabled F.O. text of the memorandum from Lansing dated Sept. 27 regarding American Expeditionary Force in Siberia.[1] It is a further attempt to define the U. S. policy towards Russia as described in my cable CXP 759 of the 21st.[2] You will observe that the plan mentioned in my CXP 767[3] has been rejected, or rather, modified. It does not seem to me that the memorandum helps matters. House recognizes the whole situation as unsatisfactory but is himself not sure what advice to offer.

I suggest that you should cable me confidentially your views based on the latest information as to the position of the Czechs in Siberia and the policy which the Allies would like the U. S. to adopt. I could then ascertain whether there was a possibility of the President modifying his policy in such a way that a common formula could be reached.

Alternatively, the whole matter might be left in abeyance until you return and can discuss the matter personally with the President.

T telegram (W. Wiseman Papers, CtY).
[1] That is, the Enclosure printed with RL to C. A. de R. Barclay, Sept. 27, 1918.
[2] W. Wiseman to Lord Reading and E. Drummond, Sept. 21, 1918, T telegram (Reading Papers, FO 800/225, PRO).
[3] It is missing.

A News Report

[Oct. 3, 1918]

SUFFRAGISTS THANK PRESIDENT;
PLEDGE AID IN WAR WORK

Washington, Oct. 3.—In addressing a delegation of Suffragists from every State in the Union which called upon him to-day to thank him for his efforts in their behalf, President Wilson is understood to have expressed himself rather forcibly regarding the "wilful thirty Senators" who voted against the Susan B. Anthony amendment.[1] The President's utterances were not made public at the White House.

The Suffragists were headed by Dr. Anna Howard Shaw and Mrs. Carrie Chapman Catt, and were with the President for half an hour. In extending the thanks of the women of the country for the untiring efforts of the President for equal suffrage, Dr. Shaw brought a tear into his eye.

"Language is too poor," she declared, "to express the emotion of the heart at such a time as this. As I am probably the oldest Suffragist in point of service, they have honored me by permitting me to express the gratitude of the women of our country to you, Mr. President, for your loyal and continued support of our amendment, and for the unequalled service that you have given to our cause and to that of humanity before the United States Senate.

"We are not only grateful, but we are proud that the leader at the head of this great nation should address the Parliament in behalf of freedom and justice for women. We can express our gratitude in no other way than by pledging our loyal support in behalf of any demand which you may make upon us which will aid you in winning this war for human liberty."

Mrs. Catt told the President that through his address to the Senate the Suffrage question occupies a higher plane than it ever did before.

Printed in the New York *World*, October 4, 1918.

[1] The resolution for a woman suffrage constitutional amendment (H.J. Res. 200) had been defeated in the Senate on October 1, 1918. With fifty-four senators in favor of the resolution and thirty opposed to it, it had failed to receive the required two-thirds majority by a margin of two votes. When Senator Andrieus A. Jones, the chairman of the suffrage committee, realized that the resolution would be rejected, he changed his vote from the affirmative to the negative so that he might have the right under the rules to move a reconsideration. Thus, as recorded, the vote was fifty-three to thirty-one. Twenty-one Democrats and ten Republicans voted against the amendment. *Cong. Record*, 65th Cong., 2nd sess., pp. 10976-88. See also the *New York Times*, Oct. 2, 1918.

Remarks to a Group of Suffragists

[Oct. 3, 1918]

I just wanted to say, Mrs. Catt and ladies, and I can say it most unaffectedly, that I do not deserve your gratitude. You know, some of you have regretted the fact that I was slow of conversion to this cause, but I do not see how any man's processes of conviction can be slow in the presence of the influences now abroad in the world. So that when my conversion to this idea came, it came with an overwhelming command that made it necessary that I should omit nothing and use the position I occupied to enforce it, if I could possibly do so. I pride myself on only one feature of it, that I did understand when circumstances have instructed me. There are some men who, I am sorry to say, have recently illustrated the fact that they will not learn. Their minds are provincial. They do not know a great influence when it is abroad. They have given themselves a lifelong task. They will have to explain for the rest of their lives. And I should like to tell some of them that, having been a historian myself, I can assure them that historians are very dull persons and do not accept ingenious explanations, and that therefore history will deal very candidly with the circumstances in which the head of a government asked the kind of support that I asked the other day, and did not get it. It is one of the serious circumstances in the history of the United States. I have to restrain myself sometimes from intellectual contempt. That is a sin, I am afraid, and being a good Presbyterian, I am trying to refrain from it.

But I had not meant to dwell on that side of it. I want to say that it has been a matter of deep gratification to me to have had the opportunity to render service, such as it was, and I want you to know that my heart not only, but my conviction and my purpose were with you, and I was speaking from knowledge. The other day, when I told the Senate that I had not been listening to the public men, I had not been listening to editors, but I had been listening to the heart of the world, which comes to me with very authentic throb, through many instrumentalities which it has set up. There are all sorts of undercurrents which are growing more and more powerful and are perceptible in the official dispatches, and come to me in all sorts of letters and communications. There seems to be growing a great voice in the world which it will be very dangerous for any statesman not to pay attention to. It was to that voice that I thought, and still think, that I had been listening, and that voice speaks with very authentic tones. So that I want to repeat again that I do not deserve your gratitude. I am only proud to cooperate with you.

T MS (WP, DLC).

To the Most Reverend Thomas O'Gorman[1]

[The White House] 3 October, 1918

I have heard with real regret of the death of Archbishop Ireland,[2] and beg to thank you for your official notification of his decease.[3] He will be greatly mourned by all who enjoyed his guidance and felt the force of his character.   Woodrow Wilson

T telegram (Letterpress Books, WP, DLC).
    [1] Bishop of Sioux Falls, S. D.
    [2] The Most Rev. John Ireland, Archbishop of St. Paul, had died on September 25, 1918.
    [3] It is missing.

To Joseph Patrick Tumulty, with Enclosure

Dear Tumulty: [The White House] 3 October, 1918.

I wish you would be kind enough to acknowledge this for me and say that I have read it and it will have my most serious and friendly consideration.   The President

TL (WP, DLC).

E N C L O S U R E

From William Harrison and Others

Mr. President: Washington, D. C. October 1, 1918.

The National Race Congress is an annual Conference of delegates from the several States, convened to consider the condition of our people in the United States and to construct a program for the development of the social, economic and spiritual life of our race. We seek to foster the aims and aspirations of a free people; and to secure to our fellows the guarantees of the Constitution of the United States, by lawful agitation, fellowship and service.

We meet this year when our country is at war. We feel with all other Americans the burdens that war imposes, and we offer to our country, not our bit, but our best. Our loyalty is unwavering, our service is whole hearted. Our history has no taint of treason. Our blood has been freely given in all our country's wars. Hence, we have earned the right to speak in our own defence if our rights are abridged.

We are grateful Mr. President, for the fine ideals you have set forth to America and the world; and we are particularly pleased with your pronouncement against mob violence. It gave encouragement to the heart of every true American, and is the harbinger of hope to all colored men in the United States. It makes us feel that the day will come when you may exercise the full power delegated to you as the chief executive of our Nation, and summon to your aid the full force of a statute of the United States Government by which such lawless acts may be suppressed.

We know that offences will be committed. We do not condone crime, but we ask for our people what is accorded to others: viz, that all individuals charged with crime, should be given a fair and impartial trial by a jury of their peers.

We now bring to your attention Mr. President, a matter that heads up under the Interstate Commerce Commission, but which we bring to you because relief has not come from that source. Our people are unfairly treated by the railroads of the South. The laws of the Southern States prescribe that "there shall be separate but equal accommodations for white and colored passengers on trains." It is a fact that while there are separate accommodations, they are in no sense equal. The treatment our people receive as passengers on railways in the South, is in open violation of the law; it is unfair, unjust and degrading. Therefore we beg that you use the authority of your exalted office to change these conditions making travel equally safe, comfortable and healthful to all who pay the same tariff.

The black soldier fights best when his mother, wife and sister are not humiliated on the common carriers of his country because of race prejudice.

Another grievance that is hindering the war spirit in our race is, the fact that in some of the administrative office[s] of the government in Washington D. C. and elsewhere, race discrimination is nullifying the letter and spirit of the Civil Service law, and delaying the winning of the war by depressing the enthusiasm of the aspiring people of our race. Our people who aspire to positions above the menial grade in some departments, are flatly denied consideration, and sometimes, if a fair official gives work to such aspirants, they are marked for insult or humiliation by boorish officials or discourteous employees. These discriminations disturb the morale of our young people and lower the efficiency of both the offender and the offended.

This species of prejudice against race and color, sometimes, nay too often, finds its way into the Army and Navy of the United States.

Our brave black boys have given a good account of themselves in the fight against the Hun and we protest against any discrimination in the Army and Navy based on race or color. We ask a fair trial in all branches of the military service.

Mr. President, we seek just and impartial dealing from the officials of our government, we believe you to be providentially directed in the guiding of our Nation at such a time as this and we beg you to give us the protection we are fighting hard to win and offer to others.

We ask you to encourage us in honoring the freedom you love. Let us be Americans in character regardless of color. Let us have no "Jim Crow Cars," no segregation, no disfranchisement, no pro[s]cription no partiality and no prejudice in the government administration of public affairs.

Finally, Mr. President; wrongs so open, weigh down the hearts and slow the movement of the people who are otherwise happy and anxious to serve their country. Now, as never before, do we as black men need to give to our people the spirit of hope, inspiration and love of country. Changing the conditions complained of will make it easier for the leaders of our race to direct and influence our people in the activities and sacrifices incident to winning the war for democracy and righteousness.

Signed: William Harrison
John R. Hawkins
Wm. Calvin Chase
I. N. Ross
H. C. Garner
W. H. Jernagin   President
J. Harvey Randolph[1]
Assistant Secretary

TLS (WP, DLC).
[1] Persons who have not heretofore been identified and who can be identified were John Russell Hawkins, former President of Kittrell College, North Carolina, at this time financial secretary of the African Methodist Episcopal Church and trustee and fiscal agent of Wilberforce University; William Calvin Chase, editor and owner of the *Washington Bee*, a leading newspaper for blacks; and the Rev. James Harvey Randolph, pastor of the Mt. Moriah Baptist Church in Washington, D. C.

To Grenville Stanley Macfarland

My dear Mr. Macfarland: [The White House] 3 October, 1918.

Thank you for your letter of yesterday.[1] Like yourself, I am daily fortified in my judgment about the part the United States government should play (or rather should not play) with regard to the public utilities throughout the country. I am even a little shy of following out the suggestion you make,[2] because I find that our commissions get sympathetically engaged and more and more deeply involved.

In haste,   Sincerely yours,   Woodrow Wilson

TLS (Letterpress Books, WP, DLC).
[1] G. S. Macfarland to WW, Oct. 2, 1918, TLS (WP, DLC).
[2] That Wilson appoint a commission with instructions to place itself at the service of

any local authorities who wanted to take over ownership and operation of their cities' public-transit systems. Macfarland added that he strongly favored municipal ownership of traction companies.

To Valentine Everit Macy

My dear Mr. Macy: [The White House] 3 October, 1918.

May I not frankly lay before you the enclosed letter from the Director General of Railroads,[1] and beg that you will get in touch with him and afford him an opportunity to present his views to your full committee before your decision[2] is finally formulated and published?

Cordially and sincerely yours,   [Woodrow Wilson]

CCL (WP, DLC).
[1] It is missing. However, it was a letter from McAdoo to Wilson of October 3, 1918, about the effect of a wage increase for machinists in shipyards upon the wages of machinists in railroad work. White House memorandum, Oct. 3, 1918, T MS (WP, DLC).
[2] That is, the decision of the Shipbuilding Labor Adjustment Board with regard to wages and working conditions of shipyard workers on the Pacific Coast. See V. E. Macy to WW, Sept. 17, 1918, and WW to V. E. Macy, Sept. 18, 1918.

From Valentine Everit Macy

My dear Mr. President: Washington, D. C. October third 1918

Your letter of the third, requesting me to arrange a conference with the Director General of Railroads before announcing our Decision, has just been received.

I have called up the office of the Director General and stated that I should be glad to meet with him any time that suited his convenience.

As explained to you in our conference some weeks ago,[1] we are bound by the agreement creating this Board to be governed in decisions by the increased cost of living. The data for establishing this increased cost is being obtained by the Bureau of Statistics. It is, of course, impossible for our Board, on its own initiative, to change the principles upon which it was found[ed]. If it should be deemed wise, in the interest of national policy, to vary from such principles, we believe it will be necessary to have such national policy authoritatively announced by the Administration. Indications of unrest, owing to the delay in rendering our Decision, are increasing, but we shall, of course, make no announcement until receiving your permission.   Respectfully   V. Everit Macy

TLS (WP, DLC).
[1] About which see V. E. Macy to WW, Aug. 20, 1918, Vol. 49, and n. 1 thereto.

From Peyton Conway March, with Enclosure

My dear Mr. President: Washington. October 3, 1918

I am sending you herewith a copy of Joint Note #37 from the military representatives of the Allied Nations at the Supreme War Council, which I have just received from General Bliss.

The note deals with the general military policy of the Allies for the autumn of 1918 and for the year 1919, and is very opportune. It is peculiarly interesting to find that the military representatives have independently come to exactly the same conclusion as has already been announced as the military policy of the United States, with reference to practically every theatre of war.

Very sincerely yours,   P. C. March

TLS (WDR, RG 120, Records of the American Section of the Supreme War Council, 1917-1919, File No. 339-1, DNA).

ENCLOSURE

SECRET.   Given at VERSAILLES on the 10th September 1918.

JOINT NOTE No. 37.

GENERAL MILITARY POLICY OF THE ALLIES FOR THE AUTUMN
OF 1918 AND FOR THE YEAR 1919.

To: THE SUPREME WAR COUNCIL.

(Study submitted by the Permanent Military Representatives to the Supreme War Council, in accordance with a Resolution of the Supreme War Council, dated 4th July, 1918).

PART I.

WESTERN FRONT.

I. GENERAL CONSIDERATIONS.

France and Italy remain, as always, the main theatres of the war. A decisive victory can only be gained by the Allies by the decisive defeat of the German Army, and its defeat would necessarily entail the total collapse of enemy resistance on the remainder of the Western front and in all other theatres of war.

The Allies must, therefore, concentrate their resources both in man power and in material on the Western front for the decisive struggle.

The decisive defeat of the enemy coalition can only be achieved on the portion of the Western front between the North Sea and Switzerland. And, even though it might appear possible to crush the Austrian Army on the Italian front, and a portion of the German Army with it, the final defeat of Germany, the real foundation of the hostile coalition, can only be brought about in the theatre of operations where the main German Armies are to be found, that is to say, between the North Sea and Switzerland.

Operations in the other theatres of war must be made to play their part in the decision sought for on the Western front by contributing to the moral and material exhaustion of the enemy. But such operations must not be allowed to absorb resources which are required by the Armies of the Entente on the decisive front. The defeat of the Central Powers in any of the subsidiary theatres of war could only be a step on the road to the defeat of Germany: it could not bring about the final decision.

A. *The front from the North Sea to Switzerland.*

By the continued arrival of American troops in increasing numbers the Allies will have from the Autumn of 1918 onwards a numerical superiority which will be appreciable. But if, in spite of the reverses he has met with during the Summer and Autumn of 1918, the enemy's fighting power still remains unbroken, it will only be in the Spring of 1919 that the Allied superiority in men, in tanks, in aeroplanes and in other material of war will justify the expectation of a great success, which would be capable of being exploited to the extent necessary to bring about a final decision.

Moreover, this superiority can only be obtained and developed:

(a) If France, Great Britain and Italy maintain their present effort, and

(b) If American troops continue to arrive in such numbers as have been demanded by the Marshal Commanding-in-Chief the Allied Armies in France.

If, however, it is evident that the fighting power of the enemy has diminished, it will be the duty of the Marshal Commanding-in-Chief the Allied Armies in France to consider if active operations can be successfully carried out before the Spring of next year.

B. *Italian Front.*

It is clear from the present situation of the opposing forces:

(a) that, for the present, the Allies could contemplate no considerable withdrawal of troops from their Armies in Italy,

(b) that so long as the Austrians are not largely reinforced by German troops, the Allied forces in Italy appear to be able not only to hold their own but, if an opportunity should occur, to hasten the exhaustion and disorganization of the enemy by offensive action.

II. GENERAL PLAN.

A. *Autumn and Winter, 1918, and the year 1919.*

  (a) *Front from the North Sea to Switzerland.*

From what has already been stated it follows that the Allies must, during the Autumn and Winter 1918-1919, first of all render their front secure against any hostile attack and, secondly, must make preparations, which are complete in all respects, for those offensive operations by which it is hoped to reach a final decision as soon as a sufficient superiority has been realised, and climatic conditions permit.

The Allied Front can only be made secure by a solid vigorous and active attitude of defence, which must include such local offensives and counteroffensive actions, as may be required, to disturb the enemy's preparations.

For the *preparation of offensive* operations it is necessary:

  (i) to ensure, to adjust, or to develop more fully, the programmes for munitions, for tanks, for aviation and other material so as to meet, as far as possible, the wishes of the Marshal Commanding-in-Chief the Allied Armies in France:

  (ii) to put the troops through a systematic course of training for offensive operations:

  (iii) to push forward the preparation of the theatre of operations as rapidly as possible, in accordance with the plans of the Marshal Commanding-in-Chief the Allied Armies in France:

  (iv) to spare no effort to accumulate in the shortest possible time the greatest possible numerical superiority. For this purpose it is very important that American troops should continue to be sent to France, to the exclusion of other theatres of operations, and to be placed at the disposal of the Marshal Commanding-in-Chief the Allied Armies in France, until such time as the Supreme War Council may decide otherwise and with this object in view the necessary tonnage should be made available.

Finally, it is necessary to think out beforehand all such operations as are calculated to improve our chances, from a military and an economic point of view, for the final decisive operations; and as are calculated to keep the initiative in the hands of the Allies; or to prevent the enemy from reorganizing his forces; or to take full advantage of any mistakes he may make or any weakness he may show. It will be the duty of the Marshal Commanding-in-Chief the Allied Armies in

France to determine the scope of such preparatory operations, having regard to the relative conditions of the Allied forces and those of the enemy, while remembering that the final decisive operations must be executed with the greatest possible force.

(b) *Italian Front.*

Similar preparations should be made for the Italian front. If the conditions in Austria render it advantageous to support an active diplomacy by military action, offensive operations in Italy might be advisable. Such operations should be executed with a concentration of resources as great as the Marshal Commanding-in-Chief the Allied Armies in France considers that the situation on the front between Switzerland and the North Sea will permit.

In order to facilitate a concentration of troops in Italy not only for offensive operations, as indicated above; but also in order to deal effectively with a possible attack by the Austro-Hungarian Army, reinforced for that purpose by a number of German Divisions, it is essential for the Allies to push forward as rapidly as possible such improvements to communications as will enable a sufficient force to be transferred from France to Italy before a hostile attack can achieve success.

B. *Year 1919.*

Although the Allied Forces will not be fully developed before the Summer of 1919, the offensive operations by which it is hoped to gain a final decision should be begun as soon as the weather permits. If this is not done the enemy might forestall the Allies and seize the initiative, thus compelling the Marshal Commanding-in-Chief the Allied Armies in France to employ his troops in a manner other than that intended.

These operations will be carried out on the front between North Sea and Switzerland with the maximum available resources.

As soon as offensive operations are begun in France the utmost vigour must characterize our operations on the front in Italy, and in every other theatre of war, so as to take advantage of any favourable developments and prevent the Germans from obtaining help from their Allies.

It must not be forgotten:

(i) that a considerable offensive operation by the Italian Armies, if carried out in conjunction with the general offensive in France, might contribute largely to the final decision by the defeat of the Austrian Army, which could not at such a time count on any help from Germany;

(ii) that the opportunity may arise for the Allied Armies to undertake in Italy in the Autumn and Winter of 1919 the offensive intended for the Autumn and Winter of 1918.

PART II.

REMAINING THEATRES OF WAR.

I. GENERAL CONSIDERATIONS.

The following are the broad principles which should guide the Entente in carrying out any operations in the subsidiary theatres of war:

(1) To retain at a distance from the Western front, those forces, which the Central Powers now maintain in the subsidiary theatres of war and, if possible, to attract additional forces:

(2) To attempt to break up the alliance of the Central Powers both by military and by diplomatic action:

(3) To prevent the Central Powers from exploiting the countries of which they are now in military occupation.

These objects demand a vigorous attitude by the Allied Armies in all the exterior theatres.

II. MACEDONIA.

The operations on this front have formed the subject of a special study which was submitted to the Governments by the Military Representatives. The following conclusions were reached:

(a) that it is desirable to make energetic preparations to enable the Allies to begin an offensive operation in the Balkans not later than 1st October, 1918, provided that these preparations do not entail the transfer of any men or material from the Western front, or the diversion of any tonnage, which would otherwise be available for the continuous transport of men and material at the maximum rate, indispensable for the realisation of the Plan of Operations on the Western front; approved by the Commander-in-Chief of the Allied Armies in France:

(b) that it is necessary, in principle, to give the General Commanding-in-Chief the Allied Armies of the East[1] a free hand to carry this offensive into execution at the moment which he may consider most favourable, provided new and unforeseen circumstances do not compel the Supreme War Council itself to fix the date, or to abandon the operation altogether.

Should this offensive be carried out in 1918, the operations to be undertaken in the Balkans in 1919 will depend on the results obtained in 1918 and on the general situation. It is not possible to

[1] Gen. Louis Félix Marie François Franchet d'Esperey.

foresee what these operations should be, on account of the uncertain political conditions in which some of our enemies are now involved.

The Commander-in-Chief of the Allied Armies in Macedonia[2] should not in preparing his offensive operations, lose sight of the necessity, which still exists, of improving his lines of communication and of establishing new bases in Old Greece, in accordance with the directions laid down by the Supreme War Council, (See Joint Note No. 4 of the Military Representatives).[3]

III. TURKEY IN ASIA.

A. PALESTINE.

The Turkish Armies in Palestine are relatively weak, they are of moderate value and are badly supplied, whilst the British Armies, in spite of reduction in number and the partial substitution of native for white troops, still possess a high military value.

If the relative position of the forces opposing one another be considered alone, the British Armies in this theatre would appear to be in a position to carry out offensive operations of considerable extent. But:

(1) as the armies progress the restricted means of communication would necessarily limit their advance:

(2) the eventual objectives, which might be assigned to these Armies, have lost much of their importance in consequence of the new lines of communication available for the Turkish Army to the Caucasus and Mesopotamia by the Black Sea, thus avoiding the Baghdad railway line.

Under these conditions it is neither possible nor opportune to fix distant objectives. But, operations of limited scope should be carried out in order to hold and attract enemy forces.

Operations of this nature would not justify a large numerical superiority of the British over the Turkish Armies. The possibility, therefore, of withdrawing troops during the winter should be considered in order to reinforce the Armies on other fronts.

B. MESOPOTAMIA & PERSIA.

The British Army in Mesopotamia is very greatly superior in numbers to the Turkish troops actually opposed to it, or which are likely to be opposed to it. It might appear possible, therefore, to operate both in Mesopotamia and in Persia; but lack of communications and means of transport would probably prevent

---

[2] That is, Gen. Franchet d'Esperey.

[3] It is printed in Ministère de la Guerre, État-Major de l'Armée, Service Historique, *Les Armées Françaises dans la Grande Guerre* (9 vols., Paris, 1922-34), VIII, Part 2, Appendix 4, pp. 460-61.

this. Consequently, the Commander-in-Chief in Mesopotamia[4] with the troops now at his disposal should spare no effort which would enable his forces to establish themselves firmly on the shores of the Caspian Sea and to render secure the Baghdad-Hamadan-Enzeli road.

A secure front, which included Baghdad and the Caspian Sea, would limit German activities in the East and would enable the Allies to stretch out a hand to such forces as could eventually penetrate into Russia from Vladivostock and the Arctic Ports. With the Allies established firmly on such a front, not only will the Germans be unable to supply themselvs from the rich resources of Turkestan, on which they could otherwise draw by means of the Caspian Sea and the railways leading East and West from it; but all the healthy elements which still exist in Russia, as well as the anti-turc and Armenian elements in the Caucasus, would be encouraged to crystallise into effective fighting bodies, which would absorb considerable enemy forces and so relieve pressure on the Western front.

The Commander-in-Chief should be free to advance to Mosul if it should appear to be advantageous to do so, provided that the necessary operations did not entail any diminution of the effort towards the Caspian Sea.

IV. RUSSIA.

Outside the Caucasus, which is directly connected with Mesopotamia and Persia, Russia contains two theatres of operations which are important to the Allies: Northern Russian and Eastern Siberia.

In both these theatres the Allies must aim at attaining the following objects:

(1) To prevent the Central Powers from exploiting such resources as may be available in Russia.

(2) To collect round nuclei of Allied forces all anti-German elements of resistance; to train these elements; to organize them, and so to make them into a force fit to fight against Germany.

(3) To bring assistance as soon as possible to the Czecho-Slovaks, who are in a critical position owing to Bolshevik propaganda; also owing to the military support given to the Bolshevik forces by the Germans and by enemy prisoners of war in increasing numbers, and whose organisation continues to expand.

(4) Finally, should circumstances permit, to build up again

---

[4] Lt. Gen. Sir William Raine Marshall.

an Eastern front by continuing the various operations undertaken in the different regions of Russia, (Northern Russia, Siberia and the Caucasus).

These objects having been defined, it is necessary to point out:

(a) *As regards Northern Russia*:

that the man-power situation of the Western Powers of the Entente precludes the transfer of any appreciable forces from the Western front in addition to those being sent in accordance with the decision taken by the Supreme War Council on the 3rd July, 1918:

that local resources being practically negligeable in this region, the maintenance of the Allied contingents depends altogether on the despatch of supplies from Overseas. Communications between Western Europe and Northern Russia are, however, very precarious:

that, under these conditions, the scope of any operations in Northern Russia must be somewhat restricted until a junction with the Czecho-Slovak contingents of Western Siberia can be assured.

(b) As regards *Siberia*:

that it is in this region that the effort of the Allies can give the greatest results on account of the presence of the Czechs; on account of the support to be obtained from Russian troops, favourable to the Allies; and also on account of the considerable resources in food and supplies of all sorts which the country affords:

that, consequently, it is expedient to increase the efforts of the Allies in this theatre; but resources necessary for the Western front, which is the decisive front, must not be absorbed elsewhere.

V. EASTERN AFRICA.

The operations in East Africa should be prosecuted with the utmost vigour with a view to their being brought to a conclusion at a very early date.

PART III.
GENERAL CONSIDERATIONS REGARDING WAR MATERIAL.

Having weighed the considerations which should govern the conduct of the operations in the various theatres of war, the Military Representatives are of opinion that the investigations into the various Allied manufacturing programmes should be followed up by determining without delay the relative proportion of raw materials, of labour and tonnage which should be allotted to each kind of manufacture according to its importance for the prosecution of the war.

The manufacturing resources of the Allies appear already to be extended to their utmost capacity. It is, therefore, essential in order to obtain the best returns that the available resources be distributed strictly in accordance with the military requirements of the operations to be undertaken. And this distribution must be made in accordance with the views expressed by the Commanders-in-Chief in the various theatres of operations as to the relative amount of manufactured products they would like to receive in the form of guns, aeroplanes, heavy tanks, light tanks, gas, railway material, etc.

The Military Representatives wish in conclusion to draw the attention of the Supreme War Council to the very great importance of ensuring that as early as possible the Allied Armies shall be made to reach their maximum strength, not only in manpower, but also in material. The Military Representatives consider that the culminating points in the development of mechanical contrivances of all kinds should coincide with the culminating point in the development of man-power.

If this coincidence of culminating points is attained, the Allies may look forward with all confidence to the operations of the year 1919, which will bring the fulfilment of their hopes, that is to say, peace through victory.　　　　Gnl Belin.

C. Sackville-West Maj-Gen.

Robilant

Tasker H. Bliss.

T MS (WDR, RG 120, Records of the American Section of the Supreme War Council, 1917-1919, File No. 339-1, DNA).

From William Kent

My dear Mr. President:　　　　Washington October 3, 1918.

I feel sure that in the press of manifold activities and responsibilities, you have not had time to consider the question of dismissal of the indictment against Theodora Pollock, concerning which I wrote you on September 26. Miss Pollock has been compelled to leave her employment in the Newark, New Jersey, Public Library to go west to stand trial. She is practically certain of conviction under the omnibus treatment afforded in such cases. As shown by certificates from medical authorities, this practically means a death sentence.

Pardon me for the suggestion, but it seems to me that cases like this, requiring Executive clemency to mitigate blundering mass-play in prosecution, are well worthy of attention.

No one denies the gentle character of this lady, and no one has any fear of her action or influence. That she should be indicted for writing a fool poem that never was published and which was unobjectionable, and that she should further be indicted for circulating a statement written by a gentle, loyal soul like Louis Post adds absurdity to a situation otherwise horribly tragic. I inclose copies of the previous letter and statement by my son-in-law, Mr. Arnold.[1]

Yours truly,   William Kent

October 7, 1918.
P.S. I have held this letter for several days, and now send it to you with a postscript to the effect that Mr. George M. LaMonte stated in a letter to Mr. Arnold the following:

"the San Francisco Judge said there was no evidence to warrant an indictment and that Miss Pollok did nothing between that time and the time of the Sacramento dragnet indictment to change the facts in the case."

TLS (WP, DLC).
[1] See W. Kent to WW, Sept. 26, 1918, n. 1.

From William Gibbs McAdoo, with Enclosure

Dear Mr. President: Washington October 3, 1918.

I enclose copy of a letter I have just sent to Senator Simmons about the revenue bill. I fear that Congress is going to adjourn without having enacted this measure. In that case, the future financial operations of the Government will be gravely imperiled. This is not an overstatement.

Cordially yours,   W G McAdoo

TLS (WP, DLC).

E N C L O S U R E

William Gibbs McAdoo to Furnifold McLendel Simmons

My dear Senator: Washington, October 3, 1918.

I am writing in deep solicitude to ask your co-operation and that of the Committee on Finance in averting a grave peril to the successful financial conduct of the war. I cannot disguise nor refrain from directing your attention to the fact that failure promptly to report and pass the new revenue bill will disorganize and endanger the national finances.

One year ago today the Revenue Act of 1917 became law. Acting thereafter with the greatest practicable dispatch, the Treasury Department was unable to frame the regulations essential to its proper interpretation, prepare the necessary forms, have them printed and properly distributed, acquaint taxpayers with their duties and responsibilities under the law and regulations, and develop the machinery necessary to secure returns on March 1, 1918, the date normally appointed by law.

The new revenue bill when enacted into law will impose a heavier burden upon a far larger number of objects than the Revenue Act of 1917. Its administrative problems will be multiplied in number and necessarily increased in complexity. Payment of income and profits taxes will begin three months earlier than in past years if the provisions of the House Bill relating to installment payments eventually become law.

The Department will make every effort to improve the administrative record of last year and it is undoubtedly in a better position to handle the administrative tasks imposed by new tax legislation than it was in the autumn of 1917. But it would be idle to deceive ourselves or you by holding out the expectation that the new income and profits taxes can be put into effect in a materially shorter time than was required last year. After the blank forms and schedules are drafted, printed and distributed, and the necessary regulations adopted and promulgated, a considerable interval of time must be given the taxpayers of the country to make out their returns and to familiarize themselves with the requirements of the laws under which they are taxed.

I shall not encumber this letter with any statement of views as to the character of the tax legislation to be adopted. My opinions on this subject have been fully set forth in my testimony before the Committee on Ways and Means of the House of Representatives. It seems unnecessary also to repeat the financial estimates which I have already furnished to the Ways and Means Committee. I have on several occasions in the past cited estimates to the effect that the actual expenditures of the Government during the present fiscal year will be at least $24,000,000,000. The actual disbursements of the Treasury since those estimates were made confirm my belief that if that estimate errs it understates rather than overstates the actual expenditures which the Government will be called upon to make during the year ending June 30, 1919. No such burden can be borne, no such financial program carried out, unless every dollar to be raised by the new revenue bill is actually collected at the time or times appointed by law. The demands of the situation are such that it would be impossible to postpone the installment dates fixed in the House Bill, and if through administrative delay the collection of the income and profits taxes should be deferred beyond those dates, it would mean financial disaster.

The necessity for revenue legislation at an early date was called to the attention of the two Houses of Congress by the President on May 27, 1918.[1] At this time the urgency of the situation has become such that I am impelled to take the liberty of urging the gentlemen of the Committee on Finance to take promptly whatever steps may be necessary for the expeditious enactment of the revenue bill, in view of the solemn truths uttered by the President in his address on that occasion:

"Definiteness, early definiteness, as to what its tasks are to be is absolutely necessary for the successful administration of the Treasury; it cannot frame fair and workable regulations in haste; and it must frame its regulations in haste if it is not to know its exact task until the very eve of its performance.

"I cannot assure the country of a successful administration of the Treasury in 1918 if the question of further taxation is to be left undecided until 1919."

Yours very truly,   W. G. McAdoo.

TCL (WP, DLC).
  [1] Wilson's address, printed at that date in Vol. 48.

From Franklin Knight Lane

My dear Mr. President: Washington October 3, 1918.

I have had a talk with Senator Lenroot regarding the Water Power Bill, and he thinks it would not be difficult to frame an amendment that would meet your mind and that would pass both houses. I therefore take the liberty of suggesting (and I do this without Lenroot's knowledge) that you send for him and ask him to present his views.[1] I would be pleased to be present myself if you desire it, but I expect to be out speaking for the Liberty Loan until next Wednesday at least.

Senator Lenroot, I have found, has the confidence of every member of the Public Lands Committee in the House, and because of his experience and fairness I think he will soon have a commanding place in these matters in the Senate. I do not suggest that Mr. Lenroot speak for you in the matter, because you have already spoken through others; but if the modification which he suggests is agreeable to you I believe it will be acceptable to Mr. Ferris and Mr. Sims.

Cordially and faithfully yours,   Franklin K. Lane

TLS (WP, DLC).
  [1] There is no record of a meeting between Wilson and Lenroot at this time.

From Josephus Daniels

My dear Mr. President: Washington. October 3, 1918.

As you know the Tenth District of North Carolina is very close and doubtful. Representative Weaver of that district was elected by a majority of nine, and we are very anxious about it. Mr. Weaver has had a better grasp of the policies in which you stand than any other member of Congress from North Carolina. He voted, as you remember, for Woman's Suffrage, the only member from North Carolina who did so. As a member of the legislature from North Carolina he led in the fight for modern child labor laws.

He is going to have a very hard fight, and we feel that he can be elected with help from you. Could you see your way clear to write a letter to him or a letter that could be used? His name is Zebulon Weaver of Asheville, North Carolina. He needs help and is worthy. Of all our members from North Carolina, he has had the true vision. Sincerely yours, Josephus Daniels

TLS (WP, DLC).

From Harry Andrew Wheeler and Elliot Hersey Goodwin

Sir: Washington, D. C. October 3, 1918.

For a year past the Board of Directors of the Chamber of Commerce of the United States has been giving some attention to various aspects of the problems of reconstruction, and has received many comments, suggestions, and resolutions from the commercial bodies included in its membership. We have just completed a meeting of the Board preceded by a meeting of the Executive Committee, in which all these suggestions and resolutions were brought together and considered as a whole, with the result that the subjoined preambles and resolutions were unanimously adopted.[1]

It has been proposed to us and we have considered a proposition for a Reconstruction Committee and a consequent reconstruction policy of the National Chamber, which would represent the views of the business interests of the country. We have decided that such a course could merely contribute to what we most fear, i.e. the formulation of class programs to which classes become committed in advance of any general and combined consideration by the proper governmental authority.

We wish to subordinate the interests of the business men as a class to the interests of the country as a whole, and with this in view, have adopted these resolutions. Should such a Commission as is here proposed be created, we believe all class antagonisms could be eliminated and an opportunity given to all interests of which business is but one, to formulate and present their ideas with the understanding that they would be fused and amalgamated by a body in which there would be representatives sympathetic to each interest but whose highest combined duty would be the interest of the public.

Should such a Commission be created, we believe we can unhesitatingly pledge the entire willingness of business interests to act in conformity with this plan and to accept the judgments arrived at without cavil.

If you should hold that it was not incompatible with any public or war policy of the Government, we should be glad to submit the proposition to a referendum vote with a view to proving this willingness of the business interests and obtaining their support.

> Very sincerely yours,   Harry A Wheeler
> President.
> Elliot H. Goodwin
> Secretary.

TLS (WP, DLC).
¹ T MS (WP, DLC). Goodwin and Wheeler paraphrase them below.

From Ruth Thomas James

My dear Mr. President: [Marion, Ky.?] October 3, 1918.

I have been too crushed until now to thank you for your splendid tribute to my dear husband,¹ and to tell you how much I appreciate your sympathy.

His loss seems too cruel but the love and tender interest of his friends and mine are most comforting.

I feel that he gave his life for his country just as much as those at the battlefront. He put every particle of his strength and energy into his service. It was a labor of love and he was untiring in its performance.

I shall always be glad of his association with you. He held you in such high esteem and admiration and valued your friendship so.

> Sincerely yours,   Ruth James

ALS (WP, DLC).
¹ WW to Ruth T. James, Aug. 28, 1918, Vol. 49.

Sir William Wiseman to Lord Reading

[New York] 3 October 1918.

No. CXP. 780. Military Attaché¹ called my attention to a passage in the President's speech to the Senate on Woman's Suffrage, September 30th: "They (the people of the United States) have seen their own governments accept this interpretation of Democracy— seen old governments like that of Great Britain, which did not profess to be democratic, promise readily and as of course this justice to women, though they had before refused it."

I have protested to Col. House in the strongest way against this passage in the President's speech. He himself agrees, and deplores it. He is writing to the President protesting, and urging him to make some public explanation pointing out what he meant to say was that governments which the people of the United States are apt to consider less democratic than their own had in this instance proved more democratic.

T telegram (W. Wiseman Papers, CtY).
[1] That is, Lt. Col. James Douglas McLachlan.

A Translation of a Telegram from Jean Jules Jusserand to Stéphen Jean Marie Pichon

Washington, New York   no date
received October 3, 1918, 10:30 p.m.

No. 1365. URGENT. CONFIDENTIAL.

I have spoken to the President about his note on Siberia and Russia,[1] not concealing from him the very painful feeling which it has caused me and which it will cause Your Excellency.

He has returned to his earlier conviction that the circumstances rendered indispensable the prudent recommendations which he had believed had to be formulated. His military advices, he said, could not have been more positive and pressing. On the other hand, not a single one of the predictions put forward by General Poole had been realized.

The irritated tone in which he spoke of the General confirmed me in the view that some clumsiness of the latter's part might well have been the determining cause for sending the note (see my telegram 1334).[2] I ask that any remonstrance to the Foreign Office about this be avoided.

I have precisely expressed our point of view: the danger to the Czechs, the opportunities lost, the encouragement to the Bolsheviks resulting from this abandonment, etc. I have concluded (one group missing) a talk with Mr. Lansing by saying: "If, (one group missing) without new aid from you but with circumstances favoring us (something that is by no means impossible), we manage to avoid this outcome that you envisage, I hope you will look upon us not unfavorably but rather the contrary."

He replied that I had nothing to fear on this point and that he had indicated that he believed what circumstances demanded were well understood and that he had no desire to prescribe them.

The door remains open to us. When I made a remark to this effect, President Wilson added, half seriously: "I cannot help being afraid that you are entering on a very risky business and then will ask for aid which I would in conscience not know how to give and which will be ghastly for me to refuse."

I assured him that we would not go beyond the point that was justified by events and by our forces.

He had not yet received the note from Masaryk which is summarized in one of my telegrams.[3] I have signaled its existence and importance to him.   Jusserand.

T telegram (État-Major, l'Armée de Terre, Service Historique, 4 N 46, FMD-Ar).
    [1] That is, the Enclosure printed with RL to C. A. de R. Barclay, Sept. 27, 1918.
    [2] J. J. Jusserand to the Foreign Ministry, Sept. 28, 1918.
    [3] J. J. Jusserand to the Foreign Ministry, No. 1368, received Oct. 3, 1918, T telegram (État-Major, l'Armée de Terre, Service Historique, 4 N 46, FMD-Ar). Masaryk's "note" strongly disagreed with the policy suggested in Wilson's memorandum of September 27 and argued at length against the proposed limitations on Czech and Allied military operations in Russia. See T. G. Masaryk, "Some Notes on the Memorandum of September 27th, 1918," Sept. 29, 1918, TS MS, enclosed in T. G. Masaryk to RL, Sept. 30, 1918, TLS (SDR, RG 59, 861.00/2900½, DNA). It is printed in *FR-LP*, II, 388-91.

From George Mason La Monte

Bound Brook, N. J.
My dear Mr. President Wilson: October 4, 1918.

It was very gratifying to me to be able to discuss with you yesterday, so frankly, the case of Miss Theo Pollok. This case justifies consideration from the standpoint of humanity as well as from the standpoint of justice, besides which I think it will give you an opportunity to make a statement to illustrate what you meant in your splendid speech condemning the mob spirit.

Miss Pollok is a thorough American—her ancestors have been such—and she has a human sympathy which is going to be required when this war is over. Therefore, if her efforts can be turned in the right channel she will be an asset to the United States, and in no sense can she possibly be considered a criminal or an enemy.

When Miss Pollok was arrested in California and taken before a Judge in San Francisco he declared there was not sufficient evidence against her to warrant an indictment. No further evidence was produced when she was indicted in the dragnet indictment in Sacramento, and in my opinion her indictment should be quashed as an act of justice, and certainly she should be given a separate trial. The first course is much preferable and much more just.

I want to thank you very much for your earnest consideration of her case, which I would not have presented to you if I had not been familiar with the facts and acquainted not only with Miss Pollok herself but with her mother[1] and her aunt, Miss Louise Connolly.[2]

Very truly yours,   Geo. M LaMonte

Miss Pollok's case is called for trial *Oct 10* and must be disposed of before that date. She is no coward and is now on the way to California to face the music.

TLS (WP, DLC).
  [1] Unidentified.
  [2] Author and editor of high-school textbooks, at various times superintendent of schools of Summit, New Jersey, and educational expert and adviser to the Newark Public Library and the Newark Museum.

To Thomas Watt Gregory

My dear Gregory: [The White House] 4 October, 1918.

I remember I wrote you the other day about Miss Pollak. I now learn that her trial is set down for the tenth of this month. So many persons whom I know and trust vouch for this young woman and for her entire loyalty and innocence of any unworthy purpose that I am going to ask you if you won't be kind enough to have a telegram sent to Preston, the District Attorney in California, asking whether the indictment as regards Miss Pollak could not be quashed without prejudice to the other cases involved. I have reason to fear that there is a rather malicious newspaper campaign on out there against Miss Pollak, and I should not hesitate to take the responsibility for dismissing the case against her, if in your judgment and Mr. Preston's there is no imperative reason against it.

Cordially and faithfully yours,   Woodrow Wilson

TLS (Letterpress Books, WP, DLC).

To Peyton Conway March

Dear Gen'l March,   The White House. 4 Oct., 1918.

Thank you for the report of the Military Council at Versailles. I have read it carefully and with not a little satisfaction. I return the copy because I have no proper place for it in my files.

Cordially   Woodrow Wilson

ALS (WDR, RG 120, Records of the American Section of the Supreme War Council, 1917-1919, File No. 339-1, DNA).

To J. Weller Long[1]

My dear Mr. Long: [The White House] 4 October, 1918.

I have received the letter of yesterday, signed by yourself, Mr. Lassater, Mr. Bouck, Mr. Owen, Mr. Slocum, Mr. Hampton, Mr. Hyde, Mr. Hagan, Mr. Anderson, and Mr. Simpson.[2] I need not say that I have read it with the greatest interest and with the closest attention.

I fully realize, and hope and believe the War Department fully realizes, the danger of too far depleting the agricultural labor of the country, and I shall from time to time try to give my personal attention to the matter. It is, as you say, of capital importance.

With regard to the suggestion that we should establish a draft for farm labor, it occurs to me that that would hardly be consistent with our ideas of the utter freedom of labor. But it would be entirely consistent with all our standards for the great farm organizations of the country to undertake to enroll a great volunteer force of men pledged to devote themselves to the industry, and the very publicity of the process, with a statement of the reasons why it was undertaken, would serve to relieve the men who enlisted of any suspicion of being desirous of avoiding the military draft.

The question of insignia has been raised again and again amongst us here in official circles, but we have always turned away from it because of unfortunate experiences of other belligerent governments, arising out of a virtual inability to prevent counterfeits and the wearing of the insignia by unauthorized persons. The whole matter is surrounded with difficulty, but it is the more necessary to treat it with the greatest care on that account.

Please express to those associated with you my appreciation of their careful and thoughful letter.

Cordially and sincerely yours,   Woodrow Wilson

TLS (Letterpress Books, WP, DLC).
    [1] Secretary-treasurer of the American Society of Equity and a member of the governing board of the Farmers' National Headquarters, the joint Washington offices of several "progressive" farm organizations.
    [2] It is missing. Those persons who have not heretofore been identified in this series were Edward Cunningham Lasater, a large cattle breeder from Texas, a member of the executive and market committees of the American National Live Stock Association, and former director of the division of livestock and farming of the Food Administration; William Bouck, Master of the Washington State Grange and a member of the governing board of the Farmers' National Headquarters; H. N. Owen of Minneapolis, publisher of *Farm, Stock and Home*; Grant Slocum, secretary-treasurer of the Ancient Order of Gleaners and a member of the governing board of the Farmers' National Headquarters; Clayton H. Hyde, chairman of the Northwestern Oklahoma Wheat Growers' Association and a member of the executive and legislative committees of the National Wheat Growers' Association; J. N. Hagan, Commissioner of Agriculture and Labor of North Dakota; John M. Anderson, president of the Equity Co-operative Exchange of Fargo, North Dakota; and John A. Simpson, president of the Oklahoma Farmers' Union. In addition, Long, Lasater, Bouck, Slocum, Hampton, Hyde, and Simpson were members of the Farmers National Committee on Packing Plants and Allied Industries.

To Franklin Knight Lane

CONFIDENTIAL

My dear Lane:				[The White House] 4 October, 1918.

I notice that Theodore Bell has been put up by some perhaps extra-legal process as a candidate for Governor in California.[1] I hope that he will get no encouragement from Washington. He certainly can get none from me. And I am writing to ask if you know of any Californians here connected with the administration who would need to be headed off in the matter. I believe I know your own judgment about Bell.

Cordially and faithfully yours,		Woodrow Wilson

TLS (Letterpress Books, WP, DLC).
[1] Theodore Arlington Bell, a lawyer of Napa, California, and an attorney for the California Winegrowers' Association. A former congressman from California (1903-1905) who had been the unsuccessful candidate of the Democratic party in the gubernatorial campaigns of 1906 and 1910, Bell was running again for governor in 1918 as an independent. Due to the peculiar provisions of California's direct-primary law and the results of the primary elections of August 27, 1918, the Democratic party had ended up without a gubernatorial candidate of its own for the November elections. Consequently, the Democratic State Central Committee had grudgingly thrown its support to Bell. As it turned out, the Republican candidate, Governor William D. Stephens, defeated Bell by a vote of 387,547 to 251,189. For a detailed discussion, see H. Brett Melendy, "California's Cross-Filing Nightmare: The 1918 Gubernatorial Election," *Pacific Historical Review*, XXXIII (Aug. 1964), 317-30.

To Samuel Vernon Stewart[1]

My dear Governor Stewart:	[The White House] 4 October, 1918.

Your letter[2] propounds a question which it is very easy and very pleasant to answer. Senator Walsh has earned for himself in the Senate of the United States a place of real distinction, and has earned it not only by being constant and diligent to promote the legitimate interests of his State and by a consistent support of the constructive measures which have during his term been enacted in the public interest, but also by very unusual legal ability and political judgment. My own feeling towards him, of course, is very warm because of his very consistent and generous support of the administration, but that ground of approbation is perhaps too personal, and I mention it only because it gives me so much pleasure to do so.	Cordially and sincerely yours,	Woodrow Wilson

TLS (Letterpress Books, WP, DLC).
[1] Governor of Montana, a Democrat.
[2] S. V. Stewart to WW, Aug. 31, 1918, about which see WW to JPT, Sept. 5, 1918, n. 1 (first letter of that date), Vol. 49.

To Josephus Daniels

My dear Daniels: The White House 4 October, 1918.

I shall be very glad to help Mr. Weaver, but I would not dare to write a letter just off my own bat to him, because that would get me in very deep water indeed by involving me in the necessity of writing letters for Congressmen without number. But it occurs to me that if someone in Mr. Weaver's district should address me a letter asking some pertinent questions about his record, it would give me an opportunity to send an answer which I would be glad to send.[1]   Always faithfully yours,   Woodrow Wilson

TLS (J. Daniels Papers, DLC).
  [1] See WW to J. H. Caine, Oct. 29, 1918.

To James Revell Lord

My dear Mr. Lord: [The White House] 4 October, 1918.

I have the letter of September 30th signed by yourself and Professor Lindsay.

Your stenographer forgot to enclose a copy of the bill to which the letter refers, but I think I know what its main provisions are, and I do not hesitate to say that I should be very glad to cooperate in its passage.

I am as anxious as others are not to clog the way for a permanent measure or to interfere with the earliest possible passage of such a measure in any way, but I should assume that the two measures could run side by side and that the one would not necessarily interfere with the other. Of course, the judgment of such men as the members of the Committee on Labor of the House of Representatives would be much better about such a matter than mine. I wonder if you have sought their opinion on that subject.

I foresee, as you do, the many difficulties that are going to surround the rapid consideration of a permanent bill, because the principle upon which it is based is necessarily disputable.

Cordially and sincerely yours,   Woodrow Wilson

TLS (Letterpress Books, WP, DLC).

To Patrick Emmet Gorman

My dear Mr. Gorman: [The White House] 4 October, 1918.

Since I feel indirectly responsible for your generous act in retiring from the congressional race in the Louisville district, I think I owe it to you to express my appreciation of the action you took. Representative Sherley has attained a place of leadership in the House of Representatives which has rendered him of the highest service to the country, and I know him so well that, in common with his many friends, I have been very much distressed to have it appear that he was in any way an enemy of the just claims of the laboring men. It is with this in view that I have taken the liberty of expressing my satisfaction with your action.

Cordially and sincerely yours,   Woodrow Wilson

TLS (Letterpress Books, WP, DLC).

From Robert Lansing, with Enclosure

My dear Mr. President: Washington October 4, 1918.

In connection with the enclosed memorandum from Mr. Phillips and my recent letter to you on the subject[1] I am now advised that of the 50,000 civilian population of St. Quentin none were found on the entry of the French troops, while the Germans had given the city over to destruction by fire. Of course the removal of the citizens and the setting fire to the city on evacuation were acts without military benefit and appear to have been inspired by malice and vandalism.

Possibly nothing we could say would have any effect in checking this wanton destruction and utterly indefensible removal of civilians who, I think we may presume, are retained for forced labor or to gratify a desire to cause needless suffering. However, it might stay these ruffians if we made a general statement that if these atrocities continued it would be necessary to hold those responsible liable therefor and that it would be impossible to restrain our troops from excesses of a like nature in the event that German cities and villages should fall into the hands of our forces.

I am not sure that this is the best way to deal with this subject, but it is difficult to avoid the conclusion that the troops, who have seen the results of this needless cruelty, will be so enraged and bitter that they will retaliate in kind if the opportunity offers which now seems probable. This would be to my mind deplorable as it would bring them down to the level of German brutality and I feel that, as we may expect such acts of revenge if the Germans do not cease their present methods, we should warn them of the consequences by some general statement which will present the possibilities to them.   Faithfully yours,   Robert Lansing.

TLS (WP, DLC).
[1] That is, RL to WW, Sept. 27, 1918 (second letter of that date).

E N C L O S U R E

To: The Secretary.   October 4, 1918
Subject: Germans devastating occupied territory as they are forced
          to retreat.

In view of the announcement that the Germans have removed
all the civilian population from Lens and have stripped and looted
the buildings of the city, it seems to me that if we are going to take
any action in the matter of your recent note to the President it ought
to be taken now. The Belgian Minister inquired again yesterday
what action if any we are going to take.

                                     Sincerely,   W Phillips

TS MS (WP, DLC).

From Lee Slater Overman

My dear Mr. President: Washington, D. C. October 4, 1918.

On the 27th of September Senator Weeks, of Massachusetts,
introduced a resolution in the Senate, a copy of which I am sending
you.[1] It occurred to me that he is playing politics; and I am satisfied
that this is an executive rather than a legislative function. I therefore went to work and prepared a bill[2] as a counter-movement so
that the Democrats rather than the Republicans should handle this
matter.

I am also sending you a copy of the bill I introduced, which I
hope you will examine and make such suggestions that may occur
to you. I notice the papers say it is an administration bill. Of course
I have had no intimation or suggestion from you or any of your
staff in regard to the matter. While it is not an administration
measure I would like to have your approval of the bill. Undoubtedly
something should be done along this line. I do not know whether
my bill will cover the matter or not, but it is subject to amendment
at all times. I am sending the bill to you for your examination, and
would like to have your views on the subject.

With sincere esteem, I am,

                        Most cordially yours,   Lee S. Overman

TLS (WP, DLC).
  [1] S. Con. Res. 21, printed copy (WP, DLC). It provided for the creation of a Joint
Congressional Committee on Reconstruction, composed of three senators and three
congressmen each from the Republican and Democratic parties. The twelve members
of the committee would be selected by the Republican and Democratic House and Senate
caucuses. The committee would investigate a large variety of problems connected with
the transition of the economic and industrial life of the nation from a state of war to a
state of peace. It would report its findings to Congress from time to time and recommend
appropriate legislative solutions.

² S. 4968, printed copy (WP, DLC). This bill, which Overman had introduced on October 3, 1918, provided for the establishment of a Federal Commission on Reconstruction, whose five members would be appointed by the President with the advice and the consent of the Senate. Not more than three commissioners could belong to the same political party, and the President could remove any commissioner for inefficiency, neglect of duty, or malfeasance in office.

From William Gibbs McAdoo

Dear Governor,   [Washington] Oct 4/18

This is clearly a matter for your decision. Overman's plan for a Commission appointed by you is best, I think.

What shall I say to Owen¹—or will you write him?

Affy   WGM

ALI (WP, DLC).
¹ Senator Owen, on September 28, 1918, had introduced a resolution (S. Con. Res. 22) for the creation of a Committee of Reorganization, composed of six senators and six congressmen who would be "fairly representative of the Democratic and Republican Parties" and who would be nominated by the party organizations of the two houses. The committee would make an immediate investigation and report to Congress not later than January 1, 1919, with suitable recommendations, on the "reorganizations required for a return to the occupations of peace of the men and women, capital investments and supplies now employed in war." In particular, the committee would investigate ways and means for the employment of returning soldiers and any other persons presently engaged in activities connected with the war; make concrete proposals for the utilization of materials, buildings, and supplies which were now used for war purposes; recommend methods by which the capital, credit, and labor of the American people could be actively employed in the production and distribution of goods at home and abroad; and report on the construction of "national hardsurfaced roads" throughout the country, the building of internal and coastal canals, the cultivation of swamp lands and arid lands, the utilization of water power, and the permanent maintenance of the American merchant marine. *Cong. Record*, 65th Cong., 2d sess., p. 10889.

From William Cox Redfield

My dear Mr. President: Washington October 4, 1918

I hand you letter from Senator Owen, with the enclosures to which he refers. I thought of answering him direct with a letter of which the enclosed is a tentative draft.¹ While drawing it, however, it occurred to me that the matter is of such importance that it should be submitted to you before anything was said or written. I should, therefore, be glad to have your counsel.

To me, the Resolution has elements of rushing in where angels fear to tread. Single phrases from the final paragraph on the second page of Senator Owen's Resolution involve great national economic policies, not hastily to be decided. For example, I should not like to have to report by the first of January in any final way upon "the permanent maintenance of the American merchant marine" or upon "the *construction of* national *hardsurfaced roads* throughout the

United States" and the "building of internal and coastal canals" has been a vexed subject for something over a century.

Awaiting the favor of your response, I am,

Sincerely yours,   William C Redfield

TLS (WP, DLC).
  [1] Owen's letter, its enclosures, and Redfield's draft reply are all missing in WP, DLC.

From Robert Somers Brookings

My dear Mr. President: Washington Oct. 4, 1918.

As probably no Administration agency of the Government occupies a closer personal relationship to you than the Price Fixing Committee, I have frequently thought that some form of report from the Committee to you, dealing with its general problems and policies, would be a justified intrusion upon your valuable time.

Failing in such a report, I would explain briefly that the Price Fixing Committe functions very much along court lines. When the condition of a commodity seems to necessitate Government control of price and probably allocation, the Price Fixing Committee proceeds to secure such evidence, through the Federal Trade Commission, as will enable it to intelligently consider the problem. This evidence usually consists of a history of the industry before the War (when available); balance sheets for the year 1917 with detailed cost sheets; and such additional cost information as will bring the data as nearly as possible up to the time set for a meeting with the interested industry.

The Chairman goes over these reports with the specialist of the Federal Trade Commission who is directly in charge of securing the information and prepares an abstract of his (the Chairman's) findings, a copy of which is sent to each member of the Committee. An Executive Session of the Committee is then called, which fully considers the problem, and a future date is arranged for a hearing of the interested industry, which is usually represented by a War Service Committee. This War Service Committee represents the different branches of the industry and sometimes numbers as many as thirty or forty persons.

At the appointed meeting of the Committee and the industry, the Chairman briefly outlines the conditions which seem to require the stabilizing of the industry, through a certain measure of Government control, and proceeds to deal with the question of what is a fair and equitable price. Without abusing the confidence necessarily involved in the many cost sheets before him, the Chairman in discussing proposed prices uses freely and frankly the cost figures in his possession, and by interrogation undertakes to develop as much additional information as possible from the representatives of the industry.

The Chairman usually explains that the Committee represents the President in studying price-fixing problems, the most important of which are referred directly to the President for his approval. This simple statement seems to fully establish the Committee's authority; and while it is naturally a constant struggle of the industries to secure the highest prices they possibly can, resulting frequently in more or less friction, in the last analysis—while the industry sometimes protests—it always concurs and agrees to do everything in its power to maintain production without reducing the price of labor, and to not only observe the maximum prices fixed but endeavor in every way to prevent speculators from defeating the Government's purposes.

We have an official stenographer who records everything that is said at these meetings, and this record, with the Federal Trade Commission's Report and all other data upon which we have based our findings, is bound together and filed, so that if at any time Congress or any other qualified authority wishes to know the grounds upon which prices have been fixed, the information is full and complete.

While prices fixed are necessarily based upon and find their reflection in the profit return on investment, it is practically impossible to establish any percentage of profit on investment that will apply to all industries. Each industry is made a separate study, the need of stimulating production taken into consideration, and a price fixed based upon a rather limited profit to the high-cost producer at the production line necessary to be maintained. If this results in a larger measure of profit for the low-cost producer than would seem to be fair, it is nearly all taken from him by the proposed Income and War Profit taxes.

As the fixing of prices has more or less bearing upon many Government activities, the Chairman is frequently consulted and uses his best efforts to harmonize conflicting interests. For example, as price-fixing and Excess Profit taxes are so closely related, the Chairman not only appeared before the Ways and Means Committee but kept in close communication with Chairman Kitchin, giving him from time to time such information as he had regarding prospective profits of manufacturers for this year.

Briefly stated, Mr. President, the present outlook indicates that manufacturing profits for 1918 will probably show somewhere between 20% and 30%. Under the proposed Income and War Profit taxes, a profit of 20% would yield the manufacturer a fraction over one-half of this amount; and a profit of 25% would yield him a fraction under one-half. From a life-time experience in many branches of manufacture, I should say this is the minimum of return necessary to maintain an industry in healthy condition. This is especially true under present conditions, when all of their replacements, additions, and inventories are based upon abnormally high costs, for which a reserve fund must be created to take care of the inevitable shrinkage after the War.

It is well understood in banking circles that the large profits shown in some lines of business are largely absorbed in their increased inventories and outstanding accounts, and as a result these concerns are more deeply indebted to the banks than ever before. A large part of these profits having been paid to the Government, I do not see how they can continue to pay any but very small dividends and maintain the necessary reserve to take care of the inevitable post-war shrinkage.

The present wide fluctuations in raw material and labor are quickly reflected in the profits of an industry and the relative profits of the different industries; as, for example,—our information indicates that the cotton goods manufacturers probably made more than double the return on investment, during the first six months of this year, than was made by the steel producers for the same period.

In conclusion, Mr. President, I would be glad to submit to you from time to time, either in person or in writing, problems involving fundamental policies, on which your judgment and advice would be invaluable to us.

Respectfully yours,   Robt. S. Brookings

TLS (WP, DLC).

A Memorandum of a Conversation by Thomas William Lamont[1]

White House, Friday, 4:30 p.m.
October 4th, 1918.

Mr. L. Mr. President, I sought this meeting with you for the purpose, as generally expressed in my letter to you of September thirtieth,[2] although that may have been somewhat vague. In order to explain more fully what I had in mind, I must, to a certain degree, be personal.

[1] Between Lamont and Wilson. It was based on notes (Hw MS [T. W. Lamont Papers, MH-BA]) which Lamont wrote during or immediately after the interview.
[2] There is no copy of this letter in either the Lamont Papers or in WP, DLC.

Mr. P. First-rate, Mr. Lamont, get at the matter in whatever way you wish.

Mr. L. I wanted to explain to you, Mr. President, about The Evening Post.[3] I bought that property very unexpectedly. I had always had in the back of my mind, the hope of some day controlling a newspaper property, this hope being based upon early associations of my family and of myself, but I had not wished the opportunity to come at present. Oswald Villard, however, came to the end of his tether. He found that he could no longer finance the proposition, losing money as it was under the handicap of his pacificist attitude in the war. If I had not bought the property, it would probably have gone to Frank Munsey, or somebody else like that.

Mr. P. That would indeed have been a calamity.

Mr. L. When I told Mr. Morgan[4] that I desired to buy the Evening Post, he considered a moment, and then said that he gave his consent provided it was clearly understood that neither he, nor any other member of the firm, nor the firm itself, had any interest in the property, and it was purely a personal venture on my part. To this condition I of course gladly assented. Then I determined to make it clear that the newspaper should be independent, in fact, as well as in form, and I trusteed the property, hoping, as I explained in my letter to you, Mr. President, that Ellery Sedgwick[5] would become active in connection with its affairs. Of course I have nothing to do with the daily management of the publication, but it has seemed to me that perhaps in the course of time I can help to accomplish two things: The first of these is the elimination of a certain fault-finding, or carping, attitude on the part of the Post that has been more or less traditional, and that has led it, as it has seemed to me, at times to make criticism without due consideration or complete study of all the facts.

Mr. P. I know just what you mean, Mr. Lamont. In the old days I always used to call the Evening Post the "whipping post."

Mr. L. The second point that I have in mind, Mr. President, is to help the publication in a constructive attitude, and here is where I come back to the subject of your Opera House speech of September 27th. Amidst all the applause that you received, I don't know whether you noticed that two sentiments of yours had little applause: one was when you said that "We must be just to those to whom we do not wish to be just." There was very little applause for that. The other was when you said that "We must conclude a

[3] That is, the New York *Evening Post*, which Lamont had purchased from Oswald Garrison Villard on August 2, 1918.

[4] Lamont was a partner in J. P. Morgan and Co. He of course referred to J. P. Morgan, Jr.

[5] Editor of *Atlantic Monthly* and president of the Atlantic Monthly Co., whom Lamont had appointed as one of the three trustees of the New York *Evening Post*.

peace satisfactory to all the belligerents." At that there was only one handclap in the whole house, and that was my wife's. I did not applaud that, because I don't see how in the world, Mr. President, you are ever going to conclude a peace satisfactory to Germany.

Mr. P. (Laughing) I am very much interested in what you say, Mr. Lamont.

Mr. L. Now Mr. President I come to the point. When you come to put into effect throughout the country the practical workings of these two sentiments of yours that I have quoted, I think you are going to have difficulty. The country is in a mood just now for war, and that mood is what is making the work of our soldiers in France so effective. We are necessarily intolerant and not ready as a whole to listen to such sentiments as you express.

Mr. P. Yes, not only intolerant, but we are growing revengeful, which, Mr. Lamont, is a very dangerous attitude and not one calculated to have us conclude the wisest sort of a peace.

Mr. L. Exactly! Now the Evening Post has considerable influence throughout the country, not because it has a wide circulation, because it has not, but because it is very largely quoted by other newspapers. And when the time comes I want to know how the Post can help you in educating the country properly. Can we, or ought we, in the near future, to undertake some sort of an educational campaign? What can we do to uphold you in your attitude in attaining a peace that is healing and permanent?

Mr. P. Well, I will answer that first by saying that, at the bottom, I believe that the peoples of all the Allies are with me in the sentiments that I have expressed. I believe that the peoples of Great Britain and of France are with me, just as well as of America. That does not, however, necessarily mean that the existing governments are of precisely the same mind. It is possible that the present administration in England has a narrower idea than I have of what should be done. For instance, you may have noticed that in their plans for an after-the-war trade, the British have appointed a lot of committees, made up of men who are ambitious to maintain Great Britain supreme commercially all over the world. They fail to "loosen up" even to us. They are reluctant to show even to America their hand on shipping questions, etc. The idea that that group of people has, in the way of a peace, is hardly one that would tend toward the permanent satisfaction of the world. For instance, take the case of the German Colonies; now we all know that throughout the world there has been a cry that England too completely dominates the sea as it is. Would not that cry be greatly intensified if these additional colonies should be placed in England's hands? Great Britain has certain ideas which she would like us to fall in with, but which we cannot. And even now she desires to put into our hands certain points of advantage, which, if we once possess them, we shall necessarily use when it comes to talking terms of peace, and, I say to you, that the United States does not desire to have any such positions of tactical advantage. Great Britain desires to have us adopt certain attitudes with respect to Russia which we do not think it wise for us to adopt. But, as I say, these are the ideas of a group of men, rather than the people of Great Britain, who, as I said before, I believe to be with me.

Now you ask how the Evening Post can assist in pointing out the dangers of a non-healing peace. In answer to that I should say that it would be wise to point out concretely from time to time precisely what the results will be of a peace concluded in any fashion other than the manner in which I have hitherto described. It is perfectly certain that if we concluded a peace that is not wholly just to every one of the large nations, then each one of those powerful nations will not rest contented until it has righted what it deems to be its wrongs. That of course means more wars. In the same way we must lean backwards in being just to the smaller nations, for equally in them lie the seeds of future trouble. If we are not careful we shall leave behind other Balkan situations in various parts of the world, smouldering fires that are banked but that will break out if we do not eliminate the cause of the fire beforehand. Get your Mr. Rollo Ogden to make a study of those banked fires. He is a student of history and editorials along this line will be most illuminating and helpful.

Mr. L. Your suggestions are very practical, Mr. President, and I thank you for them. About your league of nations, just how is it to be made effective? I am one of those who believe that economic force is about the only instrument which can serve to make a league of nations effective.

Mr. P. You mean, Mr. Lamont, to use economic force in the way of penalties?

Mr. L. No, Mr. President, not alone that, but to take economic force as the permanent constructive instrument for holding a league together and making it work. For example, let us look for a moment at the plan worked out, under your general direction, Mr. President, by Mr. Rublee and my partner Mr. Morrow[6] abroad, covering the pooling of raw materials and of shipping for the joint use of the Allies. You know even better than I that for a long time it was

---

[6] That is, George Rublee, who was at this time a member of the American delegation to the Allied Maritime Transport Council in London, and Dwight Whitney Morrow, a lawyer and a partner in J. P. Morgan and Co., at this time also an adviser to the American delegation to the Allied Maritime Transport Council.

impossible to obtain coordination among the Allies. Now they have attained it by means of the pooling of raw materials and of shipping. The plans that they have instituted cannot be cut off the moment war is over, as you know, and are likely to continue for some time anyway. Why not try to work out some scheme for their permanent continuance, a sort of international socialism on a great scale? In such event, no nation, such as Germany, would be able to pile up supplies of raw copper for years, looking forward to a war. Every member in the league of nations would have knowledge of the amount of basic raw materials produced and the general purposes for which they were being used. I mention all this purely as a possibility, no more. But it seems to me that the league of nations will not work if it is to be made dependent purely upon written rules, which our children or grandchildren can break if they see fit.

Mr. P. That's a very interesting suggestion, Mr. Lamont. Of course you understand that I have not in mind the thought of a written constitution for a league of nations. If I should go to the peace table with a written constitution for a league in my pocket, it could never be adopted, because probably no two of the nations could ever agree upon various provisions of it. It seems to me the best that we can hope to attain is to agree, at that peace time, upon certain immediate plans for conduct, arbitration of differences, etc., which we are bound to observe for a time under the shadow of the war just closed, and then adopt a plan for keeping each nation fully informed as to just what the other nation is doing. In these ways, before very long, we shall find that we have worked out a plan of procedure that will be far stronger than any written constitution would be, and such a plan will gradually become the law of the world.

Mr. L. Let me ask you again, Mr. President, reverting to your public speech at the Metropolitan Opera House, do you think that the allied governments are heart and soul with you in the various points of your speech?

Mr. P. That is very doubtful Mr. Lamont, but the people of those nations are, as I said before, and your inquiry leads me to say something to you that will sound very personal: I believe that at the present time I do enjoy extraordinary prestige abroad, and the maintenance of that prestige, I believe to be necessary to the proper handling of the peace problems. I used a phrase some months ago which has been much quoted, Mr. Lamont, I said that "Politics is adjourned." When I said that, of course I did not mean that we could do away entirely with politics. That is impossible. I did mean that any one, in the midst of war, who took some step for political advantage rather than a step destined purely for war purposes, was disloyal to his country. Now there is an election coming on, and I want to say to you that I believe it essential to the maintenance of my prestige abroad that we should re-elect a Democratic Congress. I am going to be very personal and tell you one or two little stories that will throw a little light on what I mean. In France there was a girls' school which was occupied by soldiers. I don't know whether they were American or French, but the school had quite extensive grounds, and the school girls wanted to go back and play on those grounds. The prefect refused to allow them. They took this refusal much to heart, and after a conference they sent a delegation to the prefect with the message—"Unless you allow us to do so we shall take the case up with President Wilson who is the final Court of Justice for the women of the world." There was another incident of more importance. The longshoremen in the harbor of Liverpool were on strike, and the authorities could apparently do nothing to compose the situation. Finally the harbor master called the strikers together, and said—"There are nineteen American vessels in this harbor waiting to discharge their cargoes and to be reloaded and you are holding up that work. Now I want to ask you what President Wilson will think of you when he hears what your attitude is?" And the longshoremen there and then agreed to go forward with the work. You will think me very conceited, Mr. Lamont, to quote these little stories to you, but I have a purpose in doing so, and, as you know, I am speaking to you inside these four walls. If a Republican Congress should be elected, the people of our own country would understand the matter perfectly, because we know how our constitution works. We know it is entirely possible, as in times past, for a Democratic president to have a Republican Congress on his hands. Furthermore, the members of the governments abroad would understand the situation, because they are students of history and of our political institutions. But the peoples of our Allies would never understand the matter. They would say that I had been repudiated, and such strength and power as I possess among them for the conclusion of the sort of peace that I have set my heart upon and that I see you are devoted to, would be gone.

There is another suggestion that I wish to make to you as to the domestic situation. When this war is over, Mr. Lamont, there will be great problems to settle, and I want to see them settled by professionals and not by amateurs. I call the radicals the amateurs. I want you and your associates to be assured that I am not a radical, but a moderate. I have the confidence of Labor, however, and I think that, all things considered, I am in a better position to lead in the satisfactory solution of these great problems than is a man like Theodore Roosevelt, for instance. Providentially I have been placed in a position at this time to have great power for good or ill. I see you smile, Mr. Lamont, when I use the word "providentially." I do not mean to indicate that it is necessarily a wise providence that has placed me in this position, but merely that circumstances have done so, and if these considerations that I have outlined to you appeal to you, perhaps you will wish, upon your return to New York, to bring these views to the attention of certain people over there.

Mr. L. Mr. President I am very much impressed with what you say as to your prestige abroad. That particular phase had not occurred to me, but I am a good deal impressed with that point of view. Frankly, I am not so much impressed with the consideration as to the domestic situation which you bring forward. But I am so impressed with the other point that I shall talk this over with various people in New York upon my return. Let me add, Mr. President, that I am a Republican, as you perhaps know, and I do not wish to give you the impression that my support will be given to you, thick and thin, for all time to come, but I want to have you know that you have that support to the very limit throughout the war, and I have been very much impressed with your attitude today. Thank you for receiving me so cordially and talking so freely.

Mr. P. I am indebted to you Mr. Lamont for comeing over, and I am very glad to have had a chance to see you. Good bye.

T MS (T. W. Lamont Papers, MH-BA).

To Edward Mandell House

My dear House: The White House 5 October, 1918.

I am returning these documents after giving them a very careful perusal. The scheme for the League of Nations is certainly most ambitious,[1] as is also the scheme for the study of reconstruction problems;[2] but we are tackling the matter of making the necessary studies about those problems, and I hope we shall work out some proper method which I can discuss with you later.

In haste,   Affectionately yours,   Woodrow Wilson

TLS (E. M. House Papers, CtY).
[1] Bates H. McFarland (a lawyer of St. Louis), "CONSTITUTION FOR A LEAGUE OF NA-TIONS (A Draft)," T MS (E. M. House Papers, CtY). It was indeed an ambitious plan. It created a league of nations, to be called "The Pax," which would have its own naval and military forces "to preserve peace, police the high seas, protect and regulate international communication between its members, and enforce its laws."
[2] That is, the memorandum cited in n. 1 to the extract from the House Diary printed at Sept. 28, 1918.

To Lee Slater Overman

[The White House]

My dear Senator Overman: 5 October, 1918.

I am clear, as you are, that Senator Weeks' resolution was not intended to be helpful but had a distinct political object, and a bill such as you propose is clearly better. I hope sincerely that such a bill will be matured.

Availing myself of your kind request for suggestions, let me say that I am afraid that you have made the scope of the inquiry too great for any single commission to compass. For example, the reorganization of government Departments, as you know, has been frequently studied and has required extended and minute labor on the part of commissions which have now gone out of existence. And as to the subject of the reorganization, financing, and readjustment of industries engaged in war work, this by itself would require the work of a most intelligent commission; and you know that there is already provided for by law a commission to inquire into inland transportation by rail and water.

I am taking the liberty of sending you a copy of a letter which the Secretary of Commerce wrote to Senator Pomerene on this general subject matter.[1] I subscribe to the views of that letter, for it seems to me a very wise and well-considered bit of comment and advice.

My personal advice therefore, Senator, since you have asked for it, is that the duties of the commission be stated in very general terms and be confined to the problems immediately arising out of the dislocation of commerce, industry, and labor, which have resulted from the war, and to the means which it would be wise to adopt to restore those whose economic ability has been impaired by the war to as full a participation as possible in the work of the country upon their return. I had intended in any case to appoint a commission of this sort, but I agree with the Secretary of Commerce that similar inquiries made in other countries have so far resulted in nothing that was practically useful, and that we ought to benefit by their example and merely make a premininary [preliminary] survey. Very truly yours, Woodrow Wilson

TLS (Letterpress Books, WP, DLC).
[1] It is missing in all collections.

To William Gibbs McAdoo

My dear Mac: [The White House] 5 October, 1918.

You are quite right about this resolution which you have turned over to me. I am enclosing a copy of a letter which I have just written to Senator Overman on the same subject.

Affectionately yours,   Woodrow Wilson

TLS (Letterpress Books, WP, DLC).

To Benedict Crowell

My dear Mr. Secretary: [The White House] 5 October, 1918.

The enclosed letter has given me a good deal of concern,[1] because it shows that in spite of the instructions given, somebody in your Department is still seeking out men and offering them opportunities to train for commissions.[2]

This is entirely contrary to the policy which it seems to me imperative we should follow, if we are to have a really *selective* service. Secretary Baker and I had agreed that the process of selecting men to be trained as officers was to be this: that from men of draft age who were actually drafted, there should be selected, after a brief experience of their quality, the men who seemed most likely to be serviceable as officers, and that these men and these men only should be sent to the officers' training camps.

You see how it works otherwise. Mr. Gutterson would not be drafted, but would under the principles we are following be put in one of the latest deferred classes, and yet though he would not be drafted, he is offered an opportunity to enter an Artillery Officers' Training Camp. Won't you be kind enough to look into this matter and tighten the screws all around?

Cordially and sincerely yours,   Woodrow Wilson

TLS (Letterpress Books, WP, DLC).
    [1] HCH to WW, Oct. 4, 1918, TLS (WP, DLC).
    [2] Hoover had written to Wilson about the "acute case" of Herbert Lindsley Gutterson, the head of the Division of Coordination of Purchase of the Food Administration, who had been offered admission to an artillery officers' training camp. As the only male member of a family which had been represented in every great war of the United States, Gutterson was eager to join the army. However, Hoover pointed out that Gutterson's experience and expertise made him absolutely indispensable to the Food Administration. Hoover asked Wilson to intervene, and he enclosed a draft of a letter (TL, WP, DLC) in which Wilson would request that Gutterson remain on his present job. Wilson did so in WW to H. L. Gutterson, Oct. 5, 1918, TLS (Letterpress Books, WP, DLC).

To Harry Andrew Wheeler

My dear Mr. Wheeler: [The White House] 5 October, 1918.

I appreciated very much your letter of October 3rd and am sincerely glad that the Board of Directors of the Chamber of Commerce of the United States took the position it did with regard to the proposed inquiry into problems of reconstruction.

I have for some time had in mind the appointment of such a commission as the resolutions of the Board suggest, and there is also a possibility that there will be legislative action concerning it, not along the lines of Senator Weeks' resolution, but along much saner and more practical lines.

I am very much interested in what you tell me of the attitude of business men everywhere towards difficult matters of this sort. I have no doubt that their valuable assistance would make inquiries of this sort very much easier than they would otherwise be.

Very truly yours,   Woodrow Wilson

TLS (Letterpress Books, WP, DLC).

From Robert Lansing, with Enclosures

My dear Mr. President: Washington October 5, 1918.

The report of Professor George D. Herron, enclosed in Mr. Sharp's letter of September 19th, is a most remarkable document. I started to glance through it and then began again and read every word. The correctness of Professor Herron's analysis of the psychology of the situation may be questioned, but whether it is correct or not I believe that you will find the report very interesting.

Faithfully yours,   Robert Lansing

E N C L O S U R E   I

My dear Mr. Lansing: Paris, September 19, 1918

A few days ago I received, through a gentleman coming from Geneva, a highly confidential letter from Professor George D. Herron, enclosing a report regarding the visit to him of Dr. de Fiori,[1] which he wished me to transmit to Washington.

On account of the nature of this report, as well as the Professor's letter to me, I have thought best to address to you a personal communication with regard to it rather than put it in the form of a despatch to the Department.

I am, my dear Mr. Lansing,

Sincerely yours,   W. G. Sharp.

¹ About Robert de Fiori and his earlier conversations with Herron, see WW to RL, July 8, 1918 (third letter of that date), its Enclosure, and n. 1 to the Enclosure, Vol. 48.

E N C L O S U R E   I I

George Davis Herron to William Graves Sharp

Dear Mr. Sharp: Geneva, Switzerland Sept. 12th 1918.

If you will turn to page 17 of this memorandum, you will see why I am asking you to send it, instead of sending it through our Legation at Bern, which is the usual channel of my memoranda to Washington.

I do not know if you know that, for some months past, I have been bearing the brunt of the German "peace offensives," and reporting the conversations to our State Department.

The Dr. de Fiori in question is the cleverest—and the sincerest also—of these peace messengers. He is connected with the Bavarian government, and in June and July brought direct proposals from the King and Cabinet of Bavaria for a peace initiative on their part among the German states, provided they could get a confidential encouragement from the President. Of course they could not, but I was instructed to keep the door open, even while giving no encouragement.

It was extremely important these conversations be kept strictly confidential. But, somehow, through indiscretion somewhere, rumors of them did get abroad, and Signor Sonnino sent to me to inquire about them, and other quarters knew.

So this time the messenger begged me to send my report in such way as not to have it seen by anyone in Switzerland. So I am fulfilling that request.

Should one keep strict honor with a German? some would ask. Yes, so far as I am concerned, I feel I must keep good faith with even a German. I am under a moral obligation to fulfill this man's request—especially since I am using him to get at the interior condition of Germany and report it to our government. It seems to me a matter of honor to do what he asks.

May I ask you to keep the sending of this in your own hands as nearly as possible. No one in Europe is supposed to know about these conversations except Mr. Balfour, to whom I send duplicates by arrangement.

Usually, the substance of the reports has gone by cable (coded of course) and the full report followed by the first Washington pouch.

You are at perfect liberty to accompany this report with any comments or observations of your own. Indeed, I should be very glad to have you do so.

I hope I am not putting you to too much trouble, dear Mr. Sharp, and not imposing on your conscience, by asking you to help me bear the burden which this German messenger has put upon mine. I think you, at least, will agree with me that we must keep good faith, we must fulfill a strict code of honor, even in dealing with a German.

With heartiest greetings, I remain,

Faithfully Yours,   George D. Herron

TLS (WP, DLC).

ENCLOSURE III

THE FOURTH VISIT OF DR. DE FIORI.

Geneva, September 10th, 1918.

I.

For the fourth time Dr. de Fiori, the most confidential and an[n]ointed of the German peace agents, has come and gone. This time he presented a credential from the German Foreign Office in the form of a letter addressed to himself, saying that he was authorized to carry on these negotiations, but that Germany could not go into details of what she would do until it was known what propositions the other side—that is, the Entente and especially America—had to make. It was notic[e]able, at the outset of our conversations and all through his presentations and appeals, that Dr. de Fiori was this time speaking directly for Berlin; Bavaria did not separately come into the conversations, nor was there any renewal of the former propositions from a Bavarian standpoint.

It seemed, when all was said, that Dr. de Fiori had come with a view to impressing upon me one special point, and of obtaining an answer to one special question. The point was this: *that the moment had now arrived when President Wilson, by proposing definite and reasonable terms of peace to Germany in the name of the Entente, could win a complete moral victory over the German people without the necessity of pursuing the complete military victory.* And this was the question: *Is there some way by which Germany may convey official propositions to America, either through a neutral power or through myself, and be sure that these official propositions shall*

be kept strictly confidential—not to be made public unless a fa-
vorable result should be reached, when, naturally, it would be in
order to announce such result to the world?

II.

But before taking up our discussion—(or rather his discussions, for what I said was little,)—of the point and the question with which he came, let me present several incidental matters wherewith the discussions were prefaced.

(a.) On his way to Geneva, Dr. de Fiori was in conference with Scheidemann at Bern, and came directly from Scheidemann to me. Scheidemann authorized him to say to me that Troelstra's[1] attitude and propositions did not represent the Majority Socialists of Germany. Scheidemann had never said that the question of Alsace-Lorraine was undebatable. On the contrary, he believed that an arrangement could be arrived at that would be satisfactory alike to Germany and to France, and that the German Majority Socialists were ready to discuss such an arrangement. Dr. de Fiori added that Scheidemann and Troelstra had a difference at Interlaken, and had had nothing to do with each other since. It is a singular fact, though doubtless Scheidemann would not exactly express it so, that *the separation took place because Troelstra was much too Germano-phile for Scheidemann.*

(b.) I raised with Dr. de Fiori the question of a Professor Dr. Hertz,[2] another peace messenger now in Switzerland, whose visit I was expecting. This Dr. Hertz, who is a voluminous writer on economic and sociological subjects, had previously arrived in Bâle, and from there had sent me his request for an interview, and credentials showing him to be chief of a department in the German War Office. (At the same time he is connected with the Austrian War Office: I have not been able to make out the connection between his two positions) Dr. Hertz, however, ere he reached me, fell victim to the "Spanish grippe," which affected him very seriously and sent him to the mountains to convalesce. He had just notified me to expect him, and so I inquired of Dr. de Fiori, who answered my inquiry by holding up his hands with what was at least a semblance of horror; and, finally, Dr. de Fiori begged me to be much on my guard against Dr. Hertz.

Apparently, there are two camps of German peace messengers in Switzerland, as well as in Germany itself, one representing the

[1] Pieter Jelles Troelstra, founding member and leader of the Dutch Social-Democratic Workers' Party and a member of the executive committee of the International Socialist Bureau.
[2] Friedrich Otto Hertz, professor of political science and economics, at this point without an academic position. He was later Counselor of the Chancellery of the Austrian Republic.

more liberal peace sentiment, and the other representing more distinctly the Prussian idea of peace. I say apparently, for all this may be stage-play and camouflage for my special benefit—or rather in order that I may report fictitious German differences to America. These ostensibly opposite camps may be merely two wings of the peace offensive. Perhaps I can form a clearer opinion of this when I have seen Dr. Hertz. The same thing might be surmised concerning Scheidemann and Troelstra—though I am somewhat of the opinion that an actual difference *has* taken place between these two men, and that, in one way or another, Troelstra's whole campaign has been a disastrous failure.

(c.) Dr. de Fiori said that, through an indiscretion somewhere— of which indiscretion he would speak later—rumors of our previous conversations had reached Italy and especially Sonnino, and had also gotten about Germany. But it was Italy of which he wished especially to speak. He begged me to convey to such Italians as I could, especially to Marquis Paulucci,[3] the Italian Minister at Bern, that he (Dr. de Fiori) would under no circumstances favor or promote any propositions which could be considered injurious to Italy. He wanted it known that he was Italy's good friend, and would think of her best future in all efforts he should make for peace.

(d.) He wanted to warn me that certain Americans—he would not tell me whom—had seen him in Thun, and tried to dissuade him from seeing me again, declaring that I was a person of no consequence or authority whatever—(which may all be true enough;) that it was useless to talk with me; that there were others with whom he had better talk. He intimated that these were Americans of position.* This again may be more camouflage: I do not know: I merely set it down as incident of his last visit, because I wish to make this memorandum inclusive.

(e.) He dwelt at considerable length upon a desire that I should say to the German Government through him: "I told you so." He related how little belief the German Government formerly had in America's purpose regarding the war, even when he presented my first emphatic and ample statements regarding America's purpose and preparations in June. After the second visit, when Count Hertling had become convinced, and had the fifteen or sixteen copies of de Fiori's report of his interview with me made for distribution, then the German Government began to believe and tremble before America's determination to prosecute the war with all her resources

---

[3] Baron Giacomo Paulucci di Calboli.

* *Were they the American financiers (or their representatives) who are hoping to capture the Bagdad railway concessions through procuring for Bulgaria the separate peace—and permission for further conquests—which Bulgaria is plotting for, and for which the financiers darkly plot also? Or were they a fiction?*

of men and materials. But even then, the projected offensive was not held back, but was pursued blindly and stubbornly, and to the disaster of Germany. Dr. de Fiori wanted me emphatically to point out that if Germany had asked for peace instead of pussuing [pursuing] this offensive she could have had better conditions than she will now ever again be able to obtain; and that every day she pursues the war is making harder the conditions which her enemies, and above all America, will impose. The German peoples were all against the offensive, so Dr. de Fiori says, and only the military camarilla and the dynasty persisted in it. And now the disaster is so complete that there can be no question of another German offensive. All that Germany can now hope for is a defensive war, making her long retreat as costly and exhaustive as possible to her enemies.

Dr. de Fiori seemed to imagine that if I would dwell much upon this, "I told you so," emphasizing and amplifying it, it might have some effect in turning some members of the German Government towards reason now.

I merely listened to Dr. de Fiori's request, but made no response to it beyond telling him that *he* could remind his chiefs of my former statements, and use them with as much emphasis as possible; but that I did not care to present these reminders myself.

(f.) Dr. de Fiori stated that the best and most convincing information which they had ever had in Germany concerning American determination and organization for the war had been given them through him as coming from me. I took advantage of this statement to tell him that if Germany did not immediately and unconditionally sue for peace, I feared there would not be a great deal of Germany left to sue, if she waited until American preparations were complete. I informed him that we were making between four and five hundred war-planes a day, well and powerfully equipped; that we should probably have four million American soldiers in France by early spring, amply provided for in every particular; that it would be quite impossible to stop this army, once it was on its march to Berlin; that once our war-planes had all assembled on the Rhine, it would even be doubtful if there would be any Berlin left to march to.

In this connection, Dr. de Fiori raised the question as to why the war-planes were now bombarding Cologne daily and did not fly over Essen. Of course, I did not answer his question.

(g.) He stated that in all probability Hertling would soon have to go. He was not strong enough to stand against the Great General Staff and the dynasty on one side, nor was he strong enough to take the leadership of a real movement for peace on the other. Hertling will have to go, and probably a military dictatorship will be the early result—*unless* (and this I give with his own emphasis)—*unless President Wilson can and will encourage the German people (by some personal message) to believe they can have a reasonable peace if they rise against their government. There is no use in their rising, they have no heart to do so, unless they have some assurance, or at least intimation, that their compulsory action against their own government will not result in the ruin or division or substantial imprisonment of Germany.*

III.

I will now take up our more especial conversations, at which the confidential stenographer who reported our previous conversations was present. It will be noticed that Dr. de Fiori is not altogether coherent or sequential, but I give his statements in his own order and language.

Herron: What is the general effect on the German people of the present adverse military situation? They must know that the offensive has failed, and failed disastrously.

Dr. Fiori: Those who believe in the mission of President Wilson, and were therefore against the offensive, because they wanted to protect the interests of humanity, think the same as a man thinks who has been hurt by somebody whom he loves. We looked to Wilson to save us, and Wilson seems now determined to destroy us.

You must have seen what has happened in Germany, these last days. Dr. Solf and the Kronprinz von Baden have said all that could be said.[4] Nobody has any more illusions about a new offensive: there can be no offensive after this: we only fight for our existence.

The Social-Democratic Party and the people are convinced that the war must be closed now, and that the principles I have discussed with you ought to be and shall be the real basis for peace discussions. If you examine the state of things in Germany now, you will find that those who until now have "smiled with one side of the mouth and bitten with the other," are acting very differently—facts convince even the most unwilling.

[4] In a speech to representatives of the press at the German Society in Berlin on August 20, 1918, Wilhelm Solf, the Secretary of State for the Colonies, had delivered a spirited reply to Balfour's address in the House of Commons of August 8, 1918 (about which, see the London *Times*, Aug. 9, 1918). Two days later, Prince Maximilian von Baden had addressed the Baden Diet on the occasion of the centennial of the state's constitution. Prince Max later commented on the two speeches as follows: "Solf and I both professed our adherence to the peace of understanding and to the ideals of humanity, but we appealed as earnestly as we could to the people to fight to the death against the enemy rulers whose wish was to destroy us and who would have nothing to do with negotiations. Our speeches were intended to strike a conciliatory note to the opposition parties in the enemy countries, but to be a 'fanfare' against Lloyd George and Clemenceau." Prince Max von Baden, *The Memoirs of Prince Max von Baden*, W. M. Calder and C. W. H. Sutton, trans. (2 vols., New York, 1928), I, 325. The two speeches are printed in *Schulthess' Europäischer Geschichtskalender*, LIX (1918), Part 1, pp. 254-59 and 261-64.

What is our program, and the program of the friends of Wilson in Germany? Inviolability of the Empire; arrangements of understanding in all political, economical, and ethical questions; re-consideration of all the questions of the East by the Peace Conference; the Society of Nations; Prussia and Germany democratized—(but this we shall do ourselves;)—all this can be discussed in Germany now.

There is only one question that keeps back the Volksparty[5] from acting and thereby enforcing peace: the question of the seas and of the colonies. I have already said that if President Wilson—whose principles would surely be accepted today in Germany—if President Wilson on these conditions would be ready to mediate between England and Germany, peace could be had.

I repeat: the restoration of Belgium and the evacuation of France without conditions. Arrangement concerning Alsace-Lorraine; reconsideration of the questions of the East—Poland, Russia, Asia Minor, Asia, Turkey, the Mediterranean, Serbia, Italian Austria; the Society of Nations and disarmanent—for all these we are ready, if Wilson will mediate in the colonial questions, in the questions of the sea.

But if Wilson lets himself be driven on by his military people—(though I think this is excluded because I have the highest opinion of Wilson, believing that his zest does not come of his head but of his heart, and that it is therefore metaphysical[*]) then Germany must fight till she is ruined utterly. But you may believe me that Germany, through the terrible happenings of these four years, has reached the knowledge of how necessary it is that she shall live in fellowship and equality with other peoples. You may believe me that the class that till now had the upper hand in Germany will not have it any more. Even the last speech of Count Hertling says that the pan-Germans have lost their power.[6] If President Wilson be-

---

[5] That is, the left-liberal Fortschrittliche Volkspartei (Progressive Peoples' Party).

[*] I wonder what he means by "metaphysical"!

[6] De Fiori was probably referring to Hertling's speech to the Main Committee of the Reichstag on July 11, 1918. After reaffirming Germany's adherence to the terms of the peace of Brest-Litovsk, Hertling commented at length on the Belgian question. He argued that, from the beginning of the war, Germany had never intended to annex Belgium. The occupation of Belgium had been a military necessity, and Germany was holding Belgium at present merely as a "pawn for future negotiations" and as a "safeguard against certain dangers." To Germany, Hertling maintained, the war had always been a war of defense, never one of conquest. As long as the Allies were bent upon complete destruction of Germany, the country would hold out, confident of its army, its military leadership, and the indomitable spirit of its "magnificent people." However, if serious efforts toward peace would emerge anywhere, Germany would certainly not adopt a negative attitude toward them but would pursue them in all earnestness. "If such possibilities manifest themselves," Hertling declared, "if serious inclinations toward peace show themselves on the other side, we will immediately take them up. That is to say, we will not reject them, and we will speak, to begin with, in a small circle." During a debate on Hertling's address on the next day, the Chancellor briefly reiterated

lieves this, then he will see that the power of the Sword of the Spirit which he has drawn is greater than the material sword, and that the spiritual sword will triumph in the end.

But if Wilson lets himself be led on, and does not take advantage of the present disposition of the Germans to make peace, if he listens to his militarists—who easily become the same in all countries once they are victorious—then even those among us who today would be ready for a peace of reconciliation and of freedom will take our weapons in hand and fight for the existence of Germany. Then we shall probably entrench ourselves between Lille and Maubeuge, perhaps be driven back more and more, perhaps lose the Rhine Provinces; then, when everything is ruined, not only in Belgium, but also in Germany, you will be victorious—but nothing will be left any more.

If Wilson knew that we are ready to go his way, that we have bled enough, that he only needs to say the good word and we would respond, then this would be his greatest triumph, and no monument could be found big enough for him in Germany. I am convinced that, if Wilson would do this, there could be no greater deed in history.

I might illustrate what I mean by something I saw once: an Englishman and an American were fighting together. The American beat the Englishman very badly, and with every stroke he said: "There, let it be enough and be good." The Englishman would not listen, and went on beating back, till finally the American had him on the floor. The American said: "Will you be good now?" But the Englishman answered: "No, I will not." But the American left him on the floor and went away, saying: "That will do; you have had enough."

President Wilson must know that the disposition of the German people is now such that a democratic constitution of the State could be enforced, and the participation of Germany in the League of Nations also. The restoration of Belgium and the re-considering of the Eastern questions will be no hindrance. The only hindrance of a unified action of all parliamentary parties (with exception of the Junkers to whom Hertling himself gave the death-warrant) is the uncertainty concerning the question whether President Wilson will put the inviolability of Germany, the question of the seas and of

---

his main points and concluded as follows: "We are conducting the war as a war of defense. Since we are leading a war of defense, and since any imperialistic tendency toward world domination has been far from our thoughts from the beginning of the war, our peace objectives will correspond to this. What we want is the inviolability of our territory, a breathing space for the development of our people, particularly in the economic realm, and, of course, also the necessary safeguard against difficult conditions in the future." See *Schulthess'*, LIX, 237-41.

the colonies, upon his program. All other questions will be settled peacefully by the German people. Of course, there are differences of opinion, and the formulaes will have to be found for all, otherwise precious time is lost. But the foundations I have proposed will be accepted by all: Belgium, the Eastern questions, Alsace-Lorraine, Italian Austria.

Again I ask: will President Wilson mediate in the questions between England and Germany? If President Wilson does not mediate peace, then the war will go on till we are on the floor, even should Berlin be taken.

Two things we cannot discuss: first, territorial questions; second, the question of the colonies must be settled. Shall Germany be cut into pieces? Shall her colonies be taken from her? If so we shall rather fight to the end.

Herron: Do you believe it possible that President Wilson could win a spiritual victory over Germany? If there was the right kind of appeal, would Germany surrender to this appeal?

De Fiori: Yes, if President Wilson gives out a proclamation, in which he mentions that it is not possible to come to a satisfactory peace without these two fundamental questions being solved: first, our German States shall remain what they are, providing they change their mentality; second, all nations shall have the possibilities of colonial development which they need, and according to their interests. On this foundation we are ready to begin discussions. But if he refuses it, we shall go on fighting because we must.

Herron: The feeling in America is getting to be beyond peace discussions: Germany must surrender first, and then we may talk of peace. It will be difficult to turn back this feeling that Germanism can only be destroyed by the sword. Even the President could not change this if he would.

I do not want to debate now the question as to whose fault it is that the war began. But as a matter of historical data, it was Germany who began the war. As a matter of historical data, Germany ought to take it upon herself to finish the war. Let Germany make her propositions to President Wilson in an open, regular and official way through a neutral power. You might possibly arrive, in this way, to some discussion and definite issue. But I am convinced that there is no possibility of achieving the end which you desire in any other way. I am absolutely certain that, even were I disposed to do so, it would be utterly useless for me to make the inquiry you desire of the President. I cannot conceive of the remotest chance of peace coming out of these personal discussions. If Germany wants peace, she must openly and officially say so, and state the terms upon which she is ready to make it.

De Fiori: You agreed upon another plan, some time ago. You said if a confidential question was put by a high official personality in Germany, you would find a way to send it to the President and get a confidential answer.

Herron: O no; I said I might find a way of *sending* the question to the President, but that I had not the remotest hope of getting an answer.

De Fiori: If I remember rightly, you said to me, on the fifteenth of June, on the eighth of July, and on the eighteenth of July: "If Germany wants to send an official demand in the interest of a general peace to Wilson, on the basis of Wilson's Four Principles, I am ready to send this question in the form of a confidential communication to President Wilson."

Herron: Yes, if Germany makes an *official* demand, I might find a way to send it: I do not take back the word I spoke: I can perhaps transmit such an official but confidential communication. But I am certain it would be useless and bring forth no answer. I have an overwhelming impression that the President will not listen to any overtures that are not openly made, and made through the regular diplomatic channels.

But let me revert to the East again. Do you say that Germany is willing, other conditions being fulfilled, to put the whole question of the East on the Peace Table, just as if Brest-Litovsk had not taken place?

De Fiori: There is no doubt about this. But one must not be too difficult, and not dwell too much on appearances. Hertling has, even in his own way, admitted the restoration of Belgium. Kühlmann has declared in the Reichstag that peace is not possible without a new discussion of the East. Solf has admitted directly the restoration of Belgium, and has declared that the peace of Brest-Litovsk and of Bucarest are only a "cornice" which can contain many things. Even the German Kronprinz[7] has spoken. Those are all men who have become converted, and they will declare that Germany will not make war except for her own defence. Count Hertling declared yesterday, in the Chamber of Lords, that if Prussia is not democratized, then the dynasty is in danger.[8] I should be interested to know what effect these declarations have had in America and England. After all, they are official manifestations. Why should not the other side put some equally official question. Let America ask: Is this all sincere? Then we shall answer: Certainly it is sincere.

Shall the war really go on to the destruction of Germany which,

[7] That is, Friedrich Wilhelm Viktor August Ernst, Crown Prince of Prussia and of the German Empire. For his remarks to the *Neues Wiener Journal* of September 4, 1918, see *Schulthess'*, LIX, 269-70.

[8] See *ibid.*, pp. 270-71.

according to human possibilities, is not excluded? After all, Germany is worth more than the few Junkers, and our defeat and destruction cannot be easily had. It may cost you millions of lives. Now our German peoples are ready to meet you, if you offer them the hand of peace. But if you leave the word to the soldier, then we shall be all as one man behind our front. Do you want to destroy a flourishing people which, after all, is innocent, merely in order to punish our guilty government?

Herron: I have said that, if you wish to bring me this confidential but *official* request, I will try to obtain its transmission. But I also want to repeat that the only way by which you can accomplish the end which you seek lies in persuading your government to take the initiative—proposing peace, stating the terms. There is no other way. And I see the possibility, if Germany would take this step, of opening discussions that might lead, at last, to peace; but there is no other way for accomplishing this end—except in war that leads to your deserved destruction.

De Fiori: We go round in a circle. I am convinced that, if we take this initiative, you will say to us: Give back Alsace-Lorraine, give back Prussian Poland, etc. etc.

If President Wilson does not take the initiative, then the war will go on. You will have successes; you will have reverses; we, also, shall have successes and reverses; and so together we go in the blind and red circle.

Germany cannot propose peace now. Yet it is terrible that we cannot find some form of salvation—some way to meet.

Herron: You can: surrender: ask for peace: state your terms. You began the war: the whole world has paid the price of defending itself against you: end the war, and trust the world's mercy and justice.

De Fiori: Can an official demand be confidentially sent through a neutral power?

Herron: I suppose it is possible, though I do not know. If you want to try, ask the Swiss Government to address the American Government confidentially on your behalf.

De Fiori: No, Switzerland would not do it. Ador,[9] who was opposed by the Germans, might do it. But not Schulthess and Calonder.[10] They are afraid that it might not be well looked upon by England.

Herron: What about Holland?

[9] That is, Gustave Ador, at this time head of the Domestic Department of the Swiss Federal Council (the cabinet).

[10] Edmund Schulthess, head of the Economic Department of the Swiss Federal Council, and Felix Ludwig Calonder, President of the Swiss Federal Council and head of its Political Department (the Foreign Ministry).

De Fiori: Yes, what?

Herron: I still believe that the only way that offers the smallest chance of success is that of formally, openly and officially asking for peace—or for discussion of peace upon stated terms.

De Fiori: What is your personal opinion?—if this demand goes directly to President Wilson through Holland or Switzerland, would the President take the standpoint that an understanding is possible on the basis of the Bavarian terms I discussed with you?

Herron: I can express no opinion, for I have no knowledge on which to base one. I *do* have a strong opinion that there is a chance of arriving at the discussion of peace if Germany formally and openly addresses the President, through the medium of a neutral government, asking him to address America's Allies. But it must be done before the whole world. Then perhaps President Wilson would be ready to receive the request, and to inquire of the Entente Powers if they were ready to discuss with you. A conclusion might be reached in the end. I see no chance in any other method of approach.

De Fiori: Professor Herron, I have discovered that some knowledge, or at least intimations, of the contents of our previous conversations have gotten abroad through the indiscretion of someone in Switzerland. I therefore make to you this most urgent and sacred request: That your report of this conversation, to whomsoever you report it in America, shall not be sent from Switzerland, but from Paris or London. Some person who is in close relation with the President, for instance your Ambassador in Paris, could be the channel of communication. The conditions here are now such, with the innumerable spies of all countries penetrating everywhere and even deciphering telegraphic codes, and with the overcrowding of the Legations with employees, that you yourself must see that it is nearly impossible for anything to be kept really confidential in Switzerland, or to be confidentially transmitted through any agency in Switzerland. I therefore hope you will find a way to comply with this request, in order that these conversations may not be discovered and interrupted; for I still hope, in spite of all discouragements, that we shall find a way, through these conversations, to bring this ruinous conflict to a good and reconciling conclusion. I still hope that we may make a peace of understanding, if you will keep the door open, and not let it be blocked.

IV: OBSERVATIONS AND CONCLUSIONS.

(A.) It will be noticed that Dr. de Fiori had no new terms to present, and that he added but little, in the way of direct information, to his former conversations. The significance of this visit lies in its angle of approach. Dr. de Fiori came frankly seeking to shift the moral responsibility of the German people to the shoulders of President Wilson. Of course, he was quite unaware—or was he?— of the immorality of his appeal.

The case is this: the German Government, the Junkers and the dynasty, will take no honest or open step toward peace: they will fight till the last citizen has fallen, until the last German babe dies on their behalf. The peoples of the German States begin to be aware of this: they want peace while they are still alive: but they are so accustomed to brutish docility, they are so trained to distrust all other peoples, that they have neither the force nor the courage to rise in revolt against their government, or to make an open appeal to the nations in arms against them. Will President Wilson take upon himself the burden that belongs to them? Will he take for them the initiative they ought to take for themselves? And, furthermore, will he do it in such a way as to save Germany from the appearance of having been in the wrong?

With Dr. de Fiori, as with all other Germans with whom I have conversed, the chief question is how so to end the war as to save Germany from the humiliation of repentance and confession. The conservation of Germany's national pride—I use the word advisedly, for Germany knows not the alphabet of national honor—more than the revelation of righteousness to her people, is the basis of each responsible messenger's quest for peace.

There is no use in our expecting the German mind, at its best, to revolve upon Anglo-Saxon wheels. The entire mental machinery of the German is antipodal to that of the Anglo-Saxon, and defies Anglo-Saxon analysis. The German's thinking apparatus is not built as the Anglo-Saxon's is built. The difference between the two is so great as to defy interpretative or communicative connection. Even the effort to grasp the German's mind, to get inside its processes, has the effect of deranging the intent Anglo-Saxon inquirer.

I spent the greater part of a night, at the end of January—or was it February?—trying to get Conrad Haussmann—who was at that time Acting Vice-Chancellor—face to face with one or two moral concepts as regards international relations and national decency. It was as if I were endeavoring to persuade a mid-African cannibal to read the essays of John Stuart Mill. The face of the man, as he was evidently straining for some mental connection with the idea of national righteousness, became at times like that of the lunatic one sees among the incurably but harmlessly insane. I came from this interview, as I have come from other interviews of the kind, feeling myself positively unhinged by my efforts to get somehow and vicariously inside this German mentality. Furthermore, after

each case, I always have a sense of needing to hang my soul somewhere in the sun, in order to bleach it clean of its contact with
something fundamentally unclean in the German spirit.

Men such as Dr. de Fiori, Professor Foerster and Professor Jaffe[11]
represent the German at his best. They are the very highest that
the German spirit can offer to the world today. Yet even these cannot
or will not stand erect, and manfully shoulder a responsibility for
telling the truth to the German people. They will not bid the German
peoples rise and shake off their monstrous mental and governmental tyranny. They will not ask, nor permit the German people
to ask, from the Entente powers a fellowship of help that implies
any responsibility on Germany's part for the infernal flood she has
let loose for the devastation of the world.

So whatever we do about Germany, whether or no we try to help
the German people to their moral feet before utter ruin overtakes
them, we shall have to begin with the understanding that they are
a pathological people—they are moral primitives. They are as innocent of good and evil, of even the stuff out of which good and
evil are made, as the South sea tribes that looked on the face of
the first English navigator.

(B.) Yet Something—or Some One?—forbids me to leave unasked
the question of whether or no there is a way to reach the German
peoples before they helplessly resign themselves, according to the
will of their masters, to ruin by our armies—or before the nerves
of the nation break, and a condition of national hysteria ensues,
resulting in the complete disappearance of all social order or civil
control. We have to consider, too, what will be the reaction upon
ourselves if we are forced to the necessity—as well we may be—of
Germany's utter destruction. Or we must think that [what] the
reaction will be if—as is also quite possible—the whole German
Empire becomes suddenly the sphere of an inconceivable Satur-
nalia of both ancient and original crimes.

I cannot leave unasked the question as to whether or not we
have a responsibility for dealing with these peoples—peoples yet
without moral birth or experience. Shall we treat tham [them] as
the village constable treats the mad dog loose in the streets? Or
shall we treat them somehow as the missionary treats the primitive
tribes among whom he goes, knowing that these have no knowledge
of the difference between mercy and cruelty, truth and lies—even
knowing that they may eat him tomorrow? Does there rest upon
America and the Entente Powers the duty of approaching the Ger-

---

[11] That is, Friedrich Wilhelm Foerster and Edgar Jaffé.

man peoples from something like a redemptive standpoint, and this in the face of the inferno which Germany has flung so deeply upon the world?

I would not dare to say that an appeal could not be made to the German peoples today—an appeal of such quality as to awaken in them some beginnings of a grateful and creative response, moving them to an effectual revolt against their masters and their past, paralyzing the power of these masters for further resistance. We need not make such childish propositions for peace as Dr. de Fiori and the Bavarians ask for. But we can make our own propositions, our own appeal. We can state to the German peoples their crime against the world—state it in terms of high and stern tenderness, showing them the result of the crime upon themselves, upon humanity; showing them also their present abandoned plight, and the promise of greater woe and ignominy to come. We can ask them if it is not time they waken to judgment and righteousness—if it is not time they repent and enter into the fellowship of free peoples. We can demand that they surrender the peoples who are unwillingly bound to them—Alsace-Lorraine, Prussian Poland, Schleswig-Holstein, and all the peoples that were yoked by the treaties of Brest-Litovsk and Bucarest. We can summon them to break now their Prussian yoke, to send away their Prussian dynasty—in fine, to change their minds instantly and altogether and truly.

I do not say we *should* make this appeal: I only say we *can*. I am well enough aware of the seeming absurdity of making it. But I dare not leave the question unasked. *Are* we now divinely obliged to make some such last appeal to the German peoples—ere we irrevocably march to their destruction.

I am as certain as I am of our mortal existence that if, three months ago, we had called for the Society of Nations, this offensive in France would have been paralyzed. Knowing what I do now of the inner conditions of Germany, knowing what I now know of the interrogations that are rising before every German cross-roads, I am convinced that there was a moment when, if the summons to enter the Society of Nations had then been before them, the German peoples would have refused to march, or to let their armies march, again against France.

Furthermore, the widening and menacing pacifist movement that is now deep, though more or less hidden, in England and France and Italy, would not have been—if our Governments had then made the Great Call.

That was the psychological hour—three months ago. It may not yet be too late to win a moral and political victory over Germany by the sending forth of the call. But the sands of the hour are running low. And soon the hour, with its unreturning opportunity, will have sunk into eternity. Nothing, then, is left but the sword. And, besides the sword, we shall have to forge weapons wherewith to meet that other and viler war which will then prevail—if the German masters keep their power over their peoples—that psychic war wherewith they may wrest an ultimate victory, even round the Table of Peace, from an overwhelming military defeat. Or, if not this, then we shall have to deal with the German domestic debacle of which I have spoken—a debacle disclosing undreamed-of moral abysses in our humanity.

Germany is near to breaking up, I believe. Ought we, or ought we not, give the German peoples this last opportunity for repentance?—the opportunity that would lie in such a call to the German peoples as I have indicated, or in a call for the immediate establishment of the Society of Nations? Does there rest upon us the responsibility for vicariously entering into and trying to transmute the primitive moral irresponsibility of the German peoples? Is it now our duty at this military juncture, to give these peoples a lead? Shall we make a divine gamble? Shall we take one last chance— the sort of chance God seems always taking with this sorry human pilgrimage of ours—shall we take one last chance that the German peoples may rise and righteously revolt? If we give them a divine lead and they follow it—as it is not absolutely impossible they may— then from either further stolid and suicidal obedience to their masters, or else from a bestial and really infernal anarchy, they may be at once and surprisingly saved. And we may also render to some millions of our sons careers of creative living instead of the certainty of sacrificial dying. And if the German peoples fail to respond and arise, once we have made our last effort to reach them morally— to win a spiritual as well as a military victory—then our souls will be clean of guilt, our shields will be stainless, and we shall be sure that the sword wherewith we destroy Germany is none other than the Sword of God.

I do not *say* this question should be answered or even considered: I only say I dare not leave it unasked. It is for you who read these words to ignore or to answer it: I can only obey some imperious provocation of the soul—obey it against all my predilections or conceptions of what is probable or sensible—and stand the question before you. Shall we—will you—through convoking the delegates who shall initiate the Society of Nations, or through a mighty appeal to the German peoples, give them their last and undeserved chance to repent—to repent before we move on, as we shall otherwise have to move on, to their final and utter destruction.

It may be God's question I stand before you, if you are great enough to have it so. Or it may be a question that is altogether and fatally foolish. It is for you to whom I commit this question—for you sit in the places of high decision—to consider the question or ignore or condemn it.

Respectfully submitted,   George D. Herron

TS MS (WP, DLC).

From Robert Lansing, with Enclosure

My dear Mr. President: Washington October 5, 1918.

I enclose a memorandum which contains a message from Mr. Balfour, repeated by Sir William Wiseman on the 4th to Mr. Auchincloss, in relation to the Sisson papers regarding Lenine and Trotsky which were published three or four weeks ago here and which the British Government prevented from publication in Great Britain.

In view of the fact that publication in Great Britain so long after the documents were given to the press in this country would be of no particular benefit, and, furthermore, as the whole subject has no longer public interest or comment more than a discussion as to the genuineness of the documents, I would suggest that we advise the British Government that since there has been so much delay in publishing them it would seem unwise now to do so. I am sure that this course would avoid further embarrassment and explanation.

Will you be good enough to indicate to me your wishes in the matter in order that I may reply to Mr. Balfour through Sir William?

Faithfully yours,   Robert Lansing

TLS (WP, DLC).

E N C L O S U R E

October 4, 1918.

MEMORANDUM.

Sir William Wiseman told me today that he had had a message from Mr. Balfour to the following effect:

The English experts and authorities had gone over carefully the Sisson papers and had come to the definite conclusion that they were forgeries. Consequently the British Government were very reluctant to publish them. Mr. Barclay has been instructed to advise the American Government that if the United States, in view of this information, still wish these papers to be published, the British Government would be willing to publish them after British subjects had been withdrawn from regions occupied by the Bolshiviks. The British Government will be glad if they could be advised of the reasons which influence the United States Government in requesting that these papers be published.

Mr. Balfour wished the President to be advised that he would have these papers published if he, the President, wished it, in spite of the opinion of the British authorities that the papers were forgeries.   G. A.

TI MS (WP, DLC).

From Winthrop More Daniels

My dear Mr. President: Washington October 5, 1918.

At Mr. Taft's request, some five of the Commissioners held an informal conference with him this morning in Commissioner McChord's[1] office. Mr. Taft spoke for himself and Mr. Walsh, as members of the Federal Wage Commission.[2] He expressed the hope that members of our Commission,[3] if you requested their advice, would consider favorably recommending the creation of a Federal tribunal possessing only advisory power but intended to give recommendations as to the propriety of increased fares for street railway companies in various localities.

Mr. Taft said that he was certain that in many instances street railway companies were on the verge of bankruptcy; that he and Mr. Walsh felt that in a sense they themselves contributed to the difficulties of the street railways by recommending necessary wage increases in instances where the street railroads could not get an offsetting increase in revenue. He said that their work as a Wage Commission would be very greatly helped if in a given instance, such as New Orleans where the Wage Commission recommended a specific increase in wages per hour, the suggested Federal tribunal should at the same time indicate what was a reasonable increase in passenger fares to offset the increased wages bill and other expenses.

Mr. Taft said that only about 20 of the State Commissions have power over street railway fares; and that in many of these cases the State Commissions would themselves be braced up by an expression which might emanate from a Federal tribunal even though the powers of this latter tribunal were only those of making a recommendation. Mr. Taft said also that the recommendations which such a Federal tribunal would have to make could not be based upon anything like a searching valuation of the property, but must, in the nature of things, be based upon a quick study of local conditions and confined, of course, only to war exigencies. He is evidently very strongly impressed with the fact that the maximum output, not only of munition factories but of industries generally, are going to depend upon the prompt increase of fares in proper cases to offset costs which now in many cases equal or exceed the incoming gross revenue. The Commissioners present gave an attentive ear to Mr. Taft's presentation of the matter, and while we realize that we have no jurisdiction in the case, we were impressed by the strength of Mr. Taft's presentation of the case.

I told him that the proposal to create a Federal tribunal, purporting to have lawful authority to condemn present rates and to fix future rates for local utilities, did not appeal to me; that I had favored rather an appeal to state and local commissions and consumers generally to permit increases in the rates of local utilities which were warranted by rising costs; that I had acquiesced in Mr. Cooke's plan of a tribunal to standardize contracts between Government bureaus and local public utilities,[4] and also in the expression by such a tribunal in given instances of the Federal interest in a given local situation. It seems true that certain states and localities have accorded increased rates and fares, but, on the other hand, in certain instances, as in Buffalo, an impasse was reached which has resulted, I understand, in a strike and the partial paralysis of local transportation.

In a word, Mr. Taft's position is that the Federal Wage Board is hampered in its award of higher wages in a given community if it cannot obtain at least the moral support of some tribunal to recommend to the public generally that a contemporaneous increase in revenue be permitted during war exigencies.

Commissioners McChord, Meyer and Woolley (Commissioner Aitchison is absent this afternoon)[5] authorize me to say that they favor the creation of an Advisory Board on Local Public Utilities to deal both with contracts between such utilities and the Government as suggested by Mr. Cooke and also with the larger and more general problems suggested by Mr. Taft.

Believe me, with all good wishes,

Yours very sincerely,   W. M. Daniels

TLS (WP, DLC).
[1] That is, Charles Caldwell McChord.
[2] That is, the National War Labor Board.
[3] That is, the Interstate Commerce Commission.
[4] See WW to W. M. Daniels, Sept. 23, 1918, n. 1.
[5] That is, Balthasar Henry Meyer, Robert Wickliffe Woolley, and Clyde Bruce Aitchison.

From William Kent

My dear Mr. President: Washington October 5, 1918.

I am informed that my friend, Mr. George P. Hampton, is soon to see you in connection with some agricultural questions. I wish to call to your special attention the Northwestern situation, of which Mr. Hampton is an important part. The progressive farmers of the Grange and the Nonpartisan League have been struggling to put into effect what I believe to be a sane, correct program of economic betterment. This is notably the case in the State of Washington, where, under the administration of Mr. Kegley,[1] Master of the Grange, there has been a vigorous fight made for the exact conservation measures that you have stood for—water power control and proper application of forest and other laws—which has embittered the reactionary and grabbing crowd. Mr. Kegley's successor as Master of the Grange, Mr. Bouck, has been indicted on charges of stupid and illiterate people for a certain speech he is alleged to have made concerning national finance.[2] Mr. Hampton has personal knowledge, by reason of his presence at the meeting, that Mr. Bouck said nothing at all about national finance, and has abundant witnesses to prove this contention.

Mr. Hampton was the person who at this meeting took a stand on the question of raising the largest possible part of the war expenditure through taxation rather than through bonding, a position exactly that of the Administration.

Mr. Hampton is going to Washington to testify at the trial of Mr. Bouck, and has reason to believe that he is liable himself to be indicted.

The situation in the Attorney General's office seems almost hopeless. The policy of endorsing local prosecutors, and backing them up whatever their course, is bound to produce intolerable injustice with terrible results, unless guarded against and corrected. The local prosecutor, Clarence L. Reames,[3] is, to the best of my knowledge and belief, thoroughly in sympathy with the crowd who are bent on the ruin of Bouck and the Grange and Nonpartisan League movement in the State of Washington. I have taken this matter up with the Attorney General's office, and have begged and besought an investigation of the situation by competent, unbiased people. I have urged that, in view of Hampton's evidence and his character and veracity, coupled with affidavits of other reliable citizens attendant at the meeting, that the indictment against Bouck be quashed, but nothing has been done. I wish you could realize the horror and the danger of the situation.

The Northwestern farmers have, by the investment of their sons in the war, by their response to financial appeals, by their patriotic endeavor to keep up the needed wheat supply even in the face of loss, demonstrated a complete and tested loyalty, and now, in this case, they find themselves persecuted, not through State agencies as is notorious in Minnesota, but through the office of the Attorney General.

Day in and day out they have had to bear the irresponsible, bitter, and unjust strictures of Roosevelt, urged on by reactionaries. They have looked to you and to the Administration for hope and for protection against calumny and injury.

Is there no place they can go to obtain justice and freedom from persecution? I do not believe that you can do a better thing than to talk this matter over with your friend and my friend Mr. Hampton, to the end of seeing to it that these farmers, loyal and forward-looking, may be reassured.   Yours truly,   William Kent

TLS, (WP, DLC).
    ¹ Carey B. Kegley.
    ² On August 13, 1918, the Federal District Court, Western District of Washington, Northern Division, had served William Bouck with an indictment for his remarks during a speech at Bow, Washington, on June 12, 1918. The indictment charged Bouck with interfering with the operation and success of the military and naval forces of the United States in order to promote the success of its enemies; with attempting to obstruct the recruiting and enlistment service of the United States; and with obstructing the sale of United States bonds and securities. As it turned out, the indictment was dismissed on December 21, 1918, at the request of the Wilson administration. For a brief discussion, see Harriet Ann Crawford, *The Washington State Grange, 1889-1924: A Romance of Democracy* (Portland, Ore., 1940), p. 235.
    ³ Former United States Attorney for Oregon; at this time, special assistant to the Attorney General for the prosecution of cases arising under the Espionage and Sedition acts.

From Enoch Herbert Crowder

My dear Mr. President: Washington October 5, 1918

I have given the most careful consideration to your letter of October 4th¹ in which there appears a suggestion that it may be wise to create the presumptive right to deferment on the part of anyone who can show that he is continuously engaged in real agricultural labor.

No provisions of the Selective Service Regulations have been more liberal than those accorded to agriculturists. In the first draft— and existing regulations have made little change in the procedure in respect of it—the farming class suffered far less disturbance by reason of withdrawals for military duty than any of the major industrial groups. In the first draft only 1.48 percent. of the total farming population was accepted for military service, whereas 3.12 percent. of the national total of coal miners, 4.23 percent of the ship builders, 3.79 percent. of the metal workers (except steel and iron) and 5.90 percent. of the iron and steel workers were withdrawn. These percentages will doubtless obtain in the second draft (January to October, 1918) in view of the fact that the classification rules have undergone no material change.

Not only was the agricultural class least impaired in the execution of the first draft but on March 11, 1918, ignoring both classification and order number, I directed the deferment until the end of the next quota of all Class 1 farmers who were then actively, completely and assiduously engaged in the planting and cultivation of a crop. To no other class has such a concession been made or suggested. I am certain that the farmers, as a class, have no reason to complain on the ground that an undue share of their class has been called. I am not sure but that we have gone already as far as it is safe to go and I confess my anxiety as to what may follow the adoption of a plan which approaches very closely a class exemption.

But the apprehension which I feel as to the outcome of any plan savoring of class exemption is heightened when the effect of such a procedure is viewed in the light of the contemplated military program. The 1919 program calls for the production of approximately two million seven hundred thousand men. Conservative estimates of the availables to be secured from the registration of September 12th place the total at nearly one-half million less than the requisite number. To accord a presumptive right to deferred classification to all persons continuously (time not stated) engaged in agricultural labor would so materially disturb every calculation heretofore made and would withdraw from those heretofore considered available for military service so large a number that I cannot say to what lengths we would be forced were such a procedure adopted.

I cannot believe, especially in view of the leniency already adopted toward the agricultural class and the imperative necessity of recruiting our armies to the full strength of available man power, that the present regulations should be modified or extended.

Yours very truly,   E. H. Crowder

TLS (WP, DLC).
[1] WW to E. H. Crowder, Oct. 4, 1918, TLS (Letterpress Books, WP, DLC).

From Jerome A. Myers[1]

Worthy Sir: New York October 5, 1918.

Seignor Enrico Caruso has kindly contributed to this Committee a very fine pen and ink sketch of yourself made by himself.[2] Mr

Caruso has requested that this be given to the largest purchaser of bonds at Liberty Hall, New York, N.Y. on October 18th. We have taken the liberty to add that you would personally autograph this sketch providing the denomination of bonds bought are not less than $50,000.

Hoping that this meets with your entire approval, we beg to remain,

> Yours for the 4th Liberty Loan,   Jerome A. Myers.[3]

TLS (WP, DLC).
    [1] Chief of the Outdoor Activities Division of the Speakers' Bureau of the New York Liberty Loan Committee.
    [2] For other sketches of Wilson by Caruso, see Michael Sisca, ed., *Caruso's Caricatures* (New York, 1977), p. 198.
    [3] "Dear Tumulty: Please say that the President will be very glad to comply with this request. The President." WW to JPT, Oct. 7, 1918, TL (WP, DLC).

Sir William Wiseman to Sir Eric Drummond

[New York] Octr. 5, 1918.

No. CXP 787. In reply to your CXP. 817 of the 3rd:

For your confidential information, the facts are as follows: CREEL saw the PRESIDENT without the knowledge of the State Department, and persuaded him that the SISSON papers were authentic, and that it was advisable to publish them. The State Department disapproved, but had to support the President's decision.

I have spoken to POLK, who has written a letter to the President recommending him not to press H.M.G. to publish the papers. I will advise you of the President's answer in the course of a few days.

T telegram (W. Wiseman Papers, CtY).

From Friedrich Oederlin,[1] with Enclosure

Mr. President: Washington, D. C. October 6, 1918.

I have the honor to transmit herewith, upon instructions from my government, the original text of a communication from the German government,[2] received by this Legation late this afternoon, from the Swiss Foreign Office.

An English translation of this communication is also enclosed. The German original text, however, is alone to be considered as authoritative.

Please accept, Mr. President, the assurances of my highest consideration.   F. Oederlin

TLS (SDR, RG 59, 763.72119/2113, DNA).

¹ Commercial Adviser to the Swiss legation in Washington; at this time also Chargé d'Affaires *ad interim* of Switzerland.
² T MS (SDR, RG 59, 763.72119/2113, DNA).

E N C L O S U R E¹

Washington, D. C.

TRANSLATION

of Communication from German Government to the
President of the United States,
as transmitted by the Chargé d'Affaires a.i. of
Switzerland, on October 6, 1918.

(German original text only to be considered as authoritative).

The German government requests the President of the United States of America to take steps for the restoration of peace, to notify all belligerents of this request, and to invite them to delegate Plenipotentiaries for the purpose of taking up negotiations. The German government accepts, as a basis for the peace negotiations, the program laid down by the President of the United States in his message to Congress of January 8, 1918, and in his subsequent pronouncements, particularly in his address of September 27, 1918. In order to avoid further bloodshed the German government requests to bring about the immediate conclusion of a general armistice on land, on water, and in the air.   Max, Prince of Baden,
Imperial Chancellor.²

T MS (SDR, RG 59, 763.72119/2113, DNA).
¹ The following note was also sent *en clair* and was printed, *inter alia*, in the *New York Times*, Oct. 7, 1918.
² At a conference at Supreme Headquarters in Spa on September 29, 1918, William II, Hindenburg, Ludendorff, Hertling, and Hintze had decided that Germany's desperate military situation demanded the immediate pursuit of negotiations for an armistice. However, at the same time, Ludendorff realized that a confession of collapse would rob Germany's present political and military leaders of all their authority and would throw the country into chaos. Moreover, he understood that the Entente powers would not negotiate with Germany's old rulers, and he insisted that an "alteration in the Government or its reconstitution on a broader basis" was the necessary prerequisite for the success of any peace overture. As a result of Ludendorff's sudden support for the establishment of a parliamentary system, Hertling, who had successfully resisted all demands by the majority parties in the Reichstag (the Social Democrats, the Progressives, and the Center party) for his resignation and for far-reaching constitutional changes, resigned on September 30, 1918. In what has been characterized as a "revolution from above," the Emperor, on the same day, ordered the transition toward a parliamentary system of government. He instructed Hertling to conduct the necessary negotiations with the parties in the Reichstag which would lead to their assumption of a larger share of responsibility. The outcome of the negotiations was the formation of a coalition government, composed of representatives of the three majority parties and the National Liberal party. Although the four parties worked out a common political program, they failed to agree quickly on a candidate for the chancellorship. Thus, Ludendorff, eager for an immediate cessation of hostilities, suggested that the Emperor offer the position to Prince Max von Baden. After lengthy discussions, the coalition parties acquiesced in the Emperor's choice, and Prince Max assumed his position on October 3, 1918. For detailed accounts, see Klaus Schwabe, *Deutsche Revolution und Wilson-Frieden* (Düsseldorf, 1971), pp. 88-105, and Ernst Rudolf Huber, *Deutsche Verfassungsgeschichte seit 1789, Band V: Weltkrieg, Revolution und Reichserneuerung, 1914-1919* (Stuttgart, Berlin, Köln, and Mainz, 1978), pp. 521-45. For a brief

summary, see Arthur Rosenberg, *The Birth of the German Republic, 1871-1918*, Ian F. D. Morrow, trans. (New York, 1962), pp. 243-45.

A Telegram and a Letter from Edward Mandell House

[New York, Oct. 6, 1918]

I would suggest making no direct reply to the German note. A statement from the White House saying, quote, The President will at once confer with the Allies regarding the communication received from the German Government, unquote, should be sufficient.

I would advise that you ask the Allies to confer with me in Paris at the earliest opportunity. I have a feeling that they will want to throw the burden on you, but I hope to be able to show them how unwise this would be. They should accept their full responsibility.

If the Entente permit this opportunity to go by and if the German resistance should stiffen, I am confident that there would be such a demand for peace this winter in those countries that their governments would be compelled to give Germany better terms than could now be made.

CC telegram (E. M. House Papers, CtY).

Dear Governor: New York. October 6, 1918.

It is stirring news that comes today. An armistice such as the Germans and Austrians ask for seems to me impossible, and yet a refusal should be couched in such terms as to leave the advantage with you.

If you could get the Central Powers to accept the terms of the note which you sent from here to Bulgaria it would, I believe, place you in the best possible position. The Germans will want immediate action and will probably suggest many expedients looking to an early preliminary conference. Our position I think should be one of delay without seeming so.

With Foch hammering on the west and with you driving the diplomatic wedge deeper, it is within the range of possibilities that the war may be over by the end of the year. I am fearful lest the Allies may make some diplomatic misstep. War is a terrible gamble and while everything seems with us now, something may throw the balance against us tomorrow.

With deep affection, I am,

Your devoted,   E. M. House

P.S. We are looking forward with the keenest pleasure to seeing you and Mrs. Wilson on Friday. I shall get seats for the "Follies" if they are here, and if they are not, then to "The Girld [Girl] Behind the Gun." We shall count upon you for dinner.

TLS (WP, DLC).

From Henry French Hollis

Dear Mr. President: Paris, France. Oct. 6, 1918.

I saw Baker Friday and discussed with him my idea that Germany would line up with us against France and England on the League of Nations, and impartial rights. I showed him the enclosed clipping (above). In today's L'Heure, there is proof that comment on your Sept. 27th speech was suppressed by the French government. This is on top of the other clippings I enclose *a propos* of the peace offer.[1]

All the papers publish[ed] your "Fourteen Points," your message of Feb. 12, 1918, and part of your Sept. 27 speech, and most of them expect *you* to make an early reply, saying it is "up to you" (La parole est à Wilson).

No paper but the L'Heure discusses the League of Nations or impartial rights part of your speech of Sept. 27th.

My friends think that France may be brought into line, but that England will never give up her command of the sea. The League, to be successful, must have supreme executive, judicial and military and naval power, a regular United States of the World.

Sincerely,   Henry F. Hollis.

ALS (WP, DLC).
[1] The only clipping which remains with Hollis' letter in WP, DLC, is "Le programme Wilson d'inspiration allemande," Paris *L'Intransigeant*, Oct. 4, 1918. It stated that the *Kölnische Zeitung* had just published a long article to show that Wilson's peace program was identical to that of Germany. "The war aims set forth by the government of the United States," *L'Intransigeant* concluded, "are the war aims which the German government pursues—except for the surrender of Alsace-Lorraine."

A Draft of a Note to the German Government[1]

[Oct. 7, 1918]

After formal acknowledgement * * *

Before making definite reply to the request of Imperial German Government, ⟨a reply which it⟩ and in order that that reply shall be as candid and straightforward as the momentous interests involved require, the ⟨Government⟩ *President* of the United States deems it necessary to assure ⟨itself⟩ *himself* of the exact meaning of the note of the Imperial Chancellor, in order that there may be no misunderstanding. In saying that the German Government accepts the programme of peace set forth in ⟨my⟩ *the President's* address to the Congress of the United States on the eighth of January last and in subsequent addresses does ⟨it⟩ *that Government* wish to be understood as accepting the terms there set forth and as wishing discussion only for the purpose of making them more explicit and settling the practical detail of their application? That is ⟨my⟩ *the President's* interpretation of the language which the Imperial Chancellor makes use of in the note, but ⟨I⟩ *he* does not wish to put that interpretation upon ⟨his⟩ *the Chancellor's* words without ⟨his⟩ *the Chancellor's* explicit sanction.

If that is ⟨his⟩ *the Chancellor's* meaning, the Imperial German Government will realize how unlikely it would be that the Government of the United States or the European governments engaged against the Central Powers should consent to an immediate armistice and the discussion of final arrangements of peace before at least some of the essential conditions set forth in the programme referred to had been actually complied with as an earnest of *the* purpose ⟨on the part⟩ of the German Government. ⟨I⟩ *The President* refers particularly to the evacuation of Belgium, northern France, *Russia*, Roumania, Serbia, and Montenegro. The Imperial German Chancellor will remember that in ⟨my⟩ *his* address to the Congress of the United States on the eighth of January ⟨I⟩ *the President* used this language with regard to the release of Belgium from German occupation and control: "No other single act will serve as this will serve to restore confidence among the nations in the laws which they have themselves set and determined for the government of their relations with one another," and ⟨I⟩ *he* thinks it ⟨my present⟩ *his* duty to add that nothing would so clear the air for the discussion of peace as the withdrawal of German troops from the sovereign states whose soil they have occupied. Without this it would seem impossible to bring about the temper of agreement necessary for the final accommodations of peace.

⟨I⟩ *He* feels it to be ⟨my⟩ *his* duty, also, to call the attention of the Imperial German Government with the utmost frankness to the acts with which their armies are accompanying their present ⟨gradual⟩ withdrawal from the territory they have occupied in Flanders and in France. Every city and every village, if not destroyed, is being stripped not only of everything it contained but also of its very inhabitants, a ⟨policy⟩ *course of action* which had hitherto been regarded as in direct violation of all the rules and practices of civilized warfare. Looking on, as they do, with horror at such acts of spoliation, inhumanity and desolation, the nations engaged against

Germany could hardly be expected to exact anything less than a peaceful withdrawal from their territory as a condition precedent to the discussion of a permanent and honourable ⟨peace⟩ *sattlement [settlement]*.

It is clearly impossible for ⟨me⟩ *the President* to entertain the suggestion of the Imperial German Government *with regard to armistice and discussion*[2] until ⟨I am⟩ *he is* assured that the German armies will everywhere be withdrawn to German territory and explicit assurance *is* given that the terms of peace ⟨I have⟩ *he* outlined in ⟨my⟩ *his* address to the Congress of the United States on the eighth of January, 1918, are accepted by the Imperial German Government. Is the Imperial German Government prepared to give ⟨me⟩ *him* these assurances?

WWT MS (WP, DLC).
  [1] All changes in the following document by Wilson. He deleted the words in angle brackets and added those printed in italics. About the drafting of this and the following notes, see the entry from the House Diary printed at October 9, 1918.
  [2] WWsh.

To William Kent

My dear Kent: The White House 7 October, 1918.

I have your letter of the fifth about Hampton and Bouck, and will take the matter up with the Department of Justice at once to see if something cannot be done.

In haste,   Faithfully yours,   Woodrow Wilson

TLS (W. Kent Papers, CtY).

To Thomas Watt Gregory.

My dear Gregory: The White House 7 October, 1918.

There is only too much truth in what Kent urges in the enclosed letter about the mischief that prejudice is working in the Northwest against men who are perfectly innocent of any kind of disloyalty, and I would be very much obliged if you would put some very pointed questions to your representatives out there about this particular case. As a matter of fact, we are in danger of playing into the hands of some violently and maliciously partisan Republicans, and it might have a fine effect if this whole business could be put upon the basis you and I would put it upon if we were handling it ourselves.

Cordially and faithfully yours,   Woodrow Wilson

TLS (T. W. Gregory Papers, DLC).

To Winthrop More Daniels

My dear Daniels: The White House 7 October, 1918.

I have your letter of October 5th about the conference which you and five of the other Commissioners of the Interstate Commerce Commission had with Mr. Taft on Saturday. My judgment with regard to the matter is exactly your own, and the more I study it the more imperative the conclusion seems to me to be that the Federal Govenment should not assume responsibility for the situations which have been developed with regard to public utilities.

I would be very obliged if you would express to Mr. Taft the genuine hesitation with which I differ in judgment from him, and also my entire appreciation of the delicate situation of responsibility which he and his associates on the War Labor Board are placed. I have been diligently seeking a solution of this matter, but have not been able, I am sorry to say, to satisfy myself with one.

Cordially and sincerely yours,   Woodrow Wilson

TLS (Wilson-Daniels Corr., CtY).

From Robert Lansing, with Enclosure

My dear Mr. President: Washington October 7, 1918.

Enclosed is a translation of the Austro-Hungarian note handed to me this morning by the Minister of Sweden.

It seems to me that the *offer* to conclude an armistice and enter upon negotiations can only be considered after the Austro-Hungarian Government has accepted unconditionally the principles which you have laid down and after the sincerity of the *offer* (which ought to be "request") is shown by withdrawal from all occupied territory, by denouncement of the treaties of Brest-Litovsk and Bucharest, and by a declaration that these acts will be performed regardless of the course pursued by Germany—that is on the basis of a separate peace.

The foregoing is a hasty suggestion. I hope we can make speedy answer because of the Loan Campaign.

Faithfully yours,   Robert Lansing.

TLS (SDR, RG 59, 763.72119/2536, DNA).

ENCLOSURE

No. 4978   Washington, October 7, 1918

Excellency: By order of my Government I have the honor confidentially to transmit herewith to you the following communication of the Imperial and Royal Government of Austria-Hungary to the President of the United States of America:

"The Austro-Hungarian Monarchy, which has waged war always and solely as a defensive war and repeatedly given documentary evidence of its readiness to stop the shedding of blood and arrive at a just and honorable peace, hereby addresses itself to his Lordship (*Monseigneur*) the President of the United States of America and offers to conclude with him and his allies an armistice on every front, on land, at sea, and in the air, and to enter immediately upon negotiations for a peace for which the fourteen points in the Message of President Wilson to Congress of January 8, 1918 and the four points contained in President Wilson's address of February 12, 1918, should serve as a foundation, and in which the viewpoints declared by President Wilson in his address of September 27, 1918 will also be taken into account.["][1]

Be pleased to accept etc.   W. A. F. Ekengren

T MS (SDR, RG 59, 763.72119/2536, DNA).
  [1] This note was also sent *en clair* and was printed, *inter alia*, in the *New York Times*, Oct. 6, 1918.

From Polk Lafoon[1]

My dear Mr. President: Covington, Kentucky, October 7, 1918.

The Democratic Nominee for United States Senator, Governor Stanley, attempts to justify his action in vetoing the bill prohibiting the teaching of the German language in the public schools, by the statement that he acted in accord with what he considered the wishes of the Administration, and after seeking advice from Washington. Many voters in Kentucky are interested in knowing the facts. May I be permitted to request information on this subject and statement as to whether the Administration regards as disloyal the Governor's action in this matter?

With great respect,   Polk Lafoon[2]

TLS (WP, DLC).
  [1] A prominent businessman and breeder of horses of Covington, Ky., also active in Democratic politics in his state.
  [2] Either he or his son later changed the spelling of this name to "Laffoon."

From Franklin Knight Lane

Confidential.

My dear Mr. President: Washington October 7, 1918.

I have your letter regarding Theodore Bell. I am very glad to know that you are so well aware of just what Bell is and stands for.

I certainly will give him no support, and I do not know any other Californian who will who is connected with the Administration. One of my friends in California wired me the other day suggesting that I take the matter up with you to see if you were interested, and I wrote him as follows:

"I have your telegram, and I do not think it is advisable to take it up with anybody. The President would undoubtedly say that Bell was not the Democratic nominee and let the matter go at that."

I shall let it be known that he has no Administration support.

Cordially and faithfully yours,   Franklin K. Lane

TLS (WP, DLC).

From William Bauchop Wilson

My dear Mr. President: Washington October 7, 1918.

I am glad to be able to advise you that we are making definite progress in coordinating the various governmental efforts as to the determination of rates and wages. The conference of representatives of the various wage fixing agencies initiated at your request has resulted in the establishment of a general wage committee. This is proceeding with all possible dispatch to formulate those guiding principles which should give us harmony of decisions in the determination of wage standards, the auxiliary factors such as hours, overtime and holidays (which are an integral part of the wage problem) and the relation of wage scales of the different industries to one another.

The conference of the existing wage determining agencies revealed that certain sections of the field of industry are outside any existing regulating authority except the blind and unserviceable forces of competition. Inevitably there is thus not only disorganization for the workers and the industries in those unregulated fields. There is the reflex influence of confusion and instability for the industries now subject to existing adjusting agencies.

This is particularly true of the metal trades. Within the shipyards these trades are subject to the Macy Board. Outside the shipyards— and the railroad shops which are subject to the Railroad Wage Board—the metal trades are unregulated. A resulting wasteful competition for labor therefore becomes unavoidable between the employers in the unregulated field and there is constant conflict between plants outside the shipyard and those within the yard. A highly expensive labor turnover and discontent among the workers in these industries—the primary war industries—are the results. A somewhat similar situation exists as to the building trades.

As far as possible of course we are seeking to have existing agencies cover any needed field of regulation, but many complicating factors make this impossible in all cases. What we must have is effective working relations, coordinated results attained through any single agency or singleness of effort of various agencies. Therefore, representatives of the different existing agencies have urged the need for a speedy establishment of instruments of regulation in a few of the more urgent fields now not regulated. Every attention is being given to this part of the problem and I hope before very long to bring before you definite plans to fill the gaps.

The interdependence of the limited interests entrusted to the respective agencies is now authoritatively revealed and we are acting upon the realization that the country presents a single industrial front. The mechanism of this conference committee gives us a general wage board as a natural process of evolution which will fully utilize the experience and the good-will of existing agencies with a minimum of new or disturbing machinery. Therefore, we can confidently look forward to a coordinating process by which the needs and interests of the Railroad Administration and the Fuel Administration, the Fleet Corporation, the Army and the Navy, no longer left to their conflicting independent action, will be balanced and accommodated to the single interest of the Nation.

Faithfully yours, W B Wilson

TLS (WP, DLC).

Tasker Howard Bliss to Newton Diehl Baker and Peyton Conway March

Versailles. October 7th [1918]

Number 242 Urgent.

For the Adjutant General of the Army Confidential.

To be brought to the instant attention of the Secretary of War and the Chief of Staff.

Mister Lloyd George, Mr. Clemenceau and Mr. Orlando have been in conference in Paris since last Saturday October 5th. At this moment 9 o'clock tonight I received from the British military representative the following secret document "The conference of Ministers at a meeting held on 7th October, 1918, agreed to refer to the military representatives at Versailles, with whom shall be associated representatives of the American, British, French and Italian navies, the consideration of the terms of an Armistice with Germany and Austria, on the basis of the following principles, accepted on the previous day:

Paragraph 1. Total evacuation by the enemy of France, Belgium, Luxemburg, and Italy.

Paragraph 2. The Germans to retire behind the Rhine into Germany.

Paragraph 3. Alsace-Lorraine to be evacuated by German troops without occupation by the Allies.

Paragraph 4. The same conditions to apply to the Trentino and Istria.

Paragraph 5. Servia and Montenegro to be evacuated by the enemy.

Paragraph 6. Evacuation of the Caucasus.

Paragraph 7. Immediate steps to be taken for the evacuation of all territory belonging to Russia and Roumania before the War.

Paragraph 8. Immediate cessation of submarine warfare.

(it was also agreed that the Allied blockade should not be raised.)"

The above document was handed to me with the statement that it would be considered at a meeting of Military Representatives tomorrow morning October 8th at fifteen minutes after nine o'clock, and I am requested to make arrangements for the presence of an American Naval representative. I intend to be present and shall inform the Military Representatives that I have cabled the above document to the Government in Washington and have no record of instructions. I shall cable developments but of course shall take no action whatever without formal instructions. I assume that the action of the three Prime Ministers is due to the proposal made by Germany to the Government of the United States, but I have no knowledge of whether they consulted the President before preparing the above quoted document. I have had no time to examine the document but at first glance it appears to me to be crudely drawn from a military point of view. Par. 8 is the only one which requires immediate action by the enemy, the other seven paragraphs fix no time limit. Under paragraph 2 the Germans may retire to the strong positions behind the Rhine with their armies and armaments and supplies intact. This might be completed long before the evacuation of territory in Russia and Roumania and even in Servia and Montenegro. If such a situation be created and if meanwhile all the territory which Belgium France and Italy desire is evacuated it is conceivable that one or more of the allies may refuse to fight any longer even if Germany while holding the line of the Rhine should eventually act in bad faith with respect to territory to the east of her. No guarantees are exacted of her except the evacuation of territory which she knows that she may lose anyway early next spring. I request immediate instructions.

													Bliss

TC telegram (WDR, RG 407, World War I Cablegrams, DNA).

Colville Adrian de Rune Barclay to the Foreign Office

Washington. Oct. 7th, 1918

Personal and Secret.

At an informal luncheon at the White House today in honour of Sir Eric Geddes the President said he had received this morning the German and Austrian notes proposing peace negotiations. It was interesting he said that the text of these communications were word for word the same as given out already to the Press which showed that the appeal was directed really to all peoples. He did not give any indications as to the course he might take but said with a smile that the position was a difficult one, as the Central Powers were professing to be accepting his own terms.

I hear that Colonel House is arriving in Washington this evening.

T telegram (FO 115/2428, p. 193, PRO).

A Draft of a Note to the German Government[1]

[Oct. 8, 1918]

FORMAL INTRODUCTION and then * * *

Before making definite reply to the request of the Imperial German Government, and in order that that reply shall be as candid and straightforward as the momentous interests involved require, the President of the United States deems it necessary to assure himself of the exact meaning of the note of the Imperial Chancellor. Does the Imperial Chancellor mean that the German Government accepts the terms laid down by the President in his address to the Congress of the United States on the eighth of January last and in subsequent addresses and that it wishes to enter into discussions only for the purpose of settling the practical details of their application?

If that is the Imperial Chancellor's meaning, the Imperial German Government will realize that the President cannot lay the suggestion of an armistice before the governments with which the Government of the United States is acting against Germany unless the German Government will first agree, as a condition of the armistice, that the essential foundations ⟨for the arrangements of the⟩ *of compliance with the* terms referred to be laid by the withdrawal of the German armies from Belgium, northern France, Russia, Roumania, Serbia, and Montenegro.

⟨It is clearly impossible for the President to entertain the suggestion of the Imperial German Government until these questions are answered in the affirmative.⟩

The President does not feel that he is at liberty to entertain the

*suggestion of the Imperial German Government until its meaning
and purpose are made entirely clear.*

WWT MS (WP, DLC).
  [1] This was the note which Wilson and House completed in the morning of October 8.

The Penultimate Draft of a Note to the German Government

FORMAL INTRODUCTION, and then * * *   [Oct. 8, 1918]

Before making definite reply to the request of the Imperial German Government, and in order that that reply shall be as candid and straightforward as the momentous interests involved require, the President of the United States deems it necessary to assure himself of the exact meaning of the note of the Imperial Chancellor, in order that there may be no misunderstanding. In saying that the German Government accepts the programme of peace set forth in the President's address to the Congress of the United States on the eighth of January last and in subsequent addresses does that Government wish to be understood as accepting the terms there defined and as wishing to enter into discussions only for the purpose of making those terms more explicit and settling the practical details of their application? That is the President's interpretation of the language employed by the Imperial Chancellor in the note, but he does not wish to put that interpretation upon the Chancellor's words without the Chancellor's explicit sanction.

If that is the Chancellor's meaning, the Imperial German Government will realize how unlikely it would be that the Government of the United States or the European governments engaged against the Central Powers should consent to an immediate armistice and the discussion of final arrangements of peace before at least some of the essential conditions set forth in the programme referred to had been actually complied with as an earnest of the purpose of the German Government. The President refers particularly to the evacuation of Belgium, northern France, Russia, Roumania, Serbia, and Montenegro. The Imperial German Chancellor will remember that in his address to the Congress of the United States on the eighth of January the President used this language with regard to the release of Belgium from German occupation and control: "No other single act will serve as this will serve to restore confidence among the nations in the laws which they have themselves set and determined for the government of their relations with one another"; and he now thinks it is his duty to add nothing would so clear the air for the discussion of peace as the withdrawal of German troops from the sovereign states whose soil they have occupied. Without this it would seem impossible to bring about the temper of agreement necessary for the final accommodations of peace.

He feels it to be his duty, also, to call the attention of the Imperial German Government with the utmost frankness to the acts with which its armies are accompanying their present withdrawal from the territory they have occupied in Flanders and in France. Every city and every village, if not destroyed, is being stripped not only of everything it contained but also of its very inhabitants,—a course of action which had hitherto been regarded as in direct violation of all the rules and practices of civilized warfare. Looking on, as they do, with horror at such acts of spoliation, inhumanity, and desolation, the nations engaged against Germany could hardly be expected to exact anything less than a peaceful withdrawal from their territory as a condition precedent to the discussion of a permanent and honorable settlement.

It is clearly impossible for the President to entertain the suggestion of the Imperial German Government with regard to an armistice and discussion until he is assured that the German armies will everywhere be withdrawn to German territory and explicit assurance is given that the terms of peace outlined in his address to the Congress of the United States on the eighth of January, 1918, are accepted by the Imperial German Government. Is the Imperial German Government prepared to give him these assurances?

WWT MS (WP, DLC).

Two Letters from Joseph Patrick Tumulty

Dear Governor: The White House 8 October 1918.

The editorial from the New York Post[1] expresses so clearly my own feeling toward Germany's proposal, that I hope you will get a chance to glance through it.

In my opinion, to accept the offer of Germany and Austria would be to destroy the great edifice your leadership has erected. The free peoples of the world have been inspired by the ideal of democracy which you raised and now that leadership is to meet its great test. Your record in this matter has been made up. On September 27th, you said that we had dealt with them already and we had seen them deal with other governments and that you were convinced that they were without honor and do not intend justice. If, by any chance, there should be an acceptance of these proposals, the reaction throughout this country and throughout the world, would be too terrible to contemplate. It would leave the world absolutely without hope and would destroy your leadership, which means so much at this time. A reply along the lines of your last speech will do more to end this war quickly than any attempt to deal with the present Prussian rulers of Germany. This is not a time to dally with these gentlemen.

These last proposals are a trick on the part of Germany to hold Austria and Turkey. If we stand firmly for the program of justice and peace, which you have outlined, Turkey and Austria will soon follow in the path of Bulgaria and Germany will surrender.

Sincerely,   Tumulty

TLS (WP, DLC).
  ¹ It is missing in WP, DLC; however, it was "Insincerity Already Exposed," New York *Evening Post*, Oct. 8, 1918. The editorial stated that public opinion in the countries addressed by Germany almost unanimously condemned Germany's request for an armistice as a "trick" and believed that "her professed readiness to accept President Wilson's terms of peace was a sham." As proof of Germany's insincerity, the *Evening Post* referred to a recent statement in the *Berliner Lokalanzeiger*, which had ruled out any consideration of the future of Poland and of Alsace-Lorraine during the discussions of peace terms. "When the German Government 'accepted' President Wilson's programme as 'a basis for peace negotiations,'" the editorial continued, "it intended to reserve the right to knock out any part of the basis which it did not like." By its previous conduct, the German government had already destroyed all confidence in its purposes and its good faith, and the first and justified attitude toward any German advances had to be one of suspicion. "The truth is," the editorial concluded, "that the Teutonic Powers have furnished to the Allies the one formula by which to judge them and to treat them. When they are beaten, they show signs of reason. The only way, therefore, to make them entirely reasonable is to beat them entirely."

Dear Governor: The White House October 8, 1918

I do not know what your attitude is toward the late German and Austrian offers. The record you have made up to this time, however, is so plain that in my judgment there can be only one answer and that is an absolute and unqualified rejection of these proposals.

As you said in your speech of September 27th: "They have convinced us that they are without honor and do not intend justice. They observe no covenants, accept no principle but force and their own interest. We cannot 'come to terms' with them. They have made it impossible. The German people must by this time be fully aware that we cannot think the same thoughts or speak the same language of agreement."

There is no safer counselor in this country than the Springfield Republican. Speaking of the peace program of the new German Chancellor the Republican says:

"It (referring to the offer of Prince Maximilian) does not meet the minimum requirements for the opening of negotiations. These have been variously stated, but in general may be reduced to restitution, reparation and guarantees. Under none of these heads has Germany yet come even measurably near meeting the plain requirements of the Allies, which have not been reduced in defeat and will not be increased with victory. Take, for example, the question of Belgium: now that Germany knows it cannot be kept, it makes a merit of giving it up, but beyond that Prince Maximilian is not authorized more than to say that 'an effort shall also be made to reach an understanding on the question of indemnity.' * * * What is needed first of all from Germany is a clear, specific and binding pledge in regard to the essential preliminaries. It does not advance matters an inch for the chancellor, like Baron Burian, to offer to take President Wilson's points as a 'basis' for negotiations. They will make a first-rate basis, but only when Germany has offered definite preliminary guarantees."[1]

I beg to call your attention to another editorial in the Springfield Republican, entitled "Why Germany Must Surrender," hereto attached.[2]

Speaking of Germany's promises, I mention still another editorial from the Springfield Republican which concludes by saying, "Even Mr. Wilson is not so simple-minded as the kaiser may once have thought him to be.["][3]

It is the hand of Prussianism which offers this peace to America. As long ago as last June you exposed the hollowness of peace offered under such conditions as are now set forth by the German Chancellor. Referring to the German Government, you said: ["]It wishes to close its bargain before it is too late and it has little left to offer for the pound of flesh it will demand."

In your speech of September 27th, you said:

"We are all agreed that there can be no peace obtained by any kind of bargain or compromise withe [with the] governments of the Central Empires, because we have dealt with them already and have seen them deal with other governments that were parties to this struggle, at Brest-Litovsk and Bucharest. They have convinced us that they are without homour [honor] and do not intend justice. They observe no covenants, accept no principle but force and their own interest. We cannot 'come to terms' with them. They have made it impossible. The German people must by this time be fully aware that we cannot accept the word of those who forced this war upon us. We do not think the same thoughts or speak the same language of agreement.["]

Certainly, the German people are not speaking through the German Chancellor. It is the kaiser himself. He foresees the end and will not admit it. He is still able to dictate conditions, for, in the statement which appeared in the papers yesterday, he said: "It will only be an honorable peace for which we extend our hand."

The other day you said "we cannot accept the word of those who forced this war upon us." If this were true then, how can we accept this offer now? Certainly nothing has happened since that speech that has changed the character of thos[e] in authority in Germany. Defeat has not chastened Germany in the least. The tale of their retreat is still a tale of savagery, for they have devast[at]ed the country and carried off the inhabitants; burned churches, looted homes, wreaking upon the advancing Allies every form of vengeance that cruelty can suggest.

In my opinion, your acceptance of this offer will be disastrous, for the Central Powers have made its acceptance impossible by their faithlessness.

TL (WP, DLC).
    [1] "Germany's Peace Proposal," *Springfield* (Mass.) *Republican*, Oct. 7, 1918.
    [2] *Ibid.* This editorial stated that a "complete surrender" of the German and Austrian governments, in substance as well as in form, was the necessary prerequisite for any peace talks. It was not enough that Germany admitted "privately" that it had lost the war and was ready to negotiate a reasonable peace. The crimes committed by Germany were of such a kind that it would "not do for Germany to squirm out of the war without making explicit amends for its open and shameless wrong-doing." Nor would it do to have the war end in a way which could in any sense be considered a draw. Although no particular form of victory was essential for the Allies, the fact of Germany's incontestable defeat had to be made a matter of record in order to remove all possibility of a future misunderstanding and misrepresentation. This was all the more imperative, the editorial continued, since Germany, at present, was far from beaten, unless its people followed the examples of the Russian and Bulgarian peoples and refused to continue the war. In many ways, a defeat of Germany through the refusal of its people to support their present rulers any longer would be the most satisfactory outcome. It would not only shorten the war but would have a "deeper significance than a purely military victory over a unanimous nation." However, the editorial concluded: "Whether defeat would come from the armies of the allies or from the conversion of the German people, the German government cannot be allowed to avert it by negotiations which do not start from an admitted German defeat. If and when the German government is ready to surrender, the sooner peace comes the better. But without such surrender there can be no profitable talk of making a just and lasting peace."
    [3] *Ibid.* This untitled editorial pointed out that behind the new German Chancellor, who was now appealing to Wilson, and to Wilson alone, to inaugurate peace negotiations, was the same well-known Kaiser who was responsible for the sinking of the *Lusitania*, the unrestricted submarine campaign, and the violation of international law and America's rights on the high seas. It was the same Kaiser who had come away from Brest-Litovsk with half of European Russia in his possession and who had once held the American government, and particularly Wilson, in such contempt that he believed the United States would be unable to strike back while the war lasted.

Robert Lansing to Friedrich Oederlin[1]

Sir: [Washington] October 8, 1918.

I have the honor to acknowledge, on behalf of the President, your note of October 6th, enclosing a communication from the German Government to the President; and I am instructed by the President to request you to make the following communication to the Imperial German Chancellor:

"Before making reply to the request of the Imperial German Government, and in order that that reply shall be as candid and straight-forward as the momentous interests involved require, the President of the United States deems it necessary to assure himself of the exact meaning of the note of the Imperial Chancellor. Does the Imperial Chancellor mean that the Imperial German Government accepts the terms laid down by the President in his address to the Congress of the United States of the eighth of January last and in subsequent addresses and that its object in entering into discus-sions would be only to agree upon the practical details of their application?

"The President feels bound to say with regard to the suggestion of an armistice that he would not feel at liberty to propose a cessation of arms to the governments with which the Government of the United States is associated against the Central Powers so long as the armies of these powers are upon their soil. The good faith of any discussion would manifestly depend upon the consent of the Central Powers immediately to withdraw their forces everywhere from invaded territory.

"The President also feels that he is justified in asking whether the Imperial Chancellor is speaking merely for the constituted au-thorities of the Empire who have so far conducted the war. He deems the answers to these questions vital from every point of view."

Accept, Sir, the renewed assurances of my high consideration.

Robert Lansing

CCLS (SDR, RG 59, 763.72119/2113, DNA).
  [1] The following text of the note as sent was most likely based on a fourth WWT draft, which is missing. On the other hand, it might have been prepared by Wilson and Lansing in conference.

From Robert Lansing

Dear Mr. President: Washington October 8, 1918.

We have just received the German text of Prince Maximilian's speech,[1] which, however, is so garbled that we have cabled to the Legation at The Hague to make a careful translation of it and to cable the translation in full. The German text shows that the text which we have already received through the press differs materially in certain respects: for instance, in the German text Prince Max-imilian is reported to have mentioned Alsace-Lorraine, although the text is so garbled that we are not sure just what he intended to say, (while the text as received yesterday through the press makes no mention of Alsace-Lorraine.) I shall, of course, send you the full translation of the speech as soon as it is received from The Hague.   Faithfully yours,   Robert Lansing

TLS (WP, DLC).
    ¹ In his inaugural speech to the Reichstag on October 5, 1918, Prince Max had announced his unqualified acceptance of the political program which the majority parties had drawn up on September 30. In his summary of those aspects of the program which dealt with foreign policy, Prince Max emphasized, in particular, his adherence to the principles contained in the reply of the German government to the papal note of August 1, 1917, and in the peace resolution of the Reichstag of July 19, 1917. He went on to affirm Germany's willingness to join a postwar league of nations; promised the complete restoration of Belgium's independence and territorial integrity, as well as negotiations about possible reparations; declared that the peace treaties which Germany had concluded so far would not be permitted to stand in the way of a general peace; and pledged the establishment of civil administrations and of representative bodies in Lithuania and Poland, in order to enable their people to determine their own constitutions and their relations to neighboring states. However, conspicuously absent from Prince Max's remarks was any mention of the future of Alsace-Lorraine which, according to the program of the majority parties, was to be granted full autonomy as an independent federal state within the Empire. For the full text of the speech, see *Schulthess'*, LIX (1918), Part I, pp. 325-29.

From William Bauchop Wilson

My dear Mr. President: Washington October 8, 1918.

    I have a communication from Senator Owen asking for suggestions from me relative to Senate Concurrent Resolution No. 22, introduced by Senator Owen, and Senate Concurrent Resolution 21, introduced by Senator Weeks, proposing the creation of a joint Congressional Committee on Reconstruction.

    In accordance with your suggestion I would be pleased to have you send me copies of your letter to Senator Overman and Secretary Redfield's letter, by which I may be guided in making my reply to Senator Owen.   Faithfully yours,   W B Wilson

TLS (WP, DLC).

From Thomas Watt Gregory

My dear Mr. President: Washington, D.C. October 8, 1918.

    I have received your letter of the 1st instant with its enclosure in which Mrs. Annie B. Leissler requests permission for her husband, a German alien, to come into the District of Columbia to attend to his business as a gard[e]ner and tree specialist.

    Very few exceptions have been made under the regulations excluding German alien enemies from the District and these only in cases of individuals of unquestioned loyalty who have been in this country and resided in the District for many years and honestly believed that they were actually American citizens. It is possible, in view of Mrs. Leissler's statement that her husband thought he had become naturalized and had exercised the rights of citizenship by voting and serving on juries, to bring his case within the former precedents, as these facts create sufficient doubt concerning his citizenship to justify an exception in his case and permission might be granted to him to come into the District pending the final disposition of his petition for final naturalization in the United States Circuit Court at Alexandria, Virginia.

Anticipating your approval, I have ordered an investigation and if the report is satisfactory shall advise Mr. Leissler that he may enter the District for the present.

Respectfully,   T W Gregory

TLS (WP, DLC).

From Benedict Crowell

My dear Mr. President: Washington, October 8, 1918.

I have the honor to acknowledge receipt of your letter of October 5th in reference to the selection of men for commissions and especially in reference to the case of Mr. Herbert L. Gutterson, an employee of the United States Food Administration.

I beg to assure you that the policy of the War Department is strictly the policy outlined by you and rules have been issued to restrict the appointment of officers from civil life in such a manner as to follow precisely your desires that we should have a really selective service. With this in view, orders were issued by the War Department as per the enclosed copy,[1] dated September 23, 1918. This will be seen to restrict the commissioning of men within the draft age to men of deferred classifications on grounds other than industry, occupation or employment, including agriculture, and to men in Group C, having physical disqualifications that would prevent them from being drafted as Group A men. All men, applicants for or under consideration for, commissions either in the Staff Corps or in the line, and who are qualified for general service, and are between the ages of 18 and 45, must first be inducted into the service before consideration will be given their appointment as officers. This last requirement is intended to make sure that men of the draft age and who are physically qualified for general service, shall be inducted for the period of the war and if they fail to obtain commissions, they will serve as soldiers in some later grade as long as their services may be needed.

In the particular case of Mr. Gutterson, who is, as I understand, in the draft age and physically qualified for general service, the Officers Training School would not accept him as a candidate for a commission if he is placed in the deferred classification on ground of industrial occupation or employment, either at his own instance or at the instance of the Food Administration. It would seem that all that is necessary in this case is for the head of the United States Food Administration to request that Mr. Herbert L. Gutterson be placed in the deferred classification on account of the essential work he is engaged in as head of the Division of Coordination of Purchase, United States Food Administration.   Benedict Crowell

TLS (WP, DLC).
¹ [P. C. Harris], "Appointment of Officers from Civil Life," Sept. 23, 1918, T MS (WP, DLC).

Peyton Conway March to Tasker Howard Bliss

Washington, October 8, 1918.

Number 95. CONFIDENTIAL. RUSH

Paragraph 1. Your numbers 242 and 243¹ were taken over by me to the White House immediately on receipt at 10:00 PM, October 8th and read personally by the President, who directs me to cable you in open code the answer which he has today handed the Swiss Minister for transmission to the Entente Powers as his answer to the proposals of peace from Germany. His answer is as follows: . . .²

No other instructions.   March.

TC telegram (WDR, RG 407, World War I Cablegrams, DNA).
¹ T. H. Bliss to NDB and P. C. March, Oct. 8, 1918, TC telegram (WDR, RG 407, World War I Cablegrams, DNA): "Confidential For the Secretary of War and Chief of Staff. In further reference to my Number 242 the Military and Naval representatives prepared a document today which the 3 Prime Ministers desire to have signed by 3.00 o'clock this afternoon. I declined to do this stating that I could take no action pending receipt of instructions from my Government. I shall cable a translation of the document as soon as made this afternoon. From the purely Military point of view the document removes the criticism suggested in my Cable 242 because it establishes immediate disarmament of the enemy as the basis of all other conditions. Another cable follows. Bliss."
² Here follows the text of the note embodied in RL to F. Oederlin, Oct. 8, 1918.

Tasker Howard Bliss to Robert Lansing and Others

Versailles, October 8th, 1918.

Number 244 VERY CONFIDENTIAL To be brought to the immediate attention of the Secretary of State, the Secretary of War and Chief of Staff.

In compliance with resolution of three Prime Ministers communicated to you in my number 242 the below quoted document was drawn up this morning. It was not drawn up by the Military Representatives in their official capacity as connected with the Supreme War Council but by them as individuals associated with representatives of the four navies. It is not in the form of a Joint Note but is entitled "A Joint Opinion." I do not know whether the Prime Ministers intend to communicate it to the American government or not. The Americans have taken no official part in it nor is the American government committed to it in any way by any action here. I have informed the Prime Ministers in writing that I cannot sign it in the absence of instructions from my Government. The document follows

"The Military Representatives and Naval Representatives meeting together on October 8th in accordance with the Resolution taken by the Conference of Ministers at their meeting held on 7th October, 1918, are of opinion that the first essential of an armistice is the disarmament of the enemy under the control of the Allies.

This principle having been established, the conditions specified by the Ministers at their Meeting held on 7th October, require from a military point of view to be supplemented as follows:

Paragraph 1. Total and immediate evacuation by the enemy of France, Belgium, Luxemburg and Italy on the following conditions:

Subparagraph (a) Immediate re-occupation by Allied troops of the territories so evacuated:

Subparagraph (b) Immediate repatriation of the civil population of these regions interned in enemy country:

Subparagraph (c) No "sabotage," looting or fresh requisitions by enemy forces:

Subparagraph (d) Surrender of all arms and munitions of war and supplies between the present front and the left bank of the Rhine.

Paragraph 2. Germans to retire behind the Rhine into Germany.

Paragraph 3. Alsace-Lorraine to be evacuated by German troops without occupation by the Allies, with the exception stated in Clause 18 below.

It is understood that the Allies will not evacuate the territory in their occupation.

Paragraph 4. The same conditions apply to the territory included between the Italian frontier and a line passing through the Upper Adige, the Pusterthal as far as Toblach, the Carnic Alps, the Tarvis and the meridian from Monte Nero, cutting the sea near the mouth of the Voloska (see Map of the Italian Military Geographical Institute 1 over 500,000).

Paragraph 5. Serbia, Montenegro and Albania to be evacuated by the enemy—under similar conditions to those stated in Clause 1.

Paragraph 6. Evacuation of the Caucasus by the troops of Central Powers.

Paragraph 7. Immediate steps to be taken for the evacuation of all territory belonging to Russia and Roumania before the war.

Paragraph 8. Prisoners in enemy hands to be returned to Allied Armies without reciprocity in the shortest possible time. Prisoners taken from the Armies of the Central Powers to be employed for the reparation of the wilful damage done in the occupied areas by the enemy, and for the restoration of the areas.

Paragraph 9. All enemy surface ships (including Monitors, River craft, etc.), to withdraw to Naval Bases specified by the Allies and to remain there during the Armistice.

Paragraph 10. Submarine warfare to cease immediately on the signature of the Armistice. 60 submarines of types to be specified shall proceed at once to specified Allied Ports and stay there during the Armistice. Submarines operating in the North Sea and Atlantic shall not enter the Mediterranean.

Paragraph 11. Enemy Naval air forces to be concentrated in bases specified by the Allies and there remain during the Armistice.

Paragraph 12. Enemy to reveal position of all his mines outside territorial waters. Allies to have the right to sweep such mines at their own convenience.

Paragraph 13. Enemy to evacuate Belgian and Italian coast immediately, leaving behind all Naval war stores and equipment.

Paragraph 14. The Austro-Hungarian Navy to evacuate all ports in the Adriatic occupied by them outside national territory.

Paragraph 15. The Black Sea Ports to be immediately evacuated and warships and material seized in them by the enemy delivered to the allies.

Paragraph 16. No material destruction to be permitted before evacuation.

Paragraph 17. Present blockade conditions to remain unchanged. All Enemy merchant ships found at sea remain liable to capture.

Paragraph 18. In stating their terms as above, the Allied Governments cannot lose sight of the fact that the Government of Germany is in a position peculiar among the nations of Europe in that its word cannot be believed, and that it denies any obligation of honor. It is necessary, therefore, to demand from Germany material guarantees on a scale which will serve the purpose aimed at by a signed agreement in cases amongst ordinary civilized nations.

In those circumstances, the Allied Governments demand that: Within 48 hours:

1st. The fortresses of Metz, Thionville, Strassburg, Neu Breisach and the town and fortifications of Lille to be surrendered to the Allied Commanders-in-Chief.

2nd. The surrender of Heligoland to the Allied Naval Commander-in-Chief of the North Sea.

Paragraph 19. All the above measures, with the exception of those specially mentioned in paragraph 18, to be executed in the shortest possible time, which it would appear should not exceed three to four weeks."   Bliss

TC telegram (WP, DLC).

From the Diary of Josephus Daniels

1918 Tuesday 8 October

WW came into cabinet room whistling. In response to inquiry said he whistled because he thought he had done right in answering Germans note. Only one thing troubled him. How could he have correspondence with Germany under autocracy? Then we must go into G_____ and set up a government ourselves, something unthinkable. Unless some sort of Gov. offers medium of communication, we might witness bolshevikism worse than in Russia.

Bound Hw diary (J. Daniels Papers, DLC).

From the Diary of Colonel House

October 9, 1918.

On Monday[1] after lunch I received word through Gordon that the President requested that I should come over immediately. He preferred that I should be there the same eve[n]ing, but if that was not possible, he hoped I could be there early Tuesday morning.

I did not get this message until after two o'clock but within the hour I was at the station and on the train. The White House had telephoned, and together with the State Department Secret Service, had arranged for my reservation and transportation. I was met at the Pennsylvania Station by Sharp[2] of the Secret Service, and by Egan,[3] Superintendent of the Pennsylvania Terminal and taken at

[1] October 7, 1918.
[2] Unidentified.
[3] William H. Egan.

once by private entrance to the train. Unfortunately for me, there were a good many people aboard who knew me, notably Senator Owen and Bainbridge Colby. Colby was entertaining but Owen bored me. He amused me by stating that he thought he had earned the right to be appointed a peace commissioner because he was responsible for the Federal Reserve Act and the Farm Loan Act. I promised to speak to the President, and I did much to the amusement of us both.

Bainbridge still desires to leave the Shipping Board and come with me. This, too, I mentioned to the President and he indicated a willingness, although he was loath to see him leave his present place.

And this reminds me in speaking of personalities, the President said if William Phillips' name had been suggested to him for Ambassador to London, he would have appointed him. I thought it would have been better for him and for me to have had Phillips, but that it was better for Lansing to have Davis. He agreed with this conclusion.

I arrived at the White House as the clock was striking nine o'clock. I took Colby from the station with me and sent him on to his home. The President met me and we went into his study. He said he had asked Lansing to come over and he arrived within a few minutes. The President had prepared his reply to the German Chancellor, Prince Maxmilien of Baden, and read it to us.[4] He seemed much disturbed when I expressed a decided disapproval of it. I told him I had thought of something quite different; that I did not believe the country would approve of what he had written. After arguing the matter some half hour or more, he said that I might be able to write something and embody what I had in mind, but he had to confess his inability to do so. He suggested that I have a try at it.

I said I was merely endeavoring to see the question from every angle; that it presented greater difficulties than any situation he had yet had before him. The question of going to war with Germany was easy compared with it. He appreciated this as fully as I and he was clearly not satisfied with what he had prepared.

We then began to amend his draft and before we finished with it the next day, there was not much left of the original. We worked on it steadily until nearly one o'clock Monday night. I then suggested we leave it until morning. He replied that he had thought of playing golf as he had had no exercise either on Sunday or Monday and was feeling need of it. I advised him to go to the links, and disagreed with him as to the necessity for haste in giving an answer. He evidently wished to have it ready for the Tuesday morn-

[4] That is, the draft printed at October 7, 1918.

ing papers if possible, and certainly not later than the Tuesday afternoon editions.

I took this occasion to tell him I thought his answer to the last Austrian Note was a mistake, not only in the celerity with which it was answered, but also the manner of it. He said, "What would you have done?" I replied that I would have answered it in some such way as his speech in New York, September 27th. He did not argue the matter.

Lansing took little or no part in our discussions.

After breakfast on Tuesday, Dr. Grayson came in with the expectation of playing golf with the President. When I had finished breakfast, the President appeared and announced that he had given out [up] the idea of going out and asked me to go with him to his study. We read what the papers had to say; I called attention to what the French Socialists Convention said upon the subject in Paris,[5] and the comments of the Manchester Guardian and London Daily News.[6] He, on his part, read me the debate which took place in the Senate Monday.[7]

[5] At a special national convention which met on October 6, 1918, the French Socialist party had addressed a resolution to Wilson about the peace overtures of the Central Powers. The resolution stated that, although indispensable diplomatic and military guarantees had to be exacted from the enemy, it was the duty of the Allied nations not to reject the requests of Germany and Austria without discussion. Referring to Wilson's speech of September 27, 1918, the Socialist party called upon the Allied governments for frank and clear statements of their purposes, and it concluded: "The party associates itself more than ever in all acts of President Wilson which will have the result of giving satisfaction to the masses who struggle and who have the right more than all others of having the response (to the Central Powers) not open to any misunderstanding. It is by this policy that the Socialist Party feels that it, like President Wilson, is working to bring about a just and durable peace." New York Times, Oct. 8, 1918.

[6] They were both reprinted in the New York Times, Oct. 8, 1918. The Guardian briefly commented on the recent change in Germany's system of government and argued that it had not altered the German constitution. Since the new parliamentary system was based, not upon the will of the German people, but upon an imperial decree which could be revoked at any time, the Emperor remained as absolute and supreme as ever. There was no reason, the editorial continued, why an armistice with Germany and Austria should differ from the one imposed on Bulgaria. Germany and Austria should at least withdraw their troops from all occupied territory and thus acknowledge defeat. "There ought to be an acknowledgement of defeat," the Guardian said, "and without it our work will not have been done. . . . How can we bring our armies to a standstill with their work only half done, knowing that every day of such reprieve would strengthen the German military position and add fatally to the task before us if negotiation should fail."

In its analysis of Prince Max's address to the Reichstag, the Daily News stated that the main purpose of the Chancellor's remarks had been to convince the world that he was speaking for a new Germany; that President Wilson's demand for the establishment of a democratic German government as the prerequisite for any negotiations with Germany had been met; and that the power in Germany had passed from military leaders to politicians. Although the Daily News was inclined to believe that the transformation of the German political system was genuine, its editorial pointed out that it was necessary for Wilson and the Allied leaders to receive a "guarantee of the reality of this vast revolution." "The world," the editorial concluded, "will await the reply of President Wilson with confidence in his wisdom. Whether that reply will represent the decision of the European allies we do not know. It is unfortunate that this critical moment finds the Allies without an agreed and declared policy. . . . There is no policy before the world except that of the President, and there is no other policy that would be tolerated by the democracy of any allied country. Its immediate indorsement is vital."

[7] During a debate in the Senate on October 7, 1918, about the German and Austrian requests for an armistice, the Republicans, supported by a number of Democrats, had delivered the

I found the President's viewpoint had changed during the night and he had come around to mine. He did not seem to realize before, the nearly unanimous sentiment in this country against anything but unconditional surrender. He did not realize how war mad our people have become. This, I thought, had to be taken into consideration, but not, of course, to the extent of meeting it where it was wrong.

The President thought if such an offer had been made by a reputable government, it would be impossible to decline it. After we had gotten the Note into its final form, he suggested sending for Tumulty to try it out on him. Tumulty had just written the President a letter urging that he should not give in in any particular but make a decided refusal. Tumulty's letter and the Note were not in harmony, and we were therefore anxious to see what he would

---

opening salvo of what was to develop into a fierce and concerted attack against any efforts by the Wilson administration to bring about a peace of compromise and understanding. Concerned lest Wilson might respond favorably to the overtures of the Central Powers, Senator Poindexter had initiated the debate by demanding that the members of the Foreign Relations Committee keep the Senate constantly informed about the progress of any negotiations with Germany and Austria. Poindexter then went on to reject unequivocally the overtures of the Central Powers, and he argued that the conclusion of a "premature and compromise peace" was "the most insidious danger" confronting the nation. It would rob the United States and the Allies of the fruits of their sacrifices and would be synonymous with defeat. No proposals by the Central Powers should even be considered until their troops had withdrawn from all occupied territory, including Alsace-Lorraine, and their governments were prepared to admit defeat and to pay indemnities and reparations. "The only condition of an armistice," Poindexter declared, "ought to be an allied victory; unconditional surrender of our enemies. Anything else would be approaching in a degree the betrayal of the great cause for which we are fighting, and would be action along the line of what the Bolsheviki of Russia perpetrated in a larger degree." As to Germany's professed willingness to conclude a peace based on the principles of justice, Poindexter maintained that "justice with Germany would mean the execution of some of the murderers and robbers who have laid waste Belgium and France. It would mean the trial by court-martial, or at least in some international tribunal, of the Kaiser for the crimes which he has permitted and which he has sanctioned."

Every senator who took the floor during the debate echoed Poindexter's views. Senator Lodge, for example, stated that he firmly believed in retributive and punitive justice. He argued that Germany had to be put in a position which would "physically guarantee" that she could not again enter upon a war of world conquest. "It does not matter what treaties she signs," he declared, "put her behind the bars." True peace would only come when British, French, and American soldiers were on German soil, had crushed Prussian militarism forever, and had made the world safe, "not merely for democracy, but safe against Germany." Senator Reed stated that not until Germany was "whipped" was it time for the United States and the Allies to write the terms of peace and to impose conditions which would make future treaties and agreements with Germany unnecessary. Senator Marcus A. Smith believed that peace should be considered only when the Kaiser was "absolutely on his knees," listening to the terms dictated by the Allies. Senator Ashurst declared: "A wide pathway of fire and blood from the Rhine to Berlin should be the course our Army should take; and when our armies have reached Berlin, in the city of Berlin, the German Government will be told what the peace terms will be." Even Senator Hitchcock, who had earlier argued that Wilson's Fourteen Points adequately covered all these demands, was forced to admit that the thought of suspending hostilities at the present time was "absolutely abhorrent" to every member of the Senate. The climax of the debate came when Senator McCumber introduced a resolution (S. Con. Res. 24) to the effect that there should be no cessation of hostilities and no armistice until the German government had disbanded its armies, had surrendered its arms and munitions, and had unreservedly agreed to the principles of compensation, reparation, and indemnity. *Cong. Record*, 65th Cong., 2d sess., pp. 11155-63.

think of it. Much to the surprise of both of us, Tumulty thought the country would accept the Note favorably, not enthusiastically at first but that it would appeal to the sober minded and, later, to everyone.

We all thought it essential to educate the press as to what the Note meant. We therefore drew up a little memorandum of explanation and of education. It was decided to ask Lansing to give this out when he gave out the Note to the press.[8] Lansing was then sent for and, after reading the Note, he expressed approval. He considered it much better than what we had composed the night before.

The President was not happy over this effort of ours, and neither was I, and yet it is the best that our combined judgment could produce. That it has taken with the public as well as it has makes me content. The New York Sun has an especially complimentary editorial which I attach.[9]

There was no one for lunch excepting the President, Mrs. Wilson and myself. They asked me to drive with them after lunch, but I had to go to the State Department and at three o'clock I had an engagement with Sir Eric Geddes, First Lord of the Admiralty, and I was leaving on the Congressional Limited at four.

I drove Geddes from three o'clock until I left. He came with me to the station and to the train. He gave all the inside Admiralty information, some of which is so confidential that I hesitate to record it, and it is of passing importance.

Geddes does not think the United States is doing anything like her share on the sea in European waters. He gave me the actual number of boats we had and what the British had. I was astonished at the limited number of destroyers we were using over there in comparison with the British. He said the destruction of submarines had nearly ceased, largely because the destroyers which the British Navy had formerly used to chase submarines were now being used

[8] The memorandum, which is missing, was most likely given out or read to the newspaper correspondents during Lansing's press conference of October 8, 1918, upon the understanding that it was not to be quoted. As a transcript of the press conference, dated October 8, 1918 (T MS [R. Lansing Papers, NjP]), indicates, the memorandum stated that Wilson's note applied only to Germany and that it should not be regarded as a reply but as an inquiry. See also the *New York Times*, Oct. 9, 1918.

[9] "The Answer," New York *Sun*, Oct. 9, 1918. It read, in part, as follows: "Perhaps no document proceeding from the President's capable intellectuals [intellect?] has ever gone so swiftly to the heart of the question or disposed with such candid and yet subtle dialectic skill of a dangerously plausible trick of the enemy's diplomacy as his reply yesterday, through Mr. Lansing, to Prince Maximilian's peace proposals. Ten thousand words of amplification could add naught to this incomparably effective response. It argues nothing, it promises nothing, but serenely and without the least bluster of rhetorical phrase it hamstrings the Kaiser's stalking horse. . . . That is all, but it is enough; and it is as incontrovertible in its majestic simplicity as the laws governing the movements of the heavenly bodies, and as beautiful as the American flag."

to convoy American troops. We arranged to keep in close touch with one another through Sir William Wiseman while he is here. Geddes is to lunch with me just before his departure which will be within a few days.

I had a quiet trip over from Washington. There were no old time bores, although many strangers came up to shake my hand and to say something complimentary about the work I was doing for the country.

It has been a busy day today as I have been preparing for the President's visit Friday, Saturday and Sunday of this week. In addition to that, there is always the accumulated work.

Two Letters to William Bauchop Wilson

My dear Mr. Secretary: The White House 9 October, 1918.

I am very glad to send you a copy of my letter to Senator Overman, to which you refer in your letter of yesterday, and also a copy of Secretary Redfield's letter to Senator Pomerene. I am very much obliged to you for reminding me.

Cordially and sincerely yours,   Woodrow Wilson

My dear Mr. Secretary   The White House 9 October, 1918

Allow me to acknowledge receipt of your letter of October 7th about the progress being made in coordinating the several government efforts with regard to the determination of rates of wages, and to say how much reassurance and satisfaction it has given me.

Cordially and faithfully yours,   Woodrow Wilson

TLS (LDR, RG 174, DNA).

To Henry Ford

My dear Mr. Ford: The White House 9 October, 1918.

May I not say to you upon the completion of the splendid hospital which you have put at the disposal of the Medical Department,[1] how much and how sincerely I admire your thoughtful and beneficent generosity? It is an inspiring example to those who wish in thoughtful ways to set forward the public interest and serve the highest welfare of our soldiers.

Cordially and sincerely yours,   Woodrow Wilson

TLS (MiDbF).
[1] Ford, on August 1, 1918, had turned over to the federal government the Henry Ford

Hospital, which he had acquired in 1914. It served as General Hospital No. 36 and housed some 1,500 patients until October 1919, when it was returned to Ford. See Henry Ford, *My Life and Work*, Samuel Crowther, collaborator (Garden City, N. Y., 1922), pp. 214-15.

To George Brown Martin

My dear Senator Martin: [The White House] 9 October, 1918

If I have been tardy in expressing my admiration and gratitude to you for your generous action in the matter of the suffrage amendment, it has not been because I have not been thinking of it a great deal, but because I have been waiting for an opportunity to write such a letter as I should like to write, and now I still find myself hurried and only able to say that you did a very brave and public-spirited thing. I wish with all my heart that there had been others.

Cordially and sincerely yours,   Woodrow Wilson

TLS (Letterpress Books, WP, DLC).

To William Kent

My dear Kent: [The White House] 9 October, 1918.

I am glad to say you are mistaken in your assumption that I have not taken time to look into the case of the indictment against Miss Theodora Pollok. I have had a conference with the Attorney General about the matter.

I find in the first place that the trial is not immediately at hand, but will take place in November; and I also find that there is reason to think that there is some very serious evidence against Miss Pollok. I shall know for a certainty whether this is true or not, I hope, in a very short time. In the meantime I can only assure you of my continuing interest in the case.

Cordially and sincerely yours,   Woodrow Wilson

TLS (Letterpress Books, WP, DLC).

To Josephus Daniels

My dear Mr. Secretary: The White House 9 October, 1918.

In a conversation the other day with Congressman Sherley, he brought up the subject of the construction of hospitals by the army and navy. He called attention to the fact that the authorities of the army and navy do not hesitate (and this was not a subject of criticism with him) to construct other necessary buildings whenever and wherever necessary, without always waiting for specific grants of money from the Congress for the purpose, but that they apparently did not pursue the same policy with regard to hospitals, which, at such crises as the present for example, ought to be built on the assumption that the Congress will of course assume the expense made necessary by such unusual occasions and pressing needs. He said very truly that the Priorities Board ought in the circumstances to give immediate and prompt attention to the question of according priority of supply in respect of materials to things of this sort, but that they could not do so unless the plans and action of the Departments were prompt and explicit.

It seemed to me that his suggestions in this matter were extremely wise and timely, and I hand them on to you with my entire endorsement.

Cordially and faithfully yours,   Woodrow Wilson

TLS (J. Daniels Papers, DLC).

From George Creel

My dear Mr. President,   Washington, D. C. October 9, 1918

Mr. Hearley,[1] one of our best men in Rome, had a talk on October 4 with Ceretti,[2] Papal Secretary of State, on some publicity matters. In the course of the conversation Ceretti stated that Austria was planning a reply to President Wilson and indicated that the Austrian answer would follow these lines:

"First—Appeals Wilson direct and alone as *consistent* judge conflict and above possible egotism either side.

Second—Alleges her complete acceptance 14 points and 4 principles Wilson's July 4th speech.

Third—States her territorial and popular political program.

Fourth—Asks Wilson for public conference to discuss possible peace on such basis. Austria would cease explicit ignoring Allies in her appeals but would implicitly leave opportunity for Allied participation in such conference. Austria will begin making feverish attempts democratize internally and adopt *many* popular and social democratic measures. Ceretti criticised clumsy recent Austrian note and its untimely request secret conference. Same source clearly indicates Germany will rush democracy and to extent socialization of Government and come out undoubtedly on question Belgium, agreeing to Belgium's absolute political and economical independence, restoration and indemnity and practically acknowledge criminality of invasion Belgian people. Ceretti asserted Wilson stronger among people of Austria and Germany and especially Austria than

President apparently believes and world imagines. Pope thinks and says Wilson is real master situation in all fighting countries. However, Ceretti says that President while master sovereignty central powers should not forget keep watching individually and collectively Allies."

I take it that this may be interesting to you. Hearley also states that the Pope is thinking of issuing some sort of statement largely supporting your position and that, probably, November 2, All Souls Day, will be the occasion.   Respectfully,   George Creel

TLS (WP, DLC).
[1] John Hearley, former Italian correspondent for the United Press, at this time, with the C.P.I.'s news bureau in Rome.
[2] The Most Rev. Bonaventura Cerretti, Archbishop of Corinth and Apostolic Delegate to Australasia. A former member of the Apostolic Delegation in Washington (1906-1914), he was, in fact, the Papal Secretary for Extraordinary Ecclesiastical Affairs at this time.

From Joseph Patrick Tumulty

Dear Governor: The White House. 9 October 1918

I spoke to you about the New Jersey senatorial situation yesterday.[1] Hennessy and LaMonte wish to see you this week, if possible. You probably are aware by this time that LaMonte won by only three or four hundred votes and that the next highest man was a lawyer friend of mine, named Simpson. Simpson, in a statement which he made yesterday, said he would not wait for returns from the soldier vote, but came out openly in support of LaMonte, saying that in case the soldier vote should show that he had received the nomination (and there is a strong probability that this might be so), he would decline the nomination in favor of LaMonte. This is really a big thing to do. I hope, if you let LaMonte and Hennessy come to see you, that you will permit me to ask Simpson to accompany them.[2] He has been a great admirer of yours for years. I think this would do a lot to hearten and encourage all his friends, and it would give an appearance of unity that we very much need.

                                            J.P.T.

TLI (WP, DLC).
[1] The three major Democratic contenders for the seat of the late Senator William Hughes were George Mason La Monte, Charles O'Connor Hennessy, and Alexander Simpson, a lawyer of Jersey City and the minority leader in the New Jersey Assembly. All three candidates ran for the nomination for the so-called long term, i.e. the six-year term starting on March 4, 1919. In addition, Hennessy ran unopposed for the nomination for the so-called short term, i.e. the remainder of Hughes' unexpired term until March 3, 1919. Although Hennessy won the nomination for the short term in the Democratic primary on September 24, 1918, the outcome of the race for the long-term nomination was not immediately apparent. Since La Monte led Simpson by only about 150 votes, and less than 400 votes separated Simpson and Hennessy, the nomination could not be decided until the soldier vote had been counted. As this dragged on during the

following two weeks, the contest narrowed down to a race between La Monte and Simpson. However, on October 7, Simpson declared that, since the complete returns of the soldier vote would not be known for another two weeks, he had decided to withdraw from the contest and to endorse La Monte, in order to avoid any further delay which would harm the chances of the Democratic candidate in the general election. See the *Newark Evening News*, Sept. 25, 26, and 27, and Oct. 7, 1918.

² Wilson received La Monte, Hennessy, Simpson, and other Democratic leaders of New Jersey at the White House on October 14, 1918, at 5:30 p.m.

From Herbert Bayard Swope

PERSONAL.

My dear Mr. President: [Washington] October 9, 1918.

Your reply to Germany is such a mighty stride toward peace on the basis of decision, of justice and of durability that I feel bound to express to you my deep appreciation of its value.

I am not at all certain that peace is likely to be an immediate development; I am quite certain, however, that when it comes you will have made it possible. First, you laid down the terms, and next you showed how the terms could be effectuated.

Your course was so reasonable, so elementary in its logic, that I marvel at the errors in the conjectures, preceding your statement, which pictured you as slamming the door in the face of those who sought entrance. Obviously your method would be to allow the suitors an opportunity to prove that they approached in good faith and in sincerity. This you have done.

The Teuton Allies know beyond doubt now what our terms are, and how they may obtain them. A vast obscurity has been cleared away. They can no longer pretend an ignorance of your purpose, and, through this pretense, continue the delusion of their peoples. Now that the peoples know what must be done, it will be done. You have transferred the battle from the military fronts to the hearts of the nations aligned against us. They must determine whether they are to follow you and obtain the peace they so bitterly long for, or follow their ambitious masters to destruction. The choice is theirs; it is certain which they will choose. The only doubt is as to the time that must elapse before they can make their choice—before they can free themselves from the thraldom in which you, more than any other man, have made them realize they are bound.

No man who has studied your attitude in this war, and who has been touched by your passion for justice, could think that you would do other than you have done. You could not do more; you would have been untrue to yourself had you done less.

Sometimes I wonder if you know how deep and personal, almost devotional, is the pride felt by those who know what you mean in the history of the world today. Because we are, all of us, bound by a sense of reserve in such expressions, I am the more anxious to have you learn the reaction in the minds and hearts of those who are proud to call themselves your followers, and I am certain that in this letter I am projecting, however feebly, the thoughts of those who revere, admire and love you.

With deep respect,   Faithfully,   Herbert Bayard Swope

TLS (WP, DLC).

From William Gibbs McAdoo

Dear Mr. President: Washington October 9, 1918.

The diplomatic exchanges with Germany, necessary as they are and as thoroughly as I am in accord with the course you are taking, are nevertheless having a very unfortunate effect upon the Liberty Loan campaign. The psychology of the situation is altogether unfortunate for the Loan and various adverse factors are operating at the same time.

I believe that you could help the situation immensely if you would issue a very brief statement addressed to the American people urging the importance of subscribing promptly the Fourth Liberty Loan and of not relaxing effort in any direction, but of intensifying it, in order that the full benefit of our hard earned efforts at home and on the field of battle may be pressed to a conclusive victory.

Something expressed with a punch in your own unapproachable way and gotten out in tomorrow morning's papers would be of inestimable value. I would not dare attempt to phrase anything for you.   Cordially yours,   W G McAdoo

TLS (WP, DLC).

From Robert Somers Brookings

My dear Mr. President: Washington Oct. 9, 1918.

Feeling as I am sure you do the vital importance of the steel problem which you have under consideration, I am enclosing brief abstracts of opinions that have been expressed from time to time by different members of the Price Fixing Committee, bearing directly or indirectly on the same subject.[1]

We are all conscious of the constantly increasing pressure of high prices and have exerted every effort not only to prevent further advances but, wherever possible, to reduce *existing* prices.

Wishing to avoid giving any consideration to revenue from Excess Profit Taxes, I am afraid we have failed to give full value to an important service the Excess Profit Tax renders in the price-fixing problem, as touched upon in one of the papers herewith enclosed.

Believing that our principal post-war steel competitor will be Great Britain (whose pre-war steel market was always lower than ours) I have kept in close touch with their current steel prices, which have been for some time past and are today somewhat higher than ours.

As disposing of the rail problem is of trifling importance, Mr. President, by comparison with the weighty matters of state which at this time require your attention, I feel like apologizing for sending you any further communication on this subject, and hope you will take your own time in giving it consideration.

Respectfully yours,   Robt. S. Brookings

TLS (WP, DLC).

[1] "Condition of the Steel Industry for the Last Quarter of the Year 1918, both as regards Volume of Production and Price," and "Arguments Advanced For and Against Compulsory Control of the Steel Industry," T MSS (WP, DLC). The first memorandum stated that steel manufacturers, almost without exception, had devoted the largest share of their profits for 1917 to increased facilities for production. The steel companies had made every effort to secure maximum production, and there was no reason to believe that output could be increased further by a greater measure of governmental control. The memorandum then went on to discuss the price of steel and the possibility of its reduction. It pointed out that, for the last quarter of 1918, the profits of the United States Steel Corporation, whose prices could be regarded as representative, were not likely to exceed 20 per cent, almost half of which would be absorbed by the proposed new rates of the excess war-profits tax. One way to lower steel prices, the memorandum said, was for the government to fix the profits of the steel manufacturers at approximately half their present level, which would practically eliminate all excess-profits tax for the companies and would still leave them with about the same return on their investments. However, the Price Fixing Committee agreed with the steel manufacturers that, on account of the fluctuations in costs occasioned by the decisions of the War Labor Board and other governmental agencies, the margin of profit might easily be reduced to a level which would no longer be consistent with maintaining the industry in a healthy condition. Thus, the memorandum concluded that the excess-profits tax performed an important function as an "insurance measure" which provided the steel manufacturers with the freedom of action necessary to assure maximum production, while, at the same time, it prevented them from reaping inordinate profits.

As its title indicates, the second memorandum summarized some of the arguments advanced for and against a compulsory governmental control of the steel industry. Those in favor of governmental control maintained that low prices, adequate profits for the industry, and maximum production could best be achieved by guaranteeing fair profits to low-cost producers as well as high-cost producers and by creating, in effect, a "composite pool cost and selling price." Those opposed to this policy argued that it was "bad in principle," since it would create a "cost-plus system," which was "universally rejected in its results"; that the administration of a pool scheme was impracticable in an industry as complicated as steel; that a compulsory scheme would eliminate those incentives for management which, at present, were securing maximum production; that, in light of past experience with cost-plus contracts, the government was unlikely to guarantee to manufacturers a certain return on their investments; and that a composite pooling arrangement would work against those processes which were conducive to a reduction of steel prices.

From Vance Criswell McCormick

Dear Mr. President: Washington Oct. 9th, 1918.

Referring to your request that I take up with Mr. Crowell the question of taking the votes of our soldiers in France, I desire to report that I discussed this matter with Mr. Crowell and have asked him to put in writing his conclusions, which letter I herewith enclose.[1]

I am afraid there is nothing more that we can do about this matter, as it is a difficult thing to go up against a military necessity, which apparently this seems to be.

If I can secure any more information for you I will be very glad to do so. Sincerely yours, Vance C. McCormick

TLS (WP, DLC).
[1] B. Crowell to WW, Oct. 9, 1918, TLS (WP, DLC). In response to Wilson's request for a statement by the War Department about its decision not to permit state election commissioners to take the vote of American soldiers in France, Crowell pointed out that the authorities of the A.E.F. had "strongly urged the impracticability of taking such a vote." He referred to an earlier order by the War Department which had already questioned the feasibility of such a procedure (see WW to J. S. Williams, July 8, 1918, n. 3, Vol. 48 [second letter of that date]). Since men from individual states were scattered throughout the many divisions of the A.E.F. and were now heavily involved in the actual fighting, the conditions which had initially prompted General Pershing to recommend against taking the vote had become intensified. Thus, it was not only extremely difficult but "wholly out of the question from the military standpoint for a vote to be taken by Election Commissioners in France." The alternative of a mail vote was also rejected as impractical. Whereas the states, by law, required the secret ballot, military censorship made it mandatory to inspect every letter sent from France. Moreover, the government could not guarantee either the arrival of mail from France in time for the election or the delivery of blank ballots to the men in the field. "This whole question of taking the vote of our soldiers in France," Crowell concluded, "received the careful and prolonged consideration of the Secretary of War, as well as the military establishment, and it was found entirely impossible to evolve a scheme by which the vote could be taken, even when the subject was approached with a determination to reach a solution if possible."

From William Kent

My dear Mr. President: Washington October 9, 1918.

Pardon my calling your attention to a bill, S. 2493, which passed the Senate, also the House, on October 3d. If you have not already signed it, I hope you will take time to consider the matter. It follows in regular sequence the procedure I outlined in connection with the infernal stock-raising homestead bill, which was to be corrected, but was not, by Departmental regulation. This bill permits the taking up of non-contiguous land, provided it is located within twenty miles of a partial homestead. In other words, a man at the foot of a mountain, with desert country, can take up an entirely useless, alleged arable homestead, pretend to cultivate, and then take up the balance of his claim in valuable, high summer range, where no human being could live through the year and where a home is impossible. It happens that my son, ranching in Nevada, is located in just such a place. If he were not honest, he could nail down this valuable territory. As he is honest, he will probably be run out of business by dishonest neighbors. I urgently request you to veto this measure, if it has not already been signed, or at least to hold it up until you can get expert opinion.

                                  Yours truly,   William Kent

TLS (WP, DLC).

From Helen Hamilton Gardener

My dear Mr President: Washington, D. C. October 9, 1918

Senator Martin of Kentucky urges me to try to have our own women, and also certain newspapers where we have friends, to stop trying to force Governor Stanley to come out in the open and say that if elected he will vote for the suffrage amendment.

As you doubtless know his opponent has done so. If Governor Stanley has satisfied *you* that he is "safe" we might afford to do this. If not, it places us in a position where we can hardly do so, as you will see.

If you feel that you can intrust us with such information as Governor Stanley gave to you on the topic we can act promptly as the situation now seems to demand.

                    Sincerely and gratefully yours,   Helen H. Gardener

TLS (WP, DLC).

Three Telegrams from Lord Robert Cecil to the British Embassy, Washington

CIRCULATED TO THE KING AND WAR CABINET.

                                  Paris October 9th, 1918.

No. 1229 (R). *Urgent.*

Following sent today to Washington.

Following from Lord R. Cecil.

(End of R).

Les Gouvernements Alliés ont pris connaissance avec le plus grand interêt de la réponse addressée par Monsieur le Président Wilson au Chancellier de l'Empire Allemand.

Ils reconnaissent les sentiments elevés qui ont inspiré cette réponse. Se limitant à la question la plus urgente, celle de l'armistice, ils pensent comme le Président des Etats Unis que la condition préliminaire de toute discussion sur cette question est l'évacuation par les ennemis de tous les territoires envahis. Mais pour la conclusion de l'armistice lui même ils estiment que cette condition, tout en étant nécessaire, ne serait pas suffisante.

Elle n'empêcherait pas les ennemis de tirer avantage d'une suspension d'armes pour se trouver, à l'expiration d'un armistice non suivi de paix, dans une situation militaire meilleure qu'au moment de l'interruption des hostilités. La faculté leur serait laissée de se retirer d'une situation critique, de sauver leur matériel, de réformer leurs unités, de raccourcir leur front, de se retirer sans pertes d'hommes sur des positions nouvelles qu'ils auraient le temps de choisir et de fortifier.

Les conditions d'un armistice ne peuvent être fixées qu'après consultation des experts militaires et selon la situation militaire au moment même ou s'engagent les négociations.

Ces considérations ont été fortement exposées par les experts militaires des Puissances Alliées et particulièrement par le Maréchal Foch. Elles interessent également toutes les armées des Gouvernements Associés dans la bataille contre les Empires Centraux.

Les Gouvernements Alliés appellent sur elles toute l'attention du Président Wilson.[1]

(Beginning of R).

Repeated to Foreign Office No. 1229 October 9th.

[1] "The Allied governments have taken cognizance with the greatest interest in the reply addressed by President Wilson to the Chancellor of the German Empire.

"They recognize the elevated sentiments which have inspired this reply. Limiting themselves to the most urgent question—that of the armistice—they think, as does the President of the United States, that the preliminary condition of all discussion on this question is the evacuation by the enemies of all the invaded territories. But, for the conclusion of the armistice itself, they believe that this condition, absolutely necessary though it is, would not be sufficient.

"It would not prevent the enemies from taking advantage of the suspension of arms if they found themselves, at the expiration of an armistice not followed by peace, in a better military situation than at the moment of the interruption of hostilities. The ability would be afforded them to retire from a critical situation, to save their matériel, to reform their units, to reinforce their front, and to withdraw without fatal casualties to new positions which they will have had the time to choose and fortify.

"The terms of an armistice can only be fixed after consultation of the military experts and according to the military situation at the precise moment when the negotiations occur.

"These considerations have been strongly laid out by the military experts of the Allied powers, and particularly by Marshal Foch. They concern equally all the armies of the Associated governments in the battle against the Central Empires.

"The Allied governments call President Wilson's attention to all of the above." (Our translation.)

CIRCULATED TO THE KING AND WAR CABINET.

Paris October 9th, 1918.

No. 1230 (R). *Urgent.*

Following sent to Washington today.

Following from Lord R. Cecil.

The Allied Governments venture to point out to President that time has come when decisions of supreme importance in regard to the war may have to be taken at very short notice. They therefore think it would be of very great assistance if an American representative possessing the full confidence of the United States Government could be sent to Europe to confer, when occasion arose, with the other associated Governments so as to keep them accurately and fully informed of the point of view of United States Government.

Repeated to Foreign Office No. 1230.

CIRCULATED TO THE KING AND WAR CABINET.

Paris October 9th, 1918.

No. 1231 (D). *Urgent*.

Following sent today to Washington.

Following from Lord R. Cecil.

My immediately preceding two telegrams.

The text of these telegrams was agreed to at a Conference of Prime Ministers and Foreign Ministers of Great Britain, France and Italy. As soon as your Colleagues of France and Italy are instructed you should jointly present them to President. They are to be treated as strictly confidential.

Repeated to Foreign Office No. 1231.

T telegrams (Balfour Papers, MSS Eur. F 118/90, IOR).

Sir William Wiseman to Lord Reading

SPECIAL DISTRIBUTION.

Washington October 9th, 1918.

Very Urgent. Personal and Secret.

Secretary of State sent for me this afternoon and read out to me two telegrams from General Bliss enumerating terms which Prime Ministers of Great Britain, France and Italy had agreed upon as a basis for an armistice with Germany and Austria to be referred for consideration of military representatives of Allied Governments.

Secretary of State asked me to tell you that President had been very much astounded at receiving this news and was very much perturbed and would be obliged for an explanation as soon as possible as he could not understand above action.

Secretary of State personally expressed opinion that if matter reached the ears of the public in any way a most critical situation would be created owing to effect that news would have on public opinion.

I ventured to suggest to Mr. Lansing that as the Prime Ministers had no doubt knowledge of German proposal for an armistice they had taken the opportunity, assembled as they were together at the time, to discuss terms which Allies would require should any acceptable request for an armistice be formulated in the future.

I understand Secretary of State also spoke to French and Italian Ambassadors in the same sense.

I have shown this to First Lord of the Admiralty who tells me he has also heard independently very unfavourable and alarmist comments as to attitude of Allies conveyed by General Bliss's telegram.

T telegram (Balfour Papers, Add. MSS 49748, British Library).

Sir William Wiseman to Lord Reading and Sir Eric Drummond

Washington. October 9th, 1918.

Very Urgent. Personal and Secret.

Following for Lord Reading and Sir E. Drummond from Wiseman.

A. Mr Polk showed me this afternoon two cables which the President received this morning from General Bliss.

The first cable dated 7th contained text of a document enumerating terms for an armistice with Germany.

Bliss said he was asked to agree on behalf of U. S.

He objected to certain of the terms on military grounds.

The second cable dated 8th said that the three Prime Ministers wanted the document signed by three o'clock that afternoon.

He added that his military criticisms had now been met by certain alterations in the terms.

B. Bliss uses the words "the principles of an armistice which have been accepted."

The President and the State Department interpreted this to mean that the three Prime Ministers had definitely agreed [on] the terms of an armistice.

Hence Mr Lansing's remarks to Mr Barclay, reported in his personal cable to Mr. Balfour.

Colonel House also spoke to me about the cable. Both he and the President were much disturbed about it.

C. I suggested that General Bliss' cable was not clear and a more probable interpretation was that the three Prime Ministers took the occasion of their meeting to get the views of their Naval and Military experts on the terms of a possible armistice—that the U. S. Military Representative was present and the draft terms seem to have been even modified to meet his views.

Very confidentially I learn that the State Department heard today from a source they consider reliable that the British, French and Italian Governments are bound by a secret treaty regarding Turkey and are now negotiating peace terms in accordance with the treaty though the French do not altogether approve.

Another rumour is that peace terms have been settled with Bulgaria. I mention above because a good deal of excitement prevails not only among the public but in Administrative circles.

I need not emphasize the effect on public opinion here if it was thought that steps towards peace were being taken without consulting U. S.

D. I venture to suggest a personal cable from the Prime Minister, Balfour or yourself, to the President giving him some assurance in that respect.

E. I also suggest you urge that House should be sent over at once.

Personally he is quite ready to go and I think the President would be willing to send him though possibly not at once.

T telegram (FO 115/2428, pp. 235-37, PRO).

To Hsü Shih-ch'ang

Washington, October 10, 1918.

On this memorable anniversary when the Chinese people unite to commemorate the birth of the Republic of China, I desire to send to you on behalf of the American people my sincere congratulations upon your accession to the Presidency of the Republic and my most heartfelt wishes for the future peace and prosperity of your Country and people. I do this with the greatest earnestness, not only because of the long and strong friendship between our countries, but more especially because, in this supreme crisis in the history of civilization China is torn by internal dissensions so grave that she must compose these before she can fulfill her desire to co-operate with her sister nations in their great struggle for the future existence of their highest ideals. This is an auspicious moment, as you enter upon the duties of your high office, for the leaders in China to lay aside their differences and guided by a spirit of patriotism and self sacrifice to unite in a determination to bring about harmonious co-operation among all elements of your great nation, so that each may contribute its best effort for the good of the whole, and enable your Republic to reconstitute its national unity and assume its rightful place in the councils of nations.

Woodrow Wilson

T telegram (SDR, RG 59, 893.001 H854, DNA).

To Ralph Pulitzer

My dear Mr. Pulitzer: [The White House] 10 October, 1918.

It is seldom that I have time to turn aside for a private letter, but I cannot deny myself the privilege of telling you, even in a hasty line like this, how much I appreciated the great editorial in the World of last Monday[1] and how much real service I think it is going to do.

With warmest appreciation,

Cordially and faithfully yours,   Woodrow Wilson[2]

TLS (Letterpress Books, WP, DLC).

[1] "No Divided Government," New York World, Oct. 6, 1918. The editorial, which actually appeared in Sunday's editorial section, stated that, in the midst of war, a national election was a "national misfortune" which might easily be turned into a "national calamity." In the circumstances, the only issue of the campaign was whether the Amercan people would carry on the war and establish peace through a united government or whether they would try to do it through a divided one. To be sure, the editorial continued, no question of patriotism was involved, since, on the whole, a Republican Congress would be as eager to win the war as a Democratic Congress. "Nevertheless," the editorial said, "the election of a Republican House or a Republican Senate might readily work more injury to the United States than Germany itself is capable of inflicting." The Republican leaders would be justified in interpreting a victory of their party as evidence that the country had repudiated Wilson's conduct of the war and his terms of peace, and they would act accordingly. They would try to wrest the conduct of the war from the President's hands and would put forth their own peace program in opposition to that of the President. The ensuing "political civil war" between the President and a Republican Congress would weaken the "war-making powers" of the United States and nullify the country's "peace-making power." Moreover, any political discomfiture or embarrassment to the President would be "enthusiastically welcomed" by the German government as proof of its contention that Wilson had forced the United States into the war against the will of the American people.

Still more important was the effect of the November election on President Wilson's influence on the policies of Great Britain, France, and Italy. Wilson was recognized as the leader of world democracy, yet the British, French, and Italian "imperialists" had never accepted his program for a democratic peace. Although, at present, their power was diminished by the great wave of popular support which Wilson's peace program had received, they would quickly regain their influence if it appeared that Wilson had been repudiated by a majority of the American people. There was no justification for the "dangerous and desperate expedient" of dividing the government of the United States in time of war, and all arguments which had been advanced in favor of a change had been "trivial and foolish." The editorial concluded: "The American people want President Wilson to win this war. We believe they want a peace in accordance with the President's enlightened programme which has appealed so vividly to the imagination and idealism of the common people of the whole world. If that is the case, the least they can do is to give him a Congress that will not harass him, that will not bedevil him, that will not obstruct him—a Congress that will be compelled by the unwritten law of American politics to support and sustain him in carrying through his mighty task. They cannot expect the President to succeed if they wantonly or frivolously add to his burdens by electing a Congress to oppose him. When they go to the polls they must remember that his failure will be their failure and that his success will be their success. No divided government ever marched triumphantly to victory."

[2] Wilson's letter was prompted by a note from Tumulty which read as follows: "Dear Gov-

ernor: In view of the fine editorial in the World, asking for a Democratic Congress, I think Ralph Pulitzer would appreciate a letter of thanks." JPT to WW, Oct. 9, 1918, TLS (WP, DLC).

To Helen Hamilton Gardener

My dear Mrs. Gardener: [The White House] 10 October, 1918.

Replying to your letter of October 9th, let me say that I feel reasonably confident that you can regard Governor Stanley of Kentucky as "safe."

In great haste,

Cordially and sincerely yours,   Woodrow Wilson

TLS (Letterpress Books, WP, DLC).

To Richard Irvine Manning

My dear Governor: [The White House] 10 October, 1918.

I was so deeply disappointed in the action of Senator Benet about the suffrage amendment that I am writing to ask if you will be kind enough to tell me whether you know what Senator-select Pollock's[1] views are. It is a matter of the utmost consequence that the amendment should be adopted by the Senate, and any representations that I can legitimately make to Senator-select Pollock, I should like very much to convey to him in any way that you may advise.

Cordially and sincerely yours,   Woodrow Wilson

TLS (Letterpress Books, WP, DLC).
    [1] William Pegues Pollock, a lawyer of Cheraw, S. C. Pollock was elected on November 5, 1918, to serve out the unexpired term of the late Senator Tillman until March 3, 1919.

To George Creel

My dear Creel: The White House 10 October, 1918.

Thank you for your thoughtfulness in sending me the report from Mr. Hearley at Rome. It presents a very unexpected aspect of the attitude of the Vatican.

Cordially and faithfully yours,   Woodrow Wilson

TLS (G. Creel Papers, DLC).

To George Brown Martin, with Enclosure

My dear Senator: [The White House] 10 October, 1918.

I take pleasure in sending you the enclosed reply to Mr. Lafoon's letter which you asked me to send you. I enclose also a copy of Mr. Lafoon's letter, as you requested.

Cordially and sincerely yours,   [Woodrow Wilson]

CCL (WP, DLC).

E N C L O S U R E

To Polk Lafoon

My dear Mr. Lafoon: The White House 10 October, 1918.

I answer your letter of October 7th with real pleasure. Governor Stanley did seek the advice of the Bureau of Education before vetoing the bill prohibiting the teaching of the German Language in the public schools of Kentucky, and did, in my judgment, act entirely with a view to the general educational interests, and certainly should not be considered as having in that matter been guilty of the least touch of disloyalty of any kind. I have entire confidence in Governor Stanley and should be sorry to see any misunderstanding arise as to his motives in this or any other matter.

Cordially and sincerely yours,   Woodrow Wilson

TLS (A. O. Stanley Papers, KyU).

Lord Reading to Sir William Wiseman

London, 10th October 1918.

Following for Sir W. Wiseman from Lord Reading.

Very Urgent. Personal and Secret.

Your telegram of October 10th.

(A) I have seen Mr. Balfour and the cablegram he has sent to Barclay. I am quite convinced that there is some misunderstanding caused by the language of Bliss quoted by you. I shall be in better position to send you fuller communication tomorrow when Ministers will have returned from France, but I have no doubt whatever that when properly understood it will be found that nothing has been done there to cause astonishment or annoyance on the part of U.S.G.

(B) The President's message in answer to Germany has been extremely well received here.

T telegram (Reading Papers, FO, 800/225, PRO).

From the Most Reverend John Bonzano, with Enclosure

Your Excellency: Washington, D. C., October 11, 1918.

His Eminence Cardinal Gasparri, the Papal Secretary of State, has instructed me to present to Your Excellency the enclosed message from Pope Benedict XV.

In complying with his instructions, I beg leave to avail myself of the occasion to express to Your Excellency my sense of profound respect and high esteem.

Your humble Servant   Archbishop John Bonzano
Apostolic Delegate.

ALS (WP, DLC).

E N C L O S U R E
From Benedict XV

Mr. President: [The Vatican, c. Oct. 10, 1918]

From a most ardent desire of seeing terminated as soon as possible the ruthless scourge which for too long a time has been afflicting humanity, we conjure you, Mr. President, by the Precious Blood of Jesus Christ, the Redeemer of the world, to take into kind consideration the request for armistice and for negotiations of peace which has been addressed to you. Divine Providence has reserved for you and for the great Republic over which you preside the immortal glory of restoring bleeding humanity to peace, which will mark a new epoch in the history of the world.

Benedictus XV.

TCL (WP, DLC).

From Thomas William Lamont

Dear Mr. President: [New York] October 11th, 1918.

Upon my return from Washington, I had Mr. Rollo Ogden dine with me, and went over with him some of the points of our conversation on Friday last, making to him the suggestions that you were good enough to make to me as to ways of co-operation, etc., in attaining the war and peace aims which you have in mind.

You may or may not have seen the three editorials that Mr. Ogden wrote in reference to the German peace note; one prior to the reply that you made, the second subsequent to it, and answering some of the criticisms with which it was met on many sides; the third sounding a still further note of encouragement.[1] I have had these three editorials clipped and enclose them herewith on the chance that you may not have seen them.

In regard to the last subject that we discussed, I am told that Republicans intend to make a vigorous campaign, and that their managers are encouraged to think that it will be successful. In chatting very informally with one or two of their people, I find that they are not impressed with the idea which I forwarded as to the possible effect on the people abroad of the election of a Republican Congress this Fall. I have never been active in politics and do not know the workings of the thing, but my guess is that the voters of this country will not understand the point of view that was discussed unless you find some method of telling it to them. If such a way were found I should think that they would be impressed, just as I was impressed.

I have written you very frankly and confidentially, and you must feel under no necessity of acknowledging this. I told Ogden, by the way, that I thought some time or other within the next few weeks, he ought to seek an opportunity to have a chat with you, and I felt sure you would be willing to talk with him.

Thanking you for your kind reception of last week,

Sincerely yours,　[Thomas W. Lamont]

CCL (T. W. Lamont Papers, MH-BA).

[1] Ogden's first editorial was most likely "Insincerity Already Exposed," about which see JPT to WW, Oct. 8, 1918, n. 1 (first letter of that date). The other two editorials were "The President's Demands," New York *Evening Post*, Oct. 9, 1918, and "Fresh Courage for Fearful Saints," *ibid.*, Oct. 10, 1918.

The first of the two editorials in which Ogden commented on Wilson's reply to the German government defended Wilson's note on the ground that the President had access to a good deal more information than any of his critics, including Senator Lodge. Although it was, of course, possible that Wilson had been misled, it was at least reasonable to assume that his response to the German overtures was more appropriate than that of the "casual critic in the street." The assumption that the President was both informed and sagacious in his judgment of the war situation was strengthened by the success of his previous reply to Austria. That note, too, had met with similarly severe criticism, but, as it turned out, Wilson had quite accurately gauged the "Teutonic psychology." Ogden then went on to analyze Wilson's reply to Prince Max. He stated that, by asking for a "categorical answer" as to Germany's willingness to submit to the Fourteen Points, Wilson was, in essence, asking for an unconditional surrender and a "complete capitulation." The editorial concluded: "Men reckon ill with the President who see in his note of yesterday the slightest relaxing of determination. It is not mere diplomatic fencing that he is doing. He is simply serving notice on the adversary that he will not strike if an honest surrender is intended, but otherwise—! If the Germans thought that they might find Woodrow Wilson more lenient than Lloyd George or Clemenceau, they made another terrible mistake."

In his second editorial on Wilson's note, Ogden elaborated on his previous arguments. He pointed out that the British and French press were full of praise for Wilson's "skilful diplomacy" and that the Foreign Office had entirely approved the President's course of action. It was only in his own country that men such as Lodge and Theodore Roosevelt expressed doubts and fears about the intent and the effect of Wilson's note. Yet, Ogden did not believe that a partisan motive was the true cause of this professed disquietude, for the Republicans, who had made support of the President the chief test of patriotism during the war and who had vowed to stand behind Wilson, would surely not fail him at the first good opportunity. "What we suspect," Ogden maintained, "is that there is a kind of left-over and lurking sentiment to the effect that, somehow or another, Wilson cannot be depended upon to be stanch and grim to the very end." People who, for more than two years, had been in the habit of denouncing Wilson as weak and vacillating could not easily throw off the force of old custom, and it was upon them that the note had made such a "painful impression." These "fearful saints" believed that Wilson had fallen into a German snare, that he had readily acquiesced in a German military scheme to withdraw in safety their imperiled forces behind shorter lines on German territory and then to defy the Allies to attack them. But, Ogden argued, all this was highly improbable, and he concluded: "Thus we believe that those Americans who have been so distressed lest their President had made a blunder, may compose themselves for their customary night's rest, stayed by the thought that Frenchmen and Englishmen feel their interests to be safe in Mr. Wilson's hands, and reassured by the reflection that Germany can devise no military wiles which the good sword of Gen. Foch cannot cut through."

From Henry French Hollis

Dear Mr. President: Paris, France, October 11th, 1918.

Lloyd George, Bonar Law and Robert Cecil were playing golf at St. Cloud when the papers printed your note to Germany. They read it,—and finished their game!

The world is with you, no matter hpw [how] hard it is to handle the politicians and the newspapers. Your suggestions carry such weight that the plain people, such as the French poilus and their wives, consider it settled when you announce a policy. You are so clearly right that they say to me: "I don't see how he could do any thing else." And the hour before every one was wondering what you *would* say.

The enclosed clipping from the London Daily Mail[1] is right when it says: "All nations await the decisions of one man." Your sanction comes from five years of generous, wise and humane leadership. It can not be developed over night. It is too late now for any man to develop it in time for the peace conference.

Politicians like Medill McCormick, and those of the "first circles" like Lodge, N. M. Butler and the English nobility, do not like your success nor your humane attitude toward "those to whom we do not wish to be unjust [just]." They are doing some back-biting in private, but they don't dare to come out into the open. They don't really believe in democracy any way. No newspaper here dares to oppose you. Most of them will be with you body and soul if they are permitted.

Lord Grey is out for a League of Nations, and the English papers gave it small space on the third page. The French papers ignored it. None of them have any editorial comment on the speech or the subject.

I incline to the view of H. G. Wells ("In the Fourth Year")[2] that the Peace Conference may well be continued as a permanent body and become the executive of the League of Nations. With the United States, England, France and Germany behind it, it will have enough sanction and all the other nations will be glad to join in a secondary way after they gain confidence in the way it is run.

It is too late now to have an allied conference on the allied peace program before the Peace Conference. You will do that preliminary work now before you turn it over to the others. X [It] will have been pretty well determined when you get through your lone hand. You will have blocked out the way and laid down a program acceptable to the people of the world. I assume that you will do this in a message to Congress, thus setting a good example by consulting the representatives of the people and at the same time placing these representatives in a position of *laches*[3] if they don't speak up their opposition promptly. In this way you will do the preliminary work better and quicker than an Allied Conference would do it.

You can also pick out better representatives for us at the Peace Conference than Congress could, but I hope that you will lay your appointments before *both Houses* for their formal approval in order to set a good example to other countries and to clothe them as completely as possible with all the powers delegated to Congress. You will run no danger in this, and while the Constitution and precedent do not require it, and the Senate is the treaty-making body, these are novel times and we ought to set the best possible example to others,—outside and beyond the requirements of the Constit[ut]ion.

It becomes to me increasingly evident that Germany's only hope of a fair peace rests in you. As you have said,—none but a fair peace can be permanent. I expect to see Germany throw herself on your mercy and rely on you to get her a fair peace. It will be a great role which the future will acclaim. But vengeance and the lust for conquest and commerce are so powerful in France and England that it will be difficult.   Sincerely yours,   Henry F. Hollis.

TLS (WP, DLC).
    [1] It is missing.
    [2] H. G. Wells, *In the Fourth Year: Anticipations of a World Peace* (London, 1918).
    [3] A legal term meaning "neglect to do a thing at the proper time; undue delay in asserting a right, or in claiming or asking for a privilege."

From Edward William Pou

My dear Mr. President: Washington, D. C. Oct. 11, 1918.

The election of a Republican majority to the House of Representatives would in my judgment be a national calamity. Such a majority would instantly become an obstacle in the way of the enforcement of the policies of your administration. Enough has already been said to justify the statement that such majority not only would not feel bound to follow your lead but on the contrary would attempt even to dictate to you. They would immediately construe the action of the nation in giving them a majority of the House as their justification for such course. Such a mistake by the voters of America may not be probable but, as your friend and supporter in Congress, I am going to venture to suggest that you have it in your power to render such mistake impossible.

The nation has placed upon your shoulders the heaviest burden any man has ever bourne in the history of the world. In the House and Senate you should have a majority heart and soul in sympathy with you: not a majority partly composed of men who support you on the floor to save themselves and criti[ci]ze you elsewhere, who speak one language on the floor and another in the cloak room. Now of all times there should be no divided responsibility. You know better than any one how the danger of divided responsibility should be stated.

I am proud to have taken an humble part in these world events under your leadership and I think I am in a position to appreciate the difficulties which in my judgment will inevitably spring up to annoy and harrass you in the development of the great, splendid, benign purposes of your administration. This opportunity to foresee the dangers I have ventured to mention and the further fact that I have supported you gladly, proudly at all times and in all places, constitute my apology for this note which is also prompted by a little unselfish anxiety.

Sincerely your friend,   Edwd W. Pou.

TLS (WP, DLC).

A Memorandum by Homer Stillé Cummings

10-11-18

Confidential

On Tuesday, October 1, 1918, I had a conference with President Wilson at the White House. Mr. Vance C. McCormick was present. We went to see the President primarily concerning political conditions and also because I desired some definite expression from the President relative to assuming the Acting-Chairmanship of the Democratic National Committee. I previously had several conferences with Mr. McCormick, with Mr. Burleson, with Mr. McAdoo and others, and they all wanted me to assume the responsibility.

At the conference at the White House the President expressed extreme gratification that I was willing to undertake the work and we then discussed in intimate fashion many of the outstanding questions of the campaign. It was understood that I should return to Washington on the 8th and remain here as much as possible until the end of the campaign. We discussed the situation in the various states in which a senatorial contest was involved. We also discussed the question of how far it would be advisable for cabinet officers to indulge in political campaign speeches after the Liberty Loan Drive was over, and also how far the President could go with propriety in writing personal letters of commendation for the benefit of individual candidates.

Speaking of a certain Senator, the President said,

"Now, of course, it would be ridiculous for me to commend him personally. I do not need _____, I need a Democrat, and the people in his state would be amused if I should commend him as a great statesman—he is too weak in the upper story for that."

The President then spoke of the stories being circulated in Minnesota that he had written a letter asking for the reelection of Senator Nelson. He said in substance,

"When I heard of this report I had my correspondence examined to see if, in a moment of weakness, I had written such a letter, growing out of my very great personal regard for the Senator."

He said similar stories were being told in other states, and he thought he might have to take some action to counteract the effect.

I said, "Mr. President, you might limit your disclaimers to the states in which the Democratic candidates have a chance." This remark seemed to amuse him. He thought it a wise policy.

Various other matters were discussed and the conference drew to a close.

On October 10th, at 4:15 P.M. I had a further conference with President Wilson. I was accompanied by Senator Pittman, Senator Gerry, Congressman Scott Ferris and Congressman Rouse.[1]

The principal purpose of the conference was to clear up the speakers' situation, with reference to Cabinet members and men in Departments who are awaiting word from their chiefs before making any positive engagements. The President said he had discussed this with the Cabinet and he thought that Cabinet members could make speeches, providing they do not go upon political tours but responded to individual invitations. He thought that any widespread speaking campaign by Cabinet officers might create a feeling of uneasiness and apprehension which really did not exist. I asked him whether the Cabinet officers were prepared to make straight out and out Democratic speeches or whether they were going to make patriotic speeches with Democratic leanings. The President looked at me quizically, then said,

"I supposed that every Democratic speech was a patriotic speech."
This created a laugh. I said,

"I am afraid, Mr. President, that that is exclusively a Democratic
view point."

He said,

"Anyway, I understand what you mean, and there is no reason
why the Cabinet officers should not speak very plainly."

The question of letters to individual candidates came up again,
and the Minnesota situation with its latest developments was discussed in some length. Also the situation in Montana growing out
of the disagreeable incident relative to District Attorney Wheeler
and his claimed unwillingness to prosecute certain offenders who
had spoke unpatriotically.

The question of the general policy arose early in our conference.
Mr. Pittman was the last arrival and while waiting for him I asked
the President whether we should begin or whether it would be best
to wait for the Senator. The President said he thought we had a
little time before the hour of the appointment. I looked at my watch
and said,

"Yes, we have precisely a minute and a half."

The President said,

"I will ascertain if you are correct or not."

He thereupon looked at his watch which had recently been regulated and he said,

"You are right, we have exactly a minute and a half."

I said, "That incident discloses that I am prepared to stand by
the President."

This was a remark that everyone present seemed to regard as
humorous.

With reference to speakers in general, Congressman Rouse said
there was great demand for Secretary Daniels. The President said,
"Yes, Josephus is coming into his own." This reminded him of an
incident. The President was in some particular place in the company of Secretary Daniels, Secretary Baker and Dr. Garfield. It was
at a time when Secretary Baker was particularly sensitive about
public criticism. Some incident arose which brought the matter to
forefront of the conversation, and the President said,

"Don't be discouraged, Baker. There was a time when Daniels
was so deep in the hole that I couldn't see the top of his head, but
he is now out roaming around the country, and I think I can just
begin to see the top of your head, and I even begin to have some
hope for Garfield."

We then discussed the fact that sixty-one democratic Congressmen and forty-nine Republican Congressmen had gone into the

war and that eight Democratic Senators and four Republican Senators had enlisted. I brought this subject up because if that proceeding continues it would lose us the House and the Senate, no matter how the elections turned out. The President said it was perfect nonsense for senators and congressmen to enlist. He said it implied that the whole processes of the Government might cease in order that the army might get a mere handful of men. He also said that if these men insisted on going into the army as soon as they were elected to Congress they would get out of the army mighty quick, because he would give them all an honorable discharge.

Various other political speeches were discussed, and then Senator Pittman mentioned a debate which took place in the Senate that day involving the President's last note to Germany. The President then spoke with great frankness relative to the note in question. He said that he had studied it with the utmost care—that he had not relied on the official translation, but had taken the German text and had even gotten out his dictionaries to make sure of the precise meaning of the note. He said it was exceedingly frank in terms and that if it had come from any civilized nation it would have been necessary to accept it, but knowing the German situation, he was forced into the course that he had pursued. He said,

"You may not know it, and it is not generally known, but some of our Allies are very anxious for peace, and if I had followed the course that Senator Lodge seems to desire, and had slammed the door, it might well have been possible that someone else amongst our friends would have put his foot in the door."

He said we are the real fighting nation now, and he said, "You will also observe that the war is still going on." He said the difficulty with Senator Lodge is that he wants me to be a Hun and dic[t]ate a Hun peace.

The President spoke with great earnestness, and this little glimpse of what is going on behind the scenes made one realize more clearly the cross-currents which are always at work and which any great statesman has to take into account. The President always remembers the essential thing. He possesses the rare combination of moderation and wisdom. He is the leader of the world thought at the present moment, and is taking a wider view of world affairs than any other modern statesman. It almost seems as if the destinies of the human race were in his hands. It is his task to guide the allied countries, not only to victory, but to a peace that shall endure. It is the greatest and most difficult task that has even [ever] fallen to the lot of man. I have no doubt that he is the best equipped man in the entire world to control and direct world policies at the present critical time.

The statesmen of the Old World, no matter how freely they accept liberal policies, have behind them a diplomatic tradition which exerts upon them unconsciously a potent influence, and if they were allowed to have their head unchecked and should have in their hands the fruits of victory, they would enforce a peace which would be so oppressive and so selfish that it would not endure a generation. This is precisely the failing of men like Senator Lodge in this country. It is no idle thing to say that at this time the President is the hope of the world, and it is just as important to be prepared to support his policies for permanent peace as it is to support him in the prosecution of the war. This is the essential thing that makes the present political campaign of such far reaching consequence.

Mrs. Bass and Mrs. Meredith[2] called upon me Thursday, October 10th. They seemed to be in quite a state of mind owing to some remarks that Miss Paul had recently made about the President. Mrs. Bass wanted me to decline to receive the Ladies of the Congressional Union, if they managed to locate me. She said that if I had any regard for her opinion I would show them out. I told them if they once got in I might have difficulty in getting them out. She was not in a mood to discuss the matter lightly, and quoted what Miss Paul had recently said about the President, which was to the effect that when the President appeared before the Senate and advocated the passage of the Suffrage Amendment that he was not honest about it, and he really did not want the Amendment passed. Mrs. Bass regarded this as an insult to the President and tragically appealed to me, saying, "How could any woman say such a thing." For a moment I did not quite know how to respond, but as she waited in silence for an answer I finally said, "Why do you wish to apply the processes of logic to a person bereft of reason." This was too much for Mrs. Bass who laughed heartily and went away.

T MS (H. S. Cummings Papers, ViU).
    [1] Arthur Blythe Rouse, congressman from Kentucky, a Democrat.
    [2] Ellis Meredith (Mrs. Henry H. Clement), author and journalist, director of publicity of the Woman's Bureau of the Democratic National Committee, and a member of the National American Woman Suffrage Association.

A Draft of An Appeal to Voters by Joseph Patrick Tumulty

[c. Oct. 11, 1918]

No period in the nation's history has been more critical. We are all in agreement that the war must be won; that moral triumph cannot come without military victory. Methods which will lead most surely to this victory—methods dictated by a wealth of information not always available to those outside the executive branches of the government—may be, and sometimes are, impeded by hostile critics who claim to be constructive.

Foch is powerful because those associated with him in the war recognize his leadership. If he were given aids of transce[n]dent ability, but whose military theories differed from his own, he would find himself hampered in carrying out campaigns at critical times when orders cannot be explained, discussed, debated or compromised.

Unity of command among America and the Allies has been effective not merely in a military sense, but in the political sense as well. The knowledge that its opponents were at last united helped in the demoralization of the German government. The united spirit of France, a political as well as a military unity, has measurably contributed to its success on the battlefield.

As President of the United States I claim no special attributes for myself. The position in which I find myself is one in which any American might hope for and count upon the complete cooperation of all other Americans. And it is that sort of complete cooperation which I, as an American, bespeak from my fellow citizens.

I ask no more than other Presidents, of other political faith, even in less trying times, have asked. I ask it not for myself or for a political party, but for the nation itself, so that its inward unity of purpose in this war may be wholly apparent outwardly as well.

For Congress to be turned over to the opposing party might mean one thing to America, but something quite different in enemy countries, where it would be interpreted as a reversal of the war policies of the present Administration. Even more concretely, it would open the way to conflicting legislation, based upon conceptions different from those of the administrative branches of the government.

It has been difficult enough to work out the war plans, which so far have been successful, in the face of criticism of the kind uttered by the present minority leader of the Senate.[1] The fact that such criticisms are later retracted as the continuity of an Administration policy is unfolded makes the embarrassment no less. Attempts by hostile critics to force the hand of the Administration in delicate crises—wilfull misunderstanding over day to day events which are part of larger policies—might well prove crippling, instead of merely embarrassing, if such critics at this time were given complete power over legislation.

If the present minority leaders who seek to turn isolated war moves to their own political advantage were given authority to in-

terpose their conflicting methods, I have no doubt, and they themselves have left no doubt, that they would use their power to impose
their will, and their way of doing business upon the Administration.
It would mean a return to the old political order which had to give
way under enlightened public opinion. And it was because it did
give way that sound domestic laws were passed as a prelude to the
successful participation of America in the world war.

As a minority, the Republican leaders have repeatedly uttered
criticisms and predictions of failure which have been answered by
the glorious achievements of the American army on the field of
battle in France. It is not even unjust criticism that the Administration would avoid. What should be avoided, and is vital to the
interest of the nation to avoid, is the division of responsibility and
authority between the executive branches of the government and
the legislative branch. To divide responsibility between the two
parties must inevitably lead to conflict, to a clash of methods in
waging the war, and possibly to disaster.

At this very moment when work of reconstruction after the war
is being planned as a subordinate or an attendant detail of aggres-
sive prosecution of the war itself, some of the Republican leaders
have sought to give precedence to the issue which, they profess to
believe, should be moulded according to a set political pattern of
their own. It is not only conceivable, but likely, that these leaders
will attempt, should they be restored to power, to give a political
complexion to every piece of military legislation recommended by
the Administration. Whatever is recommended by the Administration to accelerate the victory of American arms may be forced to
wait upon the transmuting processes of a party of different faith in
power in Congress.

What I ask is that the American people, at the polls, give to the
Administration supporters who will be at one with the executive
departments in Washington; supporters who will support without
critically suggesting, for political aggrandizement, a different means
to gain the same end. There are times when no great inconvenience
is suffered by the country through divided authority and responsibility. At the present time, I fear, it would cause a perceptible
slowing down of American war effort.

CC MS (J. P. Tumulty Papers, DLC).
    [1] That is, Senator Lodge, who had succeeded Jacob H. Gallinger of New Hampshire,
who had died on August 17, 1918.

A Translation of a Letter from Jean Jules Jusserand to Colville Adrian de Rune Barclay and Its Enclosure

My dear Colleague: Washington, October 11, 1918.

In order to make the information I gave you last evening complete and more precise, and because the dinner hour came earlier than I should have wished, I believe it will be helpful to send you the enclosed paraphrase of successive telegrams which I have sent to inform my government of yesterday's conversation.

Please accept, my dear colleague, assurances of my very cordial sentiments.   Jusserand

TLS (FO 115/2428, p. 223, PRO).

E N C L O S U R E

As the Italian Ambassador and the English Chargé d'Affaires were willing, just as on many earlier occasions, to have me speak to the President in their names as well as my own, I have just presented to him the two notes intended for him.

I believe that all trace has disappeared of the annoyance about which the Secretary of State informed the three of us yesterday.

The President explained anew to me the reasons for his feeling. He told me that he thought, that for himself, he did not believe there was any chance for an armistice and that, in our present circumstances, he believed it would be contrary to our real interests to obtain one. If the public here were told that the Allied Prime Ministers actually foresaw a suspension of hostilities and a drawing up of terms, the *élan* for the war would slacken, with consequences which I need not belabor.

The President recalled, as Mr. Lansing had done, that these terms had been elaborated without consulting a government which had sent an army of two million men to the western front. I replied that these remarks showed better than any argumentation on my part how far the notes which the three governments had submitted to him were justified. At the point we have reached in the war, the questions to be debated are going to multiply and become more grave; it is therefore indispensable that a country assuming a role of primary importance be represented in the deliberations not by an agent charged simply to pass along information but very much by a person who knows the President's thinking and would be in a position to take a real part in debates and decisions.

For various reasons, the President sees great difficulties in acting in this way, especially on account of the distance. The ministers of the other countries, he says, are on the spot or so close that they are in constant touch with their compatriots. For an American, contact would quickly be lost, and little by little he would be influenced by the ambience and end up incapable of giving truly American advice.

I combated this idea, saying that it ought not to be impossible to find a man having the necessary knowledge and political sense and enjoying the President's confidence, one, moreover, who could travel from time to time and maintain direct contact. In reality, however, a greater difficulty is that the President is himself the whole government, and that he is little inclined to delegate powers to a representative sent so far away.

I emphasized only the grounds which militated in favor of our requests, especially that very annoyance which he had felt at the elaboration, without consulting him, of projects with which our greatest hope was to associate him. He promised, at last, to examine the question seriously, and I believe that he will do this with good will.

In informing him that the reason for the note of the three governments was the eulogistic appreciation accorded his reply, I admitted to him that I, for my own part, had been unable, when I learned of it, to reassure myself that the door had not been opened by him to exchanges of views which our enemies, skilled as they are in working on human frailty, would exploit to frustrate our wishes.

The President assured me, in a most categorical way, that he would have none of this and that he was absolutely determined to prevent everything which could hinder a sustained and mounting effort, until together we attain definitive victory.

On this very question of the terms of an armistice, the President has told me flatly that a [German] troop withdrawal would, no more for him than for us, be a sufficient condition for consenting to the cessation of hostilities. This is only a condition to be met, so that one could *speak* of an armistice. But as for *according* one, he continued, it went without saying that the military commanders were alone competent to fix the terms.

From the interview I gained the impression that we had come very close to grave misunderstandings, and that, now, we were fundamentally in accord. There is no doubt that both parties desire a peace imposed after an absolute victory, but that each would seem to have believed and feared that the other party might give consideration to an untimely cessation of hostilities.

To remove any doubts which might remain in the President's mind, I told him that the arrangements made as to the duration of the American and Allied efforts, and, beyond these, the simple enumeration of armistice terms eventually to be set at Versailles, have demonstrated that none of us dreams of anything resembling a relaxation of the military effort; for Germany's acceptance of the kind of obligations which were envisaged at Versailles (and I know only what Mr. Lansing has told me) would in fact amount to the very *capitulation* which we want, and which she [Germany] at present seems in no way disposed to yield.

T MS (FO 115/2428, pp. 224-227, PRO).

From James Cardinal Gibbons

My dear Mr. President: Baltimore October the 12th, 1918.

I beg to inform you that I have just received a message from His Holiness the Pope, through the Cardinal Secretary of State, in which His Holiness asks me in his name to commend to your benevolent consideration the request of the Austrian Government that an armistice be granted with a treaty for peace based on the points given by you in your messages of the 8th of January and of the 12th of February. The Holy Father asks me to inform you that in this step he is actuated solely by his most ardent desire to see ended as soon as possible this disastrous war which for so long a time has desolated the world and that he feels that Divine Providence has reserved for you and for our great Republic the merciful mission of restoring peace to the world.

I would have given myself the honor of presenting this message of His Holiness to you in person, but I did not wish to trespass on your valuable time now engrossed by such weighty cares, or to offer any occasion for comment which would likely be caused by my calling on you personally.

I would be pleased to communicate to His Holiness any reply or communication which you would wish to make, assuring you that it will be treated in the strictest confidence.

With sentiments of the highest esteem and warm personal regards, I am   Very faithfully Yours,   J. Card. Gibbons.

TLS (WP, DLC).

From Thomas Watt Gregory

Dear Mr. President: Washington, D. C. October 12, 1918.

I herewith return to you a letter addressed to you by Hon. William Kent on October 5th, in regard to the indictment of Mr. Bouck in the State of Washington, having kept a copy of his letter for my own files. You wrote me on the 7th in regard to this matter and I discussed the case with you after the Cabinet meeting last Tuesday. I think, however, that in returning Mr. Kent's letter to you I should make a brief report in writing.

The Grange movement in the State of Washington is of the same character as the Non-Partisan League movement in Minnesota and the two Dakotas. It is likely that there is a rather close connection between the two. Much political animosity has been aroused and my every effort has been to prevent the Department of Justice from being involved on either side. I have taken the position from the beginning that crime was personal, that no organization would be indicted as such, and that the fact that a man was a member of the Non-Partisan League or an opponent of the Non-Partisan League would have nothing whatever to do with Federal prosecutions.

The Mr. Hampton to whom Mr. Kent alludes in his letter has visited my Department on various occasions; he is a sort of Washington representative of the movements above referred to and does not hesitate to proclaim that he has the strongest political influence, which he intimates will compel the carrying out of his ideas and recommendations.

Of course Mr. Kent's statement, that the Attorney General's office indorses local prosecutors and backs them up in whatever course they take, is entirely without foundation. The idea that the Attorney General or the Department of Justice at Washington shall sit in judgment on all indictments brought and, after trying the cases here, instruct the District Attorneys to proceed with the prosecutions or to abandon them, is utterly absurd; not infrequently I call upon District Attorneys for full reports of the facts on which indictments are based. This sometimes results in my instructing them to dismiss the prosecutions because I reach the conclusion, after hearing from both sides, that the indictment should not have been brought or that, for some reason, it would be improper to continue the prosecution.

It is a fact, as stated by Mr. Kent, that he took up this particular case with my office and insisted that the indictment should be dismissed. The Department then called for a report from the District Attorney and, after going into the situation very carefully, I concluded that I was not justified in ordering the dismissal. I not only do not accept Mr. Kent's statement that the local Assistant to the Attorney General, Clarence L. Reames, who is conducting this prosecution, is bent on the ruin of Bouck and the Grange and Non-Partisan League movements, but I am sure that it is not true.

The indictment charges Bouck with having made certain false and untrue statements, substantially as follows:

"If this war lasts three years, the war debt will amount to one hundred billion dollars; it is placing a great mortgage on our children and their children; the revenues of the United States in the years to come will not be sufficient to pay the interest on the bonds; the rich men will grab all these Liberty Bonds and they will get them all together in the rich men's pockets; the revenues of the United States for years to come will not pay the interest on the Liberty Bonds; we will be under servitude to the rich men forever as far as the United States is concerned; we will be under the reign of these rich men forever; we will never get out from under the reign of these rich men because the revenues of the United States will not pay the interest on the Liberty Bonds; the war will not end until the Nonpartisan League gets their rights; it is a rich man's war and the war will not end until the rich men get all the gold they want and then it will end; this is not a war for democracy, it is a rich man's war; the war should be based on the 'pay-as-you-go' plan, and if we cannot pay as we go, the expenses should be cut down until we can pay as we go; the war will not end until the rich people fill their pockets with gold; we are forced to fight against our will; this war will continue until the multi-millionaires make their fortunes; your children's children for years to come will have their noses to the grindstone paying off this debt of the Liberty Bonds; the capitalists brought about the war and it is all for their gain; it was not put up to the people as it should have been; the people should have had a vote on it, and we are forced to fight against our will."

The indictment charges that these remarks were made with the intent to interfere with the operation and success of the military and naval forces of the United States and to promote the success of our enemies, that in making the statements the defendant attempted to obstruct the recruiting and enlistment service of the United States, and that they were made with the intent to obstruct the sale by the United States of its bonds and securities. The District Attorney writes that six responsible and trustworthy witnesses testified before the grand jury that Bouck made the statements charged in the indictment and that these statements are more seditious than those made by William Kaufman, a prominent member of the Non-Partisan League recently sentenced to serve five years in the penitentiary. I think it very likely that when the case is tried other witnesses will deny that Bouck made the statements charged, but this would not be unusual and would not be ground for dismissing the indictment. If Bouck made the statements charged in the indictment, he should undoubtedly be vigorously prosecuted. The grand jury believed that he had made them or it would not have brought the indictment, the District Attorney says that he has six responsible witnesses to sustain the charge, and under these circumstances there is no course open for us to pursue except to let the law take its course.

To dismiss this indictment under the circumstances above set out, on the insistence of friends of Bouck, would not only be in violation of the long established rules of this Department, rules which are founded on wisdom and experience, but would be construed as, and largely equivalent to, our taking the part of the Non-Partisan League in the course of a criminal prosecution. Clearly the case is one in which the views of the grand jury and the advice of the District Attorney should be followed and the exercise of discretion by the latter acquiesced in.

Faithfully yours,   T. W. Gregory

TLS (WP, DLC)

From Scott Ferris

My dear Mr. President: Washington, D. C. October 12, 1918.

I understand you have an engagement with Senator McKellar and Congressman Keating of Colorado for Monday afternoon to discuss retirement legislation.

I have taken the liberty of suggestion [suggesting] to Mr. Keating that he say a word to you concerning the situation in his district. With the right help he can win out. He thinks he needs just a line from you, and after carefully considering all the factors that enter into the contest I am convinced he is right.

I assure you I dislike to burden you with these suggestions, but in some districts you are the only one who can give the candidates the final push which will put them across the line winners.

Very sincerely yours,   Scott Ferris

TLS (WP, DLC).

David Lloyd George to Sir Eric Geddes

[London] *12th October 1918.*

Following from Prime Minister for Sir Eric Geddes.

You should be careful to express no approval or disapproval of Wilson's attitude towards Prince Max's Note about which we were not even consulted. As you are aware we cannot accept his views about the Freedom of the Seas and our military advisers including Foch consider that the conditions he seems to contemplate for an Armistice inadequate. You can of course say that British Empire is resolute that there shall be no sham or humbugging peace. We do not mean to let them off by an armistice the terms of which will be more helpful to them than to us or to sign any peace which will give militarism a fresh lease of life. Our information as to conditions in Germany shows considerable demoralisation and panic. You ought to do your best to make America realise the extent of the effort of the British Empire including the Dominions. The naval side you know. On the military side you can say that last year our casualties were considerably more than those of our Allies, and that this year on the Western Front they have been equal to those of all the Allies combined. This last battle has been a most remarkable success for our arms.

T telegram (FO 371/3493, PRO).

Lord Reading to Sir William Wiseman

[London] 12th Oct. 1918.

Urgent.

(A) With reference to my telegram of October 10th.

You will have seen from later telegrams that the view I expressed as to misunderstanding by BLISS or of his language is right. On return of Prime Minister and other Ministers the whole situation was made quite clear. In view of possible enquiry as to terms of armistice it was thought right for the Military Advisers to study the question and arrive at an opinion, which would then have to be considered by the Prime Ministers and the President before any conclusion could be reached. That is the exact situation, and no conclusion was reached. Consequently there can be no possible ground of annoyance or grievance at Washington. I have no doubt both the President and Colonel House are now quite satisfied after the explanation of the Ambassadors given by Jusserand, and the personal telegram from Mr. Balfour. I should, however, point out that my statement in my telegram of October 10th as to impression produced here by President's reply referred to Press and public on first view. There is, however, uneasiness in some ministerial and best informed circles as to the position taken up by the President in his reply to Germany. Very confidentially there is a feeling that he should have consulted us before replying. Had he taken this course it would have been pointed out that if the Germans accepted simpliciter the conditions laid down by the President before the latter would propose a cessation of hostilities to the Allies, it would become difficult to add further conditions of armistice including amplified conditions of evacuation.

You will know how to use this comment of mine. Understand there is no uneasiness as to the President's attitude; it arises upon the form of the communications.

(B) My departure will be on October 20th. What are the possibilities of HOUSE or other political representative coming here. We fully appreciate loss to us if HOUSE were absent from America, upon which you know my views.

T telegram (Reading Papers, FO 800/225, PRO).

From the Diary of Colonel House

October 13, 1918.

The President's visit to New York on Friday the 11th,[1] and the fateful reply to his demands have made it impossible to keep the the diary day by day.

Governor Samuel W. McCall lunched with me last Thursday. I "put him through his paces" and I am quite content with the thought of him as a Peace Commissioner. I made the suggestion to the President that the Governor go over with me now as adviser. It is not that I want him in that capacity, but I believe it would have a good effect upon the country if I should take over a few men of his standing, particularly a prominent republican.

I outlined to McCall the League, as the President and I have it in mind, and he agreed to it almost without reservation. In mentioning the fact that I might ask him to go in the capacity of adviser, in the event the President should send me to Europe soon, he said he would resign as Governor of Massachusetts at once and would consider it an honor to be associated with me in such a capacity.

I had a telegram from McAdoo, saying he would reach New York at 3.30. I had planned to take Governor McCall to The Inquiry, but instead I asked Sidney[2] to do so.

McAdoo was with me from the time he arrived until 8.30. He

and Eleanor took dinner with us. He, too, is a candidate for the peace table, and mentioned many valid reasons why he should be there. He thought it would be ridiculous for Lansing to go as the head of the commission in the event the President did not go himself, and he said he would be perfectly willing to go as a member of the commission under me. McAdoo, as I have said before, is not lacking in generosity. He agrees with Frank Polk and others that the President should not go himself.

The President arrived at 3.25 on Friday the 11th. He and Mrs. Wilson and I drove from the station out Riverside. When we returned to the Waldorf we had a half hour's conference. He was much exercised over the Allies asking the Supreme War Council to give their opinion as to what should constitute a victorious armistice. He thought they should not have done this without first consulting him. He also considered it a mistake to go into details regarding the terms of the armistice at all at this time. If word of it should get out he thought it would demoralize the people of the Allies [Allied] countries as well as our own. He was indignant with Sir Eric Geddes because of an interview which appeared in the papers the day before,[3] and when I told him that Sir Eric was leaving almost at once for England and wished to say a word of farewell while he, the President, was in New York, he flatly refused. He said he had no intention of seeing him again, for he regarded Geddes' interview as a "piece of impertinence."

I did not press the matter then, but the next day I told Mrs. Wilson that it was necessary for the President to see Geddes whether he wanted to or not, and I suggested 10.45 Sunday morning as a suitable time. I explained that Geddes was one of the strong men of the British Government and his position was altogether different from that of one of the President's Cabinet.

When I saw Mrs. Wilson Saturday evening, she said she had arranged the interview as I had asked. I was present when Sir Eric Geddes and Admiral Duff[4] arrived in company with Admiral Robison[5] of our own Navy. The President was exceedingly cordial and Sir Eric went away as happy as could be. He came up to our apartment later to see me for a final word before sailing. He spoke of the President in enthusiastic terms.

The President said Sir Eric asked him what he meant by "the freedom of the seas." His reply was that it was a question that could be threshed out in "common council," but that vaguely he had in mind that any nation having become an outlaw as Germany was today, would be compelled to feel the weight of the united naval power of the world. He was distinctly opposed to any one nation exercising this power. Geddes and I discussed the question afterward and I thought if they were fair-minded we could get together on some plan which would be of benefit to all.

We dined with the President and Mrs. Wilson at the Waldorf Hotel. Just before dinner was announced, Tumulty came in with the news that Germany had accepted the President's terms.[6] Col. Churchill of the Military Intelligence Bureau had telephoned it over from Washington. We wondered whether the news was authentic, but concluded from its construction that it was. When we went in to the table the President wrote me a little note in which he said, "tell Mrs. W" and signed it "W.W."[7] I had already anticipated him in this. It was a family dinner party but rather large, consisting besides the four of us, Jessie and Francis Sayre, Miss Bones, Tumulty and Grayson.

After dinner we went almost immediately to the Italian Fete at the Metropolitan Opera House. There was an enormous crowd which cheered the President with much enthusiasm. I was so stirred by the news that had come from Berlin that I could not listen to the program. Tumulty and I went to the Directors' Room in the Opera House, called up Washington and received confirmation from Frank Polk and the Washington Post. Shortly after ten o'clock I returned home. I wished to do some telephoning and to think. I had arranged for Frank Polk to call me over the telephone at 10.30 (over the private wire), and we had a long talk. It was decided that Joe Grew should keep in touch with the Swiss Legation and let us know the official text as soon as it came in.

I did not try to sleep for a long while, for it seemed to me that the war was finished, certainly finished if the Allied statesmen have the judgment to garner victory.

Sunday morning numbers of newspaper men called me over the telephone to get my opinion and I had a busy day until the President and I left for Washington at four o'clock. He and Mrs. Wilson and Loulie lunched at Riverdale with Mr. and Mrs. Cleveland H. Dodge. The President had asked me to return to Washington with them so I had much to do.

On the way to Washington, the President had to have what he called "his does [dose] of Tumulty." Tumulty seems to have the idea that the President will do something foolish in answering the German Note.

I asked the President if he had finally decided upon the Peace Commissioners. He replied, "I thought we had done that at Magnolia. You and I, Lansing and Baker was what we thought then." I suggested Governor McCall for the republican member and told him I had "put him through his paces" and that he would be sympathetic to his, the President's ideas. The President tentatively assented to McCall.

We reached Washington at 9.15, drove immediately to the White House, and soon after went to bed.

¹ Wilson had come to New York on the afternoon of October 11 to march in the Liberty Loan parade on October 12 and to attend a concert at the Metropolitan Opera House on the latter date for the benefit of Italian soldiers blinded in the war. He also attended a performance of a musical comedy, *The Girl Behind the Gun*, with book and lyrics by Guy Bolton and Pelham Grenville [P.G.] Wodehouse and music by Ivan Caryll, at the New Amsterdam Theatre on October 11 and participated in a sale of Liberty Bonds which took place during the intermissions. *New York Times*, Oct. 12 and 13, 1918.

² That is, Sidney E. Mezes.

³ In an interview in Washington on October 9, Sir Eric Geddes asserted that the surest way to peace was to continue pounding the enemy on the battlefields. "I want a just peace," he said, "with no 'next time' written across it. My business is not to make peace, but to get on with this war. We cannot win by talking of peace. To get us all talking of peace is just what Germany wants." Geddes added that talk of peace was fatal to that enthusiasm of both soldiers and civilians necessary for the winning of the war. "The allied armies and allied navies," he declared, "will bring peace. Let the Kaiser talk while Foch shoots. 'Unconditional surrender' are words which show some understanding of the allied language. When Germany has learned that language thoroughly, including the words 'reparation,' 'restitution,' and 'good faith,' she will have gone far enough in her lesson to justify peace talk." "Geddes Deplores Peace Discussion," *New York Times*, Oct. 10, 1918.

⁴ Vice Adm. Sir Alexander Ludovic Duff, Assistant Chief of the Naval Staff.

⁵ Rear Adm. Samuel Shelburne Robison, commander of the submarine force of the Atlantic Fleet.

⁶ Tumulty's news was based upon an advance (sent *en clair* from Nauen on October 12) text of Wilhelm Solf to Swiss Foreign Office, Oct. 12, 1918, T telegram, enclosed in F. Oederlin to RL, Oct. 14, 1918, TLS, both in SDR, RG 59, 763.72119/2313, DNA. Solf had been appointed as the German Foreign Secretary on October 4. The English translation of Solf's note, provided by the German legation in Bern, reads as follows:

"In reply to the question of the President of the United States of America the German government hereby declares:

"The German government has accepted the terms laid down by President Wilson in his address of January the eighth and in his subsequent addresses as the foundations of a permanent peace of justice. Consequently its object in entering into discussions would be only to agree upon practical details of the application of these terms.

"The German government believes that the governments of the powers associated with the United States also accept the position taken by President Wilson in his addresses.

"The German government in accordance with the Austro-Hungarian government for the purpose of bringing about an armistice declares itself ready to comply with the propositions of the President in regard to evacuation.

"The German government suggests that the President may occasion the meeting of a mixed commission for making the necessary arrangements concerning the evacuation.

"The present German government which has undertaken the responsibility for this step towards peace has been formed by conference and in agreement with the great majority of the Reichstag. The chancellor supported in all of his actions by the will of this majority speaks in the name of the German government and of the German people."

⁷ Wilson's handwritten note is in the House Papers, CtY.

A Fragment of the First Draft of An Appeal to Voters

[c. Oct. 13, 1918]

ment under a unified leadership, and that a Republican Congress would divide the leadership.

The leaders of the minority in the present Congress have unquestionably been pro-war, but they have been anti-Administration. At almost every turn, since we entered the war, they have sought to take the choice of policy and the conduct of the war out of my hands and put it under the control of instrumentalities of their own choosing. This is no time either for divided counsels or for divided leadership.

The return of a Republican majority to either House of Congress would, moreover, certainly be interpreted on the other side of the water as a repudiation of my leadership. Spokesmen of the Republican party are urging you to elect a Republican Congress in order to back up and support the President, but even if that argument should impose upon some credulous voters on this side of the water they would impose on no one on the other side. It is well understood there as well as here that the Republican leaders desire not so much to support the President as to guide and direct him. The peoples of the allied countries with whom we are associated against Germany are quite familiar with the significance of elections. They would find it very difficult to believe that the voters of the United States had chosen to support their President by electing to the Congress a controlling majority of his habitual opponents, who had at every stage of the war been his active critics.

I need not tell you, my fellow countrymen, that I am asking your support, not for my own sake or for the sake of a political party, but for the sake of the nation itself, in order that its inward unity of purpose may be evident to all the world. In ordinary times I would not feel at liberty to make such an appeal to you. In ordinary times divided counsels can be endured without permanent hurt to the country. But these are not ordinary times. If in these critical days it is your wish to back me with undivided minds, I beg that you will say so in a way which it will not be possible to misunderstand either here at home or among our associates on the other side of the sea. I submit my difficulties and my hopes to you.

WWT MS (WP, DLC).

From Hsü Shih-ch'ang

Peking, Oct. 13, 1918.

Please accept my very sincere thanks for your telegram of congratulations upon my assumption of the office to which I was duly elected by the parliament of the Republic. It is my earnest desire that not only the traditional intimate friendship existing between our two countries will be maintained and strengthened but also efforts within our power will continue to be exerted towards the furtherance of the common cause in which the splendid success of the army of your country has won the admiration and respect of the world. National unity upon which the welfare of the people entirely depends is a matter demanding my first attention, and you may be assured that I will put forth my best efforts to bring about its consummation and meet the wishes of the people of the whole country that in coming councils of family of nations our country may assume its rightful place and work with your country hand in hand toward the realization of the highest ideals.

Hsu Shih Chang.

T telegram (SDR, RG 59, 893.001 H85/3, DNA).

From Henry French Hollis

Dear Mr. President: Paris, October 13, 1918.

The Embassy pouch leaves Monday and I have my letter of Oct. 11 still in hand. The papers this morning give Germany's acceptance of your terms, which was received by them too late for comment this morning. But there will be enough tomorrow morning. I will send clippings.

The French, the English and our jingo press will now say that you did not go far enough,—the usual result when a matter is compromised,—each side thinking that it might have got more. They will try to interpret the German acceptance and your propositions as favorably as possible to our side,—more favorably than you will think justified. If you are to get a fair and permanent peace, we do not want Germany beaten any worse than she is. If she should be reduced to a point where England and France should think they did not need our help any more, they would rub it in beyond all reason.

You will, I know, pay no attention to criticisms in America, and you will have in mind the pressure you can still exert on our Associates as Commander in Chief through Pershing, and through our control of essential supplies. We must feed the world for two years more.

I hope, however, that pressure of this sort will not become necessary. You will know how best to use it.

Sincerely yours,   Henry F. Hollis.

TLS (WP, DLC).

From David Lawrence

My dear Mr. President: Washington October 13, 1918

May I beg your indulgence long enough to read the analysis which I have made of our own public opinion as it is reacting on the German note of yesterday? Let me say, at the outset, that what I am setting forth is not my own advocacy of any particular course of action but what seems to be the instinctive and spontaneous desire of the people for a very well-defined course of action.

In the first place, it may not have been your opportunity as it has been mine to come in contact with the men who are engaged in feeding the people the facts and interpretation of facts on which public opinion is formed. Fortunately or unfortunately, America has been fed war-hate or rather hatred of the Kaiser and the Hohenzollerns by Liberty Loan posters, unchecked newspaper propaganda, and speeches galore. To a surprising extent the Kaiser has become the single issue. Those who have studied history know he alone is not the issue—that he may become a figurehead just as much as the King of England and that the militaristic crowd, collectively and individually, are as much responsible for this war as any single member of the Hohenzollern family. If this could be made clear to the people, they would then amplify their war cry and make it broader so as to include all the militarists. In other words, they want to see the downfall of that class in Germany which has foisted on the world its terrible system.

The man on the street today doesn't believe Germany "has been licked enough." That is a crude way to express it and I am sorry to say an unintelligent way for I believe with you in a healing peace and am as loath to believe in the knockout blow stuff as I was when the German general staff was handing it out to the German people when the shoe was on the other foot. But if we analyze "Germany hasn't been licked enough," it carries with it two implications— that the Kaiser and his family must be swept from power and that the men who broke their pledges with the United States shall never be given an opportunity to make any more pledges. It has the appearance of a personal issue but it is a fundamental principle.

Let us analyze the slogan "He kept us out of war" which caught the imagination of so many people in 1916. How absurd it would be for anyone to argue that the people of the United States were weak-kneed and spineless and selfishly wanted to avoid danger and the annoyances of war! Rather did it represent a well defined opinion that you, as the leader of our people, had the wisdom and skill to keep us out of a war in which we traditionally felt that we did not belong so long as our rights had not been trampled upon or so long as we were assured that these rights would not be again transgressed. It was a fundamental principle that gave you such wide support in 1916. The people have come to look upon you as the exponent of great principles and in the answer to the third question which you propounded to Germany may be found a principle so big that its protruding premise is inescapable. You asked, first, if Germany accepted not your program but your terms. Germany said "Yes." You asked, secondly, if Germany would withdraw from all invaded territory for purposes of an armistice. Germany said "Yes." But your basic question which was the base of the pyramid itself was number three. On its answer depended the validity of number one and number two. Without number three satisfactorily answered, the whole structure crumbled. You asked a simple question—Did the peace offer come in the name of the constituted authorities who have thus far conducted this war? The answer came back "In the name of those constituted authorities as well as in the name of a newly constructed Reichstag which represents the German people better than ever a legislature did that it has hitherto had, a legislature which had a part in selecting the chancellor, and a legislature with powers almost coordinate with that of the executive itself."

Unfortunately, our people have not been acquainted with the nature of the recent reforms and the decree of September 30th or they would see in the second clause of that third answer a very hopeful sign. If we had a free and untrammelled system of communication from the minds of the German people to the minds of our own people with no absurd censorship in between, the importance of that second clause would be obvious to everybody. But we must face the facts. Even if our people were fully acquainted with the tremendous strides that have been made toward reform, they would not be satisfied that the Thing as you so aptly christened the system of Prussianism had been totally eradicated. They would feel that the cancerous growth was still there to recrudesce when the poisons of military glory and victories won and all the other adulations showered on an army that so staunchly held the world at bay for four years were mingled with the shouts of joy over the provisions of a peace treaty that held the frontiers intact in a "war of annihilation and self-defense."

I cannot agree with the clamor for a blunt answer of the kind so many newspapers are suggesting, of the to-hell-with-the-Kaiser variety. The reform movement in Germany must be further encouraged so that the extreme socialists may come into power and bolshevize the situation in Germany. But in encouraging that movement, the indescribable spirit of the army and the navy as well as the rank and file of our people who have set their hearts on getting nothing else out of this war but the vindication of their principle that democracy must win a complete and lasting triumph over autocracy, I say the spirit of the people back of the loans and back of the troops must be given careful consideration. Judging by what I have seen and heard, I set it down most solemnly as my humble judgment that anything short of a positive definition of the issue as between the "constituted authorities who have thus far con-ducted the war" and the elimination of those authorities before conditions one and two of your inquiry can be further considered, would be disastrous not merely to the prestige of the man whom the world acclaims as its leader today but disastrous to the further application of moral force itself. No, Mr. President, rightly or wrongly, our people have been fed intolerance and personalities for eighteen months. British and French propaganda has intensified that feeling and today you have behind you a nation ready to follow you to the finish for the extermination of the men responsible for the things the people have read about. The people havent stopped to analyze events in Germany. Unfortunately those of us who have tried to keep them apace with it have not even been permitted to examine German newspapers so as to interpret intelligently the trend of affairs. As a result, America knows only that which the newspapers have been giving her and only those statements which you have made in your public speeches. You have described so splendidly the origin of this war in secret counsels and selfish groups. You have argued so effectively that such groups must never be permitted to disturb the peace of the world. You have said we cannot come to terms with the present German government and you are privi-leged now to call the attention of the German people to that section of your speech of September 30th[1] in New York in which you so described the attitude of the American people. If they accept the principles laid down in your speech of January 8th "and subsequent addresses" would it not be in order to make your answer to the German note of last night a single question, asking, in effect, if the German people read and if their answer means they have agreed to that portion of your speech of September 30th referring to the present government of Germany. All the world would applaud the interrogatory form of your answer again. You could speak with satisfaction of the straightforward answers given to questions one and two but you could advert with surprise to the failure of the Chancellor to regard sincerely your expression of unwillingness to

[1] Actually, September 27.

sign any treaty or propose any parley or submit to the Allies any proposal which is sent you "in the name of the German government" when with that government the whole world knows is *associated* the men who gave their solemn pledge after the Lusitania sank that they would not sink our ships and people without warning and then ruthlessly broke that pledge, the same people who guaranteed the neutrality of Belgium and then violated it etc.

But, Mr President, whatever your answer may be, whatever the outcome of this war may be, I believe history will associate with your name more closely than with that of any other man the championship of the league of nations. The world was ruled by absolute monarchs in the eighteenth century. The French Revolution and Napoleonic wars tended to upset their right to handle their peoples in whimsical disregard of national aspirations. Then came the Congress of Vienna and a century of intense nationalism. It was but an expansion in clever manner by the absolute monarchs of their own power—they intensified nationalism for their own purposes. A new era has come. Nationalism meant armaments and intense economic rivalries and the greatest bloodshed in human history. You have opened the eyes of the world to a new vision—internationalism and a league of nations. That is the paramount issue. That is why peace signed by the militarists would be unsafe for the league of nations. Until the Hohenzollerns are gone—and they must go anyway by the will of the German people—the American people will not be ready to accept Germany as a partner in that league. By pointing out these facts to the German people, you show them that the obstacle to peace is not indemnities, is not Alsace-Lorraine, is not anything that relates to terms for we are agreed on terms and fundamental principles; we are not in dispute about methods of arranging an armistice; we, the peoples of democracy are ready to embrace a new democracy but we cannot and will not until the last shred of autocracy is removed. Germany will see that between her and peace stands a few men and their defeated system. The German people, seeing our victorious armies at their doors, seeing that they can get a just peace through you, may at first scorn such a proposal but slowly and surely they will find ways and means of ridding themselves of the single obstacle that stands between them and peace. You have stated in one of your speeches that you were not interested in the *form* of government in Germany but the substance insofar as it represented the power to guarantee peace. You can make it clear that you are not interested in personalities but in the elimination for all times of a system that has cost the world so much suffering. The opportunity lies in that third answer and you can keep the door to peace ajar by saying that any time the third condition is satisfactorily answered, we will be ready to go ahead with the "practical details" of conditions one and two.

Pardon me for the length of this but both as a personal friend and a follower of your philosophy, I hope you will make but one answer "Not Yet."   Sincerely,   David Lawrence

TLS (WP, DLC).

From William Williams Keen

My dear Mr. President   Philada. Oct. 13, '18

Forgive me if I *implore* you not even to consider an Armistice.

That would mean that their army, now in peril but only half beaten, would be safely extricated, instead of being destroyed or captured.

Germany then would win by stoutly refusing to accept our detailed terms, for fighting would *never* be resumed after an Armistice.

We shall surely be embroiled with our Allies unless we insist on Unconditional Surrender. What a farce it is, to ask for peace and at the same moment to murder *our own* soldiers by renewed submarine atrocities; to destroy French cities as they retreat; & to deport every living human being!

As you wisely said "there can be no peace obtained by any kind of bargain or compromise with the Governments of the Central Empires. * * * They are without honor & do not intend justice. They observe no covenants* * * * We cannot come to terms with them."

Unconditional Surrender followed by terms dictated on German soil are the only possible basis for durable peace.

With Earnest prayers to God to guide you aright I am
                    Most respectfully Yours,   W. W. Keen

P.S. Literally *Everybody* I have met in the last few days are in earnest accord with these views.

ALS (WP, DLC).

Lord Reading to Sir William Wiseman

[London] 9.15. p.m. 13th Oct. 1918.

Very Urgent and Secret. NO DISTRIBUTION.

(A) The German Government's reply to the President seems to assume that his answer to the German Note contains the terms of a cessation of arms. As we know from the terms of the President's interview with the French ambassador[1] this interpretation is in direct opposition to his view which was merely to lay down an essential preliminary condition for acceptance by the German Government before the President would communicate the German proposal to the associated Governments. It appears to us vital and it is therefore suggested that the President should inform the German Government immediately and publicly, and before he makes the communication to the associated Governments that this is a wrong interpretation to place upon his language and that the terms and conditions of a cessation of arms are matters for the associated naval and military authorities and that nothing in the President's cablegram limits the terms and conditions which these authorities may think necessary.

(B) The above is intended for communication to BEACH [HOUSE] and I think you should impress upon him the difficulties in which we may be placed unless some such course is adopted, more particularly the effect upon the morale of the armies and also of our civil population from uncertainty as to whether an armistice is about to be agreed to or not.

(C) The situation now developing shows how essential it is that Colonel House should come immediately. Mr. Balfour has seen this telegram and agrees with it.

T telegram (Reading Papers, FO 800/225, PRO).
[1] See the Enclosure printed with J. J. Jusserand to C. A. de R. Barclay, Oct. 11, 1918.

Two Telegrams from Sir Eric Geddes to David Lloyd George

[Washington, Oct. 13, 1918]

[*No. 797. Very urgent.*][1] Have had full talk with President today—Sunday. His attitude now that he has received German reply appears to be hardening towards caution. He is fully alive—

(a) To the need for continuing the prosecution of the war and retaining National will for the war. Proposes shortly to announce undiminished despatch of troops and war effort of United States.

(b) Realises that the time has arrived when consultation with Allied Powers is essential and is accordingly sending House immediately to Europe.

(c) Stated that armistice terms framed by Naval and Military Officers must be viewed in spirit that undue humiliation would be inexcusable except insofar as such terms are necessary to prevent enemy taking advantage of armistice to reform their forces and better their position.

(d) Is inclined to take Germany to task for recent atrocities such as sinking "Leinster"[2] which he was excusing on ground that submarine might have been long out of touch with Germany but I assured him that Germany was able to instruct submarines daily. Am told by Wiseman that he may also take up questions of personal guilt for such murders as Fryatt and Cavell.[3]

(e) In talking of his 14 conditions conversation with me naturally turned on freedom of seas upon which his views are obviously unformed but his intention appears to be to deal with that if possible in generalities and acceptance of principle that no one Power in League of Nations shall exercise its Naval strength to crush a belligerent Power without consent of League leaving until the occasion arises any decision as to nationality of Naval police force. I ventured to explain to him that of all belligerent Nations our views would naturally be strongest on this point on account of our geographical position and overwhelming Naval superiority.

(f) President referred to the absolute necessity for break up of Austria owing to commitments to oppressed Nationalities instancing Czech-Slovaks and appeared to be of the opinion that the disintegration of Austria necessitated greater stringency in dealing with Germany in order that she should no longer be a dominant Military power surrounded by smaller impotent States.

The whole tone of the discussion was most cordial and he is evidently fully seized with the necessity for consultation with the Allied Powers but outstandingly fearful that the Naval and Military Authorities may urge an armistice so humiliating that the German people could not accept it.

Wiseman was discussing matters simultaneously with House who had just left President during my interview in adjoining rooms, and saw the President for a few minutes after I left. This telegram is dictated in his presence and embodies his own impressions of the exisiting situation.

(End of report of interview with President).

My own visit has only been partially successful owing to the really serious failure of their Destroyer building programme upon which they have been very unduly optimistic, but Admiral Duff is of the opinion that they have met us as far as their limited productive capacity permits. The negotiations and intercourse have been of a most satisfactory and cordial nature throughout.

---

[1] Addition from the copy in the D. Lloyd George Papers, House of Lords Record Office.
[2] The Irish mail steamer *Leinster* had been sunk by a German submarine in the Irish Sea on October 10. Newspaper reports immediately following the tragedy placed the death toll at approximately 450 persons, including numerous women and children. London *Times*, Oct. 11 and 12, 1918, and *New York Times*, Oct. 12, 1918.
[3] About which see, respectively, n. 9 to the Enclosure printed with RL to WW, Aug. 22, 1916, Vol. 38, and R. U. Johnson to WW, Oct. 22, 1915, n. 1, Vol. 35.

Marching in the Fourth Liberty Loan Parade in New York

Prince Maximilian von Baden

Wilhelm Solf

General Maurice Janin

Herbert Hoover

Wartime Diplomats
Clockwise, from upper left: John William Davis, William Graves Sharp,
Pleasant Alexander Stovall, Thomas Nelson Page

Unconditional Surrender!
Theodore Roosevelt and Henry Cabot Lodge

Thomas William Lamont

[Washington, Oct. 13, 1918]

I see from Barnes' Paper G. T. 5815 of 28th ultimo and recent Cabinet proceedings Minutes 481 on the same subject[1] that formulation of League of Nation proposals in detail and President's reluctance to agree to publication or discussion of Phillimore's report is concerning minds of Cabinet. The President told me to-day that he was strongly opposed to such discussions or publication because the League of Nations though a beautiful ideal which we must translate into practice would cause so much bitter controversy and so much feeling on account of the special circumstances ruling each Ally's opinion, citing as an instance the British overwhelming interest in the freedom of the seas, that he strongly deprecated confusing the issues and raising controversies on such a subject at the present time as it would divert minds of Statesmen and the public of Allied countries from a vigorous prosecution of the war. Also that publication of Phillimore's report gives opportunity for every crank to urge views to the distraction of Statesmen's minds from vital war issues, and his desire is to postpone the discussion with consequent disturbance until Peace Conference. Wiseman agrees with me that is President's attitude.

T telegrams (E. Geddes Papers, ADM 116/1809, PRO).

[1] G. T. 5815 was a memorandum by George Nicoll Barnes, dated Sept. 28, 1918 (CAB 24/65, PRO), which was considered at the meeting of the War Cabinet on October 2. Barnes, at this time the Labour party representative in the War Cabinet, argued that it was time for British and Allied discussion of a league of nations to get down to concrete, practical details concerning the nature, establishment, and operation of such an organization. Hitherto, he said, the league had been discussed only in "rhetorical terms." He feared that, if the project had not reached a more advanced stage when peace came, it would be lost sight of altogether. He believed that the Allies should come to some mutual understanding on the subject, but that each of the Allies would have to work out their own ideas before mutual discussions could take place. Balfour reminded the War Cabinet that then, as earlier, "the main difficulty in the way of Mr. Barnes' suggestion was the President of the United States." Wilson had had the Interim Report of the Phillimore Committee before him for some time but had made no move in the matter. After some further discussion of the subject, Lord Reading commented that the reason why Wilson had objected to the immediate publication of the Phillimore Report was that, if it was published, it would generally be regarded as having been issued under the aegis of the British government. This would force the hand of other governments and "raise a premature discussion." "President Wilson's view," according to Reading, "was that there must be some kind of general agreement on the subject among the co-belligerents before any Peace Conference met, and he wished in the first instance to discuss the question with the British Government, so that they might concert some agreed scheme for a League of Nations before it was submitted to the other chief *Entente* Powers." After further discussion, the War Cabinet decided to hold an "informal meeting" of the principal ministers at the Foreign Office at an early date, "not to take any formal decision, but to further explore the subject of a League of Nations, in order to give Lord Reading an opportunity to acquaint himself with the general trend of the views held by members of His Majesty's Government thereon, before his return to the United States." The War Cabinet also agreed that Reading should "take the earliest opportunity, after his arrival at Washington, of initiating private and unofficial conversations with the President, or any officials deputed by him, with a view to the free and frank interchange of views on the subject." *War Cabinet 481. Minutes of a Meeting of the War Cabinet held . . . on Wednesday, October 2, 1918. . . .*, Printed copy (CAB 23/8, PRO). See also George W. Egerton, *Great Britain and the Creation of the League of Nations: Strategy, Politics, and International Organization, 1914-1919* (Chapel Hill, N. C., 1978), pp. 78-79.

Sir William Wiseman to Lord Reading and Sir Eric Drummond

[New York] Octr. 13, 1918.

CXP 801.

VERY URGENT—CLEAR THE LINE.

PERSONAL & VERY SECRET:

(A). You will have seen today's cable from First Lord of the Admiralty to the Prime Minister, with which I entirely concur.

(B). I saw the PRESIDENT for a few minutes this morning. He is very pleased with the situation, and is friendly and cordial. The misunderstanding about VERSAILLES meeting has been explained to his complete satisfaction. He is in a mood for caution, consultation and cooperation with us. He leaves New York this (Sunday) afternoon with HOUSE. They will remain in conference at the White House until HOUSE sails on Thursday. HOUSE seems to take it for granted that I shall go with him, so I shall do so unless I hear to the contrary. It is not yet decided whether HOUSE will go first to London or Paris.

(C). I suppose you will postpone your departure at any rate until HOUSE arrives. He hopes that you will be able to do so.

(D). The President asked me to come and see him at the White House before I leave, so I shall be in Washington Tuesday, returning here Wednesday.

(E). The President has not yet decided what his next move shall be, but I think it is possible that he may send another note to the German Government asking for more explicit assurances on certain points before he submits the question of an armistice to the Allies. The general sentiment here is to be very cautious of possible German trickery.

(F). Information about HOUSE's movements is very secret. It would be most unfortunate if American officials in Europe heard of it first from us, as was the case with the appointment of DAVIS.

T telegram (W. Wiseman Papers, CtY).

From the Diary of Josephus Daniels

1918 Monday 14 October

Returned from Raleigh at 10:10. Messenger met me with message to go at once to the White House. Found Col. House, Lansing and Baker with the President discussing answer to German note.[1] I read Gov. Bicketts letter[2] wh the President thought fine. Agreed that until German submarines quit sinking passenger ships & killing non-combatants we would have no armistice & no peace with Germany until explicit acceptance of WWs Fourth of July address— no autocratic government in Germany—was accepted & put into practise. I urged [Wilson] to express these views as already accepted, if G was honest, but not to close the door to peace.

¹ See the entry from the House Diary printed at Oct. 15, 1918.
² Actually, a telegram. Bickett suggested that Wilson should demand German evacuation of all occupied territory as an essential precondition of an armistice. T. W. Bickett to JD, Oct. 7, 1918, T telegram (J. Daniels Papers, DLC).

From Joseph Patrick Tumulty

No. I Dear Governor: The White House October 14, 1918

After I left you Saturday night I went back to my hotel and drafted what I think would be an answer to the Germany [German] reply. I am sending it to you in the rough shape in which I left it.

First. I think the President ought to discuss in his message to Congress the following:

The President's conception of the responsibility of his trusteeship in time of war; the duties and obligations of that trusteeship cannot be avoided. The deep solemnity of the whole business.

Our addressing inquiries to the German government did not evidence a purpose to yield or relax our efforts over there in the least. America's spirit is invincible. The expression and demonstration of that spirit is now being vindicated in overwhelming fashion upon European battlefields. *The spirit of America will continue to express itself until the things for which she insists are written in terms that no one can distrust or misunderstand.*

Second. We wished to ascertain just what lay back of the purpose of those in Germany who claimed to desire a permanent peace. Our faith and confidence in those in authority have been sorely tested and tried. No humane man would wish this horrible thing prolonged a day if a settlement that had in it the ingredients of justice and permanency could be properly attained. Fully realizing the deep and tragic importance of this whole business, I took the liberty of addressing the following inquiry to the German Chancellor:

"Before making reply to the request of the Imperial German Government, and in order that that reply shall be as candid and straightforward as the momentous interests involved require, the President of the United States deems it necessary to assure himself of the exact meaning of the note of the Imperial Chancellor. Does the Imperial Chancellor mean that the Imperial German

Government accepts the terms laid down by the President in his address to the Congress of the United States on the 8th of January last and in subsequent addresses and that its object in entering the discussions would be only to agree upon the practical details of their application?

The President feels bound to say with regard to the suggestion of an armistice that he would not feel at liberty to propose a cessation of arms to the Governments with which the Government of the United States is associated against the Central Powers so long as the armies of those powers are upon their soil. The good faith of any discussion would manifestly depend upon the consent of the Central Powers immediately to withdraw their forces everywhere from invaded territory.

The President also feels that he is justified in asking whether the Imperial Chancellor is speaking merely for the constituted authorities of the Empire who have so far conducted the war. He deems the answers to these questions vital from every point of view."

Third. Discuss the German reply and analyze it. Is it worthy to be transmitted to those in authority in the Allied countries? Does it bear upon its face evidence of good faith? Do those who claim to speak for the German people and government clearly meet the issue? Answer. As to the acceptance of the fourteen points, since the anniuncement [announcement] of these points there has been a recurrence of the horrible things that have made the name of Germany's rulers execrated and reviled throughout the world. (Call attention to the character of the German retreat through France, to the devastation and the horrors in connection with it. Call attention to the sinking of the American ship last week upon which were wounded soldiers and women and children.) Are these evidences of the good faith of Germany. Can a peace be made lasting with those who order and direct these things of utter horror and bloodshed?

Fourth. I shall transmit this offer to the Allied governments but think it only just that as the responsible spolesman [spokesman] of this great government I should set forth just what is the attitude of this great government to these proposals, and our assessment of the good faith of those who initiated and conducted this war. I said on August 27, 1917: "We cannot take the word of the present rulers of Germany as a guaranty of anything."

(See Springfield Republican editorial) The destruction of every arbitrary power, etc.[1]

(See Borah's statement, New York Times)[2]

(See Bohn statement, especially with reference to Bismarck.[)]³

(See article in New York Times entitled "Kaiser's Dynasty Shaken by Defeat.)[4]

(See Rabbi Wise interview; Poindexter, Senator Williams, Roosevelt.)[5]

(See New York Sun editorial October 13th.)[6]

(See The President's speech at Metropolitan Opera House. "They observe no covenants, etc.")

Can they be trusted? NO. The present rulers of Germany must go. They are the enemies of democracy. They have sown the seeds of war. They shall not gather in the fruits of peace. Analogy between this and the President's pan-American doctrine. Shall those who gain control of governments by assassination be made the beneficiaries of murder? Shall those who begin war profit or be punished? *Guilt must be made personal in international affairs.* We cannot further discuss this matter until those who started and initiated this thing are entirely removed from the councils of those who desire peace.

Fifth. Cite what the Germans have done. Their ambitions, their hopes to dominate the world. Shall they be permitted to harass free peoples? Can they be trusted? Cite the Hague agreement of 1907 for mitigating the evils of war, of which Germany was one of the signatories, providing for the safety of non-combatants at sea. Violations: Lusitania case, the captain of the Lusitania rewarded by the Kaiser. "Let us tear out the roots of Hohenzollernism" (see Bohn article, New York Times). In 1813 the Hohenzollerns promised constitutional liberty to the subject people of Prussia if they would rise and fight Napoleon. With Napoleon at St. Helena, the promise was forgotten. Cite fht [the] treaty of Belgium which von Bethweg-Hollman [Bethmann Hollweg] characterized as only a scrap of paper. In 1848 Frederick the Great, in the presence of masses of revolutionists swore that he would grant every request they demanded. But the people let the villain live and received in place of reforms and liberties, imprisonments and seventy years of Bismarckism. Shall this monstrous thing once more be granted immunity? Have we a right to demand the abdication of the Kaiser? (Make the punishment fit the crime. See Borah's statement) Shall we censor other forms of Government? Answer. We are not directly concerned in the form of government which Germany shall have, but we are deeply concerned in our own security and we have a right to say that we will treat with those and those alone who can give some assurances that their treaties will be observed. (See end of Borah's speech).

"You may give back Alsace-Lorain, you may establish freedom in Poland, but if you leave the author of these conspiracies active in the field of European politics, in fifty years you will not recognize your work of peace." "Let us understand that the thing we are dealing with is a living, scheming powerful agency, arbitrary, military, fanatical, bent upon the destruction of free governments."

"We do not think the same thoughts, nor speak the same language of agreement." We cannot negotiate or come to terms with such a power, neither can we have any compassion with it. *This is not hate. It is simply the first step toward a permanent peace.*

Tumulty

TLS (J. P. Tumulty Papers, DLC).

¹ "The President and the Kaiser," *Springfield* (Mass.) *Republican*, Oct. 12, 1918. This editorial said that Wilson had consistently been opposed to the continuation of William II as the German Emperor. It cited, among other examples, Wilson's call in his speech of July 4, 1918, for "the destruction of every arbitrary power anywhere that can separately, secretly, and of its single choice disturb the peace of the world." Assuming that Wilson's words applied specifically to William, the editorial heartily endorsed the idea that he should leave his throne as a condition of peace.

² William E. Borah, "No Peace with the Hohenzollerns!" *New York Times*, Oct. 13, 1918, Sect. 8, p. 1. As the title implies, Borah argued that the imperial government of Germany would have to be replaced with a democratic government responsible to the German people before the United States and its associates could make peace with Germany. Borah also insisted that the Hohenzollern regime could not be allowed to participate in a league of nations. Tumulty paraphrases and quotes from Borah's article in the last three paragraphs of his letter, beginning with "Shall we censor other forms of government?"

³ Frank Bohn to the Editor of the *New York Times*, Oct. 5, 1918, printed in *ibid.*, Oct. 13, 1918, Sect. 3, p. 2. Bohn was a Socialist journalist and expert on labor problems and international affairs who was at this time associated with the Committee on Public Information. The editorial heading printed above his letter characterizes it well: "One Thing Needful: Central Powers Must Be Democratic, If Peace Is to Endure." Tumulty quotes extensively, although without quotation marks, from Bohn's letter in the paragraph below beginning "Fifth." The quotations begin with "Let us tear out the roots" and end with "seventy years of Bismarckism," the only reference to Bismarck in Bohn's letter.

⁴ *Ibid.*, Oct. 13, 1918. This unsigned dispatch, datelined Paris, October 12, declared that it was the common belief in that city that William II would soon abdicate and speculated as to who his successor might be.

⁵ Representatives of the *New York Times* interviewed all four of these men, as well as many others, on October 12. Rabbi Wise called for the unconditional surrender of Germany. Senator Poindexter declared that an armistice on the basis of "President Wilson's so-called fourteen propositions of Jan. 8" would mean in effect the loss of the war by the Allies. Germany's armies could then retreat within her borders without further damage, and there would be no way for the Allies to compel her to accept either Wilson's peace terms or anyone else's. Senator Williams suggested that Prince Max was trying to evade the main issues in his peace proposals and expressed doubt that the Prince in any way represented the wishes of the Reichstag. Theodore Roosevelt, as he had done repeatedly before, demanded that the war be fought to a finish and said that Germany had to be compelled to surrender unconditionally. He also set forth a long list of peace terms, all of which would have drastically reduced the size of the German, Austrian, and Turkish empires. *Ibid.*

⁶ "What Voice Is Speaking Now?," New York *Sun*, Oct. 13, 1918. As the title suggests, this editorial questioned whether the German government then negotiating with Wilson for an armistice was the discredited imperial government, or a more democratic regime which had succeeded it, or some combination of the two. The editorial suggested that the abdication of the Emperor and a renunciation of the throne by his heirs would be an acceptable sign that a real change had taken place.

A Draft of a Note to the German Government[1]

[Oct. 14, 1918]

The unqualified acceptance by the present German Government and by a large majority of the German Reichstag of the terms ⟨of peace⟩ laid down by the President of the United States of America in his address to the Congress of the United States on the eighth of January, 1918, and in [[his]] subsequent addresses justifies the President in making a frank and direct ⟨reply to the proposals of the German Government that the evacuation of all invaded territory by its armies be undertaken and that a discussion of the ap[p]lication of those terms be entered into, an armistice being in the mean time arranged on land, on the sea, and in the air.⟩ *statement of his decision with regard to the communications of the German Government*[2] [[of the eighth and twelfth of October, 1918.]]

⟨The⟩ *It must be clearly understood that the* process of evacuation and the conditions of an armistice are matters which must be left to the judgment and advice of the military advisers of the Government of the United States and the Allied Governments, and the President feels it his duty to say that no arrangement can be accepted by the Government of the United States which does not provide absolutely satisfactory safeguards and guarantees of the maintenance of the present military supremacy of the armies of the United States and of the Allies in the field. He feels confident that he can safely assume that this will also be the judgment and decision of the Allied Governments.

The President feels that it is also his duty to add that neither the Government of the United States nor, he is quite sure, the governments with which the Government of the United States is associated as a belligerent will consent to *consider* an armistice so long as the armed forces of Germany continue the illegal and inhumane practices which they still ⟨continue.⟩ *persist in.* At the very time that the German Government approaches the Government of the United States with proposals of peace ⟨—upon its own terms—⟩ its submarines are engaged in sinking passenger ships at sea [[,]] and not the ships alone but the very boats in which their passengers and crew[[s]] seek to make their way to safety; and in their present enforced withdrawal from Flanders and France the German armies are pursuing a course of ⟨cruel and⟩ wanton destruction which ⟨had hitherto⟩ [[has always]] been regarded as in direct violation of ⟨all⟩ the rules and practices of civilized warfare. Cities and villages, if not destroyed, are being stripped of all they contain not only but *often* of their very inhabitants. The nations associated against Germany cannot be expected to agree to a cessation of arms while acts of inhumanity, spoliation, and desolation are being continued which they justly look upon with horror and [[with]] burning hearts.

It is necessary, also, in order that ⟨he may excite no unwarranted hopes of peace,⟩ *there may be no possibility of misunderstanding* [[,]] that the President should very solemnly call the attention of the Government of Germany to the language and plain intent of one of the terms of peace which the German Government ⟨have⟩ [[has]] now accepted. It is contained in the address of the President delivered at Mount Vernon on the fourth of July last. It is as follows: "The destruction of every arbitrary power anywhere that can separately, secretly, and of its single choice disturb the peace of the world; or, if it cannot be presently destroyed, at least its reduction to virtual impotency." The power which has hitherto controlled the German nation is of the sort here described. It is within the choice of the German nation⟨.⟩ *to alter it.* The President's words just quoted naturally constitute a condition precedent to peace, if peace is to come by the action of the German people themselves. The President feels bound to say that the whole process of peace will, in his judgment, depend upon the definiteness and the satisfactory character of the guarantees which can be given in this fundamental matter. It is indispensable that the governments associated ⟨with⟩ against Germany should know beyond a peradventure with whom they are dealing. ⟨They will expect convincing evidence of a per-
                                              determination
manent change in the control of German public policy.⟩

The President will make a separate reply to the Royal and Imperial Government of Austria-Hungary.

WWT MS (WP, DLC).
    [1] Words in angle brackets deleted by Wilson; words in italics added by him. Words or letters in double brackets added from a second WWT draft, which was sent as RL to F. Oederlin, Oct. 14, 1918, TLS (SDR, RG 59, 763.72119/2313, DNA) and bears the same file number. For an account of the events of October 14 and of the composition of this draft, see the entry from the House Diary printed at October 15, 1918.
    [2] "with regard to the communications of the German Government" our transcript of WWsh.

From Robert Lansing, with Enclosures

My dear Mr. President: Washington October 14, 1918.

I send you herewith the paraphases of three telegrams which Mr. Barclay handed me this afternoon. I think it is important that you should see them at once.

I would particularly call your attention to the last paragraph of the second telegram, which has sufficient merit to warrant careful consideration.   Faithfully yours,   Robert Lansing

TLS (WP, DLC).

E N C L O S U R E   I

Handed me by British Chargé
Oct. 14/18. RL.

PARAPHRASE OF TELEGRAM FROM MR. BALFOUR TO MR. BARCLAY.
October 13, 1918.

Very Secret

Information has just reached us from a source which we consider to be absolutely reliable to the effect that as recently as the 9th instant the Germans, though contemplating the acceptance of the terms laid down by the President, were firmly decided not to give up all of the Polish areas nor the whole of Alsace-Lorraine. From this it must be inferred that the Germans are hoping to be able, after accepting the terms, to dispute in the Peace Conference with regard to the meaning even of these conditions, the statement of which appears to be most explicit.   BRITISH EMBASSY,
WASHINGTON,
October 14, 1918.

E N C L O S U R E   I I

Handed me by British
Chargé Oct. 14/18 RL

PARAPHRASE OF TELEGRAM FROM MR. BALFOUR TO MR. BARCLAY,
October 13, 1918.

The German reply to the President's enquiries seems to assume that his answer to their first note contains the terms of a cessation of hostilities. It is evident from the President's conversation with the French Ambassador that he never contemplated the grant of an armistice merely on the promise of Germany that she would withdraw her troops from the occupied territories. This we understand distinctly was no more than a condition essentially precedent to the communication of the German proposals by the President to the Associated Governments.

His Majesty's Government very much doubt whether the position is thoroughly understood in Germany and whether the Germans rcalize that the Associated Powers will consent to a cessation of hostilities on no other terms but such as will render any resumption of hostilities by the Central Powers impossible in the opinion not only of the military but also of the naval authorities.

His Majesty's Government accordingly regard it as of the very greatest importance that an immediate and public notification should be given to the German Government as to how the matter really stands.   BRITISH EMBASSY,
                                            WASHINGTON,
                                            October 14, 1918.

ENCLOSURE III

Handed me by
British Chargé, Oct 14/18 RL.

PARAPHRASE OF TELEGRAM FROM MR BALFOUR TO MR BARCLAY
October 13, 1918.

President Wilson's fourteen points as supplemented by his later utterances have apparently been accepted by the Germans.

His Majesty's Government fully agree with the general tenour of the President's policy but they wish to make the following observations:

(a) That there has been no discussion by the Associated Powers of the points at issue,

(b) That various interpretations can be put upon certain of these points, to some of which His Majesty's Government would object most strongly.

(c) That there are probably in existence other terms to which the President has not referred, such for instance as terms with regard to outrages on shipping, on which, if full justice is to be done, we shall have to insist.

His Majesty's Government are of opinion that in framing the conditions of armistice care must be taken to prevent the Allies from being deprived of the necessary freedom of action in the settlement of the final terms in the Peace Conference and that steps should immediately be taken by the chief belligerent Powers to discuss the doubtful points and come to some agreement amongst themselves with regard to them.

T MSS (WP, DLC).

From Richard Irvine Manning

My dear Mr. President,   Columbia Oct 14th, 1918.

I have your letter of the 10th inst. I am reliably informed that Mr. Pollock is disposed to vote for the Suffrage Amendment. My suggestion is that as soon as he takes his seat you write him a note requesting him to call upon you as you desire to discuss with him some matters of national and international importance. I am confident that this will bring the desired result.

With highest esteem, I am
                    Very sincerely yours,   Richd. I. Manning.

Permit me to congratulate you and our country on your splendid reply to Germany's peace proposal. It meets the occasion. It is enthusiastically received by our people. R.I.M.

ALS (WP, DLC).

Tasker Howard Bliss to Peyton Conway March

My dear March: VERSAILLES. October 14, 1918.

In my letter of October 9[1] (I think) I inclosed copies of the two Joint Notes submitted by the French Military Representative on the subject of a general allied policy in Russia and on the specific subject of sending additional American reinforcements to Archangel.[2] I sent you also copies of the statements which I made giving my views as to the position of the United States in the matter and the reason why I felt obliged to take no official part in the action on these proposed Joint Notes. The Notes were adopted by the other Representatives, omitting any specific reference to the United States, and submitted to their governments.

To-day the French Military Representative informs me by an official note that his government has approved the Joint Note No. 38, signed by the other three Military Representatives on the subject of "L'Orientation de la Politique des Alliés en Russie." You will observe that it is not really a Joint Note because, under the habitual procedure of the War Council, a Joint Note must be signed by *all* of the Military Representatives. What my British, French and Italian colleagues did, in reality, was to express a Joint *Opinion* to their respective governments.

Yesterday afternoon Mr. Stettinius called on me and had a long talk on the subject of the Munitions Program which he has been working on with the British and French and which he thought had reached a fairly satisfactory conclusion. He tells me that he is now running up against a decided indisposition on the part of the British and the French to give us the help which they promised. This is not suprising to me because, from various little indications that have come to my notice, it seems to me somewhat evident that the European Allies will attempt to minimize the American effort as much as possible. They think that they have got the Germans on the run and that they now do not need as much help as a little while ago they were crying for.

I think I told you sometime ago that I had heard a gentleman in high position here say that the United States was building a bridge for the allies to pass over; that the time for the United States to secure acquiescence in its wishes was while the bridge was building; that after the allies had crossed over the bridge they would have no further use for it or for its builders. This may be true or not. I do not know. *Qui vivra verra.*

I inclose two letters just received from Marshal Foch with a request that I send them to the United States. Will you kindly have your messenger drop them in the post.

With best wishes, I am

Cordially yours,   Tasker H. Bliss[3]

TCL (WP, DLC).
    [1] Cited in n. 1 to T. H. Bliss to NDB, Oct. 9, 1918, printed as an Enclosure with NDB to WW, Oct. 24, 1918 (first letter of that date).
    [2] See T. H. Bliss to NDB, Oct. 9, 1918, just cited.
    [3] The TLS of this letter is in WDR, RG 120, Records of the American Section of the Supreme War Council, 1917-1919, File No. 366-13, DNA.

From the Diary of Henry Fountain Ashurst

October 14, 1918.

When the Senate convened the galleries were empty (no visitors allowed because of influenza); the sun shone but the day was cold.

Senators charged that President Wilson had softened toward Germany and that (by opening correspondence with the German Government) he was resuming "note writing." Senators were mystified as the President had not taken any of them into his confidence. Many feared that the President's "altruism" would lead him to a reply to Germany that would lack directness. We knew that an ambiguous reply would chill the ardor of the people and depress the Liberty Loan. The strain was enormous; the rumors were that the President's mind was not made up so I resolved upon my own course; I called an automobile and went to the Executive offices of the White House where the President's Secretary, Mr. Tumulty, read me a three page letter he had just sent to W.W. urging that a firm reply be sent to the German note. Tumulty's letter was eloquent and embraced a coherent plan for future peace. I then dispatched a note to W.W. saying that I was in the Executive offices and desired an interview with him. He received me graciously; we exchanged salutations; whereupon the following dialogue took place:

Sen. HFA. "Mr. President, you might as well know in advance that I am going to say plain and unpleasant things. The time for plain talk is here."

Pres. Wilson. "Why! my dear fellow, sit down and tell me what is the matter."

Sen. HFA. "Mr. President, the Senate, the Press and the people are nervous, they expect and desire that you demand an 'unconditional surrender' of the German armies. Please give assurances that your reply to the German note will be one that will meet America's expectations? If your reply should fail to come up to the American spirit, you are destroyed. It is now widely feared, indeed charged in the Senate, that by your 'notes' to the German Government you are signing away with the pen much of the advantage that our valorous soldiers won with the sword."

Pres. Wilson. "So far as my being destroyed is concerned, I am willing if I can serve the country to go into a cellar and read poetry the remainder of my life. I am thinking now only of putting the US into a position of strength and justice. I am now playing for 100 years hence; I laid down my terms to Germany in my Fourteen Points speech to Congress on January 8th last, and in my 4th of July speech and my speech of September 27th. When Germany fully meets our terms we are through. Can it be that the people do not remember my Fourteen Points and my speeches of July 4th and September 27th?"

Sen. HFA. "No, Mr. President, they do not remember the details of those speeches."

Pres. Wilson. "Well, I remember."

Sen. HFA. "Mr. President, it is feared everywhere that an armistice would permit Germany to gain some advantage by diplomacy that she could not obtain militarily."

Pres. Wilson. "I am not making armistices, they must be left to the Commanders in the field."

Sen. HFA. "Do you intend to demand that Alsace and Lorraine shall be restored to France?"

Pres. Wilson. "Read my speech of January 8th, 1918, wherein I said: 'the wrong done to France by Prussia in the year 1871 in the matters of Alsace and Lorraine must be righted.' Now what was that wrong? It was the taking of Alsace-Lorraine."

Sen. HFA. "The Allies should demand of Germany a ship for every ship sunk by the German submarine."

Pres. Wilson. "Such matters can be left safely to the Peace Treaty."

Sen. HFA. "Mr. President, you should as a symbol, require the German Commander actually to deliver his sword to General Foch, Haig or Pershing in Berlin."
Pres. Wilson. "Why?"
Sen. HFA. "Because symbols, next to habit, most powerfully influence human beings."

He then asked me to speak in the Senate and say that the country need have no fear as to what he would do. I started to leave, and told him I was "somewhat" cheered. He said, "Why are you only 'somewhat' cheered?" and I told him that his failure to demand unconditional surrender would give him leisure in which to read poetry, and that he would read it in a cellar to escape the cyclone of the people's wrath, and then I walked out.

T MS (AzU).

From the Diary of Colonel House

October 15, 1918.

Yesterday was one of the stirring days of my life. The President and I got together directly after breakfast. I never saw him more disturbed. He said he did not know where to make the entrance in order to reach the heart of the thing. He wanted to make his reply final so there would be no exchange of notes. It reminded him, he said, of a maze. If one went in at the right entrance, he reached the center, but if one took the wrong turning, it was necessary to go out again and do it over. He said that many times in making extemporaneous speeches he had gone into the wrong entrance and had to flounder out as best he could.

I encouraged him, declaring that it could be done and we must get at it. We then began a serious discussion as to what to say and how to say it. I thought he should make one condition to a discussion of armistice, and that was the immediate cessation of all atrocities both on land and sea. He agreed to this and it stands in the Note.

We went into the question of the German Government and decided to use what he said in his Fourth of July speech about autocracies. This was his suggestion. We were anxious not to close the door, and yet we desired to make the note as strong as the occasion required. We fell back time and again on the theory which I offered when the last note was written, that was if Germany was beaten, she would accept any terms. If she was not beaten, we did not wish to make terms with her. At the same time, neither the President nor I desired to make a vengeful peace. Neither did we desire to have the Allied armies ravage Germany as Germany has ravaged the countries she has invaded. The President was especially insistent that no stain of this sort should rest upon the Allied arms. He is very fine in this feeling and I am sorry he is hampered in any way by the Allies and the vociferous outcry in this country. It is difficult to do the right thing in the right way with people like Roosevelt, Lodge, Poindexter and others clamoring for the undesirable and impossible.

The President soon formulated the points which appear in the Note, and we then decided to send for Lansing, Baker and Daniels to hear their reactions. The reason Daniels was sent for was because he wanted Baker, and the reason he wanted Baker was because he has just returned from the Western Front and we thought his knowledge would be of benefit.

Lansing and Baker arrived first and we discussed the Note for a half hour before Daniels came. Lansing started the discussion by saying that "we had to keep in mind the coming elections." I replied to this with some heat, saying if we had such a thought in mind while trying to write the note we could not do it properly or worthily. I thought the elections were not to be considered in thinking of the settlement of this great world tragedy. I was sorry I spoke so sharply for Lansing received what I said without comment. I saw that the President was eager to get to work and I facilitated the departure of the three Secretaries.

I went with them and visited the State, War and Navy Departments in succession. I told Lansing of the President's decision to name him as one of the Peace Commissioners. He was agitated and nervous over the news.

I went to Secretary Baker's office, and he told more of his experiences abroad, and of an interview he had with Lloyd George concerning our troops and their transportation. I will not go into this but I enjoyed Baker's account of it. I informed Baker that the President had him in mind for a Peace Commissioner.

I then had an interview with Daniels and asked him to lend me Admiral Benson, to which he consented with some reluctance. He said he would like to go abroad himself in November and that both could not leave at the same time. I promised to have Benson return in time to allow the Secretary to have his trip. We discussed and decided upon our means of transportation. Benson wanted to take the Great Northern over without troops, but I objected to this because I thought it was wrong to do it at this time.

I asked Hugh Wallace and T. W. Gregory to come to the White House in order to say goodbye.

There was no one at dinner excepting the President, Mrs. Wilson and myself. After dinner the President wrote a letter of credentials for me which reads as follows:

"TO WHOM IT MAY CONCERN:

Mr. Edward M. House, the bearer of this letter, is my personal representative and I have asked him to take part as such in the conferences of the Supreme War Council and in any other conferences in which it may be servicable for him to represent me. I commend him to the confidence of all representatives of the governments with which the Government of the United States is associated in the war.   Woodrow Wilson."[1]

The President certainly gives me the broadest powers. It virtually puts me in his place in Europe. I have in addition to this letter a commission from the State Department as Special Representative of the United States to the Entente Powers. This is the same as I had before when I went over as head of the "House Mission."

The President and I had a delightful evening together. We were tired and did not try to discuss serious matters.

I spoke of having arranged a secret code between us. As I was leaving he said, "I have not given you any instructions because I feel you will know what to do." I had been thinking of this before he spoke and wondered at the strange situation our relations had brought about. I am going on one of the most important missions anyone ever undertook, and yet there is no word of direction, advice or discussion between us. He knows that our mind runs parellel [parallel], and he also knows that where they diverge, I will follow his bent rather than my own.

In leaving him and going to the capitals of Europe for consultation with their leading statesmen I have a feeling that not until we are together again will I meet with a mind so sympathetic with my own. He has his weaknesses, his prejudices and his limitations like other men, but all in all, Woodrow Wilson will probably go down in history as the great figure of his time, and I hope, of all time.

I left on the midnight train arriving in New York this morning for breakfast. Grayson and Gordon came to the train to bid me goodbye. I shall not go into details of today because it all seems trivial compared with what I have gone through during the past ten days.

I have sent for Governor McCall who will be here tomorrow.

[1] The ALS, dated Oct. 14, 1918, is in the E. M. House Papers, CtY.

A Second Draft of An Appeal to Voters

My Fellow Countrymen: [c. Oct. 15, 1918]

The Congressional elections are at hand. They occur at the most critical period our Country has ever faced or is likely to face in our time. If you believe in your leader and wish me to continue to be your spokesman in affairs at home and abroad, I earnestly beg that you will give me an unmistakable vote of confidence, in the only way in which you can give it, by returning a Democratic majority to both House and Senate. If you do not believe in me, and do not wish me to continue to be your spokesman and should make that known by returning Republican majorities, I will have no cause of complaint. I am your servant, and will accept your judgment without cavil. But I would be rendered powerless by an adverse judgment and must frankly tell you so because so much depends upon your verdict. No scruple of taste must stand in the way of speaking the plain truth.

I am not one of thos[e] who believes that any party has a monopoly of the patriotism of the country, because I feel too deeply the sacrifices made by our citizens, irrespective of party, but a situation now exists for which the people are alone responsible, namely that when war was declared a Democratic President and a Democratic Congress were in control of the government, and under our constitution were entrusted with the responsibility of prosecuting the war. If the people in the coming election should change this situation and a Republican majority be returned to either House, it would be interpreted on the other side of the water as a repudiation of my leadership and give encouragement to the enemy, and greatly weaken my position with those associated with us in the war.

There is honorable precedent for what I am doing. A precedent I am not ashamed to follow. In the midst of the civil war Mr. Lincoln asked for the support of the country, as I am now asking for it. Asking it "not to swap horses in crossing a stream." He spoke not for himself but for the great interests entrusted to him. Mr. Lincoln was right then, and today if conditions were reversed and a Republican President and a Republican Congress were in power at the declaration of war and had thereafter conducted it successfully then I believe the President then in power should receive the same vote of confidence which I am now asking, in order to send across the water to our friends and foes, a message of a united people standing loyally by their leader for the winning of the war. Furthermore if the control of the House and the Senate should be taken away from my party we should live through the next two years with divided counsels. An opposing Congress if it chose could harass and darken counsel. An opposing majority could assume control of legislation and oblige all action to be taken amidst contest and obstruction. I welcome criticism which is meant to help, but at a time like this I reprobate criticism which is meant to discredit and embarrass the only executive authority the constitution provides. Unity of command is as necessary now in civil action as upon the field of battle. I need not tell you that I am asking your support not for my own sake or for the sake of a political party, but for the sake of the Nation itself, in order that its inward unity of purpose may be evident to all the world. Our war plans have so far been successfully worked out notwithstanding at times considerably embarrassed by hostile criticism which was not lessened even by the fact that that criticism has generally been retracted as the policy of the administration fully unfolded itself. The effective carrying on of the war demands that it should not be possible for the opposing leaders to turn isolated parts of the larger policies of the administration to their own political advantage and to force their own will and their own methods upon the executive. There would thus be divided authority not only but divided purpose as well between the executive and the legislative with a result that might fall little short of disaster.

In ordinary times, my fellow countrymen, I would not feel at liberty to make such an appeal to you. In ordinary times divided counsel can be endured without permanent hurt to the country, but these are not ordinary times. They are times in which we must have but one leader. If you wish other leaders please say so in unmistakable terms. If you wish me to lead you in these most critical of all years of the war, please say so in a way which cannot possibly be misunderstood either at home or over there. You have sovereign choice. The judgment is yours.

CC MS (H. S. Cummings Papers, ViU).

From the Diary of Josephus Daniels

October Tuesday 15 1918

Cabinet. WW thought not wise while discussing reduction of armament in case of peace to increase our program. Therefore did not favor Gen. Board's 7 year's program[1] to give us navy as big as Great Britain's, but approved another three year program as adopted three years ago.

McAdoo urged economy & said if war went on 2 years longer it was hard to see how the Treasury could finance it. We now finance not only our own cost of war but most of our allies.

Decided to dredge Buzzard's Bay entrance to Cape Cod canal, but not to exercise right to buy it now.

Baker said the Division in which Marines fought so valiantly at Chateau Th[i]erry saved Paris. British and French were retreating. French soldiers sifting through Marines who went forward, sustained the brunt of battle & saved Paris. Archives were ready to be moved.

What will happen in Germany.

A Princeton professor who did not believe in Democracy said the logic of a democracy would make a Negro woman President of the US

[1] The General Board of the Navy had, on September 10, 1918, recommended a building program for vessels and aircraft intended to give the United States by 1925 a navy "equal to the most powerful maintained by any other nation in the world." The plan called for the construction of over one thousand vessels, including twelve battleships, sixteen battlecruisers, 108 destroyers, and 167 submarines. See 65th Cong., 3d sess., House Committee on Naval Affairs, *Hearings . . . on Estimates Submitted by the Secretary of the Navy, 1919* (Washington, 1919), p. 495, and Harold and Margaret Sprout, *Toward a New Order of Sea Power: American Naval Policy and the World Scene, 1918-1922* (Princeton, N. J., 1940), pp. 51-52.

From Robert Lansing, with Enclosure

Dear Mr. President: Washington October 15, 1918.

I venture to invite your particular attention to the enclosed telegram from London, which shows another act of German duplicity, this time perpetrated by the German Secretary of State for Foreign Affairs Solf.

I also enclose a clipping from this morning's newspaper showing the direct result of Silf's [Solf's] instructions to General von Kress.[1]

Faithfully yours,   Robert Lansing

TLS (WP, DLC).
[1] Maj. Gen. Friedrich Sigmund Georg, Baron Kress von Kressenstein, at this time located in Tiflis as the chief of the German military and diplomatic mission to the Georgian Republic.

ENCLOSURE

London Oct 14, 1918

Greatest Urgency. 2791. Secret. Harrison from Bell. My 2756, October 12, 1 am, first paragraph.[1] Admiral Hall asks you to communicate the text of the following message to the President without delay. It is a wireless dated yesterday from Solf, German Secretary of State for Foreign Affairs to General Von Kress at (?) and reads:

"For your confidential information. In our reply to America we could not help deciding to comply in the question of evacuation; also since according to all information available here our offer of peace would otherwise have been declined. Whether President Wilson wishes to see the eastern border states also evacuated is not clear from his note. In any case the deliberations of the Commission will give us an opportunity to advance the objection that may be taken to that course.

Exclusively for your confidential information. Our opposition to a premature evacuation of the border states would be strengthened if the border states themselves would make objection thereto. In order not to expose ourselves to the reproach of double dealing we must refrain from prompting such objections ourselves. You should, however, so regulate your language as to give the best prospect that the local authorities in your area will decide upon this step of their own accord."   Laughlin.

T telegram (WP, DLC).
    ¹ I. B. Laughlin to RL, Oct. 12, 1918, T telegram (SDR, RG 59, 863.72119/2146, DNA). This telegram conveyed a message from Edward Bell to Leland Harrison. Bell reported that Prince Maximilian Klaus Wilhelm von Ratibor und Corvey, the German Ambassador to Spain, had been notified that the German government was replying "in a conciliatory tone" to Wilson's note. Ratibor had been instructed to "put it about in the Spanish press that German evacuations in the east . . . would increase the danger of Bolshevism."

From Edward Mandell House

Dear Governor: New York. October 16, 1918.

I can be reached up to eight o'clock tomorrow evening in the event you have anything important to communicate.

I want to let you know that there will be ample trustworthy people to do the coding, stenographic and other special work which you may need to have done at the Peace Conference without your having to trouble with it.

As soon as the Peace Conference is definitely in sight I would suggest that you tell at least Lansing and Baker of your decision so they may prepare themselves. They will all need a little time to get ready.

I am leaving with a deep sense of gratitude for the opportunity to serve which you are giving me. I hope I may do the work you have in mind worthily.

With deep affection, I am,

                         Your devoted,   E. M. House

TLS (WP, DLC).

From the Diary of Josephus Daniels

1918 Wednesday 16 October

WW said we must face such intolerant hatred of Germans I may have to become their advocate for justice & against American Prussianism. We must never do the things we condemn.

Baker said he heard many stories of cruelty & barbaric actions by Germans. Army traced them down & found only 2 of many cases true. Generally a man had heard that it happened in another regiment. Stories of cruelty & stories of our cruelty were exaggerated. One Am soldier did shoot a German prisoner in the back but they found he was crazy.

WW: Men tell stories they say happened to them to make it more personal when it was only a rumor they adopted

A Memorandum by Sir William Wiseman

[c. Oct. 16, 1918]

NOTES OF AN INTERVIEW WITH THE PRESIDENT
AT THE WHITE HOUSE
WEDNESDAY, OCTOBER 16TH, 1918.

VERY SECRET.

THE GERMAN NOTES:

The President had with him a few notes which he had made for me. He began at once to discuss the GERMAN NOTE. "They have said that they agree to my terms," he observed, "and if they were respectable people I should be obliged to meet them in a conference. Of course, we do not trust the present German Government; we can never trust them, and we do not want to discuss peace with them. But we must not appear to be slamming the door on peace.

You must remember that there are many honest and sincere Americans who did not want us to go into this war—who think that it should end. And again there are many (particularly among the foreign born population, such as the Italians) who did not want their sons to be drafted. They are proud now at what their boys are doing, but they are not really deeply interested in the war.

The spirit of the Bolsheviki is lurking everywhere, and there is no more fertile soil than war-weariness.

There is grave unrest all over the world. There are symptoms of it in this country—symptoms that are apparent although not yet dangerous.

We should consider too the condition of Germany. If we humiliate the German people and drive them too far, we shall destroy all form of government, and Bolshevism will take its place. We ought not to ground them to powder or there will be nothing to build up from.

I am alarmed at the temper of some of our people now. They want us to devastate Germany in the same way that Germany has devastated other countries. I should be ashamed to call myself an American if our troops destroyed one single German town. I want us all on our side to end this war as finely as we began and show the world that we are the better fellow. The people you hear shouting that we must dictate terms in Berlin are not the real Americans. Theirs is not the voice of America. I think the Germans want peace— I think even the present German Government wants peace—and I even think it would be quite safe to meet them at a Conference table now; but I am not sure—at least I am not sure enough, and I will not take any chances with them. On the other hand, we must not fall into what may prove to be a German trap by allowing our answers to be used to stimulate their own war spirit and undermine ours.

House and I have arrived at a formula which we think fairly sums up the position: 'If the Germans are beaten, they will accept any terms; and if they are not beaten, we don't want them to accept any terms.' I think it should be possible to arrange an armistice which would safeguard us against any possible treachery. It would be best for our Naval and Military experts to recommend terms for an armistice. The heads of the governments will probably have to modify the terms because the soldiers and sailors will make them too severe. We must not make them impossible, or even humiliating.["]

AN INTERCEPTED MESSAGE:

The President showed me a copy of an intercepted wireless from SOLF to some German Commander in RUSSIA. The President was immensely interested in it. Every word, he said, breathed the old Prussian trickery and deceit. It was hard to see how we could ever trust such people.

THE AUSTRIAN NOTE:

I asked the President what he proposed to do about the Note from the Austrian Government. He replied that he would write an answer as soon as he had time—probably within the next two days. He would have to say that since his speech of January 8th outlining his fourteen points, two new facts had arisen which modified his declaration as regards AUSTRIA. These were the recognition of the CZECHO-SLOVAKS and the JUGO-SLAVS. He would support to the full their just claims. Otherwise he proposed to answer Austria in the same sense as he had answered Germany. I suggested that the Austrian Government might bring with them to the Peace Conference people who would claim to speak on behalf of the various nationalities of their Empire. The President replied very promptly— "We have already recognised Masaryk, Dmowski, and their groups, and we cannot listen to anybody else."

TURKEY:

The President said he had received a request from the TURKISH GOVERNMENT to use his good offices with the Allies to persuade them to discuss a separate peace.[1] He should reply to the Turkish Government that he would communicate with the Allies; and to the Allies he should suggest, confidentially of course, that in his opinion it would be possible for them to make a satisfactory separate peace with Turkey; that such a move would materially hasten the German debacle; and that he would be glad if he could be of service in bringing about peace with Turkey.

THE FOURTEEN POINTS:

The President had with him a note of his fourteen points, some of which he discussed briefly with me, as follows:

(1). TREATIES:

There should be no more secret treaties. International negotiations should be conducted publicly for the whole world to read so that everyone might know that the treaty did not threaten international peace.

(2). THE FREEDOM OF THE SEAS:

This was a question which would naturally interest GREAT BRITAIN more than any other country on account of the preponderance of her Navy and her position as a world-wide Empire. He admitted that the British Navy had in the past acted as a sort of naval police for the world—in fact for civilization. For his part he would be willing to leave this power to the discretion of the British people, who had never abused it, but he wondered whether the rest of the world would be willing to go on doing so indefinitely. Many nations, great and small, chafed under the feeling that their sea-borne trade and maritime development proceeded only with the permission and under the shadow of the British Navy. He had always felt that the deepest-rooted cause of the present war was this feeling in Germany—an unjust fear and jealousy of the British Navy, but a feeling none the less real. I gathered that the President was searching for a remedy which he might suggest, but that he had found none; in his mind there is an idea that the great power of the British Navy might in some way be used in connection with the LEAGUE OF NATIONS and thereby cease to be a cause of jealousy and irritation.

It would be necessary, the President observed, soon after peace

[1] J. Riaño y Gayangos to WW, Oct. 14, 1918, and the enclosure thereto, printed in *FR-WWS 1918*, 1, I, 359-60.

to have a Conference to revise international law, and particularly International Maritime Laws.

Since the beginning of the war he had recognised that the submarine introduced a new element in naval warfare which must modify existing international law. That was why, in his neutral days, he had not insisted more strongly on the strict observance of international law in his dealings with the British Government. The old American theory was that the highways of the sea should be free in war as in peace. It remained to be seen how far this must be modified.

The extent of territorial waters would also have to be enlarged owing to the greater range of modern guns, and the old-fashioned definition of "blockade" must be revised.

(3). EQUAL TRADE OPPORTUNITIES FOR ALL NATIONS EVERYWHERE: and no economic boycott except as a penalty imposed by the LEAGUE OF NATIONS.

(5). GERMAN COLONIES:

With regard to the German Colonies, the President observed that he had not much faith in government by international commissions. It was clear that the Colonies must not be given back to Germany; at least until we are satisfied that their form of government is very different from the present. For his part, he would be well content to see the German Colonies administered by Great Britain, whose Colonial government was in many respects a model for the world. He must warn the British, however, of the great jealousy of the other nations—including, he regretted to say, a large number of people in America. It would, he thought, create much bad feeling internationally if the German Colonies were handed over to us as a sovereign part of the British Empire. He wondered whether there was some way in which they could be administered in trust. "In trust," I asked, "for whom?" "Well, for the League of Nations, for instance," he said.

(6). RUSSIA:

I asked the President why he would not send any political Commissioner, or join in any political conferences with the Allies regarding action to be taken in Russia. "My policy regarding Russia," he said, "is very similar to my Mexican policy. I believe in letting them work out their own salvation, even though they wallow in anarchy for a while. I visualize it like this: A lot of impossible folk, fighting among themselves. You cannot do business with them, so you shut them all up in a room and lock the door and tell them that when they have settled matters among themsevles you will unlock the door and do business." I suggested that in this case you would probably lock in a lot of Germans with them who would bolt the convention. He thought it was impossible to eradicate German influence from Russia. Hundreds and thousands of Germans had gone to live in Russia; had taken Russian names, and were apparently Russians. How could you get rid of the influence of these men? The Bolsheviki, he agreed, were impossible. He had watched with disgust their treatment of Lockhart,[2] who had tried hard to help them.

The question of RUSSIA, he thought, should also be left to the Peace Conference. I protested that would be too late; that the stage was even now being set by the Germans, and we should find forces and conditions had been created in Russia which it would be difficult, if not impossible, to alter at a Peace Conference. The President said there was a great deal in that view, and the whole question was causing him great anxiety. I gathered the impression that it is not impossible that he will modify his policy regarding Russia.

(8). ALSACE-LORRAINE:

With regard to Alsace-Lorraine, he could not imagine why his pronouncement on this subject had been misunderstood. He meant, of course, that the Germans must give back Alsace-Lorraine—just that and nothing more or less.

(9), (10), & (11).

These questions will require most careful definition. He had, however, seen the maps and arguments prepared by his advisers, and thought it was quite possible to arrive at a fair and lasting settlement on the basis of self-determination.

(14).

A LEAGUE OF NATIONS should be the very centre of the Peace agreement. The pillars upon which the house will stand.

COLONEL HOUSE'S MISSION:

I showed the President MR. BALFOUR's cable expressing his gratification at the approaching visit of Col. House.[3] "I was sure they would like me to send House," the President remarked. "He knows my mind entirely; but you must ask them to realise though how hard it is for me to spare him. On many problems he is the only person I can consult. I hope, the President added, that your Government will speak perfectly frankly to House. He will certainly be frank with them."

I suggested that it would be a good opportunity for Col. House

[2] About which see n. 2 to the Enclosure printed with RL to WW, Sept. 14, 1918. Lockhart, who had been imprisoned on September 4, was released on October 1 and allowed to cross the border into Finland on October 6 as part of an exchange arranged by the Soviet and British governments, which also included the return of Maxim Litvinov from England to Russia.

[3] A. J. Balfour to W. Wiseman, Oct. 15, 1918, T telegram (Reading Papers, FO 800/223, PRO).

to discuss peace terms generally with the Allies. The President rather demurred. He disliked the idea of settling peace terms without the enemy being present to state their case. It would give the impression of dividing the spoils amongst ourselves in advance. The same thing applied to the LEAGUE OF NATIONS—Germany ought to be present when the League of Nations is constituted. I asked if it would not be dangerous to go into conference with the enemy before we knew each other's views, and whether there would be any objection to an informal exchange of views between, say, Colonel House and the British and French Governments. The President said, on the contrary, it would be of great advantage.

PEACE CONFERENCE:

Regarding the Peace Conference, he asked whether it would be possible to have the deliberations reported fully in the press from day to day. I said it seemed to me that would be quite impossible. "We should make it as public as possible then," he said. "For my part, I am deeply committed to the policy of open diplomacy."

T MS (W. Wiseman Papers, CtY).

Sir William Wiseman to Sir Eric Drummond

Washington. October 16th. 1918.

Urgent. Personal and Secret.

The President asks me to thank Mr Balfour for his message regarding Colonel House.

He hopes that Mr Balfour will express his views to Colonel House without reserve.

The President also wishes to express his appreciation of Mr Balfour's attitude regarding the Sisson papers.

He very much regrets that U. S. Authorities did not consult H.M.G. before the papers were published here, but as the case now stands he would be grateful if Mr Balfour would permit the publication in England.

I said that as the President had made the request Mr Balfour would agree.

T telegram (FO 115/2428, p. 293, PRO).

To Joseph Patrick Tumulty, with Enclosure

Dear Tumulty   [The White House, c. Oct. 17, 1918]

Please tell me what you think of *this* version—and show it to McC and Cummings

W.W.

ALI (H. S. Cummings Papers, ViU).

E N C L O S U R E[1]

[c. Oct. 17, 1918]

My Fellow Countrymen: The Congressional elections are at hand. They occur at the most critical period our country has ever faced or is likely to face in our time. If you believe in me as your leader and wish me to continue to be your spokesman in affairs at home and abroad, I earnestly beg that you will give me an unmistakable vote of confidence, in the only way in which you can give it, by returning a Democratic majority to both the House and the Senate. If you do not believe in me and do not wish me to continue to be your spokesman and *should* make that known by returning Republican majorities, I will have no cause of complaint. I am your servant and will accept your judgment without cavil. But I would be rendered powerless by an adverse judgment and must frankly tell you so because so much depends upon your verdict ⟨in a time like this⟩. No scruple of taste must stand in the way of speaking the plain truth.

The Republican leaders have been pro-war but they have been anti-administration. Their leaders in ⟨the⟩ Senate *and House* are the same group of men whose counsel forfeited the confidence of the country six years ago. They have altered neither their principles nor their purpose, and still desire to lead the country back to policies which it has rejected. They have sought ever since we entered the war to take its conduct out of my hands and direct it by instrumentalities of their own choosing. If they should be accorded the support of a majority, we should have to limp through the next two years with divided counsels. During the past year and a half they have only harassed ⟨and⟩ action and darkened counsel; *but* they could then assume control of legislation and oblige all action to be taken amidst contest and obstruction. I welcome criticism which is meant to help, but at a time like this I reprobate criticism which is meant to discredit and embarrass the only executive authority the constitution provides. Unity of command is as necessary now in civil action as upon the field of battle. If you should *give them a majority to* back them now, there could be no united ⟨and⟩ *or* straightaway action of any kind ⟨and every critical decision would be made amidst contest and confusion⟩.

Moreover, should a Republican majority be returned to either House it would be interpreted on the other side of the water as a repudiation of my leadership. The spokesmen of the Republican party are urging you to elect a Republican Congress in order to back up and support the President, but even if that argument should impose upon some credulous voters on this side of the water, it would impose on no one on the other side. ⟨German statesmen are not⟩ *No one is really* misled as to the attitude of the Republican leaders towards the present administration. It is well understood that they wish to brush it aside and supplant it. And the peoples of the allied countries with whom we are associated against Germany are quite familiar with the significance of elections. They would find it very difficult to believe that the voters of the United States had chosen to support their President, ⟨hitherto supposed to be their spokesman,⟩ by electing to the Congress a *controlling* majority of his avowed opponents.

I need not tell you that I am asking your support, not for my own sake or for the sake of a political party, but for the sake of the nation itself, in order that its inward unity of purpose may be evident to all the world. Our war plans have so far been successfully worked out but it has been exceedingly difficult to work them out in the face of such criticism as has been constantly thrown in their way by such men as the present minority leader of the Senate. The fact that ⟨the⟩ *that* criticism has generally been retracted as the policy of the administration fully unfolded itself has not lessened the embarrassment. At every critical turn of affairs hostile critics like these have tried to force the hand of the administration. If the leaders of the present minority, who have sought upon every occasion to turn isolated parts of the larger policies ⟨to⟩ *of the* administration to their own political advantage, should be given the opportunity, they would certainly use their power to force their own will and their own methods upon the Executive. They have left no doubt of their purpose in the minds of those of us who have dealt with them. There would be divided authority not only but divided purpose as well between the Executive and the Legislature, with a result that might fall little short of disaster.

In ordinary times, my fellow countrymen, I would not feel at liberty to make such an appeal to you. In ordinary times divided counsel can be endured without permanent hurt to the country. But these are not ordinary times. They are times in which we must have but one leader. *And there ⟨are⟩ is honourable precedent⟨s⟩ for what I am doing,—a precedent I am not ashamed to follow. In the midst of the Civil War Mr.* Lincoln *asked for the support of the country as I am now asking for it, urging it "not to swap horses croosing [crossing] a stream." He spoke not for himself but for the great interests entrusted to him.* If you wish other leaders, please say so in unmistakable terms. If you wish me to lead you in these most critical of all the years of the war, please say so in a way which cannot possibly be misunderstood either at home or over there. You have sovereign choice. The judgment is yours.

WWT MS (WP, DLC).
¹ Words in angle brackets in the following document deleted by Wilson; words in italics added by him.

To the Most Reverend John Bonzano

Your Grace: [The White House] 17 October, 1918.

Allow me to acknowledge with appreciation your kindness in sending me the message from His Holiness, Pope Benedict XV, which I have received in your letter of October 11th. I shall take immediate occasion to reply to the message, and beg to convey to Your Grace an expression of my respect and esteem.

Sincerely yours,   Woodrow Wilson

TLS (Letterpress Books, WP, DLC).

To Benedict XV

Your Holiness: [The White House] 17 October, 1918.

I appreciate to the full the spirit which prompted your message to me, which I have just received through the kindness of Archbishop John Bonzano, Apostolic Delegate, and I beg in reply to assure Your Holiness that in common with the whole world the desire of the people of the United States is for peace, if peace can be founded with some prospect of permanence upon genuine and impartial justice. My every endeavor will be to pursue such a course as will bring the world the blessings of such peace. I warmly appreciate the generous confidence you express in my personal influence in this time of tragedy and travail.

Woodrow Wilson

TLS (Letterpress Books, WP, DLC).

To Walter Hines Page

My dear Page: [The White House] 17 October, 1918.

It distresses us all that you should have come home ill, and we shall wait patiently for your recovery in order that we may tell you how glad we are to have you safe on this side and how we have valued your services in your difficult post in London.

Do not distress yourself about any delay in reporting to me in person. I am in touch with your son,[1] and there is nothing that you need feel there is haste about. Only take care of yourself and get well.   Cordially and sincerely yours,   Woodrow Wilson

TLS (Letterpress Books, WP, DLC).
  [1] This was probably Maj. Frank Copeland Page, the youngest of three sons, who was with his father in England, but who came home with him when he was taken ill. This letter was written in response to JPT to WW, Oct. 17, 1918, TL (WP, DLC): "Dear Governor: Ambassador Page's son called at the office. He says his father is very seriously ill, but 'in his lucid moments' he talks about the necessity of reporting personally to the President. His son told him that he would come and report to the President for his father. His son thinks that a letter or a telegram from the President would reassure his father, and perhaps help him. I have already sent flowers with your card to the hospital. J.P.T."

To William Edgar Borah

My dear Senator Borah: [The White House] 17 October, 1918.

The influenza struck the executive offices along with every other branch of the government, and my reply to your kind letter of October 15th[1] has been delayed by the shortage of our force.

I want you to know how deeply and warmly I appreciate your generous approval of my reply to Germany. I do not feel that I should claim any credit for it, because after all it was the obvious and inevitable reply, and my only trouble in writing it was to express adequately and with sufficient dignity what I knew to be the judgment and purpose of our people. I am happy to believe from your letter that I succeeded in doing that, and I am greatly indebted to you for the reassurance you have given me.

                    Cordially and sincerely yours,   Woodrow Wilson

TLS (Letterpress Books, WP, DLC).
  [1] It is missing in both the Borah Papers, DLC, and in WP, DLC.

From Newton Diehl Baker

My dear Mr. President: [Washington] October 17, 1918.

I have just been going over with General March the extraordinary cablegrams sent by General Graves from Vladivostok during my absence. Unless you feel that it would be unwise, for diplomatic reasons, I would like to recall General Graves, send him to France and replace him with someone else; though I have not yet settled in my own mind upon his successor.

Respectfully yours,   [Newton D. Baker]

CCL (N. D. Baker Papers, DLC).

From Herbert Clark Hoover, with Enclosures

Dear Mr. President: Washington 17-October-1918

I think it will be of interest to you to glance over the attached compilations of several independent price indices in foodstuffs. The summation of these tables shows that in the first year of the Food Administration, according to the Department of Labor index, the wholesale prices have fallen 8%; according to the Times Annalist index, they have risen 8%; according to the Food Administration index, they have fallen 3.6%—a fall, averaging the three independent indices, of about 1.17%.

During the same period, according to the Department of Agriculture index, there has been a rise of 15.1% in farm produce; according to the Department of Labor index, an increase of 23%, according to the Food Administration index, an increase of 3.9%, or an average of all of about 14%. During the same period there has, on various indices, been a rise in the cost of clothing, house furnishings, etc. of from 45% to 65%. The differences of indices arise out of the different bases of calculation, but this difference of calculation adds emphasis to the fact that the currents are properly interpreted. These indices would seem to substantiate:

(a) That there has been an appreciable stabilization in the price of food and a reduction of wholesale prices.

(b) That as farmers' prices have risen and wholesale prices fallen, there has been a great reduction—about 16%—in the profits of middlemen.

There has been a coincident reduction in consumption of some 7% and there is this season apparently a 4% to 6% nutritional increase in production. There have been rises in retail prices in congested areas which give rise to much complaint, but Congress gave us no control in this matter.

I mention this as a number of theoretical economists have lately been loud in the old outcry that our interference with the sacred law of supply and demand endangers our production and that reduction of consumption can only be obtained by higher prices.

Yours faithfully,   Herbert Hoover.

TLS (WP, DLC).

Table No.1.

PRICE INDICES

1913 as 100

	*Food Administration Wholesale Price Index		Annalist Wholesale Price Index		Department of Labor Wholesale Price Index	
	Relative index.	Percentage increase or decrease.	Relative index.	Percentage increase or decrease.	Food index of prices	Percent increase over 1913
1913	100.0	0.0	100.0	0.0	100	--
1914	103.2	3.2	104.3	4.3	103	3
1915	107.6	7.6	105.8	5.8	104	4
1916	125.5	25.5	125.5	25.5	126	26
1917						
January	144.6	44.6	149.2	49.2	150	50
February	151.1	51.1	163.8	63.8	150	60
March	155.9	55.9	170.7	70.7	161	61
Average first quarter	150.5	50.5	161.3	61.3	157	57
April	177.6	77.6	187.5	87.5	182	82
May	191.5	91.5	205.9	105.9	191	91
June	183.4	83.4	197.5	97.5	187	87
Average second quarter	184.2	84.2	197.0	97.0	187	87
	Food Administration Established					
July	176.0	76.0	189.5	89.5	180	80
August	183.1	83.1	191.2	91.2	180	80
September	186.3	86.3	197.7	97.7	178	78
Average third quarter	181.8	81.8	192.8	92.8	179	79
October	186.0	86.0	200.2	100.2	183	83
November	186.7	86.7	197.7	97.7	184	84
December	188.9	88.9	199.5	99.5	185	85
Average fourth quarter	187.2	87.2	199.1	99.1	184	84
1918						
January	188.6	88.6	199.1	99.1	188	88
February	188.9	88.9	204.9	104.9	187	87
March	176.7	76.7	204.6	104.6	178	78
Average first quarter	184.7	84.7	202.9	102.9	184	84
April	178.9	78.9	208.2	108.2	179	79
May	177.6	77.6	205.8	105.8	178	78
June	185.4	85.4	201.3	101.3	180	80
Average second quarter	180.6	80.6	205.1	105.1	179	79

*Based on caloric value of food.

Statistical Division
October 11, 1918.

Table No. 2

PRODUCERS' PRICES

	Department of Agriculture Index for Crop Prices		Department of Labor Price Index		Food Administration Producers' Index 1913 as a base.	
	Relative to 1913 as 100.	Percent increase or decrease from 1913	Farm Values	Percent increase from 1913	Relative to 1913	Percent increase or decrease
1913	100.0	---	100	---	100.	---
1914	108.9	8.9	103	3	107.6	7.6
1915	110.7	10.7	105	5	109.0	9.0
1916	113.4	13.4	122	22	121.4	21.4
1917						
January	183.6	83.6	147	47	148.3	48.3
February	195.6	95.6	150	50	156.3	56.3
March	206.5	106.5	162	62	170.8	70.8
Average	195.2	95.2	153	53	158.5	58.5
April	225.2	125.2	180	80	209.3	109.3
May	280.6	180.6	196	96	215.5	115.5
June	291.3	191.3	196	96	211.3	111.3
Average	265.7	165.7	191	91	212.1	112.1
	Food Administration Established					
July	289.9	189.9	198	98	228.2	128.2
August	307.8	207.8	204	104	214.2	114.2
September	279.6	179.6	203	103	218.5	118.5
Average	292.4	192.4	202	102	220.3	120.3
October	277.0	177.0	207	107	205.1	105.1
November	261.3	161.3	211	111	195.9	95.9
December	252.8	152.8	204	114	203.7	103.7
Average	263.7	163.7	207	107	201.5	101.5
1918						
January	264.1	164.1	205	105	215.9	115.9
February	271.6	171.6	207	107	217.9	117.9
March	288.8	188.8	211	111	217.5	117.5
Average	274.8	174.8	208	108	217.1	117.1
April	288.6	188.6	217	117	218.5	118.5
May	281.8	181.8	212	112	217.3	117.3
June	271.9	171.9	214	114	212.2	112.2
Average	280.8	180.8	214	114	216.0	116.0

#-III

<u>DEPARTMENT OF LABOR WHOLESALE PRICE INDEX</u>

Period	Clothing	Percent increase or decrease from 1913
1913	100	----
1914	98	2
1915	100	----
1916	127	27
<u>1917</u>		
January	161	61
February	162	62
March	163	63
Average first quarter	162	62
April	169	69
May	173	73
June	179	79
Average second quarter	174	74
July	187	87
August	193	93
September	193	93
Average third quarter	191	91
October	194	94
November	202	102
December	206	106
Average fourth quarter	201	101
<u>1918</u>		
January	209	109
February	213	113
March	220	120
Average first quarter	214	114
April	230	130
May	234	134
June	243	143
Average second quarter	236	136

Table No. 4.

	Food Wholesale Prices			Farm Values			Clothing		
	Percent Increase over 1913			Percent Increase over 1913			Percent Increase over 1913		
	Second quarter 1917	Second quarter 1918	Increase or Decrease	Second quarter 1917	Second quarter 1918	Increase or Decrease	Second quarter 1917	Second quarter 1918	Increase or Decrease
Food Administration	84.2	80.6	-3.6	112.1	116.0	3.9			
Dept. of Labor	87.0	79.0	-8.0	91.0	114.0	23.0	74.0	136.0	62.0
Dept. of Agriculture				165.7	180.8	15.1			
Annalist	97.0	105.1	8.1						
Average			-1.17			14.00			62.0

T MSS (WP, DLC).

From William Bauchop Wilson, with Enclosures

My dear Mr. President: Washington October 17, 1918.

In connection with the labor adjustment matter you have before you, I received a letter from Mr. Taft yesterday evening which I am inclosing herewith for your consideration.

In the first draft of the proposition submitted for my consideration subsection "a" of paragraph 3 read as follows:

"a. Eight hours shall constitute a day's work. In all Government work and in all direct and sublet contracts for Government work, four hours shall constitute a day's work on Saturdays for the months of June, July, and August, but where a short workday on Saturdays has been established for a greater number of months than those specified, the number of hours heretofore constituting a day's work on Saturdays should not be increased. Any time in excess of the hours specified above is to be considered overtime."

I did not believe that was a workable proposition in the present state of our industries. A Saturday half-holiday cannot be applied to the men engaged in the movement of trains or to men employed in plants working night and day, seven days a week, without making radical changes that might seriously interfere with production at a time when we need all the production we can get. For that reason I sent it back for reconsideration, and it was changed into its present form as follows:

"a Eight hours shall constitute a day's work on all work to which the eight-hour statutes of August 1, 1892, as amended and of June 19, 1912, apply and in all direct and sublet contracts for Government work. On all work to which the eight-hour statutes of August 1, 1892, as amended and of June 19, 1912, apply and in all direct and sublet contracts for Government work, except in continuous industries and continuous occupations, and except in the production or extraction of raw materials necessary for war work, four hours shall constitute a day's work on Saturdays for the months of June, July, and August. Where a short workday on Saturdays has been established in industries excepted above or for a greater number of months than those specified, the number of hours heretofore constituting a day's work on Saturdays should not be increased. Any time in excess of the hours specified above is to be considered overtime."

The Saturday half-holiday in the building trades of the larger cities is almost universal. It has been generally applied to shipbuilding operations. It obtains in the metal trades to a considerable extent. In many of the other industries it does not exist at all, and in others only to a very limited extent. One of the serious causes of unrest has been the fact that large numbers of men have either had a Saturday half-holiday or time and one-half for the additional four hours, while others working in adjacent shops at the same trade have not had these conditions.

It would be an ideal basis for wage computation for all of the adjustment boards if the same unit of hours for the same trade could be established for all of them. It is apparent that such a basis cannot be created at this time. The question in my mind has been how to amend the present "hit and miss" system within the limits of practical application. I think that object has been accomplished in the final draft of that paragraph as it has been presented to you. There is, nevertheless, great room for doubt about the correctness of this conclusion.   Faithfully yours,   W B Wilson

TLS (WP, DLC).

Felix Frankfurter to William Bauchop Wilson

Dear Mr. Secretary: Washington October 15, 1918.

I beg to hand you herewith the final form of the report of the Conference of National Labor Adjustment Agencies, convened at your request to formulate a plan for harmony of action and the principles which guide such action by the labor adjusting agencies of the Government. This report has the approval of all who have been represented in our deliberations with two exceptions, one, the Railroad Administration has reserved a dissent of that provision of the report which provides for semi-annual revision of wages in accordance with changes in the cost of living, and two, the approval of Messrs. Taft and Walsh, acting for the War Labor Board, has not been formally made under document because they left before the document was ready for signature.

The position of the War Labor Board in regard to the proposed report was set forth by Messrs. Taft and Walsh, and in response to that a provision was added specifically reaffirming the jurisdiction of the War Labor Board and the principles under which it is operating. Mr. Walsh verbally expressed his concurrence in the document, so likewise did Mr. Taft, except as to that part of it which deals with the eight hour provision and Saturday half holiday. Mr. Taft thought that provision should be omitted.

Faithfully yours,   Felix Frankfurter

TLS (WP, DLC).

REPORT OF THE CONFERENCE COMMITTEE OF
NATIONAL LABOR ADJUSTMENT AGENCIES.

The following recommendations are submitted to serve as a basis for a National Labor Policy to be announced by the President of the United States.

I.

HARMONY OF ACTION BY LABOR ADJUSTING AGENCIES

1. A Conference of National Labor Adjustment Agencies, composed of two representatives of each Federal Labor Adjusting agency, should be established to meet at regular intervals for the purpose of promoting unified action and stability in reference to matters under their jurisdiction. Effective methods shall be established by each agency for conference with such other agencies as may be

directly concerned by a proposed award, and in no event shall a decision effecting a change in standard rates or working conditions theretofore fixed by an authorized governmental agency be deemed to be concluded, nor shall such award be promulgated until the Conference is first consulted as to its effect upon the industrial situation of the entire country.

2. It is recommended that appropriate steps be directed to be taken to secure whatever modification of existing agreements creating labor adjustment agencies is necessary to enforce the national labor policy that may be declared by the President.

3. Any complaint as to the application or operation of the principles and standards herein proclaimed shall be referred to the National War Labor Board for adjudication, in so far as its jurisdiction applies. And nothing herein is intended to repeal or amend the provisions of the Presidential Proclamation of April 8th, 1918,[1] establishing the National War Labor Board, and fixing its jurisdiction, its general procedure and the principles upon which its action and decisions should be based.

II.
STANDARDS OF WAGES AND WORKING CONDITIONS.

The following industrial standards should govern the various adjusting agencies for the purpose of securing maximum efficiency during the war, regularity of work on the part of the employe, continuity of employment on the part of the employer, and to secure stability for industry. All the provisions should be interpreted with these great ends in view.

1. *Differentials.*

The principle of wage differentials relating to emergency war construction, shipyards, loading and unloading of ships, general manufacturing and railroad shops should for the present be recognized because:

a. The transitory character of war construction and emergency shipbuilding has resulted in the establishment of rates of compensation in such occupations higher than are maintained in organizations which are part of the permanent industrial life of the Nation.

b. The supreme necessity for ships makes it necessary to attract the additional workers required for their construction from non-war industries and from localities remote from shipbuilding centers. This involves serious dislocation in the lives of workers who engage in such work. The relatively severe conditions under which shipbuilding construction is at the present time carried on entitle the

[1] It is printed at that date.

men to a payment of compensation at a rate somewhat in excess of that paid employes in similar occupations in other industries not subject to such conditions, and a sufficient number of men cannot otherwise be obtained.

c. To determine whether or not existing wage differentials should be eliminated, and if so upon what basis, will require not only extensive investigation, but the closest co-operation of employers, employes and representatives of the Government departments affected thereby. The administrative machinery to conduct such investigation and bring about such cooperation has been established and is being perfected. Pending the operation of this machinery, any radical change in existing conditions would be arbitrary, would create confusion, and would seriously embarrass the agencies which are now working toward a solution of these problems, and thus handicap war production.

2. *Principles governing wage adjustments.*

a. The national policy calls for the maintenance of proper standards of living—such standards as are appropriate to American citizens devoting their energies to the successful prosecution of a righteous war. Changes in the cost of living, therefor[e], call for adjustments in wages. In making such adjustments due regard must be accorded to securing maximum war production and to the state of the national finances, but no alteration of the national policy as to American standards should occur until the government has announced the necessity for the reduction of standards of all classes to meet the exigencies of the war. To permit the continuance of such standards we cannot too strongly urge that immediate and drastic steps be taken by all the government agencies equipped with power to prevent further increase in the cost of living.

b. The application of the broad principle of maintaining standards of living cannot be reduced to mathematical formula, but must follow the rules of reason and justice. In essence, reason and justice demand that this rule should apply in full force to those workers whose wages afford but a small margin over the amount necessary for the maintenance of their economic efficiency.

c. Reason and justice further demand that the principle of adjusting wages to changes in the cost of living should apply only where a fair and equitable wage prevails. This principle should not operate to prevent workers whose wages were below a proper standard of living from securing an equitable adjustment.

d. In the interest of stability, revisions of wage scales based upon changes in the cost of living as herein provided should be made *oftener than*[2] semi-annually. The semi-annual adjustment should be based upon a comparison of the cost of living for the current six

[2] WWhw.

months period with that of the corresponding period of the preceding year, and any change should apply to the succeeding six months.

3. *Standard Working Conditions.*

a. Eight hours shall constitute a day's work on all work to which the eight-hour statutes of August 1, 1892, as amended and of June 19, 1912, apply and in all direct and sublet contracts for Government work. On all work to which the eight-hour statutes of August 1, 1892, as amended and of June 19, 1912, apply and in all direct and sublet contracts for Government work, except in continuous industries and continuous occupations, and except in the production or extraction of raw materials necessary for war work, four hours shall constitute a day's work on Saturdays for the months of June, July, and August. Where a short workday on Saturdays has been established in industries excepted above or for a greater number of months than those specified, the number of hours heretofore constituting a day's work on Saturdays should not be increased. Any time in excess of the hours specified above is to be considered overtime.

b. In war time, on government work, overtime should be required or permitted only when the public necessity demands.

Compensation at higher rates for overtime is paid as a means of protecting workers against unduly long hours and of penalizing employers who require such hours. Under the extraordinary conditions created by the war, however, there has developed a great temptation to break down the standard work day and to work irregular hours and at undue rates in order to secure the extra compensation paid for overtime. This not only threatens all proper standards of work but has hindered war production and resulted in a serious drain on the finances of the nation. All government authorities are therefore charged to use every effort to put a stop to this abuse.

Compensation for overtime, as defined in paragraph *a*, for hourly workers shall be at one and one-half times the hourly rates and for piece workers at one and one-half times the average hourly piece-work earnings for the total number of hours worked on piece work computed at the end of each pay period, except where compensation at a higher rate is now being paid; but in no case shall compensation at a rate in excess of double time be paid.

c. On all government war work and on all direct or sublet contracts for government war work, no work shall be performed on Sundays or holidays except such as is indispensable, and in such cases the rate of compensation for such work should be not more than double the regular rates, computed as provided for in the preceding paragraph. When work on Sundays and holidays is necessary, every precaution should be taken to prevent irregular attendance on week days for the sake of the extra compensation on Sundays and holidays.

d. The Federal Government recognizes for the purpose of extra compensation the following federal holidays: New Years Day, Washington's Birthday, Decoration Day (Memorial Day), Fourth of July, Labor Day, Thanksgiving Day, and Christmas Day. On state and national election day, employes enjoying the voting privilege shall be allowed not to exceed half a day without loss of pay, in order to exercise their right of franchise.

e. For night shifts in war industries, except in continuous industries and continuous occupations, extra compensation, not exceeding ten per cent, should be added to the total earnings at day shift rates.

f. The payment of bonuses, or any extra compensation or gift, which, in the judgment of the proper government authorities have the effect of interfering with the established standards of compensation and other working conditions or which tend to promote an unnecessary shifting of employment, should be prohibited.

III.
ENFORCEMENT OF STANDARDS

1. Should any employer or worker refuse to abide by the award of an appropriate labor adjusting agency, the government will utilize all the power at its disposal, including the withdrawal of privileges, to secure compliance with such award.

2. Strict measures should be taken by the War Industries Board and all governmental agencies to prevent interference by war or non-war industries with the application of the standards herein established.   Respectfully submitted,   Felix Frankfurter[3]

October 14, 1918

TS MS (WP, DLC).

[3] This report was also signed by thirteen representatives of the various departments and agencies involved in the conference.

E N C L O S U R E   I I I

William Howard Taft to William Bauchop Wilson

My dear Mr. Secretary: Washington October 15, 1918.

I attended the conference of the Government Labor Readjustment Boards, and engaged in their discussions. A clause is introduced into their articles with reference to the 8-hour day and a

Saturday afternoon for three months in the summer. I argued with earnestness against the insertion of such a clause, first, because I think it will give rise to misinterpretation, second, because I think it will stir up throughout the country a demand for a 44-hour week instead of a 48 hour week; and, third, because, as phrased, the clause may be thought to reduce the hours of the week in time of war from 48 hours to 44 hours. The clause does not seem to me to be necessary. In cases where the Shipping Board yields to a custom of a Saturday half holiday, why not let the Shipping Board allow it and stand against it where it is not the custom? Why not take a position adverse to an unreasonable claim in war time? At any rate, why stir up the question by mentioning it in a Presidential Proclamation? It cannot be mentioned, as you will see by reading the clause, without making exceptions in respect to railroad labor and in respect to labor in the mines. The statement of such exceptions in the President's proclamation is likely to create heartburning. A rule that must have such exceptions is better not stated at all, it seems to me. I feel very sure that by the use of such a clause, we are in danger of creating far more difficulty than we are likely to allay. I beg to bring this matter to your attention and to the attention of your colleagues and the President before the order is issued.   Sincerely yours,   Wm II Taft

TLS (WP, DLC).

E N C L O S U R E   I V[1]

TO ALL PERSONS WHOM IT MAY CONCERN:

From the first we saw that this is a war in which we must bring the full power as well as the full faith of our Nation into the struggle. We have sought to release the entire industrial energies of the Nation at home, in order that our forces abroad may be effective. But the demands upon industry in time of war are dependent upon the eager and dedicated spirit of those who are engaged in it, workers and employers alike. We have, therefore, endeavored to be true to our democratic traditions in dealing with those complex aspects of human relations called the labor problem. To that end a number of distinct agencies for dealing with wages and working conditions in the different fields of industry have been evolved, each needful and effective in its own field. For the problem is many-sided—the same issues are presented under various settings, and different issues may arise in industrial conditions created by transitory war emergencies ⟨than in⟩ *from* those *which arise in* occupations that are part of the permanent industrial life of the Nation.

But experience has taught us that, after all, these issues are but separate aspects of a single problem. We must act upon the realization that the country presents a single industrial front. Therefore, at my request, the Secretary of Labor initiated a conference of representatives of the various labor adjustment agencies to secure harmony of aims and concert of action. The recommendations of this Conference are now before me, together with the concurrence of Secretary Wilson in its report.

If we translate these recommendations into action we shall assure ourselves of the full vigor of our industrial capacity. For we shall be guided by the dictates of justice and fair dealing, and we shall have the necessary administrative skill and responsibility to put our principles to the test of detailed application. I have, therefore, requested, as part of the War Labor Administration committed to Secretary Wilson, the establishment of a Conference consisting of two representatives of each of the agencies dealing with industrial relations to secure harmony and stability for industry. We shall thus have a Conference for wages and working conditions which will utilize to the fullest *extent* the experience of existing agencies, with such additional machinery as the need for regulation during war time compels. We can leave no part of the field of industry, upon which the successful prosecution of the war depends, to the blind forces of speculative venture.

I have approved the principles submitted to me by the Conference as guides for the action of the various adjustment agencies, leaving it to the Conference hereby established to modify the industrial standards now promulgated, as the ever shifting necessities of war may compel, and as new experience may recommend improvement. To evoke the amplest product from contented workers, wages must be just and working conditions right. But these are complicated matters of detail to be determined from time to time and as speedily as is consistent with adequate consultation and representation of those vitally affected before decisions are made. Suffice it for me to say that we should adhere to the cherished national policy which calls for the maintenance of sound standards of living—standards which will give us the keen spirit and the self-denial of American manhood while engaged in the august enterprise of war. Reason and justice ⟨therefore⟩ demand that changes in wage scales should be based on changes in cost of living. Such changes in the wage scale, to encourage stability, should not be made oftener than twice a year. If our social standards are to be maintained, as I hope they are to be, we must forego no effort which will prevent avoidable increase in the cost of living. No less, however, must we cheerfully lay upon ourselves the obligation of husbanding the national resources in our own daily lives.

These are the principles that must be observed if we are to strive with ever increasing vigor for the ends of justice and of right which victory will assure. These are the principles, therefore, that I desire all agencies of the Government entrusted with the administration of industrial relations to apply. Whatever steps are necessary to make their present practices or powers conform to the national policy now declared, they will, I know, speedily and cheerfully adopt. Thus, only, but thus assuredly, can we confidently expect that unity of action by which the interests of the several activities of the Government concerned with industry will no longer be left to conflicting independent effort, but will be directed to the single interest of the Nation.[2]

T MS (WP, DLC).
    [1] Words in angle brackets in the following document deleted by Woodrow Wilson; words in italics added by him.
    [2] This statement was not published, and the proposed all-American war labor board was never established due to the sudden end of the war.

From Desiré-Joseph Cardinal Mercier, with Enclosure

Monsieur le Président,   Malines Le 17 Octobre 1918.

Aujourd'hui à 3 heures, Monsieur le Baron von der Lancken,[1] Chef du Département politique allemand est venu, au nom du Gouverneur Général de Bruxelles et du Gouvernement de Berlin, m'annoncer que les détenus politiques Belges, internés soit en Belgique soit en Allemagne, et les Belges déportés en Allemagne, seront remis en liberté aussitôt que se fera l'évacuation de la Belgique. L'élargissement des prisonniers internés dans les prisons de la Belgique occupée, en dehors des étapes militaires, commencera dès lundi prochain 21 de ce mois.

J'ai l'honneur de vous remettre ci-inclus le texte d'une déclaration écrite que le délégué du Gouvernement allemand a laissé en mes mains. Les États-Unis ont si généreusement aidé notre peuple dans sa détresse; par la bravoure de leur armée, par la haute autorité et l'incomparable prestige de celui qui préside à leur Gouvernement, ils ont eu sur les événements une influence si décisive, que je considère comme un devoir de me tourner immédiatement vers Votre Excellence pour lui faire connaître la démarche bien veillante et spontanée dont je viens d'être l'objet.

Je vois dans cette démarche une preuve d'un désir sincère d'arriver a la paix, et j'entrevois, avec émotion, pour notre cher peuple belge, qui a tant et si noblement souffert, l'aurore d'une ère prochaine de calme et d'apaisement.

Puisque l'occasion m'en est offerte, je prends la confiance d'exprimer devant le Président des États-Unis l'espoir que le futur Congrès de la Paix se tiendra à Bruxelles. Mes compatriotes, les premières victimes des violences de l'invasion, accueilleraient l'honneur qui serait fait a leur capitale comme une première réparation et ils en éprouveraient une unanime reconnaissance.

Agréez, Monsieur le Président, l'hommage de mon admiration et de mon impérissable gratitude.

+ D. J. Card. Mercier, Arch. de Malines.[2]

[1] That is, Oscar Hans Emil Fritz, Baron von der Lancken-Wakenitz.

[2] This letter and its enclosure were enclosed in W. Phillips to WW, Dec. 5, 1918, TLS (WP, DLC). Lansing had sent a translation of the Cardinal's letter and its enclosure to Wilson in RL to WW, Oct. 23, 1918 (WP, DLC). Our translation follows:

"Today, at 3 o'clock, Baron von der Lancken, chief of the German political department, came, in the name of the Governor General of Brussels and of the Berlin government, to announce to me that the Belgian political prisoners, interned either in Belgium or in Germany, and the Belgians deported to Germany will be freed as soon as the evacuation of Belgium can be effected. The release of prisoners interned in occupied Belgium, outside military areas, will commence on Monday next, the twenty-first of this month.

"I have the honor to enclose the text of a written declaration which the representative of the German government has put in my hands. The United States has so generously helped our people in their distress, by the bravery of its army, by the high authority and the incomparable prestige of the one who presides over its government, and it has had so decisive an influence over events, that I consider it my duty immediately to notify Your Excellency of the most kind and spontaneous action just accorded me.

"I see in this action proof of a sincere desire to arrive at peace, and I catch a glimpse, with emotion, for our dear Belgian people, who have suffered so much and so nobly, of the dawn of an early era of calm and restored peace.

"Since the occasion offers itself, I take the liberty of expressing to the President of the United States the hope that the future peace conference will be held in Brussels. My compatriots, the first victims of the force of the invasion, would welcome the honor which would be accorded their capital as a first reparation, and they would perceive in that a unanimous recognition.

"Please, Mr. President, accept the tribute of my admiration and of my imperishable gratitude."

E N C L O S U R E

Vous incarnez pour nous la Belgique occupée dont vous êtes le pasteur vénéré et écouté. Aussi, est-ce à vous que Monsieur le Gouverneur Général et mon Gouvernement m'ont chargé de venir annoncer que, lorsque nous évacuerons votre sol, nous allons vous rendre spontanément et de plein gré les belges prisonniers politiques et déportés. Ils vont être libres de rentrer dans leurs foyers, en partie déjà dès lundi prochain 21 courant. Cette déclaration devant réjouir votre coeur, je suis heureux de venir vous la faire, d'autant plus que je n'ai pu vivre 4 années au milieu des Belges sans les estimer et sans apprécier leur patriotisme à sa juste valeur.[1]

T MS (WP, DLC).

[1] Our translation follows:

"You incarnate for us the occupied Belgium of which you are the venerated and heeded shepherd. Also, it is due to you that the Governor General and my government have charged me to come to announce that, when we evacuate your soil, we are going to return to you, spontaneously and of our own accord, the Belgian political prisoners and deportees. They will be free to return to their homes and hearths, some even beginning as early as Monday next, the twenty-first instant. This declaration, which must gladden your heart, I am happy to make to you, all the more since I could not have lived for four years in the midst of the Belgians without admiring them and without appreciating their patriotism at its true worth."

From the Diary of Josephus Daniels

October Thursday 17 1918

Discussed feeding Europe. Hoover thought we should begin now to send over food WW said a preacher said the Lord's prayer began with "Give us this day our daily bread["] & said no man could worship God on an empty stomach Similarly hunger will bring on bolshevikism & anarchy. House had proposed in Allied Council that they arrange to prevent starvation. Why [not] get Austrian ships interned in S A?

Discussing G B's selfish policy, WW said "I want to go into the Peace Conference armed with as many weapons as my pockets will hold so as to compel justice. England has agreed to trade conditions as I proposed. We must pool raw material & not permit it to be used for speculative purposes.["]

Fixing price of cotton. Baruch said committee reported it could not be done wisely. Texas man said South either wanted price fixed or not. The uncertainty had cause[d] loss of ten cents per pound

To Thomas William Lamont

PRIVATE

My dear Mr. Lamont: The White House 18 October, 1918.

I value your kindness and courtesy in sending me your letter of October 11th with its enclosures, and value also most sincerely the advice which it contains.

In haste, but with much appreciation,

Sincerely yours,   Woodrow Wilson

TLS (T. W. Lamont Papers, MH-BA).

To Newton Diehl Baker, with Enclosure

My dear Baker: [The White House] 18 October, 1918.

What do you think of *this*?

Cordially and sincerely yours,   Woodrow Wilson

TLS (Letterpress Books, WP, DLC).

E N C L O S U R E

Received at the War Department
Washington, D. C. October 18, 1918

Confidential   For the Secretary of War

Following received from Griscom:[1] "Lois [London] England; October 15th. For Commander in Chief American Expeditionary Forces. I asked Lord Milner for his views on the *present situation to communicate* to you. He said he occupied a *middle position* between those *who* insist on unconditional surrender and those who want peace immediately on the best terms obtainable. An Armistice should only be granted on condition that Germans lay down heavy guns and give some Naval guaranty such as the possession of Helgoland. He thinks it good to have the English press taking the extreme view of demanding *unconditional* surrender. He said he would like to have any views you may be willing to express to him informally during these important times as he considers the army viewpoints of great importance.

Paragraph 2. I *interviewed* General Wilson Chief of Staff who said he was not sure that it was possible to inflict a crushing military defeat on the German Army before the mud makes fighting impossible. Three reasons make the results doubtful: First, The English Army is very tired. Second, the French Army is even more tired and Third, the American Army is incapable of using its great forces to the fullest advantages. He regretted President Wilson's suggestion of German *evacuation of* occupied Allied territory because he would *prefer* to fight the German Army where they now are rather than on their own frontier with a line shortened by 165 miles. He said an Armistice should only be granted on condition that the Germans abandon their heavy guns and material and retire to the east bank of the Rhine permitting the Allied Armies to occupy the west bank and further a naval guard must be given by placing Helgoland in Allied possession and delivering some battleships and submarines into British ports. He said Armistice conditions must make it impossible for Germany to resume fighting. He said that instructions had been telegraphed today to Field Marshal Haig to continue the fighting day and night to the utmost limits of his army's capacity. General Wilson voices extreme army viewpoint but more *conservative* element in Government circles advise not pushing Germany too far for fear of having no Government there strong enough to make peace. Furthermore they fear that widespread revolution in Germany might unsettle Allied countries and imperil constitutional monarchies. Griscom"

I have expressed no opinions in the premises but have replied that the views of the President are mine. Pershing

T telegram (WC, NjP).
¹ Lloyd Carpenter Griscom was at this time serving as General Pershing's liaison with the British War Office.

To James Cardinal Gibbons

My dear Cardinal Gibbons: The White House 18 October, 1918.

You are always thoughtful and considerate, though I must say that even amidst the rush of these days it would have been a welcome relief to have the pleasure of seeing you in person once more to bring the message which you so graciously conveyed in your letter of October 12th.

I have every inclination of the heart to respond to the suggestion of His Holiness the Pope. I hope that he does not doubt that. But the whole matter of dealing with Austria-Hungary concerning peace is complicated by the change of circumstances which has taken place since my address to the Congress of thr [the] eighth of January was uttered. Since then we have recognized the Czecho-Slovaks and the national aspirations of the Jugo-Slavs, and have thereby created obligations of honor toward them. But I hope that you will express to His Holiness my very great appreciation of his message to me through you, and of the spirit which prompted it.

Cordially and sincerely yours, Woodrow Wilson

TLS (Baltimore Cathedral Archives).

To Xenophon Pierce Wilfley

My dear Senator: [The White House] 18 October, 1918.

I am distressed that I did not know that you were leaving so soon, and am not to have the opportunity to see you before you go home to take part in the campaign. I would have valued an opportunity to tell you how much I have appreciated your whole attitude since you came here, and how much I have valued your generous support. You are certainly going home on a public-spirited errand, and I bid you God-speed as well as a very regretful goodbye.

Cordially and sincerely yours, Woodrow Wilson

TLS (Letterpress Books, WP, DLC).

To Richard Irvine Manning

My dear Governor Manning: [The White House]
                                    18 October, 1918

Thank you warmly for your intimation about Mr. Pollock. I shall take pleasure in meeting him as soon as I can. I must confess I was deeply disappointed by the action of Senator Benet.

In haste, with warm regard,
                        Sincerely yours,   Woodrow Wilson

TLS (Letterpress Books, WP, DLC).

To James Viscount Bryce

My dear Lord Bryce: [The White House] 18 October, 1918.

I have your note about Page[1] and am heartily glad to have your testimony as to the fine place he made for himself in your esteem and in the esteem of others qualified to judge. The poor chap came back in pretty bad shape and is now in St. Luke's Hospital, in New York, but I hope and believe that he is going to pull through all right. It would be unspeakably distressing if he did not.

It was a real pleasure to hear directly from you. I know our thoughts are revolving about many common centers in these critical days, and it would be very refreshing to have a talk with you.
                Cordially and sincerely yours,   Woodrow Wilson

TLS (Letterpress Books, WP, DLC).
[1] J. Bryce to WW, Sept. 24, 1918, ALS (WP, DLC).

To Leslie E. Wallace[1]

My dear Mr. Wallace: [The White House] 18 October, 1918.

I cheerfully reply to your letter of October 11th.[2] You ask me whether it is true, as reported, that I am not particularly interested in the reelection of Mr. Shouse to Congress. It of course is not true. Such a statement must have been made for the purpose of misleading. Mr. Shouse has proved a most loyal and useful Member of Congress, has been very active indeed in the interest of his constituency and State, and I should feel it a real loss of valuable support if he should not be returned to the Congress. Pray ask your readers not to credit any statements with regard to my attitude which are made by the opponents of Mr. Shouse.
                        Sincerely yours,   Woodrow Wilson

TLS (Letterpress Books, WP, DLC).
[1] Editor and publisher of the Larned, Kan, *The Tiller and Toiler*, a weekly newspaper.
[2] L. E. Wallace to WW, Oct. 11, 1918, TLS (WP, DLC).

To Solomon Bulkley Griffin

My dear Friend: The White House 18 October, 1918.

I have been very much distressed to hear of your illness, the news of which has just reached me, but heartily glad to hear also that you are recovering. This is just a line to say with what sympathy I am thinking of you and how delightful it is to know that you are coming out all right.

Cordially and sincerely yours,   Woodrow Wilson

TLS (Connecticut Valley Historical Museum).

From Thomas Watt Gregory

Dear Mr. President: Washington, D. C. October 18, 1918.

I acknowledge receipt of your favors of the 1st, the 4th, and the 7th, all relating to Miss Pollock, under indictment in the United States Court at Sacramento, California.

Before receiving yours of the 1st, in which you enclosed a letter addressed to you by Hon. William Kent and one by his son-in-law, Mr. G. S. Arnold, who is attorney for Miss Pollock, I had received from Mr. Kent substantial copies of the same communications and on September 13th had written to Special Assistant to the Attorney General Preston, as follows:

"I herewith enclose copy of a memorandum made for Hon. William Kent by Mr. G. S. Arnold, in regard to the case of Theodora Pollock, under indictment in Sacramento.

"I have stated that this Department could not go over the head of the District Attorney; that this matter was in your charge and that, except under very extraordinary circumstances, no interference would be had with your handling of it.

"As I have a very high opinion of Mr. Kent, I wish you to carefully consider the enclosed memorandum and come to a conclusion as to whether the public interests would suffer by following either of the suggestions made. You are in an infinitely better position to judge of these matters than is the Attorney General. On reaching a conclusion, write directly to me and I will let Mr. Kent know what is to be expected."

On September 20th, I received from Mr. Preston a wire in reply, which is reproduced in his subsequent wire to me of October 3rd, as follows:

"September nineteenth wired you as follows: I.W.W. case cannot be reached on October eighth. Return of Pollock can be temporarily delayed until Department further considers matter. Evidence not yet sufficiently classified to give permanent opinion; can do this in about two weeks more. Pollock my own opinion is dangerous agent of I.W.W. and is guilty with others unless mental debility will shield her. Stated to me that she was an internationalist, indifferent to this Government and indifferent to war and that wage system should be abolished and proprietorship of property be abolished and she endorsed my presence statement of codefendant who said Haywood sized the war up rightly when he said the guts ought to be taken from Kaiser and used to strangle King George. She has been prominently identified with cases McNamara, Mooney, Ford, Suhr, Helstrom and the chief defense agent I.W.W. here.[1] Confession of one defendant discloses recent advocacy dynamite retaliation act of officers prosecuting I.W.W. Believed to be author many threatening letters Governors Stephens, Johnson and Spry; proof of latter charge not strong, however. Her attorney assured me of her return to jurisdiction this court when required. Think she should redeem promise. Will see that she is in no wise imposed upon. Signed Preston. Can add but little except to say Arnold letter admits active membership I.W.W. and practically admits her advocacy sabotage also other damaging admissions. Personal contact Pollock also mother convinced me she is dangerous. If she is to be dismissed half of seventy five defendants should also be dismissed. The gist of case is that organization as such is a criminal one. Am willing to recommend leniency on account of mental and physical weakness of defendant but in my judgment she has been too active in organization to be dismissed outright. Defendant reindicted last week and case will be reached about November seventh and she should be here by that time if not dismissed."

In your letter to me of the 4th, you stated you had learned that the trial was set for the 10th of this month and asked me to send a telegram to Preston, asking whether the indictment against Miss Pollock could be quashed without prejudice to the other persons involved; you likewise expressed a fear that a malicious newspaper campaign was being carried on against Miss Pollock and stated that you would not hesitate to take the responsibility for dismissing the case if, in my judgment and that of Mr. Preston, there was no imperative reason against such course. I thereupon sent a wire to Mr. Preston, as follows:

"Wire answer to following questions. First, in your opinion would dismissal of indictment against Pollock prejudice Government's case against others jointly indicted? Second, in your opinion is there

---

[1] That is, the cases of James B. and John J. McNamara, Thomas J. Mooney, Richard Ford, Herman D. Suhr, and Joseph Hillstrom (Joe Hill). The "chief defense agent I.W.W. here" cannot be identified.

imperative reason why indictment against Pollock should not be dismissed?"

While awaiting reply to this wire, I told you after Cabinet meeting last week that the case would not be called for trial on the 10th, but that it would be tried not earlier than November 7th, and that as there was, therefore, no immediate need for action, I would make a full report to you after hearing further from Mr. Preston.

Meanwhile, on the 7th, you referred to me a letter on the same subject addressed to you by Mr. George M. La Monte. Without taking time to go into Mr. La Monte's letter, I will say that I have reason to believe that he has been entirely misinformed, as indicated by his very broad assertions.

I now have Special Assistant to the Attorney General Preston's reply to my wire to him, above set out, and it is as follows:

"Think dismissal of Pollock this time would be positive injury to case. No imperative reason exists against dismissing case except the plain one of consistent action as to defendants of equal guilt. Moreover defendant arrived this jurisdiction yesterday and Mr. Denman,[2] partner of Arnold, is negotiating now about the disposition of matter. Believe arrangement about plea may be made. If not I still think she should be tried with other defendants."

I also quote as follows from a wire received in the last few days from the special investigator of this Department who took a prominent part in the development of the Chicago case against Haywood, et al., and who is thoroughly familiar with the entire I.W.W. situation. This man is now in San Francisco, helping Preston in the case in which Pollock and others are indicted. He says:

"What is back agitation to dismiss Theodora Pollock? She is old time agitator and cooperated with every anarchistic movement on Coast. Member of every defense (probably means offense) committed in last five years and we will likely prove her author of bad threat letters in Hill case."[3]

I also have a later wire from Preston, as follows:

"Am informed certain newspapers preparing attack on Department because Pollock not already been arraigned. Also because they suspect influence working Washington her behalf. Think it far better let case proceed in usual way. Mr. Kent also charged with contributing money defense I.W.W. Kent and Arnold are fine men, personal friends of mine, but judgment not best these kind of matters."

You will doubtless also notice that Mr. Kent, in his letter to you of

[2] That is, William Denman.
[3] About which, see the index references to Joseph Hillstrom and the Hillstrom case in Vols. 34 and 35 of this series.

September 26th, speaks of Mr. Preston as his friend and a man in whom he has great confidence.

In my judgment, Preston is the most effective and valuable man connected with my Department on the Pacific Coast. He is trying to sustain himself there under the most extraordinary circumstances. It is a section of the country where newspaper controversies run riot and where the yellow press on both sides seems to have no sense of proportion and little appreciation of decency. As far as Mr. Kent is concerned, he is a most estimable gentleman for whom I have a very great liking, but whose judgment in regard to matters of this kind is absolutely worthless. I have several times heard that he has contributed to the I.W.W. defense funds, and his attitude toward my Department has been one indicating tolerance, if not sympathy, for a great many persons and movements which we must continue to condemn, under the terms of the law.

This letter, I think, lays the facts very fully before you and I am of the opinion that it would be a very grave mistake to treat Miss Pollock in any other way than the other defendants in this case; that to dismiss the indictment against her would seriously shake the confidence of a large number of people on the Pacific Coast in the good faith of my Department, that it would create the impression that political influence could stay the hand of the Department, and that Preston himself and the great work he is undertaking under most adverse conditions would be seriously crippled. I think this would to an equal extent be true if Miss Pollock were not tried along with the others and in exactly the same way; by this I mean that it would be almost equally disastrous to grant her a severance and not try her when the case against the others is disposed of; in fact, if this were done it is very likely that she would never be tried at all, as the Government would perhaps not feel justified in again going to the tremendous expense of gathering witnesses from every section of the country and retrying the case against one defendant when it had previously been disposed of as to all the others.

You have no idea of the constant pressure brought to bear upon my Department by two classes of people, one being those who feel that even slight criticisms of the Government should be drastically dealt with by criminal prosecutions, if not by firing squads, and the other that the most unbridled license should be permitted in criticising and obstructing the conduct of the war, the organization of the Army, the method of raising funds, etc. The fact that our course is not satisfactory to either side is one of the best evidences that we are about right. If I am to stay the hand and overrule the judgment of my best local men, like Preston, because of general, and frequently unfounded, statements made at Washington as to what is involved in prosecutions, it would be impossible for me to maintain the strength of the Department as it should undoubtedly be maintained, under existing conditions.

I therefore must reply to the inquiry contained in yours of the 4th that in my judgment there are many good reasons why the case against Miss Pollock should not be dismissed and why she should be tried along with the others. In the event she is convicted, the matter of executive clemency can be taken up later with the sworn testimony before you for consideration. I do not feel justified in saying to you that there is an *imperative* reason against the dismissal of the indictment against Miss Pollock. I give the reasons as they appeal to me and they impress me as being very potent.

I herewith return the original letter addressed to you by Mr. Arnold, bearing date September 26th, original letter addressed to you by Mr. William Kent of the same date, and original letter addressed to you by Mr. George M. La Monte, dated October 4th, these having accompanied your letters to me on this subject. I have kept copies of these communications for my files.

Faithfully yours,   T. W. Gregory

TLS (WP, DLC).

A Memorandum by Homer Stillé Cummings[1]

Oct. 18, 1918.

First: On Page 1 omit the words, "But I would be rendered powerless by an adverse judgment, and I must frankly tell you so because so much depends upon your verdict."

And substitute the following: "But my power to fulfill the trust which under our Constitution and laws I am charged with the duty of administering, would be deplorably impaired, and I must frankly tell you so because so much depends upon your verdict."

Second: On Page 1, after the words, "plain truth" insert a paragraph reading as follows:

"I have no thought of suggesting that any political party is paramount in matters of patriotism. I feel too keenly the sacrifices which have been made in the present emergency by all our citizens, quite irrespective of party affiliations, to harbor such an idea. But when the war was declared a Democratic President and a Democratic Congress were in control of the affairs of our Government and were, of necessity, charged with the responsibility of conducting the war. The difficulty of this task has required and, up to the present moment has received, the undivided support of the nation under unified leadership."

Third: On Page 1 omit the words, "Their leaders in the Senate and House are the same group of men whose counsel forfeited the confidence of the country six years ago. They have altered neither their principles nor their purpose and still desire to lead the country back to policies which it has rejected."

Fourth: On Page 3 omit the following words, "By such men as the present minority leader."

Fifth: On Page 4 consider the omission of the reference to Lincoln, and if the reference is retained, omit the words, "As I am now asking for it."

Sixth: On Page 2, also consider omitting the words, "During the past year and a half they have only harassed action and darkened counsel; but"

T MS (WP, DLC).
¹ Cummings' comments on the draft of Wilson's appeal to voters, printed as an Enclosure with WW to JPT, Oct. 17, 1918.

An Appeal for a Democratic Congress¹

[Oct. 19, 1918]

My Fellow Countrymen: The Congressional elections are at hand. They occur in the most critical period our country has ever faced or is likely to face in our time. If you have approved of my leadership and wish me to continue to be your unembarrassed spokesman in affairs at home and abroad, I earnestly beg that you will express yourselves unmistakably to that effect by returning a Democratic majority to both the Senate and the House of Representatives. I am your servant and will accept your judgment without cavil, but my power to administer the great trust assigned me by the Constitution would be seriously impaired should your judgment be adverse, and I must frankly tell you so because so many critical issues depend upon your verdict. No scruple of taste must in grim times like these be allowed to stand in the way of speaking the plain truth.

I have no thought of suggesting that any political party is paramount in matters of patriotism. I feel too keenly the sacrifices which have been made in this war by all our citizens, irrespective of party affiliations, to harbour such an idea. I mean only that the difficulties and delicacies of our present task are of a sort that makes it imperatively necessary that the nation should give its undivided support to the government under a unified leadership, and that a Republican Congress would divide the leadership.

The leaders of the minority in the present Congress have unquestionably been pro-war, but they have been anti-administration. At almost every turn, since we entered the war, they have sought to take the choice of policy and the conduct of the war out of my hands and put it under the control of instrumentalities of their own choosing. This is no time either for divided counsel or for divided leadership. Unity of command is as necessary now in civil action as it is upon the field of battle. If the control of the House and Senate should be taken away from the party now in power, an opposing majority could assume control of legislation and oblige all action to be taken amidst contest and obstruction.

The return of a Republican majority to either House of the Congress would, moreover certainly be interpreted on the other side of the water as a repudiation of my leadership. Spokesmen of the Republican party are urging you to elect a Republican Congress in order to back up and support the President, but even if they should in this way impose upon some credulous voters on this side of the water, they would impose on no one on the other side. It is well understood there as well as here that the Republican leaders desire not so much to support the President as to control him. The peoples of the allied countries with whom we are associated against Germany are quite familiar with the significance of elections. They would find it very difficult to believe that the voters of the United States had chosen to support their President by electing to the Congress a majority controlled by those who are not in fact in sympathy with the attitude and action of the Administration.

I need not tell you, my fellow countrymen, that I am asking your support not for my own sake or for the sake of a political party, but for the sake of the nation itself, in order that its inward unity of purpose may be evident to all the world. In ordinary times I would not feel at liberty to make such an appeal to you. In ordinary times divided counsels can be endured without permanent hurt to the country. But these are not ordinary times. If in these critical days it is your wish to sustain me with undivided minds, I beg that you will say so in a way which it will not be possible to misunderstand either here at home or among our associates on the other side of the sea. I submit my difficulties and my hopes to you.

T MS (J. P. Tumulty Papers, DLC).
[1] The following appeal was released on October 25. About the final discussions concerning it, see the memorandum by Homer S. Cummings printed at Oct. 20, 1918.

A Draft of a Note to the Austro-Hungarian Government

[c. Oct. 19, 1918]

For reply to the Austro-Hungarian Government.

The President of the United States deems it his duty, in reply, to say to the Austro-Hungarian Government that he cannot entertain the present suggestions of that Government because of certain events of the utmost importance which have occurred since the President's address of the eighth of January last was uttered. Among the fourteen terms of peace which he then formulated occurred the following:

"X. The peoples of Austria-Hungary, whose place among the nations we wish to see safeguarded and assured, should be accorded the freest opportunity of autonomous development."

Since that sentence was written and uttered to the Congress of the United States the Government of the United States has recognized the belligerency of the Czecho-Slovak forces operating in Siberia and has consented to deal with the Czecho-Slovak Council as with an independent national authority and has also recognized in the fullest manner the justice of the national aspirations of the Jugo-Slavic peoples. The President is, therefore, no longer at liberty to accept the mere "autonomy" of these peoples as a basis of peace, but is obliged to insist that they, and not he, shall be the judges of what action on the part of the Austro-Hungarian Government will satisfy their aspirations and their own conception of their rights and destiny as members of the family of nations.

N.B. Will the Secretary of State not be kind enough to substitute for the above statement of the action of this Government with regard to the Czecho-Slovaks and the Jugo-Slavs a more accurate definition of exactly what was done, if he thinks the statement I have made too loose and indefinite?[1]

WWT MS (SDR, RG 59, 763.72119/2540, DNA).
[1] Lansing slightly revised Wilson's draft and sent it as RL to W. A. F. Ekengren, Oct. 19, 1918, CCLS (SDR, RG 59, 763.72119/2540, DNA). Lansing's draft, handwritten, is in the same file.

From Newton Diehl Baker, with Enclosures

[Washington, c. Oct. 19, 1918]

2 cablegrams for the President's information   Baker

ALS (WP, DLC).

E   N   C   L   O   S   U   R   E   I

VLADIVOSTOK October 18th [1918]

Number 50 SECRET

Returned Wednesday from inspection of troops to the north. Found all towns and villages occupied by what appeared to me to be ten times as many Japanese troops as are necessary. My information is to the effect that this condition obtains along the Chinese Eastern as far as Chita as well as along the Siberia Railroad from Chita to Khabarovsk and down to Vladivostok. I feel sure that there are fully sixty thousand of these troops in all. I have sent recently an officer west and he had reported there are six thousand of these troops at Verghundinsk [Verkhneudinsk][1] and also some at Irkutsk, number not reported. Our ally is evidently very much opposed to American troops going to Harbin and it looks as if I would be unable to find quarters there for one battalion as Chief Quartermaster has been there *ten days* without any success. These facts are reported because I can see no reason for such a number of troops in this country. To all intents and purposes these troops now practically in charge of railroads east of Chita.   Graves.

' Now Ulan-Ude.

E   N   C   L   O   S   U   R   E   I I

From HAEF   October 18th [1918].

Number 1809 CONFIDENTIAL.

FOR THE CHIEF OF STAFF:

The following received from American Legation, Copenhagen through Slocum. "Following is a press statement of the ban issued October 5th last by German press headquarters. Turning point of war took place July 18th. Since then Central Powers reduced to defensive on all fronts and allied offensive extended to all sectors of fronts. Entente offensive has attained its highest point and the decision of the world is nearing maturity. Struggle against half the world is increased by fact that Germany's few allies are deserting her one by one. A whole continent excellently organized has risen and America is throwing both men and materials into the fight in an incredibly short time. On the other hand Germany's resources and reserves of men are exhausted and no new hopes are in progress. War must therefore and will end before long. Ludendorff's remaining task is to stop Hindenburg line from being broken and dislocated and same is already penetrated. Belgians have made a break in Flanders 12 kilometers in depth. Question of evacuation of Lille will be acute if the front continues to be pushed back here. Furthermore there is always chance of an offensive in Alsace. This three months ago would scarcely have been believed. A sombre future awaits us if a new * * * does not bring an early peace."

Pershing

CC telegrams (WP, DLC).

From Newton Diehl Baker

Dear Mr. President: Washington. October 19, 1918.

In estimating the importance of the opinion of Sir Henry Wilson, expressed to Mr. Driscoll[1] in the cablegram which I sent you last night from General Pershing, it may be important for you to know that Sir Henry Wilson is perhaps the most unsympathetic critic the American Army has. This, however, is but a part of his general disposition as he is equally hostile to Sir Douglas Haig. I think his attitude toward the Americans is largely irritation because our divisions are not fed into the British forces. A noteworthy instance of his unreliability occurred just before the St. Mihiel drive, when the plan for that movement was shown him. He protested so fiercely to Lord Miller [Milner] against its being undertaken that Lord Miller actually adopted his opinion and committed it to writing against the movement, and was deeply humiliated and chagrined at our success at St. Mihiel which showed him the extent to which he had been beguiled by Sir Henry Wilson. Before the St. Mihiel action Sir Henry Wilson said openly in England with regard to it that one or the other of two things would take place. Either we would find less resistance than we expected, in which case our staff would be unable to manage our troops and they would rush beyond their objective and be trapped; or else we would find more resistance than we expected and get nowhere, with great losses of men and material. The event completely disappointed his predictions. The staff management of that action was admirable, and its success complete, with more than three times as many prisoners as our entire casualty list, including the slightly wounded.

You may be interested to know too why the progress on General Pershing's front in this general battle is slow. The front from the Meuse to the Argonne Forest, on which General Pershing's attack is being made, is probably as difficult ground as there is anywhere on the entire Western front, and certainly more difficult than any place where active battles are now being waged. In addition to that, the attack threatens Mezieries [Mézières], which is the great railroad center on the Sedan-Metz line. Should Mezieries fall, the

German communications for supplies would be completely cut and
the withdrawal of all their forces to the West would have to be by
insufficient and round-about railroads through Namur and other
points far to the north. It is the one place on the line where the
Germans cannot afford either to withdraw or retire, and as a consequence the heaviest enemy concentration anywhere on the line
is directly ahead of General Pershing. All this was foreseen and the
slow progress made by the American first army is to be expected
under the circumstances. In the meantime our American divisions
with the French and with the British have fought a substantial part
in the actions to the North and West, where the great gains of
territory have been made.

Lord Miller seemed to be sympathetic, cordial, and intelligent,
and I am disposed to regard most of his trouble as springing from
the counsel and advice of Sir Henry Wilson, whose political aims
and intemperance of opinion and speech seem to make him a particularly untrustworthy military adviser.

Respectfully, Newton D. Baker

TLS (WP, DLC).
   [1] He meant Lloyd C. Griscom.

From Robert Lansing, with Enclosure

PERSONAL AND CONFIDENTIAL.

My dear Mr. President: Washington October 19, 1918.

The enclosed telegram from Berne (No. 5237) you have doubtless
read with the same feeling of concern that I have, especially as it
fits in with other information which we have received as to the
political strife in Italy and the growing antagonism which exists
between the Italian and French Governments. I am surprised that
Nitti[1] is not mentioned in connection with this rivalry between
Orlando and Sonnino because I consider him one of the chief fo-
mentors of trouble at Rome as the backer of General Diaz in his
refusal to make an offensive without reinforcements from outside.

While I confess to little patience with the spirit which seems to
animate the statesmen of Italy and cannot presume to pass judgment on the wisdom of refusing troops to General Diaz from a
military point of view, I feel that the political situation demands
careful consideration.

I know how the Chief of Staff feels about dividing our military
strength and that he has thus far opposed any suggestion to send
an American force to the Italian front. He speaks as a soldier and
I would not for a moment question his military judgment for which

I have the highest regard, but this seems to me to be more than a military question. It is a question of maintaining the morale not only of the Italian army but of the Italian people as well. We know from the way that they received Germany's peace overture how weak that morale is, and I am very apprehensive of what will happen if they are forced to face another winter of war and privation without something to renew their courage.

In addition to the French military point of view, which is undoubtedly against sending troops, I believe that the increasing bitterness between France and Italy has blinded the French to the gravity of the Italian political situation and that the French Government for that reason accepted the judgment of its military advisers without questioning its wisdom.

However scheming and selfish Italy's officials may be and however unreasonable may be the attitude of her military command, it seems to me that, if anything can be done, it should be done to remove the impression that Italy is abandoned by her Allies and the belief that France is hostile to Italian interests and is not anxious to have the Italians make a successful offensive.

In view of the conditions which have, according to all our informants, been growing worse and worse during the past few weeks so far as Italy's internal affairs are concerned, it seems to me that the policy as to sending troops to that front ought to be reconsidered with due regard to political as well as military necessity. I believe that the situation is critical and that something should be done. Frankly I am by no means certain that the Italian suspicion of the French Government is entirely groundless. But whether it is or not I feel now that there is real danger in the state of affairs, although previously I was disposed to consider the pleas of the Italian Government for troops to be based only on a sentimental jealousy and not on an actual need.   Faithfully yours,   Robert Lansing

TLS (WP, DLC).
[1] Francesco Saverio Nitti, Deputy Minister of Finance.

ENCLOSURE

Pontarlier, Berne. Oct. 16, 1918.

5237. Professor Herron has communicated to me the substance of an interview with an Italian Official in Berne, a supporter Orlando's party: Followers of Orlando desire President to know that strife between them and followers of Sonnino is becoming vital and bitter. Party of former accept President as world leader, stand for the Society of Nations and forced Rome congress of nationalities.[1]

They declare Sonnino secretly and resolutely holds to pact of London putting Italy in conflict with Yugo-Slavs, that he is determined on preservation of Austria-Hungary on condition that latter country yields up the Irridenta and Dalmatia, is that in short he tends toward restoration of the Triple Alliance and is hostile to democratic ideals and American influence in Europe.

Very lately Orlando was supposed to have been received by Marshal Foch and presented to him request for Allied military aid in Italy. Clemenceau, however, refused to consider detaching American or other troops for service in Italy and a deadlock between the two Prime Ministers resulted. Orlando returned to Rome where he is said to have stated to his parliamentary group that Italy could not make any offensive now because France would not consent to the needed military help. News of this reaching Clemenceau, the latter declared it to be untrue giving Orlando practically the lie.

The result of this is a dangerous bitterness between France and Italy, the more deplorable since Orlando's followers have been devoted friends of France and the situation plays into the hands of Sonnino against the best Allied interests.

Professor Herron's informants desire that Americans should clearly understand situation and not rely on French official interpretation. Professor Herron adds: "If the waiting [war] continues to its righteous ends, I am still of the opinion that the cause of the Allies depends in part, at least upon the enabling of Italy to strike her desired decisive blow against Austro Hungarian army, the Empire."

                                                    Stovall.

T telegram (SDR, RG 59, 763.72119/2223, DNA).
  ¹ About which, see WW to RL, June 26, 1918, Enclosure II, n. 3, Vol. 48.

From Alice Wilson Page

Dear Mr. President: New York City Oct. 19, 1918

The box of beautiful roses from The White House gave to my children and me very great pleasure, as a mark of your thought of my husband in his illness. He is yet so rarely conscious that he does not realize your great kindness in thinking of him, in the midst of the tremendous questions that make so constant and insistent demand on your time. But I know so well how appreciative he would be that I add his thanks to mine.

With very deep appreciation I am

                                    Sincerely Yours,   Alice Page.

ALS (WP, DLC).

Colville Adrian de Rune Barclay to Arthur James Balfour

Washington. Oct. 19th, 1918

No. 4732 URGENT.

Your tel. No. 6180 and my tel. 4716.[1]

In the name of the British French and Italian Governments the French Ambassador this afternoon handed to the President the proposed terms of armistice with Turkey, explaining the circumstances. The President thanked him for his communication and after glancing at the paper said it was not within his competence to judge the terms—such questions were purely for the Military. He went on to say that as he must reply to the Turkish Note[2] he could if it were agreeable to the three Governments concerned recommend to the Turkish Government to apply for an armistice and also he might if we liked state our conditions. He added he would be glad for an expression of our views.

French and Italian Ambassadors are telegraphing in above sense to their Governments.

I had this morning communicated to French Ambassador views expressed in your tel. No. 6263,[3] but he told me that though they had been very useful for his guidance in conversation with the President, he had not actually advanced them.

T telegram (FO 115/2429, p. 292, PRO).
    [1] A. J. Balfour to C. A. de R. Barclay, Oct. 13, 1918, T telegram (FO 115/2428, pp. 247-48, PRO), and C. A. de R. Barclay to A. J. Balfour, Oct. 18, 1918, T telegram (FO 115/2429, p. 291, PRO).
    [2] See n. 1 to the memorandum by W. Wiseman printed at Oct. 16, 1918.
    [3] A. J. Balfour to C. A. de R. Barclay, Oct. 17, 1918, T telegram (FO 115/2429, p. 290, PRO).

A Memorandum by Homer Stillé Cummings

Oct. 20, 1918.

During the morning of October 18th I received word from McCormick that he had received a rough draft of a proposed statement to be issued by the President concerning political conditions. I went over to Mr. McCormick's office and we read the draft with great care. McCormick had quite a number of suggestions to make as to the tone and substance of the communication. In some of his views I concurred and expressed some notions of my own. I then took the draft and went to my office and examined it carefully, and prepared some proposed modifications.

In the meantime an appointment had been made to see the President and at 4:30 in the afternoon I went to the White House with Mr. McCormick. This appointment had been made several days before as I wanted to discuss with the President conditions in Minnesota, especially growing out of the fact that the chances of Calderwood in Minnesota[1] seemed to be improving and also gecause [because] it was industriously maintained and advertised in Minnesota that the President had written a letter recommending the reelection of the Republican sitting member, Senator Nelson. The President is personally fond of Senator Nelson and when it was first reported that such a letter had been written the President did not deny it, and so much time has now elapsed that it seems undesirable for him to do so, especially in view of the bare possibility that some sort of letter may have been written by the President which may have been distorted and formed some basis for the story in question. I told the President that we ought to do the best we could for the Minnesota people, especially as they have shown every evidence of a willingness to help themselves, and because John Lind and other friends of the Administration were supporting Calderwood. I read some letters from Lind and Calderwood and they seemed to create a favorable impression upon the President.

The Calderwood letter contained some sounding phrases, and the President said, "Well, he seems to be quite an orator. That phrase sounds very well." I told the President that Calderwood was reported to be the best public speaker in Minnesota with the exception of John Lind. The President then became reflective and spoke in warm terms of Lind, and then told a story which has become circulated with respect to Lind, but which I had not heard before to the effect that while Lind was a candidate for a certain office an opposition newspaper wrote a scandalous article about him. Lind did not say anything about it until the campaign was over and he had been safely elected, whereupon he went around to the editorial office and licked the editor. The point to the story especially is that Lind has only one arm. The President seemed amused at the anecdote which he, himself, related, and reflecting upon Lind's idea of the proper time to give a licking.

The method that I proposed for handling the question of the Nelson letter was approved by the President and I subsequently acted along those lines.

I then took up the draft of the proposed letter[2] and discussed it at considerable length. Mr. McCormick expressed his views quite freely, but not with entire success. The President did concur in the view that the letter might be considered too bitter. He said that he had read it to Mrs. Wilson and her comment was that it might give the impression that he had been irritated by the partisan attacks which had been made upon him. Certain suggestions of change which I made in phraseology he approved and asked me to leave the memorandum with him. I noticed that afterward in the final draft, completed the following day, he had incorporated nearly all the suggestions I had made and had adopted verbatim most of the phraseology.

The President seemed to be in high spirits. When we arrived we went into the Room of the President, adjoining the East Room, which faces the broad staircase. The President came down the staircase with the briskness of a boy, and laughingly informed us that we had interrupted his work on his reply to Austria. He then told us what the reply would be. The reply appeared in the papers the following day exactly as he had stated it would appear, so I judged he had made no change in the meanwhile and was very clear in his mind as to exactly what to say to Austria. This, naturally, led to a discussion of the previous note to Germany. The President seemed to enjoy talking about it. He said that a certain Senator, I think it was Senator Ashurst, came into his office in quite a state of excitement before the final answer to Germany was sent, and was very much concerned as to what the President should say, especially in view of the previous and famous three questions which the President had asked of Germany before preparing the final statement. Senator Ashurst seemed to be afraid that the President might give up some advantage which our Government had obtained by force of arms, and in some way weaken our position. The President told us that he had said to Ashurst, "I notice that quite a number of people are concerned about what the answer is going to be; but, Senator, it would relieve a great many people of anxiety if they did not start with the assumption that I am a damn fool." Knowing that Ashurst came from a western state and was familiar with the ways of cow boys, the President used an illustration to him to the effect that if two cow boys had been shooting at each other and one of them was finally prepared to put up his hands for the sake of discussion it would be natural for the other cow boy to require the one who was about to surrender to place his arms on the ground in front of him, and he said, "Don't you think it would be pretty safe to talk to him under such circumstances." The Senator allowed it would, and the President suggested that he did not propose to enter into any parley with the German Government, unless he was satisfied that they could not begin shooting again. Senator Ashurst went away satisfied. All of this the President related to us in the most vivacious manner.

I then asked him if he had read the Congressional Record of the day that his answer to Germany had appeared. He said he had not. I told him it was worth reading because of the solemn absurdity of it all. In the early session, before the message was published, the

Senators began discussing what it would be, what it would not be, and what it ought to be, and they talked all about it—some denouncing what they supposed the President was going to do and others defending what they supposed the President was going to do, and in this way they occupied all day in debate, and they kept the session going until the actual message appeared that afternoon and it was read to the senators and it spoiled everything that had been said all day long by everybody. This seemed to amuse the President. The President talked quite freely about certain Senators for whom he has very little respect, including Senator C and Senator H.[3]

In discussing the draft there occurred in the document a reference to Lincoln and the appeal that he made for party support during the Civil War. I had made note on my memorandum that this reference had better be left out because it had been used so much. The President agreed to this suggestion and went further and said that it might seem like an apology for his course. Apparently he did not want to cite any precedent for his course and said that the people were used to his doing unconventional things. I was also amused at another phrase that he used in discussing the language of the document which seemed to Mr. McCormick in certain places to be a little too elaborate. The President said, "I think that is all right because you see the people have gotten used by this time to a high-brow president." He said this with a grin that was quite illuminating. The net result of it all was that the President agreed to redraft the document.

The following morning, October 19th, I got a hurry call from Mr. Tumulty who had the redraft and said that the President wanted Mr. McCormick and myself to see it. We went at it again and made some additional suggestions. Tumulty, who is pretty wise in matters political, said there was one paragraph in the document which he did not like. He did not tell me which paragraph it was, but I read the document over and I said there is one paragraph in it I did not like, and curiously enough it was the same paragraph. I then prepared a substitute for it, which the President later adopted. Mr. McCormick came in while we were talking the matter over and agreed to the substitute I proposed and he also thought the President ought to retain some of the things which were in the first draft and which he had cut out. I agreed to this.

At 2:30 P.M. we say [saw] the President again. At this conference Mr. Tumulty and Mr. McCormick were present, as well as myself. The President agreed to reincorporate in the document some of the things that he had eliminated and then the document was read over pretty carefully and practically completed. There was one word in the document which seemed to me not quite the proper word—it was the word "argument" as applied to certain representations being made by certain Republican leaders. I suggested to the President that I did not think that that was quite the right word. He said that he knew it was not, but he could not think of any other. We all tried to think of a substitute and I finally said, "What we need is a book of synonyms." The President said he did not think that would help us any because we would not know what to look up. He said it was like the Irishman's dictionary—the Irishman claimed that the dictionary did not do him any good because he could never find the word he was after unless he knew how to spell it already. We then left.

T MS (H. S. Cummings Papers, ViU).
¹ Willis Greenleaf Calderwood, longtime leader of the Prohibition party and other prohibition organizations in Minnesota, had run as the Prohibition party candidate for congressman (1912), governor (1914), and senator (1916). He was at this time running for the Senate against Knute Nelson as the candidate of the National party, a coalition of Minnesota Socialists, Nonpartisans, and progressives. The regular Democratic party organization had not put up a candidate against Nelson and, hence, many Democrats were supporting Calderwood.
² That is, Wilson's appeal to voters.
³ There were six senators at this time whose surnames began with C and seven whose surnames began with H. "Senator C" was undoubtedly George E. Chamberlain; "Senator H" was probably Gilbert M. Hitchcock.

To William Kent

My dear Kent: The White House 21 October, 1918

I of course took up and discussed the matter of the indictment against Mr. Bouck, of Washington, after receiving your letter of October 5th, and I have recently received a report on the case from the Attorney General.

It seems that the Department called for a report from the District Attorney, and after going into the situation carefully at your instance concluded that a dismissal of the case was not justified in the circumstances.

The Attorney General feels confident that you are mistaken in believing that the local Assistant to the Attorney General, Clarence L. Reames, who is conducting the prosecution, is in any sense bent on the ruin of Mr. Bouck and those with whom he is associated, and reports that the indictment charges Bouck with having made certain false and untrue statements, substantially as follows:

"If this war lasts three years, the war debt will amount to one hundred billion dollars; it is placing a great mortgage on our children and their children; the revenues of the United States in the years to come will not be sufficient to pay the interest on the bonds;

the rich men will grab all these Liberty Bonds and they will get them all together in the rich men's pockets; the revenues of the United States for years to come will not pay the interest on the Liberty Bonds; we will be under servitude to the rich men forever as far as the United States is concerned; we will be under the reigh [reign] of these rich men forever; we will never get out from under the reign of these rich men because the revenues of the United States will not pay the interest of the Liberty Bonds; the war will not end until the Non-partisan League gets their rights; it is a rich man's war and the war will not end until the rich men get all the gold they want and then it will end; this is not a war for democracy, it is a rich man's war; the war should be based on the 'pay-as-you-go' plan, and if we cannot pay as we go, the expenses should be cut down until we can pay as we go; the war will not end until the rich people fill their pockets with gold; we are forced to fight against our will; this war will continue until the multi-millionaires make their fortunes; your children's children for years to come will have their noses to the grindstone paying off this debt of the Liberty Bonds; the capitalists brought about the war and it is all for their gain; it was not put up to the people as it should have been; the people should have had a vote on it, and we are forced to fight against our will."

The indictment charges that these remarks were made with the intent to interfere with the operation and success of the military and naval forces of the United States and to promote the success of our enemies, that in making the statements the defendant attempted to obstruct the recruiting and enlistment service of the United States, and that they were made with the intent to obstruct the sale by the United States of its bonds and securities. The District Attorney writes that six responsible and trustworthy witnesses testified before the grand jury that Bouck made the statements charged in the indictment and that these statements are more seditious than those made by William Kaufman, a prominent member of the Non-Partisan League recently sentenced to serve five years in the penitentiary.

It is very likely that when the case is tried, other witnesses will deny that Bouck made the statements charged, but there is no present ground for disregarding this evidence. If Bouck made the statements charged, he should undoubtedly be prosecuted. The grand jury believed that he had made them, and six responsible witnesses are ready to sustain the charge.

I think that you can rest assured that the case will be fairly conducted.

Cordially and faithfully yours,   Woodrow Wilson

TLS (WP, DLC).

To E. L. Miley[1]

[The White House] 21 October, 1918.

I earnestly desire the election of Governor Stanley to the United States Senate. I supposed that my whole-hearted support of him was well known throughout Kentucky. Woodrow Wilson.

T telegram (Letterpress Books, WP, DLC).
[1] Pastor of the First Christian Church of Hickman, Ky. The message to which Wilson was responding is missing.

To Thomas Garrigue Masaryk

My dear Dr. Masaryk: [The White House] 21 October, 1918

I need not tell you with what emotions I read the Declaration of Independence put out by the National Council of the Czecho-Slovaks,[1] and I think that my recent reply to Austria will apprise you very fully of my own attitude in the matter. You may be sure that my interest is deeply engaged.

Cordially and sincerely yours, Woodrow Wilson

TLS (Letterpress Books, WP, DLC).
[1] Enclosed in T. G. Masaryk to WW, Oct. 18, 1918, TLS (WP, DLC).

To Alexander Mitchell Palmer

My dear Palmer: The White House 21 October, 1918

I am distressed about the Busch case.[1] The Attorney General told me after the last meeting of the Cabinet that it was his unhesitating judgment that we had no legal right to retain the property. That being his judgment, it is embarrassing to resist Mrs. Busch's claim, though I agree with you that it would probably be in the public interest for us not to do so. Do you not think that it is best to avoid any possibility of error in a matter of this sort?

Cordially and faithfully yours, Woodrow Wilson

TLS (A. M. Palmer Papers, DLC).
[1] Lilly Anheuser Busch, the widow of Adolphus Busch, the late proprietor of the Anheuser-Busch Brewing Association, had in July 1918 filed a petition for the return of her property which had been seized by the Alien Property Custodian. The property included breweries in St. Louis and other cities, stocks and bonds, and real estate in New York, all of which was estimated to be worth several million dollars. Mrs. Busch, although of German birth, was a naturalized American citizen. She had been in residence on her German estate at the time of the outbreak of the war and had only returned to the United States in June 1918. Palmer's argument in justification of the seizure of her property and against its return to her was essentially that her prolonged residence in Germany during the war had in effect made her an "enemy" under the terms of the Trading with the Enemy Act of October 6, 1917. A. M. Palmer to T. W. Gregory, Oct. 15, 1918, CCL (WP, DLC); *New York Times*, July 14 and Dec. 14, 1918.

Two Letters to Newton Diehl Baker

CONFIDENTIAL

My dear Baker: The White House 21 October, 1918.

Thank you for the enclosed dispatch and for your comment upon it under date of October 19th. It is very valuable indeed for me to have these side lights in dealing with the men in authority on the other side of the water. I have again and again had occasion to regret that Mr. Lloyd George insisted upon being represented by Sir Henry Wilson.

Cordially and faithfully yours,   Woodrow Wilson

TLS (WC, NjP).

CONFIDENTIAL

My dear Baker: [The White House] 21 October, 1918.

The enclosed[1] is exceedingly disturbing, if true, and I am writing to suggest that steps be taken to probe the report very thoroughly, though I must admit I do not see just how it can be satisfactorily done.

If you would have a word with the Secretary of State about this, perhaps he would think it wise to convey some intimation to the Japanese Ambassador which would be of service.

Cordially and faithfully yours,   [Woodrow Wilson]

CCL (WP, DLC).
  [1] That is, Enclosure I with NDB to WW, Oct. 19, 1918 (first letter of that date).

From Valentine Everit Macy

My dear Mr. President: Washington, D. C. October 21, 1918

In order that you may be informed of the serious injury to the shipbuilding program, resulting from the delay in announcing our decision, I am enclosing copies of two telegrams just received.[1]

In addition, many of the shipyard owners are reporting that their most skilled men are being drawn out of the yards as the men are discouraged at not receiving the award earlier, although we have notified all districts that the award would be retroactive. The loss of men in some yards has been so great that where they formerly have had three shifts, they are now able to maintain only one shift of eight hours.

In addition, the rates provided in the award, while proper rates when the decision was formulated, will now seem very low and give little satisfaction, owing to the fact that other industries have been advancing their wages very rapidly.

Hoping that announcement may be made of the National Labor Policy, as recommended by the Conference of Wage Adjusting Agencies, so that we may issue our decision in the very near future,

Very respectfully yours   V. Everit Macy.

TLS (WP, DLC).

[1] H. W. Burnham to V. E. Macy, Oct. 20, 1918, and A. S. Shepherd to V. E. Macy, Oct. 18, 1918, both TC telegrams (WP, DLC). The writers, officials of union locals in Aberdeen and Tacoma, Washington, respectively, both declared that their members were losing faith in the Shipbuilding Labor Adjustment Board due to its failure to make public a decision in their case. They urged the board to take immediate action in the matter.

From Herbert Clark Hoover

Dear Mr. President: *Washington 21 October 1918*

The task of the Belgian Relief Commission,—the preservation of the life of 10,000,000 occupied Belgians and French over these four years—is now rapidly drawing to conclusion and questions as to what further assistance should be extended to these people and as to what organization should be set up are pressing as the Governments in Europe are taking steps on the matter.

I enclosed herewith a short memorandum on—

(a) The relief during occupation.

(b) The relief required for rehabilitation.[1]

The released French population can be best cared for by their own government through France and I do not therefore consider that we need concern ourselves therewith.

The Belgian people, while more fortunate than the Serbians and Poles in that they are all alive, come out of occupation under-nourished, under-housed, under-clothed, industrial plants ruined, without raw material and without resources in shipping and money to find a remedy.

There is immediate need for 550,000 tons of shipping of which 350,000 are now in use by the Relief Commission. The Allied governmental aid needs be at once increased from about $15,000,000 per month at present being given (of which our government furnishes $9,000,000) to about $30,000,000 per month. With these resources over twelve to eighteen months I believe the people could be made self-supporting.

Assuming this must be accomplished, the problem of organization at once arises. Certain Belgians are anxious that the Relief Commission should liquidate and be handed over to the restored Belgian government—who should undertake all further relief with loans from the Allied governments; others wish the Commission to continue to perform such functions as may be assigned by the Belgian government; others are anxious that the Commission should undertake the great problem of economic restoration, acting as hitherto, in co-operation with Belgian unofficial organizations, and drawing its support from our own and Allied governments and public charity. The British government is opening discussion with our government on the question.

From a purely Belgian point of view the direct operation by their government is a mixed argument of sturdy independence and of natural amour propre and, to some extent, of individual political ambitions; the second proposition of a continuance controlled by the Belgian government is an argument of utilization of the organization until it can be dispensed with at will; the third is an argument which I believe should be further discussed, as it has both moral and economic bearings for the American people. I need hardly mention that the selfish view of myself and my colleagues would be entirely with the first proposition. We would like to have relief from this especially poignant anxiety that has now extended over four years.

With the present misery and economic difficulties facing Europe there can be little hope of Belgian recuperation without the major help coming from the United States. The American people, under your guidance, through its citizens and with the help of its officials, took the lead in internal protection and sustenance of this population four years ago. This imposes no obligation but offers an opportunity for further service—the completion of which would confer moral values to our country not to be under-estimated.

Intangible as these values are, they cannot be gained by our people unless they are won through some bond of definite American organization participating in the labour and its consummation.

While it can be said that the Belgians are an efficient administrative people, it is my impression that security and effectiveness in the application of these funds, without religious, political or racial bias, could be much more effectively secured by American participation in organization and administration.

There will be a large outpouring of charity towards the Belgian people which could be stimulated, but in the expenditure of which, unless there is some single channel, there will be enormous waste and corruption, and re-actions will set in to the disadvantage of both Belgian and American people.

If the matter were undertaken by the Belgian government alone, they would naturally have to take their position with the other needy Allied governments under the various Allied controls; whereas, if a distinctly American organization, maintained by the American government, were to be installed for this service, such an organization could easily secure the same tenderness in obtaining priorities and supplies, and complete independence of action from other Allied control that it now possesses.

As these controls are dominated by the other needy governments I feel that the Belgians will get off much worse in shipping and in supplies than if they are particularly under our wing. If American participation in organization of rehabilitation is to be maintained it would seem logical to continue it through the Relief Commission whose organization is in action and simply requires larger resources and the use of this media would avoid discussion of any new instrumentality with the Allied governments. It would represent the rounding out of an enterprise of our people toward another in which we could have lasting pride.

One of the objectives in peace conferences must be the re-payment, in addition to other damages, to Belgium of the whole of the sums that have been spent by the Relief Commission, together with such further moneys as are spent on rehabilitation. It would appear to me that it would be a pointed and positive lesson to the world for all future time if it could be made a peace condition that the expenditures of the Relief Commission both in the past and in the future are made re-payable by the Germans, directly to the Relief Commission, and that this Commission should refund the sums advanced by the various governments.

I should be glad to have your views in the matter and if you consider the Commission should be continued to this new purpose and that it will have the support of the government, it is desirable that its relations to Belgian and other governments should be properly defined.   Yours faithfully,   Herbert Hoover

TLS (WP, DLC).
[1] "The Relief of Belgium," T MS (WP, DLC). Hoover summarizes it well.

Two Telegrams from Newton Diehl Baker to Tasker Howard Bliss

Washington. October 21, 1918.

Confidential
To be delivered on receipt night and day

Rush. "The answer of the German Government to the President's last note has been received here. Please cable me at once your own views and a summary of such official expressions, civil and military, as you have heard with reference to the situation as it now is, so that I may lay them before the President. Follow your first cablegram with any fresh expressions of significant opinion which you learn.   Baker."

T telegram (SDR, RG 59, 763.72119/6157, DNA).

                                        Washington, October 21, 1918.

The President of the United States has awarded a Distinguished Service Medal to General John J. Pershing, and directs that you act as his representative in presenting the Medal. He further directs that you say to General Pershing that he awards this Medal to the Commander of our Armies in the Field as a token of the gratitude of the American people for his distinguished services, and in appreciation of the success which our Armies have achieved under his leadership.   Newton D. Baker

TC telegram (WP, DLC).

Drafts of a Note by Robert Lansing

TENTATIVE DRAFT
(No. 1)
October 21, 1918.

From the language of the reply of the German Government[1] and of its preceding communications the assumption is unavoidable that the German Government is convinced that the United States and the Entente Powers possess the military superiority and are in a position to decide upon what terms an armistice will be granted and the German forces permitted to evacuate invaded territory, and also that the German Government must accede to such terms and furnish such guarantees for the faithful compliance therewith as the United States and the Entente Powers may require.

The President, therefore, purposes to discuss with the Entente Governments the propriety of submitting to the military advisers of the respective Governments the question of evacuation and armistice. In the event that an agreement between such Governments is reached after such submission the President will advise the German Government of the terms and guarantees which have been determined upon.

When the terms of armistice and evacuation have been complied with and the required guarantees furnished the President will be prepared to enter upon a consideration of the application of the general principles to which the German Government has given its assent.

As conditions precedent to any discussion of the detailed application of the principles of a treaty of peace as heretofore laid down by the President and unconditionally accepted by the German Government are the evacuation of all occupied territory and an armistice, and as these are necessarily of a military nature, I am instructed by the President to state that, in view of the note of October [blank], the Government of the United States, provided the Governments of the Allied Powers assent, will refer the question of terms of armistice and the necessary guarantees for their faithful performance to the Supreme War Council of the United States and the Allied Powers and the commanders of their military and naval forces. Upon the receipt of the answer of such military and naval advisers and upon its approval by the Governments of the United States and the Allied Powers the same will be forthwith communicated to the German Government.

The President instructs me to say in reply to the German Government's note of October 22d, that after careful consideration of the statements made therein he feels it to be his duty to advise the German Government in all frankness that the political changes in the constitution of the Empire and in the relative powers of the imperial authorities do not furnish sufficient safeguards and guarantees for the faithful performance of any agreement which might be entered into between the United States and the Allied Powers on the one hand and Germany on the other.

Specifically the powers of the Imperial Government and the military high command of Germany are as supreme and unlimited as they were at any time since the present war began except so far as the assent of the Reichstag is required to give validity to a treaty of peace negotiated by the Imperial Government and the German military authorities. In view of this fact one of the essential guaranties of good faith on the part of Germany would be to withdraw from the present German Government and from the German military high command all the powers which they possess and to confer the same upon a government chosen by the German people and responsible only to the popular will.

With such a guaranty of good faith as an accomplished fact the Government of the United States will give consideration in consultation with the Governments associated with it in the war as to the further guaranties necessary before the questions of evacuation and armistice are laid before the military advisers of the United States and the Allied Powers for their determination.

T MSS (WP, DLC).
    ¹ The reply of the German government of October 20, 1918, follows:
    "In accepting the proposal for an evacuation of the occupied territories the German Government has started from the assumption that the procedure of this evacuation and of the conditions of an armistice should be left to the judgment of the military advisers and that the actual standard of power on both sides in the field has to form the basis for arrangements safeguarding and guaranteeing this standard. The German Government suggests to the President to bring about an opportunity for fixing the details. It trusts that the President of the United States will approve of no demand which would be irreconcilable with the honor of the German people and with opening a way to a peace of justice.
    "The German Government protests against the reproach of illegal and inhumane actions made against the German land and sea forces and thereby against the German people. For the covering of a retreat, destructions will always be necessary and are insofar permitted by international law. The German troops are under the strictest instructions to spare private property and to exercise care for the population to the best of their ability. Where transgressions occur in spite of these instructions the guilty are being punished.
    "The German Government further denies that the German Navy in sinking ships has ever purposely destroyed lifeboats with their passengers. The German Government proposes with regard to all these charges that the facts be cleared up by neutral commissions. In order to avoid anything that might hamper the work of peace, the German Government has caused orders to be despatched to all submarine commanders precluding the torpedoing of passenger ships, without, however, for technical reasons, being able to guarantee that these orders will reach every single submarine at sea before its return.
    "As the fundamental conditions for peace, the President characterizes the destruction of every arbitrary power that can separately, secretly and of its own single choice disturb the peace of the world. To this the German Government replies: Hitherto the representation of the people in the German Empire has not been endowed with an influence on the formation of the Government. The Constitution did not provide for a concurrence of the representation of the people in decision on peace and war. These conditions have just now undergone a fundamental change. The new government has been formed in complete accord with the wishes of the representation of the people, based on the equal, universal, secret, direct franchise. The leaders of the great parties of the Reichstag are members of this government. In future no Government can take or continue in office without possessing the confidence of the majority of the Reichstag. The responsibility of the Chancellor of the Empire to the representation of the people is being legally developed and safeguarded. The first act of the new government has been to lay before the Reichstag a bill to alter the Constitution of the Empire so that the consent of the representation of the people is required for decisions on war and peace. The permanence of the new system is, however, guaranteed not only by constitutional safeguards, but also by the unshakable determination of the German people, whose vast majority stands behind these reforms and demands their energetic continuance.
    "The question of the President, with whom he and the Governments associated against Germany are dealing, is therefore answered in a clear and unequivocal manner by the statement that the offer of peace and an armistice has come from a government which, free from arbitrary and irresponsible influence, is supported by the approval of the overwhelming majority of the German people.   (Signed)   SOLF,
State Secretary of Foreign Affairs. Berlin, October 20, 1918."
Diplomatic Correspondence between the Governments of the United States and Germany,
October 23, 1918 (Washington, 1918), SDR, RG 59, 763.72119/2377A, DNA, pp. 5-6.

From the Diary of Josephus Daniels

October Monday 21 1918

German note came by radio.

Long conference at White House. WW[,] Lansing, Baker, JD & March. WW read it over and commented on it. General opinion that Germany has accepted W.W's demands. Was she in good faith. Lansing thought first should put it up to the military men as to armistice. Baker thought G. had accepted. Why not ask allies for their views? March thought W.W. ought to act without conference with allies. W.W. felt it well to sleep over it. House on way to France. Benson with him. Wish they were there now so as to get view of Prime Minister there.

Public sentiment here wants blood or to put Kaiser on St. Helena. This was regarded as "ridiculous" said W.W.

WW told how Ashurst rushed up to the White House and was afraid the Pres. would not [be] firm with the Germans. WW: "Why don't you Senators sometimes give me credit with not being a damned fool"

Ashurst was a cowboy: WW: If you & I were in a fight & you held up your hands & asked for quits & would agree to all I said, and then I made you disarm, wouldn't that be all right? Ashurst thought it would[.] Had you rather have the Kaiser or the Bolsheviks[?]

To George Mason La Monte

My dear Mr. La Monte: [The White House] 22 October, 1918.

I have read with great appreciation the statement which you and Mr. Hennessy have put before the voters of New Jersey, and I feel like adding my own appeal to them to send both you and Mr. Hennessy to the United States Senate. I particularly crave the support of New Jersey, whose people I deem it an honor to have served and whose interests I have so long had at heart, and I know how generously and truly both you and Mr. Hennessy stand for the things that I believe in, and that I believe the people of New Jersey believe in. These are times when it is particularly necessary that men who would lift affairs to a new plane of action and humane achievement should stand together and see to it that in all public counsels they are adequately and truly represented. I have had an occasion to test your quality and Mr. Hennessy's, and therefore I speak with confidence when I say that the people of New Jersey would be served by both of you in the highest way in the counsels of the nation.

May I not add my gratification that both you and Mr. Hennessy have pledged yourselves to the support of the suffrage amendment?
Cordially and faithfully yours,   Woodrow Wilson

TLS (Letterpress Books, WP, DLC).

To George Babbitt[1]

[The White House] 22 October, 1918

Congressman Hayden[2] has in every way been loyal to the country. He has supported my administration most loyally, and I should deem his defeat a distinct loss to the cause we are all fighting for.
Woodrow Wilson

T telegram (Letterpress Books, WP, DLC).
[1] Businessman of Phoenix, chairman of the Arizona State Democratic Central Committee.
[2] Carl Hayden, Democratic congressman from Arizona.

From Newton Diehl Baker

My dear Mr. President: Washington. October 22, 1918.

More than two million American soldiers have sailed from the ports in this country to participate in the war overseas. In reporting this fact to you, I feel sure that you will be interested in the following data showing the progress of our military effort.

In my letter of July 1st, 1918,[1] I informed you that between May 8, 1917 and June 30, 1918, over a million men had either been landed in France or were enroute thereto. Since July 1st, 1918, embarkations by months, have been as follows:

July	306,185
August	290,818
September	261,415
October 1st to 21st	131,398
Total	989,816
Embarked to July 1, 1918	1,019,115
Grand total	2,008,931

In our overseas operations, I feel that we have good reason to be proud and thankful of the results obtained. Our losses have been exceedingly small, considering the size of the force transported, and this is due to the efficient protection given American convoys by the Naval Forces. We also have been greatly assisted in the despatch of troops abroad by the allocation of certain vessels from our Allies, principally those of Great Britain.

Cordially yours,   Newton D. Baker

TLS (WP, DLC).
¹ It is printed at that date in Vol. 48.

To Newton Diehl Baker

My dear Mr. Secretary: The White House 22 October, 1918

I am very glad to have your letter of this morning reporting that more than two million American soldiers have sailed from the ports of this country to participate in the war overseas. I am sure that this will be a matter of deep gratification and reassurance to the country and that everyone will join me in congratulating the War and Navy Departments upon the steady accomplishment in this all-important application of force to the liberation of the world.

Cordially and sincerely yours,   Woodrow Wilson

TLS (N. D. Baker Papers, DLC).

To Gilbert Monell Hitchcock

My dear Senator: [The White House] 22 October, 1918.

In reply to your letter of October 21st,[1] let me say that it seems to me really not worth while to answer the Republican attacks on Article 3 of the peace terms I suggested in my address of January 8th. The words I used are perfectly clear to any honest mind. They leave every nation free to determine its own economic policy, except in the one particular that its policy must be the same for all other nations and not be compounded of hostile discriminations between one nation and another, such weapons of discrimination being left to the joint action of the nations for the purpose of disciplining those who will not submit to the general programme of justice and equality.

It would be impossible to follow up all the perversions and mis-representations that some of the Republicans are now indulging in, and my own judgment is that we can safely leave the matter to the good sense of our fellow-countrymen who can read English.

Sincerely yours,   Woodrow Wilson

TLS (Letterpress Books, WP, DLC).
¹ G. M. Hitchcock to WW, Oct. 21, 1918, TLS (WP, DLC).

To Valentine Everit Macy

My dear Mr. Macy: [The White House] 22 October, 1918.

Engagements which you can easily imagine have prevented my giving proper attention to the national labor policy outlined by the conference of wage adjusting agencies, but I do not think that I ought to ask you longer to delay the announcement of your award in the Western shipyards. Please feel at liberty to make the announcement.

Cordially and sincerely yours,   Woodrow Wilson

TLS (Letterpress Books, WP, DLC).

To An Unnamed Person

My dear Mrs. _____: [The White House] 22 October, 1918

You may be sure that my heart bleeds with yours over what has happened to your son, for it is a genuine tragedy, and I wish that I could comply with your prayer for your son's release and restoration. But I must in all candour as well as in sincere kindness say to you that after dealing with young men most of my life, I am convinced that the course you suggest would be much the worst and not the best, and that the boy's only salvation will come from his being brought to a full realization of what he has done by suffering the punishment.

I hope and am confident that your fears are mistaken that he will find it impossible to reinstate himself after undergoing his punishment. That will not be true if he really pulls himself together, and I believe that he would have a better chance then than he would have if excused from the penalty now.

With deep regret, and with sincere conviction that it is my duty to render this decision.

Sincerely yours,   Woodrow Wilson

TLS (Letterpress Books, WP, DLC).

From Edward Mandell House, with Enclosure

On Board U.S.S. Northern Pacific.

Dear Governor: October 22, 1918.

From the German acceptance of your terms which we received yesterday, it looks as if the Peace Conference might be close upon us.

Germany seems so nearly in collapse that I cannot believe that it will be necessary for a peace conference to continue more than two and a half to three months. It looks as if the Allies might be able to lay down their own terms, and if Clemenceau will cooperate with us as closely as he did last year at the Inter-Allied Conference, it will greatly shorten the life of the congress. It merely needs a little organization and some understanding amongst the principals to have matters expedited in a way that is quite unusual at such gatherings.

I am enclosing you a list of people which I hope you will think well to have come over to advise when these several subjects come before the congress. It will strengthen the American position and facilitate the work of the commissioners to have such a staff, and it will leave the commissioners free to discuss fundamentals.

I do not give the person[n]el of the Peace Inquiry as that is almost wholly composed of experts on technical subjects.

I am writing this on shipboard so it may return with this boat.

Affectionately yours,   E. M. House

TLS (WP, DLC).

E N C L O S U R E

Army.

General Bliss. General Pershing.

Navy.

Admiral Benson and another.

Finance. (Treasury Department)

Benjamin Strong, Leffingwell, Albert Strauss.

Labor.

Samuel Gompers and another.

Editorial Director.

Frank Cobb.

Commerce. (War Trade Board.)

Vance McCormick. Clarence Woolley.[1]

Raw *Materials.*

B. M. Baruch and another. (Summers)[2]

Food.

Herbert Hoover and another.

Merchant Shipping.

Hurley and another (Ask Benson) Whipple.

Fuel.

Garfield and another.

Aviation.

Ryan and another.

Alien Property.

Mitchell Palmer. Bradley Palmer.[3]

Railroad Transportation.

Walker Hines. A. H. Smith[4] (Consult McAdoo.)

Wire Communications.

Walter Rogers, Chas. H. Dennis.[5] (Chicago Daily News)

Peace Inquiry.

Mezes, Miller, Bowman, etc. etc.

It seems to me that it will be absolutely necessary to have a man of the dimensions of Cobb to interpret to the newspaper people the policies you stand for. It is a difficult and delicate task. The men I have suggested for Wire Communications should be under Cobb's direction. Their work should be to interpret to the world, outside of America, what Cobb interprets to the newspaper fraternity at the Conference itself. Creel, I take it, you will want to continue at home in the same capacity as now for he will never be more needed than then.

T MS (WP, DLC).

[1] That is, Clarence Mott Woolley.

[2] Leland Laflin Summers, consulting engineer, member of the War Industries Board, and at this time chairman of the W.I.B.'s mission to Europe.

[3] Bradley Webster Palmer, counsel to the Capital Issues Committee and assistant counsel to the Alien Property Custodian.

[4] That is, Alfred Holland Smith.

[5] That is, Walter Stowell Rogers and Charles Henry Dennis, managing editor of the *Chicago Daily News*.

From Homer Stillé Cummings

PERSONAL

My dear Mr. President: Washington, D. C. October 22nd, 1918.

I hope that I may be pardoned for interjecting an unsolicited word relative to the last German reply, but it occurred to me that a suggestion, having in view certain important aspects of the matter, might be of some service.

I do not for one moment anticipate that anything will be said to Germany inconsistent with our previous attitude. I have more in mind the question of the method and form of the answer. I believe that the American people have already set a just value upon the German reply. They see in it nowhere any assurance or guarantee that arbitrary and autocratic power has been destroyed; they see no repudiation of the inhumane acts of the Government which has thus far conducted the war; they see only evasions, temporary expedients and promises concerning things which have not as yet been done. They are uneasy in the belief that the note is a "play for time" and part of the military program. German autocracy is getting ready to capitulate, but it has not yet surrendered. Even on the face of the German statement power still comes from above and not from the people.

This I believe to be expressive of the almost universal temper of our people, and any answer which does not in substance, expression and form speak the word which the people want to have spoken might lead to political disaster. The time has not yet come for the unfolding of the details of the peace program, or any statement anticipating them, other than the statements which already constitute part of our record. It is a most unhappy time politically for any such considerations. A strict adherence to the logic of the previous announcements expressed with increasing vigor will carry us successfully through our political troubles and put in the hands of the President the additional power which a popular endorsement would give.

It is of the highest consequence, I might say of almost surpassing importance, that we should be successful in the November elections. Unless we win that success the whole peace program is imperiled, and the greatest conception as to the destiny of humanity which ever sprang from human brain may come to naught. It would be an unparalleled tragedy if all the sacrifices which have been made should fall short of giving the people a chance to lay the foundation of a universal, world-wide and enduring peace. The power which the President now has, and which is an ever increasing and widening power, is none too great for this superhuman task.

It is, therefore, only just and wise to take into account the effect upon this program of the coming election. If we can get by this election successfully, the President of the United States can lead the thought of the world and realize things which men have almost feared to dream.

Most sincerely yours,   Homer S. Cummings

TLS (WP, DLC).

From Robert Wickliffe Woolley

Dear Mr. President: Washington October 22, 1918.

It was my good fortune to converse with friends and foes of your administration—many of them—Monday evening and yesterday, and it has occurred to me that you would not take it amiss if I should venture to do myself the honor to say to you that, without exception, I talked to no man or woman who did not condemn the latest note of the German government as a trick subtly phrased. In most instances supreme confidence was expressed that your action following its receipt would be as swift and as adequate as were your replies to other recent notes from the German government.

With those who spoke in friendly vein, of course, I heartily agreed, but I was greatly angered by the sneeringly doubtful attitude of men who would gladly see you and all you stand for, all you have achieved for humanity, butchered to make a Republican victory; angered because more than one asserted that in saying he trusted you would not approve peace terms calculated to be humiliating to Germany, the Imperial chancellor had found a way, through your great heart, cunningly to trap the United States and her allies into peace based not upon unconditional surrender. Of course, they gave your generous spirit another name—pacifism. I presume such criminal and militant skepticism has to be, especially in republics.

As you know, I am an old hand at sounding public thought. Never have I detected greater and more vigorous unanimity of opinion on any one subject, nor have I ever seen a situation where it was generally agreed that so much was staked on the prospective utterance of one man. Some of your warm admirers expressed the gravest fears as to what the consequences of acceptance of this latest German proposal might be to your administration and to the cause of righteousness, but they did not doubt you.

I sincerely hope you will appreciate the spirit which prompted me to write you so frankly at this critical moment, and know that in doing so I discharge a duty which I feel I owe to you.

With great respect, I am,

Faithfully yours   R. W. Woolley

TLS (WP, DLC).

From James Cardinal Gibbons

My dear Mr. President: Baltimore. October 22, 1918.

I shall be most happy to convey to His Holiness, your very warm wishes, expressed in your esteemed letter of October 18th.

Be pleased to accept my own best wishes, with sentiments of high esteem.   Faithfully yours,   J. Card. Gibbons

TLS (WP, DLC).

From Harry Augustus Garfield

Dear Mr. President: Washington, D. C. October 22, 1918

The victory is yours. It is moral as well as military, and I offer you my profound congratulations. May God grant you strength to keep it where it is—in spite of the vindictive ones.

Cordially and faithfully yours, H. A. Garfield.

TLS (WP, DLC).

An Admonitory Message

Handed by British Chargé
Oct. 22/18 RL.

COPY OF TELEGRAM
FROM MR. BALFOUR TO MR. BARCLAY.
Dated Oct. 21st.

VERY URGENT.

The German reply, by concentrating attention on a single sentence in the President's first telegram, is plainly designed to obtain a conditional armistice, which would be most disastrous to the cause of the Associated Powers. About naval terms they say nothing at all. About Military terms they assume that an undisturbed retreat for the German army to their own frontier has been already accepted in principle and that nothing remains to be done but to work out under military advice a few supplementary details.

We are well aware that this is not the President's view. Our experts assure us that the effect of any such policy would be to give the Germans what they most want—time to reorganize and a short and very defensible front. Peace negotiations carried on under such conditions could never secure the terms desired by the associated Governments. If, for example, the Germans broke off on such questions as Alsace Lorraine or Poland, the Allies would be compelled to give way or else to resume hostilities against an enemy refreshed and reorganized and so situated that every German, whatever his opinion, would feel that he was fighting, not for pan-German conditions, but for the soil of the Fatherland. What would inspire his troops would discourage ours; and all the fruits of victory might be lost.

It seems to us clear that any armistice must contain securities both against the resumption of hostilities by the enemy if peace negotiations unhappily break down; and probably also against any violations of the final Treaty of Peace when that is concluded.

In the opinion of our experts these ends can only be attained if the armistice provides:

A. That some enemy territory, including at least Alsace and Lorraine, be at once occupied by Allied troops, and

B. That adequate precaution be taken against the resumption of naval warfare.

We greatly hope that the President will not commit himself on these vital questions without previous consultation with the Allies.

BRITISH EMBASSY

WASHINGTON. October 22nd, 1918.

T MS (WP, DLC).

From the Diary of Josephus Daniels

1918 Tuesday 22 October

Cabinet discussed German message.

McAdoo & Baker made strong statements. Baker left memorandum. McAdoo thought we could not go into Germany to set up government & with armistice arranged by military leaders we could accept Germany's statement it had or would comply with President's terms. Terrible responsibility to carry on war if it could be ended on our terms. Moreover there is a limit to our ability to finance this expensive war and our allies for two years more. Burleson wanted unconditional surrender, but the more discussed the more he felt this was getting what we were fighting for.

Wilson said labor was asking: What are we fighting for? They opposed war for what imperialistic England desired. McAdoo & Wilson wanted to confer with allies before answering Germany. Burleson & I felt he should answer Germany that with an armistice safeguarded we should write to Germany & agree to propose peace on the 14 propositions & addresses. To-day America can have more influence in peace meetings than in future. In July all allies approved Wilson. If we continue to win their selfish aims will begin to be asserted.

Houston wanted to fix division of districts in Reichstag so the people could rule better than in present burgh system

Redfield & Lane felt could not trust Gers

But all finally came to side of writing to Solf

A Draft of a Note to Germany by Newton Diehl Baker

[Oct. 22, 1918]

The President is obliged to assume from the statements made by the German Government that it is now ready to effect a permanent peace by the acceptance of the definite principles and propositions, enumerated by the President in the addresses and messages referred to in this correspondence. An armistice is suggested to suspend conflict while the necessary permanent arrangements are determined and effected. An armistice for such a purpose must in the nature of the case leave the United States and the powers associated with her in a position to enforce such arrangements when they are determined upon and make a renewal of hostilities impossible

The President has therefore transmitted this correspondence to the Governments with which [he] is associated with the suggestion that if those Governments are disposed to effect peace upon the principles indicated a conference of our several military advisers be asked to submit to the associated governments the terms of such an armistice, if they deem one possible from the military point of view, as will fully protect the interests of the peoples involved and assure the unimpaired power to determine and enforce the details of the peace so accepted in principle[.] Should such terms of armistice be suggested the acceptance of them by Germany will be concrete evidence of her full acceptance of the principles and proposals for peace upon which the whole action proceeds.

Hw MS (WP, DLC).

A Memorandum by Franklin Knight Lane

October 23, 1918

Yesterday we had a Cabinet Meeting. All were present. The President was manifestly disturbed. For some weeks we have spent our time at Cabinet meetings largely in telling stories. Even at the meeting of a week ago, the day on which the President sent his reply to Germany—his second Note of the Peace Series—we were given no view of the Note which was already in Lansing's hands and was emitted at four o'clock; and had no talk upon it, other than some outline given offhand by the President to one of the Cabinet who referred to it before the meeting; and for three-quarters of an hour told stories on the war, and took up small departmental affairs.

This was the Note which gave greatest joy to the people of any yet written, because it was virile and vibrant with determination to put militarism out of the world. As he sat down at the table the President said that Senator Ashurst had been to see him to represent the bewildered state of mind existing in the Senate. They were afraid that he would take Germany's words at their face value.

"I said to the Senator," said the President, "do they think I am a damned fool?" * * * Yet Senator Kellogg says that Ashurst told the Senators that the President talked most pacifically, as if inclined to peace, and that Ashurst was "afraid that he would commit the country to peace," so afraid that he wanted all the pressure possible brought to bear on the President by other Senators. At any rate, the Note when it came had no pacificism in it, and the President gained the unanimous approval of the country and the Allies.

But all this was a week ago. Germany came back with an acceptance of the President's terms—a superficial acceptance at least—hence the appeal to the Cabinet yesterday. This was his opening, "I do not know what to do. I must ask your advice. I may have made a mistake in not properly safe-guarding what I said before. What do you think should be done?"

This general query was followed by a long silence, which I broke by saying that Germany would do anything he said.

"What should I say?" he asked.

"That we would not treat until Germany was across the Rhine."

This he thought impossible.

Then others took a hand. Wilson said the Allies should be consulted. Houston thought there was no real reform inside Germany. McAdoo made a long talk favoring an armistice on terms fixed by the military authorities. Strangely enough, Burleson, who had voted against all our stiff action over the *Lusitania* and has pleaded for the Germans steadily, was most belligerent in his talk. He was ferocious—so much so that I thought he was trying to make the President react against any stiff Note—for he knows the President well, and knows that any kind of strong blood-thirsty talk drives him into the cellar of pacifism. * * *

One of the things McAdoo said was that we could not financially sustain the war for two years. He was for an armistice that would compel Germany to keep the peace, military superiority recognized by Germany, with Foch, Haig, and Pershing right on top of them all the time. Secretary Wilson came back with his suggestion that the Allies be consulted. Then Baker wrote a couple of pages outlining the form of such a Note suggesting an armistice. I said that this should be sent to our "partners" in the war, without giving it to the world, that we were in a confidential relation to France and England, that they were in danger of troubles at home, possible

revolution, and if the President, with his prestige, were to ask publicly an armistice which they would not think wise to grant, or
which couldn't be granted, the sending of such a message into the
world would be coercing them. The President said that they needed
to be coerced, that they were getting to a point where they were
reaching out for more than they should have in justice. I pointed
out the position in which the President would be if he proposed an
armistice which they (the Allies) would not grant. He said that this
would be left to their military men, and they would practically
decide the outcome of the war by the terms of the armistice, which
might include leaving all heavy guns behind, and putting Metz,
Strasburg, etc., in the hands of the Allies, until peace was declared.

I suggested that Germany might not know what the President's
terms were as to Courland, etc., that this was not "invaded territory." He replied that they evidently did, as they now were considering methods of getting out of the Brest-Litovsk treaty. He said
he was afraid of Bolshevism in Europe, and the Kaiser was needed
to keep it down—to keep some order. He really seemed alarmed
that the time would come soon when there would be no possibility
of saving Germany from the Germans. This was a new note to me.

He asked Secretary Wilson if the press really represented the
sentiment of the country as to unconditional surrender. Wilson said
it did. He said that the press was brutal in demanding all kinds of
punishment for the Germans, including the hanging of the Kaiser.
At the end of the meeting, which lasted nearly two hours, he asked
to be relieved of Departmental matters as he was unable to think
longer. I wrote a summary of the position he took, and read it after
Cabinet meeting to Houston and Wilson, who agreed. It follows:

If they (the Allies) ask you (the President), "Are you satisfied
that we can get terms that will be satisfactory to us without unconditional surrender?"

You will answer, "Yes—through the terms of the Armistice."

"By an armistice can you make sure that all the fourteen propositions will be effectively sustained, so that militarism and imperialism will end?"

"Yes, because we will be masters of the situation and will remain
in a position of supremacy until Germany puts into effect the fourteen propositions."

"Will that be a lasting peace?"

"It will do everything that can be done without crushing Germany
and wiping her out—everything except to gratify revenge."

Printed in Anne Wintermute Lane and Louise Herrick Wall, eds., *The Letters of Franklin
K. Lane, Personal and Political* (Boston and New York, 1922), pp. 293-96.

From the Diary of Josephus Daniels

October Wednesday 23 1918

War Council at White House. Long discussion of German note. McCormick rather wanted unconditional surrender. Hoover, Garfield, Hurley, Baruch, all, with McAdoo & myself favored such an armistice as our military would regard as safe. Hoover wanted note of encouragement to Germans who were trying to secure self government in Germany. Wanted to say the upper house should be changed & made popular in composition. WW said he had used a memo by Baker in the letter he thought of sending (wh. he read) but the last part he wrote himself. Like little girl whose mother said the devil put the temper & bad language & spitting in the face into her. Might [be] as to the first two "but I thought of the spitting myself" What effect on politics? On election? WW could not avoid thinking of that & he might find popular opinion so much against him he might have to go into cyclone cellar for 48 hours. But after 48 hours, the people would quit being hysterical & become reasonable & prefer getting what they are fighting for now than to fight on to Berlin & keep up war. Baruch said it was right & we must go down if necessary for right.

At 12 o'clock the President sent for Lansing, March & JD & read message to Solf. March said military opinion was to carry on war but the President could not fail to suggest armistice to the allies. Lansing thought paper OK. I suggested one verbal change. WW serious Public opinion he said was as much a fact as a mountain and must be considered

To Robert Lansing, with Enclosures

My dear Mr. Secretary,   The White House. 23 October, 1918.

Here is my idea of the form in which we should submit our correspondence with Germany to the governments with which we are associated as belligerents. What do you think of it? I dare say we should send the correspondence to each of them as promptly as possible.   Faithfully Yours,   W.W.

WWTLI (SDR, RG 59, 763.72119/2368½, DNA).

ENCLOSURE I

To the Allied Governments.

The following correspondence between the Government of Germany and the Government of the United States is respectfully submitted to the _____ Government with the request that it be taken under careful consideration and that the views and conclusions of the _____ Government concerning it be communicated at its convenience to the Government of the United States.

> Here insert the whole of the recent correspondence concerning peace and an armistice *in extenso*, including the final reply of this Government under date of the twenty-third of October.

The Government of the United States would especially appreciate an expression of the decision of the _____ Government as to its willingness and readiness to acquiesce and take part in the course of action with regard to an armistice which is suggested by the note of the Secretary of State of the United States in which, under the date of the twenty-third of October, he states the decision of the President with regard to the submission of the question of an armistice to the governments with which the Government of the United States is associated in the prosecution of the war and with regard to the manner in which the terms of an armistice are to be determined, provided an armistice at this time is deemed possible from the military point of view.

The President has endeavoured to safeguard with the utmost care the interests of the peoples associated against Germany in every statement he has made in this correspondence, and he sincerely hopes that the Government of _____ will think that he has succeeded and will see its way clear to cooperate with him in taking the steps he has suggested.[1]

[1] A paraphrase of this note was sent to the representatives in Washington of all governments at war with the Central Powers. The covering letter, RL to the Italian Ambassador, Oct. 23, 1918, is printed in *FR-WWS, 1918*, 1, I, 383.

ENCLOSURE   I I[1]

To Germany.

Having received the solemn and explicit assurance of the German Government that it unreservedly accepts the terms of peace laid down in his address to the Congress of the United States on the eighth of January, 1918, and the principles of settlement enunciated in his subsequent addresses, particularly the address of the twenty-seventh of September, and that it desires to discuss the details of their application, and that this wish and purpose emanate, not from those who have hitherto dictated German policy and conducted the present war on Germany's behalf, but from ministers who speak for the majority of the Reichstag and for an overwhelming majority of the German people; and having received also the explicit promise of the present German Government that the humane rules of civilized warfare will be observed both on land and sea by the German armed forces, the President of the United States feels that he cannot decline to take up with the governments with which the Government of the United States is associated the question of an armistice.

He deems it his duty to say again, however, that the only armistice he would feel justified in submitting for consideration would be one which should leave the United States and the powers associated with her in a position to enforce any arrangements that may be entered into and to make a renewal of hostilities on the part of Germany impossible. The President has, therefore, transmitted his correspondence with the present German authorities to the governments with which the Government of the United States is associated as a belligerent, with the suggestion that, if those governments are disposed to effect peace upon the terms and principles indicated, their military advisers and the military advisers of the United States be asked to submit to the governments associated against Germany the necessary terms of such an armistice as will fully protect the interests of the peoples involved and ensure ⟨the unimpaired power of⟩ *to* the associated governments *the unrestricted power* to safeguard and enforce the details of the peace to which the German Government has agreed,—⟨should⟩ *provided* they deem such an armistice possible from the military point of view. Should such terms of armistice be suggested, their acceptance by Germany will afford the best concrete evidence of her unequivocal acceptance of the terms and principles of peace ⟨upon⟩ *from* which the whole action proceeds.

The President would deem himself lacking in candour did he not point out in the frankest possible terms the reason why extraordinary safeguards must be demanded. Significant and important as the constitutional changes seem to be which are spoken of by the German Foreign Secretary in his note of the ⟨twenty-second⟩ *twentieth* of October, it does not appear that the principle of a government responsible to the German people has yet been fully worked out or that any guarantees either exist or are in contemplation that the alterations of principle and of practice now partially agreed upon will be permanent. Moreover, it does not appear that the heart of the present difficulty has been reached. It may be that future wars have been brought under the control of the German people, but the present war has not been, and it is with the present war that we are dealing. It is evident that the German people have no means of commanding the acquiescence of the military authorities of the Empire ⟨in their conclusions⟩ *in the popular will,* that the power of the King of Prussia to control the policy of the Empire is unimpaired; that the determining initiative still remains with those who have hitherto been the masters of Germany. Feeling that the whole peace of the world depends now on plain speaking and straightforward action, the President deems it his duty to say, without any attempt to soften what may seem harsh words, that the nations of the world do not and cannot trust the word of those who have hitherto been the masters of German policy, and to point out once more that in concluding peace and attempting to undo the infinite injuries and injustices of this war the Government of the United States cannot deal with any but veritable representatives of the German people who have been assured of a genuine constitutional standing as the real rulers of Germany. If it must deal with the military masters and the monarchical autocrats of Germany now, or *if it* is likely to have to deal with them later in regard to the international obligations of the German Empire, it must demand, not peace negotiations, but surrender. Nothing can be gained by leaving this essential thing unsaid.[2]

WWT MSS (SDR, RG 59, 763.72119/2368½, DNA).
[1] Words in angle brackets deleted by Wilson; words in italics added by him. Lansing submitted a list of suggested changes. Hw MS, SDR (RG 59, 763.72119/2368½, DNA). Those changes accepted by Wilson are printed in italics underlined.
[2] This note was sent as RL to F. Oederlin, Oct. 23, 1918, *Diplomatic Correspondence of the United States and Germany.* . . . There is an earlier draft of this note, with many WWhw and WWsh emendations, in WP, DLC.

From Bernard Mannes Baruch

My dear Mr. President: Washington October 23, 1918.

A just and continuing peace must include a just and equal access to the raw materials and manufacturing facilities of the world, thus eliminating preferential tariffs. No nation (including neutrals) must be permitted to enter into economic alliance to the detriment of any other nation or nations. This should be a part of the treaty of peace, of just as much importance as the determination of territorial and ethnological lines, and must be guaranteed the same.

Any court or league of nations which decides the questions of territorial boundaries must define and enforce this policy of economic equality of opportunity. If a scheme of this kind is not carried out, the resulting industrial inequalities will cause dissatisfaction and revolution within countries or force wars to relieve intolerable conditions.

This agreement should cover both dependent colonies like India, Phillipine Islands, Porto Rico; self-governing colonies like Canada, Australia, etc.; and the so-called spheres of influence.

Each and every nation (including neutrals) shall have access on the same terms to the raw materials and manufactured goods of all other nations.

This will not prevent the making of tariffs so long as the tariff affects the export to or import from other nations equally. It is not contemplated by this that nations shall always be equal, but that they shall receive equal opportunity. It is no more possible to keep nations upon an equality than it is to keep individuals upon an equality, except the equality of equal opportunity. The individual within the nation will thus have an opportunity through ingenuity and application to work out his own salvation, only under such restrictions as may be imposed upon him by the nation of which he is a part.

With these principles determined upon, (and I cannot see how right-thinking people can think otherwise), there will be no difficulty in setting up the machinery to carry them into effect. The concurrence of Great Britain, France, Italy and the United States would immediately make them operative, and a plan of operation can be worked out. Acceptance at the Peace Table will naturally follow.

Arrangements for the Period of Transition.

The Germans have removed from the factories of Northern France and Belgium, and Poland (and it is probable also Roumania and Servia), practically all raw materials and all manufacturing facilities.

The objects of the war will not have been achieved if the devastated countries are not rehabilitated and as far as practicable, restored to the condition previously existing. Otherwise a nation like Belgium, which was a factor in the competitive markets of the world for manufactured products, could never regain its place in the trade of the world, except after years of unequal struggle.

There should be immediately gathered a list of the things which are necessary to rehabilitate the countries affected, and each nation should guarantee to do its determined share towards replacing immediately these things at some set or guaranteed price, at some set or guaranteed time, not exceeding two years after the war. Pursuant to your request, I have asked this information from Roumania, Servia and Belgium.

Yours very truly, Bernard M Baruch

TLS (WP, DLC).

From Henry French Hollis

Dear Mr. President: Paris, France, October 23rd, 1918.

Your note of October 14th was hailed with joy by the press and the people of England and France. If there were any moderate voices they were lost in the shouts of praise. You added greatly to the prestige you already had in Europe. On every side you were acclaimed as the greatest man in the world. If it becomes necessary later to defend "those to whpm [whom] we do not wish to be unjust [just]," you will have only to point to your firmness at this juncture to prove that you may be implicitly trusted not to be fooled.

Since the receipt of this note by Germany, there has been no wholesale destruction of property in French and Belgian towns. I enclose clippings[1] from the Paris Edition of the New York Herald showing that Lille was left intact, and that her shops had enough goods to remain open: that the people showed no signs of great privation: that Iseghem "escaped with hardly a scratch": that the "enemy shows almost almost [sic] ostentatious care in avoiding the destruction of buildings within the limits of Courtrai": that "the city (Lille) appears rather normal * * * the shops seem to be provisioned reasonably": that one officer said "We are playing up to President Wilson."

I spent last Thursday and Friday in the devastated region, visiting Montdidier, Roye, Ham, St. Quentin, Noyon and Tergnier. Practically every building was destroyed. Wherever there was a building standing, it sheltered troops or horses. Not mant [many] fruit trees were cut.

It may be said with some justice that fruit trees furnish food, and excellent hiding places from airplanes. I doubt whether the destruction was more thorough than the destruction inflicted by Sherman on his march to the sea.

But since Germany has failed, she should be made to pay indemnity. My point is that she has kept pretty nearly within the rules of war in destroying property, and she is now being very punctilious, hoping for better terms of peace. The French newspapers do not give any news of such improvement. It seems to me that the deportation of citizens and the drowning and killing of ship passengers are a very different matter.

The German reply of October 20th is out. I enclose commentaries by the press.[2] They are not so sure that this reply should be rejected. There is a division of sentiment. If you should now conclude to submit the case to the Allies, I think that you would be solidly backed in that action, but that the papers would divide (probably a majority against) on the question of acceptance. If, on the other hand, you reject it you will probably be unanimously supported.

Since I wrote last I have talked with Dr. Rappard of Switzerland, now on the way to the United States with Mr. Sulzer, where he hopes to talk to you about a League of Nations. He is a cultivated and high-minded man with two years lecture experience at Harvard. I hope that you will see him. I did not assume to know what sort of League you have in mind.

Mr. Rublee went with me to see some members of the French administration who are doubtless sincere in their desire for a League of Nations. They say that Clemenceau will be for it, but I am not convinced. They say that he has discouraged talk about it, as he has thought it necessary to centre every thing on winning the war, and to avoid division of sentiment on other subjects.

I still believe that Lloyd George and Clemenceau are opposed to a League of Nations, and that France will come to it slowly, but much more readily than England.

Just one paper in Paris (L'Information) mentions the fact that Lord Brice "delivered a remarkable speech" yesterday on the League of Nations, before the Inter-Allied Parliament, but no part of it has got into print. A speech by the King of England at the same meeting was played up strong.   Sincerely yours,   Henry F. Hollis.

TLS (WP, DLC).
¹ They are missing.
² These enclosures are also missing.

Two Letters from Valentine Everit Macy

My dear Mr. President: Washington, D. C. October 23, 1918.

Your kind letter of the 22nd leads us to feel that we have not made it clear to you that the basis of our forthcoming decisions was hearings in connection with which the international presidents appeared before us on behalf of the shipyard workers of the entire country, and that the principal characteristic of these decisions is that they deal with the wage problem not sectionally but for all of the shipyards of the country.

The consequence of this policy is that the wage scales determined upon should be announced for all districts at the same time and not merely for the "Western shipyards," so that we may have the full support of the international officers of the unions in connection with any local dissatisfaction with them which may develop on the ground that they are lower than was anticipated in certain districts.

Another aspect of the situation is that conditions of employment have grown up in shipyards in certain localities as regards excessive compensation for overtime which do not conform to the standards recommended by the Conference of Wage Adjusting Agencies as a national policy. These local conditions have become too well established to permit of a change except in connection with the adoption of a national labor policy and we fear that the announcement of our award continuing these local conditions will make it very difficult to change them later.

We hesitate very much to obtrude this problem further on your attention at this time but feel that any announcement now made must include all shipyards and not merely those of the Pacific Coast. Our only desire is to place the situation clearly before you so that we may act in full accord with your wishes.

Very respectfully yours,   V. Everit Macy.

Washington, D. C.

My dear Mr. President: October Twenty-third, 1918.

Realizing that your time is fully occupied with important international problems and wishing to avoid troubling you with unnecessary questions, upon receipt of your letter of the 22nd, I tried to reach the Secretary of Labor in order to ask whether he would assume that in authorizing the announcement of our award for the "western shipyard," you meant to release the award for all shipyards.

Unfortunately, the Secretary was out of the city and therefore, I reluctantly wrote you on the 23rd. Today I have been able to reach the Secretary and he has advised me under the circumstances that he thinks we should release our award as applying to all shipyards and we are therefore, mailing the award today.

I am writing you of our action so that you may not be troubled to reply to my letter of the 23rd.

Very respectfully,   V. Everit Macy.

TLS (WP, DLC).

From Gilbert Monell Hitchcock

My dear Mr. President: [Washington] October 23, 1918

I thank you for your letter of October 22d and I agree with you that the language of Article III of your peace terms bears the interpretation you put upon it. In order that you may see a sample of what the Republican leaders are using broadcast, I quote the following from matter just sent out by the Republican Committee:

"This is a positive declaration that the treaty of peace must guarantee to Germany free trade with the United States without any tariff safeguards whatever to protect the American laborer, manufacturer, farmer and business man from foreign competition in his home markets. * * *

"No one doubts that in an open and unrestricted American field Germany with her cheaper labor will be able to dominate markets for many manufactured products in the United States, and will drive similar American products out of those markets, with the ruin of American manufacturers and harm to American labor swiftly following."

In a recent statement Leslie M. Shaw[1] made substantially the same declarations, asserting that the issue should be tested at the election in November, and concluded by saying:

"In my opinion the rejection of this treaty is the paramount issue of this campaign."

I call the matter to your attention because I assume that in the press of important matters you had not realized the extent to which Republican managers have gone in perverting this issue for the purpose of gaining control of Congress. Thousands of Republican newspapers throughout the country are using this matter.

Yours very truly,   G M Hitchcock

TLS (WP, DLC).
   [1] Leslie Mortier Shaw, Secretary of the Treasury in the cabinet of Theodore Roosevelt, 1902-1907; at this time a writer and lecturer resident in Washington.

To Isaac M. Shaine[1]

My dear Rabbi Shaine: [The White House] 24 October, 1918.

I am very glad to reply to your letter of October 21st.[2] Mr. Donovan[3] has supported the present administration in the finest spirit and has always stood for the progressive and humanitarian legislation in which we all believe, and I am glad of this opportunity to confirm your judgment of him.

Cordially and sincerely yours,   Woodrow Wilson

TLS (Letterpress Books, WP, DLC).
   [1] Rabbi of the Congregation Agudath Achim of Harlem.
   [2] I. M. Shaine to WW, Oct. 21, 1918, TLS (WP, DLC).
   [3] Jerome Francis Donovan, Democratic congressman from New York.

To Homer Stillé Cummings

My dear Cummings: The White House 24 October, 1918.

You may be sure I greatly appreciated your letter of the 22nd about the reply to Germany, and I hope with all my heart that the reply I made seems to you the right one.

Cordially and sincerely yours,   Woodrow Wilson

TLS (H. S. Cummings Papers, ViU).

To Henry French Hollis

My dear Senator: [The White House] 24 October, 1918

Your letters are highly valued and have furnished me some extremely valuable information, and you may be sure I am very appreciative of your kindness. But I am writing now to say how deeply distressed I am by the death of your son.[1] I know the pain that the tragedy must have given you, and I want you to know that my heart is with you at this time when you are called upon to face so great a grief.   Cordially and sincerely yours,   Woodrow Wilson

TLS (Letterpress Books, WP, DLC).
[1] See H. F. Hollis to WW, Oct. 2, 1918 (second letter of that date).

From Newton Diehl Baker, with Enclosure

Dear Mr. President: Washington. October 24th, 1918.

I think you have seen the papers attached to the enclosed letter from General Bliss, but you have not seen the letter itself. I feel quite sure you will be interested to read it.

As these are all copies, none need be returned to me.

Respectfully yours,   Newton D. Baker

TLS (WP, DLC).

E N C L O S U R E

Tasker Howard Bliss to Newton Diehl Baker

No. 28.

My dear Mr. Secretary: Versailles. October 9, 1918.

I have just written a letter to General March, No. 27,[1] in the

[1] T. H. Bliss to P. C. March, Oct. 9, 1918, TLS (WDR, RG 120, Records of the American Section of the Supreme War Council, 1917-1919, File No. 366-12, DNA). This letter is

same series as those which I have been writing to you. You may remember that I told you while you were here that as these letters of mine to the Secretary of War and the Chief of Staff are on the same general line of subjects I have numbered them in the same series.

I am sending an additional copy of my No. 27 of today addressed to General March, in order that you may put it in your file if you so desire. General March can give you copies of the others that I have written to him during your absence from Washington, or I can have them made here and send them to you.

I assume that you will be in Washington when this courier reaches there.

You were at my house on the afternoon of Thursday, October 3d (a few hours prior to your departure for home), when I was considering the attitude which I ought to take on the drafts of two Joint Notes proposed by the French Military Representative and at the request of M. Clemenceau, one of them on the general subject of a policy to be pursued by the allies in Russia and the other on the specific subject of sending American reinforcements to Archangel. I had set forth my general views in a letter which you read at the time and to which you gave your approval. In that letter I called attention to the fact that the United States, so far as I knew, had not entered into a formal alliance with any European power but was merely associated with the European allies in the prosecution of the war against Germany and in doing so was actuated by a spirit of the utmost cordiality and co-operation; but that it plainly reserved the right to use its military forces as seemed best to it, yielding only to the views and desires of the European allies when those views were in accordance with a well considered and conscientious policy on the part of the United States. As I told you that I intended to do, I made a concise draft of the views expressed in my letter to you and submitted it to the Military Representatives at their meeting on Monday, October 7th. But I decided to omit any specific reference to the fact that the United States was not in formal alliance with any one here, because it seemed to me wiser not to put in anything more than was absolutely necessary to make perfectly clear the policy of the United States.

It seems difficult to make some people here understand that the United States is actuated by any *principle* or that it has any conscientious policy. I think that the reason is that some of them do

---

essentially the same in content as Bliss's No. 28 to Baker, printed above, through the paragraph beginning "However, I declined to sign it. . . ." The material following that paragraph is omitted in the letter to March.

not believe there is any connection between "policy" and their conscience. At any rate, one of the Representatives quite ignored the
fact that I had made clear that the allies were pursuing a policy
which ran counter to the one adopted by the United States for itself,
and insisted on knowing whether I would sign the note provided
there was stricken out of it all reference to the sending of American
reinforcements to Archangel and to using American troops to push
through Siberia the entire length of the Trans-Siberian Railway
and in the general pacification of the country. If they were stricken
from the draft of the note, and the note were still presented for
approval to the President of the United States it would be tanta-
mount to an attempt to force from him an approval of a policy
adopted by the allies which he had already decided (and I know as
yet nothing to the contrary) that he could not and would not adopt.
Therefore, of course, I could not sign the note in any event. I
therefore submitted a second statement to make my reason for this
clear.

I have submitted the statement of the whole case to March in
my letter to him of this date, together with copies of the documents,
which he will show you.

While you were on the water a very important subject came up
here, which is explained in my official cablegrams to the War Department Nos. 242,[2] 243,[3] and 244.[4] The three Prime Ministers,—
of Great Britain, France, and Italy,—have been in session here in
Paris (not at Versailles), together with various members of their
respective cabinets. It is understood that the first object of their
meeting was to try to come to some agreement about the Balkans.
What agreement, if any, they reached is not known. They find
themselves now in the situation which pretty much all of us have
anticipated for a good while. The British Section here at Versailles
has been, for a long time, urging its government to get together
with its allies and try to thrash out in advance all of the points
which will have to be settled when the resistance of the Central
Powers collapses. But none of them believed that that resistance
would collapse in certain quarters so completely and suddenly as
it has, or that there would be such evidence of a general collapse
of it everywhere, before at least next year. They have dreaded to
get together and try to settle the "after-the-war" difficulties. They
have foreseen the possibilities of the discord that would result from
throwing the golden apple into the ring. They have feared (and

[2] T. H. Bliss to NDB and P. C. March, Oct. 7, 1918.
[3] T. H. Bliss to NDB and P. C. March, Oct. 8, 1918, printed in n. 1 to P. C. March
to T. H. Bliss, Oct. 8, 1918.
[4] T. H. Bliss to RL et al., Oct. 8, 1918.

perhaps wisely) that it might bring about a lack of cohesion in their alliance or entente which would weaken them and encourage the enemy. At any rate, they have done nothing and now suddenly find themselves confronted with the fact that the settlement of some of these difficult questions is pressing them.

The other thing that occupied the attention of the Ministers, as I learned late in the evening of Monday, October 7, was the question of a general armistice with the Central Powers. At 9 o'clock on the evening of Monday, October 7 I received a copy of the resolution arrived at at a conference of the Ministers that same day putting up for consideration certain questions to the Military Representatives at Versailles in association with representatives of the four navies.

I inclose a copy of this resolution marked "A." Immediately on its receipt I cabled it to Washington in my No. 242, with a request for instructions. I was informed that a meeting of the Military Representatives, with the associated representatives of the four navies, would be held at 9.15 the following morning.

It is not too much to say that I was somewhat appalled at the idea of having such an important subject "sprung" upon me at night in bed, and to be told at the same time that it was to be settled at 9.15 the next morning. However, it had the one good effect of curing me of my illness! I thought over the matter long that night, perplexed because of my absolute ignorance of what might have been done already between the respective governments on this subject, because of my ignorance of the attitude that had been or would be taken by the United States, and also because of the underlying meaning which seemed to me to be involved in this action of the three Prime Ministers. I had taken note of the fact announced in the daily journals that a proposal had been made direct from Germany to the government of the United States. I did not know to what extent, if any, that government was conferring on the subject with its European associates in the war. I had to assume that, even if such had been the case, no definite common agreement had been arrived at; else, why should the three Prime Ministers take this matter up by themselves? It is evident that they were not acting as members of the Supreme War Council of which the President of the United States is the fourth member. The document which they presented to me, as well as to the other Military Representatives, was prepared at a "Conference of Ministers at a Meeting, etc." It was not merely a conference of *Prime* Ministers but one in which other ministers of the respective governments took part. It was not acted on by the Military Representatives at Versailles in their capacity as Military Representatives on the Supreme War

Council, but was acted upon by what was in reality a committee of those representatives together with certain naval representatives who have no connection whatever with the Supreme War Council.

Nor could I determine in my own mind what was intended to be done with the opinion which might be rendered by this committee of military and naval representatives after it had been given to Mr. Lloyd George and M. Clemenceau and M. Orlando. I asked myself the question, "Did they intend to submit this opinion (if they approve it themselves) to the President of the United States?" If so, it would look as though they intended it to be a declaration to the government of the United States as to their determination on a subject which they knew was under consideration in Washington. If they did not intend to do this, I again asked myself the question, "Did they intend that it should indirectly get before the government in Washington through a report which they had every reason to know would be made by me?" If so, it would look still more as though they intended to influence the decision of the government in Washington on the question which they knew was then pending before it. I felt sure that if they did not intend or want that I should make such a report, they would not have attempted to associate me with the matter but would have called for the opinion of their own military and naval representatives.

The meeting was held at 9.15 a.m. on Tuesday, October 8th. I was not present, although the night before I had intended to be there. I sent word that the doctor did not want me to go out until he gave me permission, which was the exact fact. He came in on the evening of the same day and gave me permission to go out today. I allowed my Chief of Staff and the Secretary of the American Section,[5] together with Captain Jackson of the Navy,[6] to be present, but told them in advance that no official action could be taken by the Americans in the absence of instructions from Washington.

Shortly after the meeting was over there was submitted to me a copy of the "Joint Opinion" drawn up by the Committee, and of which I inclose two copies as contained in my telegram No. 244 of last night to the War Department. Later in the day the British Military Representative called at my house and I then learned from him that the matter had been under consideration by his Section during the day and the night before; and that they had drawn up a draft which was the one adopted, substantially, by the Committee. He said that it had been discussed with the British Chief of Staff, General Sir Henry Wilson, and that it was prepared, as he consid-

[5] Brig. Gen. P. D. Lochridge and Col. Ulysses S. Grant, 3rd, respectively.
[6] Richard Harrison Jackson, special representative of the Navy Department at the Ministry of Marine and Naval Attaché at the American embassy in Paris.

ered it, from the purely military point of view, but that he did not know whether his government would approve it nor whether the other governments would approve it. He expressed surprise when I told him that the French Military Representative had sent to me at my house for signature copies of the document with the statement that the Prime Ministers wanted it signed before three o'clock. He said that he had had no understanding that such was the request of the Prime Ministers.

However, I declined to sign it and immediately addressed a note to the three Prime Ministers telling them that I could not do so without instructions from my government. Of course, they all understand why I cannot sign it without such instructions and I am sure that they did not really expect me to do so.

The document will have been under consideration in Washington before you reach there. It will have been discovered there, as you will note when you see it, that it is couched in such terms as make inevitable and to be intended to make inevitable the reply which Germany must make. Of course, it may be that she feels beaten to such a degree that she will accept such conditions as a precedent to an armistice, but I doubt it. But of course it is not an armistice in the ordinary sense of the word. It looks to me as though it were intended to say, "We will not treat with you on the terms of President Wilson's fourteen propositions or on any other terms. Surrender, and we will then do as we please." It looks to me as though it were intended to say to the United States that these are the conditions which the United States must inform Germany are the necessary precedent to considering any proposition for an armistice.

I myself believe that the laying down of arms by Germany is a necessary precedent to any conversation with her. Whether it is wise to impose such other conditions as may make it impossible for her to lay down her arms, even though by her doing so she puts herself in such a position that we can demand from her all of our war aims, I leave it for others to decide. Judging from the spirit which seems to more and more actuate our European allies, I am beginning to despair that the war will accomplish much more than the abolition of *German* militarism while leaving *European* militarism as rampant as ever. I am one of those who believe that the absolute destruction of all militarism, under any of its evil forms is the only corner stone of the foundation of any League (I like better the French term "Société") of Nations. I think that the present war will prove a doubly hideous crime if it does not result in *something* that will make another such war, or anything faintly approaching it, an impossibility for a hundred years to come. I look no further than that, because if the world, the civilized world, can be made to stop fighting for a hundred years there is some hope that it may stop fighting forever.

What is that "Something"? There are some who say that it is the destruction of Prussian militarism; others, that it is a League of Nations. There are few, so far as I can find here, who lay stress on the Third (I think it is the third, but I have not the document by me) of President Wilson's declaration of fourteen war aims,—the limitation of armaments to the necessities for the maintenance of internal order. Yet I think that that third declaration will be found to be the very essence, the health-giving principle, of any attempted remedy for the cure of this war-sick world and without which the remedy will prove nothing but well-meant quackery. It will be an attempt to cure an ulcer without purifying the poisoned blood.

In looking to the future peace of the world it is a mistake I think to lay so much stress on Prussian militarism. It may soothe our guilty souls by doing so, by saying that "Prussia did it first." That kind of plea was first made in the Garden of Eden, and it no more clears our skirts of sin to-day than it did then. Looking to the future, the curse of the world to-day is "*European* militarism." Prussia, or rather a Prussianized Germany, has given us a present exhibition of what this curse can be; but it is a German ulcer on the European body growing out of the rotten European blood. And for practical purposes, for the purposes of the scientific physician, it makes no difference that it was Prussia that introduced into the European system the evil, blood-putrifying germ. It is there, in the blood of all Europe, and it must be gotten out.

And, that what I have said is in the back of the head of the average American at the plough-tail, at the counting office desk, at the throttle of a million engines, would, I believe, appear if you were to announce that our main war aim is to destroy German militarism. I believe they would say, "We are in this war to destroy MILITARISM not merely militarism 'camouflaged' as German or French or Russian, or under any other of its evil aspects. We want to guarantee ourselves against the necessity of having to take up the burden under which Europe, and not Germany alone, has been staggering. What guarantee have we that if we crush one giant out of a dozen some one of the others may not acquire his powers and with his powers his spirit and use his giant's strength like a giant? If we take his revolver away from one man on Pennsylvania Avenue or Broadway because he has misused it and leave theirs in the hands of 99 other men, what guarantee have we that one of these, by himself or in combination with others, may not misuse his revolver? After having determined that none of them *needs* a revolver we will take it away from all of them; and unwillingness of any one to submit will be an evidence of his intent to misuse it."

And when the time comes for cold blooded international politicians to sit around a table to consider the future conditions of the world it is possible that we will see some unexpected developments if their discussions are not to be conducted on the basic fact that all militarism in its present development is definitely a thing of the past. There has been, as it seems to me, a curious revival of French ambitions. She has a growing desire for possessions in the East or near East; and the ultimate disposition of German colonial territory is as much a subject of anxious thought with her as it is with England and Japan and even Italy. She looks to a reconstituted Russia under a government that will make her what she was before. This may be a dream; but dreams sometimes come true,—especially with sufficient time. And world-politicians look a long ways ahead. But with Germany reduced to a military nullity and every other nation militarized or navalized or both, who is to stand between her and a reconstituted Russia? Who can she play off against England in disputes, backed by force of arms, about over-sea possessions? What reason have we in history for believing that if world conditions continue as they have been, except that Germany will have been reduced to military helplessness, the alliances and ententes which have grown out of fear of Germany's overweening strength will not dissolve and that other alliances will not grow out of other fears and with like results? Countless questions will arise which never would arise if this war could end with the abolition of military power in a form that can be directed readily and quickly by one nation against another.

But, it is when we come to consider the *practicability* of a League of Nations, that is to say a League for Peace, that a radical change in existing world conditions, as respects world-militarism becomes especially evident. What can be more inconsistent, even absurd, than to imagine a League of Nations for the maintenance of peace composed of nations all armed to the teeth—against whom?—against each other? That cannot give the slightest guarantee of peace. That will not relieve the world of its present intolerable burden. And what do we want such a League for unless it be to relieve us from this burden? Suppose such a League had been formed five or six years ago. Germany and Austria would have been members of it. What would prevent them from saying, just as they did say to each other, "We want certain things that the League will not let us have. We, together, are stronger than they; we have more and better trained soldiers, better weapons, and a greater accumulation of military stores, than they. We can whip the League, we can whip the world; let us do it." Suppose, as a result of this war, that Germany is reduced to military powerlessness for a generation to come while other world conditions remain unchanged; what guarantee have you that some other nation, or combination of them, may not do what Germany and Austria have done? What agreement, what form of Constitution or Articles of *Federation* can be made by the nations of a League that will prevent this? Have Constitutions prevented rebellions? Have articles of Confederation prevented Secession?

But, you will say, our war aims look to the prevention of larger military establishments than are necessary to maintain internal order. *Rem acu tetegisti!*[7] I come back to what I said before, that the realization of the President's declaration as to the reduction of armaments is absolutely vital to any proposition for the destruction of militarism and the effective creation of a League of Nations. It seems, off-hand, a declaration easy to realize; but it is not. We have to hammer the idea into the minds of the world while the common peoples are in a receptive mood for it, or the governments of the world will defeat it. It is now, while the prestige and influence of the United States are predominate that we should do this. The peoples just now are sick of the whole thing. I do not mean, of course, that they want to stop, because they realize the necessity of going to the end. But they are sick of the conditions that cause this necessity. Now is the time to hold out hope for the future and to create a popular sentiment that will dominate the Congress that is to adjust affairs after the war.

Very cordially yours,   Tasker H. Bliss.

TCLS (WP, DLC).
[7] "You hit the nail on the head!" He should have said "*tetigisti*."

From Newton Diehl Baker, with Enclosure

Dear Mr President   [Washington, Oct. 24, 1918]
This is the complete Bliss cablegram. You have already seen the first 5 pages   Respectfully Baker

ALS (WP, DLC).

E N C L O S U R E

Versailles. October 23rd [1918].

2 THB Confidential.

For the Secretary of War.

In further reference to my number 1 THB dated October 22nd[1] I make following preliminary report of views.

Your telegram dated October 21st through Department of State calls for summary of official expressions, civil and military. Just now it is difficult to obtain official expressions because all officials hesitate to speak definitely of the aims for publication. I doubt if anything definite will be obtained until Government of the United States makes request for conference with all its associates with view to reach definite detailed agreement. I think European allies want this and are waiting for it.

The nearest approach to official opinion by the three prime ministers is contained in my number 242 dated October 7th. I am informed that this agreement was the result of mutual concessions.

The nearest approach to an official expression of military opinion is contained in my number 244 dated October 8th. This also was the result of mutual concessions but is far more drastic than the views of the three prime ministers referred to above. I am informed that Marshal Foch also submitted confidentially his recommendations at the same time to the three prime ministers and that they were more drastic than those of the three military representatives contained in my number 244. I am informed that he demanded that the Germans should retire at the rate of 30 kilometers per day until they reached a line 50 kilometers east of the Rhine and that they should surrender to the allies four bridge heads on the Rhine to be occupied by the Allies. You will observe that the views expressed by the military men as to conditions of so called armistice are quite as much political as they are military and probably foreshadow peace demands that will be insisted on by the military parties of the Allies. These demands show a tendency to increase with each day's success in present military operations.

I think that foregoing facts show that much trouble is to be apprehended if military men alone are to determine conditions of armistice. This is because the so called armistice is not an armistice but a demand for a complete surrender accompanied by a plain indication of the political demands that will be made after the surrender. If the purely military conditions for the so called armistice were the absolute laying down of arms by Germany the military men will have perfect guaranty(ies) against the possibility of a resumption of hostilities. It seems to me that that is all the military men should be permitted to say. It would be a complete surrender on the part of Germany but would leave them with the hope that some mercy would be shown them. I believe that to be the only way in which we can get a complete surrender. And if we get such complete surrender what more need we ask? The Government of the United States and its associates in the war can then determine calmly and without passion what it is right and just to do now and what will conduce to the future peace of the world. The present attitude of Germany as indicated in her last note to the Government of the United States is probably sincere because, if for no other reason, she believes the United States and its associates are standing together. Notwithstanding this Germany hopes that possibly through the influence of the United States an unnecessary humiliating peace will not be forced on her even though she now surrenders her arms and makes it impossible for her to resume hostilities. But if under the guise of conditions for an armistice Germany thinks that the European Allies intend to force upon her an unnecessary humiliating peace (which means taking from her everything that can be taken under any conditions) it may mean at least another year of war with certain possible chances involved. If we can now secure the surrender of Germany under conditions that will make it impossible for her to resume hostilities and thus enable the Allies to determine in cool blood what is right and just and wise, why should this not be done? It probably can not be done by imposing in advance unnecessary humiliating conditions. If this be not done the German people may accept complete surrender, the influence of the United States to prevent unnecessary humiliation in subsequent terms to be imposed on them.

If such a peace as the United States and her associates have a right to demand can possibly be obtained without the necessity of beating Germany into the ground it seems most probable that she will agree to some form of permanent disarmament. There will then be hope that other nations will disarm also. But if the peace comes with Germany beaten into the ground I think that it means Europe armed indefinitely to try to maintain such a peace. If a league of armed nations is then formed, the United States must be armed like the rest. It is one of our war aims to prevent this. To sum up:

First, attempt to secure complete military disarmament of Germany so that there can be no hope of her resuming hostilities. I think there is hope that this can be done if the great powers associated against Germany make *this their* united demand without the imposition of any other terms for cessation of hostilities.

Second, say to Germany that there will be no relaxation in our war aims but that they will be subject to full and reasonable discussion with our associates in the war and that Germany herself will be heard in these matters but that she must submit to whatever the United States and her associates finally agree upon. Some of these things must necessarily be the subject of discussion.

For example, every military man in Europe knows that there are two sides to many of the stories of wanton devastation for which compensation may be asked. But all of these things can be safely discussed provided Germany is first put in a position where she cannot resume hostilities if she does not like the discussion. And with it all Germany will have the hope that her punishment will not be greater than common justice requires. Finally, it seems to me that the danger of a great successful war is close at hand. I mean the building up of an allied military party as strong as any that has ever cursed Germany. To avoid this, what better object can the Government of the United States set for itself than together with its associates to secure the disarmament of Germany and then after full discussion agree as far as possible upon what it is wise to demand for the present and for the future peace of the world.

I feel a very grave responsibility in making the foregoing suggestions and I do so only because of your instructions.

In connection with my cablegram Number One THB October 22d, it is suggested that the following method of communication be adopted to insure handling by proper parties. All cablegrams in my new series indicated in my Number 1 THB and all cables to me from War Department on similar subject to be enciphered from Military Intelligence Code Number 5, using the number groups in connection with series AA encipherment tables, issued semimonthly. Please wire me your decision.[2]   Bliss.

TC telegram (WP, DLC).
    [1] T. H. Bliss to NDB, "Number 1 T.H.B.," Oct. 22, 1918, T telegram (T. H. Bliss Papers, DLC):
    "For my cables which I do not intend to put on the official records of the American Section of The Supreme War Council but which will be recorded in Washington I shall use separate serial numbers beginning with Number One and followed in each case by the letters T.H.B. If you will follow a similar system in cables to me on subjects which are not for discussion I have made arrangements that will guarantee absolute secrecy at this end of the line which is of great importance. . . ."
    [2] It was P. C. March to T. H. Bliss, No. 98, Oct. 24, 1918, TC telegram (WDR, RG 407, World War I Cablegrams, DNA), which reads as follows:
    "Reference to your number one and number 2 THB, last page of number 2 being received at 9:50 p.m. October 24th. Your recommendation as to cipher to be used approved. Your number 2 arrived too late to be of immediate use but is very valuable anyway. State Department had promised unusual prompt delivery to you of original cablegram but apparently failed on the other side. No great harm done. March."

From Joseph Patrick Tumulty

Dear Governor: The White House 24 October 1918.

I know how you feel about Senator Watson,[1] but every indication points to his election, if he can get some support from this end. The argument the Republicans are making is that you do not want him and every line I read in the West Virginia papers tends to convey this impression. The party is united there and I think it would help very much if you would write to John McGraw[2] and say that you hope for Senator Watson's election, as between Elkins,[3] a bitter partisan, who hates the administration and Watson, I s[h]ould prefer Watson by all means.   Sincerely,   Tumulty

I'm afraid my general statement will have to do   W.W.[4]

TLS (J. P. Tumulty Papers, DLC).
    [1] That is, Clarence Wayland Watson.
    [2] That is, John Thomas McGraw.
    [3] Davis Elkins, Republican, coal mine owner of West Virginia, at this time serving with the A.E.F. in France.
    [4] WWhw. Elkins defeated Watson in the general election by a vote of 115,216 to 97,711.

From Herbert Clark Hoover

Dear Mr. President: Washington 24 October 1918

I feel that despite the great burden of anxiety which you must entertain, it is necessary for me to present for your consideration one or two phases of the after-war situation in food, for peace-making might catch us suddenly. Until peace, even though it be deferred until next harvest, the Western Allies and neutrals can get along without drawing appreciably on supplies otherwise than North America. You are of course aware that considerable accumulations have taken place in the Far East and the Southern Hemisphere as the result of short shipping. These accumulations are of course available as additional support to the German occupied area after peace. If peace should come before Christmas, even with these accumulations referred to, there will be an international shortage in several vital commodities if consumption is to be restored to normal pending next harvest. If peace did not come until, say, April, then these accumulations would carry the burden.

The principal reason why this problem arises at the moment is that some members of the Allied Food Council are putting forward suggestions for international control of world distribution of food after peace. My own instinct is entirely against any such agreements or entanglements for, at least morally, any international body on this subject in which we participated would involve us in acceptance of their views and, practically, in acceptance of their distribution of our supplies.

If peace arrives at any time during the next few months, we will have the dominant supplies and my own view is that we should maintain a complete independence and, upon information that we are to obtain, distribute our resources so as to fill in the gaps in supplies that are not secured by the various nations from other countries. In other words, we could use our food supplies to level up, in a rough manner, the deficiencies that will utlimately arise from the general grab for the balances of the world's food. If we maintain our independence we can confer favours instead of complying with agreements and we can use our resources to make economic exchanges which will maintain justice all round. For instance, our best implement to restore government and order in Russia is through food and raw material relief. Another instance lies in that our Army would need rapid transport home and if we maintain control of our own foodstuffs and other materials we could make it a requirement that for every ton of these materials, England, France, Germany, Austria and the neutrals should furnish us a certain amount of transportation for this purpose.

I think it would be desirable if you could consider whether such a policy should not be extended to the raw materials. There will be a shortage of many of these materials for European manufacturing purposes and the control of them could be used to maintain some sort of justice. For instance, Germany has wantonly destroyed the enitre spinning industry in Belgium, Northern France and Poland, with a view to acquiring the markets in these industries subsequent to the war. If we took in hand the control of our distribution of cotton, we could no doubt ration Germany in such manner as to allow the other localities to again get on their industrial feet.

Another phase of the matter lies in the fact that we will require some imports of raw material and if we maintain control of our own supplies of food and raw material we will be in position to make such arrangements as will insure our own interests.

I should be glad indeed if I could have your views in this matter, for if you hold the view that we shall enter no entanglements whatever I shall take steps at once to maintain such a stand.

Yours faithfully,   Herbert Hoover

TLS (WP, DLC).

From Robert Latham Owen

My dear Mr. President: Washington. Oct 24. 1918

I send you my heartfelt blessing for your absolutely perfect reply to William's government.

I am so delighted I can not refrain from telling you that the World will forever bless you for your wisdom justice patience and clear vision.

When I answered on the Senate Floor Senator Lodge's criticism I fully foresaw the issue & had the completest confidence in your ability to handle it to the very best advantage which you have so splendidly done.

You have brought the desired end much nearer. Diplomacy and Force are both of supreme importance in winning a war like this, and I wish you to know of my ardent approval & support.

Yours Cordially   Robt L Owen

ALS (WP, DLC).

From Sherman Leland Whipple

My dear Mr. President: Washington October 24, 1918.

I have wanted for some days to make known to you how deeply impressed I have been with your handling of the grave questions involved in the German suit for peace. At the risk of intrusion, may I now express my admiration for all that you have done, and my complete accord with your final and decisive word?

I had feared that the startling intensity of the desire for blood-thirsty vengeance that has been sweeping the country might make it impracticable, if not impossible, just now, to do the thing that is wise and the thing that at the same time is right and just. But you had the courage to do just this thing, and it is in this courage that I deeply and sincerely rejoice. I believe that the people whose opinion you value will all support you with enthusiasm. By your wise leadership you have completely won the popular confidence. They will follow you here, I believe, as they will in whatever course your conscience and wisdom may lead you to adopt.

I venture further to express the belief that Germany has met your terms of peace with sincerity and without reserve, because it would be folly for her to do otherwise. I think it pretty clear that her government now realizes that in the American people and their President is the supreme hope of the German Nation for just conditions of peace. While you have not concealed your contempt for the artifice and trickery of the German people, and while your expressions of condemnation have been stern and humiliating, yet they believe that in your ultimate decisions you are always just and that you will not wittingly permit injustice to be done. I think, too, that they will understand that while our people are outraged and indignant yet they are instinctively fairminded and even chivalrously generous.

It must be quite clear to the German Nation that if she fails to convince you of her sincere purpose to make such a peace as will meet your approval, her single alternative will be to stand helpless before her ancient enemies to do their will upon her, to suffer fearful vengeance for fearful wrongs. She therefore can profit nothing by insincerity or deceit toward you. She has every reason to be sincere and open with you, and no reason to be otherwise.

Although, therefore, you have made the conditions very humiliating, I believe that they will be accepted, and that through your unfailing wisdom a just peace will come.

Sincerely yours,   Sherman L. Whipple

TLS (WP, DLC).

From Bainbridge Colby

My dear Mr. President: Washington October 24, 1918.

I have followed with spell-bound interest the series of utterances, which have proceeded from you, beginning with the speech of Sept. 27th, and culminating in yesterday's reply to the overtures from the German government.

Your speech was a bold challenge to the established habitudes of men's thinking. Was it Utopian? Could it be made to fit the gnarled and incorrigible old world? I asked myself these questions. The more I reflected upon it, the more clear it became to me, that you had stated with precise logic the only alternative, if alternative there is to be, to the unending succession of futile wars, broken treaties, secret alliances and all the countless duplicities that have made up the course of history.

As to your replies to the German notes, this can be said: You have preserved unimpaired every potentiality for good in the situation, and have done the utmost possible, to hasten, to help and to encourage the forces making for a just and permanent settlement. This has not been easy. The German communications were not lacking in subtlety, but you emerged from each exchange with increased authority and prestige. I fancied I could hear the rustle of the Chancellor's silk in yesterday's note. It was like a final decree.

All the points were covered. There are no exceptions of value in the record. All that the defendant can do is to settle.

I think your countrymen are happy and proud today—proud of your work and proud of you.

Sincerely yours,   Bainbridge Colby

TLS (WP, DLC).

From William Byron Colver

My dear Mr. President: Washington 24 October 1918

Herewith is a new draft of the proposed Meat Packer legislation.[1]

This draft seeks to place the fullest discretion in the hands of the President and to suggest such means and methods as may be employed without disturbance of existing governmental agencies.

A primary consideration was to give this legislation a permanent character as distinguished from war or emergency measures. Thus, this draft includes in permanent form, numerous powers now being exercised by temporary agencies or by permanent government agencies.

The President is authorized through such agencies as he may designate, to do all things, and as much or little as he may from time to time deem needful, to insure free competitive markets and an open, free channel of commerce for meat animals and the products thereof, unentangled with commerce in any other commodity.

The President is empowered—

(1) To acquire and operate any or all rolling stock especially equipped for the transportation of live-stock or its products, and stock-yards, cold-storage and freezing plants and the necessary appurtenances thereof and

(2) to acquire and license the operation of any or all of such facilities,

(3) to license the use of all such facilities without acquiring them, and

(4) to license all persons, partnerships, associations and corporations engaged in meat packing in interstate commerce, with respect to such business and with respect to any interest, direct or indirect, which the licensee may have in any other sort of interstate commerce.

The five large packers substantially control the marketing of live-stock and of products derived from live-stock.

In the interest of producer and consumer the Government must effectively regulate them so far as they are or tend to be a monopoly;

must prevent the extension of this monopoly, and must destroy it as rapidly as practicable by opening the doors to competition.

The problem is the difficult one of restoring competition in an industry which has once been brought under monopolistic control.

The Packers have usurped the functions which properly belong to the railroads as common carriers by furnishing refrigerator cars and other specially equipped cars. If a shipper cannot secure from the carrier, the type of car he needs, he must either buy or hire such cars.

The present Railroad Administration regulation of special-type cars naturally does not go to the difficulty of the small packer, for, as the Interstate Commerce Commission says, ("In the Matter of Private Cars, No. 4906. p. 673):

"So far as the carrier is concerned it can make no difference whether the shipper is owner or lessee. So far as the shipper or the relation of one shipper to another is concerned, there may be a marked difference between an owner and a lessee." (p. 673-4).

While it makes no difference to the carrier, it makes a vital difference to an independent shipper whether he can obtain necessary special equipment cars from one who has no financial interest in the products transported, or whether he must use cars owned or controlled by others who are directly engaged with him in competition.

The control of the terminal facilities by the large packers is even more pernicious, because it restricts competition in buying and thereby affects prices.

The same is true of the refrigerated storage for meats.

Competition can most effectively be encouraged by relieving prospective competitors of the packers of the burden of monopolistic control at the market where they buy their animals, and the market where they dispose of their product and insuring safe-conduct on equal terms and with equal facilities on the high-way of interstate commerce.

All of the steps suggested in the draft of bill, might be taken immediately as war measures, and probably without additional legislation. Many of them are already in operation as war measures but not coordinated as a check upon or cure of monopoly.

So far as possible, and in advance of permanent legislation, these remedies, as temporary war expedients, might well be extended so that conditions may be created which, in the interest of the public, cannot lightly be destroyed at the close of the war.

However, it is the permanent remedy rather than the temporary one to which the accompanying draft of a bill is addressed.

Its theory and purpose is to empower the President to control, by license, the use of the instruments for carrying on the packing business and, if need be, to supplement the licensing power by outright dispossession, by lease or purchase.

Similarly, discretionary license control is given to the President over the business conduct of all engaged in this commerce and, finally, the power to meet, by license control, the sinister tendency toward monopoly of related and unrelated commodities looking to an ultimate control of the nation's food supply.

By direction of the Commission.

Faithfully,   William B. Colver.

TLS (WP, DLC).
    [1] "A BILL TO provide transportation, storage and marketing facilities for, and to regulate the commerce among the States in, live stock, meats and other products derived from live stock or the slaughtering of live stock," Oct. 24, 1918, T MS (WP, DLC). Colver summarizes it well.

From Cleveland Hoadley Dodge

My dear President: New York October 24, 1918.

I was just on the point of writing you to congratulate you upon your last reply to Germany, when I received a call from a man who was in Washington yesterday conferring with Mr. Harding, of the Federal Reserve Board. Mr. Harding is anxious to have a good man appointed on the Federal Reserve Board to take the place of Mr. Delano, and seemed to think that if you should now appoint Tom Jones, of Chicago, for the position, owing to the settlement of the Harvester suit, the objections which prevailed against him formerly would not be made now. Of course Tom Jones would make a splendid man for the Board, and I am simply suggesting this to you as I know you are probably considering the matter carefully.

In spite of some of the criticisms which the hide-bound Republicans feel they have to make against anything which you do, I think the whole country will heartily approve of your last message to Germany, and the more I study it, the more admirable it seems. You are certainly educating the German people, and I sincerely trust that the inevitable end may come speedily.

With warm regards

Yours affectionately,   Cleveland H. Dodge

TLS (WP, DLC).

To Ben La Fayette[1]

[The White House] 25 October 1918.

I venture to express to the voters of Oklahoma my very profound interest in the constitutional amendment for Woman Suffrage upon which they will act on the fifth of November, and I beg that they will permit me to express to them, as I did to the Congress of the United States, my deliberate judgment that the adoption of woman suffrage is a necessary part of the great programme of justice and reconstruction which the war has convinced the nations of the world that they should undertake in the interest of justice and peace.[2]   Woodrow Wilson.

T telegram (Letterpress Books, WP, DLC).
    [1] Chairman of the Oklahoma Democratic State Committee. Wilson sent an identical telegram on the same day to James Joseph McGraw (T telegram, Letterpress Books, WP, DLC), chairman of the Oklahoma Republican State Committee. Maud Wood Park had suggested that Wilson send a message to the voters of Oklahoma urging them to vote for a suffrage amendment to the state's constitution. Maud W. Park to WW, Oct. 21, 1918, TLS (WP, DLC).
    [2] Oklahoma ratified the state constitutional amendment for woman suffrage.

From John St. Loe Strachey

Private & Confidential.

My dear Mr. President,   Guildford. Friday, October 25th, 1918.

I hope you will not think me an impertinent intruder on the time of one who now has a larger weight of responsibility on his shoulders than has any other man in the civilised world, or, indeed, than any man has ever had in recorded history. I want to ask you to look at an attempt I have made in my paper, "The Spectator," to draft the constitution of a League of Nations on the basis of preserving the sanctity of Treaty contracts.[1] You were kind enough to express your interest in the idea in a letter with which you honoured me some two or three months ago.[2] This must be my excuse for troubling you.

It may interest you to note that I have based the drafting of the greater part of my constitution on that wonderful document, the Articles of Confederation of 1777,—a monument of wisdom and statesmanship as well as of clear and nervous[3] English.

I feel I cannot end a letter written on the day of the publication of your reply to the German Government, without expressing my admiration of its firmness and plain speaking. The reply is perhaps the most important state paper that any ruler of a free people has ever had the responsibility of writing. You have had to speak, not only for the American nation, but for the whole civilised world. It is not for me to bandy compliments with the President of the United States, but perhaps, without treading upon ground on which I have no right to encroach, I may at least speak as one man of letters to another. The style in which the reply is conveyed is worthy of the great occasion and worthy of the greatest language in which human intent has ever been expressed. For the last forty years it has been part of my life to study very fully the public utterances of English speaking statesmen, not only here, but in the United States, and I can say without flattery or exaggeration that in the matter of dignified word and phrase your reply may fittingly stand with the noblest examples.

Believe me, dear Mr. President, with profound respect,

Yours sincerely,   J. S. Loe Strachey

TLS (WP, DLC).
¹ "Topics of the Day: The League of Nations," London *Spectator*, CXXI (Oct. 26, 1918), 444-45. Strachey proposed a league of nations whose members could end treaties among themselves or with nations outside the league, or leave the league, only after a year's notice. Any nation going to war without such notice was to be punished by a decree of nonintercourse adopted by the league. The league was also to appoint international commissions to resolve disputes among nations.
² WW to J. St. L. Strachey, April 5, 1918, Vol. 47.
³ That is, vigorous, forcible.

From Alexander Mitchell Palmer

Dear Mr. President: Washington, D. C. October 25, 1918.

I have your note of the twenty-first instant, in regard to the claim of Lilly Busch.

It was for the very purpose of avoiding "any possibility of error" that I advised against allowing her claim. The allowance of such a claim under the Act is discretionary. Section 9 provides that the "President, if application is made therefor by the claimant, *may*, with the assent of the owner of said property and of all persons claiming any right, title, or interest therein, order the payment" &c. We clearly had the legal right to take this property, because Mrs. Busch was admittedly in the enemy class when the property was taken over. That being so, we must have the legal right to retain the property until the discretion of the President is exercised, or until judgment is obtained in suit against the Alien Property Custodian, as provided for in the Act. I think for the reason stated in my letter of the fifteenth instant to the Attorney General that we would be on much safer ground if we allow Mrs. Busch to sue, if she desires to do so, enter a defense and abide by the decision of the United States Court.

I am enclosing, for your information, a letter which I am writing to the Attorney General to-day,[1] calling attention to my view of the law. For the reasons therein stated, I cannot agree with him that we have no legal right to retain the property, but, of course, that is a matter for him and not for me. I have stated my position in the matter only because the Department of Justice asked for my views, and I still think that the claim ought not to be allowed. If, however, the Attorney General thinks otherwise, and you concur, it is needless to say I shall cheerfully acquiesce in the decision.[2]

Respectfully yours,   A Mitchell Palmer

TLS (WP, DLC).
   [1] A. M. Palmer to TWG, Oct. 25, 1918, CCL (WP, DLC).
   [2] Palmer returned Mrs. Busch's property to her in December. See the *New York Times*, Dec. 14, 1918.

From William Gibbs McAdoo

Dear Mr. President: Washington October 25, 1918.

As I understand the result of our conversation of yesterday, you are going to read again my letter of September 18, 1918 in reference to the Mexican situation and give me a definite reply. This is merely a reminder.   Cordially yours,   W G McAdoo

TLS (WP, DLC).

From Robert Lansing, with Enclosure

My dear Mr. President: Washington October 25, 1918.

May I trouble you to read these letters which I have received from Mr. Dmowski in relation to a definite recognition of the Polish National Committee, of which he is the head? As I understand it Mr. Paderewski and his faction, which is by all odds the largest and most influential, support Mr. Dmowski's Committee. You will note in Mr. Dmowski's letter of today[1] that he quotes a letter from Mr. Balfour giving recognition of the Polish Army by the British Government.

Will you be good enough to advise me as to your wishes in this matter?   Faithfully yours,   Robert Lansing

Approved W. W.

TLS (SDR, RG 59, 763.72/12496, DNA).
   [1] R. Dmowski to RL, Oct. 25, 1918, TLS (SDR, RG 59, 763.72/12497, DNA).

From Roman Dmowskí

Sir: Washington, D. C. October 18, 1918.

In the course of our conversation this morning, I had the honor of presenting to you the subject of the Polish Army in France, the position of which has undergone an essential change within the last few weeks.

On the Fourth of June, 1917, the President of the French Republic issued a decree creating an autonomous Polish Army, fighting under its own national colors.

The French Government undertook the organization of that Army by the French Military Authorities and out of its own funds. As there was at that time no Polish political body which could exercise the supreme authority over that Army, and no Polish ranking officers who could command it, the Army, though composed of Poles, remained under the authority of the French Government, and all appointments were made by the French Ministry of War. Under these conditions, the successful organization of the Army, its thorough training and the introduction of a model discipline was accomplished. But from the national and political point of view, the situation of the Army remained abnormal.

This situation changed gradually as a result of the constitution of the Polish National Committee now recognized as the Polish official organization by the Governments of France, Great Britain, Italy and the United States.

On the basis of an agreement with the French Government, the Polish National Committee undertook the direction of the political side of the Army. Lastly, some ranking Polish officers, among them General Joseph Haller, arrived in France and offered their services to the Polish National Committee. This made possible to accomplish the organization of the Polish Army, as an autonomous National Army, under the Polish political authority and Polish Military Command.

On August 7th, 1918, the Polish National Committee addressed to the French Government a proposal that the Polish National Committee be recognized by France and other governments as the supreme political authority of the Polish Army and that the said Committee should appoint a Commander-in-Chief of the Polish Army in France and of all Polish military forces wherever they might be organized.

The French Government agreed to the proposal of the Committee: The Polish National Committee has been recognized by France as the supreme political authority of the Polish Army, and General

Joseph Haller appointed by the Polish National Committee as Commander-in-Chief of the Polish Army, took oath on the Polish colors on October 6th 1918. The military representatives of France, of the United States, Great Britain, and Italy were present at the ceremony.

The Government of Great Britain by an official act of October 15th, 1918, recognized the Polish National Army as autonomous, allied and co-belligerent.

I have the honor to beg the Government of the United States to associate itself with the Governments of France and Great Britain by recognizing the Polish Army, under the supreme political authority of the Polish National Committee, as autonomous, allied, and co-belligerent.

I am, Sir,   Most respectfully yours,   Roman Dmowskí

TLS (SDR, RG 59, 763.72/12496, DNA).

William Sidney Graves to Peter Charles Harris

CONFIDENTIAL.   [Vladivostok] October 25, 1918.

From: The Commanding General.
To: The Adjutant General of the Army.
Subject: Intelligence Detachment.

1. I find there is some difficulty in handling the Intelligence Detachment sent here for service in Siberia. The idea of most of these officers is that they should operate on the same general principles as are used in France. As my guide in determining what is desired in Siberia, I have taken the unsigned "aide memoir" of the Department of State, dated July 17th, which was handed to me by the Secretary of War in Kansas City. In this "aide memoir" one of the objects mentioned was "to render such aid as may be acceptable to the Russians in the organization of their own self-defence."

This limiting phrase, "as may be acceptable to the Russians," of course hampers all activities. I think, however, it is a very wise limitation. These intelligence officers are energetic, competent and very ambitious to accomplish what they think is for the good of the United States, and their desire, I am sure, is to be hampered as little as possible by the limitations placed upon me. I have been trying to use them to aid the Russians who have been selected to supervise in Vladivostok censorship of mail and telegraph and for the examination of passports, but, with the greatest of caution and the most specific instructions, I find they take the lead and soon it appears to the onlooker that the Americans have taken over these activities.

I am going to send these officers out to various points in Siberia, with very specific and definite instructions, with the idea of getting all information possible on military, political and economic conditions, with a view to helping in any way we can in the regeneration of Siberia. This information will be valuable in helping distribute American supplies sent here. The Russians cannot be depended upon to do things according to our ideas. This is particularly true now when all Russians are uncertain as to what political faction will be on top when a government is established in Russia.

As to the censorship of the press, mail and postoffice, it is impossible for it to be made effective. The Japanese want to handle their own boats and their own people, and so do other representatives of foreign governments, to a greater or less extent. If such control be established in Vladivostok alone, it becomes a farce, because any supervision here can be easily evaded by sending news from other parts of the country just a short distance from Vladivostok. To take complete charge would be most offensive to the Russians and would not be in accordance with War Department instructions.

2. The Japanese have practically filled all empty barracks east of Lake Baikal. I cabled recently that, in my judgment, they had 60,000 troops east of Lake Baikal, and I feel sure my estimate is not above what they actually have. I have just received word from Verhnudinsk[1] that they have 8,000 Japanese there, and that we will be unable to get any quarters there. Under the guise of combined operation, and the need for troops at certain places, I have practically been sewed up to the railway line between Vladivostok and Habarovsk;[2] and the Japanese have more troops at practically every station occupied by United States troops than I have. It is evidently their desire to keep American troops from being stationed alone at any station in Siberia, and they have already accomplished their desire by occupying all of the places.

I understood from the Secretary, when in Kansas City, that the Japanese were to send 10,000 or 12,000 troops to Siberia. I think they undoubtedly now have 40,000 in Siberia, and about 20,000 in the Seventh Division between Chita and Pogranitchnaya[3] on the Chinese Eastern Railway. Apparently, our Government keeps the Japanese well informed as to all orders given me, but I am kept in the dark as to any agreements between the Japanese government and the United States Government. I think, generally speaking, it would be well to give me such information, especially such as affects the strength of Allied troops in Siberia, and limits as to movements. The Japanese character is sufficiently well known in the War Department to make it unnecessary for me to state that it is impossible for me to find out their intentions or strength here. Two or three days ago a detachment of 600 Japanese landed at Possiet Bay,[4] which action apparently very much excited the Russian people.

3. Yesterday General Ivanoff-Rinoff, Minister of War for the new Russian government at Omsk,[5] called upon me. He seemed to be a man of moderate convictions, for a Russian. He stated to me that he had just arrived from Omsk, and from all information that he could gather and from what he had seen on the railways he was convinced the Japanese were permanently establishing themselves in this part of Siberia. He said their flags were flying from all railway stations; Japanese sentinels were stationed at these railway stations; and that in some cases they had thrown the Russian troops out of Russian barracks. In reply, I informed him that public announcement had been made by the United States and Japan as to their objects here, and I felt sure there were no good grounds for his anxiety. He then replied that the Japanese were encouraging factions in this part of Siberia, and he could come to no conclusion other than that it was their desire to prevent the Russian people from getting together. He cited the case of Ataman Kalmikoff at Habarovsk.[6] He said that he was being encouraged and, in his judgment, given money by the Japanese, and it is a well known fact that he is a murderer and a robber, and naturally the Russians could not understand why such a man was being encouraged by the Allies. I replied that I had no evidence as to these facts and, consequently, had absolutely nothing to say other than that the policy of the United States was not to interfere in the internal squabbles of Russia, and I believed it should be possible to make any man in Russia comply with their laws.

The President of the Zemstvo and the Mayor of the city,[7] who were in office prior to the Bolsheviki regime, also came to me and made practically the same complaints. They all said that they must look to America to see that the announcement of the Allies as to their intentions when coming here was carried out.

As to the object of these Russians in coming to me with these stories, I cannot be absolutely sure. The Russian seems to thrive on controversy, and I have to be particularly guarded in my conversation with them, because of fear of exaggeration as to what I said, and also because I am always looking for an intent on the part of certain Russians to stir up trouble between the Allies. My relations with Japanese Headquarters have been very cordial, and they have always, apparently, desired to cooperate with me in matters within our respective authorities. I am beginning, however, to believe that the Japanese soldiers and junior officers are very high-handed in their dealing with the Russian people. Feeling is undoubtedly growing more bitter against them all the time, and the feeling toward the American soldiers is becoming better all the time. This probably has something to do with two or three unfortunate incidents which occurred recently.   Wm. S. Graves

TCL (WP, DLC).
  [1] That is, Verkhneudinsk.
  [2] That is, Khabarovsk.
  [3] That is, Pogranichnaya, now called Suifenho.
  [4] That is, Posyet Bay.
  [5] Pavel Pavlovich Ivanov-Rinov. About the Ufa, or Omsk, Directorate, see n. 1 to Enclosure II with RL to WW, Sept. 24, 1918 (second letter of that date).
  [6] Ivan Pavlovich Kalmykov, a Cossack, anti-Bolshevik military leader who had taken control of Khabarovsk on September 5. He had a reputation for brutality extreme even for the Russia of this period.
  [7] A. S. Medvedev and one Ogarev, respectively.

To George Mason La Monte

My dear La Monte: [The White House] 26 October, 1918

I have now gone very carefully over the case of Miss Pollok with the Attorney General, and am sorry to tell you that I think you have got the wrong impression about the evidence against her. It is very considerable in volume and very serious in character. To dismiss the charges against Miss Pollok would involve dismissing charges of the same sort against others who have been justly indicted and would, I am afraid, be an act of unjustifiable discrimination.

I am sorry to make this report but am convinced by what I have learned through the Department of Justice that I can make no other.
          Cordially and sincerely yours,   Woodrow Wilson

TLS (Letterpress Books, WP, DLC).

To Sherman Leland Whipple

My dear Mr. Whipple: [The White House] 26 October, 1918

Your letter of yesterday has given me very genuine gratification. I know the value to attach to your judgment, and it reassures me mightily to have such support from your own mind and judgment.
          Cordially and sincerely yours,   Woodrow Wilson

TLS (Letterpress Books, WP, DLC).

To Edward Beale McLean

PERSONAL

My dear Mr. McLean: [The White House] 26 October, 1918

I sincerely hope that you approve of what I have done in making a frank appeal to the people of the country to support me, and I hope most sincerely that if you do approve, you will take occasion to say so. There is so evident an intention to create a false impression about the whole thing that this, it seems to me, is the time for my friends to strike hard in defence of the frank and right course.

I know I can appeal to you in confidence to see that the just view of the matter is presented.

With much esteem, and sincere appreciation of the generous attitude of the paper.

Cordially and sincerely yours,   [Woodrow Wilson]

CCL (WP, DLC).

To Charles O'Connor Hennessy

My dear Mr. Hennessey: [The White House] 26 October, 1918.

May I not say how deeply interested I am in the contest you are conducting? I cannot but feel that in ignoring my earnest appeal with regard to the suffrage amendment,[1] made in the public interest and because of my intimate knowledge of the issues involved both on the other side of the water and here, Senator Baird has certainly not represented the true feeling and spirit of the people of New Jersey. I am sure that they must have felt that such an appeal could not and should not be ignored. It would be a very great make-weight thrown into the international scale if his course of action while in the Senate could be reversed by the people of our great State.   Cordially and sincerely yours,   Woodrow Wilson

TLS (Letterpress Books, WP, DLC).
  [1] See WW to D. Baird, July 31, 1918, and D. Baird to WW, Aug. 5, 1918, both in Vol. 49.

To Edward Parker Davis

My dear E.P.:   [The White House] 26 October, 1918

Thank you for your verses "Fight and Hold Fast,"[1] for certainly no one is more determined in that matter than I am, but do you not think, my dear fellow, that we are on the verge of yielding to the sort of hate which we are fighting in the Germans? I am beginning to be fearful lest we go too far to be in a mood to make an absolutely and rigorously impartial peace, and God knows the disposition to make a peace of that sort is growing less and less on the other side of the water.

Affectionately yours,   Woodrow Wilson

TLS (Letterpress Books, WP, DLC).
    [1] E. P. Davis, "Fight and Hold Fast," T MS, enclosed in E. P. Davis to WW, Oct. 10, 1918, ALS, both in WP, DLC. As Wilson's comment in the above letter suggests, Davis' poem called for an implacable determination to defeat "the lying Hun."

To Bainbridge Colby

My dear Colby: The White House 26 October, 1918.

Your letter of yesterday has cheered me mightily. I work along sometimes with hardly more than instinct for a guide, and it is deeply reassuring to me to have those with vision standing outside say that the instinct was right. I thank you with all my heart.

Cordially and sincerely yours,   Woodrow Wilson

TLS (B. Colby Papers, DLC).

To Robert G. Withers[1]

[The White House] 26 October, 1918

You tell me[2] that the people of Nevada are showing that they would be assisting me by returning Senator Henderson[3] to the Senate. They are quite right in that assumption. I have formed the highest opinion of Senator Henderson and his assistance has been indispensable.   Woodrow Wilson

T telegram (Letterpress Books, WP, DLC).
    [1] Lawyer of Reno, Nev., active in Nevada Democratic party politics. Withers had been a fellow student with Wilson in the law department of the University of Virginia in 1879-1880. At that time, his home was in Staunton, Va. See R. G. Withers to WW, Nov. 12, 1910, and Nov. 12, 1912, both TLS (WP, DLC).
    [2] Withers' communication is missing.
    [3] Charles Belknap Henderson, Democrat, who had been appointed to the Senate in January 1918 to fill the vacancy created by the death of Francis G. Newlands on December 24, 1917.

From Newton Diehl Baker, with Enclosure

Oct. 26, 1918 10:30 P.M.

Just received from Gen Pershing   Respectfully   Baker

ALS (WP, DLC).

E N C L O S U R E

London October 26, 1918

RUSH CONFIDENTIAL [No. 5]

Paragraph 1 At a conference of the British, French and American Commanders in Chief, called today, the 25th, by Marshal Foch to discuss the terms of an armistice with Germany pursuant to the indications contained in the President's recent letter to the German Government, each Commander in Chief expressed his views on the Military situation and the conditions that should be demanded of Germany. My own views are expressed in the following paragraph.

Paragraph 2 To begin with I agree with the opinion expressed by the Commanders in Chief of the British and French armies and with President Wilson as to the general conditions of an armistice which should provide a guarantee against a resumption of hostilities, giving the Allies a decided advantage and be unfavorable to Germany in case hostilities should be resumed. If the German Government is really sincere in its desire to end the war, then neither the German Government nor the German people should object to strict conditions regarding an armistice. I think that the damage done by the war to the interests of the powers with which the United States is now associated against Germany has been so great that there should be no tendency toward leniency with Germany and her allies in fixing the terms of an armistice.

Subparagraph The military situation at present is very favorable to the Allies. The German forces since the beginning of the counter-offensive on July 18th have been constantly in retreat and have not been able to recover since that counter-offensive was begun. The situation of the French and British Armies can best be judged by pointing out the fact that they have been continuously on the offensive since then, and that they are now attacking with as much vigor as ever. As to the American Army, the part it has taken in the great counter-offensive since July 18th has not been inconsiderable. It is constantly increasing in strength and training, its staffs, its services and its higher commanders have improved by experience, so there is every reason to suppose that the American Army will be able to take the part expected of it in the event of resumption of hostilities after an armistice. In consideration of these facts and of our favorable situation, the terms we demand should not be light. I therefore propose: First, The evacuation of France and Belgium within 30 days and of all other foreign territory occupied by Germany without delay. Second, The withdrawal of the German armies from Alsace Lorraine and occupation of those territories by the

Allied Armies. Third, Withdrawal of the German armies to the east of the Rhine and the possession of such bridge heads on the eastern side of the Rhine by the Allies as may be necessary to ensure their control of that river. Fourth, The unrestricted transportation of the American Army and its material across the seas. Fifth, the immediate repatriation of all *native troops* of foreign territory now or heretofore occupied during the war by Germany. Sixth, Surrender of all U-Boats and U-Boat Bases to the control of a neutral power until their disposition is otherwise determined. Seventh, Return to France and Belgium of all railroad rolling stock that has been seized by Germany from those countries.

Paragraph 3. The proposal of Marshal Haig are included generally in paragraphs Numbers 1, 2, 5 and 7 of the above, omitting all others, his opinion being that the terms should not be too severe. The views of General Petain are covered practically by paragraphs 1, 2, 3 and 7 of the above, omitting the others. The opinion of Marshal Foch was not given definitely, but it is presumed will be communicated to Washington through the French Prime Minister.

Pershing

T telegram (WP, DLC).

From Newton Diehl Baker

Dear Mr. President: [Washington] October 26, 1918.

I do not like Mr. Roosevelt, and therefore I mistrust my judgment. But should you not take some occasion to point out that your fourteen-point address was made on January 8 and that it is scandalous for Mr. Roosevelt to remain silent about it for nine months, until our Allies rely upon it, our own country approves it, our enemies in professed good faith accept it—until our national good faith is pledged to it as a statement of our war aims, and then seek to repudiate it by writing to Republican Senators in an effort to make a partisan row?[1] Surely he is estopped now, even if his bloodthirstiness has been whetted by our victory into an appetite for demands which he did not have the courage to make when your address was made and accepted throughout the world.

Respectfully yours,   Newton D. Baker.

CCL (N. D. Baker Papers, DLC).
[1] Baker refers to T. Roosevelt to H. C. Lodge, Oct. 24, 1918, a telegram printed in Elting E. Morison *et al.*, eds., *The Letters of Theodore Roosevelt* (8 vols., Cambridge, Mass., 1951-54), VIII, 1380-81. The full text of this telegram made public on October 24, reads as follows:
"I am sending this telegram in triplicate to you and to Senators Miles Poindexter and Hiram Johnson, because I make my appeal to the Representatives of the American

people from one ocean to the other. As an American citizen I most earnestly hope that the Senate of the United States, which is part of the treaty-making power of the United States, will take affirmative action as regards peace with Germany and in favor of peace based on the unconditional surrender of Germany. I also earnestly hope that on behalf of the American people it will declare against the adoption in their entirety of the fourteen points of the President's address of last January as offering a basis for a peace satisfactory to the United States.

"Let us dictate peace by the hammering guns and not chat about peace to the accompaniment of the clicking of typewriters.

"The language of the fourteen points and of the subsequent statements explaining or qualifying them, is neither straightforward nor plain, but if construed in its probable sense many and possibly most of those fourteen points are thoroly mischievous and if made the basis of a peace, such peace would represent not the unconditional surrender of Germany but the unconditional surrender of the United States. Naturally they are entirely satisfactory to Germany and equally naturally they are in this country satisfactory to every pro-German and pacifist and socialist and anti-American so-called internationalist.

"The only peace offer which we should consider from Germany at this time is an offer to accept such terms as the Allies without our aid have imposed on Bulgaria. We ought to declare war on Turkey without an hour's delay. The failure to do so hitherto has caused the talk about making the world safe for democracy, to look unpleasantly like mere insincere rhetoric. While the Turk is left in Europe and permitted to tyrannize over the subject peoples, the world is thoroly unsafe for democracy.

"Moreover we should find out what the President means by continually referring to this country merely as the associate, instead of the ally of the nations with whose troops our own troops are actually brigaded in battle. If he means that we are something less than an ally of France, England, Italy, Belgium and Serbia, then he means that we are something less than an enemy of Germany and Austria. We ought to make it clear to the world that we are neither an untrustworthy friend nor an irresolute foe. Let us clearly show that we do not desire to pose as the umpire between our faithful and loyal friends and our treacherous and brutal enemies, but that we are the staunch ally of our friends and the staunch foe of our enemies. When the German people repudiate the Hohenzollerns, then, and not until then, it will be time to discriminate between them and their masters. I hope the Senate and the House will pass some resolution demanding the unconditional surrender of Germany as our war aim and stating that our peace terms have never yet been formulated or accepted by our people, and that they will be fully discussed with our allies and made fully satisfactory to our own people, before they are discussed with Germany."

Two Letters from Robert Lansing

My dear Mr. President: Washington October 26, 1918.

In reference to a reply to the Turkish appeal for our intervention in the matter of an armistice, the Italian Ambassador states that he has received a reply from his Government in which it is suggested that we answer the Turkish note by proposing to the Turkish Government that it should address itself directly to the Allied Military Authorities.

The French Ambassador has not received anything positive from his Government, but from telegrams which have just arrived he has the impression that it will be acceptable to his Government if the President should suggest to Turkey that she ask for an armistice directly to the Allied Military authorities.

Mr. Barclay has received no definite reply as yet but he shares the view of the French Ambassador as to what would probably be his Government's judgment.

Faithfully yours,   Robert Lansing

My dear Mr. President: Washington October 26, 1918.

I send you a memorandum handed to me yesterday by the Japanese Ambassador,[1] together with two memoranda by Mr. Miller, Chief of the Division of Far Eastern Affairs.[2]

My own disposition is to accede to the suggestion of the Japanese Government that a joint representation be made to China by the Powers relative to the desirability of settling the factional differences between the North and the South. I can see no harm in this action at the present time and it undoubtedly offers the possibility of impressing the antagonistic elements in China with the idea that neither can gain independent support from this or that Power. I believe that each of the factions hopes to obtain foreign support for itself. Joint action will dispel such hope and will show that the Powers are united in the desire for political tranquility in China. At the same time it will check any effort by one of the Powers to favor one faction, which might cause a serious situation.

In ordinary circumstances I am opposed to joint action of any kind, but in this particular case a common desire expressed jointly is the only effective method of influencing the two Chinese parties to settle their quarrel.

Will you be good enough to indicate your wishes in this matter?
Faithfully yours,   Robert Lansing

TLS (WP, DLC).
   [1] K. Ishii to RL, Oct. 25, 1918, T MS (WP, DLC). As Lansing's letter above indicates, Ishii suggested on behalf of his government that Japan, the United States, Great Britain, France, and Italy make a joint representation to the leaders of the factions in North and South China urging them to arrive at an amicable settlement of their differences.
   [2] Ransford Stevens Miller to RL, Oct. 24 and Oct. 25, 1918, both TLI (WP, DLC). Miller's first letter outlined the factional conflict in China and the widely differing views of Allied and American diplomats as to what, if anything, should be done about the situation. His own recommendations were that the United States, Great Britain, France, and Japan should make any new loans to China only with strict agreements upon, and supervision of, the purposes for which the funds were to be used and that Hsü-Shih-ch'ang, the new President of the Peking government, should be supported in his efforts to reach a settlement with the southern factional leaders in Canton. Miller's second letter discussed the Ishii memorandum cited in n. 1 above and supported the action suggested therein.

From Herbert Clark Hoover, with Enclosure

Dear Mr. President: Washington 26 October 1918

I enclose herewith two memoranda[1] about which I spoke to you on Thursday. The first of these I would be glad if you could see your way to address to me so as to give me a measure of authority and standing in undertaking this problem. I find that the matter is even more necessary than I contemplated on Thursday as already there have sprung up various attempts in this country to formulate important trade relations with the Belgians, some of which, at least,

I feel could not but have a bad reflection on the whole situation. Doubtless it is desirable to secure the rehabilitation of trade with the United States, but if we are to prevent advantage being taken of the distress of this people, it must be under firm control.

I have formulated this memorandum so that I can use it as a basis for approach to the state departments of the other governments, indicating the future attitude so far as this government is concerned and, therefore, a basis for them to agree to.

The second memorandum I would like, if you approve, to have addressed to the various departments which are indicated in the heading, for it will be necessary to have the co-operation of these departments and that they should act from a common center in all matters of trade and shipping, if we are to direct our energies to the great objective, that is, economic rehabilitation rather than trade.   Yours faithfully,   Herbert Hoover

TLS (WP, DLC).
¹ One is the Enclosure. The other is missing; however, Wilson sent it as WW to E. N. Hurley *et al.* Nov. 6, 1918.

E N C L O S U R E

Dear Mr. Hoover: 26 October, 1918.

The probable early evacuation of Belgium brings us face to face with the problems of this distressed people, not only in continued food relief, but in the broad issues of economic rehabilitation. The initial task of preserving the bare lives of the people during German occupation, undertaken four years ago under your direction, is now nearing completion. I conceive that the American people will willingly accept a large share of the burden in their continued assistance to reconstruction and rehabilitation, pending their re-payment for injury by Germany.

In order that such assistance should be exerted in the most liberal, efficient and comprehensive manner, I feel that it should be organized under a single agency, that it may coordinate the whole effort of the American people or the government, in the furnishing of supplies, machinery, finance, exchange, shipping, trade relations and philanthropy. I also feel in this matter that such an agency, in addition to being the sole vehicle of supplies, should also have some proper participation in the expenditure and distribution of this assistance. Such consolidation should give much greater assurance of proper assistance and prevent any profiteering in this situation.

The large experience of the Belgian Relief Commission, the character of its organization without profit, its shipping and the sympathetic bond which it forms, after four years of co-operation, with the Belgian people, point to its continuation and enlargement as the logical agency for this purpose. I should therefore be glad if you and your colleagues would undertake this extended work.

I understand that the sentiment of the English and French people is to also participate in this burden. It would seem to me desirable to inquire if these governments would not therefore continue and enlarge their present support to the Commission to these ends, so that we may have a comprehensive and efficient agency for dealing with the entire problem on behalf of all.

It is of course primary that our assistance in this expenditure and organization shall be built upon co-operation with the Belgian government and the use of such internal agencies and methods as may be agreed with them, to whom our whole solicitude is directed.

It is also of first importance that the expenditure of all philanthropy of the American people toward Belgium, of whatever character, should be conducted by or under the control of the Commission, if duplication and waste are to be avoided.

With view to the advancement of these ideas, I have addressed a note to the various departments of this government, indicating my direction that all matters relating to these problems should be undertaken under your guidance and that they should give to you every co-operation.

I wish for you to proceed at once with the undertaking so far as it relates to the United States and I should be glad if you would, through the proper agencies, take up a discussion of these matters with the Belgian government and with the English and French governments as to their relationship and participation.

Yours etc.[1]

T MS (WP, DLC).
[1] Wilson's edited version of this draft is WW to HCH, Nov. 7, 1918. Wilson's hand-written changes are on Hoover's draft.

From Grosvenor Blaine Clarkson

My dear Mr. President: Washington 26 October, 1918.

This is entirely a personal expression. I wish to say that I believe your statement to the country asking that it return a Democratic congress is wholly justified. It means a little something for me to say that. I was raised in the rock-ribbed Republican faith. My father, the late James S. Clarkson,[1] was chairman of the Republican National Committee, served on its executive committee throughout four national campaigns, and six times sat in national conventions as delegate-at-large from the state of Iowa. I have been through three national campaigns myself in a confidential capacity. I believe that it will interest you to know that my father, almost up to the day of his death last June, had no patience whatever with the Republican criticisms of your conduct of the war and invariably said, "Support the President." My father, however, spent his entire life and his entire fortune in doing and saying what he believed to be right; he simply didn't know any other road.

For myself, party ties as such no longer interest or hold me. I believe in you and in your direction of this country's part in the war. One of the things that makes me say that is that in twenty months of war-time service in the Council of National Defense, I can not recall a single action on the part of the Council bearing on administrative matters which has had a political flavor. I have never heard even raised the question of the political faith of an appointee of the Council either during the terrific days when that body made its now historic mobilization of the industries of the Nation, or later. Frankly, before coming to Washington I would not have believed such a non-partisan attitude possible. That is one reason, among very many others, why it has been easy for me, of a totally different affiliation in the past, to give my undivided loyalty to your administration, and I shall continue to do so.

I hope that you will not misunderstand the purpose of this letter. There are no reservations of any nature in my mind. There is nothing whatever that I seek at the hands of the Democratic party or at the hands of the Administration. My chief desire is to get back into business when the war shall have ended. I feel very strongly on the question of the undivided support of yourself in the prosecution of this war; feeling as I do, I could make no other expression than that which I have here made, even though I burn a good many bridges as I do so.   Faithfully yours,   Grosvenor Clarkson

TLS (WP, DLC).
  [1] James Sullivan Clarkson, 1842-1918, operator of a station on the Underground Railway, 1856-1862; editor in chief and coproprietor of the Des Moines *Iowa State Register*, 1868-1889; member of the Republican National Committee, 1880-1896.

From Joseph Patrick Tumulty, with Enclosure

Dear Governor: The White House. 26 October, 1918

I sincerely hope that you will not let this letter go out in the way that Scott Ferris suggests.[1] I was present in the House while this gentleman denounced the war resolution. No one could have been more bitter or have shown more vindictiveness. I am afraid that the Republicans will take this letter and other letters that you have written for men that have voted against the war and make an argument against us that would deeply embarrass us.[2]

The conclusion "By the way, I congratulate you on your renomination and hope you may be reelected to further aid the twenty million toilers of the country," if published throughout the country, would look like a class appeal. Mr. Keating is in no way entitled to such praise at your hands.

I think you should insert a paragraph like this: "I sincerely hope that I may have the benefit of your cooperation in these matters at the next session of Congress.[3]   J.P.T.

TL (WP, DLC).
   [1] S. Ferris to WW, Oct. 23, 1918, TLS (WP, DLC). Ferris urged Wilson to write a letter to Edward Keating in support of his bid for reelection to Congress and specifically suggested the sentence which Tumulty quotes in the second paragraph of the above letter.
   [2] The enclosure was not sent.
   [3] For the letter sent, see WW to E. Keating, Oct. 29, 1918.

E N C L O S U R E

My dear Mr. Keating: The White House 25 October, 1918.

May I not turn aside from the hurry of the day to congratulate you on your good work in behalf of labor legislation, childrens' bureau, needed civil pensions, etc.? You are certainly engaged in a good cause and are following it with admirable diligence.

By the way, I congratulate you on your renomination and hope you may be reelected to further aid the twenty million toilers of the country.   Cordially and sincerely yours,

TL (WP, DLC).

From William Gibbs McAdoo

Dear Mr. President: Washington October 26, 1918.

The Treasury has been recently approached as to methods of financing the requirements of the civil population in that part of Belgium now being evacuated by the Germans and in regard to reconstruction. The Treasury immediately consulted Mr. Hoover concerning these matters. Mr. Hoover replied by saying that he had taken the subject up with you, but he did not send me a copy of his letter. I, therefore, do not know what suggestions he is making.

The problem, from the financial standpoint, to say nothing of its other features, is of very great importance and needs careful consideration. I, therefore, venture to express the hope that you will take no action upon Mr. Hoover's letters or any suggestions that may be made to you in this connection until I have had an opportunity to present the views of the Treasury.

Cordially yours,   W G McAdoo

TLS (WP, DLC).

Two Telegrams from Edward Mandell House[1]

[Paris, Oct. 27, 1918]

Urgent. Number one.

Have already seen French Prime Minister, British Minister for War, Haig, and many others. I hope to get at the bottom of the situation before the meeting of Supreme War Council on Tuesday. Haig and Milner are exceedingly reasonable.

I understand by the press French Prime Minister would be doubtless (?) influenced by Foch who believes Germany is absolutely beaten. Haig and Bliss disagree with me on this point and advise a reasonable armistice. French Prime Minister has given me and I presume to you Foch's confidential memorandum to him stating what, in essence, the armistice should contain. He disclosed that no one has seen this and begs that you will keep private until after the meeting of the War Council. The French Prime Minister says that Pershing is handling our men badly and is (landing ?) more men than necessary and is not making the progress he should, and which the other allies are making. This is for your confidential information. It evidently reflects Foch's opinion. I would be pleased if deemed advisable advise me before Tuesday of anything you may have in mind.   Edward House[2]

T transcript of WWsh decode (WP, DLC).

[1] In reproducing these telegraphic exchanges between Wilson and House, the Editors will reproduce the texts which each man sent and the texts as he decoded the telegrams received. When the texts of decoded documents are badly garbled, we will print both the garbled decode and, usually in a footnote, the sender's text. In most cases, however, we will repair in square brackets significant mistakes and omissions in received telegrams and decodes of them from the copies of the telegrams as they were sent. These mistakes occur most frequently in the telegrams from House to Wilson. In a few cases, we have made corrections in square brackets from copies in the State Department's files, and we always call special attention to this source of corrections.

[2] House's copy of this telegram reads as follows:

"I have already seen Clemenceau, Milner, Haig and many others. I hope to get at the bottom of the situation before the meeting of the Supreme War Council on Tuesday. Haig and Milner are exceedingly reasonable. George, I understand, is not. Clemenceau would be but is influenced by Foch who believes Germany is absolutely beaten. Haig and Bliss disagree with him on this point and advise a reasonable armistice.

"Clemenceau has given me and I am transmitting to you Foch's confidential memorandum to him stating what in his opinion the armistice should contain. He declares no one has seen this and he begs that you will keep it private until after the meeting of the War Council.

"Clemenceau says Pershing is handling our men badly and is losing more men than is necessary and is not making the progress he should and that which the other allies are making. This, too, is for your confidential information. It evidently reflects Marshal Foch's opinion.

"I would be pleased if you would advise me before Tuesday of anything you may have in mind." EMH to WW, Oct. 27, 1918, TC telegram (E. M. House Papers, CtY).

[Paris, Oct. 27, 1918][1]

[No. 2]

Referring my [No. One] following are the essential points of Foch's proposed military conditions for an armistice:

1. Immediate evacuation France, Belgium, Alsace-Lorraine, Luxemburg, repatriation of their inhabitants and abandonment of part of enemy material in region evacuated. Following time limits should be set for evacuation in order to prevent enemy from withdrawing great part of war material and provisions of every character:

At end of four days from signature of armistice enemy shall have withdrawn to a line running roughly west of Veteren, Mons, Maubeuge, Mezieres, Metz, Colmar. At end of eight days to a line running west of Antwerp, Malines, Brussels, Charleroi, Luxemburg to the Rhine near Carlsruhe. At end of fourteen days to a line entirely liberating Belgium, Luxemburg and Alsace-Lorraine.

Enemy shall abandon 2500 heavy guns, 2500 field artillery, 30,000 machine guns, 3,000 mine throwers, to be delivered at certain points under specified conditions. This constitutes about one-third of the artillery and mine throwers and one-half of the machine guns of the German Army.

The allied troops shall follow the march of evacuation of which the details will eventually be regulated.

2. Enemy shall evacuate left bank of Rhine, this territory to be administered by local authorities under control of allied troops of occupation. Occupation to be ensured by garrisoned bridge-heads at Mainz, Coblence, Cologne and Strassburg, each bridge-head thirty kilometers in radius. Strategic points of the region also to be held. A neutral zone to be established on right bank of Rhine forty kilometers wide from Swiss to Dutch frontiers.

Time limits for evacuation of Rhine territory: to the Rhine, eight days from time limits indicated above, making twenty-two days from signature of armistice; to the neutral zone, three days more, making twenty-five days in all

3. In all the territory evacuated by the enemy, no destruction of any kind shall be caused, nor any damage or prejudice to the persons or property of the inhabitants.

4. The enemy shall deliver 5,000 locomotives and 150,000 railways cars in good running order. Among this quantity 2,000 lo-

comotives and 135,000 cars represent the material carried away from Belgium and France; the surplus is necessary for the railroad service in the territory on left bank of Rhine.

5. German Commander shall be required to announce all mines or measures taken to cause delay in evacuated territory and to facilitate the searching out of acts of destruction.

6. As a guarantee, the blockade of Germany shall be maintained until the evacuation shall have been completed.

7. Allied prisoners shall be returned within shortest time possible under specified conditions.

Following naval conditions suggested:

Delivery of 150 submarines, representing approximately the number actually in commission.

Entire German surface fleet shall gather in Baltic ports. Port of Cuxhaven and Island of Heligoland to be occupied by allied fleets.

Enemy to indicate positions of all his mine fields excepting those anchored in his territorial waters. Allies to have the right to remove the latter where they consider it necessary.

TC telegram (E. M. House Papers, CtY).
¹ Wilson decoded the first portion of this telegram in his own shorthand, up to the word "Maubeuge." Then Close decoded it in longhand up to the words "territory evacuated." Wilson then completed the decode in his own shorthand.

From Edward Beale McLean

My dear Mr. President: Washington, D. C. Oct. 27, 1918.

I beg to assure you that I am honored by your letter of Oct. 26, and to say that if The Post has not discussed in detail every one of your public policies, domestic as well as those connected with the war, it has not been because of any lack of ardent sympathy with you in your great tasks. Indeed, for the last three years I have constantly endeavored to make The Post and the Cincinnati Enquirer sympathetically helpful to you, but I am compelled to say that when I have advised members of your official family, who appeared to be clothed with some authority, of my desire to be of service to you, my offers have fallen upon deaf ears.

Notwithstanding this fact, Mr. President, I trust you will accept my hearty assurance of deep appreciation of the many great problems with which you are so successfully dealing in this present national crisis. I am, with great respect,

Sincerely yours,   Edward McLean.

TLS (WP, DLC).

From William Gibbs McAdoo, with Enclosure

Dear Governor,   [Washington] Oct 27 [1918].

Please read this *first*. The letter is 4 pages only. The exhibits are also worth reading.[1]   WGM

ALI (WP, DLC).
[1] WGM to WW, "MEMORANDUM ON THE FINANCIAL SITUATION, EXISTING AND PRO-SPECTIVE, BETWEEN THE GOVERNMENTS OF THE UNITED STATES AND FRANCE," Oct. 22, 1918, TS MS; WGM to G. Clemenceau, July 3, 1918, CCS MS; and G. Clemenceau to WGM, June 9, 1918, T translation of telegram, all in WP, DLC.

E N C L O S U R E

From William Gibbs McAdoo

Dear Mr. President: Washington October 26, 1918.

I have heretofore discussed with you the French financial situation, but I think it of great importance that you should be fully informed concerning it, and I enclose a memorandum which has been prepared for me dealing with the subject. I also enclose a copy of M. Clemenceau's message of last June, and a copy of my reply which was sent with your approval.

You will recall that when M. Clemenceau's message was under discussion I felt that it was the desire of the French Government through the financial aid then requested of the United States Treasury to obtain credits in this country to provide for post-war expenditures in connection with the reconstruction of France. I have now been informed by M. de Billy that M. Tardieu is expected to reach here next week and during his short stay in this country desires to discuss with me the provision of credits to aid in the reconstruction of France and the dates to be fixed for the maturity of the French obligations held by the United States Government.

I feel it to be of great importance that we should be assured of a supply of francs for our Army in France during the war and after hostilities shall have ceased until the return of our troops, and it is clear that no discussion of this subject will be possible without entering on the questions which M. Tardieu desires to take up, even if we should otherwise prefer to postpone consideration of those questions. For reasons which I shall explain it seems essential that the British representatives should also participate in the discussions.

Unless the francs needed by our Army in France are obtained from the French Government resort would have to be had either to an offering of United States franc obligations or to the foreign exchange market. I should not want to be dependent upon floating a United States loan in France as such a step might seriously injure the credit of the United States. If we should be obliged to purchase on the market the exchange needed to produce the francs we require the dollar would speedily go to a discount as compared with the franc, and our whole foreign exchange situation would be badly disorganized. True, we might demand payment of the French obligations we hold to correct exchange, but such demand probably ought not to be made and might not be met if made, and our requirements for francs would nevertheless have to be supplied, be the consequences what they might. I am therefore most anxious to secure from the French Government an agreement to continue to supply the francs needed by our Army until their return home, against reimbursement in dollars, to be applied by the French Government only to the repayment of France's debt to the United States or other purposes specified or approved by the United States Treasury.

If the French Government does continue to so supply the francs for our Army it is to be anticipated that by the time peace is declared the French government will become entitled to a large amount of dollars in this country in excess of its war expenditures during the same period, and the amount will have been largely augmented by the time our Army reaches home, unless applied to the repayment of the French obligations held by the United States. These dollars France will be most anxious to use to pay for the commodities which it must purchase without its territory to provide for the reconstruction of the invaded portions of France. France must have foreign credits to meet these expenditures, as for some time after the war it is not likely to have either gold or commodities to meet all its foreign balances, and consequently no doubt will object to applying its accumulated dollars towards the payment of the loans heretofore made to it by the United States Government unless assured of the foreign credits needed for reconstruction purposes. In view of the provisions of the First Liberty Bond Act the United States can hardly refuse to exchange the demand obligations of the French Government acquired under the authority of that Act (about $550,000,000 in amount) for long time obligations, and without the acquiescence of the French Government a demand for the payment immediately after the war of the indebtedness of France to us incurred before our Army participated in force in the battles upon the western front could not be made with very good grace nor would it appeal to our people as fair treatment.

It is obvious that, to relieve us of the burden of foreign expenditures to support our Army as well as for other and even more urgent reasons, we must make every effort to have our forces returned home as speedily as practicable. How quickly this can be done depends partly on the progress of our shipbuilding before peace is declared, but in part also on whether we can obtain the use of foreign ships. If British ships are used for commercial purposes while our ships are engaged in bringing home our Army, and if British Empire products are sold for cash while ours are to a large extent sold against dollar credits established in exchange for francs supplied to our Army, the inevitable result will be that Great Britain will secure an undue share of the cash markets of the world. It is most necessary that we arrange to secure such use of British or other foreign ships as may be requisite to bring our soldiers home expeditiously, and that Great Britain should share with us in supplying the credits required to defray the cost of the commodities needed for the reconstruction of France. I have no reason to believe that Great Britain will not be willing, in cooperation with the United States, to provide credits for the reconstruction of France, but in view of the loans made by Great Britain to the Allied Governments before we entered the war—its loans to France since the commencement of the war to the present time being upwards of £400,000,000 or, say, $2,000,000,000—a discussion with Great Britain may involve a general discussion as to the war indebtedness incurred by the various Allied Governments to the British government, and the indebtedness (now amounting to $3,652,000,000) of the British Government to the United States.

The dimensions of the British problem of bringing home her army in France and of obtaining the francs needed for its support until its return are so much less formidable than our problem that I merely refer to it.

I am sending you this letter for your information so that you may be informed of the questions which are about to be brought up for discussion by M. Tardieu upon his arrival next week. No action upon your part is required at this time unless, indeed, you have some directions to give me concerning the matter.

Cordially yours,   W G McAdoo

TLS (WP, DLC).

From William Gibbs McAdoo, with Enclosure

Dear Governor,   [Washington] Oct 27 [1918].

Please read this *Second*—

WGM

ALI (WP, DLC).

E   N   C   L   O   S   U   R   E

From William Gibbs McAdoo

Dear Mr. President: Washington October 26, 1918.

In my letter of this morning I called to your attention the financial questions which it is anticipated will form the subject of discussions almost immediately between the United States Treasury and the representatives of the French and British Governments. These discussions cannot but lead to further questions being raised which will have a bearing on peace negotiations.

I feel I should draw your attention to some of the financial phases of the peace problem and the importance of insuring adequate presentation of the views of the United States on these questions at the Peace Conference.

As settlements at the Peace Conference may involve supplying France with gold or foreign credits, the use of the German mercantile fleet and other matters that will have a vital bearing on the questions indicated in my previous letter to you of this date I do not anticipate that any final settlement of these questions can be effected until the Peace Conference. I do think, however, that it may be possible at the discussions about to take place to establish some general principles for dealing with these matters and in any event such discussions will go far to clarify the situation.

The financial questions referred to in my letter of this morning are sure in some form or other to crop out about the peace table in spite of any tentative arrangements made before that time. There are other questions of finance that must then be determined, in many of which our country is vitally concerned and in all of which we are at least indirectly interested. A permanent and satisfactory peace can scarcely be realized if the financial conditions are not such as to permit the various nationalities to prosper materially and to reap the rewards of industry and frugality.

Among the other financial questions that will no doubt receive consideration at a Peace Conference are—

(1) Those arising from territorial readjustments, involving considerations of war and pre-war debt, character and purposes of past borrowing, relative wealth and resources of different territorial areas, currency and banking.

(2) Those arising from reparation, involving consideration of war expenditures, extent to which they have a permanent residual value, extent of damage by the enemy, both in the ordinary course of war and in violation of international law, including seizures of money and securities, destruction at sea as well as on land, payments exacted in occupied territory for legitimate purposes or for spoil[i]ation, and also a study

of the sources of wealth and financial limitations of nationalities so as to determine the amount of any payments that
can safely be required without impairing financial resources
beyond the safety point.

(3) Those arising regarding reconstruction, involving consideration of the extent to which neutral countries should be
required to participate in the reconstruction of devastated
areas by the supply of materials, the wealth and financial
resources of such neutral countries, and the methods of financing the actual work of reconstruction in the devastated
areas.

(4) Those arising regarding the use and disposition of seques-
tered property in the various belligerent countries. It is reported that the Alien Property Custodian holds a large amount
of property, and delicate and important financial questions
may be involved in the disposition of this and similar funds
held in other countries.

(5) Those arising from demands that will no doubt be presented
by some of the associated governments in regard to restoring
gold reserves, involving a consideration of the present and
pre-war gold and currency situation of the belligerent countries.

(6) Those arising in respect of the war indebtedness of governments *inter se*. It may be anticipated that questions of a
general readjustment of this debt will be raised by the nations
which have been both borrowers and lenders and with which
the United States, as one of the principal lending nations, is
preeminently concerned from a financial standpoint. Such
questions would involve studies from the financial standpoint
concerning the international trade and finance during the
pre-war period of the countries concerned, their earnings
and expenditures on account of shipping, capital investment,
internal and external debt, and other data required to form
a judgment as to the ability of the debtor nations to pay
interest on their indebtedness and to amortize the principal.
From the standpoint of our own financial safety the importance of holding the obligations of the foreign governments
which we have acquired I think must be apparent in any
consideration of the questions I have presented, and I cannot
too strongly deprecate the suggestion that we should cancel
the indebtedness of the Allied Governments which we hold,
which is being made by various individuals who are not
charged with any responsibility and who are necessarily ignorant of the complicated problems involved.

I am not attempting to state all of the financial questions which may arise at the Peace Conference, nor to go into them in detail. Those mentioned will serve to indicate the importance of the financial problems to the United States and the desirability—if not the necessity—of the Treasury's being represented on any Peace Commission that may be constituted. The magnitude of the task of preparing the statistical information and studies which are necessary if the Commission is to be fully equipped for its work will readily suggest itself to you, and I recommend that the Treasury, working in close cooperation with the inquiry being conducted under Colonel House, should be charged with the preparation of the financial information necessary to equip the Peace Commission to deal effectively with the financial phases of the peace negotiations. I have every reason to believe that such an arrangement would be welcomed by those in charge of the inquiry.

Cordially yours,   W G McAdoo

TLS (WP, DLC).

A Draft of a Telegram from Newton Diehl Baker to John Joseph Pershing

[Washington] October 27, 1918.

Replying to your cablegram from London, October twenty-six, the President directs me to say that he is relying upon your counsel and advice in this matter, and in making the following comments he will be glad to have you feel entirely free to bring to his attention any consideration he may have overlooked which in your judgment ought to be weighed before settling finally his views.

In general, the President approves of your Number One, in sub-paragraph, but suggests wisdom of retention of at least part of German heavy guns in pledge, and specific enumeration of territory to be evacuated other than France and Belgium. This has to do especially with territory to the east and southeast, but should not Luxemburg be also included?

With regard to your Second in sub-paragraph, the President raises the question as to whether it is necessary for Allied or American Army actually to occupy Alsace and Lorraine when evacuated under armistice.

With regard to your Third in sub-paragraph, the President doubts advisability of requiring Allied or American occupation on eastern side of the Rhine, as that is practically an invasion of German soil under armistice.

The President concurs in your Fourth in sub-paragraph.

With regard to your Fifth in sub-paragraph, the President assumes this to mean repatriation of troops now in German army which have been recruited from non-German soil occupied by Germans. In this sense he approves.

With regard to your Sixth, the President believes it would be enough to require internment of U-boats in neutral waters, and a further pledge and also to further unrestricted transportation of American army and material referred to in your Fourth, but does not think terms of armistice should suggest ultimate disposition of such U-boats, nor that U-boat bases should be occupied under armistice, as that would mean Allied or American occupation of German soil not now in their possession.

Your Seventh in sub-paragraph, the President approves.

In general, the President feels the terms of the armistice should be rigid enough to secure us against renewal of hostilities by Germany but not humiliating beyond that necessity, as such terms would throw the advantage to the military party in Germany.

The President would be glad to have you confer with Colonel House, who is now in France, showing him copy of your dispatch and this answer, and generally discussing with him all phases of this subject. Newton D. Baker

CC telegram (WP, DLC).

From Newton Diehl Baker, with Enclosure

Dear Mr. President: Washington. October 28, 1918.

I enclose a corrected copy of the dispatch as sent. The change made with regard to General Pershing's Number 4 necessitated a corresponding change with regard to his Number 6.

With regard to General Pershing's Number 5, the word which was translated "native troops" in the code also reads "nationals." I therefore added the underlined words to cover the other interpretation of that part of the message.

Do you not think it would be wise to send a copy of General Pershing's cable and this reply, confidentially, to General Bliss?

Respectfully yours, Newton D. Baker

TLS (WP, DLC).

E N C L O S U R E

Washington. October 27, 1918.

Replying to your cablegram from London October 26th, the President directs me to say that he is relying upon your counsel and advice in this matter, and in making the following comments he will be glad to have you feel entirely free to bring to his attention any consideration he may have overlooked which in your judgment ought to be weighed before settling finally his views.

In general, the President approves of your first, in subparagraph, but suggests wisdom of retention of at least part of German heavy guns, in pledge, and specific enumeration of territory to be evacuated other than France and Belgium. This has to do especially with territory to the east and southeast, but should not Luxemburg be also included?

With regard to your Second in subparagraph, the President raises the question as to whether it is necessary for Allied or American Army actually to occupy Alsace and Lorraine when evacuated under armistice.

With regard to your Third in subparagraph, the President doubts advisability of requiring Allied or American occupation on eastern side of the Rhine, as that is practically an invasion of German soil under armistice.

The President concurs in your Fourth in subparagraph to the extent of continuing transportation for supplies of troops then in France but would not insist on right to increase American force during armistice.

With regard to your Fifth in subparagraph, if this means repatriation of troops now in German army which have been recruited from non-German soil occupied by Germans, *or repatriation of civil population deported from occupied territory*, the President approves.

With regard to your Sixth, the President believes it would be enough to require internment of U-boats in neutral waters, as a further pledge and also to further unrestricted transportation of American material referred to in your Fourth, but does not think terms of armistice should suggest ultimate disposition of such U-boats, nor that U-boat bases should be occupied under armistice, as that would mean Allied or American occupation of German soil not now in their possession.

Your Seventh in subparagraph, the President approves.

In general, the President feels the terms of the armistice should be rigid enough to secure us against renewal of hostilities by Germany but not humiliating beyond that necessity, as such terms would throw the advantage to the military party in Germany.

The President would be glad to have you confer with Colonel House, who is now in France, showing him copy of your dispatch and this answer, and generally discussing with him all phases of this subject. Baker.   P. C. March

T telegram (WP, DLC).

From Edward Mandell House

Paris 28/10/18

[Three urgent] Things are moving so rapidly that the question of the place of the peace conference is upon us. The French are urging Paris, the Belgians Brussels. The only objection to Paris is that if a sharp difference should arise between one of the Allies and the French it might be embarrassing. Otherwise it is desirable. Will you not advise as to your preference. Supreme War Council will not meet until Wednesday.   Edward House

T transcript of WWsh decode (WP, DLC).

Two Telegrams to Edward Mandell House

For House. No. One.   [The White House, Oct. 28, 1918]

My deliberate judgment is that our whole weight should be thrown for an armistice which will prevent a renewal of hostilities by Germany but which will be as moderate and reasonable as possible within those limits, because it is certain that too much success or security on the part of the Allies will make a genuine peace settlement exceedingly difficult if not impossible. The position of Haig and Milner and Petain as reported by our commander-in-chief is therefore safer than Foch's. See Baker's despatch of today to commander-in-chief. Foresight is wiser than immediate advantage.
          Wilson.[1]

WWT telegram (WP, DLC).
[1] The text of this message as House decoded it reads as follows:
"My deliberate judgment is that our whole weight should be thrown for an armistice which will not permit a renewal of hostilities by Germany but which will be as moderate and reasonable as possible within that condition, because lately I am certain that too much severity on the part of the Allies will make a genuine peace settlement exceedingly difficult if not impossible.
"The position of Haig and Milner and Petain as reported and Pershing is therefore subordinate to Foch. See Baker's despatch of today to Pershing. Foresight is wiser than immediate advantage." WW to EMH, Oct. 29, 1918, T telegram (E. M. House Papers, CtY).

No. Two.   The White House. October 28/18
[In reply to your despatch No. 3.]

Much as I should enjoy Paris I think neutral place of meeting much wiser care being taken not to choose a place where either German or English influence would be strong. My preference is for Lausanne.   Wilson.

WWhw telegram (WP, DLC).

Naval Terms of An Armistice[1]

Recommendations by Sims[2]   [Oct. 28, 1918]

1. Enemy submarines to cease hostilities immediately upon the signing of the armistice.

2. Enemy to lay no mines outside his territorial waters during the armistice. ⟨Allies to continue to have the right to lay mines outside of enemy territorial waters.⟩

3. Enemy to do no mine sweeping outside his own territorial waters. ⟨Allies to be free to sweep for mines anywhere except in enemy territorial waters.⟩ Enemy to disclose the location of all mine fields laid by him outside his own territorial waters⟨.⟩ *near allied or neutral shores.*

4. Allied blockade aod [and] restrictions on ocean-borne commerce to continue as at present.

⟨5. Allied naval vessels to be employed outside enemy territorial waters in any manner desired not involving attack on enemy territory, vessels, or property.⟩

⟨6. Same restrictions and privileges to apply to our own aircraft as to naval vessels.⟩

⟨7⟩ 5. Enemy naval forces to evacuate (a) all coasts and ports of ⟨*neutral,*⟩ occupied ⟨, or allied⟩ countries; (b) all ports and coasts of disputed territory which by the terms of the armistice military forces are to evacuate, including (c) the ports and coasts formerly included in the Empire of Russia.

⟨Note: Coasts and ports of countries under (b) and (c) not to be occupied by the Allies during the armistice.⟩

⟨8⟩ 6. No damage of any kind to be done by the enemy to any of evacuated coasts or ports ⟨before evacuation⟩ and no military *or naval* stores, provisions, or munitions to be destroyed or to be removed before evacuation.

⟨9⟩ 7. All enemy naval surface craft of all classes shall withdraw for the duration of the armistice to enemy waters or bases as follows: Enemy vessels now in the North Sea, Baltic, or German home ports to the German Baltic ports; enemy vessels in the ⟨home ports to⟩ *Mediterranean, Adriatic,* Aegean and adjacent waters, excepting the Black Sea and its tributaries, to the Austrian Adriatic ports; Enemy vessels in the Black Sea and its tributaries to remain in that Sea; vess[e]ls formerly belonging to Russia and now in the possession of the enemy to be surrendered to the Allies at such place or places and under such conditions as may be prescribed by the allied commanders in chief in the North Sea and Mediterranean. No damage of any kind to be done to these vessels by the enemy.

⟨before surrender.⟩ Final disposition of these vessels to be determined by the treaty of peace.

⟨10⟩ 8. All enemy submarines, except only such of those under construction as are not yet launched, to be interned in ⟨allied⟩ *specified neutral* ports for the duration of the war *under such conditions as would ensure their detention.* ⟨Final disposition of these to be determined by the treaty of peace.⟩

⟨11⟩ 9. All enemy naval aircraft to be concentrated at enemy base specified by the Allies, and to remain there during the armistice.

⟨12. All naval and mercantile marine prisoners in the enemy's hands to be returned in the shortest possible time, without reciprocity, and authorization to be given by enemy for the immediate release of naval and mercantile marine prisoners of the Allies and of the United States interned in neutral countries.⟩

⟨13. The merchant ships of all nations at war with Germany now in enemy control to be handed over to the Allies, without reciprocity, in ports or bases to be specified by the Allies.⟩

⟨14⟩ 10. All the above measures to be executed in the shortest possible time.

⟨15⟩ 11. In the above proposals wherever the word "Allies" or its derivative was used it should be interpreted to include all the powers actively associated in the war against the Central Powers.[3]

WWT MS (WP, DLC).
[1] Secretary Daniels, on October 15, had requested Sims and his aides to suggest the naval terms of an armistice. Sims replied on October 25. David F. Trask, *Captains and Cabinets: Anglo-American Relations, 1917-1918* (Columbia, Mo., 1972), pp. 328-30.
Wilson copied Sims' terms and then edited them in the following document. Words in angle brackets deleted by Wilson; those in italics added by him.
[2] Transcript of WWsh.
[3] Wilson's edited version was sent (via Sims) as Opnav to EMH and W. S. Benson, No. 3998, Oct. 28, 1918, T telegram, enclosed in W. V. Pratt to WW, Oct. 29, 1918, ALS, both in WP, DLC.

To Gilbert Fairchild Close, with Enclosure

Dear Close,   [The White House, Oct. 28, 1918]

Please copy the enclosed (revised) draft letter to Senator Simmons and send it over for my signature as soon as you can. Please send it to Mr. Hoover, the Head Usher, and ask him to present it to me for signature at the earliest possible opportunity.

W.W.

WWTLI (J. P. Tumulty Papers, DLC).

E N C L O S U R E[1]

Dear Senator:

⟨Of course,⟩ I am glad to respond to the question addressed to me by your ⟨interesting⟩ letter of October 26th.[2] The words I used in my address to the Congress of January 8, 1918, were:

"The removal, so far as possible, of all economic barriers and the establishment of an equality of trade conditions among all the nations consenting to the peace and associating themselves for its maintenance."

⟨Under this paragraph every sovereign nation always would have the right to determine its own economic policy. There can be no doubt about that. But⟩ *I of course meant to suggest no restriction upon the free determination by any nation of its own economic policy, but only that,* whatever tariff any nation might deem necessary for its own economic ⟨existence⟩ *service,* be that tariff high or low, *it* should apply equally to all foreign nations: ⟨In⟩ *in* other words, *that* there should be no discriminations against ⟨certain⟩ *some* nations that ⟨do⟩ *did* not apply to others ⟨countries⟩. This leaves every nation free to determine for itself its own <u>internal</u> policies ⟨,but such policies must not be⟩ *and limits only <u>its right</u> to* compound⟨ed⟩ *those policies* of ⟨purely⟩ hostile discriminations between one nation and another. Weapons of economic discipline and punishment should be left to the joint action of all nations for the purpose of punishing those who will not submit to a general program of justice and equality.

The experiences of the past among nations have taught us that the attempt by one nation to punish another by exclusive and discriminatory trade agreements has been a prolific breeder of that kind of antagonism which oftentimes results in war, and that if a permanent peace is to be established among nations every obstacle that has stood in the way of international friendship should be cast aside. It was with that fundamental purpose in mind that I announced this principle in my address of January 8th. To pervert this great principle for partisan purposes, and to inject the bogey of free-trade, which is not involved at all, is to attempt to divert the mind of the nation from the broad and humane principle of a durable peace by introducing an internal question of quite another kind. ⟨Indeed, America has always stood in the past for this very thing under administrations, Republican as well as Democratic, when we have made treaties with nations embodying what is known as the Favored Nation Clause, through which the United States was always willing to apply to every nation the same tariff that it found necessary for its own protection to impose on every other nation.⟩ American business has in the past been unaffected by a policy of ⟨this⟩ the kind⟨,⟩ *suggested* and it has nothing to fear now from a policy of simple international justice. It is *indeed* lamentable ⟨, indeed,⟩ that the momentous issues of this solemn hour should be seized ⟨in the designing⟩ *upon in an* effort to bend them to partisan service. To the initiated and discerning, the motive is transparent and the attempt fails.[3]

T MS (J. P. Tumulty Papers, DLC).
[1] Tumulty wrote the draft of this letter. Words in angle brackets deleted by Wilson; those in italics added by him.
[2] F. M. Simmons to WW, Oct. 26, 1918, TLS (WP, DLC).
[3] The edited version was sent as WW to F. M. Simmons, Oct. 28, 1918, TLS (Letterpress Books, WP, DLC).

To Edward Parson Smith[1]

The White House 28 October, 1918

I cannot refrain from expressing my deep interest in the election of Mr. Morehead[2] to the United States Senate. I not only know something of his quality but I have more particularly in mind the delicate and difficult tasks immediately ahead of the Congress and am convinced that it would be of the utmost value not only to Nebraska but to the country to have a man of his quality and principles in the Senate. We need men with just his steadfast loyalty to the cause which now stands in need of unfaltering support.

Woodrow Wilson

T telegram (Letterpress Books, WP, DLC).
[1] Mayor of Omaha, Neb.
[2] John Henry Morehead, Governor of Nebraska, 1913-1917; at this time running against Senator George W. Norris.

To Zachary Taylor Malaby[1]

[The White House] 28 October 1918.

I am glad to say in reply to your inquiry[2] that Mr. Randall's[3] course in Congress has proved of the highest value to the country and that I should deem it a distinct loss at this critical time if he were not returned.   Woodrow Wilson.

T telegram (Letterpress Books, WP, DLC).
[1] Physician of Pasadena, Calif.; active in Democratic party affairs in southern California.
[2] The communication to which Wilson is replying is Z. T. Malaby to G. R. Cooksey, Oct. 26, 1918, T telegram (J. P. Tumulty Papers, DLC).
[3] Charles Hiram Randall, Democratic and Prohibition congressman from Los Angeles.

To William Penn Metcalf[1]

[The White House] 28 October 1918.

Your question[2] whether I would be willing to depend upon Senator Fall's support in settling our foreign relations is easily answered. I would not. He has given such repeated evidence of his entire hostility to this Administration that I would be ignoring his whole course of action if I did. No one who wishes to sustain me can intelligently vote for him. If that is the issue the voters of New Mexico wish to vote upon it is easily determined.

Woodrow Wilson.

T telegram (Letterpress Books, WP, DLC).
  [1] A real estate and insurance broker of Albuquerque, Socialist candidate for the United States Senate in New Mexico.
  [2] It is missing in WP, DLC, but it was W. P. Metcalf to WW, Oct. 26, 1918, telegram printed in *Cong. Record*, 65th Cong., 2d sess., p. 11525. Wilson's reply is also printed in *ibid.*

Basil Miles to Robert Lansing, with Enclosures

Washington October 28, 1918

MEMORANDUM for the Secretary of State:

CONTROL OF SIBERIAN RAILWAYS

The attached telegram from Ambassador Morris would seem to indicate that what he suggested some time back as possible has now actually happened; namely, that the Japanese General Staff has gone ahead with plans of its own in North Manchuria, including practical absorption of the Chinese Eastern Railway, and left it for the Foreign Office to explain the accomplished fact.

Mr. Stevens says divided operation of the railway and any of its branches is impossible; Mr Morris believes the successful operation of the railways is fundamental to all our plans to assist the Russian population.

We propose some kind of joint supervision, with Stevens directing operations and representing Russia and not the United States. Time presses. I regard the Japanese action as at variance with the President's expressed views and purposes; it conflicts sharply with what you have proposed to the Japanese Government.

We do not wish to exclude Japan from any joint action or assistance; but I think we are equally committed to prevent any separate action and recommend that this fact be made clear to the Japanese Government.   Basil Miles

TS MS (WP, DLC).

E N C L O S U R E   I

Tokio. Oct. 25, 1918.

My visit to Harbin has enabled me to confirm the following facts:

First. During the last six weeks 40,000 Japanese troops have passed through Northern Manchuria. These figures are taken from careful examination compiled separate from the railway service corps.

Second. Of these troops 6,000 as estimated by our army officers, are located in barracks at Harbin. All the available barracks, about 19 in number, have been taken over by the Japanese and although several of the large barracks are merely guarded and not occupied, it has thus far been impossible to obtain any quarters for the American troops which General Graves had planned to send. Friendly efforts of Russian and Chinese officials to obtain from the Japanese military authorities one of unoccupied barracks for American use have been unsuccessful.

Third. The stations and yards of the Chinese Eastern at Harbin are virtually under the control of the Japanese singly, who supervise the movement of all freight and the distribution of all cars.

Fourth. The Russian railway officials are permitted to remain at the stations but are compelled, by show of force, to submit to the directing of the Japanese garrison commanders.

Fifth. Outside of Harbin, Japanese garrisons have been placed at the following stations along the Chinese Eastern: Pogianichnaya 150, Moline 153, Handaohedzy 500, Imianpo 200, Ancon 60, Tsitsihar 210, Djalantoon 50, Boohedoo 100, Hailar 200, Manchuli 4, Kuanchentzie 100, intermediate stations, 100.[1]

Sixth. The total number of Japanese troops thus stationed on the main line, including Harbin, is approximately 12,000. In addition, I am informed that 20,000 are preparing to winter at Chita, commanding the junction of the Amur Railway, which is being carefully policed with Japanese soldiers. Japanese garrisons are also being placed at strategic points on the railway between Harbin and Vladivostok.

Seventh. During the last month, and while the Japanese troops have been occupying the railway, practically no freight except that intended for Japanese use have been allowed to move. All Japanese supply train[s] are carefully sealed and guarded by soldiers. No railway or other official is permitted to approach or examine them. This has naturally given rise to rumors that large quantities of Japanese goods are being shipped into Manchuria and Siberia for commercial purposes and free from customs inspection.

Eighth. Within the last few days Colonel Emerson has confirmed the following additional facts: A. The Japanese flag is being raised on the various stations, or on the adjoining railway property occupied; B. In several authenticated cases Russian railway employees have been evicted from the living quarters provided for them by the railway authorities, and Japanese soldiers have taken possession; C. Russian stationmasters and trainmen have been threatened unless they promptly recognized the authority of Japanese officers. As a result Colonel Emerson is informed that many of the Russian engineers are leaving and that there are Japanese railway men assembled at Changchuen prepared immediately to replace them.

Ninth. General Horvath has frankly admitted to Stevens that control of the operation of the Chinese Eastern has passed entirely out of his hands. The remnant of the Russian military guard is of course ignored. The Chinese soldiers are holding their ground at the various stations but are helpless before the Japanese garrison commanders and are being forced gradually to surrender their quarters.

Tenth. With the exception of a few American troops operating under Japanese senior command north of Vladivostok and seventy-five soldiers sent by General Graves to Harbin and quartered in the Red Cross offices there, the American forces are still in barracks at Vladivostok. I do not think they could at present move to any point along the entire length of the Chinese Eastern as all the available shelters have been appropriated by the Japanese authorities.

Eleventh. Colonel Emerson and his men are continuing their efforts to retain the position of instructors to the Russian personnel of the Chinese Eastern but Japanese interference is daily narrowing their field. They have been definitely excluded from assisting in any way the operation of Japanese troop or supply trains and are hampered in aiding the despatch of the few remaining passenger trains which the Russians are still permitted to run. These men of experience and capacity have met the situation with patience and judgment.

I submit this statement for the consideration of the Department as it forms the actual background of the present negotiations. Unless some clear understanding can be reached with the Japanese Government in regard to the meaning and purpose of this military occupation of the Chinese Eastern Railway, any assent to our proposed plan of operation would, I fear, be artificial and dangerous, and Mr. Stevens's position would rapidly become untenable.

Morris.

[1] The standard forms of the place names listed in this sentence are as follows: Po-

granichnaya (now Suifenho), Muling, Hengtowhotze, Imienpo, Antachan, Tsitsihar, Chalantun (now Yalu), Bukhedu (or Pokotu), Hailar, Manchouli, and Kwanchengtze (now Changchun).

E N C L O S U R E   I I

Tokio. Oct. 27, 1918.

The Japanese Government has refused the recent request of the British Government to send additional forces into Siberia to support the Czech[s] in the Volga region. The French Charge d'Affaires[1] was instructed to join in the request but did not receive his instructions until after the answer of the Japanese Government had been handed to my British colleague.   Morris.

T telegrams (WP, DLC).
[1] Unidentified.

To Robert Lansing

CONFIDENTIAL

My dear Mr. Secretary: The White House 29 October, 1918.

Thank you for letting me see the enclosed.[1] I think you have made an admirable reply.[2]

Cordially and sincerely yours,   Woodrow Wilson

TLS (R. Lansing Papers, DLC).
[1] This no doubt referred to Lansing's reply to a telegram sent from Harbin by Morris through Charles K. Moser, Consul at Harbin, in which Morris summarized the political situation in Siberia as it appeared to him after a month of daily conferences with "representative Russians and other careful observers." Morris found that there was no central government in Siberia which exercised real authority. The leading aspirant to power, he went on, was the group organized at Omsk, which had the support of Prince L'vov and was in touch with the Horvat regime. The group at Omsk had the sympathy of the British and French representatives, Morris continued, largely because it had cultivated close relations with the Czech forces in that region. There was intense jealousy in the local governments against any central organization, and Morris added that there was a strong and bitter Bolshevik sentiment in the larger towns along the Trans-Siberian Railway. For the present, he suggested the following policy: "One, that no recognition or assistance be accorded to any of the so called all Siberian Governments; two, that aid and advice be given by our representatives whenever possible to local governments in their efforts to improve local conditions; three, that in the proposed operation of the railways, no recognition be accorded to any one of the several Ministers of Way and Communications, who are now making futile efforts to exercise their jurisdiction, but that every assistance be given Mr. Stevens to introduce modern equipment and spirit of [co]operation; four, that our military forces be spread in groups over as large a part as possible of the Chinese Eastern and Trans-Siberian Railways with strict instructions to avoid all political entanglements and simply to maintain order along the line of the Railway." Morris thought that this policy would require some modification later, but he hoped that, by providing efficient and evenhanded operation of the railways and by retaining sufficient Allied and American troops for protection and support, "we can begin our economic and social program and at the same time permit the free development of local self-government out of which may grow a central Siberian authority which will be truly representative." R. S. Morris and C. K. Moser to RL, Oct. 18, 1918, T telegram (SDR, RG 59, 861.00/3008, DNA).
[2] Lansing replied as follows: "Department appreciates very helpful summary contained

in your October 18 eight p.m. from Harbin. Regarding your recommendations: First: The Russian Ambassador here has already been informed that this Government is not yet prepared to recognize any new government in Russia, although this decision must not be construed as a lack of sympathy with efforts to restore a stable government which will be able to protect individual rights and fulfil its international obligations. Second: The Consul General at Irkutsk has been authorized to have consular representatives in Siberia give aid and advice to local governments in efforts to improve local conditions wherever opportunity offers. Third: Department concurs and would like to know whether this question cannot be met for the present by dealing with the management of the Ussuri, Chinese-Eastern, Trans-Baikal and other sections of the Siberian system. Four: Will advise you later how, if at all, it may be practicable to follow your recommendation.

"The Department concurs in views expressed in last paragraph of your telegram excepting employment of troops which under consideration and wishes to inform you have fulfilled admirably the purpose of your visit to Vladivostok." RL to R. S. Morris, Oct. 23, 1918, T telegram (SDR, RG 59, 861.00/3008, DNA).

To Edward Keating

My dear Mr. Keating: [The White House] 29 October, 1918.

May I not turn aside from the hurry of the day to congratulate you on your good work in behalf of labor legislation, children's bureau, needed civil pensions, etc.? You are certainly engaged in a good cause and are following it with diligence.

I sincerely hope that I may have the benefit of your cooperation in these matters at the next session of Congress.

Cordially and sincerely yours,   Woodrow Wilson

TLS (Letterpress Books, WP, DLC).

To James Hall Caine[1]

My dear Mr. Caine: [The White House] 29 October, 1918.

In reply to your inquiry,[2] which I am glad to answer, let me say that I should regard the loss of Mr. Weaver from the Congress a very serious one indeed. Alike by his services and by his quality he has won the admiration of those who have the public welfare most at heart, and I hope most sincerely that the voters of the Tenth District appreciate his quality as we do.

Cordially and sincerely yours,   Woodrow Wilson

TLS (Letterpress Books, WP, DLC).
  [1] Editor of the Asheville, N. C., *Citizen.*
  [2] It is missing.

To Harry Clay Adler[1]

My dear Mr. Adler: [The White House] 29 October, 1918

I have your letter of October 26th[2] telling me that it is being stated in Tennessee that I desire the election of the Hon. H. Clay

Evans,[3] Republican, and the defeat of the Hon. John K. Shields, Democrat, for the United States Senate, and asking me whether the statement is true. Of course, it is not. I do not know that the people of Tennessee will wish to be guided by my preference in a case of this sort, but I do feel that I am at liberty to deny this unfounded and absolutely unwarranted statement.

Cordially and sincerely yours,   Woodrow Wilson

TLS (Letterpress Books, WP, DLC).
[1] General Manager of the *Chattanooga Daily Times*
[2] H. C. Adler to WW, Oct. 26, 1918, ALS (WP, DLC).
[3] Henry Clay Evans, a manufacturer and former Mayor of Chattanooga; former congressman, United States Commissioner of Pensions, and Consul General in London.

To Albert Sidney Burleson, with Enclosure

My dear Burleson: The White House 29 October, 1918.

I cannot help having a good deal of sympathy with Mr. Gavit's letter enclosed. What is your own judgment?

Cordially and faithfully yours,   Woodrow Wilson

TLS (A. S. Burleson Papers, DLC).

E N C L O S U R E

John Palmer Gavit to Joseph Patrick Tumulty

PERSONAL

Dear Joe: [New York] October 25, 1918.

What do you suppose would have happened to "The Masses" or to Rose Pastor Stokes, or even to Oswald Garrison Villard, had they published this cartoon?[1] Personally, I have no interest in or sympathy with the business of punishing people, little or big, for the expression of ideas, however abhorrent to me. But I do believe in fair play, and so far as this particular matter is concerned, I have only contempt for that "enforcement of the law"—save the mark!— that is ruthless toward the little fellows, but is palsied, its bowels turned to water, in the presence of precisely the same conduct on the part of the great ones. I understand perfectly that there will be a claim that there is a difference between this case and the others, but I think the claim is piffle.

I'll bet four dollars you agree with me!

Affectionately, as ever,   John P. Gavit

TLS (WP, DLC).
[1] "Their Only Hope," *The North American Review's War Weekly*, I (Oct. 19, 1918), 8-9. The cartoon, undoubtedly inspired by George B. M. Harvey, the editor, depicted worried German warlords having a vision of Wilson at his typewriter.

From Sherman Leland Whipple

Dear Mr. President: Washington October 29, 1918.

While I do not assume that my opinion can merit your too kindly expressions, may I yet have the indulgence of saying one other thought that I have carried heavily and anxiously in my mind?

I earnestly hope that the present occasion will not be permitted to pass without a firm insistence upon a frank and explicit expression of the war aims of each of our associated nations—especially Great Britain.

A reputable journal has recently stated that it would be embarrassing for England to state her war aims with Germany's army in the field. This is a most suggestive statement. What difference whether England expresses her views now or after Germany's army is demobilized or helpless? England's failure to declare herself is at least susceptible of the inference that she entertains designs which Germany's army in the field might check or interfere with.

What these designs are has never been fully disclosed, but the intimations given out are disquieting. Mr. Balfour has just stated that England could never permit Germany's colonies to be restored to her—and intimates pretty plainly that England herself will take them over. But a few days ago either Mr. Balfour or some other English statesman put out the suggestion that Germany's war fleet should be divided among the Allies in proportion to their naval losses,—which means that practically the whole fleet would go to England. Will she also demand the German commercial fleet, including, perhaps, the interned ships which we now hold?

With the German army broken, I see no nation or combination of nations who, if they desired, could deny England's demands. We certainly would be helpless, with three or four million soldiers three thousand miles across the sea, practically hostages, because they could be fed only by England's grace.

It may be said that England's sense of gratitude would never permit her to make or insist upon unrighteous or unfair demands; but if this be true, why should she not be willing now to state her demands frankly and fully, as you have stated ours?

I feel sure of your pardon for writing thus. I am certain you have thought it all out, yet I am very, very anxious about it, and so I have taken the liberty to write—perhaps too much for my own mental relief.

Pray do not trouble to answer. You must have so many letters that you feel constrained to reply to. It is quite enough to be assured that the thought is certainly in your mind.

                              Sincerely yours,   Sherman L. Whipple

TLS (WP, DLC).

To Sherman Leland Whipple

My dear Mr. Whipple: [The White House] 29 October, 1918.

Thank you for your letter of October 29th. You may be sure I am keenly alive to the dangers upon which it very properly dwells.

Cordially and sincerely yours,   Woodrow Wilson

TLS (Letterpress Books, WP, DLC).

To Edward Beale McLean

My dear Mr. McLean: [The White House] 29 October, 1918

I sincerely appreciate your kind letter of the twenty-seventh. I am distressed that you should feel that you do not always get the guidance you ask for. I am sure that the omission is never intentional or from any lack of the most cordial feeling, but I beg that if you care to apply to me directly at any time, you may be sure that I would be very glad indeed to answer.

Cordially and sincerely yours,   Woodrow Wilson

TLS (Letterpress Books, WP, DLC).

To Joseph Patrick Tumulty

Dear Tumulty: [The White House] 29 October, 1918

Of course I feel it awkward to acc[e]pt a gift of this sort.[1] I would accept it from Fairbanks if from anybody. Perhaps you might just suggest to him to do it without asking anybody's consent but your own.   The President

TL (J. P. Tumulty Papers, DLC).
[1] Douglas Fairbanks, the motion-picture actor and producer, had offered to give Wilson a "projecting machine," which could be set up in any room. "Any picture or star picture or weekly review," Fairbanks wrote, could be ordered from the local exchange and sent to the White House within an hour. He thought that, "during the stress of these times, together with the 'Flu,' the President might enjoy a little recreation." D. Fairbanks to JPT, c. Oct. 29, 1918, TCL (J. P. Tumulty Papers, DLC). Tumulty commented: "Dear Governor, This would be a great entertainment. I know Fairbanks very well. He has no desire to advertise himself in this way. It is an act of real friendship. Sincerely Tumulty." JPT to WW, c. Oct. 29, 1918, ALS written on *ibid.*

To Grosvenor Blaine Clarkson

My dear Mr. Clarkson: [The White House] 29 October, 1918

Through the courtesy of the Secretary of War, I have received your generous letter of the 26th of October. I know that you will understand that I have time only for a brief acknowledgment, but

I hope you will understand also how genuine a gratitude and appreciation goes with these few lines.

Cordially and sincerely yours,   Woodrow Wilson

TLS (Letterpress Books, WP, DLC).

To Cleveland Hoadley Dodge

My dear Cleve: The White House 29 October, 1918.

Thank you for your letter of the 24th. Of course there is no one I would be more delighted to have in the Federal Reserve Board than Tom Jones. I am interested to know that Mr. Harding thinks there would be no renewal of the old objection in the Senate. I will try to find out what makes him think so.

In great haste,   Affectionately yours,   Woodrow Wilson

TLS (WC, NjP).

To Mary Owen Graham[1]

My dear Miss Graham: [The White House] 29 October, 1918.

I have heard with the deepest sorrow of the death of Dr. Graham. I counted him among my valued personal friends not only, but I know how great a service he was rendering the University and the State and how sadly he will be missed. By gift and character alike he was qualified to play a distinguished part and was playing it to the admiration of all who knew him.

With warmest sympathy,

Cordially and sincerely yours,   Woodrow Wilson

TLS (Letterpress Books, WP, DLC).
[1] Sister of Edward Kidder Graham, President of the University of North Carolina, who had died from influenza on October 26, 1918. Miss Graham was President of the Peace Institute in Raleigh, N. C.

A Memorandum by Franklin Delano Roosevelt, with Enclosures

Washington [c. Oct. 29, 1918].

Memorandum for the President

1. The written addition to the first line shows that the decisions were reached prior to receipt of your message.
2. I enclose memorandum to me from Capt. Pratt.[1] I cannot wholly agree.

3. I think we must remember that the naval terms must to a large extent follow the *tenor* of the army terms, for the latter are unquestionably more vital to the situation.

4. I agree with Pratt that to gain time before sending terms to Germany would be of benefit. But if we are going to send army terms we must send Naval terms also—and in my judgment it will be less difficult for Germany to accept harsh Naval terms than harsh army terms.

5. I do not believe the terms to Germany should differ materially from the terms to Austria—except in regard to the right to maintain order in Austria if that becomes necessary.

Franklin D Roosevelt

HwS MS (WP, DLC).
¹ That is, William Veazie Pratt, Assistant Chief of Naval Operations.

E N C L O S U R E   I

MEMORANDUM FOR THE SECRETARY.

Please note the addition to the first line of cable, which changes its entire complexion.

As I read the cable, these are the decisions arrived at by the Allied Naval Council, but subject to the approval of the governments concerned.

Where the purely naval features involve no departure from governmental policies or conceptions of future policy it might be wise to accept those decisions. But where they do, it seems wiser to pause and consider the situation more thoroughly.

The within terms of armistice do represent a view point which is at variance with the terms indicated by the President.

Attention is invited to the paragraph beginning with line twenty, first page, the Allied Council's assumptions, special reference to last clause.¹

The result of these terms as apart from the intent, will be, I feel to drive Germany, now perhaps in the transition stage from one form of stable government to another form of stable government, to some last desperate move. There is nothing constructive in these terms, nothing which paves the way for a more amicable future settlement.

Perhaps Germany has played her last military card, but she has not played her last naval card. And while in the end defeat on sea, as on land, and quickly too, is sure to overtake her, she, I think is bound to play the card, if the controlling destinies of Germany are still those that have been in power. If they have changed or are changing, would it be wise to push Germany so far during the armistice. Do we wish to overload such a government?

Therefore it would seem wiser to me not to force the issue with Germany too drastically now, but (1) to gain time, (2) secure a German government acceptible to deal with, and the absolute guarantee of same, (3) Use the time gained to render Turkey and Austria impotent, and eliminated from the war.

Following the above course it would seem that every effort might be made to force the right form of government in Germany as the prelude to armistice (While such negotiations are on there will probably be no danger of Germany sacrificing her fleet)

Having secured this aim, I feel that the President's terms of armistice, are far simpler but stronger, and easier of accomplishment. During this period Turkey and Austria can be made to surrender, and in this regard I feel that Austria can and should be pushed, according to the terms of armistice laid down in the cable.

Her case is different and needs different treatment. How can we hope to combine the various elements into a strong government, strong enough to deal with. Rapid action in her case seems necessary.

Meanwhile, the psyc[h]ological effect of our action towards Austria and Turkey will have time to filter into the German mind.

                                                        Pratt

TS MS (WP, DLC).
    ¹ That is, the paragraph beginning "Allied Naval Council puts forward . . ."

E N C L O S U R E   I I

To: Secretary of the Navy
     Chief of Naval Operations
From: Admiral Benson

Previous receipt of your message regarding naval terms of armistice question had been thoroughly discussed by Inter-Allied Naval Council in which I was present. Decision reached was on basis conditions laid down by President as follows:

Quote The only armistice it would feel justified in submitting for consideration would be one which would leave the United States and Powers associated with her in position to enforce any agreement that may be entered into and make renewal hostilities on part of Germany impossible unquote.

In order to carry out fully the principles involved it was considered necessary to reduce naval power of Germany to such state that she could not attack any of the Powers associated in the War against her. Final decision of Inter-Allied Naval Council is embodied in following terms: Quote

Naval conditions of armistice with (A) Germany, (B) Austria-Hungary.

Allied Naval Council puts forward following terms of armistice for Germany and Austria-Hungary in belief and understanding: (1) That military authorities are in position to continue to press the enemy and prosecute vigorously on land. (2) That enemy's morale and materials collapsing, and his general position is such that he must in fact submit to terms which would only be accepted by a beaten foe; and (3) That the associated Governments desire only terms of this nature, and not such armistice as could be expected from an enemy still capable of powerful and effective resistance. Should these assumptions be wrong, Allied Naval Council would require considering question further. It should be borne in mind that if War is prolonged through refusal of armistice terms by enemy a severely active submarine offensive is materializing, and at sea— as apart from on land—enemy may be able to cause material loss of men and property to the associated countries.

A. Naval conditions of armistice with Germany.

PREAMBLE

It is understood that any armistice resulting as consequence of exchange of notes between President Wilson and German government will on signature carry with it the immediate cessation of hostilities at sea, and that in the event of German government being unable to convey immediate orders to that effect to any submarines, raiders or other ships which may be operating on seas, they will communicate immediately with Allies and governments associated with them in war against Germany, the latest information in their possession as to location and movements of all such vessels.

Further, all neutral countries shall be informed of assent of German government to the free navigation of all territorial waters by naval and mercantile marine of Allies and associated governments, and that Germany waive all questions of neutrality which may arise from any arrangements made with neutral Powers by Allies and associated Powers in regard to such use of their territorial waters,

1. German submarines to number of 160 (including all submarine cruisers and mine laying submarines) with their complete armament and equipment, are to be surrendered to Allies and United States government, in ports which will be specified by them. All other submarines are to be paid off and completely disarmed.

2. All German surface war vessels (including monitors and river craft) are to return to German Naval bases to be specified by Allies,

and with exception of vessels which are to be surrendered they are to remain there during armistice.

Following ships and vessels of German fleet with their complete armament and equipment are to be surrendered to Allied and United States governments in ports which will be specified by them namely—

BATTLESHIPS

Battle Squadron Three. KONIG, GROSSER KURFURST, KRON-PRINZ [WILHELM], MARKGRAF and BAYERN.

Battle Squadron Four. FRIEDRICH DER GROSSE, KONIG ALBERT, KAISERIN, PRINZREGENT LUITPOLD, KAISER.

BATTLE CRUISERS

HINDENBURG, DERF[F]LINGER, SEYDLITZ, MOLTKE, VON DER TANN, MACKENSEN.

LIGHT CRUISERS

BRUMMER, BREMSE.

CRUISERS

KOLN, DRESDEN, EMDEN, FRANKFURST [FRANKFURT], NURNBERG, WEISBADEN [WIESBADEN].

DESTROYERS

Fifty of most modern destroyers.

All other battleships, cruisers and destroyers are to be paid off immediately. And only retain on board nucleus crews. Number which will be fixed by Allies.

All vessels of auxiliary fleet (trawlers, motor vessels, etc.) are to be disarmed.

3. Crews of ships and vessels surrendered under paragraphs one and two will be repatriated to Germany if surrender obligations have been faithfully carried out.

4. Allied and United States fleets and ships are to be given free access to and from the Baltic, and to secure this the Allied and United States governments shall be empowered to occupy all German forts, fortifications, batteries, torpedo batteries and other defenses of all kinds at all entrances from the Cattegat into Baltic. And further for that purpose the associated governments shall be empowered to sweep all mines and obstructions of all kinds laid by Germany between Danish and German coast on the one side Norwegian and Swedish coast on the other side. And also any mines or obstructions laid in Baltic outside German territorial waters, and position any such are to be notified to associated governments by Germany and appropriate plans of the positions are to be furnished.

5. The existing blockade conditions set by associated governments are to remain unchanged, and all German merchant vessels found at sea remain liable to capture.

6. Otherwise than is provided in paragraph four the position of

all mine fields or obstructions laid by Germany are to be indicated with the exception of those laid in German territorial waters and associated governments shall have the right at their own convenience to sweep up German mines or other obstructions outside German territorial waters during continuation of armistice.

Germany shall also agree to waive all questions of neutrality in connection with any mine sweeping or other warlike operations in Baltic or elsewhere which associated governments may arrange with neutral governments to carry out them[selves] or jointly with such neutrals in neutral territorial waters.

And Germany shall so inform all neutral governments.

7. All German aircraft are to be concentrated in German base to be specified by Allied and United States governments and are to remain immobilized and stationary during armistice.

8. All Black Sea ports are to be evacuated by Germany, all merchant vessels belonging to associated governments in these ports seized or taken over by Germany are to be handed back to associated governments at ports designated by them, and all neutral merchant vessels seized are to be released. All warlike and other material of all kinds seized those ports, together with all German material as specified in paragraph nine in connection with Belgium, are to be handed over to Allied and United States governments.

9. Germany shall in evacuating all of Belgium coast leave behind all merchant vessels, tugs, lighters, cranes and other harbor material, all material for inland navigation, all aircraft and air material and stores, all arms and armament and all stores and apparatus of all kinds, all of which are to be abandoned by her.

10. All merchant vessels in German control belonging to associated governments are to be restored in ports to be specified by them, without reciprocity on part of associated governments.

11. No destruction of vessels and material specified in preceding paragraphs is to be permitted before evacuation, surrender or restoration.

12. All above measures shall be executed by Germany in shortest possible time, within period for each item which will be laid down before armistice is signed.

13. German naval prisoners shall be dealt with on similar lines to those laid down for military prisoners, but in no case will prisoners who have formed parts of crew for German submarines be released.

Note: All vessels and property belonging to enemy which under the armistice terms are to be surrendered or handed over, are to be held in trust for final disposal at conferring of allied and United States governments representatives on conclusion armistice. Note by United States Naval representative.

Naval representative of United States wished to reserve for further instructions from his government the question of disposition of surrendered vessels.

End dated October 29th.

Naval conditions of armistice with Austria-Hungary.

PREAMBLE

It is understood that any armistice which may result from exchange of notes between President Wilson and Austro-Hungarian government will, on signature, carry with it the immediate cessation of naval hostilities at sea and that in event of Austro-Hungarian government being unable to convey immediate orders to that effect to submarines, raiders, and other vessels which may be operating on seas, they immediately communicate to Allies and governments associated with them in war against Austria-Hungary, latest information in their possession as to location and movements all such vessels.

Further, all neutral countries shall be informed of assent of Austro-Hungarian government to navigation of all territorial waters by naval and mercantile marine of allied and associated governments, and that Austro-Hungarian government waive question of neutrality which may arise from any arrangements made with neutral powers by associated Allied Powers in regard to such use of their territorial waters.

1. Austro-Hungarian submarines completed between 1910 and 1918 to number of fifteen and all German submarines which are in or may after signature of armistice enter territorial waters of Austro-Hungarian Empire, with complete armament and equipment, are to be surrendered to the Allied and United States governments in ports which will be specified by them. All other submarines are to be paid off and completely disarmed.

2. Following ships of the Austro-Hungarian fleet, with complete armament and equipment, are to be surrendered to the Allied and United States governments in ports which will be specified by them, namely:

Battleships.

PRINZ EUGEN, TEGETTHOF, VIRIBUS, UNITIS, ZRINYI, RADETZKY, ERZHERZOG FRANZ FERDINAND, KAISER KARL VI, HELGOLAND, NOVARA, SAIDA, ADMIRAL SPANN [SPAUN].

Destroyers.

ORJEN, BALATON, TATRA, LOVCEN, LIKA, USZOK [USKOKE], DUKLA, TRIGLAV, OSEPEL [CSEPEL].

Mine vessels.

CHAMALEON, DANUBE.

Monitors.

ALMOSSAVA, BAGUSA, TEMES, ENNS, INN.

All other Austro-Hungarian surface battleships (including monitors and river craft) or [capable?] of going to sea are to be handed over similarly to the Allied and United States governments.

All remaining battleships, cruisers, destroyers and DANUBE monitors are to return to naval bases to be designated by the associated governments and to be paid off and disarmed immediately, and they are to be rendered useless or to be disabled in accordance with such instructions as Allied and United States governments may give. Associated governments are to be at complete liberty to appoint representatives to supervise and inspect fulfilling above measures.

3. Crews of ships and vessels surrendered under paragraph one and paragraph two will be repatriated to Austria-Hungary after surrender, if surrender obligations have been faithfully carried out.

4. Fleets and ships and vessels of the associated governments are to be given free access to and from Adriatic and up river Danube and tributaries throughout Austria-Hungary territory, and to secure this Allied and United States governments shall be empowered to occupy all Austria-Hungary fortifications, batteries, torpedo batteries and other defenses of any kind on Danube, or to dismantle them at their option, further Allied and United States governments shall be empowered to sweep minefields and obstructions of all kinds laid by Austria-Hungary in the Danube, and positions of any such mines and obstructions are to be notified to the Allied and United States governments by Austria-Hungary and appropriate plans of the positions are to be furnished.

5. Existing blockade conditions set up by the associated governments are to remain unchanged, all Austro-Hungarian merchant vessels found at sea are to remain liable to capture.

6. Position all mine fields or obstructions of any kind laid by Austria-Hungary are to be indicated, including those laid in Austro-Hungarian territorial waters, and the associated governments shall have right at their own convenience to sweep up any of these mines or obstructions.

7. All Austro-Hungarian aircraft are to be concentrated in Austro-Hungarian bases to be specified by the Allied and United States governments and are there to remain immobilized and stationary during armistice.

8. Austria-Hungary to evacuate whole of Italian coast and all ports they have occupied outside their national territory, leaving behind all merchant vessels, tugs, lighters, cranes and all other harbor equipment, all equipment for inland navigation, all aircraft

and air equipment and stores, all arms and armament and all stores, all apparatus of all kinds, all of which are to be abandoned by her.

9. Allied and United States governments may occupy during armistice the naval and land forts of Pola, including the islands that constitute an integral part of the place and of the forts and dockyards at that base, limits of the occupied territory being defined by the allied and United States governments having regard to the necessity of the defense of the base from the land side. Mine fields and other obstructions at the entrance of Pola within these limits are to be included in provision paragraph six.

Note: Allied Naval Council dealing with this question solely from naval viewpoint without prejudice to any political or military reasons for the occupation of other parts of Austro-Hungarian territory.

10. All merchant vessels in Austro-Hungarian control belonging to the associated governments are to be restored, in ports to be specified by them without reciprocity on part of associated governments.

11. No destruction of the ships and equipment specified in the preceding paragraph is to be permitted before evacuation, surrender or restoration, except as provided in paragraph two.

12. All above measures shall be executed by Austria-Hungary in the shortest possible time, within the periods for each item which will be laid down before armistice is signed.

13. Austro-Hungarian naval prisoners shall be dealt with on similar lines to those laid down for military prisoners, but in no case will prisoners who have formed part of crews of Austro-Hungarian or German submarines be released.

Note: All vessels and property belonging to the enemy which under the terms armistice are to be surrendered or handed over, are to be held in trust for final disposition at conference of the Allied and United States representatives on conclusion of the armistice.

Note by the Naval representative of the United States.

Naval representative of the United States wished to reserve for further instructions from his government question of the disposition of surrendered vessels.

End. Dated October 29, 1918. Unquote.

While you did not definitely state it, it is implied that ownership of war vessels referred to would not change hands. The message implied this by stating definitely in paragraph seven what should be done with German warships. I therefore changed my previous agreement with the following Quote All vessels and property belonging to enemy which under the terms of the armistice are to be surrendered or handed over are to be held in trust for final disposition of conference of Allied and United States representatives upon completion of the armistice. The representative of the United States wishes to reserve question of disposition of surrendered vessels for further instructions from his government unquote.

My professional opinion is that in order to fully comply with President's conditions the measures recommended by the Inter-Allied Naval Council must be carried out. Immediate decision requested.

I have consulted with Colonel House. He approves my action in referring this matter for decision. Benson. Unquote.

CC MS (WP, DLC).

Three Telegrams from Edward Mandell House

Urgent Number five.   [Paris via] London October 29, 1918.

Following for the President from Colonel House "At my request Cobb and Lippmann have compiled the following respecting your fourteen points. I shall be grateful to you if you will cable me whether it meets with your general approval. Here follows memorandum.

'One. Open covenant of peace, openly arrived at, after which there shall be no private international understandings of any kind, but diplomacy shall proceed always frankly and in the public view.

The purpose is clearly to prohibit treaties, *sections* [of][1] treaties or understandings that are secret, such as the Triple Alliance, et cetera.

The phrase "Openly arrived at" need not cause difficulty. In fact, the President explained to the Senate last winter[2] that the phrase was not meant to exclude confidential diplomatic negotiations involving delicate matters. The intention is that nothing which occurs in the course of such confidential negotiations shall be binding unless it appears in the final covenant made public to the world.

The matter may perhaps be put this way: it is *not* proposed that in future every treaty be part of the public law of the world, and that every nation assume a certain obligation in regard to its enforcement. Obviously, nations cannot assume obligations in matter of which they are ignorant of, and therefore any secret treaty tends to undermine the solidity of the whole structure of international covenants which it is proposed to erect.

Two. Absolute freedom of navigation upon the seas, outside territorial waters, alike in peace and in war, except as the seas may

---

[1] Corrections and additions from the copy in SDR, RG 59, 763.72119/8979, DNA. There is no copy of this telegram in the House Papers.
[2] See WW to RL, March 12, 1918, Vol. 46.

be closed in whole or in part by international action for the enforcement of international covenants. This proposition must be read
in connection with number 14 which proposes a League of Nations.
It refers to navigation under the three following conditions: One.
General peace: Two. A general war, entered into by the League of
Nations for the purpose of enforcing international covenants: Three.
Limited war, involving no breach of international covenants. Under
one (general peace) no serious dispute exists. There is implied
freedom to come and go on the high seas.

No serious dispute exists as to the intention under two (a general
war entered into by the League of Nations to enforce international
covenants). Obviously such a war is conducted against an outlaw
nation and complete non-intercourse with that nation is intended.

Four (A limited war, involving no breach of international covenants) is the crux of the whole difficulty. The question is, what are
to be the rights of neutral shipping and private property on the
high seas during a war between a limited number of nations when
that war involves no issue upon which the League of Nations cares
to take sides. In other words, a war in which the League of Nations
remains neutral. Clearly, it is the intention of the proposal that in
such a war the rights of neutrals shall be maintained against the
belligerents, the rights of both to be clearly and precisely defined
in the law of nations.

Three. The removal, so far as possible, of all economic barriers
and the establishment of an equality of trade conditions among all
the nations consenting to the peace and associating themselves for
its maintenance. The proposal applies only to those nations which
accept the responsibilities of membership in the League of Nations.
It means the destruction of all special commercial agreements, each
putting the trade of every other nation in the league on the same
basis, the most favored nation clause applying automatically to all
members of the League of Nations. Thus a nation could legally
maintain a tariff or a special railroad rate or a port restriction against
the whole world, or against all the signatory powers. It could maintain any kind of restriction which it chose against a nation not in
the league. But it could not discriminate as between its partners
in the league. This clause naturally contemplates fair and equitable
understanding as to the distribution of raw materials.

Four. Adequate guarantee given and taken that national armaments will be reduced to the lowest points consistent with domestic
safety. "Domestic safety" clearly implies not only internal policing,
but the protection of territory against invasion. The accumulation
of armaments above this level would be a violation of the intention
of the proposal. What guarantees should be given and taken, or

what are to be the standards of judgment have never been determined. It will be necessary to adopt the general principle and then institute some means to prepare detailed projects for its execution.

Five. A free, open-minded and absolutely impartial adjustment of all colonial claims, based upon a strict observance of the principle that in determining all such questions of sovereignty the interests of the populations concerned must have equal weight with the equitable claims of the government whose title is to be determined. Some fear is expressed in France that this involves reopening of all colonial questions. Obviously it is not so intended. It applies clearly to those colonial claims which have been created by the war. That means the German colonies and any other colonies which may come under international consideration as a result of the war. The stipulation is that in the case of the German colonies the title is to be determined after the conclusion of the war by "impartial adjustment" based on certain principles. These are of two kinds: One. "Equitable" claims: Two. The interest of the population concerned. What are the "equitable" claims put forth by Great Britain and Japan, the two chief heirs of the German Colonial Empire, that the colonies cannot be returned to Germany? Because she will use them as submarine bases, because she will arm the blacks, because she uses the colonies as bases of intrigue, because she oppresses the natives. What are the "equitable" claims put forth by Germany? That she needs access to tropical raw material, that she needs a field for the expansion of her population, that under the principles of the peace proposed, conquest gives her enemies no title to her colonies.

What are the "interests of the populations?" That they should not be militarized, that exploitation should be conducted on the principles of the open door, and under the strictest regulation as to labor conditions, profits and taxes, that a sanitary regime be maintained, that permanent improvements in the way of roads, et cetera, be made, that native organization and custom be respected, that the protecting authority be stable and experienced enough to thwart intrigue and corruption, that the protecting power have adequate resources in money and competent administrators to act successfully.

It would seem as if the principle involved in this proposition is that a colonial power acts not as owner of its colonies, but as trustee for the natives and for the interests of the society of nations, that the terms on which the colonial administration is conducted are a matter of international concern and may legitimately be the subject of international inquiry and that the peace conference may, therefore, write a code of colonial conduct binding upon colonial powers.

Six, The evacuation of all Russian territory and such a settlement of all questions affecting Russia as will secure the best and freest cooperation of the other nations of the world in obtaining for her an unhampered and unembarrassed opportunity for the *independence* [independent] determination of her own political development and national policy and [assure] her of a sincere welcome into the society of free nations under institutions of her own choosing; and more than a welcome, assistance also of every kind that she may need and may herself desire. The treatment accorded Russia by her sister nations in the months to come will be the acid test of their good will, of their compensation [comprehension] of her needs as distinguished from their own interests and of their intelligent and unselfish sympathy.

The first question is whether Russian territory is synonymous with territory belonging to the former Russian Empire. This is clearly not so, because proposition thirteen stipulates an independent Poland, a proposal which excludes the territorial reestablishment of the Empire. What is recognized as valid for the Poles will certainly have to be recognized for the Finns, the Lithuanians, the Letts, and perhaps also for the Ukrainians. Since the formulating [formulation] of this condition these subject nationalities have emerged and there can be no doubt that they will have to be given an opportunity of free development.

The problem *on* [of] these nationalities is complicated by two facts: One. That they have conflicting claims. [Two.] That the evacuation called for in the proposal may be followed by Bolshevist revolutions in all of them. The chief conflicts are: A. Between the Letts and Germans in Courland: B. Between the Poles and the Lithuanians on the Northeast: C. Between the Poles and the White Ruthenians on the East: D. Between the Poles and the Ukrainians on the Southeast (and in Eastern Galicia). In this whole borderland the relations of the German Poles to the other nationalities is roughly speaking that of landlord to peasant. Therefore the evacuating [evacuation] of the territory, if it resulted in class war, would very probably also take the form of a conflict of nationalities. It is clearly to the interests of a good settlement that the real nation in each territory should be consulted rather than the ruling and possessing class.

This can mean nothing less than the (∗) [recognition] by the peace conference of a series of de facto Governments representing Finns *Esths*, Lithuanians, Ukrainians. This primary art[3] of recognition should be conditional upon the calling of national assemblies

(∗) Apparent omission.

[3] That is, act.

for the creation of de facto governments, as soon as the peace conference has drawn frontiers for these new states. The frontiers should be drawn so far as possible on ethnic lines but in either [every] case the right of unhampered economic trade interests [transit] should be reserved. No dynastic ties with German, Austrian or Romanoff Princes should be permitted and every inducement should be (∗) [given] to encourage federal regulations [relations] between these new states. Under proposition three, the economic sections of the treaty of Brest Litovsk are obliterated [abolished] but this proposition should not be construed as forbidding a customs union, a monetary union, a railroad union, et cetera, of these states. Provision should also be made by which Great Russia can federate with these states on the same terms.

As for Great Russia and Siberia, the peace conference might well send a message asking for the creation of a government sufficiently represented [representative] to speak for these territories. It should be understood that economic rehabilitation is offered provided a government carrying sufficient credentials can appear at the peace conference. The Allies should offer this provisional government any form of assistance it may need. The possibility of extending this will exist when the Dardanelles are opened.

The essence of the Russian problem then in the immediate future would seem to be: One, the recognition of provisional governments: Two. Assistance extended to and through these governments.

The Caucasus should probably be treated as part of the problem of the Turkish Empire. No information exists justifying an opinion on the proper policy in regard to Mohammedan Russia—that is, briefly, Central Asia. It may well be that some power will have to be given a limited mandate to act as protector.

In any case the treaties of Brest-Litovsk and Bucharest must be cancelled as palpably fraudulent. Provision must be made for the withdrawal of all German troops in Russia and the peace conference have a clean slate on which to write a policy for all the Russian peoples.

Section seven. Belgium, the whole world will agree must be evacuated and restored without any attempt to limit the sovereignty which she enjoys in common with all other free nations. No other single act will serve as this will to restore confidence among the nations in the laws which they have themselves set and determined for the government of their relations with one another. Without this healing act the whole structure and validity of international law is forever impaired.

The only problem raised here is in the word "restored." Whether restoration is to be in kind or how the amount of the indemnity is to be determined is a matter of detail, not of principle. The principle that should be established is that in the case of Belgium there exists no distinction between "legitimate" and "illegitimate" destruction. The initial act of invasion was illegitimate and therefore all the consequences of that act are of the same character. Among the consequences may be put the war debt of Belgium. The recognition of this principle would constitute "the healing act" of which the President speaks.

Eight. All French territory should be freed and the invaded portions restored and the wrong done to France by Prussia in 1871 in the matter of Alsace-Lorraine [which has unsettled the peace of the world for fifty years] should be righted in order that peace may once more be made secure in the interest of all.

In regard to the restoration of French territory it might well be argued that the invasion of northern France being the result of the illegal act as regards Belgium was in itself illegal. But the case is not perfect. As the world stood in 1914 war between France and Germany was not in itself a violation of international law and great insistence should be put upon keeping the Belgian case distinct and symbolic. Thus Belgium might well, as indicated above, claim reimbursement not only for destruction but for the cost of carrying on the war. France could not claim payment, it would seem, for more than the damage done to her northeastern departments.

The status of Alsace-Lorraine was settled by the official statement issued a few days ago. It is to be restored completely to French sovereignty.

Attention is called to the strong current of French opinion which claims "the boundaries of 1914"[4] rather than of 1871. The territory claimed is the valley of the Saar with its coal fields. No claim on grounds of nationality can be established but the argument leans on the possibility of taking this territory in lieu of indemnity. It would seem to be a clear violation of the President's proposal.

Attention is called also to the fact that no reference is made to status of Luxemburg. The best solution would seem to be a free choice by the (∗) [people of] Luxemburg themselves.

Nine. A readjustment of the frontiers of Italy should be effected along clearly recognizable lines of nationality.

This proposal is less than the Italian claim; less of course than the territory allotted by the treaty of London; less than the arrangement made between the Italian Government and the Jugo-Slav state.

In the region of Trent the Italians claim a strategic rather than

(∗) Apparent omission.

4 That is, 1814.

ethnic frontier. It should be noted in this connection that (*) [Italy] and Germany will become neighbors if German Austria joins the German empire. And if Italy obtains the best geographical frontier she will assume sovereignty over a large number of Germans. This ia a violation of principle. But it may be argued that by drawing a sharp line along the crest of the Alps, Italy's security will be enormously enhanced and the necessity of heavy armaments reduced. It might therefore, be provided that Italy should have her claim in the Trentine but that the northern part inhabited by Germans should be completely autonomous and that the population should not be liable to military service in the Italian army. Italy could thus occupy the uninhabited Alpine peaks for military purposes but would not govern the cultural life of the alien population to the south of her frontier.

The other problems of the frontier are questions between Italy and Jugo-Slavia, Italy and the Balkans, Italy and Greece.

The agreement reached with Jugo-Slavs may well be allowed to stand although it should be insisted for the protection of the hinterland that both Trieste and Fiume be free ports. This is *especial* [essential] to Bohemia, German-Austria, Hungary as well as to prosperity of the cities themselves.

Italy appears in Balkan politics through her claim to a protectorate over Albania and the possession of Valona. There is no serious *rejection* [objection] raised to this; in this case [although the] terms of the protectorate need to be vigorously controlled. If Italy is protector of Albania the local life of Albania should be guaranteed by the League of Nations.

A conflict with Greece appears through the Greek claim to Northern Epirus or what is now Southern Albania. This would bring Greece closer to Valona than Italy desires. A second conflict with Greece occurs over the Aegean Islands of the Dodekanese but it is understood that a solution favorable to Greece is being worked out.

Italy's claims in Turkey belong to the problem of the Turkish empire.

Article ten. The peoples of Austria-Hungary whose place among the nations we wish to see safeguarded and assured should be accorded the freest opportunity of autonomous development.

This proposition no longer holds; instead we have to *veto* [today] the following elements: one, Czecho-Slovakia. Its territories include at least a million Germans for whom some provision must be made.

The independence of Slovakia means the dismemberment of the northwestern countries of Hungary; two, Galicia. Western Galicia is clearly Polish. Eastern Galicia is in large measure Ukrainian (or Ruthenian) and does not of right belong to Poland.

There also are several hundred thousand Ukrainians along the

(*) Apparent omission.

north and northeastern borders of Hungary and in parts of Buko-
wina (which belongs to Austria). Three, German Austria. This territory should of right be permitted to join Germany but there is
strong objection in general because of the increase of population
involved. Fourth. Jugo-Slavia. It faces the following problems: A.
Frontier questions with Italy in Istria and the Dalmatia coast; with
Roumania in the Banat. B. An international problem arises out of
the refusal of the Croats to accept the domination of the Serbs of
the Servian kingdom. C. A problem of the Mohammedan Serbs of
Bosnia who are said to be loyal to the Hapsburgs. They constitute
a little less than one third of the population. Five. Transylvania.
Will undoubtedly join Roumania but provision must be made for
the protection of the Magyars, Szeklers[5] and Germans who constitute a large minority. Six. Hungary. Now independent and very
democratic in form but governed by Magyars whose aim is to prevent the detachment of territory of nationalities on the fringe.

The United States is clearly committed to the program of national
unity and independence. It must stipulate, however, for the protection of national minorities, or freedom of access to the Adriatic
and the Black Sea, and it supports a program aiming at a confederation of southeastern Europe.

Eleven. Roumania, [Serbia] and Montenegro should be evacuated; occupied territories restored; Serbia accorded free and secure
access to the sea; and the relations of the several Balkan States to
one another determined by friendly counsel along historically established lines of allegiance and nationality; and international guarantees of the political and economic independence and territorial
integrity of the several Balkan States should be entered into.

This proposal is also altered by events. Serbia will appear as Jugo-
Slavia with access to the Adriatic. Roumania will have acquired the
Dobrudja, Bessarabia and probably Transylvania. These two states
will have eleven or twelve million inhabitants and will be far greater
and stronger than Bulgaria.

Bulgaria should clearly have her frontier in the southern Dobrudja as it stood before the second Balkan war. She should also
have Thrace up to the Enos-Midia line and perhaps even to the
Midia-Rodosto line.

Macedonia should be allotted after an impartial investigation. The
line which might be taken as a basis of investigation is the southern
line of the "contested zone" agreed upon by Serbia and Bulgaria
before the first Balkan war.

---

[5] That is, Szeklers, Magyars living in present-day Rumania.

Albania could be under a protectorate, no doubt of Italy, and its frontiers in the north might be essentially those of the London conference.[6]

Twelve. The Turkish portions of the present Ottoman Empire should be assured a secure sovereignty, but the other nationalities which are now under Turkish rule should be assured an undoubted security of life and an absolutely unmolested opportunity of autonomous development, and the Dardanelles should be permanently opened as free passage to the ships and commerce of all nations under international guarantees.

The same difficulty arises here as in the case of Austria Hungary concerning the word autonomous.

It is clear that the Straits and Constantinople, while they may remain nominally Turkish, should be under international control. This control may be collective or be in the hands of one power as mandatory of the league.

Anatolia should be reserved for the Turks. The coast lands, where Greeks predominate, should be under special international control, perhaps with Greece as mandatory.

Armenia must be [given] a port on the Mediterranean, and a protecting power established. France may claim it, but the Armenians would prefer Great Britain.

Syria has already been allotted to France by agreement with Great Britain.

Great Britain is clearly the best mandatory for the Palestine, Mesopotamia and Arabia.

A general code of guarantees binding upon all mandatories in Asia Minor should be written into the treaty of peace.

This should contain provisions for minorities and the open door. The trunk railroad lines should be internationalized.

Thirteen. An independent Polish state should be erected which should include the territories inhabited by indisputably Polish populations, which should be assured a free and secure access to the sea, and whose political and economic independence and territorial integrity should be guaranteed by international covenants.

The chief problem is whether Poland is to obtain territory west of the Vistula, which would cut off the Germans of East Prussia from the Empire, or whether Danzig can be made a free port and the Vistula internationalized.

On the East, Poland should receive no territory in which Lithuanians or Ukrainians predominate.

[6] The London Conference of December 17, 1912-May 30, 1913, which ended the first Balkan War.

If Posen and Silesia go to Poland, rigid protection must be afforded the minorities of Germans and Jews living there, as well as in other parts of the Polish state.

The principle on which frontiers will be limited is contained in the President's words "indisputably." This may imply the taking of an impartial census before frontiers are marked.

Fourteen. A general association of nations must be formed under specific covenants for the purpose of affording mutual guarantees of political independence and territorial integrity to great and small states alike.

The principle of a League of Nations as the primary essential of a permanent peace has been so clearly presented by President Wilson in his speech of September 27th 1918, that no further elucidation is required. It is the foundation of the whole diplomatic structure of a permanent peace.   Edward House.

Urgent. Six.   Paris, October 29, 1918.

For the President. I have had Cobb direct the interpretation of your fourteen points. I am cabling this to you for your correction and revision. It is very essential that I should have this at the earliest moment for I am constantly asked to interpret them myself and the wires may become crossed.   Edward House.

Urgent. 7.   Paris, October 29, 1918

Strictly confidential. Cobb has reported to me the following. "General opinion of all American correspondents in Paris is that the one definite policy of the Allies at this time is to take the control of the peace negotiations out of the * [hands] of President Wilson. The same opinion is expressed by correspondents who have just returned to Paris from London. That also is the tone of a large section of the French papers."   Edward House

T telegrams (WP, DLC).

To Edward Mandell House

HOUSE. III.   [The White House, Oct. 29, 1918]

Can be no real difficulty about peace terms and interpretation of fourteen points if the Entente statesmen will be perfectly frank with us and have no selfish aims of their own which would in any case alienate us from them altogether. It is the fourteen points that Germany has accepted. England cannot [get away from or] dispense with our friendship in the future and the other Allies cannot without our assistance get their rights as against England. If it is the purpose of the Allied statesmen to nullify my influence force the purpose boldly to the surface and let me speak of it to all the world as I shall. League of nations underlies freedom of the seas and every other part of peace programme so far as I am concerned. I am ready to repudiate any selfish programme openly, but assume that the Allies cannot honorably turn the present discussions into a peace conference without me. Please do not use wireless.[1]

WWT telegram (WP, DLC).
[1] Auchincloss explained in a telegram, sent as EMH to RL, Oct. 31, 1918 (WP, DLC), that some cablegrams had been sent by wireless for test purposes by the naval communications office without his knowledge and that he had ordered the practice discontinued.

Wilhelm August Ferdinand Ekengren to Robert Lansing

T R A N S L A T I O N

Excellency: Washington, D. C., October 29, 1918.

By order of my Government, I have the honor to beg you to transmit to the President the following communication from the Imperial and Royal Government of Austro-Hungary.

"In reply to the note of President Wilson to the Austro-Hungarian Government dated October 18 of this year, with regard to the decision of the President to take up with Austro-Hungary separately the question of Armistice and Peace, the Austro-Hungarian Government has the honor to declare that it adheres both to the previous declarations of the President and his opinion of the rights of the peoples of Austro-Hungary, notably those of the Czecho-Slovaks and the Jugo-Slavs contained in his last note. Austria Hungary having thereby accepted all the conditions which the President had put upon entering into negotiations on the subject of Armistice and Peace, nothing, in the opinion of the Austro-Hungarian Government, longer stands in the way of beginning those negotiations. The Austro-Hungarian Government therefore declares itself ready to enter, without waiting for the outcome of other negotiations, into negotiations for a peace between Austria-Hungary and the Entente States and for an immediate armistice on all the fronts of Austria-Hungary and begs President Wilson to take the necessary measures to that effect.["]

Be pleased to accept Excellency the assurances of my high consideration.   W. A. F. Ekengren.[1]

T MS (SDR, RG 59, 763.72119/2392, DNA).
    [1] The French-text TLS, in the same file, bears the notations: "Handed me by Swedish Min. Oct. 29/18 4:20 pm RL" and "Copy of note and translation sent to the President 5:10 pm. RL."

From Robert Lansing, with Enclosures

My dear Mr. President: Washington October 29, 1918.

I am sending you at once a letter from Professor Masaryk dealing with the Austro-Hungarian note, which I have hastily scanned. Will you be good enough to return it to me after reading?
                    Faithfully yours,   Robert Lansing

TLS (SDR, RG 59, 763.72119/2464, DNA).

E N C L O S U R E   I

Thomas Garrigue Masaryk to Robert Lansing

Mr. Secretary,   [Washington] October 29, 1918.

You will allow me to express my views on the last Austro-Hungarian note, as it primarily concerns our nation, and I can claim a fairly good knowlege of all questions involved.

The note again reveals the Austro-Hungarian and Hapsburg meanness and duplicity. The note says that the Austro-Hungarian Government "adheres to the same *point of view contained* in the last (President's) note"; that means that they accept some general views, which can be deduced or inferred from the President's note. But the President clearly stated that our National Council is a *de facto* government, clothed with proper authority to direct not only the military, but also the *political* affairs of the Czechoslovaks. That means that Austria-Hungary must negotiate with us. President Wilson says so expressedly in his note, insisting, that not he, but our nation shall be the judge of how Austria-Hungary can satisfy our aspirations and rights. The National Council is not only the recognized representative of the Czechoslovak Nation, but also authorized to act as such by the Nation herself (repeated declaration of the Czech leaders, (Stanek, Stransky)[1] who explicitly stated that the Austro-Hungarian Government must deal not with them, but with the National Council in Paris, also the action of the Czech deputies in leaving the Parliament on October 9th, with the declaration that they forever sever all relations with Austria-Hungary.

It is for this reason that I think the President cannot answer the Austro-Hungarian Note without weakening his position; it is quite evident that Austria-Hungary, like Germany, is trying to continue the discussion. Austria-Hungary apparently deserts Germany, but I am not quite sure whether this desertion is not made in Germany; at any rate even when we accept the services of a traitor, we do not respect him. The Hapsburgs betraying their Ally, who in this war twice saved them from destruction (first against the Russians, then against the Italians), will betray their opponents.

I do not see any other possibility than that you, Mr. Secretary, notify the Austro-Hungarian government that the President cannot enter into further parleys with them, giving the reasons.

In the question of "overtures" it is evident that Austria-Hungary, like Germany, is trying to induce the President to begin the overtures in a way which would enable them to say that America is war-weary.

Finally, I must emphasize the fact that up to the present, Austria-Hungary was ruled in a quite absolute manner: if America cannot enter into negotiations with the absolute masters of Germany, she cannot enter into negotiations with the absolute masters of Austria-Hungary, who declared the war without ever thinking of asking for the sanction of Parliament or the people. That is required by political consistency and by President Wilson's repeated utterances. In case of Germany, it means negotiation with representatives of the German people, in case of Austria-Hungary with representatives of the different peoples of the Empire.

I enclose a copy of what I think should be included among the conditions under which an Armistice could be granted.

Believe me, Mr. Secretary,

Most sincerely yours,   T. G. Masaryk

TLS (SDR, RG 59, 763.72119/2464, DNA).
¹ František Staněk, Czech leader in the Austrian Reichsrat; and Dr. Adolf Stránský, editor of *Lidove Noviny (Peoples' Newspaper)*, Czech deputy in the Reichsrat.

E N C L O S U R E   I I

CONDITIONS OF A POSSIBLE ARMISTICE.

1. Evacuation of all occupied territories.
2. Occupation of German and Austro-Hungarian territories, else the Allies will have no means of pressure to secure the reorganization in the East. In the West there will be no great difficulties; it is the East which must be reorganized.
3. Demobilization in Germany, Austria-Hungary, and Turkey.

4. If Germany must negotiate thru a democratic government, Austria-Hungary must negotiate thru her nations.

5. Constitutional reforms in Germany and Prussia are not sufficient; the constitution of the component German states must be democratized. The position of the Kaiser and all Kings (3) and the rest of the smaller dynasts (20) must be clearly changed, so that they derive their power from the people and not by divine grace. The same holds good for Austria-Hungary (and Turkey). Prussianism, dynastical absolutism in Germany emanates not only from the Emperor but from the 23 dynasties.

T MS (SDR, RG 59, 763.72119/2464, DNA).

From Edward Parker Davis

My dear Woodrow,   Philadelphia Pa. Oct. 29th 1918

I cannot hate any human family, and the German nation is such. But they are hated for carrying matters to the extreme of a logical conclusion, and can they be convinced of the failure of brute force unless they are gripped by a force greater than theirs, but restrained by a soul more noble than theirs? I believe the German people will yet come to recognize your great service to mankind, and applaud you for it. The soul of the German people is not stolid, but highly passionate, for good or bad.

I am more concerned about our country than about Europe. We are in the greatest of crises. I wonder and am thrilled by your courage, in leading the people against the Republican bosses; you must and will succeed! You are winning your war of arms and ideals in the old world; and now for the New.

As ever,   Affectionately Yours,   E. P. Davis.

ALS (WP, DLC).

From Georgii Vasil'evich Chicherin

Christiania October 29, 1918.

No. 1290. The following English translation of a note in Russian handed by the Russian Commissariat for Foreign Affairs to the Norwegian Legation at Petrograd was telegraphed by that Legation to the Foreign Office under date of October twenty-sixth with the request it be forwarded to this Legation for transmission to President Wilson:

"In your note to the congress of the Russian Government on the eighteenth of January [of 8 January to the Congress of the United

States of North America],[1] point six,[2] you expressed the deep sympathy which you felt toward Russia, which at that moment was facing the necessity of carrying on negotiations with the powerful German Imperialism. You said that your program consisted in the [evacuation of all Russian territory and the] clearing of all questions concerning Russia. You said that Russia should be guaranteed an absolutely effective assistance from the other nations in her effort to be able to take an independent decision concerning her own political development and her national policy. This would assure her a hearty welcome from the so-called union of free nations, whatever the form of government that she may elect for herself would be. You would also give Russia every kind of support that would answer to her wishes. You added that the relations assumed toward Russia by all great powers during the coming months would be the proof [acid test of] their good feelings towards her, the proof of their comprehending of Russia's needs, even if these might not be in accordance with their own interests, and also a proof of their wisdom and the disinterestedness of their sympathy. The supreme struggle we had with German Imperialism in Brestlitovsk apparently increased your sympathies towards Soviet Russia since you sent your greetings to the Congress of Councils which ratified the Brest predatory peace under the threat of a German offensive and assured it that Soviet Russia could depend on the support of America.[3] This was six months ago, and the Russia people have had ample time to experience *de facto* the good feelings of your Government, the good feelings of your Allies, the realization on the part of the Allies of Russia's needs and the wisdom and the disinterestedness of their sympathy. These feelings have been expressed firstly through the fact that with financial assistance on the part of your [French] Allies, and with the diplomatic support of your Government, the conspiracy of the Czecho-Slovaks was organized on Russian territory, and to this conspiracy your Government showed every assistance. During a certain period attempts were made to create a catastrophe between the United States and Russia by spreading rumors about the German occupation of the Siberian railway. Your own officers, however, and after them the head of your Red Cross Mission, Colonel Robins, could convince themselves of the libelous nature of these rumors. The Czecho-Slovak movement was organized under the pretext of protecting these unfortunate misguided individuals from being delivered into the hands of Germany and Austria. You can however learn among other things from the open letter of Captain Sadoul, member of the French Military Mission, how much this lacked any actual foundation.[4] The Czecho-Slovaks had not left Russia at the beginning of the year only because the French Government had not given them any ships for their use. For several months we waited in vain for Allies to grant them a possibility for leaving the country; apparently their presence in Russia was more desirable for these governments than their families [their departure] to France to take part in the war on the French frontier. Ultimate events have made clear the truth of the motives. The best proof of the true Czecho-Slovak revolt is the fact that, having occupied the Siberian railway, they did not profit by this means of departure, but at the order of the Government of the Allied Powers, who were directing them, preferred to become the basis of the Russian counter-revolution. This counter-revolutionary revolt which has made all transport of food and naphtha [petroleum] on the Volga impossible, which has cut off all the peasants and workman of Russia from the bread and other supplies of Siberia, and which has exposed these peasants and workmen to hunger." Foreign Office announces continuation to follow which will be stated as soon as received.[5]

Schmedeman

T telegram (SDR, RG 59, 861.00/3102, DNA).

[1] Corrections in brackets are from the quite different translation printed under the date of October 24, 1918, in Jane Degras, ed., *Soviet Documents on Foreign Policy* (3 vols., New York, 1951-53), I, 112-20. Variations not materially affecting the sense are not noted here. Degras' text is from a documentary collection by I. V. Kluchnikov and A. Sabanin, which was published in three volumes in Moscow, 1925-1928. A German translation, entitled "an open letter" from Chicherin to Wilson, was published in Berlin, presumably in 1918 or 1919. There is a copy of it in the Rare Books Collection, NjP.

[2] That is, of Wilson's Fourteen Points Address of Jan. 8, 1918.

[3] WW to the Fourth All-Russia Congress of Soviets, March 11, 1918, Vol. 46.

[4] Not found.

[5] G. V. Chicherin to WW, Nov. 2, 1918.

To Henry French Hollis

My dear Senator: [The White House] 30 October, 1918.

Your letter of October 6th puts me under additional obligation to you for very valuable direct and side lights on the difficult situation into which we are now running and assists not a little in the formation of my judgment. Thank you very warmly. I hope you are keeping well.

Cordially and sincerely yours,   Woodrow Wilson

TLS (Letterpress Books, WP, DLC).

To Edward Mandell House

[The White House, Oct. 30, 1918]

IV Analysis of fourteen points satisfactory interpretation of principles involved but details of application mentioned should be regarded as merely illustrative suggestions and reserved for peace conference. Admission of inchoate nationalities to peace-conference most undesirable.

WWhw telegram (WP, DLC).

Two Telegrams from Edward Mandell House

[Paris, Oct. 30, 1918]

The English, I think, will accept your 14 points with some changing, such as military commander

Open the question of reparation at sea and the making of the freedom of the seas

Conditional upon the formation of a League of Nations

The French are inclined not to accept your terms but will formulate their *demands* (?)

There will be a meeting between Lloyd George Clemenceau _____ myself this afternoon. Wiseman informs me that—*Hackler? futier?* and Foch have now agreed to terms for an Armistice but I have not the details[1]

EBWhw decode (WP, DLC).
    [1] The copy of this telegram in the House Papers, CtY, dated Oct. 30, 1918, reads as follows:
    "The English I think will accept your fourteen points with some modification such as leaving open the question of reparation at sea and the making of the freedom of the seas conditional upon the formation of the league of nations.
    "The French are inclined not to accept your terms but to formulate their own. There will be a meeting between Lloyd George, Clemenceau and myself this afternoon.
    "Wiseman informs me that Haig and Foch have now agreed upon terms for an armistice but I have not the details."

Paris Oct 30, 1918

Urgent. Number 8. Secret. For the President. Lloyd George, Balfour, and Reading lunched with me today and George stated that it was his opinion that if the Allies submitted to Germany's terms of Armistice without more (∗) [discussion][1] Germany would assume that the Allies had accepted President Wilson's fourteen points and other speeches without qualification. So far as Great Britain was concerned George stated point two of speech of January 8th, 1918, respecting freedom of the seas, could not be accepted with[out] qualification. He admitted that if point two was made a part of point fourteen concerning League of Nations and assuming League of Nations was such a one as Great Britain could subscribe to, it might be possible for Great Britain to accept point two. He said that he did not wish to discuss freedom of the seas with Germany and (*) [if] freedom of the seas was a condition of peace Great Britain could not agree to it. Before our discussion ended it seemed as though we were near an agreement concerning this matter along the lines of interpretation of point two heretofore cabled you in cable number five to the Department. We then went to conference at Quay d'Orsay attended by Clemenceau, Pichon, George, Balfour, Sonnino and myself. Conference opened with discussion of fourteen points enumerated in President's address of January eighth last. Clemenceau and others balked at number one until I read them interpretation thereof as cabled to you in telegram number five. They then all accepted number one. After number two had been read George made a short speech worded so as to excite Clemenceau. He reversed his position taken a short time before with me privately and said respecting point two: "We cannot accept this under any circumstances. It takes away from us the power of blockade. My view is this, I want to see character of League of Nations first before I accept this proposition. I do not wish to discuss it with Germany. I will not make it a condition of peace with Germany." I stated that if these views were persisted in the logical consequences would be for the President to say to Germany: "The Allies do not agree to the conditions of peace proposed by me and accordingly the present negotiations are at an end." I pointed out that this would leave the President free to consider the question afresh and to determine whether the United States should continue to fight for the principles laid down by the Allies. My statement had a very exciting effect upon those present. Balfour then made a forceful speech to the effect that it was clear that the Germans were trying to drive a wedge between the President and the Allies and that their attempts in this direction must be foiled. It was [[I]] then suggested that France, England, and Italy confer together and submit tomorrow drafts of the proposed answers to the President's communication asking whether they agree to his terms of peace, stating where they can agree with the President and where they disagree. I then offered to withdraw from the conference so that they would feel at liberty to discuss the matter between themselves. They all stated that they had no secret[[s]] from America and that they wished me to remain. Accordingly it was agreed after further discussion and after the reading of the terms agreed upon by the Inter-Allied Naval Conference now in session in Paris for the naval armistice that we should meet [[together]] Wednesday afternoon to consider draft answers by the Allies to the President's communication transmitting correspondence between the President and Germany. French Prime Minister and Italian Prime Minister [[*Sonnino*]] are not at all in sympathy with the idea of League of Nations. Italian Prime Minister [[Sonnino]] will probably submit many objections to fourteen points. French Prime Minister, George, and I agreed to meet Wednesday morning without Italian Prime Minister [[Sonnino]] for the purpose of further discussion. It is my view that privately George and Balfour believe that the proposed terms of the naval armistice and those of the military armistice are too severe. They wish to get just as much as they can but they wish to be able to continue negotiations in the event that Germany refuses to accept the terms proposed. An exceedingly strict censorship by the French War Office makes it impossible for American correspondents to send any communications to the United States respecting the progress of the present conference. I am examining into this matter and it may be advisable to take drastic steps in order that the United States can arrange [[determine]] for herself what news of political character shall be communicated to her people. Edward House.

(*) Omissions

T telegram (WP, DLC).
  [1] Corrections and additions in square brackets in this telegram from the copy in SDR, RG 59, 763.72119/8992, DNA; corrections in double square brackets from the copy in the House Papers.

To Edward Mandell House

V.   [The White House, Oct. 30, 1918]

I feel it my solemn duty to authorize you to say that I cannot consent to take part in the negotiation of a peace which does not include freedom of the seas because we are pledged to fight not only to do away with Prussian militarism but with militarism everywhere. Neither could I participate in a settlement which did not include league of nations because peace would be without any guarantee except universal armament which would be intolerable. I hope I shall not be obliged to make this decision public.

WWhw telegram (WP, DLC).

Four Telegrams from Edward Mandell House

Paris. Oct. 30, 1918.

9. Secret for the President. It is my intention to tell Prime Ministers today that if their conditions of peace are essentially different from the points [conditions] you have laid down and for which the American people have been fighting that you will probably feel obliged to go before Congress and state the new conditions and ask their advice as to whether the United States shall continue to fight for the aims of Great Britain, France and Italy.

The last thing they want is publicity and they do not wish it to appear that there is any cause for difference between the Allies. Unless we deal with these people with a firm hand everything we have been fighting for will be lost.

I told the British privately you anticipate [yesterday] that their policy would lead to the establishment of the greatest naval program by the United States that the world had ever seen. I did not believe that the United States [American people] would consent *for any [nation] to interpret* for them the rules under which American commerce could traverse the sea. I would suggest that you quietly diminish the transport of troops giving as an excuse the prevalence of influenza or any other reason but the real one. I would also suggest a little later that you begin to gently shut down upon money, food and raw material. I feel confidential [confidence] that we should play a [very] strong hand and if it meets with your approval I will do it in the gentle and friendly (?) almost certain [gentlest and friendliest way possible] (?) (?).   House.

Paris, Oct. 30, 1918.

10. Secret for the President. In my private conversation with Lloyd George yesterday he said that Great Britain desired the United States to become trustee for German East African Colonies. That Great Britain was unwilling that they should be turned back to Germany for the reason that the Germans had used such inhuman methods in their treatment of the natives. He said by right [Southwest] Africa and the Asiatic Islands belonging to Germany must go to the South African Federation and to Australia respectively; that unless this was done Great Britain would be confronted by a revolution in those dominions.

He added that Great Britain would have to assume a protectorate over Mesopotamia and perhaps Palestine. Arabia he thought should become autonomous. France might be given a sphere of influence in Syria.

My (?) (as seen from?) [feeling as to] his suggestion regarding German East Africa, is that the British would like us to accept something so they might more freely take what they desire.

George also thought the Allies should get together before the Peace Conference and thresh out their differences. He believed the Peace Conference itself need not last longer than one week. The preliminary conference he thought could be finished in three or four weeks.

I strongly advise against their procedure and for reasons which will be obvious to you.   House.

Paris. Oct. 30, 1918.

Urgent. 12. Secret for the President.

Lloyd George, Clemenceau and I met for forty-five minutes this morning alone at the office of the Minister of War. Just before we entered Clemenceau's office George handed me a proposed answer to the President which the British authorities had drafted. I quote the draft in full.

"The Allied Government's have given careful consideration to the correspondence which has passed between the President of the United States and the German Government. Subject to the qualifications which follow, they declare their willingness to make peace with the Government of Germany on the terms of peace laid down in the President's address to Congress of January 8, 1918, and the principles of settlement enunciated in his subsequent addresses. They [must] point out, however, that clause two, relating to what is usually described as the freedom of the seas, is open to various interpretations, some of which they could not accept. They must therefore reserve to themselves complete freedom on this subject when they enter the peace conference.

"Further, in the condition[s] of peace laid down in his address to Congress of January 8, 1918, the President declared that invaded territories must be restored as well as evacuated and freed. The Allied Governments feel that no doubt ought to be allowed to exist as to what this provision implies. By it they understand that compensation will be made by Germany for all damage done to the civilian population of the Allies, and their property (by the forces of Germany ?), by land, by sea, and from the air."

I told George that I was afraid his attitude at yesterdays meeting had opened the flood gates; [and that] Clemenceau, Sonnino would have elaborate memoranda to submit containing their objections to the President's fourteen points, and that I doubted whether Clemenceau would accept (another version?) [answer as] drafted by

British which was in marked contrast to the position taken by George yesterday. It (?) developed at the conference that Clemenceau was having prepared an elaborate brief setting forth France's objections to the President's fourteen points. I promptly pointed out to Clemenceau that undoubtedly Sonnino was preparing a similar memorandum and that if the Allied Governments felt constrained to submit an elaborate answer to the President containing many objections to his program it would doubtless be necessary for the President to go to Congress and to place before that body exactly what Italy, France, and Great Britain were fighting for and to place the responsibility upon Congress for the further continuation of the war by the United States in behalf of the aims of the Allies. As soon as I had said this George and Clemenceau looked at each other significantly. Clemenceau at once abandoned his idea of submitting an elaborate memorandum concerning the President's fourteen points and apparently accepted the proposed answer drafted by the British. I suggest[ed] that the word "illegal" be placed before the words "damage done to the civilian population of the allies," in the last sentence of draft of proposed answer. George accepted this suggestion but Clemenceau stated preferred that the draft should be left as it was. I believe that the suggestion would be accepted by all if the President sees fit to insist upon it. I am not entirely clear yet that this is necessary. I ascertained that George and Clemenceau believed that the terms of the armistice both naval and military were too severe and that they should be modified. George stated that he thought it might be unwise to insist on the occupation of the east bank of the Rhine. Clemenceau stated that he could not maintain himself in the Chamber of Deputies unless this was made a part of the armistice to be submitted to the German forces and that the French army would also insist on this as their due after the long occupation of French soil by the Germans, but he gave us his word of honor that France would withdraw after the peace conditions had been fulfilled. I am inclined to sympathize with position taken by Clemenceau. I pointed out the danger of bringing about a state of Bolshevicism in Germany if terms of Armistice were made too stiff and the consequent danger to England, France and Italy. Clemenceau refused to recognize that there was any danger of Bolshevicism in France. George admitted it was possible to create such a state of affairs in England and both agreed that anything might happen in Italy. I asked Clemenceau where he thought it would be wise to hold the peace conference. He answered Versailles, but however, did not argue with us when George stated that he and I had agreed on Geneva. I stated that I thought this matter should be discussed later. Upon leaving the conference, George and I again agreed that the conference had better be held in neutral territory than in a belligerent country and I still have in mind to urge Lausanne. It was agreed that this afternoon we would discuss, first, results [the terms] of an armistice with Austria; second, the terms of the armistice with Turkey, (with this I explained we have nothing to do); three, the terms of the armistice with Germany. It was agreed that there should be a meeting at my headquarters tomorrow morning of Clemenceau, George, Orlando, Marshal Foch, and myself, with Geddes at hand to advise concerning naval questions. Uninterruptedly [Of course], I am in constant consultation with our military and naval authorities. In the event that answer drafted by British and quoted above is adopted by Allies as their answer to your communicaton I would strongly advise your accepting it without alteration.   House.

                              Paris October 30, 1918

Number 13, urgent. Secret. For the President.

At the meeting this afternoon practically entire time was consumed with a discussion between George and Clemenceau as to who should accept the surrender of the Turks, the British or the French Admiral. Discussion was *not* [most][1] bitter at times and of course I did not participate in it. It was virtually agreed by French, British, and Italians that the proposed answer to the President's communication as drafted by the British and as cabled you this morning should be adopted as the answer of the Allies, so far as Germany was concerned. It was agreed that the terms of the military and naval armistice to be offered Austria should be reviewed [revised][2] by the Allied generals and admirals, and when completed should be transmitted direct through General Diaz to the Austrian Commander-in-Chief. This has the advantage of avoiding political discussion respecting Italian and other claims before capitulation of Austria [is completed.][3] Conference set for tomorrow at eleven thirty at my headquarters, of George, Clemenceau, Orlando, Foch and myself. Full meeting of Supreme War Council called for three P.M. tomorrow afternoon at Versailles.   Edward House

T telegrams (WP, DLC).
  [1] Changes from the copy in SDR, RG 59, 763.72119/8986, DNA.
  [2] Correction from the copy in the House Papers, CtY.
  [3] *ibid.*

From Robert Lansing, with Enclosures

My dear Mr. President: Washington October 30, 1918.

I enclose a copy of a note received today from the Chargé of Switzerland, enclosing a memorandum from the German Government dated the 27th. I intend to give the changes which it is asserted have been made careful study in connection with the German Constitution.   Faithfully yours,   Robert Lansing.

TLS (WP, DLC).

E N C L O S U R E   I

Friedrich Oederlin to Robert Lansing

SIR: Washington, D. C. October 30, 1918.

By direction of my Government, I have the honor to transmit herewith the original text of a memorandum from the German Government, supplementary to its communication of October 27, 1918, and indicating the amendments passed by the Reichstag to the German Constitution, as received by cable from the Swiss Foreign Office.

Accept, Sir, the renewed assurances of my highest consideration.
                                            F. Oederlin

TCL (WP, DLC).

E N C L O S U R E   I I

MEMORANDUM
supplementary to the communication
from the German Government

dated October 27, 1918.

"The amendments to the German constitution, as passed by the Reichstag, signify nothing less but a complete change of the system in German constitutional life. Germany has, thereby, entered the family of States by parliamentary government. The most striking changes are as follows:

First: The declaration of war and the conclusion of peace as well as the conclusion of all treaties are subject to the decision of the Reichstag;

Second: The position to [of] the chancellor is completely changed. Whilst hitherto the chancellor was merely a minister appointed by the confidence of the Emperor, henceforward, according to a new and explicit clause of the constitution, he can assume office only with the confidence of the Reichstag, and hold office as long as the confidence of this body is assured to him. Contrary to other states where such rules are merely observed by custom, it is in Germany now established by the constitution that a vote of non-confidence on the part of the Reichstag obliges the chancellor as well as any other responsible member of the government of the empire to resign.

Third: Another important change is the following: Whilst hitherto the chancellor was only responsible for the orders and decrees of the Emperor as far as countersigned by him, the amended constitution now holds him responsible for all acts and actions of political significance including even the personal utterances of the Emperor, made in speeches or letters, as far as they are liable to influence interior politics or the foreign policy of the empire;

Fourth: The position of the Emperor as the supreme war lord of the German army and navy has been completely abolished. No longer can military acts of political consequence be performed without the consent of the chancellor. The subordination of the military power under the civil power goes so far that even the commission, appointment and dismissal of all offices of the army and navy, done thus far by advice of the constitutionally irresponsible chiefs of the military and naval cabinets, now require the countersignature of the Minister of War, or the Secretary for the Navy, respectively, who, thereby, assume responsibility to the Reichstag;

Fifth: The former clause of the constitution, providing that a representative accepting an office, paid out of the Treasury, lost his mandate, wherefore no representative was able to be a member of the government, has been abolished. In consequence the leaders of the majority parties of the Reichstag have already been appointed to the posts of secretaries and undersecretaries of State within the new government. In this connection an entirely new departure has been made by the appointment of secretaries of State without portfolio. Moreover, the influence of the secretaries of State, chosen from among the members of the Reichstag, has been considerably increased by the fact that, together with and under the presidence of the chancellor, they form the War Cabinet;

Sixth: The introduction, now definitely assured, of the universal, equal and secret electoral law for the Prussian Landtag precludes in future that undemocratic influences may be exercised by the Prussian government on decision of the executive of the empire;

Seventh: By the amendments to the constitution of the empire as well as of Prussia, it has now been secured for all times that in the same degree as in other states, governed since long by parliamentary government, the popular will embodied in parliament, will be decisive within all spheres of public life, in peace as well as in war. Any possibility for personal government is, thereby, definitely eliminated and precluded."

T MS (WP, DLC).

From William Kent

My dear Mr. President:　Kentfield, Marin Co., Cal. Oct. 30, 1918

It was very kind of you to write me at such length concerning the Bouck case. The form of the indictment is to my mind specific evidence that Bouck was not correctly reported. No man capable of filling his position in the community would or could be guilty of such imbecile remarks.

My friend and your friend, George P. Hampton of the Farmers' Open Forum, who is available at all times in Washington, was at the meeting and testifies that Bouck said nothing at all about war finance and that the charges made against him were therefore absurdly false. After personal knowledge of Hampton for six or eight years I have absolute confidence in his statements.

I am sorry to be obliged to reiterate the statement that I believe there is a serious weakness in the Attorney General's office in that the Attorney General, whom I esteem and respect, has determined upon an obstinate policy of absolute trust in the subordinate prosecutors despite any evidence that may be brought as to their disqualification or disqualification of the evidence upon which they are acting.

When you address queries to the Attorney General you merely get a repetition of the charges which in the case of Bouck and the case of Miss Pollock I believe to be unfounded and growing out of prejudice. I ask in this case that someone not subject to the hallucination that the subprosecutors of the Department of Justice can do no wrong, be asked to investigate and report as in the Mooney case.　　　　　　　　　Yours truly,　William Kent

TLS (WP, DLC).

From Albert Sidney Burleson

My dear Mr. President:　　　　　Washington October 30, 1918.

I have examined the cartoon in The North American Review's War Weekly of recent date, enclosed with your note of the 29th instant.

Of course every one not actuated by personal malice or extreme partisanship will agree that a cartoon of this character as well as the article appearing in the same issue[1] which it supplements are out of place at this serious time. The cartoon, however, as well as the article referred to can be viewed in no other light than very harsh criticism. No conduct of these publishers during the war, so far as I am advised, indicates disloyalty to the Government, in fact, they, like Mr. Roosevelt and others of like kidney have the reputation of being extreme advocates of extermination of the Central Powers, and are not only unable to appreciate the good work done by you in the prosecution of this war, but are apparently blind to the consequences which might follow if government in Germany was too much weakened. There can, therefore, be no presumption of disloyal intent in a case of this kind however severe the reflection may be upon one charged with important duties with respect to the conduct of the war.

In fact I do not think the terms of the Espionage Act applies to matter of this character, and I am very sure from the discussion of the measure when it was pending in Congress that the Senators and Members did not intend that the Law should cover this class of matter. If you will remember, there was an amendent proposed to the Bill in the Senate which prohibited criticism of the President, but this was either withdrawn after some discussion or voted down.

I can understand the disgust expressed by Mr. Gavit of this cartoon in his letter to Mr. Tumulty of the 25th instant attached to your communication, but cannot agree with him in the statement that this matter is of the same character as that published by The Masses, which was declared nonmailable by this Department and which ruling was sustained by the courts. I emphatically dissent from the insinuation contained in his letter that there has been ruthless enforcement of the Espionage Act against "the little fellows" but that action has been palsied in the presence of "the great ones." In the discharge of my duty under this law the weak and the strong, the poor and the rich have been accorded like treatment.

Cordially and faithfully yours, A. S. Burleson

TLS (WP, DLC).
  [1] "Negotiations," *The North American Review's War Weekly,* I (Oct. 19, 1918), 2-6. This was a savagely satirical attack, almost certainly written by George B. M. Harvey, on Wilson's recent communications to the German government and upon all those in the administration and in the press who supported the President's personal diplomacy. The article suggested that Wilson's negotiations were anathema to the Allies and to most of the American people and that they were enthusiastically accepted only by Germany and her allies.

From Francis Patrick Walsh

Dear Mr. President: Washington October 30, 1918.

I beg to present the following situation, which I consider extremely important:

War necessities in industry, combined with other narrower economic reasons, have increased the number of women and girls in industry in the United States by approximately 1,650,000, according to our best available information. Every case which comes before the National War Labor Board is impressed deeply with the necessity of handling this new and complicated situation.

Requests have come to me from organizations of women in different parts of the country from sources that might be divided as industrial, political and social, requesting and in some cases insistently demanding that recommendations be made to you to the effect that two women be added as full voting members to the National War Labor Board. In my opinion, this demand has a substantial basis, in reason, justice and the effective working out of the principles which govern the Board. The abnormal influx of women in industry frequently meets with opposition, sometimes extremely violent, on the part of the men workers. In many cases I have observed that the women in the presentation of their grievances are not fairly and vigorously represented by the men. This is due, in my opinion, partly to this prejudice and in part to the lack of understanding of the peculiar problems applying to women in industry. The women as a rule are wholly uninformed as to their rights and, undoubtedly, advantage is being taken of them to their very serious detriment by many employers.

I feel sure that our Board could act with much more intelligence if we had the advice and co-operation of two women who could act with us in the settlement of controversies constantly coming before us in which conditions surrounding women workers are among the principal issues.

Formal requests in writing have been made to the National War Labor Board to recommend to you that you appoint two women to membership on the Board. Inasmuch as the members of the Board, with the exception of Mr. Taft and myself, were nominated by the industrial organizations which they represent; i.e., the representatives of employers by the National Industrial Conference, and the representatives of employees by the American Federation of Labor, by vote of the Board, the matter was referred to these two organizations for their action. This decision of the Board was made during my absence from the city. Had I been present, I would have strongly urged that the Board make a direct recommendation to you that the two women be appointed. From information which I have at hand, I think I am safe in advising you that the organizations will not take any action in the matter or, if they do, will delay so long as to gather additional complications.

Considering this as I do a most vital and pregnant question, I am making bold to suggest that you call upon the National Industrial Conference of which Mr. Frederick P. Fish,[1] 15 Beacon Street, Boston, Mass., is President, and upon the American Federation of Labor of which Mr. John R. Alpine,[2] Washington, D. C., is Acting President in the absence of Mr. Samuel Gompers, requesting each organization to nominate a woman to serve upon the National War Labor Board, and intimating, perhaps, that if the nominations are not promptly made you may, on account of the urgency of the matter, feel compelled to make the appointments by executive order.   Respectfully and sincerely,   Frank P Walsh

TLS (WP, DLC).
    [1] Frederick Perry Fish, corporation lawyer of Boston, former president of the American Telephone & Telegraph Co.
    [2] Former president of the United Association of Plumbers and Steam Fitters of the United States and Canada and a vice-president of the American Federation of Labor.

From Edward Mandell House

Paris Oct 31, 1918

Number 14. Urgent. Secret. For the President. Five minutes before I entered into conference this afternoon of Prime Ministers and Foreign Secretaries and without previous notification General Pershing handed me a copy of the communication I quote herewith, the original thereof having already been sent to the Supreme War Council at Versailles and when George read this his comment was "Political not military. Some one put him up to it." When Clemenceau read it his comment was "theatrical and not in accordance with what he has said to Marshal Foch." No allied general has ever submitted a document of this character to the Supreme War Council without a previous request having been made by the civilian authorities.

I have written the following letter to General Pershing: "In regard to the communication which you sent in to the Supreme War Council this afternoon will you not let me know whether your views are shared by any of the other allied generals." He sent me a verbal answer saying he had not gotten the views of the other allied commanders on this question.

"Paris, October 30th, 1918. To the Allied Supreme War Council, Paris.

Gentlemen:

In considering the question of whether or not Germany's request for an Armistice should be granted, the following expresses my opinion from the military point of view: One. Judging from their excellent conduct during the three months, the British, French, Belgian and American armies appear capable of continuing the offensive indefinitely. Their morale is high and the prospects of certain victory should keep it so.

Two. The American army is constantly increasing in strength and experience, and should be able to take an increasingly important part in the allied offensive. Its growth, both in personnel and material, with such reserves as the Allies may furnish, not counting the Italian army, should be more than equal to the combined losses of the Allied armies.

Three. German man power is constantly diminishing and her armies have lost over three hundred thousand prisoners and over one thousand pieces of artillery during the last three months in their efforts to extricate themselves from a difficult situation and avoid disaster.

Four. The estimated strength of the Allies on the western front, not counting Italy, and of Germany, in rifles is: Allies, one million five hundred sixty four thousand; Germany one million one hundred thirty four thousand; an advantage in favor of the Allies of thirty seven percent. In guns: Allies—twenty two thousand, four hundred and thirteen; Germany-sixteen thousand, four hundred and ninety five; advantage of thirty five percent in favor of the Allies. If Italy's forces should be added to the western front we should have a still greater advantage.

Five. Germany's morale is undoubtedly low, her Allies have deserted her one by one and she can no longer hope to win. Therefore we should take full advantage of the situation and continue the offensive until we compel her unconditional surrender.

Six. An Armistice would revivify the low spirits of the German army and enable it to organize and resist later on and would deprive the Allies of the full measure of victory by failing to press their present advantage to its complete military end.

Seven. As the apparent humility of German leaders in talking of peace may be feigned the Allies should distrust their sincerity and their motives. The appeal for an Armistice is undoubtedly to enable the withdrawal from a critical situation to one more advantageous.

Eight. On the other hand the internal political conditions of Germany, correctly reported, are such that she is practically forced to ask for an armistice to save the overthrow of her present Government a consummation which should be sought by the Allies as precedent to permanent peace.

Nine. A cessation of hostilities short of capitulation postpones, if it does not render impossible, the imposition of satisfactory peace terms, because it would allow Germany to withdraw her army with its present strength, ready to resume hostilities if terms were not satisfactory to her.

Ten. An armistice would lead the allied armies to believe this the end of fighting and it would be difficult if not impossible to resume hostilities with our present advantage in morale in the event of failure to secure at a peace conference what we have fought for.

Eleven. By agreeing to an armistice under the present favorable military situation of the Allies and accepting the principle of a negotiated peace rather than a dictated peace the Allies would jeopardize the moral position they now hold and possibly lose the chance actually to secure world peace on terms that would insure its permanence.

Twelve. It is the experience of history that victorious armies are prone to overestimate the enemy's strength and too eagerly seek an opportunity for peace. This mistake is likely to be made now on account of the reputation Germany has gained through her victories of the last four years.

Thirteen. Finally I believe that complete victory can only be obtained by continuing the war until we force unconditional surrender from Germany but if the Allied Governments decide to grant an armistice the terms should be so rigid that under no circumstances could Germany again take up arms. Respectfully submitted. John J. Pershing, Commander in Chief American Expeditionary Forces."

Edward House.

T telegram (WP, DLC).

From Newton Diehl Baker

Dear Mr President: Washington. October 31, 1918

General March read the enclosed[1] with amazement and frank expressions of distress. He also makes the political suggestion by way of explanation and points out that it is not only at variance with your instructions to him but also at variance with Gen Pershing's own message to you as to what he had said at the Foch-Haig-Petain-Pershing conference where he advised terms and injected no political advice.[2] He is obviously on record one way with you and another way with the Supreme War Council! It is really tragic   Respectfully yours,   Newton D. Baker

ALS (WP, DLC).
¹ The enclosure was J. J. Pershing to the Adjutant General, received Oct. 31, 1918, 5:10 p.m. (repeating Pershing's letter to the Supreme War Council), T telegram (WP, DLC), another copy of which Baker sent to Wilson on November 1.
² See the Enclosure printed with NDB to WW, Oct, 26, 1918.

From Robert Lansing, with Enclosure

My dear Mr. President: Washington October 31, 1918.

I enclose to you a copy of a note which I was handed this morning by the Swedish Minister, containing a communication from Count Andrássy,¹ which has already appeared in the public press. Would you be good enough to indicate what course you deem advisable in connection with this communication?

Faithfully yours,   Robert Lansing

TLS (SDR, RG 59, 763.72119/2600, DNA).
¹ Julius, Count Andrássy von Csik-Szent-Király und Krasznahorka, whom Emperor Charles had appointed Foreign Minister of Austria-Hungary on October 24, 1918.

E N C L O S U R E

Wilhelm August Ferdinand Ekengren to Robert Lansing

Handed me by Swedish Minister
October 31, 1918. RL

Excellency,   Washington, October 30, 1918.

At the request of the Imperial and Royal Austro-Hungarian Government I have been ordered to transmit to Your Excellency the following communication:

"Mr. Secretary of State,

Having taken charge of my office, I have immediately dispatched an official answer to your note of October 18th, by which you will find that we in all respects accept the principles which the President of the United States has expressed in his various declarations.

In full accord with Mr. Wilson's efforts to prevent future wars, and to create a family of nations, we have already made preparations, in order that the peoples of Austria-Hungary may, entirely without hindrance, decide upon, and complete their future organization, according to their own wishes.

Since the accession of Emperor and King Karl, it has been His Majesty's undaunted endeavor to bring, in every way, an end to the war.

More than ever before, this is today the wish of the monarch and of all the peoples, who are dominated by the conviction that the future destiny of the peoples of Austria-Hungary can only be formed in a peaceful world free from the disturbances, the trials, the privations and the bitterness of war.

I, therefore, address to you directly Mr. Secretary of State, an appeal that you use your good offices with the President of the United States to the end that, in the interest of humanity, as well as in the interest of all the peoples living in Austria-Hungary, the entering upon negotiations of peace and an immediate armistice of all the fronts of Austria-Hungary may be brought about.

(Signed) Andrássy."

Accept, Sir, the renewed assurances of my highest consideration.

(Sd) W. A. F. Ekengren.

TCL (SDR, RG 59, 763.72119/2600, DNA).

A Memorandum by Robert Lansing

October 31, 1918.

The Minister of Sweden, at my request, called upon me at 6:15 p.m. at my residence.

I informed him that, after conferring with the President relative to the communication of the Austro-Hungarian Government addressed to the President in relation to peace negotiations and an armistice, I wished to inform him that the communication would be submitted to the Governments with which this Government is associated in the war for their consideration and that he was at liberty to so advise his Government.

The Minister thanked me for the information and said that he would immediately cable his Government to that effect.

Robert Lansing

TS MS (SDR, RG 59, 763.72119/2392, DNA).

From Robert Lansing, with Enclosure

My dear Mr. President: Washington October 31, 1918.

I think you will be interested in reading the attached telegram from London.

Information from this source has, as you know, been most reliable in the past and I am inclined to give full credence to this information. It should be read in connection with reports we have received from other sources indicating that the German military regime has not been eliminated, that it is still all-powerful and that it intends to resume control in the event of the failure of the present negotiations looking to an armistice and peace.

Faithfully yours,   Robert Lansing.

TLS (WP, DLC).

E N C L O S U R E

London Oct 30, 1918

Urgent. 3219. Most secret. Harrison from Bell. Polo[1] has reported to his Government from Berlin that the continued cessation of submarine attacks on passenger ships is dependent on the conclusion of an Armistice and that if the negotiations are abortive a recrudescence of such activity may be expected.

Our friends tell me that when Austria's collapse appeared inevitable, the German Government ordered the German submarines in the Mediterranean to the number of about thirty to take in fuel *and* the nearest Austro-Hungarian Adriatic port and to come north.

Regarding the present apparent cessation of German submarine activity and similar reports from Scandinavia that submarines are returning to German ports, Hall informs me that these reports are untrue and are being put about by the enemy to put us off our guard with respect to submarine concentration in certain localities which is now taking place. Am privately informed Sims is fully informed on this point.

Finally Ambassador [Admiral] Hall informs me that he has learned from an absolutely sure source that at a recent council in Berlin the German Emperor said: "During peace negotiations or even after peace, my U boats will find an opportunity to destroy the English fleet."

Hall asked to be excused from divulging the source of this astonishing piece of information but he assures me that it is as certain as the wireless to Madrid and he dictated what I have quoted as being the exact words used by the Emperor.   Laughlin.

T telegram (WP, DLC).
   [1] That is, Luis Polo de Bernabé, the Spanish Ambassador to Germany.

From Robert Lansing, with Enclosure

My dear Mr. President: Washington October 31, 1918.

I enclose to you a letter which I received yesterday afternoon from the Italian Ambassador, which makes a request as to our taking a position relative to an armistice with Germany separate from Austria-Hungary. I presume the Ambassador will want an answer promptly and I would like to have your views as to what I should say to him. I would be very much obliged if you would give me your views as to what reply I should make to him.

Faithfully yours,   Robert Lansing.

TLS (SDR, RG 59, 763.72119/2554½, DNA).

ENCLOSURE

Count Macchi di Cellere to Robert Lansing

Personal and Confidential

Regia Ambasciata D'Italia

My dear Mr. Lansing: October 30, 1918

Baron Sonnino cabled yesterday to me pointing out that it is vital to Italy that any armistice to be granted to Germany should be coupled with an Austro-Hungarian armistice. I brought this matter late in the afternoon to the attention of Mr. Polk, asking him whether it would be possible for the government of the United States to instruct accordingly their representatives at Versailles. Mr. Polk was good enough to say that he would take up the matter with you this morning. Menawhile [Meanwhile] I have received another cable from my Government which gives expression to the thought of the Italian Government in regard to the questions you put to them in your note of the twenty-third to me, and bears largely on the subject of the German and Austrian armistice. I thought it advisable, consequently to let you know confidentially its contents at once, thus conveying also to you in advance the views of the Italian Government on the note in question.

Baron Sonnino, having stated that on the twenty-ninth of October there was called at Paris an interallied meeting to discuss the conditions of an armistice, points out in his cable that it would seem to him premature to give now an official answer to questions which have been addressed also to the other governments and in regard to which there will be a joint discussion in the presence of the American delegate. This the more, inasmuch as Italy, who faces almost alone the whole Austro-Hungarian army, has to safeguard herself against the very serious consequences which might arise from an armistice with Germany alone, which Mr. Wilson has now submitted to the Allies.

Baron Sonnino, however, authorizes me to let the President know at once that in so far as the Italian Government are concerned they are willing to participate in the exchange of views of the allied powers at war against the Central Empires regarding a possible armistice, as suggested in the note of the President of the United States of October 23, 1918. The Italian Government fully agree concerning what is said in this note in respect to the manner with which the conditions of such armistice are to be determined. They acknowledge the wise care with which the President of the United States has endeavored in his statements to safeguard the interests of the peoples at war against Germany, and hope that the allied powers proceed at the same time to a determination of the terms which are to be requested for an armistice of the Austro-Hungarian Empire. Because of the very high aims the President put forth in his note of the twenty-third of October, the Italian Government do not deem that an armistice may be in any way taken into consideration and, much less, granted to Germany and to Austria-Hungary separately. An armistice granted only to Germany, even when accompanied by the highest guarantees, would make it possible for the Austro-Hungarian army to reenforce, with the divisions freed from the western front, its forces in Italy, which are already superior in number and position. The Austro-Hungarian army would also thus retain in its rank and file German troops disguised as soldiers of the Austro-Hungarian monarchy, as they have already done in the past. And the geographical conditions are such that internal communications are made more easy between Germany and Austria than between France and Italy, so that it would be impossible for the allies to parry in time the danger by the transferring of arms and troops from one front to the other.

I thought it was important, on account of the urgency of the matters involved, to bring to your kind attention the aforesaid, and I earnestly hope that you may see the way clear to accede to my Government's point of view, not only in the interests of Italy, but of the allied cause.

Accept, my dear Mr. Lansing, the assurance of my highest consideration.   Very sincerely yours,   Macchi di Cellere

TLS (SDR, RG 59, 763.72119/2554½, DNA).

From Thomas William Lamont

Personal

Dear Mr. President: [New York] October 31st, 1918.

Referring to my letter to you of October eleventh and your kind acknowledgment of the eighteenth, I am venturing, almost without warrant, to address you again to explain a sense of some personal discomfiture which I feel, because of an editorial which appeared in the Evening Post of October twenty-fifth, questioning your wisdom in issuing your appeal for the election of a Democratic Congress.

When I returned from my talk with you in Washington on October fourth, I went over with Mr. Ogden certain points of the conversation, desiring that he should have the benefit of the views that you expressed to me, as to ways in which the Evening Post might co-operate in assisting to bring about a just and permanent peace. You may remember that you made some very practical suggestions on that line. I mentioned further that you felt it important that a Democratic Congress should be returned, but I said nothing further on that point.

So Ogden's editorial ("An Unnecessary Risk") which appeared on October twenty-fifth, was without my knowledge. His position was: Has not the President assumed an unnecessary risk at this time when "his position is supreme and unchallenged"?

I haven't any idea that you have ever read the editorial in question, but it has occurred to me that in case you should, you might think it more than curious that it should have appeared. I often wish that time were afforded me so that I could take an active part in the daily councils of Mr. Odgen and his associates, and later on I may be able to do so, but at present it is quite out of the question.

I feel that in writing you I am making almost too much of an unimportant matter, but I could not rest easily under even a remote apprehension that you might have read Mr. Ogden's editorial and have gained the erroneous impression that it was written with my knowledge.

Let me take this opportunity to say that if, at any time, any way occurs to you in which I can serve the Government's interest in any direction, I trust you will command me with complete freedom.

With great respect,

Sincerely yours,   Thomas W. Lamont

TLS (WP, DLC).

From Edward Mandell House

Paris October 31, 1918.

Urgent, number 23, Secret for the President. The three Prime Ministers Marshal Foch, and myself met this morning and practically agreed upon terms for the armistice with Austria in order that we might facilitate matters when we met at Versailles this afternoon. At conference this afternoon at Versailles terms of naval and military armistice to be proposed to Austria were formally agreed upon. Views of military and naval authorities were somewhat modified. Full text of proposed armistice is being cabled.[1]

Following resolution was adopted by Supreme War Council

"The Supreme War Council decided [decide]:

A. To approve attached terms of armistice with Austria-Hungary.

B. That General Diaz on behalf of the associated Governments shall on the arrival of accredited representatives of Austrian Supreme Command communicate to them approved terms of an armistice.

C. That the Italian Government on behalf of the Supreme War Council shall be responsible for communicating this decision to General Diaz.

D. To invite Colonel House on behalf of the Supreme War Council to communicate this decision to *the* President Wilson.

Versailles, October 31, 1918."

Fortunately *I was able* present [to prevent] discussion of political questions. I regard this feature as most favorable. It is not very probable [my opinion] that the submission of terms of armistice to Austria under the circumstances and without any express qualifications may be construed as acceptance on the part of the Allies of the President's proposals. I thought it best not to bring on a discussion of this matter at this time. Clemenceau, George, Orlando, Foch and myself are to meet again tomorrow at my headquarters and the Supreme War Council is to meet again tomorrow at ten [three] oclock at Versailles. At these meetings terms of the military and naval armistice to be offered Germany are to be discussed. It is my understanding that when the terms of armistice to be offered Germany have been agreed upon, they will be cabled to the President. The Allies will at the same time formally *agreed* [agree] to the President's fourteen points with the reservations cabled you in our number twelve. If the President accepts this they then propose to send word to Germany that Foch is prepared to receive their military authorities and to transmit to them the terms of armistice agreed upon by the Allies and the United States. The plan is not to publish the terms of the armistice until Germany has accepted them. They insist that publication should not be made because if published, public opinion would not permit modification.

House

T telegram (WP, DLC).
  [1] House conveyed these in EMH to RL, Nos. 15 and 16, Oct. 31, 1918, T telegrams (E. M. House Papers, CtY).

To Edward Mandell House

The White House, October 31, 1918.

[No. 6] Referring to your No. twelve,[1] I fully and sympathetically recognize the exceptional position and necessities of Great Britain with regard to the use of the sea for defence, both at home and throughout the Empire, and also realize that freedom of the seas needs careful definition and is full of questions upon which there is need of the freest discussion and the most liberal interchange of views. But I am not clear that the reply of the Allies, quoted in your No. twelve, definitely accept[s] the principle of freedom of the seas and means to reserve only the free discussion of definitions and limitations.

Please insist that it be made clear before I decide whether it must be altered, or go again to Congress who will have no sympathy or wish that American life and property should be sacrificed for British naval control. I cannot recede from the position taken in my No. 5 though, of course, I depend on your discretion to insist at the right time and in the right way on terms, one, two, three and fourteen as essentially American terms in the program and I cannot change what our troops are fighting for or consent to end with only European arrangements for peace.

Freedom of the seas will not have to be discussed with the German Government if we agree among ourselves beforehand, but will be if we do not. Blockade is one of the many things which will require immediate re-definition in view of the many new circumstances of warfare developed by this war. There is no danger of its being abolished.

Replying to your No. 10, Oct. 30, I cannot agree to Lloyd George's program of a general settlement among ourselves before the peace conference. I am entitled to take a personal part in the beginning of the real settlement and in such preliminaries as would make the final conference a mere form.

Would suggest that Council refer Pershing's letter to me and so inform him.

I am proud of the way you are handling situation.

Wilson.

T telegram (E. M. House Papers, CtY).
[1] Of October 30, 1918. There is only a WWsh partial decode of this telegram in WP, DLC.

From Edward Mandell House

[Paris, Oct. 31, 1918]

Everything is changing for the better since yesterday and I hope you will not insist upon my using your cable he[re] referred to as I listened to [except as I may think best.]

If you will give me free hand in dealing with these immediate negotiations assure you that nothing will be done to embarrass you or to compromise any of your peace principles. You will have as free a hand after the Armistice is signed as you now have. It is exceedingly important that nothing be said or done at this time which may in any way halt the Armistice which will save [so many] thousands of lives. Negotiations are now proceeding satisfactorily.

Edward House

EBWhw decode (WP, DLC).

From George Foster Peabody

Dear Mr President   New York Octo 31, 1918

I enclose a clipping respecting Mr Roger Baldwin[1] who is as will be seen of a very intense nature but his passion for real service to others and to be true to himself is a nobly fine thing. There is surely something wrong with a democracy that so impinges upon a mans conscience as does this action of the Judge. I think few things are more undermining to the spirit that you have manifested with such healing power to a world in travail to know the truth and how—as such a conviction. I doubt not that you have sent for the papers in the case already and will as soon as possible exercise the righteousness which is an essential part of mercy at an early date. I am writing this to say that I know personally of Mr Baldwin's invaluable work in many directions and how he has strained family ties in the past to be true to his conscience. He says he "deliberately violated the Draft act"—but that depends upon the spirit of the act respecting the conscience of the individual and not upon Mr Baldwin's acceptance of the interpretation taken by the District Attorney. I ventured some months since to urge upon my long time friendly acquaintance Dist Attorney Caffey that he was not strengthening the power of the administration to win the war and conclude a permanent because constructive peace by insisting upon a second trial of Max Eastman but he was in spite of himself a victim to the normal disease of the District Attorney determined to convict.

I hope that your quite marvelous temper of wisdom will lead to your granting a pardon to Mr Baldwin. I believe it will be in line with the work you desire the country to help you carry forward to complete success. I shall hope that I may have the honor of trying out the loyalty to you of some of my neighbors at Glens Falls in which heavy Republican district we are trying to send Mr Rogers an earnest Democrat in place of Mr Parker.[2] We are to have a large meeting on Saturday third when for the first time I shall plead for a Tammany mans election as Governor too,[3] that New York may give you the fullest support.

I will trust to have the high privilege after the election of congratulating you in person and speaking with you of some of the issues that stir our souls.

You evidently failed to realize how few of the Republican leaders can "understand English." Their failure on your candid and most modest statement of simple facts about the advantage of "undivided counsels" certainly brought out the failure of some parts of our educational system.

I am with ever increasing admiration and strongest pride
Faithfully Yours George Foster Peabody

ALS (WP, DLC).
[1] "R. N. Baldwin, Draft Violator, Sentenced," New York *Evening Post*, Oct. 30, 1918. This news report stated that Baldwin had been sentenced to serve one year in a federal penitentiary after pleading guilty to a violation of the Selective Service Act. Baldwin had refused to submit himself to a physical examination for the draft. He was quoted as saying that he considered "the principle of conscription of life as a flat contradiction of all our cherished ideals of individual freedom, democratic liberty, and Christian teaching." He also declared himself opposed to the Selective Service Act because it was for the purpose of conducting war.
[2] James Southworth Parker, the incumbent Republican congressman, defeated Gustavus Adolphus Rogers, a lawyer and businessman of Glens Falls and New York, by a vote of 11,841 to 6,682 in the election held on November 5.
[3] That is, Alfred E. Smith.

From Edward Graham Elliott

Dear Mr. President: San Francisco October 31st, 1918.

In the course of my revision of The State, I have come to the enclosed paragraphs, to-wit, 1457 and 1458, regarding International Law. In view of the great changes that have taken place in the thirty years since these paragraphs were first written, and also in view of the need of a correct presentation of your views at the present time with respect to this subject, I have thought it best to send you the originals and a tentative revised statement,[1] in order that you may re-write these paragraphs or make what changes seem desirable in my revision. I should much prefer to have you do the former, but, knowing the great demands upon your time, I hesitate even to broach the question to you.

I may say that the publishers contemplate issuing the appropriate parts of The State as a text for possible use by S.A.T.C. students in American Universities, and, in the revision, I have sought to retain the work, as nearly as might be, in its original form, though I have taken the liberty of modifying certain criticisms made of France and certain statements apparently in commendation of Germany,[2] having in mind always the desire that your present unrivalled position should not be rendered liable to criticism by what was said so long ago under other circumstances.

In consultation with the publishers, it has seemed wise to omit the section numbers.

Margaret joins me in love and fond greetings to you all.

Very truly yours,   Edward Elliott

P.S. In view of the need for haste, I would be glad to have you forward your revision, or mine, with corrections direct to D. C. Heath & Co., 231-245 West 39th St., New York City.

TLS (WP, DLC).
    [1] Wilson accepted all of the revisions mentioned by Elliott in this letter, making only a few stylistic changes before sending Elliott's text to the publisher. See WW to E. G. Elliott and to D. C. Heath and Company, Nov. 11, 1918. Elliott refers to paragraphs 1457 and 1458 of the revised edition of *The State* (Boston, 1898). These are virtually identical to paragraphs 1216 and 1217 of that portion of the original version of *The State* printed in this series at June 3, 1889, Vol. 6. Elliott's revision of these paragraphs reads as follows:

"International Law.—International Law may be described as law in an incomplete state. It is law without a forceful sanction such as exists for the ordinary law of the land. There is no earthly power to which all nations are subject; there is no power, therefore, above the nations to enforce obedience to rules of conduct as between them, yet International Law is not lacking in sanction altogether; it rests upon those principles of right action, of justice, and of consideration which have so universal an acceptance in the moral judgment of men that they have been styled the Laws of Nature. Back of it in the first instance is the common public opinion of the world. When this public opinion is flouted, and the principles and practices of international Law are disregarded, then the physical force of individual states or groups of states may be brought to bear upon the law-breaker. International Law is the law of the international community of states; its principles are those upon which the successful life of that community depends. The society of states is not yet fully organized and International Law is incomplete just to the extent that this society lacks organization; its courts, its judges, its legislatures are rudimentary and are wanting as yet in that definiteness of constitution and authority which we find in individual states.

"Early writers like Grotius and Vattel embodied it in distinct statements of what they conceived to be the almost self-evident principles of the Law of Nature. In process of time, the practice of nations has been recorded in state papers and in learned treatises by hosts of scholars; principles of international action have been agreed to in treaties by which states acting in pairs or in groups have agreed to be found in their relations with each other, and both practice and agreements have found their way into the statutes or established judicial precedents of enlightened individual states. More and more international conventions have come to recognize certain elements of right, of equity and comity as settled, as always to be accepted in transactions between states. The practice of concerted action by the states of the world in formulating International Law is best exemplified in the First and Second Hague Conferences of 1899 and 1907, where much of the practice of International Law was formulated and definite rules accepted by the great body of states as binding upon them.

"The formation of a 'League of Nations' to bring pressure to bear upon a state unmindful of its international obligations will go far towards supplying the sanction of regulated force which International Law has hitherto lacked." *The State*, "Special Edition Revised to December, 1918 by Edward Elliott, Ph.D.," (Boston, 1918), pp. 85-86.

[2] Most of Elliott's revisions in the chapter on "The Government of France" involved sections in which Wilson had strongly criticized the character and activities of the Chamber of Deputies. For example, Elliott cut out the last sentence of paragraph 418 of the edition of 1898, which reads as follows: "The later presidents [of the French Republic] have been men of so little commanding force and the Senate has played so timid a part in affairs that their position of advantage has been altogether sacrificed; and the unbridled license of the Chamber constitutes one of the chief menaces to the success and even to the existence of the Republic." For other examples of Elliott's revisions, compare paragraphs 429 and 430 of the edition of 1898 with pp. 161-62 of the Elliott edition; paragraph 432 of the former with p. 163 of the latter; and paragraph 435 with p. 164. Elliott also cut out paragraph 446 of the edition of 1898: this was an attack on the "spoils system" in the distribution of public offices in France.

Elliott actually made very few substantive changes in the chapter on "The Governments of Germany," undoubtedly because Wilson himself had made far fewer value judgments in that chapter than in the one of France. Elliott cut out two paragraphs (numbers 569 and 570 in the edition of 1898) praising the role played by political scientists in the development of German institutions and one (number 615 in *ibid.*) comparing favorably the flexibility of Prussian local organizations with the allegedly "forced uniformity" of local institutions in France. Beyond this, Elliott's chief alteration was to shift the entire discussion of German political institutions from the present to the past tense, explaining in a new final paragraph that "all Germany" was then (December 1, 1918) in a "state of revolution" (Elliott edition, p. 489).

From Lydia Wickliffe Holmes

New Orleans La Oct 31-18

State woman suffrage amendment will be submitted Nov 5 governor[1] with us. Col Ewing[2] national committeeman has finally endorsed it. With light vote in state on account of war and no campaign city has determining voice organization controlled by Mayor Behrman[3] who is hostile. We have put it up to him and matter of loyalty to you and democracy without result. You alone can save situation. Lydia Wickliffe Holmes,
State Chairman Womans Suffrage party
of Louisiana

T telegram (WP, DLC).
[1] Ruffin Golson Pleasant, Governor of Louisiana, 1916-1920.
[2] That is, Robert Ewing.
[3] That is, Martin Behrman.

From Joseph Patrick Tumulty

Dear Governor: The White House 31 October, 1918

There are three applications before you for letters of endorsement in the cases of Candidate O'Shaunessy[1] of Rhode Island, Mr. Jameson[2] whose vote on suffrage is needed, in New Hampshire, and Senator Watson of West Virginia. Vance McCormick and Homer Cummings last night urged me to again put the matter before you. A vicious attack is being made on O'Shaunessy by the Republicans, and the suffragists are asking your intervention in Jameson's behalf. I know how deeply sensitive you feel about Watson, but every indication points to his election in West Virginia. Telegrams are pouring in here from our friends, like John T. McGraw, asking a final word from you in Senator Watson's behalf. They claim that your letter to Chilton,[3] which was published, in which you seemed to prefer Chilton, has given the impression to the people of West Virginia that you do not want Watson. As I see this campaign growing more desperate from day to day and realize that every effort is being made to defeat Democrats who have openly declared themselves to be your friends, I do not think you ought to hesitate very long before granting the request in these cases. Certainly Watson is to be preferred to Mr. Stephen B. Elkins,[4] who represents everything that is opposed to our principles. I hope that you will send brief telegrams in all of these cases.   J.P.T.

TL (WP, DLC).
    [1] George Francis O'Shaunessy, Democratic congressman from Rhode Island, 1911-1919; at this time a candidate for the Senate against the Republican incumbent, LeBaron Bradford Colt.
    [2] John Butler Jameson, life insurance executive of Concord, N. H., and chairman of the New Hampshire Committee on Public Safety; at this time the Democratic candidate for the Senate seat vacated by the death of Jacob H. Gallinger.
    [3] WW to W. E. Chilton, June 27, 1918, TLS (Letterpress Books, WP, DLC). Chilton had lost to Watson in the Democratic senatorial primary election on August 6, 1918.
    [4] Tumulty was confused. The Republican candidate for the Senate was Davis Elkins, son of Stephen Benton Elkins, Senator from West Virginia from 1895 until his death in 1911.

Roy Wilson Howard to William Walter Hawkins[1]

Paris. Oct. 31, 1918.

Urgent. Number 18. Following for Hawkins, United Press, New York City:

"Confidential. Following not to be published but should furnish basis and tone for United Press despatches. Allies negotiation of armistice terms, military not political matter. British and the French have insisted upon airtight censorship all press despatches to United States. Only permit cable matter appearing French and British press, wherein only militarist unconditional surrender articles permitted appear. Both French and British politicians are showing junker tendencies. Despite politicians short vision, masses France, Great Britain overwhelmingly support Wilsons program. Socialists to-day placarded Paris denouncing politicians attempt thwart Wilsons program to which pledge full support. Impossible to state this now because evidence discord among Allies would strengthen German junkers enfeebled generals but utmost important our despatches in the United States be handled with foregoing constantly in mind regardless of text of such matter as can be sent through censorship. Inexpedient House make fight now to abolish existing political censorship but will do so when time comes. Understand Wilson will win in Peace Conference, in any event *at* [as] he now commands confidence of laboring masses in both England and France. Greater virulency German militarism however makes it impossible force showdown until Germans completely defeated. House now contending for armistice terms that will make immediate German surrender possible instead of junkeristic allied demands which would assure bloody German last ditch stand. Important you avoid any suggestion allied discord, equally important cable desk Washington staff, beware insidious propaganda movement about United States becloud Wilson's aims. Howard."   Edward House.

T telegram (WP, DLC).
    [1] First vice-president and general manager of the United Press Association.

Lord Robert Cecil to Colville Adrian de Rune Barclay

[London] 31 October, 1918.

No. 6526. My telegram No. 6360.[1]

Text of declaration[2] has now been decided upon and is being telegraphed to your French colleague.

We have had some difficulty with the French Government over the wording of the second paragraph giving areas in which we undertake to encourage and aid establishment of Native Governments and Administrations. Clause defining this area should read: "En Syrie et Mesopotamie actuellement liberées par les Alliés et dans les territoires dont ils poursuivent la libération." You should make sure that version telegraphed to your French colleague is worded as above.

It is left to you and to your French colleague to decide upon the method of communication to the President and as soon as we learn that this communication has been made the text will be communicated to the Arabs.

It has also been decided that the agreements of 1916, 1917 and 1918 and any other documents bearing on the Middle Eastern situation should be brought confidentially to the President's notice, and you should make arrangements accordingly in concert with your French colleague. As intimated in my telegram marked Personal of October 10th,[3] I have already explained to him privately and personally the agreement of 1915, under which Italy entered the War as also the agreements of 1916 and 1917. Lord Reading will bring copies of these and of papers respecting recent arrangement with France, and will then be ready to take up the whole matter with the President in concert with the French Ambassador.[4]

In the meantime should French Ambassador be already in possession of the several documents and desirous of your co-operation in making a preliminary confidential communication to the State Department or to the President, you are authorised to act with him. But communication should be in any case purely private and unofficial.

T telegram (FO 115/2429, pp. 321-22, PRO).
[1] A. J. Balfour to C. A. de R. Barclay, Oct. 23, 1918, T telegram (FO 115/2429, pp. 318-20, PRO). This telegram summarized the diplomatic discussions between Great Britain and France which led to the declaration quoted in n. 2 below.
[2] "The aim of France and Great Britain in carrying on in the Near East the war let loose by Germany's ambitions is the complete and final liberation of the peoples so long oppressed by the Turks and the establishment of governments and administrations deriving their authority from the initiative and the free choice of the native populations.
"In view of following out this intention, France and Great Britain are agreed to encourage and help the establishment of native governments and administrations in Syria and Mesopotamia actually liberated by the Allies, and in the territories they are now striving to liberate, and to recognize them as soon as effectively established. Far from seeking to force upon the populations of these countries any particular institution, France and Great Britain have no other concern than to insure by their support and their active assistance the normal working of the governments and institutions which the populations shall have freely adopted, so as to secure just impartiality for all, and also to facilitate the economic development of the country in arousing and encouraging local initiative by the diffusion of instruction, and to put an end to discords which have too long been taken advantage of by Turkish rule.
"Such is the role that the two Allied Governments claim for themselves in the liberated territories." T MS (FO 115/2429, p. 325, PRO).
[3] A. J. Balfour to C. A. de R. Barclay, Oct. 10, 1918, T telegram (FO 115/2428, pp. 231-33, PRO).
[4] See C. A. de R. Barclay to R. Cecil, Nov. 3, 1918.

To John Thomas McGraw

[The White House] 1 November, 1918

In response to your letter,[1] I am very glad to confirm your impression that in supporting Colonel Clarence W. Watson for the Senate of the United States you are directly aiding in the winning of the war and the securing of a peace that will satisfy the ideals of the Nation. Any reports that the administration does not favor the election of Col. Watson are of course utterly without foundation.

Woodrow Wilson

T telegram (Letterpress Books, WP, DLC).
[1] J. T. McGraw to WW, Oct. 16, 1918, TLS (WP, DLC).

From Edward Mandell House

Paris. Nov. 1, 1918.

Very urgent. Number 27. Secret. For the President. Meeting has been called for Saturday morning ten a.m. at French War office. Purpose is to discuss what steps should be taken if it becomes necessary on account of serious internal condition of Austria to police that country. Telegram has been intercepted from Austrian authorities at Pola to naval attaché Constantinople stating that naval stores establishment and all other naval property will be handed over to Yugo-Slav national council at Agram through medium of provision [local] committees. Telegraph [Telegram] also states that "the handing over of *contribute* [dangerous] flotilla to the royal Hungarian Government will take effect under the same conditions." The word *contribute* [dangerous] may mean "Danube." I should appreciate immediate expression of your views for my guidance at conference.   House.

T telegram (WP, DLC).

To Edward Mandell House

The White House [Nov. 1, 1918].

VII. Referring to your number twenty-seven strongly advise the most liberal possible concurrence in transfer of actual armed force to Czecho-Slovak and Jugo-Slav local authorities as the best proof of our utter good faith towards them, but more caution with regard to Hungary. Local control of course infinitely better than foreign on every account. On principle and for the sake of the incalculable difficulties of the future keep hands off the pieces of Austria-Hungary and reduce outside intervention to minimum.

This is the time to win the confidence of the populations there and the peace of Europe pivots there.

WWT telegram (WP, DLC).

Two Telegrams from Edward Mandell House

Paris Nov 1, 1918

29. Secret. For the President. Admiral Benson handed me the following memorandum: "In view of possibility of desperate action being attempted by German naval forces or a part of it upon receipt of Armistice terms,[1] strongly recommend sailing of troops be delayed until definite information is received. End."

                                          Edward House.

¹ The "desperate action" had already been "attempted." Obsessed by a desire to preserve the honor of the German navy, and especially that of its officer corps, Admiral Reinhard Karl Friedrich Heinrich Scheer, chief of the Admiralty Staff, Commodore Magnus von Levetzow, Scheer's chief of staff, Admiral Franz von Hipper, commander of the High Seas Fleet, and Admiral Adolf von Trotha, Hipper's chief of staff, had, in early October, conceived a plan to send the High Seas Fleet, then at Kiel, out to make a final, and almost certainly suicidal, attack on the British Grand Fleet. The German admirals carefully concealed the project from the civilian government and even from Emperor William himself. They hoped to carry out their plan by assembling the German fleet from October 27 to October 29 at Schilling Roads off Wilhelmshaven. The enlisted men, however, having heard rumors of the proposed sortie, refused to man the ships. This action soon mushroomed into a full-scale mutiny and takeover of the city of Kiel and its naval base on November 3. These events in turn set off revolution throughout Germany. See Daniel Horn, *The German Naval Mutinies of World War I* (New Brunswick, N. J., 1969), pp. 198-266.

Paris Nov. 1, 1918

Number 30. For the President. We made satisfactory progress this morning regarding terms for German Armistice. Both Clemenceau and George now moderate as Foch will permit. They realize that the terms somewhat [should not be] harsher than is necessary to fulfill your conditions regarding the making of it impossible for Germany to renew hostilities. We are modifying the naval program in the interest of commerce [the same way].

Edward House.

T telegrams (WP, DLC).

From Robert Lansing, with Enclosure

My dear Mr. President: Washington November 1, 1918.

The Russian Ambassador handed me today the enclosed pro memoria relative to the reported purpose of a massacre by the Bolsheviks on November 10th.

I told him that I would lay the document before you for your consideration and would advise him as soon as possible as to your views.   Faithfully yours,   Robert Lansing.

TLS (WP, DLC).

E N C L O S U R E

Handed me by the Russian Amb.
Nov 1st/18 RL.

PRO MEMORIA

November 1, 1918.

September 21, in its efforts to check Bolsheviki terrorism in Russia, the American Government addressed an appeal to the Allied and neutral Governments, inviting them to join in an expression of abhorrence against barbarism and to impress upon the perpetrators of the crimes their aversion and horror.

Events have proved since, that the reign of terror has not subsided. On the contrary later reports indicate, that the Bolsheviki now openly declare November 10, as a general St. Bartholomew night, with wholesale slaughter of the Bourgeoisie and the intellectual classes.

The past records of the leaders of the Red Guards rend[er] futile any illusions with regard to this threat. It is useless as well to qualify these unheard acts from the point of view of humanity and civilization. Facts are to be taken as they stand.

The Russian people are not responsible for this indiscriminate barbarism. A gang of men, foreign to the Russian people, using for their bloody crimes hoards of hirelings, composed mostly of elements not Russian.

The relations between the Bolsheviki rulers and Germany have been openly established. The leaders of the Red Guards are mere instruments in the hands of the German agents. German detachments, formed of prisoners of war and officered by Germans, are operating on Russian territory in close contact with the Bolsheviki forces.

The terrorism and the annihilation of the intellectual classes may be a part of a nefarious German scheme. In any case, the crimes and terrorism are committed with approbation, even if silent, of the German foremen in Russia.

In order to stop terrorism it is useless to appeal to the conscience of the instigators. Massacre can be stopped only through a direct threat to the perpetrators. The Bolsheviki leaders, both in central and local organizations, should be made to understand that they will be held personally accountable for their crimes. Strict personal responsibility ought to be applied as well to German agents and military commanders now in Russia.

The leaders of the Red Guards and their German masters must be made to feel, unmistakably and unequivocally, that they will have to answer for their crimes before a Court of organized humanity, from which no leniency is to be expected. Extradiction [Extradition] of these criminals should be made part of the future peace agreements.

T MS (WP, DLC).

From Newton Diehl Baker, with Enclosures

Dear Mr. President: Washington. November 1, 1918.

I enclose—

No. 1. A cablegram received late last night from General Pershing. Please note the paragraph marked with red pencil;[1] the rest of it you have seen.

No. 2. A cablegram just received from General Bliss.

No. 3. A cablegram which I have sent General Bliss. This I thought it wise to send to make quite sure that General Bliss understands the situation and will not be misled by what he would perhaps assume to be your views unless warned as shown in the underscored sentence.

No. 4. A cablegram which I think I should send General Pershing, since this matter has now been brought officially to my attention by him. Respectfully yours, Newton D. Baker

TLS (WP, DLC).
[1] "Reporting my view terms of armistice with Germany, views were expressed under circumstances as reported and upon conditions that it should be deemed wise to grant an armistice. Question now seems undetermined and therefore have handed Allied Supreme War the following communication which I hasten to report to Secretary of War. Have not had full opportunity to discuss with Mr. House nor with Allied Commanders in Chief but am inclined to believe that Marshal Foch would hold same views and that Marshal Haig would not approve. No doubt Mr. House will report action of Council." J. J. Pershing to P. C. Harris, Oct. 31, 1918, T telegram (WP, DLC). The remainder of this telegram quoted Pershing's communication to the Supreme War Council, Oct. 30, 1918, which is quoted in full in EMH to WW, Oct. 31, 1918 (first telegram of that date).

ENCLOSURE I

Versailles. October 31st [1918].

3-THB Confidential. For Secretary of War and Chief of Staff.

Supreme War Council tonight agreed on terms of armistice with Austria-Hungary and charged Colonel House with communicating it to the President. Considered important that this should precede armistice with Germany. Bliss.

ENCLOSURE II

November 1, 1918.

RUSH Bliss Amsec Versailles.

Your 3 THB just received and communicated to the President. I have not been sending you information or instructions because Colonel House has direct communication with the President and you are doubtless conferring with him fully. General Pershing has just sent me a copy of a letter sent by him October 30th to Supreme War Council. The letter was not previously submitted to the President and you will rely on Colonel House for the President's views in such matters. Cable me freely your own views if you desire any points especially considered by the President. Baker.

P. C. March

TC telegrams (WP, DLC).

E N C L O S U R E   I I I

November 1, 1918.

CABLEGRAM to General John J. Pershing:

"I have received your number B-13-CO, October thirty-first, reporting letter sent by you to the Supreme War Council. The subject of the letter is plainly beyond my province as Secretary of War, and I have therefore laid your telegram in full before the President, who directs me to say that he will make known his further views on the subject through Colonel House, his special representative, and General Bliss, his military representative on the Supreme War Council.

Please cable me whether you had received my cablegram of October twenty-seventh, giving the President's views on armistice,[1] prior to your sending this letter to Supreme War Council; and also whether you had acted upon President's direction as explained in last paragraph of that cablegram.   Baker."

I entirely approve of this W.W.

CC MS (WC, NjP).
[1] It is printed as an Enclosure with NDB to WW, Oct. 28, 1918.

From Frank J. Hayes and Others

Indianapolis, Ind., Nov. 1, 1918.

Since last July the representatives of the United Mine Workers of America have been asking Dr. Garfield, Federal Fuel Administration, for an increase in mining prices for the miners of the United States. On October first Dr. Garfield permitted the anthracite mine workers to present their reasons for an advance in wages and later on, October fourteen, he allowed them an increase. But, on October twenty fourth, he denied an increase to the bituminous miners. We regard this decision, affecting the bituminous miners of the United States, as unfair; therefore, we appeal to you from the decision of

Dr. Garfield. In appealing to you we ask only that the same treatment be accorded the bituminous miners of the United States as that given the anthracite mine workers and the employees of the shipbuilding industry. We ask for the privilege of presenting the claim of the bituminous miners for an increase in wages in the same way and in the same manner as that which Dr. Garfield authorized as affecting the anthracite mine workers. It is not sufficient when Dr. Garfield states that the bituminous mine workers are not entitled to an increase in mining prices. In making such a statement he denies to them the fundamental right of presenting facts and the reasons why they feel they are justified in seeking an increase in wages. Surely such an important body of our citizenship cannot be denied the right to present their case to the proper authority. The claim of the bituminous miners for an increase in wages is based upon an increase in the cost of living amounting to more than twenty per cent during the last year, as shown by statistics gathered from reliable sources in mining communities throughout the United States. In addition the bituminous mine workers are prepared to present additional facts to sustain their contention. This appeal to you is ordered by the bona fide representatives of the five hundred thousand bituminous miners assembled in conference from every coal mining state in the union. They deeply resent the treatment accorded the spokesman of the miners of the miners [sic] of the United States by Federal Fuel Administrator Garfield, in that they were deprived of the opportunity of a proper hearing and the bituminous miners of the United States were denied an increase in wages commensurate at least with the increase in the cost of the necessaries of life. If his decision is to stand it will jeopardize the policy of the Federal Government in standardizing rates in essential war industries. Such a position is arbitrary autocratic and unfair and will destroy confidence in the plans and policies of the government to stabilize wages in industry.

We feel that the splendid record of the coal miners of the United States during all the period since our country has been involved in war is of such a character as to commend this appeal to your favorable consideration. The miners have responded to every call our nation has made; at no time or period have they either slackened or failed. In making this appeal to you we are but exercising the inherent right of groups of citizens within the republic, to petition to the highest authority within the nation for the redress of grievance and the correction of wrongs. We ask for no other privilege than to be accorded our day in court; the right to present reasons to the proper authorities in support of the miners claim for an increase in mining prices. The miners of America have confidence in you; therefore, we will wait your early and favorable consideration of this appeal. We will gladly come to Washington and meet you at your convenience, for the purpose of presenting the request of the bituminous miners and the reasons for an increase in wages.

Frank J. Hayes, President;

John L. Lewis, Vice President;

William Green, Secretary-Treasurer,

The United Mine Workers of America.

T telegram (WP, DLC).

From Harvey MacCauley[1]

Dear Dr. Wilson: Newark, N. J. November 1, 1918.

Fifteen years ago while a member of the class of 1904 I came to you for assistance in a distressing matter. On the last day I had lost forty-four dollars ($44.00) entrusted to me by friends to purchase tickets for the Yale and Princeton football game. With a kindness that I have never forgotten you loaned me the money. For many years I have been totally unable to pay this money. I did not feel that I could send it to you in small installments. I now return it to you with simple thanks, the depth and sincerity of which I am unable to fully express. I will not add to your duties by asking for an acknowledgment of its receipt.

Will you permit me to say that, although I vote for Republicans (mostly) for local offices, I am and always have been a firm believer in your policies and clearly expressed program. My wife[2] and little daughter[3] are also firm believers in "Standing by the President." This is not the blind following of a "Life long Democrat" but the sincere respect and confidence of a thinking, reading and independent voter.

It has occurred to me that in these times of criticism an expression of confidence in the President, even if it is only one in many, may have its part in strengthening his courage for the still greater problems that are ahead.

Respectfully and sincerely yours,   Harvey MacCauley.

TLS (WP, DLC).

[1] Princeton 1904, at this time assistant treasurer of the Anti-Saloon League of New Jersey.

[2] Nell Carolyn Deatrick MacCauley.

[3] Alice Bournonville MacCauley.

A Memorandum by Franklin Knight Lane

November 1, 1918

At last week's Cabinet we talked of Austria—again we talked like a Cabinet. The President said that he did not know to whom to reply, as things were breaking up so completely. There was no Austria-Hungary. Secretary Wilson suggested that, of course, their army was still under control of the Empire, and that the answer would have to go to it.

Theoretically, the President said, German-Austria should go to Germany, as all were of one language and one race, but this would mean the establishment of a great central Roman-Catholic nation which would be under control of the Papacy, and would be particularly objectionable to Italy. I said that such an arrangement would mean a Germany on two seas, and would leave the Germans victors after all. The President read despatches from Europe on the situation in Germany—the first received in many months.

Nothing was said of politics—although things are at a white heat over the President's appeal to the country to elect a Democratic Congress. He made a mistake. * * * My notion was, and I told him so at a meeting three or four weeks ago, that the country would give him a vote of confidence because it wanted to strengthen his hand. But Burleson said that the party wanted a leader with *guts*— this was his word and it was a challenge to his (the President's) virility, that was at once manifest.

The country thinks that the President lowered himself by his letter, calling for a partisan victory at this time. * * * But he likes the idea of personal party-leadership—Cabinet responsibility is still in his mind.

Printed in Lane and Wall, eds., *Letters of Franklin K. Lane*, pp. 296-97.

A Translation of a Telegram from Viscount Kikujiro Ishii to the Foreign Office

No. 652 (Confidential)   Washington, [c. Nov. 1], 1918

I visited the President at his request on November 1. After remarking that he had invited me for consultation on a few matters, he turned to the Siberian problem. He reminded me that, after the agreement between the United States and Japan concerning the dispatch of armies to Siberia, Japan had sent an unnecessarily large number of troops (reportedly as many as sixty thousand) to that area. Although he did not intend to criticize this fact at the present occasion, he said that he had heard that a difference of opinion between our civil and military officials had arisen and as a result Japan had sent more troops than had been previously agreed between the two governments. Saying that I did not need to address the problem if I did not want to, he set it aside and proceeded. He stated that, when the United States army had found no task to fulfill in Vladivostok, an attempt was made to move its main portion to Harbin in order to expedite relief activity to Russia. The Japanese officials there declined this move on the ground that there were no extra buildings in Harbin for the use of American officials because all of them were already allotted. In addition, he continued, it was said that Japan had also declined Britain's request to advance her army to the west to Irkutsk. Referring to the Secretary of State's note to the international powers previously,[1] the President denied the United States' intention to further extend its military activities. However, as a relief measure for Russia, the United States planned gradually to send such goods as shoes and clothing to the west of Irkutsk, and also intended to dispatch a few troops along with these goods in order to prevent them from falling into the hands of the Bolsheviks. The President complained that even these transports had been hindered because Japan had already occupied all important points east of Irkutsk and enjoyed the sole use of almost all the railway lines. Thus the United States was unable to fulfill its task to send relief to Russia. The foregoing was said to be the crux of the reports which the President had received thus far. He remarked that if the reports were indicative of the attitude of the dispatched Japanese army (despite the indisputable fact that the United States did not intend to do more than to help the Czech army and innocent Russians) he could not but feel "friendly uneasiness"[2] in his heart.

To this I replied that I had not been aware of the Siberian military situation since the time of the mishap of our military attaché.[3] I promised to send a telegram to the home government promptly and to give a detailed explanation later. But I hastened to call the President's attention to the report I had once received stating that the activities of the United States army or railway corps in Siberia had displeased our officials time and again. I said that, although I could not confirm the report, it was necessary for the home government to take into account that such a report would tend to be exaggerated due to mutual misunderstandings caused by a bona fide confusion. The President asked me to relate the content of the report I said I had received. After warning him that, because of his friendly and frank assertion, I would myself try to be candid in return, I used as an example the report that Americans had disconnected locomotive engines from trains in use by the Japanese army, attached two locomotives to their own train, and fled away. The President thanked me for my statement and showed his appreciation for such a frank exchange. He promised to give the secretaries of the army and the navy informal instructions to put the authorities at the outpost under stricter supervision in order to avoid further conflict. Concerning the President's inquiry about our officials, I request you to telegraph a reply.

The President next referred to the plan for reconciliation between the South and the North of China which had been proposed by the Imperial Government.[4] Although he approved the purpose of the proposal, he said that, as a matter of principle, China should not have two Presidents, and that, at the present time, all the powers recognized the incumbent President[5] and the Peking government as the legitimate representatives of China. He then expressed concern over the inevitability that the reconciliation would naturally result in the South's favor and thus defeat its own purpose. I asked whether he believed that the incumbent President should be given aid. After pondering, he affirmed that a small amount of aid was necessary and that this was an opinion propounded in the cable from the American Ambassador to China,[6] with which he himself agreed. Because I felt that his stand was not clear enough, I tried to ask further questions. But the President begged me to talk directly with the Secretary of State about the matter, since some details of the question had slipped from his memory. I said that, since the President was now facing such a grave situation, forgetting a relatively trivial matter like that was fully understandable.

Breaking off the discussion about China, the President proceeded to the present [international] situation, which, he said, was very critical, more critical than expected. He said that leading the nation to a victory in the war would be a much easier task than the one lying ahead after such a victory. I told the President that I had not known that he had had such a difficulty in reconciling differences of opinion among the Allied powers. Although the President said that he had had difficulty, he emphasized that it would not be insuperable.[7] When the victorious powers became so selfish that they forgot justice and made unreasonable demands, the costly peace of today would lack a permanent foundation even if the harmonious relations between the powers might be maintained. We would have to face a second world war before long. "I will never yield on this point,"[8] he said. Finally, in reply to my question, the President said that a peace conference should not be held in a belligerent country but rather in a neutral one, because in the former (especially in a country like the United States), where war fever was still prevalent, it would be difficult for both hostile and Allied powes to overcome this fever and obtain satisfactory results. In his opinion Switzerland, especially Lausanne[9] in French Switzerland,[10] might be the most preferable.

These are the outlines of the conference which lasted for about forty minutes. Based on this meeting, I believe that the United States Government is bewildered by powers such as Britain, France, and Italy, which are suffering from a raging vengeful fever. This message has been wired to each Ambassador. I think it will be possible to request a meeting with the President after I receive your telegram requested above. If there is anything I should relate to him at that time, please instruct me.[11]

Hw telegram (MT 163247, pp. 95-108, JFO-Ar).
[1] See WW to RL, Sept. 26, 1918, and the Enclosure printed with RL to C. A. de R. Barclay, Sept. 27, 1918.
[2] In English in the telegram.
[3] Maj. Gen. Kazutsugu Inouye.
[4] About which see RL to WW, Oct. 26, 1918 (second letter of that date), n. 1.
[5] That is, Hsü Shih-ch'ang. The military group, with headquarters at Canton, which controlled much of southern China, had refused to recognize Hsü's election by the National Assembly at Peking and had declared that the "Military Government" at Canton would perform the functions and duties of the President of China for the time being. Wu Ting-fang to Dean of the Diplomatic Corps, Oct. 12, 1918, FR 1918, p. 117.
[6] P. S. Reinsch to RL, Oct. 30, 1918, ibid., p. 116.
[7] In English in the telegram.
[8] ibid.
[9] ibid.
[10] "French Switzerland" in English.
[11] Apparently, Ishii received no such instructions. In any event, he did not have a further meeting with Wilson.

To Charles William Eliot

My dear Dr. Eliot: The White House 2 November, 1918.

I cannot deny myself the privilege of saying to you how deeply I appreciate your letter of October 29th in the New York Times concerning my appeal to the voters.[1] It is a matter of peculiar gratification to me to be so supported by your judgment and approval.

Cordially and sincerely yours,   Woodrow Wilson

TLS (C. W. Eliot Papers, MH-Ar).
[1] "President Wilson's Appeal," C. W. Eliot to the Editor, Oct. 29, 1918, New York Times, Oct. 31, 1918. Eliot's opinion of Wilson's appeal was mixed. On the one hand, he expressed doubt that a Republican victory in the election would "affect unfavorably" the influence of the Wilson administration on European opinion. On the other hand, he conceded that the recent public statements of Taft and Roosevelt on Wilson's appeal and on appropriate terms for an armistice tended to confirm Wilson's opinion about the effects of a shift in the control of Congress to the Republican party. "At the very moment," he wrote, "when the Administration is making an indispensable effort to unite all the nations which are now contending against Germany in a common statement of the objects of the war and the inevitable terms of peace, these Republican leaders are attempting themselves to dictate the terms of peace which shall be advocated by the responsible representatives of the American people. If they think and act in that way

at a very critical moment while they represent a minority party in Congress, how would they treat the Administration if they came to represent the majority party? If they meddle in such an irresponsible and passionate manner concerning the comparatively simple questions of the right way to bring the actual fighting to an end, what will they do when the solutions of the very complicated geographical, racial, industrial and commercial questions which will arise out of the war come before them for discussion?"

From Joseph Patrick Tumulty

Dear Governor: [The White House] 2 November, 1918

Senator Weeks in a speech last night said that Mr. Walsh[1] could not procure an endorsement from you. Mr. Morgenthau, Mr. Grossiere of the Post,[2] and the State Chairman[3] have had me on the phone this morning and say that Walsh is going to be elected, and that they have Weeks in a corner. Secretary Daniels, who has returned from Massachusetts, confirms this.

I have also a telegram from Frank Peabody[4] asking the question whether Medill McCormick[5] would be acceptable to you. Our friends out there say that if you will send a telegram to Peabody, saying "I know that Mr. McCormick could not support me and that he is out of sympathy with the things I believe in," and expressing your high appreciation of what Jim Ham[6] has done in supporting you, that this would settle the business.

Tom Scully[7] is also in trouble. Mr. J. Lisle Kinmouth, of Asbury Park,[8] and the State Chairman of New Jersey[9] join in this request. Scully is a queer fellow, but there is no doubt of his loyalty to you and his support of you at every turn. If you can do these things, it will close the whole matter of endorsements.   J.P.T.

TL (WP, DLC).
    [1] That is, David Ignatius Walsh, the Democratic senatorial candidate in Massachusetts.
    [2] Edwin Atkins Grozier, editor, publisher, and chief proprietor of the *Boston Post*.
    [3] Michael A. O'Leary.
    [4] That is, Francis Stuyvesant Peabody of Chicago.
    [5] Joseph Medill McCormick, the Republican senatorial candidate in Illinois, who was running against James Hamilton Lewis.
    [6] That is, James Hamilton Lewis.
    [7] That is, Thomas J. Scully.
    [8] He meant J. Lyle Kinmonth, editor and publisher of the *Asbury Park Evening Press*.
    [9] That is, Charles F. McDonald.

To Edward Albert Filene

[The White House] 2 November 1918.

Your telegram,[1] calling my attention to statement in Senator Weeks' speech at Fitchburg, Mass., received. If any doubt exists as to my attitude toward Mr. Walsh I am glad to have an opportunity to say

I would feel confident of his support and Mr. Weeks has given me every reason to be confident of his opposition.

Woodrow Wilson.

T telegram (Letterpress Books, WP, DLC).
¹ It is missing.

To Francis Patrick Walsh

My dear Mr. Walsh: [The White House] 2 November, 1918.

Just a hasty line in a crowded day to say that I fully appreciate the importance of the matter you call my attention to in your letter of October 30th, and that it will have my most serious consideration without further urging.

Cordially and sincerely yours,   Woodrow Wilson

TLS (Letterpress Books, WP, DLC).

From Newton Diehl Baker

My dear Mr. President: [Washington] November 2, 1918.

May I suggest for your consideration the possibility of your issuing a statement for circulation through Berne, or otherwise, into the constituent countries of the Austro-Hungarian Empire expressing the hope that the peoples of these nascent nations will observe orderly processes in these revolutionary days and refrain from acts of violence in order that their candidacy to admission in the family of nations will not be blemished at the outset by disorders which would tend to throw doubt upon their capacity for self-government in the eyes of the nations whose ordered civilizations have made this era of freedom possible for them.

I have two things in my mind about it—first, I think your voice in such a statement would have more weight in restraining disorganizing revolution than anybody else's, and if such a statement could be supplied to those who are attempting to preserve order in those countries it would have a great appeal with the people; and second, I think it would be a very tragic thing if a lot of regicides and political assassinations were to take place in those countries at this time, and if you could be quoted as disapproving and warning against such conduct it would be weighty. There may be people in those countries in large numbers who have so little comprehension of us as to believe that they would gain favor with us by killing their kings.¹   Respectfully yours,   [Newton D. Baker]

CCL (N. D. Baker Papers, DLC).
¹ For Wilson's response to this suggestion, see RL to P. A. Stovall, Nov. 5, 1918.

Herbert Clark Hoover to Frederic René Coudert

My Dear Friend,   [Washington] Nov. 2, 1918.

I have yours of Nov. 2 in front of me.¹ My own views are summarized in a word—that we must have united support for the President. In the issues before us there can be no party policies. It is vital that we have a solid front and a sustained leadership.

I am for President Wilson's leadership not only in the conduct of the war, but also in the negotiation of peace, and afterward in the direction of America's burden in the rehabilitation of the world. Our object in this war is to see the establishment of Governments in the Central Empires that are responsible to their people. This is the vital safeguard to permanent peace. The passing of their militaristic autocracies must be and is rapidly being marked by such treatment as to put that system out of action forever.

There is no greater monument to any man's genius than the conduct of negotiations with the enemy by the President. There has been a steady growth of realization by the German people and her deluded allies of the debauchery into which they and the world have been plunged by militarism. The President has by his conduct and word stimulated this realization. He has assured them justice if they themselves will throw off their yoke, and he has not hesitated in application of our every resource in force against their military dictators.

If the final overthrow and surrender of autocracy can be accomplished through the German and their allied peoples themselves, the President will not only save the lives of a million American boys and countless innocent women and children, but will have attained more complete victory and a more permanent guarantee of peace than any other means. The President's leadership has gained gigantic strides in this course. The terms of surrender are being made by Marshal Foch and our military leaders. The action of the Bulgarian, Turkish, and Austrian people has or is forcing the acceptance of these terms. The German people will sooner or later do so.

Our objects in the overthrow of all autocracies in Europe and the establishment of government by the people is but part of our great burden, for beyond this, when these immediate objects are attained, we still have before us the greatest problem that our Government has ever faced if we are to prevent Europe's immolation in a conflagration of anarchy such as Russia is plunged in today.

We must nurse Europe back to industry and self-support and we must ourselves avoid entanglement in the process. This can be accomplished only by this same leadership which has the confidence of the great mass of people in Europe. The President has spoken throughout this war the aspirations of the vast majority of the American people. There is no other leadership possible now if we are to succeed in these great issues.

Yours faithfully,   Herbert Hoover

Printed in the *New York Times*, Nov. 4, 1918.
    [1] F. R. Coudert to HCH, Nov. 2, 1918, printed in the *New York Times*, Nov. 4, 1918. Coudert had asked Hoover to discuss the question of whether or not the people of the United States could and should continue the unity of purpose which they had achieved during the war in order to bring about a just and lasting peace settlement.

From Georgii Vasil'evich Chicherin

Christiania Nov. 2, 1918

1297. My telegram number 1290, Oct. 29, 8 p.m. Note of Russian Commissariat continues as follows: "This is the first fruit which the workmen and peasants of Russia have reaped from your Government or the Allies. This is the result of your promises given in the beginning of the year. And then the Russian people were made subject to the offensive of Allied troops, including American, in the North. Russian territory has been invaded without cause or declaration of war. Russian towns and villages have been occupied, Soviet officials have been executed, and acts of violence have been directed towards the peaceful Russian population. You had given the promise, President, to offer Russia your assistance in her aim of taking an independent decision concerning her own political development and her national policy. Actually, however, this assistance has found expression in the attempts made in Archangel, Murmansk, and the Far East by Czecho-Slovak troops and later on your Allies to impose by force on the Russian people the power of the subjugators, the exploiting classes, the supremacy of which classes was overthrown in Oct. of last year. The Russian people, instead of an assistance in the independent expression of their will, which was promised to them, President, in your declarations, have met with a revival of the Russian counter-revolution which had already become a corpse, and attempts to establish in a predatory way its sanguinary supremacy over the Russian nation. You had also promised the Russian people, President, to offer your support in their struggle for independence. Actually, however, when the Russian nation was struggling on the southern front with counter-revolution which had sold itself to German imperialism and threatened their independence, when on the western front the Russian people were using all their forces in their effort to organize a defense of their territory, they were compelled to move their troops to the east against the Czecho-Slovaks who were bringing back the undefended yoke and subjugation, and to the south [north][1] against the intruders in the shape of your troops and those of your allies and the counter revolution organized by them. The touching story [acid test] of the relations between the United States and Russia have not given quite the results which could be expected from your address to Congress. But we have reason not to be entirely displeased with these results, for the violence of the counter-revolution in the East and North has opened the eyes of the workmen and peasants of Russia as to the aims of the Russian counter-revolution and of its foreign assistants. Through this experience has been carried the iron will for the protection of the freedom acquired by the revolution for the protection of the land that the latter has given to the workmen. After the fall of Kazan, Simbirsk, Suzran, Samzpa, you must have realized, President, what results the actual suppressions of your promises of the 18th of January have had for us. [The fall of Kazan, Simbirsk, Syzran, and Samara should, at last, make it clear to you, Mr. President, what were the consequences for us of what in fact came of the promises you made on 8 January.] What we have gone through has assisted us in creating a disciplined united Red Army which grows daily, renews its strength and power and learns to defend the revolution. Your relations to us, shown by your Government's actions, have not been capable of annihilating us. American cruisers helped us to become [On the contrary, we are now] stronger than we were a few months ago; and the international negotiations on general peace which you propose now find us vital and strong and allow us to express in the name of Russia our consent to take part in them. As an interlude [a precondition] for the armistice during which the peace negotiations are to begin you have placed on Germany the condition of withdrawing troops from the occupied territory. We argue [are ready], President, to conclude an armistice on these conditions and beg you to inform us as to when do you and your allies intend to withdraw yours troops from Murmansk, Archangel, and Siberia. You will not consent to an armistice; [unless] Germany, in withdrawing the troops, will indulge in [will stop] violence and robbery etcetera. We presume that this means as well that you and your allies will order the Czecho-Slovaks to return us that part of our gold fund that they robbed us of in Kazan, that you will forbid them during compelled withdrawal in which we will assist them, without awaiting your orders, to continue their predatory actions and the violence they inflicted upon the workmen and the peasants. As regards your further conditions of peace, namely that the Governments con-

[1] About the textual corrections in this document, see the first part, G. V. Chicherin to WW, Oct. 29, 1918, n. 1.

cluding peace must be the representatives of the will of the people, our Government, as you know, answers to it fully. Our Government expresses the will of the Councils of the workmen, peasants, and Red Army, deputies, which represent at least eighty percent of the Russian people, which cannot be said, President, of your Government. But in the name of humanity and peace we do not place as the basis for the general peace negotiations that all the participating nations should be represented by councils of the people's commissaires elected at congresses of councils of workmen, peasants' and soldiers' deputies. We learn [know that] this form of governing nations will soon become a general form, and that only general peace will protect nations from the threat of intrusion and will give them the liberty of dealing with the form of government and the gangs which have thrust humanity in this international slaughter and will naturally exult their will. [We know that this form of administration will soon be the universal form, and that precisely a general peace, when nations will be liberated from danger and destruction, will leave them free to bring to justice the system and the cliques that forced this world-wide slaughter upon mankind, and will, in spite of themselves, surely lead the tortured peoples to create Soviet Governments, which give exact expression to their will.] Though consenting to participate at present in negotiations even with such governments which do not yet express the will of the people, we, on our side, would like to learn in detail from you in what you figure to yourself the union of nations which according to you ought to crown the work of peace. You demand the independence of Poland, [Serbia,] Belgium, freedom for the people of Austria-Hungary. Presumably you mean that at first the people will have to come to the decision of their future development for themselves and then join in a union of nations. But strangely enough you do not mention in your demands the freedom of Ireland, Egypt, India, or even the Philippines; and we would greatly regret if these nations would be deprived of the possibility to participate with us in the organization of a union of nations through their freely elected representatives. We would like to learn too, President, before starting negotiations concerning the creation of the union of nations how you figure to yourself the solution of the many questions of economic nature which have a profound importance for the work of the future peace. You do not mention the war expenses which will become spread with their whole abnormal weight on the people if the union of nations will not abolish the payment of war loans to the capitalist[s] of all the world. You know as well as we do that this war is the result of the policy of all capitalistic governments, that the governments all over the world competed in their mutual armament, that

all governing groups of civilized nations participated in this predatory policy, and that therefore it would be highly (?) [unjust] if
the people who have paid for this policy with the blood of millions,
have settled accounts at the expense of an economic disaster, should
pay a tribute to the groups actually responsible for this policy that
has led them to ruin. We propose thereafter, President, that the
union of nations should be based on the refusal [cancellation] of
payment of war loans. As regards the restoration of the territories
ruined by the war we find it just that all nations ? participate in
assisting unfortunate Belgium, Poland, [Serbia]; and, as exhausted
as Russia may appear, she is ready on her side to do her utmost to
assist them, and she expects that American capital which has not
suffered from the war but acquired many a million of profit will on
its side come to the assistance of the nations. But the [league of]
nations has not only to settle the present war, it has to render further
wars impossible. You can not ignore that the capitalists of your
country intend to continue the policy of requiring super profit in
China and Siberia and that, fearing the competition of the Japanese
capitalists, they prescribe a military power which enables them to
offer resistance to any measures undertaken by Japan. You are
undoubtedly aware of similar plots on the side of capitalist governing circles in other countries in relation to other territories and
other nations. Knowing this you can not refrain from agreeing with
us that we cannot leave factories, banks, mines in the hands of
private individuals who always use the great means of the industry
created by the people in order to export the products and the capital
to foreign countries and in return for these favors obtain a super
profit, which involves the countries struggles in imperialistic wars.
We propose therefore that expropriation of the capitalists provides
for world the basis of the union nations. [that the league of nations
be based on the expropriation of the capitalists of all countries.] In
your country banks and industry are in the hands of such a small
group of capitalists that, according to the statement of your personal
friend, Colonel Robins, it would be sufficient to arrest twenty leaders capitalistic group [of capitalist cliques] and deliver into the hands
of the people all that, by means of the methods usual to the capitalists world, they have concentrated in their hands and in that way
abolish the chief source of new wars. If you consent to this, President, if in that manner the sources of wars will be settled with for
the future, there is no doubt that there will be no difficulty in
breaking down all economic barriers and that all nations finding
themselves in possession of all means of industry will be intensely
interested in the exchange of what they need. The matter will then
be confined to an exchange of products between nations according

to their capacity of production, and the union of nations will become a union of mutual support of the working classes. It will not be a difficult matter for them to diminish military forces to the limits necessary for interior safety. We learn well that the grasping class of capitalists will view with (alarm?) [will attempt to create] this interior danger just as now the necessity for safekeeping landowners, Russian capitalists, with the support of American, English and French armed forces, try to withdraw factories from the workmen and land from the peasants. But if American workmen, led by the idea of a union of nations, will break the resolution of American capitalists in the same way that we have broken the resistance of Russian capitalists, in that case neither German capitalists nor any other capitalists will present a sufficiently serious danger for a victorious labor class; and it will be sufficient then if any member of society, working six hours at the factory, will learn to use arms during two hours a day for several months, and then the whole nation will know how to deal with the interior danger. As it is in spite of having experienced what your promises mean, we have nevertheless accepted the basis of your proposals concerning an international peace and a union of nations, but we strive to cooperate with your proposals in order that the results should not contradict your promises as it happened with your support of Russia. [And so, Mr. President, although we have had practical experience of your promises, we nevertheless accept as a basis your proposals about international peace and about a League of Nations. We have only tried to elaborate them in order to avoid results which would run counter to your promises, as happened with your promise of assistance to Russia.] We have tried to formulate your proposals concerning a union of nations so precisely that a union of nations should not become a union of capitalist nations. If you do not agree with us in detail, President, we shall not protest against an open discussion of your peace proposals as is stated in the first point of your peace program. We will find a way of agreeing in detail as long as you accept the basis of our proposals. There is another possibility; we have had to deal with the President of the Archangel and Siberian invasion, we have also had to deal with the real President actually. What if the policy of the capitalistic American government should turn out of old the President of the Archangel and Siberian invasion. [We have had dealings with two Presidents, the President of the Archangel attack and the Siberian invasion, and the President of the League of Nations peace programme. Is not the first of these the real President, actually directing the policies of the capitalist American Government?]. What if the American government should prove to be the Government of American limited companies, American industrial, commercial, and railway trusts, American banks, in one word the government of American capitalists. And what if the proposals issuing from such a government concerning the creation of a union of nations should lead only to thrusting new chains on the people organizing an international trust for the exploitation [of] helpless workmen. In that case, President, you will be incapable of answering our questions and we will say to the workmen of all the countries: beware, millions of your fellow brothers are still shedding their blood in this war, thrown against one another by the bourgeoisie of all the countries, and leaders of capital are already appearing to hasten to a final arrangement in order to crush those remaining alive, when they will demand an answer from those who are responsible for this war. However, as we by no means wish to fight with America, even if your government is not yet replaced by a Soviet of people's commissaires and your place is not yet occupied by Eugene Debs, who is still kept in prison. As we do not wish to fight with England, although the cabinet of Mr. Lloyd George is not yet replaced by a council of people's commissaires with Machona [MacLean][2] as head, or with France although as Clemenceau's government is not yet replaced by a labor government of Merhieu [Merrheim][3]; in the same way as we concluded peace with an imperial German government, Emperor William, second, at the head—towards whom you are not better disposed than we—we propose to discuss together with your allies all the following questions and give us clear, precise, and business like answers: do the governments of America, England, and France intend to stop shedding the blood of Russian citizens if the Russian people consent to pay ransom? In that case what payment do the governments of America, England and France expect from the Russian people? Do they demand concessions, delivery of railways on certain conditions, mines, gold mines, etc., or territorial concessions, part of Siberia or the Caucasus, the Murman coast? We expect you, President, to declare decidedly what are your demands and those of your allies. We also should like to know whether the alliance between your government and those of the other allied powers has the character of a union which could be compared to a limited company for the reception of dividends from Russia or does your government and the other governments of allied powers put up separate demands and what are these? It would interest us particularly to know what do your French allies demand in exchange for the milliards of roubles with which Paris bankers

[2] John MacLean, Scottish revolutionary Socialist, at this time in prison for sedition and incitement to riot.

[3] Charles Merrheim, French syndicalist and leader of the metalworkers' union.

subsidized the subjugators of Russia, the enemy of their own people, the criminal tsarist government? You are aware as well as your French allies that the Russian nation is exhausted by war and not yet capable of profiting by the efforts of the peoples Soviet authorities which are endeavoring to augment the national economy. You therefore know that Russia will not be enabled to pay fully to the French bankers the milliards spent for the nation's ruin by the government of the Tsar even if you and your allies succeed in invading all the territory of Russia which our heroic revolutionary Red Army will not allow. We therefore put you the following questions: Do your French allies consent to a payment in part, and if so, in what measure and do they foresee that their demand further will lead to similar ones on the part of all other creditors of the shameful government of the Tsar overthrown by the people. We cannot admit [hardly think] that your government and that of your allies should not have a ready answer to this question at the moment when your and their troops attempt to advance on our territory with the evident aim of invading our country. The Russian people represented by the national Red Army are keeping guard on their territory and fight splendidly against your invasion and the advance of your allies. But your government and the governments of the other allied powers have undoubtedly prepared plans according to which you are shedding the blood of your soldiers. We wait for you to state clearly and decidedly all your demands. If our questions remain unanswered we will then presume that we are not mistaken in supposing that your government and the governments of your allies expect from the Russian nation a payment with Russia's natural (?) [resources] as well as a monetary one and also territorial concessions. We will announce [this] to the Russian people and the working classes of other countries that the absence of an answer on which conditions already a silent answer. [countries, and the absence of a reply from you will serve for us as an unspoken reply.] The Russian people will realize that the demands of your government and those of your allies are so limitless and heavy that you cannot present them to the Russian Government."

Schmedeman.

T telegram (SDR, RG 59, 861.00/3151, DNA).

Three Telegrams from Edward Mandell House

Paris Nov 2, 1918

Number 35. Secret. For the President.

At meeting yesterday afternoon at Versailles terms of military armistice to be offered Germany were discussed, but no final conclusion[s] reached. At meeting this morning at French War Office general discussion was had respecting steps to be taken by Allies and the United States in the event that: Terms of armistice are accepted by Austria; two, terms of armistice are refused by Austria. These matters were referred to the military and naval authorities and I am in constant conference with Generals Pershing and Bliss and Admiral Benson regarding the position of the United States respecting them. After consulting with military authorities, it was decided to give Austria until Sunday midnight, November third to accept terms of armistice. It was agreed that we should wait until we receive Austria's answer before finally determining the terms of armistice to be offered Germany. Meeting at Versailles this afternoon to discuss terms of naval armistice to be offered Germany.

Edward House.

Paris, November 2, 1918

Number 36. Secret. For the President.

Please advise the President that the matter mentioned in my telegram number 14[1] to the President (?) [Secretary of State] has been adjusted in a manner entirely satisfactory and I consider that no further action is advisable.   Edward House

[1] Of October 31, 1918.

Paris, November 2, 1918

Number 37. Secret. For the President.

The following telegram was despatched this morning. "Messrs Trentic, Pavisic, Bugsck, Koch,[1] commander of the fleet at Pola. In reply to your telegram with salutations of friendship we notify you to proceed immediately to Corfu under a white flag to place yourself at the disposal of the Commander in Chief of the Allied forces. Notify the commander in chief at Corfu by wireless of the moment of your departure and your arrival. Signed Clemenceau, House, Lloyd George, Orlando."

This telegram is addressed to the Jugo-Slav committee at Pola.

At the same time it was agreed that each [of] the French, British, Italian, and the United States Governments should send the following instructions to their naval commandants [commanders] in chief in the Adriatic: "Until further notice you are not to attack the ships of the Austro-Hungarian fleet in port. Take measures to insure the passage of those ships which may come to Corfu under the white flag to place themselves at your disposal. You may expect to receive (?) [from] Pola a confidential [radio-]telegram advising you of their departure." Edward House

T telegrams (WP, DLC).
[1] Ante Trešić-Pavičić, Vilim Bugšeg, and Capt. Metod Koch. Trešić-Pavičić and Bugšeg were members of the local Yugoslav National Committee at Pola, or Pula, the site of the major base of the Austro-Hungarian navy. Koch was the commander of the Yugoslav navy. The telegram from the Supreme War Council to these men was necessitated by the fact that Vice Adm. Miklós Horthy de Nagybánya, on behalf of the Austro-Hungarian government, had, on October 31, signed with Trešić-Pavičić, Bugšeg, and Ivan Čok a convention surrendering the fleet and naval facilities at Pola to the Yugoslav National Council at Zagreb. See Victor S. Mamatey, *The United States and East Central Europe, 1914-1918: A Study in Wilsonian Diplomacy and Propaganda* (Princeton, N. J., 1957), pp. 364-66.

A Memorandum by William Christian Bullitt

November 2, 1918.

MEMORANDUM FOR MR. LANSING

SUBJECT: THE BOLSHEVIST MOVEMENT IN EUROPE

SUBSTANCE: I. Recent information indicating increase of Bolshevism.

II. Methods of combating Bolshevism.

I. RECENT INFORMATION INDICATING INCREASE OF BOLSHEVISM

1. Reports from Russia indicate that the Bolsheviki have crushed all substantial opposition within the confines of Great Russia.

2. Reports from the Baltic Provinces, Poland and Ukraine indicate that an outbreak of Bolshevism is expected when the German army of occupation is withdrawn.

3. A peasant socialist Republic has been established in Bulgaria under the leadership of Stambuliwsky,[1] a peasant socialist leader who was in jail throughout the Radislavov regime.[2] This new Government of Bulgaria may or may not become Bolshevist in character.

4. Press reports from Turkey indicate that the country is being

[1] Aleksandŭr Stambuliiski, head of the Bulgarian Agrarian Union (Peasants' party) and future Prime Minister of Bulgaria. A strong supporter of the Allied cause, Stambuliiski had been sentenced to life imprisonment at the beginning of the war. Following the defeat of the Bulgarian army, he had been released from prison, had become the nominal head of a rebellion within the army, and, on September 27, 1918, had proclaimed the so-called Radomir Republic. However, contrary to Bullitt's contention, Stambuliiski's attempt to overthrow the Bulgarian government had failed when his troops were defeated near Sofia on October 2, 1918. See Nissan Oren, *Revolution Administered: Agrarianism and Communism in Bulgaria* (Baltimore and London, 1973), pp. 7-9.
[2] That is, the government of Vasil' Radoslavov, who had been Prime Minister from July 1913 to June 1918.

overrun by deserters who subsist by robbery, and that Constantinople is on the verge of starvation.

5. The disorganized flight of the Austro-Hungarian army threatens all the western portions of the Dual Monarchy with anarchy.

A. The Committee of Public Safety of Trieste has been so alarmed by the sudden arrival of fleeing soldiers from Venetia that it has asked the Commander of the Allied Fleets in the Adriatic to occupy the city.

B. Troops of soldiers are marching northward in South Tyrol and Croatia burning and looting.

C. Vienna is threatened with famine. At present the city is in the hands of the new Government formed by the Austro-German National Assembly.[3] The dominant figure in this new Government is Victor [Viktor] Adler, the leader of the Austro-German Socialist Party.[4] Adler is a thoroughly moderate socialist of great courage and ability. He has supported the international policies of President Wilson, in and out of season, and is in no sense a Bolshevist. Indeed, he has repeatedly restrained the younger leaders of the party when they have advocated revolutionary tactics. Adler is a thoroughly safe man and is the chief hope of those who hope to avoid Bolshevism in Austria. His hold on the situation is, however, precarious. The younger leaders of the Socialist Party are more radical than he. And although the soliders now in Vienna are at present supporting him, the most recent reports indicate that a Provisional Soldiers' Central Committee has been formed and that the troops have been invited to elect soldiers committees, which in turn will elect a permanent Soldiers' Central Committee. This smacks distinctly of the early days of the Soviet in Petrograd, and it is quite probable that the wave of returning soldiers, which shortly will pour over Vienna, will place all real power in the hands of the Soldiers' Central Committee and

[3] On October 21, 1918, three days after Emperor Charles had announced the federalization of Cisleithanian Austria and paved the way for final dissolution of the Austro-Hungarian Empire, 208 members of the *Reichsrat* who represented the German-speaking parts of the empire met in Vienna and formed a "provisional national assembly of a German-Austrian state." Dominated by Social Democrats and Christian Socialists, the assembly elected an executive committee of twenty members, later called the *Staatsrat*, as a provisional government and, on October 30, chose the Social Democrat, Karl Renner, as its first Chancellor. Following the renunciation by the Emperor of his executive powers, the provisional assembly, on November 12, proclaimed the establishment of a democratic German-Austrian republic. The *Staatsrat* remained the *de facto* government of the new republic until February 16, 1919, when general elections for a constituent national assembly were held. For a brief discussion, see Walter Goldinger, *Geschichte der Republik Österreich* (Munich, 1962), pp. 1-34.

[4] In fact, the provisional assembly had appointed Adler as Secretary of State for Foreign Affairs. He died on November 11, 1918.

end the Adler regime. The soldiers now in Vienna are being harangued daily by Bolshevist orators many of whom are returned prisoners who imbibed Boshevism in Petrograd.

6. President Kramarz[5] of the Czecho-Slovak National Council who is now in Berne reports that "there is grave danger of Bolshevism in Bohemia, not from Radical Socialism, but from famine."

7. There have been serious riots in Budapest, but they have not yet become Bolshevist in character. Count Karolyi at present controls the situation,[6] but the following excerpt from the [Berlin] *Vossische Zeitung* of October 31 will give some idea of the power of the Budapest mob:

"The Budapest eastern railway station was occupied by the crowd where two battalions leaving for the front joined the mob. Civilians were also arrested by the mob, which having pillaged the arms factory had enormous amounts of arms and munitions. Budapest infantry regiment number 32 mutinied and placed itself at the disposal of the Republic. The military prison was stormed and all political and military prisoners released. The Commandant of Budapest was put in prison by Hungarian soldiers."

8. Liebknecht, Franz Mehring and other ultra-radical socialist leaders in Germany are speaking everywhere denouncing Scheidemann and attempting to incite the German proletariat to immediate revolution. They have sent greetings to the Bolsheviki and Liebknecht has announced that the Soviet Government has promised him all possible assistance.

9. Dr. Herron reports that propaganda agents of the Bolsheviki with millions of dollars at their disposal have been sent to Italy and France.

10. The Milan Chamber of Labor has begun a movement to promote a general strike, which would be Bolshevist in character.

11. At the meeting of the Socialist Federation of the Seine on September 29, the former Minority of the French Socialist Party, which is led by Longuet[7] and is semi-Bolshevist in character, became the Majority, obtaining 5,999 votes for its resolution, whereas the former Majority led by Renaudel[8] obtained only 2,896 votes and

[5] Karel Kramář, president of the Czech National Committee of Prague and Prime Minister Designate of Czechoslovakia.

[6] Count Mihály Károlyi, the head of the revolutionary Hungarian National Council, had been appointed by Emperor Charles on October 31 to head a coalition government made up of members of that council. On November 1, Charles freed the Károlyi government from its oath of allegiance to the Hungarian crown and thus opened the way to the proclamation of a republic. This took place on November 16.

[7] Jean Longuet, the leader of the radical pacifist wing of the French Socialist party and a grandson of Karl Marx.

[8] Pierre Renaudel, a leader of the French Socialist party, a longtime member of the Chamber of Deputies, and the former editor of *L'Humanité*.

the "40" led by Albert Thomas and Varenne[9] obtained only 4 votes.

12. The South Wales Coal Miners have announced that they will strike on November 18.

II. METHODS OF COMBATING BOLSHEVISM

It is evident from the foregoing facts and the history of Russia during the past year, that economic disorganization and famine are the parents of Bolshevism. If the central sections of Europe are allowed to dissolve into economic chaos and to starve, no leaders on earth can prevent the establishment of a dictatorship of the proletariat with attendant pillage and murder. It is, therefore, respectfully suggested that as soon as the Government of Austria and the Government of Hungary surrender unconditionally, the President should announce that the United States will take steps at once to alleviate the distress of the civilian population of the former Habsburg Monarchy. It is respectfully suggested that food should be shipped to Vienna and to Bohemia to be distributed by an American directorate acting through local administrative agencies such as the Adler Government in Vienna and the National Council in Bohemia.

If it should be possible to do this, the administrative organizations which controlled the food distribution would automatically obtain the greatest power over the proletariat. And the American directors would control the Governments.

(Note: If such a statement should be made by the President just before the Allies' statement of armistice terms, it would greatly increase the demand of the German proletariat for an armistice at any price; for it would hold out to them the hope of immediate economic assistance.)

In dealing with the Bolshevik movement in Europe it is necessary to distinguish with the utmost care between the Socialists who advocate the immediate establishment of a dictatorship of the proletariat created by force and maintained by murder and terror, and the Socialists who advocate the establishment of democratic governments by peaceful means and the domination by reason of "all who work by hand or brain." The latter variety of moderate socialist is the bitterest opponent of the Bolshevik. And at present it seems that the Bolshevik movement in Europe can be combated successfully only by cooperation with the moderate socialist and labor leaders of Europe: Henderson, Webb, Albert Thomas, Renaudel, Scheidemann, David, Victor Adler, etc., etc.

[9] Alexandre Claude Varenne, a lawyer and journalist, a member of the Chamber of Deputies, and a leader of the moderate wing of the French Socialist party.

The movement for social democracy is beginning to occupy much the same place in the political arena of the twentieth century that the movement for political and national democracy occupied during the nineteenth century. And it has become an axiom of political history that popular movements can be suppressed for a period by force, but that their victory is only retarded and that the effect of such suppression is to intensify the violence of the outbreak when it finally comes.

(Note: The following instances support this contention:

1. *Eighteenth century France—French Revolution*

Strong movement (intellectual and economic) for destruction of special privileges of upper classes. Had the government *led* this movement all historians agree that it could have controlled it; evolution would have been gradual and safe. The Government attempted to suppress it by force. The result was revolution, taking violent form in massacres and the Reign of Terror.

2. *Settlement of Europe, 1815*

The Congress of Vienna attempted to suppress the popular desire for national union of peoples, independence, and democracy.

A. Belgium—annexed to the Netherlands.

Effect: Revolution in 1830.

B. Poland—placed under Tsar.

Effect: Revolutions in 1830 and 1863.

C. Italy—disintegrated, chiefly under Habsburg control.

Effects: Revolutions in 1824, 1830; revolutionary wars in 1848, 1859.

D. Spain—put under autocratic rule.

Effect: Revolution in 1822.

Final success of popular movement.

3. *Austria-Hungary.*

Popular movement for democracy and autonomy of nationalities—suppressed forcibly by Metternich.

Effect: Revolution of 1848—exile of Metternich—Again suppressed by German Magyar coalition. Effect: Present revolution in Austria-Hungary.

4. *Russia.*

Movement for democracy. Revolutions averted by moderate reforms of Alexander II. Suppression by force under Alexander III, and Nicholas II.

Effect: Revolutions of 1905 and 1917.

The history of England on the other hand points the way by which the present movement for Social Democracy may be turned into tranquil channels. The British policy has always been to meet and to compromise with radical elements in order to cut the ground from under the feet of anarchy—as a result there has been no armed revolution or movement of violence in England since 1649.

It is respectfully suggested that today in order to break the strength of the Bolshevik movement it is necessary to support the moderate socialists throughout Europe. The international policy of President Wilson has gone far to accomplish this; for he has voiced fully the international aspirations of the moderate socialists. It seems necessary now, however, to establish closer communication with the moderate labor and socialist groups. It is respectfully suggested that, for this purpose, Labor Attachés should be attached to the Embassies and Legations of the United States throughout Europe, whose duty would be to interpret the labor movements of the various European countries to the Government of the United States and to interpret the aims of the United States to the moderate socialists of Europe.

> Very respectfully submitted,   William C. Bullitt.

TS MS (SDR, RG 59, 840.00 B/1, DNA).

Two Telegrams from Edward Mandell House

Paris. Nov. 3, 1918.

Number 38. Secret for the President. Yesterday afternoon we had a meeting of the Supreme Council at Versailles in which we made further progress on the military terms of armistice for Germany. We did not reach the naval terms because both Lloyd George and Clemenceau wanted to wait for Austria's reply which *much* (must?) come in by Sunday midnight. I disagreed with this procedure believing it a waste of time.

The Belgians are protesting articles three and five of the fourteen points. The Italians are protesting article nine.

The three Prime Ministers meet this afternoon at three o'clock at my headquarters to discuss the fourteen points. As a matter of fact Clemenceau and Orlando will accept anything that the English will agree to concerning article two. I have spent almost every minute outside my conference[s] discussing this article with the British. I am insisting that they must recognize the principle, that it is a strong case [subject] for discussion at the peace conference or before, and I am having the greatest difficulty in getting them to admit even that much.

I have contended that they might notwithstanding [as well] refuse to accept the principle that laws governing war upon land was not a subject for discussion. I believe if I could get the matter postponed until you come that some satisfactory solution might be arrived at.   Edward House.

Paris November 3, 1918.

Number 41, Priority A. Secret for the President. My entire time outside of the scheduled conferences of Prime Ministers has been spent in working for a solution of the difficulties mentioned in my number 38. It had become very clear that the conference to be held at my headquarters at three o'clock this afternoon was to be a critical one and I was fully prepared to exert strong pressure in order to secure from the Allies an acceptance of the President's fourteen points set forth in his speech of January eighth 1918 and of his subsequent addresses. At three o'clock this afternoon Lloyd George, Clemenceau, Orlando and Hymans[1] (representing the Belgian Government) met with me at my headquarters for a talk over the fourteen points. George opened the discussion by stating that he was prepared to stand by the proposed answer cabled in my number 12.[2] I pointed out that the following phrase of this answer was not satisfactory to the President inasmuch as it was not clear that the Allies accepted the principle of the freedom of the seas "They must therefore reserve to themselves complete freedom on this subject when they enter the Peace Conference." I then read to the conference a paraphrase of the President's telegram to me dated October 31, in answer to my number 12. Clemenceau then stated "We accept the principle of the freedom of the seas" and turning to George he said "You do also do you not" George answered "No, it is impossible for any British Prime Minister to do this" He then stated "We are quite willing to discuss the freedom of the seas in the light of the new conditions which have arisen by reason of the war." I stated "Why do you not say so" He said "I am perfectly willing to say that to the President and I will instruct the British Ambassador in Washington to so inform the President" I said "I would prefer to have you so inform me and I will inform the President" I am now in receipt of the following letter

"British Embassy Paris, November 3rd., 1918. My dear Colonel House. I write to confirm the statement I made in the course of our talk this afternoon at your house when I told you that 'We were quite willing to discuss the freedom of the sea in the light of the new conditions which have arisen in the course of the present war' In our judgment this most important subject can only be dealt with satisfactorily through the freest debate and the most liberal exchange of views.

"I send you this letter after having had an opportunity of talking the matter over with the Foreign Secretary who quite agrees. Ever sincerely D. Lloyd-George."

The Belgian Representative proposed a number of modifications of point number three. None of these received approval. One change, however, was requested by the Allied Representatives to Point three. They wish it to be understood that the words "required, must carry out" ["so far as possible"] qualify the entire point. This they suggest[ed] could be accomplished by transposing them to the beginning of the point, so that point three would read "So far as possible the removable, et cetera, et cetera." I assented to this suggestion and stated that I thought it would probably be unnecessary for the President to point out this change to Germany. All other points were agreed upon without reservation. Situation now is therefore as follows. The proposed answer cabled you in number 12 will be sent to the President along with the terms of the military and Naval armistice to be offered to Germany. The President will then send the answer received from the Allies to the German Government with the statement that the military authorities of the Allies and the United States are prepared to receive the German military authorities and to communicate to them the terms upon which an armistice will be granted to Germany. The letter quoted above that I received from George must not be published unless it becomes necessary. If I do not hear from you to the contrary, I shall assume that you accept the situation as it now is. This I strongly advise. Any other decision would cause serious friction and delay. A conference will be held at my headquarters Monday morning *it* (at?) eleven o'clock. In the afternoon at three o'clock a full conference to be held at Versailles. At these meetings the terms of the naval and military armistice to be offered Germany will be finally agreed upon.   Edward House

T telegrams (WP, DLC).
   ¹ That is, Paul Hymans.
   ² Of Oct. 30, 1918.

From Newton Diehl Baker, with Enclosure

[Washington, Nov. 3, 1918]

For the President's information
Interesting from Gen Bliss   Baker

ALS (WP, DLC).

ENCLOSURE

Versailles November 3d [1918].

4 T.H.B. Secret
For Secretary of War

Your NDB One received. In accordance with March's 96[1] I reported to Colonel House and under my understanding of his instructions I ceased making reports except as to the Purely military questions. The Armistices that have been and are under discussion should be purely military questions but they are not. They should in my judgment contain nothing but the military conditions which the associated powers believe will make it perfectly safe for themselves to cease hostilities without fear of their resumption while these powers confer on the terms of Peace. The powers can then safely allow their differences to be known and can discuss and adjust them without danger of resumption of war. The difficulty is to avoid writing approximate Peace Terms in the Armistice. Mr. Clemenceau claimed in conference yesterday that if some concessions were not made on this point it meant the downfall of his Government. He did not use those (words) in the open conference but his meaning was clear. The Council accepted Marshal Foch's conditions for Armistice with Germany on land but did not agree about naval Armistice. Mr. Lloyd George secured postponement of action till Monday saying that if Austria accepts Armistice proposed to her the British and French demand in the Armistice for delivery of German naval ships to Allies will be much more severe. From personal interview and their statements in open Council I think that Mr. Balfour, Mr. Bonar Law, Lords Reading and Milner are of opinion that the Armistice should be military and other terms left to Peace conference. Marshal Foch has proposed plans for the occupation of positions in Austria threatening Munich and Bavaria. Understand that it will be considered by the Council tomorrow. This plan is also intended to put Allies in position to meet possible revolution in Austria. In view of its possible political bearing and its possible use of the American regiments now in Italy I shall ask Mr. House to cable it as soon as it is presented.   Bliss

T telegram (WP, DLC).
    [1] "When Colonel House arrives with his party report to him and cooperate with him in any way he may desire. March." P. C. Harris to Amsec, Versailles, Oct. 18, 1918, T telegram (WDR, RG 120, Records of the American Section of the Supreme War Council, 1917-1919, File No. 366-14, DNA).

From Joseph Patrick Tumulty, with Enclosure

Dear Governor: The White House. November 3, 1918.

We have just finished the attached advertisement, which will be printed in all the leading papers of the United States Monday afternoon and Tuesday morning. I hope it meets with your approval.

J.P.T.

TL (WP, DLC).

E N C L O S U R E

**WHEN THE BIG GERMAN DRIVE BEGAN LAST MARCH,
PREMIER LLOYD GEORGE SAID:**
"It is a race between Wilson and Hindenberg."
WHO IS WINNING?
The armies of the Kaiser are still fighting—will you take a chance on postponing their surrender by refusing to back up the Commander-in-Chief of our Army and Navy?
REMEMBER VOTERS WHEN YOU GO TO THE POLLS TUESDAY,
you will not be voting for Republicans or Democrats as *individuals* but for the *leaders* who will control them when they go to Congress.
THE ISSUE IS LEADERSHIP!
Whose leadership do you prefer? That of Senator Lodge, Senator Penrose and Colonel Roosevelt, who would dominate a Republican majority and block the President, or the leadership of Woodrow Wilson? What is the difference? The Republican leaders are on record against President Wilson's fourteen war aims which have been applauded by public opinion throughout the world, and constitute the basis of an enduring peace. Our President's fourteen terms do not help the SELFISH classes in any country but they favor all the MASSES of people. They seek to put an end to war AND THE THINGS THAT BREED WAR.

With Colonel Roosevelt denouncing the whole basis of these peace terms and Senator Lodge rejecting all the fundamentals NOW what could the country expect the Republican leaders to do with a peace treaty if they came into control of congressional committees? Having condemned such a treaty in advance they could not ratify it without stultifying themselves, and by their speeches Colonel Roosevelt and Senator Lodge have served notice on the country that they will not approve a peace treaty based on the Wilson principles of peace.

This is the issue which is now squarely before the country. The people have to decide whether they will follow President Wilson or

Colonel Roosevelt, whether they want a peace of liberalism and justice, or a peace of imperialism, standpatism, militarism that leaves all the old causes of war exactly where they were before we undertook to root out militarism and the rule of force and war itself.
YOU VOTERS MUST DECIDE THESE ISSUES FOR YOURSELVES AND FOR YOUR CHILDREN.
President Wilson stands for
WINNING THE WAR AND DESTROYING MILITARISM AND KAISERISM.
He insists "that adequate guarantees be given and taken that national armaments will be reduced to the lowest point consistent with domestic safety."

The President stands for a LEAGUE OF NATIONS. This League will protect nations, large and small, and permit every people desiring freedom to determine their own destiny. EVERYBODY WANTS THIS EXCEPT THOSE WHO WILL PROFIT BY THE OLD ORDER.

Now that the hour when the triumph of President Wilson's program for the liberation of the world is at hand, shall our President be politically discredited?

The most momentous diplomatic conference in all history is *now* being held in France. Show the world, by your vote of confidence in President Wilson, that he speaks as President of the United States for a united country.

Never mind what political party you are ordinarily affiliated with. The big question is:

Are you behind your President in the most critical moment of the world's history?
AUSTRIA:HUNGARY, BULGARIA, AND TURKEY HAVE CRUMBLED.
GERMANY IS NEXT.
Let us stand behind our leader, so that we may complete our victory and obtain a conclusive and enduring peace.

Do not vote to hamper the President, as surely would be the result if one branch of the Government is Republican and the other Democratic. President McKinley in the Spanish-American War asked for a united nation through the medium of a Republican majority, and was supported in this appeal by former President Harrison, Colonel Roosevelt, Senator Lodge, Senator Penrose, as well as Democratic voters—by the people of the country without respect to party lines.

VOTE TO SUSTAIN THE PRESIDENT WHO HAS APPEALED TO THE PATRIOTISM OF REPUBLICANS AS WELL AS DEMOCRATS TO CONSIDER COUNTRY ABOVE PARTY—TO SAY WHETHER THE PEOPLE SHALL HAVE THE LEADERSHIP OF PRESIDENT WILSON, OR OF HIS POLITICAL OPPONENTS.

BACK UP YOUR PRESIDENT WHO IS RECOGNIZED EVERYWHERE AS THE TRUE SPOKESMAN OF LIBERALS AND PROGRESSIVES THROUGHOUT THE WORLD.

DO NOT VOTE TO EMBARRASS THE PRESIDENT. HOLD UP HIS HANDS. VOTE TO SUSTAIN HIM BY ELECTING DEMOCRATIC SENATORS AND REPRESENTATIVES TO SPEAK FOR YOU.

CC MS (WP, DLC).

Colville Adrian de Rune Barclay to the Foreign Office

Washington. November 3rd, 1918.

No. 4963. Urgent. Secret.

Your telegram No. 6526.[1]

Text of Anglo-French declaration was presented to the President this afternoon by the French Ambassador. Wording of passage mentioned by you was as stated in your telegram.

In handing it to the President, M. Jusserand alluded to various agreements saying that they had been negotiated at a time when there was a very exacting Russia to deal with and that he supposed they might be subject to some revision. He did this knowing that the President objected to them.

After reading the translation of the text which M. Jusserand handed to him at the same time as the original, the President praised the sentiments which had inspired the declaration and which he said were the same as those he had expressed so often himself. He seemed concerned however as to the prospects which would lead, he thought, through the force of circumstances to the creation of spheres of Influence. M. Jusserand remarked that there were many sorts of spheres of influence some resulting from assistance rendered, others from community of interests, and yet others from proximity, all of which were legitimate.

The President then referred to a scheme, which he said was in his mind, though without definite form, whereby the League of Nations should assume the care of regions such as those that formed the object of our declaration, and entrust their welfare and development to the care of a small neutral nation acting as it were as trustee.

M. Jusserand pointed out that whatever the practicability of such a scheme it might well happen that local populations would prefer to deal with Great Powers whom they knew than with a neutral they did not know, and that to impose a neutral upon them against their will would be in opposition to the President's own tenets. The President saw the justice of this remark.

French Ambassador gathered the firm impression that the President will propound such a scheme as roughly described above at the Peace Conference.

The French Ambassador is not in possession of the various documents mentioned by you and consequently does not propose to make any further communication to the President or the State Department for the present.

T telegram (FO 115/2429, pp. 340-41, PRO).
    [1] R. Cecil to C. A. de R. Barclay, Oct. 31, 1918.

From the Diary of Josephus Daniels

1918 Sunday 3 November

Benson had wired for definite instructions as to naval terms of an armistice to be proposed. The President had cabled that any ships taken over should be held in trust, but given no specific instructions. After return to Washington I went to the White House—had a talk with the President—and in accordance with his views sent this telegram:

"In advising Col. House with regard to the terms of armistice, you are authorized to use your judgment, but the President's judgment is clear that it ought to be distinctly understood that all armed vessels taken should be held in trust and that it is quite possible to goo [go] too far in demanding excessive security"

Two Telegrams to Edward Mandell House

[The White House, Nov. 4, 1918]

VIII [Referring to your Number 36] I suggest that you urge that if the British cannot, relying upon our friendship and good faith, accept the principle of the freedom of the seas, they can count upon the certainty of our using our present great equipment to build up the strongest navy our resources permit, as our people have long desired.   Wilson.

T transcript (WC, NjP) of WWsh (WP, DLC).

The White House, November 4, 1918.

[No. 9] I accept the situation in your No. 41.   Wilson.

T telegram (E. M. House Papers, CtY).

To Thomas William Lamont

My dear Mr. Lamont: [The White House] 4 November, 1918

It was certainly very kind of you to write me your letter of October 31st and I warmly appreciate it. I quite understand that you could have had no personal connection with the editorial to which you refer, and it really caused me no annoyance. I have been frankly amused at the idea of some of the newspapers that it was out of taste for the President, who after all is only the elected servant of the people, to appeal directly to the people to know their judgment about what he is doing and gain their continued support if he could. I have no idea that the President is sacrosanct in any way, and being the leader of the country and under our system necessarily the leader of a party, he certainly ought not be rendered dumb on a point of taste at a critical moment.

Cordially and sincerely yours,   Woodrow Wilson

TLS (Letterpress Books, WP, DLC).

To Vittorio Emanuele III

The White House [Nov. 4, 1918].

Message to the King of Italy

May I not say how deeply and sincerely the people of the United States rejoice that the soil of Italy is delivered from her enemies.[1] In their name I send your Majesty and the great Italian people the most enthusiastic congratulations.   Woodrow Wilson

WWhw MS (received from T. W. Brahany).

[1] Representatives of the Italian and Austro-Hungarian armies signed an armistice at Villa Giusti, near Serravalle, Italy, on the afternoon of November 3. It was to take effect at 3 p.m., central European time, on November 4. For an authoritative English text of the armistice, see Charles I. Bevans, comp., *Treaties and Other International Agreements of the United States of America, 1776-1949* (13 vols., Washington, 1968-76), II, 1-8.

To Robert Lansing, with Enclosure

My dear Mr. Secretary: The White House 4 November, 1918

I entirely agree with Mr. Hoover in what he says in the enclosed letter, and if you think it not too irregular a course of action, I beg that you will request the Chargé of the Swiss Legation to convey through his government in the form you deem best our very earnest protest against any such action as is here forecast.

Cordially and faithfully yours,   Woodrow Wilson

TLS (SDR, RG 59, 763.72/12495, DNA).

ENCLOSURE
From Herbert Clark Hoover

Dear Mr. President: Washington 2 *November 1918*

I am informed through our correspondents this morning that the Germans in Belgium have given notice to the coal mines to the effect that all men and animals should be brought out of the pits, all raw materials in possession of companies to be delivered to the Germans and that the mines will be destroyed at once. They have already started in two places in Belgium.

I can scarcely express the concern that I feel over this matter. It means the loss of an absolutely vital necessity to these people over the coming winter. It will result in enormous loss of human life. It seems to me hardly in accord with the professions recently made by the German government in their communications to you.

I have not a great deal of faith in protests but it does seem to me that if you could see your way to point out in a note to the Germans that this does not accord with their professions; that it means the most terrible of human hardships; that it is absolutely wanton and that the continuation of this policy will necessitate the imposition of a greater burden upon the German people at the hands of the Allies. It might be that it would cause them to hesitate and at least appears to me could do no harm.

Yours faithfully,   Herbert Hoover.

TLS (SDR, RG 59, 763.72/12495, DNA).

To André Tardieu, with Enclosure

My dear Mr. Tardieu: [The White House] 4 November, 1918.

I am indeed delighted to get the photograph of Marshal Foch which you have been kind enough to bring to this country for me,[1] and I am very much complimented that he should have prepared it for me in so thoughtful a way.

Will you not be gracious enough, at the first opportunity, to forward to Marshal Foch the enclosed letter?

Cordially and sincerely yours,   Woodrow Wilson

TLS (Letterpress Books, WP, DLC).
[1] Wilson was replying to A. Tardieu to WW, Nov. 2, 1918, TLS (WP, DLC).

ENCLOSURE

To Ferdinand Foch

My dear Marshal Foch: [The White House] 4 November, 1918.

May I not express the very great pleasure with which I have received at the hands of M. Tardieu the photograph of yourself which you were kind enough to send me by him. I hope that at some not distant time I may have the pleasure of thanking you in person, for I am anxious to grasp the hand of the man who has so admirably directed the combined forces associated against Germany, and to whom we all take pride in looking up, as our Commander-in-Chief.

Cordially and sincerely yours,   Woodrow Wilson

TLS (Letterpress Books, WP, DLC).

To Herbert Clark Hoover

My dear Hoover: [The White House] 4 November, 1918

Your letter to Mr. Coudert has touched me very deeply, and I want you to know not only how proud I am to have your endorsement and your backing given in such generous fashion, but also what serious importance I attach to it, for I have learned to value your judgment and have the greatest trust in all your moral reactions. I thank you from the bottom of my heart.

Cordially and sincerely yours,   Woodrow Wilson

TLS (Letterpress Books, WP, DLC).

To Harvey MacCauley

My dear Mr. MacCauley: [The White House] 4 November, 1918.

Thank you for your letter of November 1st. It was certainly a fine piece of faithfulness for you to return the money I loaned you fifteen years ago. You may be sure I had no hard thoughts about the matter in the meantime, and that this letter carries with it my best wishes and my sincere appreciation of your generous words about the political support which ought to be given the administration.   Sincerely yours,   Woodrow Wilson

TLS (Letterpress Books, WP, DLC).

From Frederick Dixon

Dear Mr. Wilson: Boston, Massachusetts November 4, 1918.

I have carefully thought over my conversation with you the other day,[1] and have deliberately come to the conclusion that the way to accomplish the end is a two-fold one. First, a campaign of education editorially in the Monitor, and second, a visit to the other side. The campaign I will initiate here immediately we know the result of the armistice proposals. I think for reasons which I need not go into, it is better to wait until then. I can conduct it from this side or the other equally easily, as editorials are not a matter to depend on minutes for their publication. In any case I can get it under way here before it will be worth my while to cross.

I believe that both of these methods can have a great effect, and I am only too glad to be able to help you in the way you indicated.

Now there are one or two things that I want you to do for me if you will, so as to help me in these rather difficult days. One thing is that I want to take my secretary, who is an American and of draft age, with me. He is the only man I shall have over there whom I can trust implicitly, and whom I should not be afraid of leaking in any way. And nobody will understand better than you how desirable it is that what I hope to do should not leak out in any way. His name is Henry Newmark, and his address is The Braemore, Commonwealth Avenue, Boston. In any case I shall apply for his release from the draft as essential to an essential industry. This brings me to the other point, and that is the question of the men essential to the paper. With me in England it is more than ever essential that the reliable men should be at my disposal here, and not picked up for the draft. Beside I imagine that the days of fighting are really over, and that Germany will give in long before any of the present draft could be trained and taken across. That, however, has, of course, nothing to do with it. Although General Crowder has ruled that newspapers are essential industries, there is a curious sort of set here against them or at all events against the Monitor. The idea of the boards seems to be to make us as ineffectual as possible by the withdrawal of our men, an act which is entirely against the spirit and letter of General Crowder's rulings, for which they profess a supreme contempt.

When Mr. Warner[2] applied for assistance in Washington, he was told that if I would forward a list of the indispensable men to you direct, you would help us in the matter. I am therefore enclosing such a list to you,[3] and have not included a single man who can be spared, no matter with how much difficulty, from the paper.

Will you do one other thing to help me? Will you let somebody

unobtrusively warn the people here who grant the permits for the
OK[4] departure of aliens to let me and my wife pass, without undue
inquiry. My experience is that all sorts of questions are put very
often which make it a little difficult to explain one's reasons for
departure, and, of course, a word from anybody in your office will
put this right. The Embassy in Washington have promised to make
the shipping question all right for both of us, and of course there
is no real difficulty about the permits, only I would like the wheels
oiled a little. This should include Mr. Newmark.

I shall put in my application for a permit to depart in a few days,
just leaving time for you to help me, if you can and will. I shall
then of course have to wait for a boat, but that will be all right as
I would like to initiate the other campaign in the meantime. As
soon as I get to the other side I will get in touch with Colonel
House. And then I shall have to trust to my own discretion and
judgment.   Yours very sincerely,   Frederick Dixon

TLS (WP, DLC).
   [1] October 30, 1918, at 5 p.m. at the White House.
   [2] Charles D. Warner, chief of the Washington bureau of the *Christian Science Monitor*.
   [3] Not printed. There are twelve names on the list.
   [4] WWhw.

Two Telegrams from Edward Mandell House

Paris. November 4, 1918.

Number 42. Priority A. Secret for the President. A meeting was
held at my headquarters this morning at eleven o'clock attended
by Lloyd George, Clemenceau, Orlando, Doctor Benes (representing the Czecho-Slovaks) and myself. Marshal Foch and the Allied
military and naval authorities were in attendence also.

The conference agreed to the following resolutions:

"One: To approve the plan of operations against Germany through
Austria proposed by Marshal Foch, General Bliss, General Wilson
and General DiRobilant.

Two: That Marshal Foch shall have the supreme strategical direction of operations against Germany on all fronts including the
southern and eastern.

Three: That the military advisers of the British, French and Italian and the United States Government[s] shall immediately examine the following [questions]:

A. The possibility of taking immediate steps to send a force which
shall include the Czecho-Slovak forces on the French and Italian
fronts to Bohemia and Gallicia with the following subjects [objects]:
to organize these countries against invasion by Germany; to prevent

the export to Germany of oil, coal or any other material, and to render these available to the Allied forces; to establish airdromes for the purpose of bombing Germany.

B. The immediate cooperation of General Franchet d'Esperey in these objects."

The procedure to be adopted by the Supreme War Council this afternoon was agreed upon as follows: "The Supreme War Council decide as follows. A. To approve the attached terms for an armistice with Germany.[1] B. To communicate the terms of armistice to President Wilson inviting him to notify the German Government that the next step for them to take is to send a parlementaire to Marshal Foch who will receive instructions to act on behalf of the Associated Governments. C. To communicate to President Wilson the attached memorandum [of] observations by the Allied Governments on the correspondence which has passed between the President and the German Government, in order that they may be forwarded to Germany together with the communication in regard to an armistice. D. To invite Colonel House to make the above communications on their behalf to President Wilson. E. To authorize Marshal Foch to communicate the terms as finally approved to envoys properly accredited by the German Government. F. To associate a British admiral with Marshal Foch bearing on naval aspects of the armistice. G. To leave to the direction [discretion][2] of Marshal Foch and the British admiral in regard to minor technical points in the armistice."

The memorandum of observations by the Allied Governments on the correspondence which has passed between the President and the German Government; memorandum one supra now reads as follows:

"The Allied Governments have given careful consideration to the correspondence which has passed between the President of the United States and the German Government. Subject to the qualifications which follow they declare their willingness to make peace with the Government of Germany on the terms of peace laid down in the President's address to Congress of January [8] 1918, and the principles of settlement enunciated in his subsequent addresses. They must point out, however, that clause two relating to what is usually described as the freedom of the seas, is open to various interpretations, some of which they could not accept. They must therefore reserve to themselves complete freedom on this subject when they enter the peace conference.

"Further, in the conditions of peace laid down in his address to Congress of January 8th, 1918, the President declared that invaded territories must be restored as well as evacuated and freed. The Allied Governments feel that no doubt ought to be allowed to exist as to what this provision implies. By it they understand that compensation will be made by Germany for all damage done to the civilian population of the Allies and their property (by the forces of Germany) by the aggression of Germany by land, by sea and from the air."

Main [The only] change in this from draft cabled you in my number twelve is that [the] insertion of the words "by the aggression of Germany" in the last sentence. This with Lloyd George's letter quoted in my number 38 makes the situation quite satisfactory for the moment. The terms of the military and naval armistice will be finally adopted this afternoon at Versailles and will be cabled you in full as soon as they have been adopted. Lloyd George leaves today at two o'clock for England, accordingly he will not be present at the conference this afternoon.   Edward House.

¹ The military and naval terms were transmitted in EMH to WW, No. 46, Nov. 4, 1918, T telegram (WP, DLC). Wilson repeated the text of this telegram, *mutatis mutandis*, in the address to a joint session of Congress printed at Nov. 11, 1918.
² This and other corrections from the copy in SDR, RG 59, 763.72119/9052, DNA.

Paris Nov 4, 1918

Number 47. Secret for the President. In order that there may be no misunderstanding I venture to repeat the procedure agreed upon for the handling of the Armistice negotiations with Germany. The terms of the Armistice to be offered Germany and the memorandum of the observations of the Allied Governments on the correspondence which has passed between the President and the German Government both having been communicated by me to the President and having been accepted by him, the President is expected to proceed as follows: One. To notify the German Government to send a parlementaire to Marshal Foch who has been advised of the views of the Allied and United States Governments respecting the terms of the Armistice to be offered Germany. Two, to forward to Germany together with the communication mentioned in one supra the memorandum of observations by the Allied Governments on the correspondence which has passed between the President and the German Government. It must be clearly understood that the terms of the Armistice to be offered Germany are not to be made public until these terms have been accepted by Germany.

Edward House.

T telegrams (WP, DLC).

From Newton Diehl Baker, with Enclosure

Dear Mr. President:　　　　　　　Washington. November 4, 1918.

I transmit a letter from General Bliss, the early part of which will undoubtedly interest you. I attach, also, copy of a memorandum which I have caused to be filed with the Air Service for its guidance in connection with the proposed formation of an Inter-Allied independent air force.[1]

Respectfully yours,　Newton D. Baker

TLS (WP, DLC).
[1] NDB to P. C. March, Nov. 4, 1918, TC MS (WP, DLC).

ENCLOSURE

Tasker Howard Bliss to Newton Diehl Baker

No. 31.
My dear Mr. Secretary:　　　　　Versailles. October 23, 1918.

I am sending hasty lines to you and March[1] by to-day's courier.

I received your telegram about the presentation of the Distinguished Service Medal awarded by the President to General Pershing. General Pershing happened to be here the day of its receipt and I conferred with him on the subject and we arranged to have the presentation take place at his field headquarters very shortly after the arrival of Mr. House who is expected in Brest the day after to-morrow (Friday).

General Pershing wants me to bring Mr. House with me on that occasion. At the same time he impressed upon me the fact that Mrs. House must not accompany her husband. He says there are absolutely no accommodations for ladies. We have arranged for a special train to meet Mr. House and his party and it will leave here to-morrow morning about eight o'clock for Brest. I hope to be able to go there and meet him in person. I think that we have made satisfactory arrangements for his accommodation on arrival. But it is for him to decide when he gets here.

I also received your cablegram of October 21st[2] which came to me through the State Department, signed by Mr. Lansing below your signature, and through the American Embassy in Paris. I received it yesterday too late to reply to it that day.

You ask me not only for a summary of official civil and military

[1] T. H. Bliss to P. C. March, Oct. 23, 1918, TLS (WDR, RG 120, Records of the American Section of the Supreme War Council, 1917-1919, File No. 366-14, DNA).
[2] It is missing, but see T. H. Bliss to NDB, Oct. 23, 1918, printed as an Enclosure with NDB to WW, Oct. 24, 1918 (second letter of that date).

expressions as I may have heard with reference to the present situation, but also for my own views, in order that you may lay them before the President. If any weight is to be attached to my views, this imposes a very grave responsibility upon me which, however, I shall shoulder as best I may. I have not expressed officially my opinion on subjects which are so largely international-political in character except when I have been expressly directed to do so,—as, for example, when my opinion was asked about military intervention in Siberia. In that case, however, the subject was about as much military as it was political.

I wish to God that the President himself could be here for a week. I hear in all quarters a longing for this. The people who want to get a rational solution out of this awful mess look to him alone. I have already told you that I have heard it repeatedly said that he alone can settle in any permanent way the Balkan questions. I have even heard my British colleagues say that they believe the only solution will be an American Protectorate there. In this dark storm of angry passion that has been let loose in all quarters I doubt if any one but he can let in the light of reason. It will be "ex Occidente lux," and not "ex Oriente lux."

I hope to get off a telegram to-day, as I promised in my cable to you last night. I have begun it and torn it up several times. It is a perplexing question to handle, at this stage, in writing. My views are, I think, pretty well understood here by *inference* although not by direct statements on my part. There are so few people with whom one can reason and state views without leading to an outbreak of passion. I think that the English are by far the most reasonable and that it is with them that our government can most probably come to an agreement as to what is right and just for the present and which will tend to the future peace of the world. The trouble is that the military element is on top, and if they are allowed to work their will they will do that which, if done by Germany, would shock the sense of justice of the world. And the worst of it is that what they would do would lead to a perpetuation of armaments and the standing threat of war.

When I send my telegram you will note that I do not believe that, in this peculiar case, the question of conditions of a so-called armistice should be left to the military men *alone*. The trouble is that it is not an armistice. It is an absolute surrender that we must have. But in order to get that surrender the conditions which are to follow it should be determined in advance and made known. All of the military propositions for an armistice that I have seen plainly embody or point to the political conditions which will exist after the so-called armistice is agreed to. These political conditions, imposed in the armistice, will be doubtless demanded by the political people in the discussion of final terms. At the same time, these political conditions imposed by military men alone may be such as to keep the world in turmoil for many years to come.

If the President's idea of rational disarmament can only be realized it will simplify the whole problem. If all the nations will disarm to the extent that they properly can, there will be no necessity of taking away this or that or the other part of the defeated nation merely for the purpose of rendering it militarily weak. An international sense of justice can readily agree on taking away of such territory as does not justly belong to that nation whether it is armed or disarmed.

But no two men think alike, apparently, about these things. Everything is drifting. The military party is demanding more and more with every day's success. There is nobody to impose any check. There is no free speech here and no free press, in our sense of the word. I think that the time is ripe for our government to immediately take the lead; to recognize that there are certain things that it is right and just and conducive to future peace to now demand; to recognize that there are other questions which can only be settled by the prolonged and earnest consideration and discussion of honest, reasonable, intelligent, and just persons.

If in this bewildering darkness a way can be pointed out and accepted by all, which will put a stop to the fighting under such conditions that it cannot be resumed I believe that Germany, still with a formidable army at her disposal, will agree to rational disarmament. Then there will be hope that all will disarm. But if certain elements of the military party have their way I fear that the rest of Europe will have to remain armed for an indefinite time in order to keep Germany in the position in which it is desired to put her, and in order to defend their own spoils against each other.

In my opinion the time has come for the United States to act swiftly and determinedly. I think that it should formulate its own views of what is right, right not only now but also for all time to come, and boldly put these up to its associates as a basis for their own agreement. In these, I think, should be included the doctrine of rational disarmament. I doubt if the governments are ripe for this but I believe that the common people are. And I think that the governments, knowing this, will listen to reason.

I shall try to write more logically and consecutively on this complicated subject the next time.

I inclose herewith the original document which I have received from the French Military Representative on the subject of the formation of an Inter-Allied Aerial Force.[3]

You will notice that he asks me to send it in order to obtain the ratification of the project by the American Government as soon as possible. It shows the curious way in which business is done here. The document relates to an agreement drawn up between the British Government and the French Government. I have no doubt of its being in correct form from the French point of view, but you will note that there is absolutely no authentification of the document. Why a document drawn up between two governments should be sent to me for transmission to my government, instead of having it go from the proper official bureau of those governments I do not see. I have told my French colleague that I have forwarded it because of his request that I should do so; but that I doubt very much if I shall hear further from it until it shall have been transmitted by either the British or French governments or both.

Please note paragraph 1 of the document, which states that the object of this aerial force is to carry the war into Germany by attacking its industry, its commerce, and its *population*. You will note that there is not a word to indicate that this proposed use of the aerial force is by way of reprisal. When, in some future year, the document is withdrawn from the archives of some State Department, it will look as though the governments which drew it up regarded bombing attacks upon *populations, as such*, to be a perfectly legitimate object of warfare. Even the Germans have maintained that their bombing raids on London, Paris, and other centers of population have been made only because those places were the centers of all kinds of war industries, or that they were places where large numbers of troops were concentrated, and they claim that those industries or troops are the objects of their raids and that injury to populations is incidental. But the document herewith makes the *population, per se*, to be the object of attack.

I inclose also a copy of a memorandum handed to me by Mr. W. B. Poland, Director for Europe of the Commission for Relief in Belgium, in regard to the problem of revictualling those portions of French territory and Belgian territory evacuated by the Germans.[4] You will find it interesting.

I am also sending you a copy of the personal and secret instruc-

[3] E. E. Belin to the American and Italian permanent representatives on the Supreme War Council, Oct. 18, 1918, enclosing "POINTS PRINCIPAUX de l' ACCORD RELATIF A LA CONSTITUTION DE LA FORCE AERIENNE INDEPENDANTE INTERALLIEE," dated Oct. 3, 1918, both T MS (T. H. Bliss Papers, DLC).

[4] W. B. Poland, "Memorandum . . . regarding the conduct of the Ravitaillement of the occupied territories of Northern France and Belgium in the event of their whole or partial evacuation by the Germans," T MS (WDR, RG 120, Records of the American Section of the Supreme War Council, 1917-1919, File No. 366-14, DNA).

tions to General Franchet d'Esperey, Commanding the Allied Armies of the East, and to General Berthelot, sent on a special mission to Roumania, both of them signed by Mr. Clemenceau.[5]

I also send you (in connection with your request in a former letter) the last report that I have received on the subject of the Haviland planes fitted with Liberty motors.[6] You will note that final trials have not been made and it looks now as though they would not be made. You will also note that the report states that the American aviators at the front agree in stating that the Haviland plane gives satisfaction.

I hope that you had a pleasant trip on your return home and that you have found your family in the best of health, to whom I hope you will present my kindest regards.

Hastily but cordially yours,   Tasker H. Bliss

TCL (WP, DLC).
[5] Not found.
[6] Not found.

From Andrew Furuseth

Mr. President: Washington, D. C., Nov 4, 1918.

Even though I should incur your displeasure by this my act of addressing you at this time and on this subject my sense of duty compells me.

Great Britain is registering all her merchant seamen, their age, rating when at sea, their present employment, their addresses etc for the purpose of being able to man her merchant fleet when the war shall be ended. My information is that she is to dispense with all the Chinese now employed and most of the Lascars. This is done in complete co-operation with the Unions Seamen.

The U. S. Shipping Board is discussing the question of sending instructions, which if sent will drive a very large number of the seamen now and in the past sailing in American vessels out of this service.

In order that you may understand and take such action as you shall think wise and proper I am sending you inclosed a letter which I have sent to Commissioner Charles R. Page, who is by the Shipping Board entrusted with the relations between the Board and the seamen.[1]   Most Respectfully   Andrew Furuseth.

TLS (WP, DLC).
[1] A. Furuseth to C. R. Page, Nov. 4, 1918, CCLS (WP, DLC).

From Homer Stillé Cummings, with Enclosure

[Washington]

My dear Mr. President: November the Fourth 1918.

I have endeavored during the progress of the present political campaign to avoid troubling you with any matters except of the highest consequence. Now that the campaign is drawing to a close I thought I would drop you a note which would indicate in a general way the situation as I view it.

The work of the Democratic National Committee, closely affiliated, as you know it has been, with the Senatorial and Congressional Committees, has, on the whole, been well conducted. We have obtained a larger campaign fund than at one time seemed possible and I hope that the deficit (chiefly represented by a note for $130,000 given by ten of us), will not be too large or too burdensome. The exigencies of the situation made it imperatively necessary to secure and disburse a much larger campaign fund than we have ever before used in an off-year election.

The speaking campaign was very largely abandoned on account of the influenza. This made it necessary to devise alternative methods of publicity, and I think that in this regard we have been somewhat ingenious and really effective. Every possible agency of publicity open to us has been employed. The great number of interviews from prominent men all over the country which have found their way into the public press have been, in a large measure, due to the activities of the Committee. At the present time I do not know of any of the customary work of the National Committee which has been neglected. I think also it may be said that we have stimulated the state committees and local organizations to unusually effective work. The Committee has also been in touch with a very large number of individuals throughout the country. We have thrown everything that we had into the scale.

Your appeal to the country for a Democratic majority in the House and Senate has had a wonderfully wholesome effect. It went directly to the mark, and the wisdom of issuing such an appeal is more and more apparent every day.

I look forward with the utmost confidence to a highly satisfactory result. I am receiving reports hourly of the most encouraging character. These reports would justify the prediction of a land-slide. Making every allowance for errors due to overconfidence and resolving all reasonable doubts against us, I feel justified in saying that we shall control the House by a very substantial majority, probably between fifteen and forty; I do not think that the present Democratic majority in the Senate will be much changed. I enclose herewith a brief statement as to the Senatorial situation in some of the states in which we are chiefly interested. I have, I hope, avoided extravagant claims, though the newspaper reports on the international situation are of such a character as to make it likely that the impending Republican defeat will be converted into a rout.

I have been most happy to have been of some service in this matter and regret only that I could not have done more. I am
Very sincerely yours, [Homer S. Cummings]

CCL (H. S. Cummings Papers, ViU).

E N C L O S U R E

MEMORANDUM CONCERNING SENATORIAL SITUATION

November 4, 1918.

The present Democratic majority of eight in the Senate is, on the whole, not likely to be much changed, though there will probably be some losses which will be off-set by corresponding gains.

It would not be surprising if we lost the senatorial contests in Illinois and Kansas—this would lose us two votes in the Senate.

In New Hampshire there is a vigorous fight—the result will probably be very close. We must win there or lose another Democratic vote in the Senate. It looks, however, as if we would win by a narrow margin.

There is a hard fight on in Delaware, but Senator Saulsbury ought to be reelected.

In Montana I look for the reelection of Senator Walsh.

In Nevada we ought also to be successful.

In Idaho and Missouri every indication points our way. We will hold our present Democratic representation.

With reference to Kentucky, I am still somewhat disturbed. The situation has been very complicated and very unsatisfactory. I think, however, your appeal to the country has been especially potent in that state. Without that appeal I do not think it would have been possible to carry Kentucky. I have myself sent out several thousand individual letters to Democratic workers and leaders in that state. I believe we shall come through all right.

With reference to Colorado, the fight there seems to be a desperate one and somewhat in doubt. The present difficulties are largely the outgrowth of Democratic dissension beginning in Denver through a change in leadership there and extending throughout the state. I cannot rid myself of the notion, however, that Senator

Shafroth will be reelected, although it is only fair to say that the result is very much in doubt as the matter stands now.

I think it quite likely that we shall be successful in South Dakota and in Nebraska.

This would be a net gain of two Democrats in the Senate, and while the margin is not great in either place, it seems to be reasonably safe.

The foregoing statement if justified by events would leave the Senate precisely as it now stands.

I do not look for the election of any Democratic Senators in New Jersey, and while Minnesota and Michigan may be classed as doubtful, the chances favor the Republicans.

This leaves five states, all now represented by Republicans, and in every one of these states there is a chance of Democratic success. I think the chance is much more than a fighting chance, and it would not be at all surprising if we made some gains. The states referred to are Massachusetts, Rhode Island, West Virginia, Wyoming and New Mexico.

To put it another way, I think the chance of Democratic success in this group of five states is fully as great, if not greater, than the possibility of any unexpected Democratic losses elsewhere.

I think a general survey of the situation, therefore, justifies the view that in all probability there will be little or no change in the Senate.

CC MS (H. S. Cummings Papers, ViU).

A Memorandum by Frank Irving Cobb

Paris, November 4th, 1918.
Confidential Memorandum for Colonel House
In the matter of the President coming to Europe.

The moment President Wilson sits at the consul [council] table with these Prime Ministers and Foreign Secretaries he has lost all the power that comes from distance and detachment. Instead of remaining the great arbiter of human freedom he becomes merely a negotiator dealing with other negotiators. He is simply one vote in a Peace Conference bound either to abide by the will of the majority or disrupt its proceedings under circumstances which, having come to a climax in secret, can never be clearly explained to the public. Any public protest to which the President gave utterance would thus be only the complaint of a thwarted and disappointed negotiator.

The President's extraordinary facility of statement would be lost in a conference. Anything he said to his associates would be made mediocre and common place by the translators, and could carry none of the weight of his formal utterances.

Furthermore, personal contact between the President and these Prime Ministers and Foreign Secretaries who are already jealous of his power and resentful of his leadership in Europe must inevitably develop new friction and endless contraversey. They would miss no opportunity to harass him and wear him down. They would seek to play him off one against the other, a game in which they are marvelously adroit, since it has been the game of European diplomacy, since the days of Metternich and Tallyrand. The President cannot afford to play it.

In Washington, President Wilson has the ear of the whole world. It is a commanding position, the position of a court of last resort, of world democracy. He cannot afford to be manoeuvered into the position of an advocate engaged in personal dispute and altercation with other advocates around a counsel table. In Washington, he is a dispassionate judge whose mind is unclouded by all these petty personal circumstances of a conference. If his representatives are balked by the representatives of the other powers in matters which he regards as vital to the lasting peace of the world, he can go before Congress and appeal to the conscience and hope of mankind. He can do this over the head of any Peace Conference. This is a mighty weapon, but if the President were to participate personally in the proceedings, it would be a broken stick.

The President, if he is to win this great battle for human freedom, must fight on his own ground and his own ground is Washington. Diplomatic Europe is all enemy soil for him. He cannot make a successful appeal to the people of the world here. The official surroundings are all unfavorable. The means of minimizing its effect are all under the control of those who are opposed to him. One of his strongest weapons in this conflict is the very mystery and uncertainty that attach to him while he remains in Washington.

When we left New York, I believed that it was not only desirable but necessary for President Wison to come to Europe. Since our arrival here, my opinion is changed completely, and I am wholly convinced now that the success of the Peace Conference from the American point of view depends on the President's directing the proceedings from Washington where he can be free from immediate personal contact with European negotiators and European diplomacy.

T MS (WP, DLC).

From the Diary of Josephus Daniels

November Monday 4 1918

Had message to come to White House at 8:30. Lansing and Baker there. President had message from House. Supreme War Council agreed, but Great Britain raised question of freedom of the seas—did not understand exactly what is meant by it—and wished that left open for discussion. WW had cabled House if E[ngland] took course in opposition we would use our facilities to build the greatest navy. France accepted principle. Decided to accept inasmuch as G. B. agreed to all other 13 points & did not actually dissent from that in order to have unity. But he is resolved in later conference to win over the other countries to our point of view, and secure it from League of Nations. Great disappointment to me. Lansing & Baker thought it would work out all right. L _____ does not believe in doctrine of blockade & thinks new conditions must make a change in it.

Baker told of Hughes, in War Drive speech, saying "unconditional surrender." Bourke Cochran: "I approve of that doctrine first enunciated by WW who said there could be no compromise with autocracy[."]

To Homer Stillé Cummings

My dear Cummings: The White House 5 November, 1918

Thank you for your letter of yesterday about the campaign. My thoughts have of course been engrossed by other matters, but I have not failed to follow the work that you and the rest of the committee have been doing, and I want you to know how sincerely I admire it and how highly I value the thoughtfulness and enthusiasm with which it was done. I am hoping with you that the results will be very unusual and surprising to our opponents.

Cordially and sincerely yours,   Woodrow Wilson

TLS (H. S. Cummings Papers, ViU).

To Robert Lansing

My dear Mr. Secretary: [The White House] 5 November, 1918

In the interview I had the other day with the Japanese Ambassador I suggested to him that any joint action such as he had proposed should be in accord with this pronouncement of the President of China.¹ I also asked the Ambassador to have a frank consultation with you. I am simply writing this for your information.

Cordially and faithfully yours,   Woodrow Wilson

TLS (Letterpress Books, WP, DLC).
¹ For the complete text of which, see P. S. Reinsch to RL, Nov. 8, 1918, *FR 1918*, pp. 117-19.

To Charles R. Page

[The White House]

My dear Mr. Commissioner: 5 November, 1918

This is just a line to express my very profound sympathy with the views of Mr. Andrew Furuseth concerning the general policy we should pursue towards our seamen, and to express the hope that the Shipping Board will not take any action with regard to the seamen without first learning the views of the Secretary of Labor, with whom I have discussed this matter more than with any other person, and whose guidance I think it indispensable to follow.

I am sure you will understand that I am writing only after considerable experience in at least the analysis and discussion of these matters, and because I have so much at heart the development of a real virile body of American seamen.

Cordially and sincerely yours,   Woodrow Wilson

TLS (Letterpress Books, WP, DLC).

To Andrew Furuseth

My dear Mr. Furuseth: [The White House] 5 November, 1918

I have been glad to write Mr. Page, of the Shipping Board, a letter urging him to give the fullest consideration to your views, and also to follow the counsel of Secretary Wilson in any policy that may be adopted with regard to the seamen.

Cordially and sincerely yours,   Woodrow Wilson

TLS (Letterpress Books, WP, DLC).

To Henry French Hollis

My dear Senator: [The White House] 5 November, 1918

Again I have to thank you for a very instructive letter, yours of October 13th. We are in the midst of great things, and the sidelights you throw on matters of the first consequence make them much easier for me to see in their whole proportion.

With best wishes,

Cordially and sincerely yours,   Woodrow Wilson

TLS (Letterpress Books, WP, DLC).

Two Telegrams from Edward Mandell House

[Paris, Nov. 5, 1918]

From House, No. Six. I consider that we have won a great diplomatic victory in getting the Allies to accept the principles laid down in your January eighth speech and in your subsequent addresses. This has been done in the face of a hostile and influential junta in the United States and the thoroughly unsympath[et]ic personnel constituting the Entente governments. I doubt whether any other [of the] heads of the governments with whom we are have been dealing[1] [quite] realize how far they are now committed to the American peace programme. As far as the question of the freedom of the seas is concerned, I think it [fair to] say that Balfour agrees with me and so in a lesser degree did Eric Geddes. It is only that mischievous and reactionary blue water school that drove George to take his extraordinary attitude. Reading, I think, treated the matter from the lawyer's view point and felt that George was his client. Motive for what he said did not impress me as being his own convictions.[2] Both French Prime Minister and George wanted [want] to make the League of Nations an after consideration, and not make it a part of the Peace Conference. [Curiously] enough your speech of September twenty-seventh as published here was clearly open to this interpretation (par excellence?) I set them right about [it] but did not press it further at the moment, for in accepting your terms they automatically accept this also.

If Germany accepts the conditions of our armistice, the Peace Conference should be called for December eleventh [or] thereabouts. It would be necessary for you [to] leave as soon as possible in order to have some preliminary conferences here with [Great Britain] France and Italy. This is essential. If Germany accepts by November tenth, could you not sail on the eighteenth? I think Oxford may offer you degree of DCL. This would give a reason for landing in England and also for making an address. Impossible to do anything at present;[3] [I am now] busy bringing every force to bear to help win a peoples' victory, and your landing in England is an essential part of it. I send (?) [Cobb] to London to-night. Wiseman has been splendidly helpful. House.

WWT MS (WP, DLC).
    1 Wilson typed "have been" over the line and failed to delete the "are."
    2 This sentence in House's copy reads: "What he said did not impress me as being his own convictions."
    3 These words not in House's copy.

Paris Nov 5, 1918

Number 50. For the President. At the conclusion of the meeting of Supreme War Council yesterday [afternoon] I proposed a resolution in the following sense and the same was adopted: "The Supreme War Council in session at Versailles desire to cooperate with Austria, Turkey and Bulgaria in the making available as far as possible food and other supplies necessary for the life of the civilian population of those countries."

You may use your discretion in making this resolution public.

Edward House.

T telegram (WP, DLC).

From Newton Diehl Baker, with Enclosure

Dear Mr. President: Washington November 5, 1918

A bad matter is made much worse by this cablegram from General Pershing. It does not seem possible to let it rest in this situation and I am preparing a letter about which I shall hope to speak to you at your convenience and of course before I send it.

Further cablegrams on the subject are apparently unnecessary since the General is now in a proper relation to Colonel House.

Respectfully Newton D. Baker

ALS (WP, DLC).

E N C L O S U R E

RUSH Number 1869 [Paris] November 4th [1918].

Personal and Confidential for the Secretary of War.

Reference your cable November 2d, President's comments as set forth in former cablegram had been received and it was because of his wishes as expressed in first paragraph therein[1] that I thought it desirable from a military standpoint to lay before him fully my views as to advisability of granting armistice. On account of my illness with grippe for some days was unable to discuss the matter with Mr. House, and also unable to present views to War Council, so I gave the letter personally to Mr. House whom I saw for only a moment and letter was presented by him to the War Council. I left immediately for the front where I remained two days when I was called back to Paris together with Allied Commanders in Chief and met with War Council on Saturday. While there had full opportunity to go over the whole situation with Mr. House and we are working together in perfect harmony. Shall give him all assistance possible in his difficult task. For your personal information, War Council decided withhold reply to Germany until answer from Austria shall be received. Armistice conditions have been discussed by Supreme War Council and views of the military obtained. As Mr. House reports direct to President on this whole question further report by me to War Department would now seem unnecessary.

Pershing.

T telegram (WP, DLC).
  ¹ See the Enclosure printed with NDB to WW, Oct. 28, 1918.

From Newton Diehl Baker, with Enclosure

My dear Mr. President: Washington November 5, 1918.
    I think I ought to send this letter to General Pershing, and a copy of it to Colonel House with copies of the cablegrams between General Pershing and me which he has not seen.
Respectfully yours,   Newton D. Baker

    P.S. I would only send so much of Colonel House as is pertinent, omitting comments by Mr Lloyd George Mr Clemenceau &c.

TLS (WP, DLC).

E N C L O S U R E
Newton Diehl Baker to John Joseph Pershing

My dear General Pershing: Washington. November 5, 1918.
    On October 31 Colonel House sent the President a confidential dispatch of which I enclose a copy.
    On the twenty-seventh of October I had sent you a cablegram of which paragraph 1 conveyed the direction of the President that you "feel entirely free to bring to *his* attention any consideration" which in your judgment should be weighed before finally settling his

views; and in the last paragraph I conveyed the President's wish to have you confer with Colonel House, "showing him a copy of your dispatch and this answer, and generally discussing with him all phases of this subject."

On October 31 you cabled me a copy of your letter dated October 30, 1918, addressed to the Allied Supreme War Council, Paris, and your cablegram tells me that you "have handed the Allied Supreme War Council the following communication."

You will observe from the cablegram of Colonel House to the President that Colonel House understood that you were giving him a copy of the communication, "the original thereof having already been sent to the Supreme War Council at Versailles," and did not understand that the copy handed to him was intended to be communicated through him or in any case subject to his discretion.

When I laid your cablegram of October 31 before the President he was unable to understand why your views were communicated to the Supreme War Council instead of to him, or at least to Colonel House, his special representative, and General Bliss, his military representative at Versailles, in view of the directions contained in my previous cablegram, and in further view of the fact stated by Colonel House that "no Allied General has ever submitted a document of this character to the Supreme War Council without a previous request having been made by the civilian authorities."

It would seem plain that your relation to this question would be through the President, just as that of Marshal Haig would be through Mr. Lloyd George and that of General Petain through M. Clemenceau, and that independent expressions of opinion by you on questions involving both military and political considerations might at some time produce the deep embarrassment of a variance of opinion between you and your Commander-in-Chief. Obviously, the views of the United States upon any question of national policy could be expressed only by the President.

Your cablegram of November 4 indicates that your letter was drawn up for the President's information, rather than that of the Supreme War Council, and was presented to the latter body by Colonel House, while the cablegram of Colonel House's indicates that he received only a copy of a document previously transmitted by you directly.

It is, of course, unimportant now to discuss any of the views set forth in your letter to the Supreme War Council, since the issues to which they were addressed have for the time being been settled by that body; but I am sure you will share my earnest desire to have the misunderstanding cleared up, which on the face of these cablegrams mystifies me by seeming to present conflicting statements of fact with regard to the mode of presenting a letter to the Supreme War Council. Obviously, there is a misunderstanding which at this distance and with the insufficiency of cable correspondence seems insoluble, but which of course a letter will be able to set right.   Cordially yours,

TL (N. D. Baker Papers, DLC).

From Robert Lansing

My dear Mr. President: Washington November 5, 1918

The telegrams we have from Mr. Morris give a clear idea of the problems to be met in Siberia as far as he has been able to ascertain them without visiting the country. They tally closely with what we have been able to gather from other sources. I am confident that the material and economic aid which we can offer will be supplied to best advantage by the plans which Mr. McCormick is formulating so rapidly. I believe Mr. Stevens and the American Engineers of the Russian Railway Service Corps will also do a great deal with the railway workers, quite aside from the improved railway service they will introduce, by effecting fair shop practice in railway repair shops and by cultivating a spirit of justice in industry.

At the same time, these very measures seem to me to open a way for increased activity by the Young Men's Christian Association and the Red Cross. The army medical units will gradually—and in fact have already begun to do so—absorb the activities necessary for the military requirements both of the Czechs and of the Russians. But there will remain the civilian population. The townspeople in Siberia have felt little of the terror which exists in European Russia. But a considerable industrial and social uneasiness persists, fraught with danger for the future. It would seem timely to me if we should consult with the Young Men's Christian Association and the War Council of the Red Cross, as to whether they feel prepared to extend the admirable efforts which have already been made as a beginning. I believe the Red Cross could extend its work in the cities and the Young Men's Christian Association, by the selection of mature representatives, do much to further its work among both civilians and soldiers.   Faithfully yours,   Robert Lansing.

TLS (WP, DLC).

From Charles William Eliot

Dear Mr. President: Cambridge, Mass., 5 November 1918.

Your cordial note of the second of November received this morn-ing gives me solid satisfaction; but I think I ought not to withhold from you the fact that I wished, and still wish, you had not written that appeal to the voters. I support you and the Democratic party with every ounce of weight I can carry. For instance, I have just voted for all the Democratic candidates on the ballot, in spite of the fact that a considerable proportion of them are to my knowledge inferior to the Republican candidates for the same offices. Never-theless, I cannot but think that your appeal to the voters was an unnecessary and inexpedient departure from the position you have previously held, namely, that you are the President of the United States, claiming and having the support of the entire people.

May I avail myself of this opportunity to express the opinion that the only League of Nations which ought to be contemplated at present is a league consisting of Belgium, Great Britain, the United States, France, Italy, and Japan, and that this league ought to be made in the firmest way *now* before peace negotiations actually begin, but not before those nations have agreed not only on terms of surrender—which seem to be developing very well—but on the objects and aims in the reconstruction of the map of Europe and of the industrial and commercial policies of the civilized nations? This preliminary league, from which Germany must be of course excluded because she is faithless, ought to have power to set up a council, an executive commission, and an international court, and to admit other nations to the league as fast as seems safe. To save the fruits of the War we need such a League of Nations forthwith very urgently; and out of such a League of Nations might grow in time a league of all the nations which have proved themselves capable of seeking, speaking, and carrying into their action the Truth.

I chance to live in a community or society which contains many more well-educated Republicans than Democrats. The recent talk of these Republicans satisfies me completely that the Democratic party as a whole is much more to be trusted to manage the legis-lation and administration of the country wisely during the next ten years than the Republican party in respect to all industrial, com-mercial, financial, and social arrangements; so that I hope very much you will succeed in building up the Democratic party in all the States where it is now weak, and in making the policies of the Democratic party in those States where it is strong liberal and fair.

I hope that the vote today will show a substantial increase in the total Democratic vote of the country; but whether it does or not, I believe you have at your back for all War purposes almost the entire people of the United States, including almost all those of foreign birth. Even the German ruling class seems to see that. They seem likely to console themselves for their defeat with the reflection—it was those Americans that did it.

I am, with the highest regard,

Sincerely yours   Charles W. Eliot

TLS (WP, DLC).

From James Cardinal Gibbons

My dear Mr. President: Baltimore. November the fifth, 1918.

I have received a cable from Rome asking me to convey to you the thanks of the Holy Father for your courteous reply to his last message, and to assure you that at this moment, all Humanity places the most absolute confidence in your ability and impartiality. The Holy Father sees with great joy your attitude on the question of Peace, and he is of the opinion that to gain such a peace the other Allies should clearly consent to the conditions you may lay down; secondly, that the peace should be stable and permanent, which can not be if it is to be a merely punitive peace, and thirdly, that whatever may be decided upon as the terms of the armistice, should be the basis of the ultimate agreement.

I am, my dear Mr. President,

Yours most sincerely,   J. Card. Gibbons

TLS (WP, DLC).

From Thomas Nelson Page

Confidential

My dear Mr. President: Rome November 5, 1918.

As the epic events of these past weeks have succeeded each other, I have felt almost as though I were close beside you and saw, not only felt, unfolding the work which you have accomplished.

How tremendous this accomplishment has been many may know, and in time many more will know. But how vast and complicated the difficulties, and the problems of solving them, few, I believe, can know so well as I who have been close to some of the most complex and difficult portions of the problems which you had to solve.

For the present, in Italy at least, the actual war has entered on a phase so new that it seems here on the outside to be over. We know that it is not over, and the people will come to know it, but they will be ready now to endure further sacrifices since they feel that the end is so near, and are realizing that the victory has been won.

Yesterday was one of the great days in which I have lived. All day long the people of Rome marched and counter-marched through the streets acclaiming victory, and winding up in a demonstration in the Corso and in the Piazza Venezia at the foot of the Victor Emmanuel Statue, the Arapatrae and at the Campidoglio, which was one of the most extraordinary manifestations of popular joy that I have ever seen. It was the more impressive because it had in it something that was very solemn.

Three times during the day great demonstrations took place under the windows of the Embassy offices, and I was called on to address the crowds on behalf of America and yourself whom they were acclaiming. I was glad to speak to them because it gave me the opportunity to impress on them the necessity for continued resolution and for the preservation of order. Your name was not only applauded wildly, but was continually shouted. In fact, you have become to the people here not only the representative of the power of America, but also of what America stands for and this, I think, is worth more than the other.

I would say, if called on to define the feeling here, that you are tremendously respected and somewhat feared by public men generally, whom you have mystified no less than impressed, but that by the common people you are adored. I might even cite instances in which this is carried to a practical extent, as of soldiers placing candles beside your picture in their barracks and dugouts. And this will interest you no less than amuse you: I was told a few days ago of an old woman saying that she had heard that over in America there was a great saint (che bel Santo quel Santo Americano) who was making peace for us.

Perhaps I use only a different terminology, for I feel that you have, under the providence of God, made peace for us, and have made a peace which will be well worth preserving.

I know very well that in the presence of this great upheaval of the world all personal ambition has become merged in the sense of duty, and even pleasure in personal declarations of appreciation becomes attenuated to nothing. But I want you at least to know that, as one who believes in the principles which you have enunciated,—and I may say codified into a system for the guidance of humanity in the new world which is forming under forces which you have done so much to co-ordinate and guide,—I have always followed with such ability as I could command the course which you have laid down, and that I believe that you have been the directive power which has saved Christian civilization and order for the future generations of men.

The war, in its military phase at least, seems now almost on the point of coming to a close, though doubtless there will be many terrible battles, or rather one great and continuous battle, to fight before Germany is brought to acknowledge her decisive and complete and final defeat. But even when the military phase shall close, or appear to close, there will be problems to solve, and no less tremendous and no less perilous should they not be solved right, in which you must play the controlling part which you have played in the actual direction of the war. On the sound solution of these problems will rest the future peace and the future prosperity and the future civilization of the world. In many of these problems Italy is involved, and in many others while not actually involved she will undoubtedly be a potent influence. The whole Balkan Peninsula, the eastern Mediterranean and the entire Near East must continue a field in which the ambitions of governments and the commercial interests of peoples will come in conflict in the present as they have been in the past. Into these ambitions and interests Italy will without doubt enter in the future in some form. Her vital interests cannot be entirely walled off from the interests of those great regions which lie to the northeast and the east of her. The break-up of Austria to any extent such as appears likely at present, introduces a whole new system of problems in Europe, and those problems are in themselves new, at least in the form which they now promise to bear. One of the consequences of the break-up of Austria will be the throwing into the arms of Germany some twelve millions of Germans—formerly Austrian subjects—besides some millions of Magyars whose hatred of other races will Germanize them. This brings German enterprise and power of organization down towards the Adriatic, and opens up the whole field of Balkan problems. Besides this, the next danger, as I see it, is that the German people, under whatever form of Government they may profess to start their new career, have already got a start in the Ukraine and in the other western Russian provinces, extending up to the Baltic. Unless something be done to oust Germany therefrom, and secure some measurable amount of independence, Germany is likely to annex all of western Russia, at least commercially and financially and to spread her influence gradually all over Russia and possibly once more become a menace to the world.

These are some of the things which stare me in the face as I try to work out what the future will be. There are many more problems than these to face in the near future, especially that overwhelming one of starting the new world to work under its new conditions when the twenty odd million of men under arms shall be de-mo-bilized.

I rejoice for more reasons than one that I am an American. One of the chief of them, however, is that I feel that we have in you a leader who has shown a vision which if not prophetic has been broad enough to take within its scope all the problems which have hitherto arisen and solve them in a way to give promise that those which arise hereafter will also be solved with courage and wisdom.

I am writing Colonel House once or twice a week now and am sending him copies of the important telegrams bearing on conditions here in accordance with a telegram that I received from the Department. I have written him urging him to come here at the first opportunity, and I am glad to know that he thinks he will be able to do so before a great while. I consider it of great importance that he should come.

Always, my dear Mr. President,
Sincerely yours,   Thos. Nelson Page

TLS (WP, DLC).

Robert Lansing to Pleasant Alexander Stovall

Washington, November 5, 1918.

3275 Department sends you herewith an appeal by the President to be issued through Compub's office in Berne to the peoples of the constituent nations of Austria-Hungary that have achieved liberation from the yoke of an Austro-Hungarian Empire. Please hand to Mrs. Whitehouse[1] and say that the President directs that she have the necessary translations prepared and widest possible distribution given this appeal. The appeal follows:

Quote "May I not say, as speaking for multitudes of your most sincere friends, that it is the earnest hope and expectation of all friends of freedom everywhere and particularly of those whose present and immediate task it is to assist the liberated peoples of the world to establish themselves in genuine freedom, that both the leaders and the peoples of the countries recently set free shall see to it that the momentous changes now being brought about are carried through with order, with moderation, with mercy as well as firmness, and that violence and cruelty of every kind are checked and prevented, so that nothing inhumane may stain the annals of the new age of achievement. They know that such things would only delay the great things we are all striving for, and they therefore confidently appeal to you to restrain every force that may threaten either to delay or to discredit the noble processes of liberty. Signed Woodrow Wilson."[2]   Lansing

TS telegram (SDR, RG 59, 763.00/106a, DNA).
    [1] Vira Boarman (Mrs. Norman de R.) Whitehouse, at this time Director for Switzerland of the Committee on Public Information. See Vira B. Whitehouse, *A Year as a Government Agent* (New York and London, 1920).
    [2] There is a WWsh draft of this message in WP, DLC.

From the Diary of Josephus Daniels

1918 Tuesday 5 November

Election day—very quiet

Cabinet discussed German situation. WW said it would take months for people to get over passionate hate. Some wanted to get things— some special treaty—& even approved brutal treatment of Germans. I was a boy at Columbia & heard near relatives tell of outrageous deeds of Sherman's troops. The mob spirit of vengeance gets into some soldiers. Baker said certain stock stories were current in Europe—awful cruelty but told of other regiments. Only two were substantiated. Most stories exaggerated. . . .

No Prussianism. Must not do the things we condemn.

Met in Cummings room at the Shoreham to hear election returns. First news was encouraging, but later left us in gloom.[1]

    [1] The Democratic party was about to lose control of both houses of Congress. In the Sixty-sixth Congress, the Senate was to consist of forty-nine Republicans and forty-seven Democrats. The House of Representatives was to include 239 Republicans and 193 Democrats. For a detailed discussion of the election results, see Seward W. Livermore, *Politics Is Adjourned: Woodrow Wilson and the War Congress, 1916-1918* (Middletown, Conn., 1966), pp. 224-47.

A Memorandum by Franklin Knight Lane

Election Day. November 5, [1918]

At Cabinet some one asked if Germany would accept armistice terms. The President said he thought so. ∗ ∗ ∗

The President spoke of the Bolsheviki having decided upon a revolution in Germany, Hungary, and Switzerland, and that they had ten million dollars ready in Switzerland, besides more money in Swedish banks held by the Jews from Russia, ready for the campaign of propaganda. He read a despatch from the French minister in Berne, to Jusserand, telling of this conspiracy. Houston suggested the advisability of stopping it by seizing the money and interning the agitators. After some discussion, the President directed Lansing to ask the Governments in Switzerland and Sweden to get the men and money, and hold them, and then to notify the Allies of what we had done and suggest that they do likewise. Lansing suggested a joint Note, but the President vetoed this idea, wanting us to take the initiative.[1] He spoke of always having been sympathetic with Japan in her war with Russia, and thought that the latter would have to work out her own salvation. But he was in favor of sending food to France, Belgium, Italy, Serbia, Roumania, and Bulgaria just as soon as possible; and the need was great, also in Austria.

He said that the terms had been agreed upon, but he did not say what they were—further than to say that the Council at Versailles had agreed to his fourteen points, with two reservations: (1) as to the meaning of the freedom of the seas, (2) as to the meaning of the restoration of Belgium and France. This word he had directed Lansing to give to the Swiss minister for Germany—and to notify Germany also that Foch would talk the terms of armistice. * * * He is certainly in splendid humor and in good trim—not worried a bit. And why should he be, for the world is at his feet, eating out of his hand! No Caesar ever had such a triumph!

Printed in Lane and Wall, eds., *The Letters of Franklin K. Lane*, pp. 297-98.
[1] The Editors have not found any documents relating to this matter.

To Edward Nash Hurley

My dear Mr. Hurley: The White House 6 November, 1918.

In view of the approaching evacuation of Belgium and the new problems that confront this unfortunate people, I have asked Mr. Hoover to expand the activities of the Commission for Relief in Belgium to cover the entire relationship of this government, and possibly that of other governments, together with all American public charity, to the whole business not only of food but also clothing, raw materials, tools, machinery, exchange and other economic relief involved in the reconstruction of Belgium.

I would be obliged if your Department would give him all support and cooperation in this matter and refer to him for guidance in all questions of an economic order that arise in any connection between Belgium and this country.

Faithfully yours,   Woodrow Wilson[1]

TLS (E. N. Hurley Papers, InNd).
[1] Wilson sent the same letter, *mutatis mutandis*, to RL, NDB, B. M. Baruch, H. P. Davison, and WGM, all dated Nov. 6, 1918, and all TLS (Letterpress Books, WP, DLC). The TLS of the letter to Lansing is WW to RL, Nov. 6, 1918, TLS (SDR, RG 59, 855.48/820, DNA).

From George Mason La Monte

My dear President Wilson: New York November 6, 1918.

I have your letter of the 26th of October, which I have read with serious concern.

I think that you know as well as I do that these are the times that we must beware of false witnesses and I explained to you when I was in Washington that a case was being built up against Miss Pollok to satisfy the hungry wolves in California. I still think that this is true and that she is entitled to a separate trial. I know her family and her connections so well that I cannot bring myself to believe that she is a guilty person. Certainly she is not an enemy of the country or of humanity. In fact, she is a friend of human beings, such as your daughters are and my daughter is, and is to be commended for that reason and not condemned.

I enclose you a letter and memorandum I just received from Miss Connolly,[1] which I think merits your most earnest consideration.

I say nothing about yesterday's election[2] because the case of Miss Pollok is of much greater importance. There is no use at all in fighting for humanity unless we mean what we say, as I do and I know that you do.   Very truly yours,   Geo M La Monte

TLS (WP, DLC).
[1] It is missing.
[2] Walter E. Edge had defeated La Monte for the full term in the Senate by a vote of 179,022 to 153,743.

From Edward Mandell House

[Paris, Nov. 6, 1918]

#7. When Lloyd George was here I spoke to him and the French Prime Minister about the number of delegates each country should have in the peace conference. French Prime Minister remarked that half of France wanted to be present and Lloyd George replied that he was lucky for all England wished to attend. Lloyd George said he would be compelled to appoint among others a man from the colonies and a labor representative. We agreed to postpone final discussion until they had time to think about it further. I suggested that England, France, Italy, and United States should each have 5 places at the table, the other belligerent powers to have representation varying from one to 3 places according to their relative importance. This seems to meet with their approval. I had in mind [that Germany should also have] 5 places. It is essential that the sittings should contain only limited number for we have found it difficult to transact business satisfactorily at Versailles, and it was necessary for the Prime Ministers to meet in advance in order that business might be expedited. The smaller countries like Belgium, Serbia, and Greece have been quite content to have one place each at the Versailles sittings. I would appreciate an expression of your opinion (concurring?).

T transcript (WC, NjP) of WWsh decode (WP, DLC).

From Newton Diehl Baker, with Enclosure

[Washington, Nov. 6, 1918]

For the President   Baker

ALS (WP, DLC).

E N C L O S U R E

New York, N. Y.
Nov. 6, 10:30 a.m. [1918]

BY TELEPHONE

Chief Cable Censor reports:

Outbreak of revolution in Germany begun Kiel by sailors on the dreadnought KAISER, later spread to rest of fleet in harbor, finally spreading through the entire province of Schleswig. The sailors mounted the red flag and took possession of the town after seizing ships. A soldiers' and sailors' council was organized. Four companies of infantry were sent against the rebels, three companies fraternizing with them and the fourth company being disarmed.

Heavy artillery fighting continues in streets of Hamburg and rebels have seized Altona.

Peace riots in Munich, Stuttgart, Nuremburg and Erlangen. Rebels in Schleswig wore red cockades.

Later despatch states revolution has spread to part of Holstein. Number of garrisons on south coast deserted and soldiers have gone to Kiel. Aerd[r]ome at Kiel seized and airmen arrested.

Prince Max announced that Germany has asked for an armistice and a delegation has been sent to obtain the terms.

German authorities have decided to suppress revolution in Kiel district and ordered several thousand soldiers from Fehmain [Fehmarn] Island to Kiel. None of the garrisons at Kiel would act against the sailors.

T MS (WP, DLC).

From Newton Diehl Baker, with Enclosure

Dear Mr. President: Washington. November 6, 1918.

I enclose copy of a letter received from General Graves which contains several interesting suggestions with regard to the Siberian situation. I heartily wish it were possible for us to arrange affairs in such a way as to withdraw entirely from that expedition.

Respectfully yours, Newton D. Baker

TLS (WP, DLC).

ENCLOSURE

[Vladivostok] October 1, 1918.

Subject: Situation in Siberia.

1. I have now been here four weeks, and have tried as best I could to form an estimate of the situation as it exists here today.

2. My instructions as to helping the Czechs under the changed condition, and specific instructions, are clear to me.

3. As to what can be done for the Russian people in helping them reestablish a government, is a very difficult question. I have not been able to see any starting point in rendering any assistance from a military standpoint. General Simeonoff[1] has been in the pay of the Japanese government. In fact, his Supply Officer has informed my Intelligence Officer of this fact. He now claims that he does not desire longer to receive assistance from the Japanese government, but desires the United States government to back him. I am inclined to think this attitude is due, on his part, to the fact that probably the Japanese government will no longer give him the backing he desires. It is common gossip, and I believe it is true although I am unable to establish it, that General Horvat has been receiving pay from the Japanese government.

4. General Dietrichs, who appears to me to be one of the best Russian officers I have met, is being backed in a small way by the French government. I was requested by General Paris to ask the United States to combine with the Allies in giving General Dietrichs arms, clothing, equipment, munitions, etc., for about 85,000 men. I informed General Paris that before I could submit such a question I would have to know what General Dietrichs' plans were and for what purpose he contemplated using this force; and I also desired to know if General Dietrichs claimed to be entirely independent of all the Russian authority, or if he felt that he was subordinate to and acting under the authority of the Central Siberian government with headquarters at Omsk. I have never received this information

from General Paris, who has now gone west with General Guida. I feel that, undoubtedly, the object of General Paris was to get the backing of the Allies in organizing a force for the purpose of forming an Eastern Front.

5. It appears to me that the Russians who have been in power are becoming so disappointed with their situation that they are ready to do anything suggested which would get them relief from the terrible conditions under which they are living now. Reports from all over Siberia show conclusively that the Russian people feel more confidence in the statements of the United States than in any of the other Allies, and feel more friendly toward the United States troops than toward the troops of any of the other Allies.

6. I fear that our close cooperation with the Japanese on the Ussuri line at the north will tend to remove some of the good feeling which the people have toward America. We have cooperated fully with the Japanese during their movements toward Habarovsk and Blagovestchensk. The custom of the Japanese army seems to be different, in some respects, than the customs we follow when entering a town. I have been told by the Commanding Officer of the 27th Infantry that Russians come to him asking for redress on account of the actions of the Japanese troops. It is very likely, and I believe such will be the case, that the actions of the Japanese troops with whom we are so closely associated will soon be considered by the Russian people as the actions of the Allied troops and it will not be long before no distinction will be made, whether such acts are committed by Japanese or American troops. If the opportunity is presented to go to Harbin, as mentioned in your 26, I hope to get out of this difficult situation by removing the troops now with the Japanese to Harbin.

7. Unless the railroad is opened and run on a business basis, I am unable to see how the people are to get along during the winter. This fact apparently does not worry the Russians and one does not find them making any strenuous or determined effort to prepare for the winter.

8. These few thoughts are submitted with a full realization that there are no helpful suggestions or information for the War Department, but I desire to submit them so that the Department will be in possession of the situation as I see it, and I submit them at this time because I have an opportunity to send this mail direct to the States on the Sheridan, which leaves Thursday.

Wm. S. Graves
Major General, Commanding.

TCL (WP, DLC).
[1] That is, Grigorii Mikhailovich Semenov.

From Charles R. Page

My dear Mr. President: Washington 6 November, 1918.

Permit me in acknowledgment of your note of yesterday's date to assure you that I too, am in entire accord with the development of a virile body of real American seamen. Mr. Andrew Furuseth and I have possibly differed over the form rather than the substance of that which we all have at heart, and I am glad of the opportunity to be able to reassure you that the entire matter will have the most impartial and careful consideration of the Shipping Board before any action is taken.

I shall gladly avail myself of an immediate opportunity to ascertain the views of the Secretary of Labor and am highly appreciative of the suggestion.   Faithfully yours,   Chas. R. Page.

TLS (WP, DLC).

From Bernard Mannes Baruch, with Enclosure

My dear Mr. President: Washington November 6, 1918.

I am enclosing herewith a statement which was dictated by Dr. Page and Mr. Brand.[1] The report of the Cotton Committee will be ready for submittal to you in a few days.

In view of the fact that a large part of the information related to foreign countries and had to be collected through conference with agents of those countries who were sent over after the Committee was appointed, may I say that I think the time consumed in getting together this report has been remarkably short.

I wish you would consider the advisability of permitting the statement herewith submitted to be released by Dr. Page, as Chairman of the Cotton Committee.

In connection with this I would like to draw your attention to the fact that cotton today reached the price of thirty cents a pound, which shows a recovery of something over three cents from the low point of last week. My personal opinion is that it will be governed more by the question of shipping than any other factor.

Very truly yours,   Bernard M Baruch

TLS (WP, DLC).
[1] Thomas Walker Page, Professor of Economics at the University of Virginia, a member of the United States Tariff Commission, and chairman of a special committee of inquiry appointed by the War Industries Board to investigate the cotton situation (about the appointment of which, see White House Staff to WW, Sept. 14, 1918, n. 1). Charles John Brand was chief of the Bureau of Markets of the Department of Agriculture and chairman of the Committee on Cotton Distribution appointed by the W.I.B. at the same time as the committee of inquiry.

ENCLOSURE

To avoid misinterpretation of the statements made concerning the stabilization of the cotton industry, the President authorizes the following:

The demand for high grade cotton which is out of proportion to the available supply, and the fact that the Government, through early agreements with the Allies, must act as a common buyer for Allied purchases, make it necessary to secure some basis of distribution of all grades of cotton. Based on the standard grades established by the Department of Agriculture, an effort will be made to provide a way by which the low grade cotton will be brought to sale and use along with the high grade cotton at reasonable and just prices.

It is believed that by this course, both the producer and consumer will be better protected than by continuation of the present chaotic conditions of the market.

The plan is to create, subject to the approval of the President, a cotton committee to devise methods for (a) broadening the channels of distribution and use of the great stock of low grades now practically unmarketable, (b) eliminating speculation and hoarding, and (c) apportioning the foreign orders.

It may be part of this committee's duty to recommend basic prices on cotton. If, after investigation, it is found necessary, a fair price will be fixed.

During this investigation and in order to avoid stagnation, a separate committee of three is being set up with authority to buy cotton for the use of the United States Government and the Allies, at prices to be approved by the President.

T MS (WP, DLC).

From Key Pittman

My dear Mr. President: Washington, D. C. [Nov. 6, 1918]

Just now, as I was sitting in the National Committee room, the window-curtain was blown aside and your picture which was hanging on the wall was flooded with sunlight. I take it as a good omen. At no time did we give up the fight, and now, judging from the latest returns, we may confidently look forward to maintaining our organization in the Senate, and to re-organizing the House. The post-election events bear strong resemblance to those of 1916.

From those more remote sections of the Country—where men are more free from the corrupting influences of money and misrepresentation—are coming reports of loyalty that give us heart. The votes from such sections in each state are steadily reducing the Republican lead where they now have an apparent majority.

Senator Nugent's manager has just wired that the Senator is re-elected by a safe majority.

In Nevada, we have not only re-elected Senator Henderson, but have won a new Congressman.

Reports from Montana, while indicating that the race is close, warrant us in believing that Senator Walsh will be returned.

New Mexico reports a Democratic Senatorial candidate as 1,000 votes behind; but the remote districts of the state, which are overwhelmingly Democratic, have not yet been heard from.

We are assured of the election of Mr. Ford by direct communication from Mr. Ford's son. This assurance, however, is based partially on estimates as to further returns.

Senator Shafroth is 4,000 votes behind, with one-third of the votes of the state to be heard from. We have a right to expect that Senator Shafroth will have a large majority of the unreported votes, as they will come from those more remote sections of the state that are least affected by the influences which I have referred to.

Folk of Missouri is steadily gaining, and the Committee has not given up hopes of his election.

If we lose Illinois, Missouri, Colorado, Delaware, and New Hampshire, we will still maintain the organization of the Senate by an equal membership, if we win in Idaho, Montana and Michigan. We have heard nothing definite from Minnesota or West Virginia.

We are all sick at heart because of the results. It is our fault— not yours. You did your share and more. We did not do ours. The Republican leaders successfully deceived the people of the United States, with regard to your attitude towards Peace with Germany. They have been carrying on a powerful and brazen propaganda, teaching the people to believe that you were endeavoring through negotiations to reach a compromise peace with Germany.

Even upon the occasion of your last message to Germany, they had the audacity to construe it as a partial surrender of what we had won so gloriously with our arms. And in this criticism they bemoan the fact that you did not demand "unconditional surrender." They made the issue between unconditional surrender, as advocated by the Republican leaders, and compromise peace, alledged to be advocated by you.

A few of us, on the floor of the United States Senate, combated these base and unpatriotic slanders, but our words, of course, reached few of the people. The terms of the Austrian armistice refuted these slanders; but the armistice came late, and even then few of the people could construe the meaning and intent of an armistice.

The people have been deceived. They have thoughtlessly done you and the cause of humanity a serious injustice; but the American people will soon understand, and when they do they will right all of these wrongs in their own peculiar and forceful way.

If we have not destroyed the re-actionaries at this election, we will renew the fight immediately and pluck victory from them in 1920.

You and those who are supporting you are right; and we know that right will win, if the people are permitted the opportunity to understand. The situation as it is now, in my opinion, is better understood in Europe than it is in the United States. I believe we are going to lick them now, and I am sure we are going to lick them under your leadership hereafter.

With every expression of the highest respect and loyal friendship, I am   Very sincerely yours,   Key Pittman

TLS (WP, DLC).

A Memorandum by Frank Irving Cobb

[c. Nov. 6, 1918]

The key to the diplomatic situation in respect to Great Britain lies in the economic and financial situation.

Great Britain is practically bankrupt and its economic condition is desperate. In all high governmental circles there are grave fears of a Bolshevik movement among the laboring classes unless British industry can be rehabilitated soon, and the armies reabsorbed at good wages into the producing population.

British diplomacy at this time seems to be shaped almost wholly by the interest and demands of the financial, commercial and industrial elements.

The country lives off its foreign trade and has been felicitating itself that whatever the cost of the war might be in money, Germany would be destroyed as an over-seas competitor, and hence the account could be squared without difficulty. Suddenly, as the war ends, the United States emerges as an overseas rival more powerful and more to be feared than Germany ever was. Hence the hysteria over the "freedom of the seas," which is neither more nor less than the ultimatum of the maritime and exporting classes that if the United States persists in building what Mr. Hurley called "the greatest merchant marine in the world," the American ships must sail under the fiat of the British Navy, and that fiat is to be the law of the sea.

This is a very serious affair, because it touches everybody's daily bread in Great Britain, and in resisting any restrictions upon the power of the British Navy, the British Government can gain a measure of popular support which it could command on no other issue.

The British Government has handled its propaganda with great skill and adroitness. The freedom of the seas controversy is never presented as a dispute between Great Britain and the United States. Such it is, but always as a dispute between Great Britain and Germany.

By virtue of this propaganda most Englishmen really believe that in demanding the freedom of the seas the President has been tricked into supporting a German proposal. What is equally sinister, British officials in general believe that the Republican party in the United States is squarely behind them and that a Republican Congress, representing a majority of the American people, will sustain them against the President. This belief is strengthened daily by the news from the United States.

When I speak of the British Government in this matter I mean the Lloyd George Government, and particularly Lloyd George himself. I am unable to discover that he has any particular convictions on the subject—or on any subject—but he knows that British shipping is the most powerful single interest in the Empire, and that its support is vital to him. By promoting and encouraging their extreme propaganda he is every day making it more difficult for himself to arrive at any understanding whatever with the United States.

France, of course, will support Great Britain's contention in the matter of the freedom of the seas. It is anti-Wilson, and therefore appeals to Clemenceau. But the British in exchange will sustain the French claims for reparation as far as it is possible to do so, and these claims for reparation are the principal concern of the French Government.

The Japanese will also support Great Britain—for a price—but part of the price is the removal everywhere of all restrictions against Japanese immigration and on this issue it is not easy for Great Britain to deal with Australia and Canada.

At the same time if the President sticks to his thesis that this is a war to end war, and that the peace must be a people's peace, he will have an enormous popular following everywhere, but he will have to be patient in awaiting results. It is necessary to remember too, that everybody's nerves are raw after four years of war, and it is doubly difficult to make any appeal to reason effective.

Anything the President attempts here must fail completely unless the American people can be induced to take a pro-American view of the issue. They have been so active and ardent for four years in championing the cause of various European countries, that most of them seem to have forgotten that the United States exists or that it has any particular excuse for existing. The immediate result of all this folly and foolishness is to block the way to anything resembling a peace of progress. Indeed the situation within the United States is more serious for the United States than the situation here, and unless means can be found to make the Americans realize it, the war has failed in its larger and more humanitarian aspects.

I do not see yet how the President can meet this question of division at home, but unless it is met, he can never convince these governments that he has the American people back of him on any point. They know that if he is not supported at home they can beat him here, and the tragic aspect of the situation is that a sordid and reactionary European diplomacy is relying upon Americans to help it defeat the larger issues of the war and make peace merely a matter of dividing the spoils among the victors.

CC MS (WP DLC).

From the Diary of Josephus Daniels

November Wednesday 6 1918

War Council. Discussed getting food to Austria to feed starving people. Cannot use money for that purpose. Could we lend to Jugo-Slavs? Lansing to be asked to furnish statement as to whether we had power. If so, could be supplied to them and then we could send food-stuffs.

Hoover to go to Europe and Hurley too—Hoover on food and Hurley about ships—to try to get Austrian ships in S. A. ports & others tied up to transport food. Hoover thought as this country would have to furnish money direct or lend it to England & France we ought to undertake it, and let it have our brand

Baruch said France wanted much steel, England wanted many things. [WW] "I wish no ships & nothing done till peace. I intend to carry as many weapons to the peace table as I can conceal on my person I will be cold & firm. G B selfish.["] He looked for League of Nations to settle freedom of the seas

A Memorandum by Franklin Knight Lane

November 6, 1918

Yesterday we had an election. I had expected we would win because the President had made a personal appeal for a vote of confidence, and all other members of the Cabinet had followed suit, except Baker who said he wanted to keep the Army out of politics. The President thought it was necessary to make such an appeal. He liked the idea of personal leadership, and he has received a slap in the face—for both Houses are in the balance. This is the culmination of the policy Burleson urged when he got the President to sign a telegram which he (Burleson) had written opposing Representative Slayden, his personal enemy, from San Antonio,[1] and, in effect, nominating Burleson's brother-in-law for Congress.[2] We heard of it by the President bringing it up at Cabinet. Burleson worked it through Tumulty. The President said that he did not know whether to write other letters of a similar nature as to Vardaman, Hardwick, *et al.* I advised against it, saying that the voters had sense enough to take care of these people. Burleson said, "The people like a leader with guts." The word struck the President's fancy and although Lansing, Houston, and Wilson also protested, in as strong a manner as any one ever does protest, the letters were issued.[3] * * * Even before the Slayden letter was one endorsing Davies, in Wisconsin, as against Lenroot.[4] * * * Then came the letter to the people of the whole country, reflecting upon the Republicans, saying that they were in great part pro-war but not pro-administration.[5]

Printed in Lane and Wall, eds., *The Letters of Franklin K. Lane*, p. 299.

[1] See WW to H. L. Beach, July 24, 1918, Vol. 49.
[2] About this, see the extract from the Daniels Diary printed at July 30, 1918, *ibid.*
[3] See WW to M. S. McNeil, Aug. 5, 1918, and WW to C. Howell, Aug. 7, 1918 (second letter of that date), both in *ibid.*
[4] See WW to J. E. Davies, March 18, 1918, Vol. 47.
[5] Wilson's appeal to voters, printed at Oct. 19, 1918.

Edward Mandell House to Robert Lansing

Paris. Nov. 7, 1918.

Number 57. Monsieur Pichon, French Minister for Foreign Affairs, informed me that General Diaz had sent the following telegram to the Italian military representative at Versailles:

"The Austrian Government through its plenipotentiary General Weber[1] requests the Entente to allow the Austrian troops to remain in the Ukraine until the arrival of the troops of the Entente, on account of the Bolshevism which prevails in that region." Monsieur

Pichon stated that both he and the Prime Minister thought that this request should not be granted because it would constitute a point which the Germans might make use of. He stated that he had telegraphed to London to ascertain the views of the British Government. He asked me what my view was. I informed him that in my opinion we ought to make them no promises, but allow them to remain for the moment until we knew more about the situation.

Edward House.

T telegram (WP, DLC).
¹ Gen. Victor Weber, Edler von Webenau, head of the team of military leaders which negotiated the Austro-Hungarian armistice.

Two telegrams to Edward Mandell House

[The White House, Nov. 7, 1918]

X. Referring to your number 7 I concur in your views with regard to representation at the Peace Conference.

WWhw telegram (WP, DLC).

[The White House, Nov. 7, 1918]

XI On second thought it [In reply to your No. 11, the thought] occurs to me that Versailles may be the best place for the Peace Conference where friendly influences and authorities are in control rather than Switzerland which is saturated with every poisonous element and open to every hostile influence in Europe.

Referring to your Number 57, your reply to the French Minister of Foreign Affairs about Austrian forces in the Ukraine I altogether approve.

T transcript of WWsh (WP, DLC).

To Newton Diehl Baker,

CONFIDENTIAL

My dear Mr. Secretary: The White House 7 November, 1918.

In returning the enclosed,¹ I remember, with apologies to you, that I received a cablegram from House in which it was somewhat laconically stated that this whole matter had been straightened out and in his judgment had better be let drop.² I am wondering whether in view of that cablegram we would not perhaps be embarrassing House in his relations with General Pershing if you were to send a letter like the enclosed, a letter which in itself I entirely approve. What do you think?

Cordially and faithfully yours,   Woodrow Wilson

TLS (N. D. Baker Papers, DLC).
   [1] That is, the Enclosure printed with NDB to WW, Nov. 5, 1918 (second letter of that date).
   [2] See EMH to WW, Nov. 2, 1918 (second telegram of that date).

To Robert Lansing

My dear Mr. Secretary: [The White House] 7 November, 1918.

Replying to your letter of November 5th, you are no doubt right in thinking that the time is at hand when thoughtful men representing the Y.M.C.A. and the Red Cross could very well go to do very useful work in Siberia, but I am afraid we must still wait upon our pending settlement with Japan before going forward with that part of the business.

Cordially and sincerely yours,   Woodrow Wilson

TLS (Letterpress Books, WP, DLC).

To Charles Evans Hughes

My dear Mr. Hughes: The White House 7 November, 1918.

I write to express to you my sincere thanks for the painstaking and exhaustive examination you personally gave to the aircraft production situation, in cooperation with the Attorney General.[1] I appreciate as much as the Attorney General does the thoroughness of the investigation and feel confident that the results of it put the country in possession of all the pertinent facts.

Sincerely yours,   Woodrow Wilson

TLS (C. E. Hughes Papers, DLC).
   [1] Hughes' report, dated October 25, 1918, was made public on October 31. Hughes had found incompetence, confusion, and a lack of central responsibility in the aircraft program. He had also found some minor violations of law by governmental and military officials active in the program but no thievery or major corruption. The report is printed in full in the *Official Bulletin*, II (Nov. 6, 1918), 16-48. TWG to WW, Oct. 31, 1918, printed in *ibid.*, pp. 14-16, was the letter of transmittal and provides a convenient summary of the report.

To Herbert Clark Hoover[1]

Dear Mr. Hoover: The White House 7 November, 1918

The probable early evacuation of Belgium brings us face to face with the problem of this distressed people, not only in regard to continued food relief, but also with regard to the many questions of economic rehabilitation. The initial task of preserving the bare lives of the people during German occupation, undertaken four years ago under your direction, is now nearing completion. I believe that the American people will willingly accept a large share of the burden of assisting in the now all important work of reconstruction and rehabilitation, pending re-payment by Germany for the injury done.

In order that such assistance should be exerted in the most liberal, efficient and comprehensive manner, I feel that it should be organized under a single agency, which may coordinate the whole effort of the American people and government, in the furnishing of supplies, machinery, finance, exchange, shipping, trade relations and philanthropic aid. I also feel that such an agency, in addition to being the sole vehicle of supplies, should also have some proper participation in the expenditure and distribution of assistance. Such unity of administration would give much greater assurance of proper assistance and should be effective in preventing profiteering.

The large experience of the Belgian Relief Commission, the character of its organization without profit, its established use of shipping, and the sympathetic bond which it now forms with the Belgian people point to its continuation and enlargement as the natural agency for this purpose. I should therefore be glad if you and your colleagues of the Commission would undertake this extended work.

I understand that it is also the wish and purpose of the English and French people to participate in carrying this burden. It would seem to me desirable to inquire if these governments would not therefore continue and enlarge their present support to the Commission to these ends, so that we may have a comprehensive and efficient agency for dealing with the entire problem on behalf of all.

It is of course of primary importance that our assistance in this expenditure and organization shall be built upon cooperation with the Belgian government and the use of such internal agencies and methods as may be agreed upon with them, to whom our whole solicitude is directed.

It is also of first importance that the expenditure of all the philanthropic aid of the American people toward Belgium, of whatever character, should be conducted by or under the control of the Commission, if duplication and waste are to be avoided.

With a view to the advancement of these ideas, I have addressed a note to the various departments of our government, indicating my wish that all matters relating to these problems should be undertaken under your guidance and that they should give to you every cooperation.

I wish you to proceed at once with the undertaking so far as it relates to the United States and I should be glad if you would, through the proper agencies, take up a discussion of these matters with the Belgian government and with the English and French governments as to their relationship and participation.

Cordially and sincerely yours,   Woodrow Wilson

TLS (Hoover Archives, CSt-H).
[1] The following letter represents Wilson's extensive editing of a T draft by Hoover dated Oct. 26, 1918, printed as an Enclosure with HCH to WW, Oct. 26, 1918.

To Key Pittman

My dear Senator: The White House 7 November, 1918.

Your letter of yesterday gave me peculiar pleasure and touched me very deeply. It is generous to me beyond my deserts and assumes an altogether unfair burden of blame (if any blame be involved) for yourself and your colleagues. Personally I do not feel that there is any blame resting anywhere. All sorts of causes have contributed to the result, but none of these ought either to discourage us or to divert us for a moment from our purposes. America is the leader of the liberal thought of the world, and nobody from any quarter should be allowed to interfere with or impair that leadership without giving an account of himself, which can be made very difficult.

Gratefully and faithfully yours,   Woodrow Wilson

TLS (K. Pittman Papers, DLC).

To Scott Ferris

My dear Ferris: [The White House] 7 November, 1918.

I am heartily sorry that you and Mrs. Ferris have been caught by the influenza, and I am all the more appreciative of your generous telegram of yesterday[1] because it was sent from your sick room. You may be sure that the stubborn Scotch-Irish in me will be rendered no less stubborn and a[g]gressive by the results of the election, and I do not want you or any of the other fine men who conducted this campaign in the best possible way to feel that anybody is at fault.

Please get well and come back soon.

With warmest regard,

Cordially and faithfully yours,   Woodrow Wilson

TLS (Letterpress Books, WP, DLC).
[1] S. Ferris to WW, Nov. 6, 1918, T telegram (WP, DLC).

To Ferris Greenslet

My dear Mr. Greenslet: [The White House] 7 November, 1918.

Answering your letter of November 4th,[1] may I not express the very strong preference not to receive any royalty at all from the copies of "Congressional Government" which you are going to supply to the Y.M.C.A. or the A.L.A.,[2] to be used in the cantonment libraries in this country. I am very much obliged to you for consulting me about this matter.

Sincerely yours,   Woodrow Wilson

TLS (Letterpress Books, WP, DLC).

[1] F. Greenslet to WW, Nov. 4, 1918, TLS (WP, DLC).

[2] That is, the American Library Association, which supplied books for the cantonment libraries.

From Samuel Gompers

Enroute to Chicago,
Pittsburgh, Pa., Nov. 7, 1918.

In this gladsome hour[1] of the country's and the world's history may I not indulge myself in the pleasure of tendering to you my congratulations upon the triumphant conclusion thus far reached in the world struggle for freedom justice and democracy under your inspired leadership. Every liberty loving man, every true humanitarian, every devotee of the spirit and fact of peace and good will have been proud to follow, to do and to sacrifice. Glory and progress for America, for the peoples of the world. Honor, long life and a superb immortality are yours,   Samuel Gompers.

T telegram (WP, DLC).

[1] Editions of some newspapers published in New York and other American cities in the early afternoon of November 7 carried reports that an armistice had been signed between Germany and the Allies. The reports of this "false armistice," as it came to be called, set off orgies of celebration in many parts of the United States. Dispatches arriving in the evening of November 7 denied authoritatively that an armistice had been signed. Investigation soon revealed that the story of the false armistice had originated from a cablegram sent that morning from Brest by Roy W. Howard to the United Press in New York. Howard's cablegram in turn had been based upon a telegram from the American Naval Attaché in Paris, Lt. Commander William R. Sayles, who had incorrectly stated that an armistice had been signed. See Harry R. Rudin, *Armistice 1918* (New Haven, Conn., 1944), p. 319n26, and Mark Sullivan, *Our Times: The United States, 1900-1925* (6 vols., New York, 1926-35), V, 513-17. Rudin incorrectly identifies the Naval Attaché as "one Capt. Jackson."

From Robert Lansing, with Enclosure

My dear Mr. President: Washington November 7, 1918.

For your information I enclose to you a memorandum on the Bolshevist Movement, prepared by Mr. Bullitt. It is not comprehensive as other memoranda have preceded it.

Faithfully yours,   Robert Lansing

TLS (WP, DLC).

E N C L O S U R E

November 6, 1918.

Memorandum for the Secretary:
Subject: The Bolshevist Movement in Europe.

Germany has demanded the withdrawal of all Russian representatives in the German Empire, and has recalled the German representatives in Russia, according to an Associated Press despatch of this afternoon. This action unquestionably was the result of the repeated proofs that Joffe, Bolshevik Ambassador at Berlin, was the center of the Bolshevik propaganda organization, and that he was flooding Germany with revolutionary literature, imported in his official pouches, and with revolutionary organizers imported as couriers.

The straw which broke the back of the German Government's patience was the following incident described by the Nauen wireless of this morning:

"On the evening of November 4, the regular evening courier of the Bolshevik Government arrived at Friedrichstrasse Station with a large amount of luggage. One of the pieces of luggage was damaged so that the papers in it fell on the platform. These papers were circulars printed in German calling upon German workmen and soldiers to bring about a bloody revolution! One of the circulars was signed by the 'Gruppe Internationale (Spartacus Gruppe),' i.e., the Liebknecht, Mehring group of Independent Socialists.[1] Another circular which gave precise directions for a revolutionary attack demanded assassination and terror. At the instance of the railway authorities all the luggage of the courier was locked in a room in the station."

Although Joffe has been dismissed from Berlin, the Bolshevik propaganda organization for other European countries will not be disrupted by his removal. For the Bolsheviki have a central revolutionary staff established in Switzerland, which, according to a report of the French Ambassador in Berne,[2] plans to start Bolshevik revolutions at once in Germany, Hungary and Italy, and later in Switzerland. The French Ambassador reports that this central organization has at its disposal fifty-two million francs transferred to Switzerland by the Bolsheviki.

Mr. Stovall reports that Switzerland is deeply concerned over the possibility of a Bolshevist outbreak, and that the President of the Republic considers the danger serious but not imminent. Mr. Stovall asks the permission of the Department to inform the President that the American Government hopes the Swiss Government will use every effort to prevent Bolsheviki from coming to Switzerland and will stop the activities of those who have been admitted.

The Counsellor of the Austrian Legation at Berne[3] has asked that American troops be sent to occupy Vienna to prevent Bolshevik uprisings. Prince Hohenlohe, who is also attached to the Austrian Legation at Berne, has repeated his appeal for immediate supplies of food, saying that if such supplies do not come, the triumph of Bolshevism in Austria will be immediate.

Mr. Schmedeman reports that the Norwegian Government has been asked by the British and French to assist in protecting the Baltic provinces against the spread of Bolshevism after the Germans withdraw, and that the Norwegian Government is unwilling to acquiesce on the ground that such action might provoke internal trouble in Norway.

Mr. Grant-Smith reports by despatch from Copenhagen dated October 1, that Bolshevist agents, some of them Danes, are endeavoring to convert to Bolshevism all Russian prisoners who have escaped to Jutland. It appears that these agents have had some success, particularly among the soldiers interned at Horserød.

Very respectfully submitted,   William C Bullitt

TS MS (WP, DLC).
    [1] That is, the Spartacus Association, or the Spartacists, the radical, revolutionary wing of the German socialist movement, led by Karl Liebknecht, Franz Mehring, and Rosa Luxemburg.
    [2] Paul Eugène Dutasta.
    [3] Probably Léon Freiherr de Vaux.

From Jouett Shouse

Dear Mr. President: Kinsley, Kansas, 7th November, 1918.

The only deep regret I have over election results is that you will be deprived of a Democratic Congress. I hope my fears may prove not well founded, but, despite their repeated promises, I apprehend that many of the Republicans who have been chosen will do all they can to embar[r]ass and impede your administration.

In Kansas your appeal for a Democratic Congress had the unfortunate effect of solidifying Republican opposition more strongly than in ten years. My district, for example, has elected a Republican representative by ten thousand although I ran ten thousand ahead of my ticket. Lacking newspapers in this State and prohibited from making a campaign because of the influenza epidemic, it was impossible to get the facts before the people in the proper light, while the opposition did not hesitate to indulge in deliberate misrepresentation and perversion of the truth.

I am writing primarily to express my deep loyalty to you at all times and under all circumstances. It has been a wonderful privilege to be permitted to serve with you during the stirring times of the past four years. May your strength and health be spared to continue the unsurpassed work you are doing for America and for the world.

In friendship and admiration, I am

Most sincerely yours,   Jouett Shouse

TLS (WP, DLC).

From Andrew James Peters

Dear Mr. President: Boston November 7, 1918.

The election of Mr. Walsh as Senator by the Democrats of Massachusetts is an endorsement of yourself and your administration. This is particularly apparent by the defeat of the Democrat candidate for Governor by a majority of over seventeen thousand votes.[1]

Your appeal to the people for support and your approval of his candidacy as evidenced by the presence of Mr. Daniels here were, in my opinion, without any reflection on the candidate, the main factors that brought about Mr. Walsh's election. The change in public sentiment after your announcement and the interest in the campaign following the presence of Mr. Daniels here made this clear beyond a doubt.

With best wishes, I am

Sincerely yours,   Andrew J. Peters

TLS (WP, DLC).
[1] Richard Henry Long, a shoe manufacturer of Framingham, Mass., had been defeated by the Lieutenant Governor, Calvin Coolidge.

From Louis Marshall

The President,   New York November 7, 1918.

It is generally recognized that one of the most important subjects to come before the Conference of Nations to be held at the close of the war, is the restoration of Poland. It necessarily affects the future of all of the inhabitants within the area of the re-created Polish State. Assuming it to be coextensive with the boundaries proposed by the Polish National Committee, of which Mr. Roman Dmowski is the Chairman, approximately four million Jews who now dwell within that territory, will be directly concerned. Hence, whatever the geographical extent of the new State or its form of government, the civil, political and religious rights of these Jews must be safeguarded.

The American Jewish Committee has long sympathized with the aspirations of the Polish people for independence and the right of self-government. It heartily approves of the establishment of a State which shall, as far as practicable, be re-possessed of those lands which composed Poland during the Seventeenth Century and which are essential to its industrial and economic rehabilitation.

Unfortunately, however, in 1912, there was inaugurated by the leaders of the Polish National Committee, and has ever since been carried on in that country, a policy looking to the practical destruction of the Jews of Poland through the medium of a most virulent economic boycott, which is still in full operation and has grown in intensity from year to year. In substantiation of this statement attention is called to the annexed report of a conversation between Mr. Dmowski and the President of the American Jewish Committee, which took place on October 6th, 1918,[1] and which explains the existing status of the Jews of Poland and the attitude maintained toward them by Mr. Dmowski and his party.

The mere statement of the facts discloses an intolerable condition and bodes unspeakable evil unless immediate remedial action is taken by those who are seeking the recognition of an independent Polish State, to end this policy of extermination for which many of them are avowedly responsible, and unless the Constitution of the new Poland shall contain guaranties adequate for the protection of the Jewish inhabitants of Poland.

The Polish National Committee has recently intimated that the proposed Constitution of the Polish State would provide that "Polish citizens, without distinction as to origin, race or creed, must all stand equal before the law." Admonished by the unhappy experience of the Jews of Roumania, who were promised similar rights by the Treaty of Berlin of 1878, pursuant to which Roumania was

created a kingdom and which for forty years has wantonly disregarded the terms of that treaty by withholding from the Jews of
that country the rights which were sought to be secured to them,
and warned by the frank avowal of Mr. Dmowski as to his past and
present attitude toward the Jews, the American Jewish Committee
regards the proposed pronouncement as wholly inadequate.

When it speaks of "Polish citizens" it affords the same loophole
for evasion as that by which Roumania has hitherto successfully
nullified the conditions of the instrument which called it into being—
the lack of a definition of the term "citizen."

It also fails to forbid discrimination or restrictions or the imposition of disabilities.

Nor does it confer the right to employ any language other than
Polish, commercially, socially or educationally.

The necessity of such a right is shown by the attitude of Mr.
Dmowski and the terms of a law enacted during the Polish revolution of 1862, which while purporting to grant to the Jews of Poland
equal rights with all other citizens of the state, did so under the
following condition:

"In consideration for their admission to the enjoyment of equal
rights the Jews shall renounce the use of a language of their own
in speech as well as in writing, * * * After the promulgation of this
act, no legal act, no will, no contract or guaranty, no obligation of
any sort, no accounts or bills, no books or commercial correspondence shall be written or signed in Hebrew or Yiddish. All such
documents shall in that case be held to be invalid."

The significance of this enactment lies in the fact that upwards
of ninety per cent. of the Jews of Poland speak and write and are
deeply attached to their Yiddish tongue. As is well known, their
religious services are conducted exclusively in Hebrew, as they
have been for centuries. This legislation, though superseded by the
Russian law, is still regarded by the Polish National Committee as
being in full force.

This proposed declaration also disregards the fact that the new
Poland is to include Austrian Jews, German Jews and Russian Jews
who in all likelihood will not desire to retain the status of Austrians,
Germans or Russians and who will expect to be recognized as Polish
citizens.

Hence, the American Jewish Committee most earnestly prays
that it be made a condition of the organization of the new Poland,
that its Constitution shall contain specific provisions to the following effect:

(1) All inhabitants of the territory of the Polish State, who are
not subjects of other states, shall for all purposes be recognized as

of Polish nationality, provided, however, that those who have heretofore been subjects of other states and who are now domiciled in
Poland who desire to continue their allegiance to such states may
do so by a formal declaration to be made within a specified period.

(2) All Polish subjects, without distinction as to origin, race or
creed, shall enjoy equal civil, political and religious rights, and no
law shall be made or enforced which shall abridge the privileges
or immunities of any of them, or impose upon any of them any
discrimination, disability or restriction on account of race or reli-
gion, or deny to any person the equal protection of the laws.

(3) Polish shall be the official language, but no law shall be passed
restricting the use of any other language, and all existing laws
declaring such prohibition are repealed.

(4) The Jews shall be accorded autonomous management of their
own religious, educational, charitable and other cultural institutions.

(5) Those who observe the Jewish Sabbath shall not be prohibited
from pursuing their secular affairs on any other day of the week
so long as they shall not disturb the religious worship of others.

   Respectfully submitted: American Jewish Committee
                     by Louis Marshall President.

TLS (WP, DLC).
   [1] "REPORT OF CONVERSATION BETWEEN MESSRS. ROMAN DMOWSKI AND LOUIS MARSHALL
AT THE PLAZA HOTEL, NEW YORK CITY, ON SUNDAY, OCTOBER 6, 1918," TS MS (WP,
DLC).

From Homer Stillé Cummings, with Enclosure

                                           Washington, D. C.
My dear Mr. President: November the Seventh 1918.

   I have taken the liberty of hastily dictating a few observations
and conclusions relative to the recent election. I submit them to
you for what they may be worth.

   I am deeply grieved and distressed that the result was not more
satisfactory, but I have an invincible faith in your leadership and
in the future of our party. It is needless to say that I am always at
your service.

   I am   Sincerely yours,   Homer S. Cummings

TLS (WP, DLC).

E N C L O S U R E

COMMENTS ON RECENT CONGRESSIONAL ELECTION

The depression, which we naturally feel as the result of Tuesday's election, arises out of the fact that we expected too much. The result is practically a drawn battle, instead of the substantial victory which we had expected. We had every apparent reason to expect a victory, not only because of the merits of our case, but also because our preliminary reports, especially from the East, were both encouraging and reliable. If we had known before election that we were to elect a Senator in Massachusetts, carry New York State, reduce the Republican majority in Connecticut and New Jersey almost to the vanishing point, and make net congressional gains in the East, we would have felt supremely confident of the outcome. The slump occurred in the Middle West and far West. The loss of Missouri and Colorado, both primarily due to internal party dissensions, was a severe and unexpected blow.

MINOR ADVERSE CAUSES

There are, of course, many causes of a minor nature which contributed to the result. These minor causes may be described as follows:

1. Lack of sufficiently effective organization.
2. More effective organization in the Republican party due to continuous effort along that line for a period of more than a year.
3. Healing of party dissensions in the Republican party.
4. Persistence of belief in many quarters, particularly amongst manufacturers and business men, that the Republican party is a better representative of their ideas than the Democratic party, especially in the matter of tariff legislation, financial affairs and reconstruction policies.
5. Discontent among the farming population of the West, owing to the regulation of the price of wheat, coupled with a failure to regulate the price of cotton.
6. Discontent which develops when any political party is long in power.
7. Business disturbances and readjustments during the war period which have affected adversely certain lines of industry and employment.
8. Persistent criticism of public officials by the opposition party.
9. Dissatisfaction of organization Democrats with Federal and war appointments.

All of the foregoing, and perhaps other minor matters, had a substantial effect upon the result and would inevitably have quite a potent effect in such a close election.

CONTROLLING CAUSES

It must not be forgotten that in 1916 the popular vote throughout the country, calculated on a basis of senatorial contests, where there were such contests, and gubernatorial contests in the remaining states, indicated that about one-half million more votes were cast for Republican candidates than for Democratic candidates. Undoubtedly, more Democratic votes were cast for Democratic candidates than would have been the case in 1916, except for the fact that President Wilson was a candidate. This, no doubt, added many thousands to the Democratic vote througout the country.

It is fair to say, therefore, that the Democratic party was in the minority in 1916 by about one-half million votes, and it was only owing to a fortunate distribution of these votes that we carried the House and the Senate. In order to win, therefore, it was necessary to overcome this initial handicap. This initial handicap was, in all probability, very nearly overcome. The figures of the popular vote are not before us and any conclusions on that score must necessarily be a mere guess. It is quite likely, however, that the popular vote throughout the country was pretty evenly divided between the two parties. If this is true, we have made a great gain, which ought to be encouraging as we look forward to the election of 1920.

While a great deal of criticism from opposition sources was directed against the appeal made by the President for a Democratic Congress, I am confident not only that the appeal was justified but that it had a very wholesome and beneficial effect. There is no evidence that it injuriously affected our vote in any part of the country, but there is much evidence that it was very helpful. For instance, I do not believe it would have been possible to have carried Kentucky, Montana or Idaho without such an appeal. The appeal also had the effect of making the President and his policies an issue of the campaign—this was the strongest issue that we had, and if the lines of political battle had not been drawn accordingly, I think that we should have been very badly defeated. Indeed, so just was our cause in this respect and so increasingly satisfactory was the international news that there is no reason to doubt that we were on the verge of a great and sweeping victory.

I now come to the three points which I think are expressive of the three great causes which deprived them [us] of the great victory to which we were entitled:

1. THE LAVISH USE OF MONEY BY THE REPUBLICAN ORGANIZATION.

We knew that vast sums were being used and now there is beginning to develop tangible proof of the misuse of these funds. This aspect of the matter is being run down by the National Committee and other agencies with a view to assembling all possible proof on the subject. This may be helpful now, and certainly ought to be helpful later. We know enough now to make it clear that safety requires that a more stringent Federal Act should be passed covering the matter of campaign expenditures.

2. SECTIONAL QUESTION AND LEADERSHIP IN HOUSE AND SENATE.

These matters had very far reaching effects. It is unnecessary to go into details as the facts are so generally understood and recognized. The country had no great confidence in the Congressional leaders, especially in the House, many of whom have disclosed invincible provincialism in almost all matters of national consequence and it was generally believed that the Selective Draft Law would have failed utterly had it not been for the Republican support. The fact that many of these leaders were from the South did not help the situation any.

3. MISREPRESENTATION OF THE ATTITUDE OF THE PRESIDENT.

It was an essential part of the Republican campaign to misrepresent the attitude of the President. The leaders of the Republican party misrepresented his appeal to the people for popular support and alleged that it was an attack upon the patriotism of Republicans who had loyally supported the war. Every effort that ingenuity could suggest was employed with that end in view. More important and more injurious, however, were the falsehoods industriously circulated concerning the attitude of the President toward Germany. A campaign based upon the catchwords "Unconditional Surrender" and "No Negotiated Peace" was surprisingly effective. The very vigor with which these banalities were uttered undoubtedly caused a great many unwary voters to think that the President was prepared to make easy terms with Germany.

Mr. Taft in a statement published November 7th in the "Public Ledger," speaking of the general desire for unconditional surrender, said:

"It was unfortunate for the President and his party that his opening note to Germany and the correspondence alarmed the people, lest he might make a peace by negotiations."

Mr. Taft, of course, was too just to suggest that such was the attitude of the President. He merely states that the people were "alarmed" and that the situation was "unfortunate for the President and his party." I think this essentially states the truth.

The dastardly part of the whole business was that the Republican leaders, with the aid of a large part of the public press, created the alarm by deliberate misrepresentation. It seemed incredible to us that such a campaign could have succeeded in disturbing so many people, but there can be no doubt that it had a very wide-spread effect. Had the good news from Europe broken a little earlier, it would have constituted a most complete refutation of these charges and have satisfied the public mind. Indeed, such seems to have been the effect in communities easily accessible to newspaper publicity. There was no time, however, for the full significance of the President's handling of the diplomatic situation to dawn upon the minds of a troubled and anxious people.

CONCLUSION

A desperate political conflict awaits us in 1920. Without the leadership of President Wilson the Democratic party today would undoubtedly be in a hopeless minority. As matters now stand we are upon even terms with them. We shall have the benefit of the President's leadership. It is too much to expect that leadership alone can be depended upon to win the contest. There ought to be many opportunities during the next two years to organize public opinion in behalf of the policies of the President and to enforce a more faithful cooperation upon the part of public men of our political faith. No time should be lost in passing an effective Corrupt Practice Act.

The Democratic National Committee can be made, under proper organization, a more effective instrument than it ever has been. There ought to be some just ground upon which to base proper relationship between the party organization and Democratic public officials. Between elections they apparently have very little in common, though the friendship becomes intensive about two weeks prior to election. The situation is a delicate one, but it can be managed. There are ways also of bringing additional independent support to the party management. I do not under rate the good work done by the party organization, I merely suggest that it can be made very much more effective. It should be possible also to nurture a spirit in Congress which would lead to effective and outspoken support of Administration policies from now on. I have in mind various ways in which this can be accomplished. It is pitiable to note how barren the Senate record is of Administration speeches and how full it is of speeches of criticism.

A further consideration should be given to some of the numerous adverse causes heretofore referred to. Many of them can be eliminated all together. It has too long been the custom to regard party organization as a sporadic thing requiring attention only biennially.

ADDENDA

In the foregoing statement I made no reference to a number of factors which ordinarily have to be taken into account, because I was, more or less, comparing the present election to the results two years ago, and the omitted factors were for the most part either equally or more favorable to us than they were two years ago, or had practically disappeared all together as issues or elements in the problem.

Amongst the factors referred to are the following: namely, the attitude of the women voters, the attitude of the voters of foreign parentage, including Germans, Italians, Poles, etc., etc., the attitude of Jewish voters, the attitude of labor, questions concerning the Eight Hour Law, criticism of individual members of the cabinet, etc., etc., as well, of course, as the question of Mexico.

ADDENDA #2.

I have just made a calculation of the estimated pluralities in the various states, based on the senatorial votes in states where there were senatorial contests and on the vote for Governor in the remaining states. It would seem from this calculation that the pluralities in Democratic states were practically equal to the pluralities in Republican states, which indicates that the popular vote throughout the country is almost evenly divided between the two political parties on party lines. It must also be remembered that this being an off year the pluralities in the Southern states were much lower than they would have been in a Presidential election.

I have also made a calculation of the electoral vote, on the foregoing basis, and I find the result to be as follows:

REPUBLICAN STATES		DEMOCRATIC STATES	
California	13	Alabama	12
Colorado	6	Arizona	3
Connecticut	7	Arkansas	9
Delaware	3	Florida	6
Illinois	29	Georgia	14
Indiana	15	Idaho	4
Iowa	13	Kentucky	13
Kansas	10	Louisiana	10
Maine	6	Maryland	8
Michigan	15	Massachusetts	18
Minnesota	12	Mississippi	10
Missouri	18	Montana	4
Nebraska	8	Nevada	3
North Dakota	5	New York	45
New Jersey	14	North Carolina	12
New Mexico	3	Ohio	24

New Hampshire........... 4	Oklahoma................... 10
Oregon......................... 5	South Carolina 9
Pennsylvania 38	Tennessee.................. 12
Rhode Island 5	Texas 20
South Dakota............... 5	Utah.............................. 4
Vermont........................ 4	Virginia...................... 12
Washington 7	
West Virginia............... 8	
Wisconsin................... 13	
Wyoming 3	
269	262

This calculation also shows how evenly divided in strength the two parties are throughout the country. Another significant feature is the large number of states in which the margin, either way, was exceedingly small. It is also apparent that had President Wilson been running for President he would have been elected by a very large popular and electoral vote.

T MS (WP, DLC).

A Memorandum by Sir Eric Geddes

[London] 7th November, 1918.

MEMORANDUM TO THE WAR CABINET.

The Cabinet may remember that as a sequence of my recent visit to the United States, I gave verbally as my view that the President was looking to the exercise of sea power to enforce, in the ultimate resort, anything which the League of Nations, as he sees it, wish to enforce.

I also drew attention to the fact that America was continuing to build capital ships, at a time when the whole of her energies ought to have been thrown into building destroyers for convoying and escorting her own Army across the Atlantic.

In Paris, the one outstanding feature which I detected in the American Naval Representatives' attitude at our Meetings, was that nothing that we did there should in any way pre-judge or have any influence upon the disposal of any war ships of which Germany may ultimately be deprived after Peace.

My sequence of thought in observing these various happenings, has been that President Wilson wishes to create a sea power other than ours.

(a) By building in the United States at the present time.

(b) By the allocation of the ships of which Germany is to be deprived at the Peace Conference; and

(c) By combination with other nations, jealous of our sea power, which will, in combination, be the equivalent of, or greater than, the sea power of the British Empire.

In other words, he is pursuing the "Balance of Power" theory, which has hitherto so much influenced European policies, and is applying it in sea power only to world politics.

I called to say good-bye to Colonel House before I left Paris, after the conclusion of all the Meetings, and I got an interesting but rather unaccountable confirmation of this view. Colonel House told me that the President had realised how sea-power had built up and maintained the British Empire, and how the absolutely essential importance of it had been demonstrated by the present War, and that the League of Nations would control recalcitrant members in the future by the exercise of sea-power.

I can hardly think why Colonel House made this statement to me. He is the last man to suspect of thoughtlessly indiscreet utterances, but I am convinced that by the methods I have set out above, it is the aim and purpose of the President to reduce comparatively the preponderance in sea power of the British Empire.

Eric Geddes

TS MS (ADM 116/1771, PRO).

To Robert Lansing, with Enclosures

My dear Mr. Secretary: The White House 8 November, 1918

I think the suggestions of Mr. Hoover in the enclosed, about sending a copy of the dispatch to House and stating that it was sent with my authorization and approval should be complied with, and I would be glad if you would convey our attitude in this matter to House in the sense contained in the closing lines of Hoover's letter.   Cordially and sincerely yours,   Woodrow Wilson

ENCLOSURE   I

From Herbert Clark Hoover

Dear Mr. President: Washington 7 *November 1918*

Please find enclosed herewith a telegram which I am despatching to Mr. Cotton[1] in respect to the proposals for the world's food and shipping supplies to be vested in the Inter-Allied Food Council and the Inter-Allied Maritime Council.

I believe this cable is in accord with the conclusions of our conference yesterday and I am wondering if you could see your way to despatch this same telegram to Colonel House, informing him that it has been sent to Mr. Cotton by myself and that it is with your authorization and, furthermore, if you could state to Colonel House that I will be leaving within the next few days for Paris and that no arrangements looking forward to the handling of food for liberated populations should be undertaken until after my arrival and consultation with him.

Yours faithfully,   Herbert Hoover

TLS (SDR, RG 59, 103.97/837, DNA).
¹ That is, Joseph Potter Cotton.

E   N   C   L   O   S   U   R   E   I   I

7 November

Your 35 For your general advice this government will not agree to any programme that even looks like interallied control of our economic resources after peace (stop) After peace over one half of the whole export food supplies of the world will come from the United States and for the buyers of these supplies to sit in majority in dictation to us as to prices and distribution is wholly inconceivable (stop) The same applies to raw materials (stop) Our only hope of securing justice in distribution proper appreciation abroad of the effort we make to assist foreign nations and proper return for the service that we will perform will revolve around complete independence of commitment to joint action on our part (stop) I understand no provisions have been made in armistice such as recommended your 35 (stop) As to any intermediate action during armistice this can be handled as to its political aspects simply as a relaxation of blockade under present arrangements as to cooperation in this matter (stop) As to commercial aspects of feeding Austria Bulgaria Turkey and Serbia the efficient thing is to organize a duplication of Belgian Relief organization Such machinery can determine the needs arrange for the relaxation of blockade necessary Can find help from Allied governments Can secure credits from liberated governments or municipalities or banks Can operate Austrian or other shipping Can buy and sell and distribute food and take independent action generally of commercial character impossible to the Interallied Food and Maritime Councils (stop) The representation of the Allies in such commission could be proportional to the actual resources in food and money that they find for its support (stop) Such a commission can cooperate with the Food

Administration here directly in food purchases where they will be coordinated with other buyers and in case of purchases in other localities can cooperate through existing agencies to avoid competition thus the international disorganization outlined in your 35 will be avoided and above all the extension of the functions and life of Interallied Food and Maritime Councils either now or after peace will be prevented (stop) We cannot consent to the delegation of neutral buying in the United States to the Interallied Food or Maritime Councils We must continue to act with entire independence in our commercial relations with all neutrals and Belgian Relief I trust therefore you will in representing this government discourage any attempts to carry out the proposals of your 35.

Herbert Hoover[1]

T telegram (SDR, RG 59, 103.97/837, DNA).
    [1] This telegram was sent on November 8, 1919, as No. 62.

To John R. Mott

My dear Dr. Mott: [The White House] 8 November, 1918.

I am sure the people throughout the country will understand why it is that I am unable to fulfill the desire of my heart to make a public address at this time in the interest of the approaching campaign.[1]

It has been with sincere gratification that I have observed the whole-hearted cooperation of the Young Men's Christian Association, the Young Women's Christian Association, the National Catholic War Council, the Jewish Welfare Board, the War Camp Community Service, the American Library Association and the Salvation Army in response to my request that they combine their respective financial drives in one United War Work Campaign, November 11-18, to secure the sum of at least $170,500,000 for their invaluable work. The wise economy of money and effort, the increased efficiency which will result from a blending of experience, the creation of an atmosphere of truer understanding, the unmistakable evidence of a growing unity of spirit and the influence of all this in strengthening the national solidarity is reassuring in the extreme.

As you now stand on the threshold of presenting your appeal to the entire American people, I wish to renew the expression of my conviction that the service rendered by these welfare agencies is indispensable, and my earnest hope for the abundant success of the Campaign. The inevitable growth of the Army and Navy, and the multiplying demands for our help from France, Italy and Russia, make it clear that a generous oversubscription is highly desirable.

No matter how distant the day of peace may prove to be, it will be followed by a long period of demobilization, during which the opportunity and need for the constructive work of these organizations will be quite as great as in war time, and I am glad to note that your plans contemplate serving the soldiers and sailors in this critically important period. I am particularly pleased to know of the comprehensive program of education to be carried out during the coming months.

Gifts that provide the service which this Campaign makes possible are not so much gifts to organizations as gifts,—invaluable gifts,—to our soldiers, sailors and marines and constitute an appropriate expression of our gratitude for their patriotic and unselfish devotion. The whole plan of the United War Work Campaign is inspiring and is most emphatically in the interest of the nation and of all the lands with which we are associated in these momentous days.   Cordially and sincerely yours,   Woodrow Wilson

TLS (Letterpress Books, WP, DLC).
  [1] This sentence was added at Mott's suggestion. See White House Staff to WW, Nov. 7, 1918, TL (WP, DLC).

To Charles William Eliot

My dear Dr. Eliot: The White House 8 November, 1918.

Thank you for your frank letter of November fifth. It distresses me that you thought I committed a mistake in putting forth my appeal to the country. If I erred, it was merely under the impulse to be frank with the people I am trying to serve.

I note with the greatest interest your suggestions about cooperation between Belgium, the United States, Great Britain, France, Italy, and Japan. My thoughts are very much engaged upon this perplexing problem of the best way to secure a world's peace, and you may be sure your views in the matter are of the greatest service to me.

With warm appreciation, in unavoidable haste,
        Cordially and sincerely yours,   Woodrow Wilson

TLS (C. W. Eliot Papers, MH-Ar).

Two Telegrams from Edward Mandell House

Paris Nov 8, 1918

Number 61. Secret for the President and Secretary of State. We are getting a mass of misinformation respecting present conditions in Austria, Bohemia and the Ukraine, practically all of which is being provided us by the English, French and Italians. We have no American sources of information. The reports received are, as they are often, colored by the self interest of the persons furnishing them. I regard it as exceedingly important that we send at once to these countries agents who will be in a position to furnish us with accurate and unbiased information respecting conditions. This work should be under the general direction of a man who is entirely familiar with German and Austrian affairs. I suggest that you constitute Grew a special representative of the Department of State to do this work. Of course he should have a number of assistants whom I can secure for him over here. If you approve of this suggestion I will take the necessary steps to set up the organization. This matter I believe is most urgent.   Edward House.

Paris November 8, 1918.

Number 66, priority A. Secret, for the President. Probably the greatest problem which will be presented to us upon the cessation of hostilities is the furnishing of food and other essential supplies to the civilian populations of Servia, Austria, Bohemia, Germany, Belgium and Northern France. This relief work, together with the reconstruction of devastated regions, will have to be done almost entirely through American effort and with the use of American food, raw materials, and finished products. Difficult questions of priority and the allocation of tonnage will be presented. At one of the meetings of the Supreme War Council Mr. Balfour proposed that as a condition of the armistice to be offered Germany the large amount of German merchant tonnage now in German and neutral ports be handed over during the armistice for operation by the Allies and the United States under the general supervision and control of the Allied Maritime Transport Council now sitting in London. I advised that this be not made a condition of the armistice but be taken up as soon as the armistice was signed and Mr. Balfour acquiesced in this suggestion. I now advise that instead of adopting Mr. Balfour's suggestion, which presents obvious objections, that you, as soon as the armistice with Germany is signed, propose to Allies and Germany the immediate formation of the "International Relief Organization." I suggest that Hoover be placed at the head of this organization and that McCormick and Baruch be associated with him as American representatives and that two representatives each be named by England, France, Italy, and Germany. Germany should at once be asked to place at the disposal of this organization until the final peace treaty is signed the entire German merchant marine now in German or neutral ports. The organization should then be charged with securing food and other supplies immediately required for the civilian populations of the countries above set forth and in determining the priority of the needs presented. These supplies would necessarily have to be furnished by the United States and the Allies. It should be pointed out to Germany that only in this way will it be possible for her merchant marine to be placed in service from the inception of the armistice until the final peace treaty is signed and that her willingness to enter wholeheartedly into such a scheme of relief, which would include her own civilian population, would be the best possible evidence of her desire to alleviate the sufferings caused the civilian populations of all countries by the exigencies of the war. In this way also the whole question of relief pending the signing of the final treaty of peace can be kept separate from the very keen struggle which will arise immediately following the signing of the armistice between the various belligerent nations for selfish trade advantage. *It is very clear* [It is true] that the terms of the armistice provide that the blockade shall be continued. The impracticability of this so far as food and other essential supplies are concerned, has already become apparent. Conditions in Austria and in Bohemia are of such a character as to make relief on a large scale imperative if serious disturbances are to be averted. I should appreciate very much an expression of your views on this most urgent matter.   Edward House

T telegrams (WP, DLC).

To Edward Augustus Woods

My dear Friend,   [The White House] 8 November, 1918

I had, as you may imagine, a bit of a pang in reading your letter of November 5th,[1] because expectations so confidently expressed in it had not been realized, but you may be sure that my Scotch-Irish spirit has rallied from the disappointment of Tuesday. I realize that it will require all the more steadfastness and strength to withstand the efforts which the Republican leaders will undoubtedly make to embarrass my course to the utmost, but I accept the additional burden without demur, and comfort myself with the thought that splendid friends like yourself will at every turn of the critical business stand by me.

Cordially and sincerely yours,   Woodrow Wilson

TLS (Letterpress Books, WP, DLC).
[1] E. A. Woods to WW, Nov. 5, 1918, TLS (WP, DLC).

To George Mason La Monte

My dear La Monte: [The White House] 8 November, 1918.

It was a fine race gallantly made, and there is certainly nothing for you to regret. I feel like congratulating you.

I will of course turn again to the case of Miss Pollok in the hope that I may still find something to relieve the doubts about her, and I beg that in the meantime you will not think that any of us supposes that Miss Pollok in what she did was more than merely misled and carried away by impulses to which she yielded without realizing the portentous results that might ensue.

Thank you for having let me see the enclosed papers, which I return. Cordially and sincerely yours, Woodrow Wilson

TLS (Letterpress Books, WP, DLC).

To Thomas Francis Logan

My dear Mr. Logan: [The White House] 8 November, 1918.

That was a singularly generous letter you wrote me on November 6th.[1] It has more than cheered and pleased me; it has touched me very deeply.

I am of course disturbed by the result of Tuesday's elections, because they create obstacles to the settlement of the many difficult questions which throng so on every side, but I have an implicit faith in Divine providence and I am sure that by one means or another the great thing we have to do will work itself out, and you may be sure that letters such as yours do not a little to clear the mists away.

Cordially and sincerely yours, Woodrow Wilson

TLS (Letterpress Books, WP, DLC).
[1] T. F. Logan to WW, Nov. 6, 1918, TLS (WP, DLC).

To Robert Bridges

My dear Bobby: The White House 8 November, 1918

You know my cousin, Helen Woodrow Bones, but perhaps you do not know that before she came to Washington to help Mrs. Wilson and my daughters, she had had long experience in many forms of proof reading. Our little household has now been so reduced by the marriage or absence of the girls that it has of late hung heavy on my cousin's mind that she no longer really had anything to do. She has besides been prudently looking forward to the time when we shall all leave the White House, and she is very anxious to get settled down to some new appointment at the work to which she is accustomed and which she knows she can do. I am therefore writing to you to ask if you or the publishing house have any vacancy into which you could take her, useful to yourself? It would be a great joy to me to know that she had been placed among friends, but I know that it would displease her if she thought I was putting you to any inconvenience in the matter. I am merely asking a frank question.

If you should happen to wish to get in touch with her, she is just now staying with my daughter, Mrs. Francis B. Sayre, at 490 Riverside Drive.

We have been deeply distressed down here by the false news of the last day or two. So far as I can find out, it is nobody's fault in the strict sense of the word, and yet it is manifestly impossible that it should be true because the commissioners did not meet General Foch until nine o'clock (French time) this morning. I am hoping most earnestly that the news may presently be turned from false to true.

In haste, Affectionately yours, Woodrow Wilson

TLS (Meyer Coll., DLC).

A Translation of a Letter from Benedict XV

Mr. President, The Vatican, November 8, 1918.

We are happy to profit by the arrival in America of Archbishop [Msgr.] Bonaventure Cerretti to offer to Your Excellency all our greetings and our thanks for the gracious letter in which you were pleased to reply to our telegram and at the same time to beg you again, in the unfortunate times through which we are passing, to become the champion of peace and of a just and lasting peace.

The news published by the newspapers that Your Excellency has recognized the independence of Poland, gave us very great satisfaction: the great injustice of more than a century's duration is at last about to be redressed. Your Excellency is not unaware that the Holy See, whilst all others bowed down before might, has always upheld the claims of right and has never despaired of Poland's resurrection. The documents preserved in our archives will show still more clearly, when they are published, that the solicitude of the Holy See for Poland was continually increasing as its martyrdom became more cruel. The last letter We sent to the people of Poland, on October 15 last, in the name of the Archbishop of Warsaw, is a fresh proof of this. Your Excellency would make his humanitarian work complete in the East if he would extend his protection to other nationalities formerly subjects of Russia, demanding that to them also, as it is just, be accorded the right of disposing of themselves and to develop and prosper according to their genius.

In addition to Poland, there was and is still another nation which deserves the sympathy of Your Excellency and of all men of heart— we mean Armenia. It is needless to recall how much this unfortunate nation has suffered, especially during the last few years! Although the Armenian people, for the greater part, do not belong to the Catholic faith, the Holy See on different occasions has interested itself in their defence, either by special mention as in its Note to the Belligerent Powers of August 1, 1917, or by writing to the Sultan to obtain in favor of the poor Armenians, the cessation of the massacres, or by sending material assistance to alleviate a little their sufferings. But all this is useless if the independence of united Armenia is not recognized, which she has merited from every point of view. That is why humanity has its eyes fixed on the great President of the greatest democracy in the world.

We pray to the Saviour to bless the efforts of Your Excellency to set up a just and lasting peace in the world. However, it is Our personal conviction, as it is also of Your Excellency, that peace cannot be lasting if conditions are imposed which leave deep-sown seeds of rancour and projects of revenge. The history of the past is the master of the future.

In wishing, on the part of Heaven to Your Excellency and the great Republic over whose destinies you preside, all kind of prosperity, We offer you, Mr. President, fresh assurance of Our highest esteem.   [Benedictus XV][1]

T MS (WP, DLC).
[1] The HwLS, in French, is in WP, DLC.

From Robert Lansing, with Enclosure

My dear Mr. President: Washington November 8, 1918.

I have received the petition regarding the Russian situation, signed by Mr. Gompers, Oscar Strauss, and others, which you sent me today for an expression of my views.

Every since the receipt of a report that a general massacre was being planned in Russia for November 10th, I have been giving this matter serious consideration, and have come to the conclusion that there are no steps we can take which would be effective in minimizing any acts of this kind which the Bolsheviki may have in contemplation. Our dealings with this group would necessarily have to be indirect, and it has been our experience that they resent suggestions from the outside, and any protest on our part might even have the effect of inducing increased acts of violence, and thus bring about the very thing we seek to prevent. I would, therefore, advise against doing anything in regard to the report.

Faithfully yours,   Robert Lansing

E N C L O. S U R E
From Samuel Gompers and Others

New York, November 5, 1918.

On September 21st the Secretary of State issued a telegram in which he called the attention of American Ambassadors and Ministers abroad to information received from reliable sources which revealed an openly avowed campaign of mass terrorism, followed by wholesale executions of thousands of Russian citizens, without even a form of trial. He requested that inquiries be made to ascertain whether the Governments to which they were respectively accredited would be disposed to take some immediate action to impress upon the perpetrators of these crimes the aversion with which civilization regarded these acts, in the hope of successfully checking the further increase of this indiscriminate slaughter.

Your petitioners respectfully represent that, in spite of all protests thus far so impressively made in the cause of humanity and of the Russian people, this reign of terror not only continues unabated, but the press has within the past few days published alarming reports, apparently authentic, purporting to emanate from those now exercising political power in Russia, which show that it has been openly proclaimed that on the coming Sunday, November 10, 1918, the extermination of the intellectual classes and of the so-called bourgeoisie of Russia will be deliberately undertaken by means of what has been fitly termed a general St. Bartholomew's massacre.

Were it not for recent occurrences which have demonstrated the blood thirstiness of the leaders of the Bolshevist party in Russia and the disposition of their followers to indulge in atrocities unparalleled in history, the possibility of such a holocaust would be inconceivable. But the stern reality, the gruesome details of which are as yet unknown, inevitably compels the conviction that unless the entire civilized world shall at once give public expression to its condemnation and abhorrence of the contemplated barbarity, such scenes of horror will ensue as will stagger the imagination.

Impelled by sympathy for the unfortunate people of Russia, and especially for those men and women who have in the past made the greatest sacrifices for their country and who have now been doomed to destruction at the hands of hireling murderers, to whom a free hand has been accorded for the satisfaction of bestial passions, we turn to you, though fully appreciating the practical difficulties of successfully staying these wanton assassinations at this late hour, to appeal not only to the conscience of the world, which, as always, will give immediate response to your call, but to make the instigators of this dreadful conspiracy thoroughly understand that, if they persist in their unholy project, a day of reckoning is sure to come, when they shall be held personally accountable for every life sacrificed by their savage hate, and that every agent and officer of Germany who has it in his power to render nugatory this threatened outbreak of terrorism and fails to intervene, shall likewise be made to answer, as an accessory to these wholesale murders, for their consequences. The deeds about to be perpetrated are offenses against humanity, of such a nature as to call imperatively for condign punishment whenever the terms of the peace which shall end the world war are formulated. They are crimes for which neither pardon nor amnesty will be tolerated.

And thus your petitioners most earnestly pray.

Saml. Gompers.	
Oscar S. Straus }	American Russian League
Herbert L. Carpenter	
Cleveland H. Dodge	
Alton B. Parker[1]	
Louis Marshall	American Jewish Committee
Morgan J. O'Brien	
Alfred E. Marling	President of Chamber of Commerce of State of New York.
Frederick Lynch	Editor of The Christian Work
Lee Kohns	President, New York Board of Trade and Transportation
Henry L. Slobodin[2]	Social Dem. League

TLS (WP, DLC).

[1] That is, Alton Brooks Parker.

[2] Persons not hitherto identified in this series or fully identified in the text above are Alfred Erskine Marling, president of Horace S. Ely & Co., real estate brokers and managers; Frederick Henry Lynch; and Lee Kohns, member of the importing firm of L. Straus & Sons and a vice-president of Abraham & Straus, the Brooklyn department store.

From George Creel

My dear Mr. President,   Washington, D. C. November 8, 1918

You have indeed made this war a war to "make the world safe for democracy." But it was not that sort of war when it began. And it was not that sort of war when we entered it.

Before we got into it, our entrance had its chief impulsion from our most reactionary and least democratic elements. Consequently nearly all our most progressive and liberal leaders had marked themselves as opposed to it. The Republican representatives of Big Business made a clear record of patriotic support of what was then, in outward appearance, a reactionary trade-imperialistic war. Many radicals, progressives and Democrats spoke and voted against it.

When you raised it to the level of a war for democracy, you rallied, to the support of the war, all the progressive and democratic elements. The Big Business patriots went with you, ostensibly on your own terms, because they saw that only on your terms could the war be won. They came into conspicuous leadership as Red Cross executives, as heads of State Councils of Defense, as patriotic dollar-a-year men. They stood out as pure patriots, like Phipps in Colorado[1] as against Keating. They prevented men like Tynan or Lindsey[2] from getting an opportunity to show patriotism in Red Cross campaigns and the like. And they persecuted men like Steffens and organizations like the Nonpartisan League, who tried to stand for the democratic non-imperialist objects of the war.

All the radical, or liberal friends of your anti-imperialist war policy were either silenced or intimidated. The Department of Justice and the Post Office were allowed to silence or intimidate them. There was no voice left to argue for your sort of peace. The Nation and the Public got nipped. All the radical and socialist press was dumb.

When we came to this election, the reactionary Republicans had a clean record of anti-Hun imperialistic patriotism. Their opponents, your friends, were often either besmirched or obscure. No one had been able to tell the public what was really at issue in the elections. The reactionaries knew, but they concealed it. They could appeal, to their patriotism, against what looked like a demand for a partisan verdict for the Democrats. The Democrats, afraid of raising the class issue, went on making a political campaign. Secretary Daniels and you spoke too late.

It seems to me if the defeat is to be repaired, the issue as between the imperialists and the democracy will have to be stated. The liberal, radical, progressive, labor and socialist press will have to be rallied to the President's support. You will have to give out your program for peace and reconstruction and find friends for it. Otherwise, the reactionary patrioteers will defeat the whole immediate future of reform and progress.

I feel that as soon as possible steps should be taken to demobilize the Council of National Defense so that the Chauvinistic, reactionary state organizations may be put out of business.

Respectfully,   George Creel

TLS (WP, DLC).
¹ Lawrence Cowle Phipps, a Republican, had defeated John F. Shafroth in the senatorial contest. Guy Urban Hardy, also a Republican, had defeated Edward Keating in the race for Keating's seat in the House of Representatives.
² Thomas J. Tynan, warden of the Colorado State Penitentiary, famous for his work in prison reform, and Benjamin Barr Lindsey.

Oswald Garrison Villard to Joseph Patrick Tumulty

Dear Mr. Tumulty: New York November 8, 1918

I hope you will find time to read these articles.¹ It is just because of these things which the President could at any moment have stopped that he is today without the liberal support he needs in this trying hour when the real victory of the war is still to be won. I am dismayed by the defeat, because you in the White House have not built up a liberal party and have permitted Burleson and Gregory to scatter and intimidate such liberal forces as have existed.

In this connection the Nation has added 4,750 readers (without special effort) since I took hold July 15th. It is not a personal following, but a spontaneous response to the liberal ideas we are preaching and our upholding of the President's fourteen peace terms. As we, because of the paper famine, have undertaken no circulation campaign, I consider this proof of the existence of a great body of liberal opinion waiting to be led. Shall it go to the Bolsheviki or the reactionary Republicans? That the President himself and no one else will decide.

Faithfully yours,   Oswald Garrison Villard.

TLS (WP, DLC).
¹ "Woodrow Wilson, Politician" and "Why Is Roosevelt Unjailed?" *The Nation*, CVII (Nov. 2, 1918), 503, 546.

A Memorandum by Homer Stillé Cummings

[Washington] About November 8th or 9th 1918.

I had a meeting with Mr. Wilson at the White House after the elections of November 1918. He was very much saddened by the result. He told me frankly that it made his difficulties enormously greater. He felt that it would encourage opposition at home to the policies that he contemplated abroad. He felt grieved that the people had not responded to his appeal which he had hoped and attributed it to the misrepresentations which had gone on during the campaign and to the failure on the part of the public generally to realize the real problem which confronted him. I wish I could recall all that he said at this interview. He was very kind and generous in his attitude toward me. He knew that I was deeply grieved by the result of the campaign. He did not blame anyone in particular. He felt that I had done everything that was humanly possible and that it was simply one of those things that had to be. He was not bitter toward anyone. I think under the circumstances that he was rather gentle toward those who had most misunderstood him and who had most violently and unreasonably attacked him. I shall never forget that interview. I wish that I had made a memorandum of all that had occurred at the time. I have never known him to talk more freely nor more at length. I was with him nearly an hour during which time he talked almost continuously. I did not have very much to say. He knew that I was fully in sympathy with his program and I had had rather the feeling that it was a sort of relief to him to pour out his heart. He certainly did so. It was an unforgettable experience.

His discussion ranged over the whole field of American politics, dealing with the attitude of public men, occasional flashes of description concerning various outstanding figures, the problems of the Democratic Party, and interrelated questions. Most of all, however, his mind dwelt on world problems and the part the United States ought to play in the readjustment of the world. He talked of the statesmen of Europe, of the problems of France, Italy, England, Germany, Belgium, Poland, Czechoslovakia, Greece and indeed covered the whole field. He dwelt on the problems of Germany and the German people. He had a feeling that they had shaken off the imperialistic rule and the military autocracy and that being an industrious people, and naturally orderly, they might, if properly treated, ultimately be a bulwark for peace in Europe. He was very much concerned as to labor conditions. He spoke of the various labor leaders who were prominent throughout the world. He discussed economic problems, key industries and innumerable other subjects. It was a most amusing [amazing] panorama that he spread before me. I have never witnessed in any one individual a more complete and masterly understanding of such wideflung interests and such complicated problems. We conversed for nearly an hour without interruption in the quiet of his study. Although disappointed by the result of the election and fully comprehending what use might be made of it, he had not abated one whit of his determination to carry on to the limit of his strength and ability.

T MS (H. S. Cummings Papers, ViU).

ADDENDA

To Paul Lendrum Blakely

My dear Mr. Blakely: Princeton, N. J. December 17th, 1907.

Thank you most sincerely for your letter of the 14th.[1] I did not see the copy of The Literary Digest to which you allude,[2] and therefore cannot be sure that the quotations you saw from my address before the Association of Colleges and Preparatory Schools of the Middle States correctly reported my meaning or not. But from what you say in your letter I judge it likely that they did.

The address was reported stenographically and will be printed in full in the Proceedings of the Association, of which Professor A. H. Quinn[3] of the University of Pennsylvania has charge. Just how promptly these proceedings are issued I do not know.[4] I only know that I have not yet had an opportunity to revise the stenographer's report.

I very much appreciate what you say about your agreement with me in the main points touched upon, and I certainly heartily agree with you that the unnamed University President, while he did a great deal to liberalize, has certainly done a vast deal to confuse and weaken our education. I think, however, that the whole educational world is slowly awakening to that fact, and I cannot help hoping that we are upon the eve of an era of sane reconstruction.

With much regard,   Sincerely yours,   Woodrow Wilson

TLS (Special Colls. Div., DGU).
[1] P. L. Blakely to WW, Dec. 14, 1907, Vol. 17.
[2] Cited in n. 2 to the letter just cited.
[3] Arthur Hobson Quinn, at this time Assistant Professor of English at the University of Pennsylvania.
[4] Wilson's address is printed in Vol. 17, pp. 529-45.

To Archibald Stevens Alexander

My dear Mr. Alexander,   Lyme, Connecticut, 20 July, 1910.

Thank you most warmly for your kind letter of the sixteenth.[1] I appreciate it deeply. It reassures me in many particulars. I was in great doubt what I ought to do about the suggested nomination if it should come. It was hard to see it a duty to allow myself to be drawn away from Princeton at this critical time, when so much important work is only half done there. But in view of what I have always preached about the duty of educated men in politics I saw that I had no choice, if it should turn out that there was a genuine demand and a real need that I should consent, even upon the chance. Your letter confirms my impressions. It confirms also several things that were told me upon what I feared was doubtful authority. It has done me a real service.

I shall hope to be associated with you in many ways in this, to me novel, business. I beg that you will let me hear from you whenever there is anything in your mind that you think I ought to know.

With much regard,

Sincerely yours,   Woodrow Wilson

What is the animus of the *Observer*?[2]

WWTLS (WC, NjP).
    [1] A. S. Alexander to WW, July 16, 1910, Vol. 21.
    [2] That is, the Hoboken *Observer*. About its opposition to Wilson's candidacy for the Democratic gubernatorial nomination, see A. S. Alexander to WW, July 22, 1918, Vol. 21.

INDEX

NOTE ON THE INDEX

THE alphabetically arranged analytical table of contents at the front of the volume eliminates duplication, in both contents and index, of references to certain documents, such as letters. Letters are listed in the contents alphabetically by name, and chronologically within each name by page. The subject matter of all letters is, of course, indexed. The Editorial Notes and Wilson's writings are listed in the contents chronologically by page. In addition, the subject matter of both categories is indexed. The index covers all references to books and articles mentioned in text or notes. Footnotes are indexed. Page references to footnotes which place a comma between the page number and "n" cite both text and footnote, thus: "418,n1." On the other hand, absence of the comma indicates reference to the footnote only, thus: "59n1"—the page number denoting where the footnote appears.

The index supplies the fullest known form of names and, for the Wilson and Axson families, relationships as far down as cousins. Persons referred to by nicknames or shortened forms of names can be identified by reference to entries for these forms of the names.

All entries consisting of page numbers only and which refer to concepts, issues, and opinions (such as democracy, the tariff, the money trust, leadership, and labor problems), are references to Wilson's speeches and writings. Page references that follow the symbol Δ in such entries refer to the opinions and comments of others who are identified.

Three cumulative contents-index volumes are now in print: Volume 13, which covers Volumes 1-12, Volume 26, which covers Volumes 14-25, and Volume 39, which covers Volumes 27-38.

INDEX

Abbott, Grace, 181-82,n1,4
Abbott, Lawrence Fraser, 15-16
Abraham & Straus, 644n2
Acid Test of Our Democracy (Thomas), 12n2
Adler, Harry Clay, 482-83,n1
Adler, Viktor, 564,n4, 566
Admiral Spaun, S.M.S., 492
Ador, Gustave, 240,n9
African Methodist Episcopal Church, 168n1, 193n1
agricultural bill: and prohibition, 28,n2, 105
agriculture: prices and, 118n1, 126-27,n1,2; *see also* farmers and farming
Agriculture, Department of, 357
Agudath Achim Congregation (Harlem), 424n1
aircraft program, 15-16,n1, 38, 618,n1
Airplane Scandal (*The Outlook*), 15,n1
Aitchison, Clyde Bruce, 248,n5
Alabama: politics in, 632
Albania, 43, 274, 501, 503
Albert, King of the Belgians, 184
alcohol: *see* prohibition
Alexander III, Tsar of Russia, 567
Alexander, Archibald Stevens, 649-50
Alexander, Thomas Mathew, 113,n2, 115
Alien Property Custodian: and Busch case, 395n1, 445, 469
Allen, Benjamin Shannon, 113-16,n1
Allied Food Council: *see* Inter-Allied Food Council
Allied Maritime Transport Council, 94, 223n6, 638
Allied Military Council at Vladivostok, 25, 86n1
Allied Naval Council: *see* Inter-Allied Naval Council
Allies, 8; Sharp on, 22; Bliss on political issues and policy making and, 40-45; and possible German peace proposals, 46-47; Czechs' plea for assistance from, 51n2; and U.S. food program, 89; and tonnage issue, 94-95; WW on U.S. military policy and, 121-22; and Bulgaria, 145, 163; and conduct of operations in various theaters of war, 195-203; importance of consultation with on peace terms, 254, 289,n1, 307-309, 411-12, 413, 414-15, 416-17, 427-29, 514-17; Bliss on discord among, 427-28; and Polish National Army, 447-48; and Turkey, 456; acceptance of WW's peace terms with qualifications, now willing to make peace with Germany, 580-82; and delegates to peace conference, 606-607; *see also* Supreme War Council, and under the names of the individual countries
All-Russian Provisional Government, 102n1
Almossava, S.M.S., 493
Alpine, John R., 523,n2
Alsace-Lorraine, 21n1, 47, 106n7, 156n2, 232, 236, 240, 244, 255n1, 262, 265n1, 269,n1, 273, 277n7, 331, 335, 339, 351, 385, 411, 412, 454, 463, 470, 472, 500

American Association for Labor Legislation, 165n1
American Defense Society, Inc., 147n1, 161, 162, 175
American Expeditionary Force, 61, 139-41, 188; *see also* United States Army
American Federation of Labor, 149, 165,n1, 522-23,n2
American International Shipbuilding Corporation, 13-14
American Jewish Committee, 644; on rights of Polish Jews, 625-27
American Library Association, 621,n1, 636
American National Live Stock Association, 212n2
American Red Cross, 4,n3, 598, 618
American Russian League, 644
American-Slavic legion (proposed), 178,n1,2
American Society of Equity, 212n1
American Telephone & Telegraph Co., 523n1
America's Siberian Adventure, 1918-1920 (Graves), 8n2
Amur Railway, 479
Anatolia, 503
Ancient Order of Gleaners, 212n2
Anderson, John M., 212,n2
Andrássy, Count Julius (Andrássy von Czik-Szent-Király und Krasznahorka), 526,n1, 526-27
Andrews, James W., 4,n3, 18n1
Anglo-American relations: *see* Great Britain and the United States
Anglo-Soviet Relations, 1917-1921: Intervention and the War (Ullman), 4n2
Anheuser-Busch Brewing Association, 395n1
Answer, The (New York *Sun*), 279,n9
Antachan, Manchuria, 479,n1
Anti-Saloon League of New Jersey, 547n1
Appropriations, Committee on (House of Reps.), 138
Arabia, 503, 514
Archangel, 31, 32, 141; *see also*: Russia—Murmansk and Archangel, intervention in
Archangel-Vologda-Ekaterinburg Railway, 52
Arguments Advanced For and Against Compulsory Control of the Steel Industry (memorandum), 285,n1
Arizona: politics in, 404,n1,2, 632
Arkansas: politics in, 632
Armées Françaises dans la Grande Guerre, 200n3
Armenia, 503, 642
Armenian massacres, 62
Armistice 1918 (Rudin), 621n1
Armour and Company, 92n1
Army (U.S.): *see* United States Army
Arnold, George Stanleigh, 125,n1, 172, 204, 376, 377, 378
Arraga, Mr., 76n1
Asbury Park Evening Press, 552n8
Asheville, N.C., *Citizen*, 482n1

WOODROW WILSON

APPOINTMENT SUGGESTIONS, APPOINTMENTS AND RESIGNATIONS

WITHDRAWN

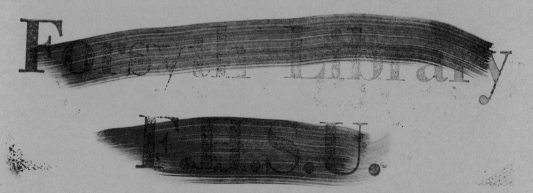